1990

REALITY IN FOCUS

Contemporary Readings on Metaphysics

Edited by Paul K. Moser

Loyola University of Chicago

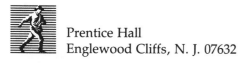

Prentice Hall
Englewood Cliffs, N. J. 07632

Library of Congress Cataloging-in-Publication Data

Reality in focus : contemporary readings on metaphysics / edited by
  Paul K. Moser.
      p.   cm.
    Bibliography: p.
    Includes index.
    ISBN 0-13-762410-7
    1. Metaphysics.   I. Moser, Paul K., [date].
  BD111.R23   1989
  110—dc20   89-8742
                                                                        CIP

Editorial/production supervision and
  interior design: Fred Dahl and Rose Kernan
Cover design: Photo Plus Art
Manufacturing buyer: Carol Bystrom

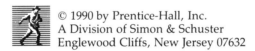 © 1990 by Prentice-Hall, Inc.
A Division of Simon & Schuster
Englewood Cliffs, New Jersey 07632

Printed in the United States of America
10 9 8 7 6 5 4 3 2 1

ISBN   0-13-762410-7

Prentice-Hall International (UK) Limited, *London*
Prentice-Hall of Australia Pty. Limited, *Sydney*
Prentice-Hall Canada Inc., *Toronto*
Prentice-Hall Hispanoamericana, S.A., *Mexico*
Prentice-Hall of India Private Limited, *New Delhi*
Prentice-Hall of Japan, Inc., *Tokyo*
Simon & Schuster Asia Pte. Ltd., *Singapore*
Editora Prentice-Hall do Brasil, Ltda., *Rio de Janeiro*

Contents

IV
Universals, Essences, and Natural Kinds, 307

V
Reality and God. 391

Preface

This book includes thirty-three important 20th-century essays on most of the prominent topics of metaphysics and, therefore, can serve as a comprehensive textbook for any college course dealing with the questions and problems of metaphysics. Readers who have had prior exposure to the perennial issues of philosophy will get maximal benefits from this book. But none of the essays is inherently technical in nature, and all should be accessible, at least for the most part, to middle-level undergraduate philosophy students. Yet, each essay is sufficiently substantial to be beneficial reading for graduate-level philosophy students as well. The essays fall into these main categories: Reality and an External World (Part I); Space, Time, and Causation (Part II); Persons, Minds, and Free Will (Part III); Universals, Essences, and Natural Kinds (Part IV); and Reality and God (Part V).

My general introduction gives the nonspecialist a rough idea of some of the prominent approaches to metaphysics by providing a general orientation for students with no prior work in the field. My section introductions summarize the various selections to follow. My summaries should give students some signposts to watch out for on their long journey through the readings. Each of the book's main sections concludes with a list of recommended readings.

My work on this book has benefited from discussions with several colleagues in the philosophy department at Loyola University of Chicago, especially Arnold vander Nat, Kenneth Thompson, and Thomas Sheehan. My research assistant, Bradley Owen, provided indispensable assistance in the preparation of the book's manuscript. And several anonymous referees, provided helpful comments on my initial proposal for the book. I thank all these people for their help.

Paul K. Moser
Chicago, Illinois

General Introduction: Metaphysics and Reality

Paul K. Moser

SOME NOTIONS OF METAPHYSICS

The term *metaphysics* comes from the Greek phrase *meta ta physika*, meaning "after the things of nature." This phrase was first used by some ancient Greek commentators on the works of Aristotle (384–322 B.C.) to refer to his philosophical writings that we now call the *Metaphysics*. The traditional story is that an ancient Greek librarian, Andronicus of Rhodes (first century B.C.), was the first to use this phrase to refer to the location of these writings in the cataloged arrangment of Aristotle's works (the books located on the shelf after the books on nature, i.e., Aristotle's *Physics*). Contemporary historians disagree, however, about the original sense of this Greek phrase. Some still support the traditional story, while others believe that the phrase originally connoted Aristotle's works that were intended to be studied only after one studied Aristotle's *Physics*. For present purposes, we need not pursue this historical matter.[1]

Aristotle himself called the subject of the *Metaphysics* "first philosophy" and "wisdom" (*sophia*). He understood first philosophy to be the science of first principles, i.e., principles assumed by, but not provable by, the special sciences. On Aristotle's view, first philosophy investigates things apart from the classifications peculiar to the special sciences; it is the science of being as such: being *qua* being. In effect, Aristotle reduced metaphysics to the science of substances and the causes thereof. He took it to be the science of things that have independent existence and of how they causally interrelate.

1

(Aristotle distinguished three main kinds of substances: destructible sensible substances, indestructible sensible substances, and immovable substances.) He regarded metaphysics not as mere speculative opinion, but as a body of *knowledge* about independent existence. On his view, metaphysics is no less a science than is mathematics or physics.

Apparently, the influence of *neoplatonic philosophy* (a post-Aristotle revival of Plato's philosophy) accounts for the early use of the term 'metaphysics' to designate simply the study of things that transcend, or exist independently of, physical reality: things such as God and souls. This use of the term is narrower than its earlier use in referring to Aristotle's first philosophy. His first philosophy has much to say about the nature of physical substances, although it also concerns nonphysical substances. The neoplatonic use of 'metaphysics' carries over into modern as well as medieval times. Some philosophers and theologians still use the term to refer simply to the study of what transcends physical reality.

A somewhat different use persists, as well. Under the influence of Immanuel Kant (1724–1804), many 19th- and 20th-century philosophers have used the term 'metaphysics' to signify a sort of thinking whose judgments cannot be verified by sensory experience. Kant regarded metaphysics as an area of philosophy involving *pure reason* (reason independent of sensory experience). In his *Prolegomena to any Future Metaphysics* (1783), Kant claimed that some nondefinitional, synthetic truths "carry with them necessity which cannot be obtained from experience." One of Kant's examples comes from mathematics: A straight line is the shortest path between two points. Kant held that synthetic truths of this sort can be known *a priori*, that is, solely by pure reason without any evidence from sensory experience. Such synthetic *a priori* knowledge, according to Kant, is genuine *metaphysical* knowledge.[2]

Kant denied that metaphysics can provide knowledge of things that transcend possible experience. On Kant's view, metaphysics is a science only when it applies to the objects of possible sensory experience; otherwise we have mere speculation or dogmatism. So Kant's use of 'metaphysics' differs from the aforementioned neoplatonic use. The Kantian use signifies a kind of knowledge that is restricted to objects of possible sensory experience, but that cannot be supported by sensory experience. In general, Kant himself seems to have thought of metaphysics as the science of what makes synthetic *a priori* knowledge possible.

In light of Kant's approach to metaphysics, P. F. Strawson has drawn a general distinction between *descriptive* metaphysics and *revisionary* metaphysics.[3] Descriptive metaphysics aims to describe the actual structure of our thought about the world. It aims to clarify the actual functioning of our basic concepts without revising those concepts. In Strawson's words, the goal of descriptive metaphysics is "to show how the fundamental categories of our thought hang together and how they relate, in turn, to those formal notions (such as existence, identity, and unity) which range through all categories."[4]

Revisionary metaphysics, in contrast, aims to identify the actual constituents of reality, and thereby aims to revise any mistakes or inadequacies in our actual thought about the world. The goal of revisionary metaphysics is to specify how we can *correctly* think about the world. Strawson lists Descartes, Leibniz, and Berkeley as proponents of revisionary metaphysics, and Aristotle and Kant as proponents of descriptive metaphysics. Strawson himself evidently shares Kant's skepticism about our ability to identify the reality that lies beyond what we experience. He recommends descriptive metaphysics on the ground that it needs no special justification beyond that of inquiry in general.

Many philosophers now use the term 'metaphysics' to refer to the philosophical study of:

1. the kinds of things that exist, and

2. the ways in which things exist in general (e.g., how they came to exist, how they interrelate, how they are similar and dissimilar, and how they cease to exist).

This approach to metaphysics involves, among other things, a systematic clarification of the concepts of existence, substance, essence, event, kind, property, universal, mind, body, external world, relation, and causation, The list goes on, but the main point should be clear—the present approach to metaphysics is wide ranging. On this approach, metaphysics is simply the philosophical investigation of reality in general, whatever that may include.

Kant's approach was a metaphysics of *experience*, but the present approach is a philosophy of *what there is*, or *how things are*, in general. The relevant notion of how things are is basically the notion of what items (e.g., objects, features of objects, relations between objects and/or features), if any, exist. Conceivably, reality does not transcend experience, but our *notion* of metaphysics should be neutral on this controversial matter. Whether reality does or does not transcend experience, metaphysics can persist. In either case, we can have a philosophical account of what there is or how things are, in general. Let us call this *the broad construal of metaphysics*.

The broad construal makes metaphysics a congenial discipline for a wide range of philosophical positions. Even if one claimed that no physical objects exist, one might pursue a metaphysical account of our perceptual and sensory experiences, or of whatever else one claimed to exist. Broad construal metaphysics should be agreeable even to those 20th-century logical positivists often thought to be enemies of metaphysics.[5] Here I have in mind such philosophers as Bertrand Russell, Rudolf Carnap, and A. J. Ayer. The central tenet of these positivists in the 1920s and 1930s was the *verification principle*. This principle states that a nonanalytic, nondefinitional statement is meaningful if and only if it is verifiable or falsifiable solely on the basis of sensory experience and logic. (These positivists took the meaning of analytic statements to be a simple matter of logic.)

Given the verification principle, we would have to shun metaphysics understood as an effort to acquire knowledge of nonanalytic statements having no basis in sensory experience. We would regard such metaphysics as a hopeless science of meaningless statements. But the verification principle, however questionable (and self-referentially inconsistent), poses no threat to the broad construal of metaphysics. For even if experience-transcendent statements were meaningless, we still could aspire to a philosophical account of what there is, or how things are, in general. We still could seek a general philosophical account of experience-relative items.

OBJECTIONS TO THE BROAD CONSTRUAL

Some philosophers would object that the broad construal of metaphysics is unjustifiable on the ground that the very notion of how things are (or what there is) independent of conceivers is unintelligible.[6] According to these philosophers, we can understand the notion of how things are "as conceived by certain conceivers," but we cannot understand the notion of how things are apart from conceivers. One might look for support for such a view in this argument:

1. Every intelligible concept is conceiver-relative.
2. The concept of how things are apart from conceivers is not conceiver-relative.
3. So the concept of how things are apart from conceivers is unintelligible.

Clearly, if this argument is sound, the broad construal of metaphysics needs revision.

Fortunately for the broad construal, the foregoing argument commits the fallacy of equivocation. It equivocates on the key term *conceiver-relative*. A concept can be conceiver-relative in the sense that it is "possessed by a conceiver," and it can be conceiver-relative in the sense that it "makes essential reference to a conceiver." Our concept of a tree, for example, is possessed by many conceivers, but it does not make essential reference to a conceiver. We could have the concept of a tree without having the concept of a conceiver. In that respect, the concept of how things are is similar to our concept of a tree. Nonetheless, we still can hold that a *contingent* feature of how things are is that there are mental entities such as conceivers.

Premise (1) of the argument above seems to be false if construed as the claim that every intelligible concept makes essential reference to a conceiver. We have no reason to think that for every concept, one's possessing that concept requires one to have the concept of a conceiver. But premise (1) is arguably true if construed as the claim that every intelligible concept is possessed by some conceiver or other. (A plausible non-Platonist view of concepts states that a concept exists only as the psychological feature of some conceiver or other.) But on the latter construal, premise (2) seems to be false or at least question-begging. We have no reason to think that the concept of how things are is not possessed by some conceiver or other. Premise (2) seems to be true only on the construal where to be conceiver-relative is to make essential reference to a conceiver. Thus, once we remove equivocation, it seems that if premise (2) is true, then premise (1) is false, and that if premise (1) is true, then premise (2) is false. So the argument (1)–(3) is unconvincing.

Here is another noteworthy argument against the justifiability of the broad construal:

1. A concept is intelligible only if its exemplification conditions (i.e., conditions under which it is exemplified or under which it is not exemplified) are verifiable.
2. The exemplification conditions for the concept of how things are are not verifiable.
3. So the concept of how things are is unintelligible.

This argument derives from the positivist view that the intelligibility of a concept requires the verifiability of the conditions for that concept's being exemplified or not being exemplified. Positivists such as Carnap and Ayer used this view to argue for the meaninglessness of various traditional metaphysical notions, including the metaphysical notion of how things are.[7]

However, premises (1) and (2) are unconvincing because of the vagueness of the term *verifiable*. If only for the sake of argument, let's grant, regarding premise (1), that a concept is intelligible only if one could in principle be justified in believing that it is exemplified (or that it is not exemplified). The foregoing argument provides no reason to think that one cannot be justified in believing a proposition stating how things are. So premise (2) lacks support. And it is quite unclear how one might provide the needed support. If verifiability requires only *overridable justifiability* (i.e., justifiability that can be undermined by new evidence), premise (2) will be implausible or at least question-begging. And if a stronger notion of verifiability is relevant, premise (1) will be implausible. Thus, the foregoing argument is far from compelling.

One still might be uneasy with the notion of how things are because of general worries concerning how we can *find out* that a proposition really describes how things are. Such worries are common, but we must avoid a serious confusion here: a confusion of (1) a definition of a general concept, and (2) a criterion for finding out whether something exemplifies that concept. The failure of a definition to provide the latter sort of criterion does not undercut the definition, and does not distinguish it from most definitions of general concepts. (Consider, for example, our definitions of the concepts of animal, conscious being, and sentient being.) We can define the notion of how things are by the notion of what items, if any, exist; but this does not mean that the latter notion can provide a criterion for our finding out how things actually are. The search for such a criterion is an important task of *epistemology*; it need not be accomplished by a merely definitional characterization of the notion of how things are.

Suppose we grant the objector's claim that the concept of how things are is unintelligible. Given this claim, we must ask whether it itself is a claim about how things are. If it is, we must wonder whether it itself is intelligible *given what it claims*. And if it is not a claim about how things are, we must ask what sort of claim it is.

One likely response is that it is a claim not about how things are, but only about what we are *justified in accepting*. On this response, we have the view that we are justified in accepting that the concept of how things are is unintelligible. But we can ask of that view also whether it itself is a claim about how things are. If it is, we must then wonder whether we can reasonably regard it as intelligible, given its own claim. And if it is not a claim about how things are, we need again to ask what sort of claim it is.

If it is a claim only about what we are justified in accepting, we have the iterative view that we are justified in accepting that we are justified in accepting that the concept of how things are is unintelligible. But if we take this approach, and continue the foregoing line of questioning, we face a potentially endless regress of increasing levels of iteration regarding what we are justified in accepting. Such a regress raises serious problems, mainly because we apparently do not have the sort of complex iterative evidence it requires.

It is unclear, then, how one can justify the claim that the concept of how things are is unintelligible. If we reject the threatening implausible endless regress, we must wonder whether that claim presupposes the very concept it affirms to be unintelligible. And so far as the foregoing objections go, it seems that we plausibly can persist with our use of the notion of how things are. So, the broad construal of metaphysics appears not to be threatened by those objections.

A final noteworthy objection to the justifiability of the broad construal comes from what may be called *naturalized philosophy*. This is the view that the natural sciences provide the *only* justifiable account of how things are.[8] On this view, philosophical accounts outside the natural sciences are unjustifiable and so metaphysics, broadly construed, is also unjustifiable.

We can handle this objection with a twofold reply. First, nothing I have said so far commits the broad construal of metaphysics to justifiable philosophical accounts outside the natural sciences. Second, the objection needs to be supplemented not only with a clear statement of what constitutes a "natural science," but also with a rationale for its assumption that only the natural sciences provide a justifiable account of how things are. This latter requirement is not easily met.

If we revise the objection at hand to concern simply the scope of the term 'metaphysics', rather than the justifiability of the broad construal, then we must notice another point. Even if all justifiable philosophical accounts come from the natural sciences, there surely are in circulation unjustifiable philosophical accounts of how things are; and we can plausibly call the latter accounts *metaphysical* even if they cannot be justified relative to our current evidence. Just as there can be unjustified psychological theories, for example, so also there can be unjustified metaphysical accounts. The mere fact that a philosophical account cannot be justified relative to our current evidence does not entail that the account is not metaphysical. There can be good, or justified, metaphysical accounts; and there can be bad, or unjustified, metaphysical accounts.

But the objection at hand forces us to confront an important and difficult question: what is the exact difference, if any, between a *philosophical* account of how things are and a *scientific* account of how things are? Let us briefly discuss this issue.

One philosophically (and historically) naive outlook proposes that the natural sciences properly have a monopoly on legitimate accounts of how things are because the natural sciences alone have a method (*the scientific method*) that guarantees objectivity (i.e., reliable access to reality). Even a passing acquaintance with the history of shifting scientific views should save one from such an outlook.

If the natural sciences possess a method that guarantees objectivity, the history of those sciences does not disclose such a method. And the contemporary scientist certainly does not wear such a method on his or her sleeve. Perhaps the natural sciences' reliance on experimentation and empirical testing provides for a sort of reproducibility of experimental results. But the assumption that such reproducibility guarantees objectivity overlooks the fact that the relevant procedures for experimentation and testing themselves rely on a considerable amount of theory about reality. (For example, consider the theory concerning how the relevant experimental devices represent, or otherwise relate to, the world.) And there is, of course, no obvious guarantee that the underlying theory is itself correct.

The natural sciences, however, do provide an arguably unsurpassed, if fallible, model of a fairly comprehensive explanatory account of how the world is (or at least how the perceptual world is). On the plausible assumption that an explanatory account of the relevant sort involves an answer to a question concerning why something is as it is (i.e., a why-question), we can say that the natural sciences provide answers to the questions of why various aspects of the perceptual world are as they are.[9] Yet, it seems that these scientific answers are *logically contingent* in the sense that it is logically possible that each one is false. For example, it seems that quantum theory and the theory of the big bang might be false. Quantum theory and the theory of the big bang apparently are not necessarily true in the way that the principle of noncontradiction—it is not the case that both P and not-P—seems to be necessarily true. One way to illustrate this is to ask whether you can imagine that quantum theory and the theory of the big bang are false. If you can, those theories are not necessarily true.

Many philosophers hold that the contingency of scientific explanations prevents those explanations from being metaphysical. These philosophers hold that metaphysical theses essentially have some sort of necessity: either logical necessity or a special sort of nonlogical metaphysical necessity (e.g., the sort of necessity characterizing synthetic *a priori* propositions).[10] Typically, these philosophers also hold that philosophical theses, in general, essentially have a sort of necessity that is not had by scientific claims. And they also typically hold that metaphysical claims, like all other philosophical claims, must be justifiable *a priori* (i.e., independent of perceptual and sensory experience).[11] Naturally, given such views, one would draw a sharp contrast between metaphysics and science. A metaphysical account, on the present approach, is necessary in some suitably demanding sense and is justifiable *a priori*, whereas a scientific account is contingent and is justifiable only by perceptual and sensory experience.

We now have two general options:

1. regard metaphysics as an *a priori* discipline, or
2. free metaphysics, and thereby a large part of philosophy, from an exclusive connection to what is *a priori*.

Generally, philosophers in the rationalist tradition of Descartes take the first option, whereas philosophers in the empiricist tradition of Aristotle and Locke take the second. With either option, however, we can pursue metaphysics broadly construed. For the broad construal, option (2) provides for a wider domain of metaphysics than does option (1). Given option (2), much of theoretical natural science (e.g., cosmology and particle physics) may very well count as metaphysical. But option (2) need not make metaphysics all inclusive (as the old saying goes: a night in which all cows are black). We still could distinguish metaphysics broadly construed from much of ethics, epistemology, and philosophy of science, for example.

We should acknowledge a difficult problem that is closely related to choosing between options (1) and (2). If broadly construed metaphysics is the philosophical account of what there is, or how things are, in general, what provides the evidential basis for such an account? That is, what sort of evidence underlies a legitimate metaphysical account and enables us to say that we have an account of reality rather than fantasy.

An empiricist answer would state that legitimate metaphysics must be constrained in an appropriate way by what is presented to us in perceptual and sensory experience. Otherwise, according to empiricist metaphysics, we have mere speculation or dogmatism.

A rationalist answer to our question would deny any necessary constraints from perceptual and sensory experience. According to rationalist metaphysics, pure reason provides evidentially relevant input that goes beyond what we find in perceptual and sensory experience (and perhaps even beyond what we find in logic and mathematics). Conflicts between variations on rationalist metaphysics and variations on empiricist metaphysics constitute one of the perennial philosophical disputes. Whichever side we take in these conflicts, it seems doubtful that the natural sciences themselves can provide a resolution. Perhaps we have here, then, a special task for philosophy that is not accomplished by the natural sciences.

In any case, we can effectively treat the foregoing problem-issues only after we have acquired considerable familiarity with the major problems and positions of metaphysics. This book's selections aim to provide such familiarity. The selections treat most of the traditional prominent topics in metaphysics, such as:

reality and an external world (Part I);

space, time, and causation (Part II);

persons, minds, and free will (Part III);

universals, essences, and natural kinds (Part IV); and

reality and God (Part V).

The introductions to the individual sections summarize the selections themselves.

A book of this type cannot adequately represent all the topics of metaphysics. Some topics in metaphysics are fairly technical and require considerable background work in philosophy or in some other specific discipline. Here we might mention, for example, some of the metaphysical issues involved in *cosmology,* in the *philosophy of mathematics,* and in the *theory of necessity.* Such issues are philosophically important, but need to be reserved for more advanced work.

The selections should provide an accessible starting point for independent thinking about most of the major topics in metaphysics. They might even enable the reader to resolve some of the problems we have identified in this introductory discussion. Only time and serious metaphysical thinking will tell.

F. H. Bradley, a British idealist philosopher, once remarked that metaphysics is but the finding of bad reasons for what we believe upon instinct. Readers should ask, at the least, whether this book's selections prove Bradley wrong.

NOTES

[1]On some of the early history of the term *metaphysics,* see Anton-Hermann Chroust, "The Origin of 'Metaphysics'," *The Review of Metaphysics* 14 (1961), 601–16. For a broad historical survey of prominent notions of metaphysics, see Roger Hancock, "Metaphysics, History of," in *The Encyclopedia of Philosophy,* ed. Paul Edwards (New York: Macmillan, 1967), Vol. 5, pp. 289–300.

[2]Kant's thesis of the synthetic *a priori* is still a topic of philosophical controversy. For contrasting treatments of it see the essays by A. J. Ayer, Roderick Chisholm, and Richard Swinburne in *A Priori Knowledge*, ed. P. K. Moser (Oxford: Oxford University Press, 1987).

[3]Strawson, *Individuals: An Essay in Descriptive Metaphysics* (Garden City, N.Y.: Doubleday, 1959), pp. xiii–xv, and "Analysis, Science, and Metaphysics," in *The Linguistic Turn*, ed. Richard Rorty (Chicago: University of Chicago Press, 1967), pp. 317–20.

[4]Strawson, "Analysis, Science, and Metaphysics," p. 318.

[5]For a useful historical discussion of logical positivism see Milton Munitz, *Contemporary Analytic Philosophy* (New York: Macmillan, 1981), chapter 6.

[6]Such an objection receives support from Nelson Goodman, *Ways of Worldmaking* (Indianapolis: Hackett, 1978), pp. 3–4; Hilary Putnam, *Reason, Truth, and History* (Cambridge: Cambridge University Press, 1981), pp. 49–54, 60–64; and Richard Rorty, *Consequences of Pragmatism* (Minneapolis: University of Minnesota Press, 1982), pp. xxvi, 14–15, 192. See also the essays by Putnam and Carnap in Parts I and IV of this book.

[7]See Carnap's essay in Part IV of this book, and Ayer, *Language, Truth, and Logic*, 2d ed. (London: Victor Gollancz, 1946). See also the essays in Part I of *The Linguistic Turn*, ed. Richard Rorty (Chicago: University of Chicago Press, 1967).

[8]Naturalized philosophy is simply a generalization of W. V. Quine's view in "Epistemology Naturalized," in Quine, *Ontological Relativity and Other Essays* (New York: Columbia University Press, 1969), pp. 69–90.

[9]For defense of the view that scientific explanations are answers to why-questions, see Bas van Fraassen, *The Scientific Image* (Oxford: Clarendon Press, 1980), chapter 5. For some support for the view that the natural sciences aspire to explanatory accounts of natural phenomena, see Brian Ellis, "What Science Aims to Do," in *Images of Science*, eds. P. M. Churchland and C. A. Hooker (Chicago: University of Chicago Press, 1985), pp. 48–74.

[10]For a helpful survey of prominent approaches to necessary truth in classical modern and contemporary philosophy, see Arthur Pap, *Semantics and Necessary Truth* (New Haven: Yale University Press, 1958), Part I. For related discussion, including remarks on Saul Kripke's influential notion of metaphysical necessity, see Hilary Putnam, *Realism and Reason* (Cambridge: Cambridge University Press, 1983), pp. 46–68. And, for emphasis on the conceptual distinction between the *logical* category of the necessary and the *epistemic* category of the *a priori*, see my Introduction and the essay by Kripke in *A Priori Knowledge*, ed. P. K. Moser (Oxford: Oxford University Press, 1987).

[11]One recent endorsement of such a view can be found in George Bealer, "The Boundary Between Philosophy and Cognitive Science," *The Journal of Philosophy* 84 (1987), 553–55. Cf. Alvin Goldman's "Cognitive Science and Metaphysics" in the same issue. For a general discussion of the relation of metaphysics to the natural sciences, and of the method of philosophy in general, see C. I. Lewis, *Mind and the World Order* (New York: Charles Scribner's Sons, 1929), chapter 1. It is regrettable that contemporary philosophers rarely investigate this important topic.

I

Reality and an External World

This section consists of two subsections: *Realism versus Anti-Realism* and *On Scientific Realism.* The first subsection contains three essays on the controversial notion of an *external* world (a world existing independently of how we perceive it and think about it). Can we make sense of the notion of an external world, and if so, do we have reason to believe that there is an external world? Such questions motivate the essays in the first subsection. The *realist* claims that there is an external world; the *anti-realist* claims that there is not, or that we cannot even make sense of the notion of an external world.

In "Yes, Virginia, There is a Real World," William Alston defends realism. He generally characterizes *realism* as the view that "whatever there is, is what it is, regardless of how we think of it." And he identifies this realist notion of truth: "we have said what is true if and only if what we were talking about is as we have said it to be." Alston focuses on this version of realism: our statements are issued with a claim to truth in the realist sense. He contrasts this version with 19th century *idealism* (the view that all reality is somehow mind dependent) and with *pragmatism* (the view that truth consists in usefulness of some sort). And he defends this version of realism against various contemporary anti-realist arguments. Alston claims that we do not yet have a coherent alternative to realism.

In "Why There Isn't a Ready-Made World," Hilary Putnam opposes realism of the sort defended by Alston. Specifically, Putnam opposes the *correspondence notion of truth* typically invoked by the realist (roughly, the notion that truth consists in an objective correspondence relation between the two sides of a world/language duality). One question motivating Putnam's opposition is: "How can we pick out any *one* correspondence between our words (or thoughts) and the supposed mind-independent things if we have no direct access to the mind-independent things?" Putnam argues that an act of will or intention will not work, and that the realist faces serious problems if he or she denies that things have essential or intrinsic properties. (See Putnam's essay for the reasons why he thinks this is so.)

Putnam notes that some modern materialists of a realist persuasion have endorsed the existence of intrinsic similarities and dissimilarities between physical objects. Putnam argues that this mixture of *materialism* and *essentialism* is inconsistent. In the end, Putnam rejects essentialism, and endorses a version of pragmatism (or internal realism) that does without a correspondence notion of truth. On Putnam's view, truth is whatever it is ideally rational to believe.

In "Realism vs. Anti-Realism," Nicholas Wolterstorff defends realism against Putnam's attack. Wolterstorff characterizes the realist's correspondence notion of truth as follows: a sentence is true, in a particular use, because what was asserted to be the case by that use is, in fact, the case. He adds that according to the realist, the facts that make our assertions true are (for the most part) independent of human intellectual activity, such as our acts of assertion or conceptualization. Wolterstorff argues that Putnam's alternative to such realism generates a vicious regress of *truth-ascertainings* (or our affirmations) since what determines the truth of a belief, on Putnam's view, is never its content's being a fact, but rather is its being rationally held. Wolterstorff also points out that a basic issue in the debate between the realist and the anti-realist is whether our concepts are (a) graspings of actual properties in the world or, as the anti-realist suggests, (b) simply rules that we follow to introduce certain divisions into reality. Wolterstorff endorses option (a), an option rejected by Putnam and other anti-realists.

The second subsection of Part I focuses on *scientific realism*. A general statement of scientific realism is that the natural sciences give us a true account of reality. Scientific realism implies that the entities postulated by the natural sciences really exist. If scientific realism is true, we should look to the natural sciences for a correct account of what there is.

In "The Scope and Language of Science," W. V. Quine endorses a version of scientific realism. Quine claims that "we cannot significantly question the reality of the external world or deny that there is evidence of external objects in the testimony of our senses; for, to do so is simply to dissociate the terms 'reality' and 'evidence' from the very applications which originally did most to invest those terms with whatever intelligibility they may have for us."

Quine's outlook is explicitly empiricist: our knowledge of the external world derives solely from sensory stimulations. Quine claims that natural science has the task of "specifying how reality 'really' is." He identifies this task with that of "delineating the structure of reality as distinct from the structure of one or another traditional language. . . ." Quine also argues that natural science is an extension of common sense. He claims that the layman and the scientist share the same general sort of evidence (i.e., sensory stimulation), but that the scientist is more careful with his or her use of such evidence. Another aim of Quine's essay is to characterize the sorts of existence claims (i.e., the *ontology*) common to the natural sciences, and to explain how our common, often mentalistic, idioms relate to the physicalist ontology of the natural sciences.

In "Arguments Concerning Scientific Realism," Bas van Fraassen contrasts scientific realism with *constructive empiricism* (the view that "science aims to give us theories which are empirically adequate, and acceptance of a theory involves a belief only that it is empirically adequate"). Van Fraassen endorses constructive empiricism and rejects the view that science aims at literally true accounts of the external world.

He argues that the traditional observation/theory distinction in the philosophy of science has no ontological significance on the ground that the term *observable* classifies putative entities, and does not imply *actually exists*. The underlying assumption seems to be that even observation is not theory-neutral. On van Fraassen's view, "to accept a theory is (for us) to believe that it is empirically adequate—that what the theory says about what is observable (by us) is true." Van Fraassen defends his anti-realism against several influential arguments claiming that the principles of rational inference in the natural sciences require scientific realism. He also opposes the argument that only scientific realism can adequately explain the success of the natural sciences.

In "Scientific Realism vs. Constructive Empiricism: A Dialogue," Gary Gutting constructs an exchange between the scientific realist and the anti-realist of van Fraassen's stripe. At one point in the exchange, the scientific realist claims that if we have good reasons to believe that atomic theory is needed to explain certain observable data, we have good reasons to believe that atoms exist. This is, in effect, an inference from the explanatory necessity of a theory to the existence of the theory's posited entities. The anti-realist questions such an inference. He claims that the only role for theoretical postulation is the improved description *of observable phenomena*.

On the anti-realist view, the truth of claims involving postulated entities is quite irrelevant. What is all important is a theory's ability to account for observable phenomena. Here, the exchange turns to the alleged need for scientific realism in order to explain the success of science. The anti-realist claims that we do not need to appeal to truth to explain this success; he claims that an appeal to empirical adequacy will do the job. This leads the scientific realist to argue that the anti-realist presupposes a sharp epistemic distinction between the observable and the unobservable.

This argument moves the exchange to a discussion of observability, and of whether the anti-realist assumes that mere observability is relevant to our beliefs about what exists. The exchange does not resolve the disagreement between the realist and the anti-realist, but it clearly identifies some of the key underlying assumptions.

Realism versus Anti-Realism

Yes, Virginia, There is a Real World*

William P. Alston

My topic this evening is realism, which I come not to bury but to praise. More specifically, I shall be casting a critical eye on some recent divagations from the straight and narrow path of realism, and I shall be considering whether these tempting byways do really exist. My contention shall be that there is, in truth, but the one path through the forest, and that what have been taken as alternative routes, are but insubstantial phantoms.

I

But first I must explain what view this is that will be so earnestly commended. Many a position wears the name of "realism", and with most of them I shall not be concerned.

As a first shot, let's say that Realism is here being understood as the view that whatever there is is what it is regardless of how we think of it. Even if there were no

human thought, even if there were no human beings, whatever there is other than human thought (and what depends on that, causally or logically) would still be just what it actually is.

As just stated the position is quite compatible with there being nothing except human thought and what depends on that. So watery a potion is unsuitable for this high occasion. Let's turn it into wine by a codicil to the effect that there is something independent of human thought.

Realism, so stated, is a bit hard to get hold of. It will prove useful to concentrate instead on a certain consequence around which many of the historic battles have raged. If there is a reality independent of our thought it obviously behooves us to find out as much about it as possible. This means that our thought and discourse will be (largely) directed to thinking (saying) it like it is. Believing (saying) what is true rather than what is false will be the primary goal of cognition; *where we have said what is true iff what we were talking about is as we have said it to be.*[1] I shall call this the realistic conception of truth, and where 'true' and its cognates are used in the sequel without further qualification this is the intended meaning. So the consequence in question is: *The primary goal of human thought and discourse is to believe (say) what is true in the realistic sense.* Although this is the full statement of the consequence, I shall be working with a somewhat less inflated form:

Our statements are issued with a (realistic) truth claim (a claim to truth in the realist sense).

I agree with Hilary Putnam[2] that a distinguishing feature of the realistic sense of 'true' is that it is logically possible for even the best attested statement to be false, where the attestation is in terms of "internal" criteria like coherence with the total system of beliefs, being self-evident, being a report of current experience, or being the best explanation of something or other. That is what is "realistic" about this concept of truth. In the final analysis what makes our statement true or false is the way things are (the things the statement is about); not the reasons, evidence, or justification we have for it.

Our thesis is marked by exemplary modesty. It only requires that we hold our statements subject to assessment in terms of truth and falsity. A bolder thesis would be that we sometimes succeed in making statements that are true rather than false. I shall not be so rash this evening; it will not be necessary, since the issues I will be considering concern the viability of the realistic *concept* of truth and its attempted substitutes. Therefore it will be sufficient to consider whether we can, and whether we must, make statements with that kind of claim.

But even within this ambit we can distinguish more and less modest claims. Let me illustrate this point with respect to singular subject-predicate statements. Suppose I assert that this cup is empty. According to the above formulation of the realist thesis, that statement is true or false, depending on whether what the statement is about is as it is said to be. That formulation *presupposes* that I have succeeded at least to the extent of picking out a particular referent about which to make a statement. But even if I had

failed in that referential task (there is nothing that I would be prepared to recognize as what I was saying to be empty), I would still be saying something intelligible that could be assessed for its success in "saying it like it is". There is, notoriously, controversy over whether, in that case, I said anything that could be evaluated as true or false. Be that as it may, a realistic thesis more modest than ours could be formulated as follows: a statement is put forward with the claim that what it is about, if there is anything it is about, is as it is said to be. I shall not carry modesty to those lengths in this paper; I shall be rash enough to assume that we often do succeed in making a statement about something. If anyone feels that this unfairly begs an important question against the antirealist, he may substitute the more guarded formulation without disrupting the ensuing discussion.

Here are a few additional exegetical notes.

(1) I have presented the thesis in terms both of thought and discourse (beliefs and statements). To sharpen the focus I shall henceforward restrict the discussion to statements. I do this not because I consider statement more fundamental than belief; my bent is the opposite one. It is rather that statements are more "out in the open" and, hence, the structure is more readily identified and denominated.

(2) My formulation is limited to statements that can be said to be about something(s). This will take in a wider territory than is sometimes supposed, e.g., not only singular statements but also universal and existential generalizations if we can think of the latter as being "about" all the values of the variables. Other kinds of statements, e.g., subjunctive conditionals, will be harder to fit into this model. But enough statements clearly do fit to give our discussion a point.

(3) Whether my version of realism boils down to a "correspondence" theory of truth depends on how that term is construed. If correspondence theory of truth merely holds that the truth-value of a statement depends on how it is with what the statement

is about, rather than on, e.g., its relations to other statements, then of course this is a (the) correspondence theory. But that term is often reserved for theories that take truth to consist in some structural isomorphism, or mirroring or picturing relation between statements (propositions) and facts. Nothing of that sort is implied by my thesis.

(4) In espousing realism in this fundamental sense I am not committed to acknowledging the independent reality of any particular kinds of entities—material substances, numbers, classes, properties, facts, propositions, quanta, angels, or whatever. The thesis is quite neutral as to what is real; it merely holds that our attempts at knowledge are to be evaluated in terms of whether we succeed in picking out something(s) real and saying them to be as they are. Thus it is not tied to most of the views called "realism"—"Platonic" realism about abstract objects, perceptual realism about common-sense physical objects, "scientific" realism about theoretical entities, and so on. These are all much more specific doctrines than the one being defended here.

Because of this my thesis is not necessarily opposed to many of the positions with which realism is commonly contrasted—idealism (in most uses of that term), phenomenalism, verificationism, even conventionalism as applied to some restricted domain, such as scientific theories. If idealism is the view that reality is basically mental or spiritual in character, whether this be a Berkeliean, Leibnizian, or Hegelian[3] version of that thesis, then idealism allows particular statements (about spirits, monads, the Absolute, or whatever) to be true or false in a realistic sense. If you're attributing to the Absolute characteristics it really has you are speaking truly; if not, not.

I note in this connection that in the March, 1979 issue of *The Journal of Philosophy* an excellent article by Colin McGinn, entitled "An A Priori Argument for Realism" begins with the sentence:

Except in the vulgar sense, one is not a realist *tout court;* one is a realist with respect to some or other type of subject matter—or better, with respect to particular classes of statements.

As Thomas Reid said, in connection with Hume's contrast between the vulgar and the philosophical opinions concerning the immediate objects of perception, "In this division, to my great humiliation, I find myself classed with the vulgar".

Realism, as I have defined it, may seem to the uninitiated to be so minimal as to be trivially true. But notoriously even so minimal a doctrine as this has been repeatedly denied; and the denials supported by elaborate and ingenious argumentation. Nineteenth-century idealism and pragmatism were in good part devoted to attacking realism and searching for an alternative. Thus F. H. Bradley tells us that truth is "that which satisfies the intellect"[4], "an ideal expression of the Universe, at once coherent and comprehensive"[5] and Brand Blanshard that a proposition is true if it coheres with an all comprehensive and fully articulated whole.[6] From the pragmatist side, C. S. Peirce's well known view is that "the opinion which is fated to be ultimately agreed to by all who investigate, is what we mean by the truth",[7] while William James writes that "true ideas are those that we can assimilate, validate, corroborate, and verify".[8] John Dewey holds true ideas to be those that are instrumental to "an active reorganization of the given environment, a removal of some specific trouble and perplexity . . ."[9] Such philosophers would make the truth of the statement that snow is white to consist in something other than snow's *being* white. More recently Hilary Putnam, who for years had been presenting a highly visible target to the anti-realist, has now been kind enough to turn the other cheek and present an equally prominent target to the realist. In his recent Presidential Address to the Eastern Division,[10] he argues that it is incoherent to suppose that a theory that satisfies all epistemic criteria might be false.

After having dominated the field for some time the idealist and pragmatist movements provoked a vigorous realist reaction in the late nineteenth and early twentieth century in the redoubtable persons of Frege, Husserl, Moore, and Russell. It is not my intention this evening to do an instant replay of these epic battles, even though it might result in changing some earlier calls by the arbiters of philosophic fashion. Rather I shall look at some recent anti-realist tendencies. Though these are by no means unconnected with their distinguished precedents, they also present some apparently new features.

My procedure will be as follows. First, I shall look at some anti-realist arguments, or trends of thought, and find them lacking in merit. Second, I shall consider some attempts to work out a nonrealist position, and conclude that no coherent alternative has been provided. At that point the defense will rest.

II

A

Under the first rubric I will begin by taking a very brief look at the Quinean theses of indeterminacy of translation and inscrutability of reference. I have no time to enter the formidable thickets of Quinean exegesis, and so I refrain from asking whether Quine is a realist, or whether Quine himself takes these theses to have an anti-realist thrust. But they have frequently been so taken, a tendency encouraged by Quine's use of the label "Ontological Relativism". Just what bearing do these celebrated doctrines have on the matter? It seems to me somewhat less direct than ordinarily supposed. They don't exactly contradict realism; rather they strike at a presupposition of the question for which realism is one possible answer. They make, or seem to make, it impossible to raise the question. What indeterminacy of translation and inscrutability of reference most directly imply is that our thought and discourse is irremediably indeterminate in a thoroughgoing and shocking fashion. To wit, there is no particular determinate content to any assertion. Because of the indeter-

minacy of translation there are indefinitely many versions of what it is I am saying about an object in any assertion I make. And because of inscrutability of reference there are indefinitely many versions of what I would be saying it about if there were any particular thing I were saying. Viewed in a larger context, this is simply an extreme version of forms of indeterminacy that have long been recognized as affecting much of our speech. It is uncontroversial that people frequently use words in an ambiguous or confused manner, so that there is no precise answer to the question: "What is he saying?". And again it is uncontroversial that there are breakdowns in reference in which it is in principle indeterminate to what the speaker meant to be referring. Quine is simply holding, with what justice I shall not inquire, that such indeterminacies ineluctably affect all speech. Now it has long been recognized by realists that a statement will have a definite truth-value only to the extent that it has a definite content. If I am not saying anything definite it will be correspondingly indefinite whether what I say is true or false. If, e.g., the meaning of 'religion' does not involve precise necessary and sufficient conditions for something's being a religion then there is no definite answer to the question whether the Ethical Culture movement is a religion. Since the Quinean doctrines under consideration imply that all our utterances are in this condition, they imply that the issue of realism cannot arise anywhere in human discourse. Anti-realism goes down the drain along with realism. For the remainder of this section I shall concentrate on arguments that have been thought to support an anti-realist answer to the question to which realism is another answer.

B

Next let's take a brief look at some echoes of Nineteenth Century Idealism—the attack on the "Given". This familiar theme of Hegelianism and Pragmatism has reappeared in partially novel garb in the work of Quine, Sellars, and others. As in the previous century, it is denied that there are any fixed immutable certainties, any statements totally immune to revision or rejection, any points at which an objective fact itself is directly given to us, so that all we need to is to note it. Since it is assumed, wrongly in my opinion, that unless a statement satisfies these descriptions it cannot be justified save by its support from other statements, these denials issue in some form of a coherence or contextualist epistemology. Insofar as there is novelty in the recent attack on fixed, isolated, intuitive certainties, it comes from the "linguistic turn", e.g., the resting of epistemic status on conditions of assertability in a language community.

So far this is epistemology. What does it have to do with truth and reality? Not all the recent opponents of the given have followed their idealist and pragmatist forebears in rejecting a realist conception of truth. The story of where Sellars, e.g., stands on this matter is too complex to be gone into here. But at least one contemporary thinker has drawn antirealist morals from this epistemology. In his recent book, *Philosophy and the Mirror of Nature* (Princeton University Press, 1979), Richard Rorty writes:

> Shall we take . . . "S knows non-inferentially that *p*" . . . as a remark about the status of S's reports among his peers, or shall we take it as a remark about the relation between nature and its mirror?[11] The first alternative leads to a pragmatic view of truth . . . (on) the second alternative . . . truth is something more than what Dewey called "warranted assertability": more than what our peers will, *ceteris paribus*, let us get away with saying . . . To choose between these approaches is to choose between truth as "what it is good for us to believe" and truth as "contact with reality".

Why should we suppose realism to depend on the existence of fixed intuitive certainties? Perhaps the argument goes like this. If we are to have any reason for supposing that any of our statements are realistically true, there must be some points at which we have direct access to the way things are in themselves. If some objective states of affairs are directly presented to consciousness, so that here we have the fact itself and not just our own "interpretation", then at those points at least, we can tell whether a statement is telling it like it is. But if we never enjoy any such intuitive apprehensions of objective reality, how could we ever tell whether any statement is or is not in accord with the facts. And if it is in principle impossible to determine this, it is idle, meaningless, or empty, to claim such an accord or to wonder whether it obtains.

This argument is in two stages. (1) Without fixed intuitive certainties we have no way of telling whether any statement is realistically true. (2) Hence it is unintelligible, or otherwise out of order, to employ this dimension of evaluation. Both steps seem to me unwarranted.

The first stage is, at best, question begging. The basic issue here is the status and evaluation of epistemic principles. The argument obviously assumes that a valid (reasonable, justified) set of epistemic principles might be such that a statement could satisfy sufficient conditions for acceptability without our having any reason to think it realistically true. But that is just what a realist would deny. From a realist point of view, epistemic justification is intimately connected with truth; not necessarily so closely connected that justification entails truth, but at least so closely connected that justification entails a considerable probability of truth. An epistemic principle that laid down sufficient conditions of justification such that we could know that a statement satisfied them while having no reason to think it true, would *ipso facto* be unacceptable.

Another way of putting this last point. This first stage of the argument is one form of the old contention that "we can't get outside our thought and experience to compare it with reality". Therefore we had better renounce any ambition to make our thought conform to "reality" and concentrate instead on tidying up its internal structure. But from a realist point of view this picture of being trapped inside our own thought, unable to get a glimpse of what it is like outside, is radically misleading—even if we do lack fixed intuitive certainties. For whenever we have knowledge, that is *ipso facto* a case of getting a glimpse of the reality "outside". However we get this knowledge, it wouldn't be knowledge unless the belief in question were conformed to its referent(s).[12] It is unfortunate picture-thinking to suppose that only some specially direct or intuitive knowledge constitutes finding out what something is really like.

The second stage of the argument is plain unvarnished verificationism. If there is no way of telling whether a given statement is realistically true, then we can attach no sense (or, if you prefer, no cognitive or factual meaning) to the supposition that it is true. It would be pleasant to suppose that verificationism is now in such ill repute that to tar the argument with this brush would be condemnation enow. But, alas, such is not the case. The verificationist criterion has conclusively and repeatedly been found wanting; but perhaps excessive attention to technical details has obscured the basic point of these criticisms. If the underlying causes of the disease are not clearly identified, relapses are to be expected. The basic point is simply this. Except for such statements as are directly testable, no statement can be empirically tested in isolation. We must conjoin it with other statements if we are to derive any directly testable consequences. And for any sentence, no matter how meaningless, we can find some set of sentences that together with the former will yield observation sentences not derivable from that set alone. Thus the capacity of a sentence to contribute to the generation of directly testable consequences completely fails to discriminate between the meaningful and the meaningless. We do, of course, make distinctions between those sentences that do, and those that do not, enter *fruitfully* into empirically testable systems, though it is either very difficult or impossible to formulate precise criteria for this. But this distinction also fails to coincide with the distinction between meaningful and meaningless, as is shown by the fact that one and the same statement, e.g., "Matter is composed of tiny indivisible particles", will enter into such combinations fruitfully at one period but not at another.[13]

C

Rorty's argument can be generally characterized as moving from epistemology to ontology, from considerations concerning the epistemic status of statements to conclusions concerning their capacity to "reveal" reality. I now want to consider some further arguments of this general sort, which differ from the argument just discussed in being of a relativistic character. Although Rorty's argument depends on rejecting classical foundationalism, it does not question (1) the existence of a single set of epistemological principles that (2) yield a unique result in each individual instance. The two lines of thought I shall now consider each deny one of these assumptions.

The first assumption is rejected by, e.g., the language-game approach that stems from the later work of Wittgenstein and is found full-blown in Peter Winch and D. Z. Phillips. Here the idea is that there are radically different criteria of justification and rationality for different spheres of discourse—common sense-talk about the physical environment, talk about personal agents, moral discourse, religious discourse, scientific theorizing, reports of dreams, experiential reports, etc. Observation is crucial for physical-object talk, the authority of sacred books and holy persons for religious discourse, and the sincere asseveration of the subject for reports of experience. It is a piece of outrageous imperialism to suppose that any single requirements for justification applies across the board.

What bearing is this supposed to have on realism? Well, first there is a straight verificationist argument from the fact that different language games have different criteria of truth to the conclusion that they employ different concepts of truth. This argument pre-supposes a stronger form of verificationism. Rorty's argument only required us to suppose that being empirically testable is a necessary condition of meaning-fulness for sentences. But here we need the additional assumption that the mode of verification constitutes the meaning. We need this stronger thesis if we are to infer a difference in the meaning of 'true' in different language-games from differences in the *way* of verifying truth-ascriptions in different language-games. This stronger verificationist thesis can hardly be in a more favorable position than the weaker one, since it entails the latter.

The language-game approach also generates arguments of a more distinctive sort, though I cannot see that they fare any better.

(1) The irreducible plurality of language-games militates against the realist position in another way. The ontologies of different language-games do not all fit into any single scheme. There is no place in physical space for minds, sense-data, or God. Agency cannot be located in the interstices of the physiological causal network. Nor is there any overarching neutral position from which particular language-games can be criticized and their subject-matters integrated into a single framework. Therefore it seems quite unjustified to suppose that the success of a statement in some particular language-game depends on whether it conforms to the constitution of something called "reality".

This argument also depends on verificationism. It argues from our inability to see whether, or how, different sorts of entities fit into one scheme, to the unintelligibility of supposing that they do. But, more basically, the argument suffers from a naively simplistic conception of reality. Why suppose that reality, if there be such, must fall into some single pattern? Why shouldn't reality be as many-mansioned as you like? Why should there not be even more kinds of entities in heaven and earth than are dreamt of in our language-games? And if there is some significant degree of unity to it all, why should we expect to be able to discern it? Even if we can't integrate agency and physical causation in a single "space", they may, for all that, be what they are apart from our attempts to conceptualize them. The argu-ment suffers from a grievous lack of ontological imagination.

(2) We find in the writings of Sprachspielists, as well as in their historical relativist forebears, the insistence that *our* concepts of truth and reality are rooted in *our* forms of life, *our* practices—linguistic and non-linguistic. From this the inference is drawn that truth cannot consist in conformity to the way things are "outside" our thought and practice. But this is just the old question-begging argument that we "can't get outside our own thought and experience to compare it with reality". Of course when we use the term 'true' or any other term we are using *our* language, if we know what we are talking about. Who else's language might we be using? (I could have been speaking French or Bantu instead, but that is presumably not to the point.) But this has absolutely no implications for the *content* of what I am saying, nor for the ways in which it is properly evaluated. The fact that when I say anything I am using the language I am using, which is rooted in the social practices it is rooted in, is a miserable truism that has no bearing on our problem. It leaves completely open the question of whether, in saying what I say, I am claiming to refer to something that exists independent of our discourse, and whether this is an intelligible or reasonable claim to make.[14]

D

Although Sprachspielism is relativistic in the sense that it takes any particular cognitive success to be relative to some particular language-game, it is not so relativistic as to suppose that different language-games yield mutually incompatible results. On the contrary, it considers different language-games to be too different to be in competition for the same prize. We now turn to a more extreme relativism, which denies the second of the assumptions listed earlier—that our epistemological principles yield a unique result in each application.

This line of thought has taken many forms from the ancient Greek sophists to the present. Its most prominent recent incarnation is in the work of Feyerabend and Kuhn. Here is a highly over-simplified version. In the development of a science we have a succession of "theoretical (or conceptual) frameworks" or "paradigms". Each of these paradigms is self-enclosed in something like the way Winch and Phillips think of a language-game as being self-enclosed. The constituent terms get their meanings by their place in the framework; observations are conceptualized and reported in these terms; and hypotheses are evaluated in terms of how well they explain data so construed, and in terms of how well they solve the problems generated by that paradigm. Hence we are unable to choose between rival theoretical frameworks in terms of one or another contestant.

The position is usually not held in so extreme a form, but I wanted to present it as such so as to see what bearing it would have on realism. The obvious argument is this. All our conclusions are relative to the assumptions and conceptual framework of a given paradigm, which has indefinitely many alternatives. Therefore we can never have reason to think that any of our conclusions are in conformity with reality itself. Hence the realist notion of truth is inapplicable to our discourse. Clearly this is but another rerun of the same old verificationist argument. And again the same comments are applicable.

These, I take it, are the epistemological arguments against realism that are most prominent on the current scene. I have not contested their epistemological premises, though I do not accept them in every case, but instead have concentrated on showing that even with these premises the arguments are far from cogent.

E

Finally, there is the direct application of verificationism to the crucial implication of realism mentioned above, viz., that however well confirmed, justified, or rationally acceptable a statement may be, it is logically possible that it be false. The argument is very simple. We have, *ex hypothesi*, ruled out any possible reason for supposing the statement false. Therefore we cannot attach any meaning to the denial that it is true. This is clearly not just an argument against realism, but also an argument for the equation of 'true' and 'justified' (or 'could be justified'), or at least for the substitution of the latter for the former. In only slightly different garb it is the main argument of Peirce, James, and Dewey for their several pragmatic conceptions of truth. It is given a fancy logical dress in Hilary Putnam's recent Presidential address to the Eastern Division, but the verificationist underpinning is the same in all its versions. And about this enough has been said.

I conclude from this discussion that the recent opponents of realism have failed to shake our common-sense confidence in that doctrine. They have not done significantly better than Hegel, Bradley, James, and Dewey; in fact, their arguments turn out to be warmed over scraps from the idealist, pragmatist and positivist traditions, masked by a few ingenious sauces from La Nouvelle Cuisine.

III

However, on this solemn occasion I am not content with simply shooting down the arguments of opponents. A more fitting aspiration would be to show that there is no coherent alternative to realism. Unfortunately, I can see no way to do this other than by examining all sufficiently promising alternatives. This is, of course, a very large task, and I shall only be able to make a start.

The most obvious move for the anti-realist is to *define* truth in terms of whatever he takes to be the appropriate standards for accepting a statement. A common thread in the arguments we have been considering is the verificationist objection to the idea that there is something involved in a statement's *being* true over and above the grounds we can have for regarding it as true. Such arguments naturally lead to an identification of a statement's being true with there being adequate grounds for taking it to be true (not, of course, with anyone's seeing that there are adequate grounds). Thus the truth of a statement, S, will be identified with S's cohering with the rest of one's beliefs, with S's leading, or having the capacity to lead, to fruitful consequences, with S's satisfying the standards of the particular language-game in which it is a move, with S's being one of the survivors at the ideal limit of scientific inquiry, or whatever.[15]

Instead of proposing a non-realist analysis of 'true' the anti-realist may instead (more candidly, in my view) propose that we abandon the concept of truth and talk instead of justification, confirmation, or verification. Thus Dewey once advocated dropping 'true' in favor of 'warrantedly assertable'. It will be easier to focus the discussion if I stick with the version in which some non-realist analysis of 'true' is given.

As is implicit in the list just given, these non-realist theories differ along various dimensions. They may be atomistic or holistic; i.e., they may attach justification conditions to individual statements or only to larger systems; in the latter case what it is for a particular statement to be true is to belong to a system that, as a whole, satisfies certain constraints. Again, they may seek to give a single account of justification for *all* statements, like the traditional coherence theories, or they may hold, like Sprachspielism, that different accounts are to be given for different realms of discourse. The question I want to explore is whether *any* verificationist account of truth can be intelligibly and coherently spelled out (while not completely losing touch with its subject matter), without involving or presupposing the realist concept of truth.

A

The first place a realist will look for a chink in the armor is the status of the higher-level epistemic judgments like S_1—'S would be included in the ultimate scientific theory'.[16] Isn't Peirce implicitly thinking of this as true in the realist sense? In asserting S, isn't he thinking that it is really the case that if scientific inquiry were pushed to the limit S would still be there? If so, we have

extruded (real) truth from first-level statements, only to have it reappear on a second-level.[17] But suppose that Peirce retorts that he is prepared to treat these second-level statements in the same way, i.e., hold their truth to consist in their membership in the ultimate scientific theory. In that case he will be faced with an infinite regress. For this will set up a still higher-level statement—S_2:'S_1 would be included in the ultimate scientific theory'. And if that in turn is treated in the same way. . . .

I am uncertain as to the force of this realist criticism. It is unclear to me whether this regress is any more vicious than a variety of other infinite regresses with which we are saddled anyway, e.g., the regress of truth levels, or the regress of levels of justification. Hence I will pass on to difficulties that seem to me to be clearly fatal.

B

The real crusher for the anti-realist is the question "How are we to interpret the statements to which you apply your concept of truth?" What is crushing about this question? Well, the point is that on a natural, intuitive way of understanding statement content [of specifying what is being asserted in a given statement], that content carries with it the applicability of the realist concept of truth. Let's continue to restrict the discussion to those statements that can plausibly be thought of as being "about something(s)". For such a statement, the natural way of specifying content, of making explicit what statement it is, is to specify the referent(s), and to make explicit what is being asserted of that referent(s). But if that is what makes the statement the statement it is, then there is no alternative to supposing that the statement is true *iff* the referent(s) is as it is being said to be. If what I did in a certain utterance was to refer to snow and say of it that it is white, what alternative is there to holding that my statement is true *iff* snow is white?[18] You can't in one and the same breath construe the statement as a commitment to X's being φ, and also deny that the statement is true *iff* X is φ. To understand statement content in this familiar way *is* to subject it to realistic truth conditions. It is incoherent to say "What I asserted was that snow is white (or what I did in my assertion was to refer to snow and say of it that it is white), but the truth of my assertion does not ride on whether snow *is* white". This is to take away with one hand what was offered with the other. The realistic concept of truth is indissolubly bound up with this familiar way of specifying statement content.[19] If I am correct in this, the anti-realist will have to provide some other way of specifying *what* is being asserted—other than "The speaker referred to snow and said of it that it is white."

If we ask whether anti-realists have recognized the necessity for an alternative reading, the picture appears to be a mixed one. I believe that idealists in the Hegelian tradition have generally been alive to the issue. Consider Bradley's view of the nature of judgment, as involving a separation of the 'that' and the 'what', and a vain attempt to reunite them in the forms of predication, together with the view that the essential aim of thought is to produce a comprehensive, coherent totality that would be identical with reality. This is an attempt to give an account of what we are up to in statement making that is fundamentally different from the familiar account and that is in harmony with a coherence account of the nature of truth. Again, we can see Dewey's emphasis on the "instrumental" function of ideas and judgments as the germ of a different kind of alternative account. If what we are up to in statement making is not attempting to tell it like it is with particular referents or classes thereof, but rather providing effective guidance to our active commerce with the environment (allowing, as I would not, that the latter can be separated from the former), then it might be not incoherent to hold that the fundamental dimension of evaluation for statements is their effectiveness in this role. In many cases, however, one is left with the impression that the anti-realist takes individual statements in the same old way, but simply proposes to change the account of what it is for them to be *true*. If the

above argument is correct, this is just what she cannot do.

A thoroughgoing anti anti-realist argument would involve a careful scrutiny of all the noteworthy attempts, actual and possible, to devise a mode of statement interpretation suitable for their purposes. However I fear that an examination of such darkly labyrinthine authors as Bradley and Dewey would be beyond the bounds of this lecture even if we were at the beginning rather than, as I hasten to assure you, in the latter half. Instead, I shall consider some moves that are more in accord with the dominant temper of Anglo-American philosophy of the last half-century, moves that might well tempt anti-realists, and in some cases actually have.

1. The anti-realist may try to turn the above argument back on her opponent in the following manner. "The argument depends on the claim that statemental content is tied to truth conditions. Well and good; two can play at this game. If a realist construal of statements yields realist truth conditions, then non-realist truth conditions can be associated with a corresponding mode of assigning statement-content. If what it takes for a statement, S, to be true is that it belong to the ultimate scientific theory (call that 'T') then we will simply assign to S the content—*S belongs to T.*"

However tempting this may sound in the abstract, as soon as it is stated explicitly it clearly displays its absurdity. How could it be that asserting that *S* is asserting that *S* has some property or other? How could S *be* some higher-level statement about S, i.e., be a higher level statement than itself? How can a statement be a statement about itself, rather than itself?

A contemporary anti-realist like Dummett, or (the most recent) Putnam, would not be moved by this. They would just take it as illustrating the futility of working with *statements* or *propositions* as our basic units, instead of sentences in a language. Of course we can't regard a statement as being a statement about itself, instead of being itself. But we do not find the same absurdity in the suggestion that each of our statements makes a claim about a certain sentence, even the very sentence used to make that statement. Let's follow recent fashion and take a theory to consist of a set of sentences. Then we may formulate the following Peircean view of statement interpretation. When I assertorically utter 'Lead melts at 327 degrees F.', what I am claiming is: "The sentence 'Lead melts at 327 degrees F.' will (would) be included in the final scientific theory, T".[20]

But though this escapes the absurdity of denying that a statement is identical with itself, it suffers the same unhappy fate that befalls other attempts to substitute sentences for beliefs, propositions, or statements. Here, as elsewhere, it turns out that even the closest possible statement about language will fail to have the same force as the original. In this case (passing over the *parochiality* involved in supposing that the *ultimate* scientific theory will consist of English sentences) the difficulty is that whether the sentence in question figures in T depends, *inter alia*, on what that sentence will mean by the time the final consummation is achieved. If the sentence means something different from what it means now, it may not be included, even if T does include a statement to the effect that lead melts at 327 degrees F. Thus on this interpretation, when we assert "Lead melts at 327 degrees F.", we are, in part, making a claim about the future history of the English language. This radically distorts our intent. Sometimes we are talking about language, but most of the time we are not.

Of course, this view may be so construed that our statement has to do not with a mere phonological string (which might receive various semantic interpretations) but with the semantically interpreted sentence 'Lead melts at 327 degrees F.' But that is to throw us back on the absurdities of treating a statement as being about itself. For a semantic interpretation of an assertoric sentence is precisely designated to determine a statement content; it specifies *what* is asserted when the sentence is used assertorically. Therefore this latest proposal amounts to assigning two different contents to the statement:—the one determined by the presupposed semantic interpretation, and the one built on that—to the effect that the sentence used to express the first content will be in T. Again we lapse into incoherence.

2. The moral of this story is that we can't identify a statement with a statement about *itself*, whether about its epistemic status or about the sentence used to make it. But the diagnosis suggests a simple remedy. Why not take S to be, not the statement that S satisfies certain epistemic conditions, but rather the statement of those conditions themselves? For each statement, S, we will choose conditions the satisfaction of which will guarantee that the statement has the desired epistemic status; but we will construe S not as the statement that S has that status, but rather as the affirmation of those conditions.

It would seem that this kind of first-level interpretation is not available for holistic theories that identify the truth of S with the way it fits into some system—[the final scientific theory, the most coherent and comprehensive theory of truth, or the ongoing enterprise of coping with the environment.] Here a blanket statement that makes reference to S (to the way S fits into some system) is all we have to work with. But an empirical verifiability theory of truth looks more promising. If we can specify conditions under which S would be verified, why not identify what is stated by S with the satisfaction of those conditions?

Interpretations like this were prominent in twentieth-century phenomenalism and in early logical positivism. ("The meaning of a statement is its method of verification.")[21] And recently Michael Dummett has suggested the possibility of replacing (realist) truth-conditions with "verification-conditions" in giving a semantic description of a language. Let's use as our example an oversimplified statement of C. I. Lewis' version of phenomenalism.[22] A singular attribution of a property to a physical object, like 'This container is made of glass', is to be construed as the assertion of an indefinitely large conjunction of subjunctive conditionals like the following:

1. If I were to seem to dash this container to the floor, I would seem to see the container shattering.
2. If I were to seem to thump this container with my finger, I would hear a certain kind of ringing sound.

Each of these "terminating judgments" is supposed to have the virtue of being decisively verified or falsified by "sensory presentations". And the verification of the whole set would *be* the verification of the original statement, since they are one and the same.[23]

It has been frequently argued, and, I think, to good effect, that projects like Lewis' cannot be carried out, that no purely phenomenalistic statement is equivalent to any physical-object statement. I don't want to get into all of that. I merely want to ask whether, assuming that some such project can be carried through, it enables us to avoid the realistic concept of truth. And here I am not asking whether the concept of verification can be cut loose from dependence on the concept of truth, as it would have to be if it is to be used in an analysis of truth. Clearly the ordinary meaning of 'verify' is simply—*show (ascertain) to be true.* But this is not to the present point, since the second-level concept of verification does not enter into the proposed interpretation of first-level statements like *This container is made of paper.*

The crucial point, rather, is this. Let's say that S is taken to be the assertion that p,q, . . . , where these are verifying conditions, whether stated in Lewis' way or in some other. We have given a propositional content to S that differs from the familiar one. But in giving it this new content, are we not thereby committed to realistic truth conditions for that content as firmly as we were with the earlier one? Instead of simply attributing a property to the object referred to by 'this container', we are asserting a number of contingencies in sense experience. But with respect to each of those contingencies are we not asserting that it in fact

obtains—that if I were to seem to dash this container to the floor it would seem to break? But if so, then again I am saying something that is true *iff* that consequence would result from that activity.[24] Once more I cannot both be making that claim and denying that whether the claim is true rides on whether things would come out that way under those conditions. In fact, this is the way in which the matter has been viewed by most phenomenalists and other verificationists. They were far from wanting to jettison the realistic concept of truth. They simply wanted to put restrictions on what sorts of statements are susceptible of (realistic) truth and falsity.

One might think that the failure to slough off realistic truth-conditions comes from making the verificationist interpretation match the original too closely. By insisting on conditions of conclusive verification, we have guaranteed that the translation says just the same as the original, and that is why we wind up with realistic truth-claims after all. This suggests that we should follow the pilgrimage of logical positivism from conclusive verification to "confirmation". Perhaps we should interpret our statements in terms of what would provide (more or less strong) confirmation, rather than in terms of what would conclusively verify. But this suggestion is even more incoherent than its predecessor. We cannot judge a certain condition to be merely providing some evidence for S, rather than conclusively verifying it, except against the background of a conception of what would render S *true,* or, if you like, of what would conclusively verify S. Why do we suppose that determining that X is malleable is only some evidence for X's being gold, but does not conclusively establish that it is gold? Because we have enough of an idea of what it is for X to *be* gold to see that it is possible for something to be malleable and yet not be gold.

Contrariwise, if we simply take some "confirmation condition" as giving the content of a statement, then it follows that we can't be taking it to be merely non-conclusively confirming. If what I am asserting when I utter 'X is gold' is that X is malleable, then it cannot be denied that the malleability of X makes my assertion true. A set of conditions cannot be merely confirming evidence, and also constitute the content of what was said.

Nor will it be more efficacious to construe our interpretation as made up of conditions of "acceptance". Again, if we mean to contrast conditions of acceptance with conditions of truth or verification, we still have the latter in the background; we have neither eliminated them, nor dissolved their tie with statement content. If, on the other hand, we are serious in taking our so-called "conditions of acceptance" to specify statement content, we are thereby precluded from regarding them as conditions of acceptance rather than of truth.

Thus these verificationist moves are to no avail. When we identify statement-content in terms of test, verification, or confirmation conditions, we do not evade realistic truth conditions; rather we introduce certain restrictions on what can be asserted, thereby generating parallel restrictions on what it takes to make statements true. When all the smoke has cleared it is still a matter of what is talked about being as it is said to be.

The language-game, and other relativistic approaches such as Quine's "ontological relativism", may *seem* to provide a different way out. Instead of trying to get away from interpreting statements in terms of the familiar machinery of reference, predication, and truth, we simply hang onto all that, but regard it, in each instance, as relative to a certain language-game (paradigm, scheme of translation). In a normal utterance of 'snow is white', we are, indeed, referring to snow and predicating whiteness of it; and so what we say is true *iff* snow is white. But this is all relative to the "commonsense physical world language-game". We can only pick out a referent, identify a property predicated, and adjudge truth, by the standards internal to that language-game. There is no way in which we can raise the question, absolutely, as to what is referred to in that statement, or as to the conditions under which it is true. All such semantic notions exist only in relativized forms. When we try to drop the qualification the concept dissolves.

But what does it mean to say that 'snow is white' is true *in the commonsense physical world language-game,* rather than just true *tout court?*

(1) There is an innocuous interpretation according to which it is in L that S is true, because L is where S is. That is, S is constructed from the conceptual resources of L; that statement-content emerges from the conceptual practice. Clearly on this interpretation 'S is true in L' will be true for some L, for any true statement, S, assuming that every statement can be assigned to at least one language-game. But this is innocuous because the relativity does not affect the notion of truth. On this reading 'S is true in L' is just a conjunction of 'S is in L' and 'S is true (*tout court*)'.

(2) It could mean—we're just pretending, rather than claiming that S is *really* true, as in 'It is true that Bunter is Lord Peter's butler in Dorothy Sayers' mysteries.' But presumably this is not what is intended, for this reading depends on a contrast with "really true" (absolutely). Not to mention the fact that a Sprachspielist would not be prepared to assimilate all language-games to fiction.

(3) What is left to us? Only the obvious, straightforward suggestion that 'S is true in L' means—'S passes the tests of L for being true'. But the second occurrence of 'true' has to be taken as employing the *verboten* absolute concept. For if we try to make that occurrence express a relativistic concept of truth in some L, that will require a similar explanation, and an infinite regress looms.

These all too brief considerations indicate that notions like 'true' and 'refers' stubbornly resist relativization. Once admitted, they point inevitably to what there is, whatever webs of thought we weave.

3. The non-realist interpretations that emerge from currently fashionable modes of thought have all backfired. The moral I draw from this cautionary tale is that most non-realists have seriously underestimated the magnitude of their task. They have failed to appreciate how violent a break is required with our customary ways of viewing thought and discourse. They have failed to grasp the central point that if they are to abandon the realistic concept of truth, they must give up thinking of our thought and discourse in terms of reference, and the other semantic notions based on that—saying this or that *of* what is referred to, quantification over what is (or could be) referred to, and so on. They have supposed that they can continue to construe discourse in these terms, while attaching a relativistic rider to these semantic notions, or by substituting some specially tailored propositional content for the more familiar ones. But it just doesn't work. To repeat the main point once more, so long as we think of our utterances as being about something(s), there is no escape from the realistic truth formula. So long as it is correct to say that you are talking about this container, or dogs, or the quality of mercy, then there is no escape from the recognition that what you say is true *iff* what you are talking about is as you say it to be. If, on the other hand, it could be made out that it is a mistake to think of statemental utterances as being *about* anything, then clearly the realistic truth concept does not apply. If there is nothing I am talking about, my utterance can hardly be evaluated in terms of whether what it is about is as I say it to be. If the non-realist is to make her position stick, she will have to find some adequate non-referential account of statemental discourse.

How might this be done. Well, there is the Bradleian idea that the aim of thought is to develop a comprehensive, coherent system of concepts, where this aim is so conceived that if it were fully realized the system would *be* Reality as a whole. Here the relation with reality is not secured by way of reference to particular objects in each judgment (belief, statement), but rather by way of the fact that Reality is what would constitute the complete fulfillment of the aim of thought. Whether this is a radically non-referential conception depends on whether we can understand the incomplete stages of this quest without thinking of ourselves as referring either to the concepts themselves, or to their extensions or instances. A still more radical alternative would be an explicitly non-intentionalistic account of speech as complexly conditioned behavior, as in B. F. Skinner's book, *Verbal Behavior*. Whether *this* is really a radically non-referential account will depend, *inter alia*, on whether the account itself can be an account of speech without itself being about something, viz., speech.

Obviously I can't discuss these putatively non-referential accounts at the tag-end of this paper. I shall have to confine myself to the following remark. Even if doubts of the sort just expressed could be stilled and one or more such accounts could be formulated without embodying or presupposing references at some point, the question would still remain whether reference is being sold at too dear a price. We would have to give up such cherished ideas as that we can pick out objects of various sorts and characterize them, correctly and incorrectly, and that in the course of this enterprise we sometimes communicate information about the world that guides our behavior as well as satisfies our intellectual curiosity. Unless the arguments against realism are considerably stronger than I found them to be earlier in this essay, the game, clearly, is not worth the candle.

IV

Yes, Virginia, there is a real world. Not, or not only, in the hearts and minds of men. Not, or not only, in the language-games we play, in the schemes of translation we devise, or in the epistemic standards we acknowledge. But in that ineluctable, circumambient web of fact to the texture of which we must needs do homage, lest, though we speak with the tongues of men and of angels, and have not truth, our logos is become as sounding symbols or as tinkling paradigms.

NOTES

[1] I take this to be simply a slightly more explicit formulation of the view classically expressed by Aris-

totle in *Metaphysics* (1011b, 27) as ". . . to say of what is that it is, and of what is not that it is not, is true".

[2]See his "Realism and Reason", *Proceedings and Addresses of the American Philosophical Association*, Vol. 50, No. 6, p. 485.

[3]To be sure, Hegel's philosophy as a whole contains elements that are incompatible with realism in my sense. Here I am only concerned with the Hegelian or "absolute" version of the particular thesis that reality is basically spiritual in character.

[4]*Essays on Truth and Reality* (Oxford: Clarendon Press, 1914), p. 1.

[5]Ibid., p. 223.

[6]*The Nature of Thought* (London: George Allen & Unwin Ltd., 1939), Vol. II, p. 264.

[7]"How to Make Our Ideas Clear", in *Collected Papers*, ed. C. Hartshorne & P. Weiss (Cambridge, Mass.: Harvard University Press, 1934), p. 268.

[8]*Pragmatism* (Cambridge, Mass.: Harvard University Press, 1975), p. 97.

[9]*Reconstruction in Philosophy* (New York: Henry Holt & Co., 1920), p. 156.

[10]*Op. cit.*

[11]This last is Rorty's picturesque way of saying, "taking it as involving an immediate awareness that *p*, or as involving the fact that *p*'s being directly presented to consciousness."

[12]Hence the well-advised tendency of some anti-realists to renounce the concept of knowledge for justified belief, or warranted assertability.

[13]In this connection we may note that the verifiability criterion forces us into a caricature of the process of scientific inquiry. Often this involves generating some hypothesis ('Electric current is a flow of tiny particles') and then looking around for some way to test it. Free of verificationist blinders, it seems obvious that this process is guided throughout by our understanding of the hypothesis we do not yet see how to test. (We haven't yet found a promising way of imbedding it in a larger system that will generate directly testable consequences.) But verificationism would have it that what we were doing was looking for a meaning to bestow on a certain sentence! And if that were what we were doing, why should it matter which of indefinitely many empirically respectable meanings we chose?

[14]We might also note that though this argument is found principally in the writings of Sprachspielists, it does not in any way depend on the multiplicity of language-games. These truisms would be equally true if our discourse were restricted to a single language game.

[15]It may be suggested that I should have taken "redundancy" or "disappearance" theories as equally obvious alternatives for the anti-realist. These theories deny that the statement 'It is true that S' has any more "cognitive" or "assertoric" content (makes any further truth claim!) than S. The function of 'It's true' is simply to endorse someone else's statement that S, or to assert that S in a specially emphatic way, or the like. But the relation of the redundancy theory to realism is unclear. It does *look* anti-realist; if we aren't asserting anything (over and above S) in saying 'It's true that S', then we aren't asserting, among other things, that what S is about is as it is said to be in asserting S. Nevertheless the opposition might be only skin deep. If the redundancy theory is merely a view as to how the *word* 'true' or phrases like 'It's true' are used, then it is quite compatible with the view that realism is right about the primary aim of thought, and about the most fundamental dimension of evaluation of statements; the disagreement would only be over whether the word 'true' is properly used to express this.

[16]We might also raise questions about the status of epistemic principles like 'The ultimate scientific theory must satisfy the following constraints . . .'.

[17]This realist rejoinder is reminiscent of a variety of *tu quoque*'s in which one who denies that there are X's is charged with assuming X's himself. Thus the sceptic who denies that anyone knows anything is charged with himself claiming to know something—viz., that no one knows anything. Again, the mechanist or behaviorist who writes books to prove that men are not actuated by purposes, is charged with displaying an example of what he is claiming not to exist. It is generally true in these cases that the denial of X's on a first level is held to involve the admission of X's on a higher level.

[18]The use of the Tarskian paradigm is not inadvertent. Unlike those who see the whole Tarskian treatment of truth as a series of technical gimmicks, I feel that Tarski's criterion of adequacy embodies a fundamental feature of our concept of truth. But I read it somewhat differently from many other admirers. The fact that ' 'S' is true *iff* S' is a conceptual truth is often taken to show that the former doesn't say anything more than the latter, and that truth-talk is eliminable. But in opposition to this reductive reading, I prefer to concentrate on the other direction of equivalence and give it an inflationary reading. That is, the notion of what it takes for the statement to be true is already embodied, implicitly, in the statement-content; in explicitly saying that S is true we are just bringing to light what is already embedded in the first-level statement.

[19]This contention can be rerun for the question "What is it to *understand* a given statement or to know what statement is being made on a given occasion?" For what one has to know to know that, is precisely

what we have been calling statement-content. So again we cannot say: "In order to know what statement P asserted at *t*, what we have to know is that P referred to snow and said of it that it was white; and yet the truth of what P said does not ride on whether snow is white".

[20]Hilary Putnam considers an interpretation like this in the second of his John Locke lectures, *Meaning and the Moral Sciences* (London: Routledge and Kegan Paul, 1978).

[21]To be sure, the mid-twentieth century advocates of this mode of interpretation were not concerned to reject a realist theory of truth, and rightly so, as we shall see. Nevertheless their verificationist brand of statement-interpretation might well appear attractive to an anti-realist who is grappling with the problem currently under consideration.

[22]See his *Analysis of Knowledge and Valuation*, La Salle, IL.: Open Court, 1946, Ch. VIII.

[23]Of course there are many alternative ways of stating verification conditions for statements. They may be stated in terms of what would have to be experienced in order to verify it, or, as with Lewis, in terms of the experiencing of it. On the former alternative the conditions may be phenomenalistic or physicalistic. They may or may not be such as to provide a practicable possibility of complete verification or falsification. And so on.

[24]It must be admitted that conditionals, especially subjunctive conditions, pose special difficulties for the determination of realistic truth conditions. But these are problems that arise for any view that allows conditionals (and how can they be avoided?). It is just that subjunctive conditionals loom much larger on the view under discussion.

Why There Isn't a Ready-Made World*

Hilary Putnam

Two ideas that have become a part of our philosophical culture stand in a certain amount of conflict. One idea, which was revived by Moore and Russell after having been definitely sunk by Kant and Hegel (or so people thought) is metaphysical realism, and the other is that there are no such things as intrinsic or 'essential' properties. Let me begin by saying a word about each.

What the metaphysical realist holds is that we can think and talk about things as they are, independently of our minds, and that we can do this by virtue of a 'correspondence' relation between the terms in our language and some sorts of mind-independent entities. Moore and Russell held the strange view that *sensibilia* (sense data) are such *mind-independent* entities: a view so dotty, on the face of it, that few analytic philosophers like to be reminded that this is how analytic philosophy started. Today material objects are taken to be paradigm mind-independent entities, and the 'correspondence' is taken to be some sort of causal relation. For example, it is

said that what makes it the case that I refer to chairs is that I have causally interacted with them, and that I would not utter the utterances containing the word 'chair' that I do if I did not have causal transactions 'of the appropriate type' with chairs. This complex relationship—being connected with x by a causal chain of the appropriate type—between my word (or way of using the word) and x constitutes the relevant *correspondence* between my word and x. On this view, it is no puzzle that we can refer to physical things, but reference to numbers, sets, moral values, or anything not 'physical' is widely held to be problematical if not actually impossible.

The second doctrine, the doctrine that there are no essential properties, is presaged by Locke's famous rejection of 'substantial forms'. Locke rejected the idea that the terms we use to classify things (e.g., 'man' or 'water') connote properties which are in any sense the 'real essences' of those things. Whereas the medievals thought that the real essence of water was a so-called substantial form, which exists both in the thing and (*minus* the matter) in our minds, Locke argued that what we have in our minds is a number of conventional marks (e.g., being liquid) which we have put together into a descrip-

*Reprinted with the permission of Cambridge University Press, from Putnam, *Realism and Reason* (Philosophical Papers, vol. 3), pp. 205–28. Cambridge: Cambridge University Press, 1983.

tive idea because of certain interests we have, and that any assumption that these marks are the 'real essence' of anything we classify under the idea is unwarranted.

Later empiricists went further and denied there was any place for the notion of an essence at all. Here is a typical way of arguing this case: 'Suppose a piece of clay has been formed into a statue. We are sure the piece of clay would not be what it is (a piece of clay) if it were dissolved, or separated into its chemical elements, or cut into five pieces. We can also say the *statue* would not be what it is (*that* statue) if the clay were squeezed into a ball (or formed into a different statue). But the piece of clay and the statue are *one* thing, not two. What this shows is that it only makes sense to speak of an "essential property" of something *relative to a description*. Relative to the description "that statue", a certain shape is an essential property of the object; relative to the description "that piece of clay", the shape is *not* an essential property (but being clay is). The question "what are the essential properties of the thing *in itself*" is a nonsensical one.

The denial of essences is also a denial of intrinsic structure: an electron in my body has a certain electrical charge, but on the view just described it is a mistake to think that having that charge is an 'intrinsic' property of the object (except *relative to the description* 'electron') in a way in which the property of being a part of my body is not. In short, it is (or was until recently) commonly thought that

A thing is not related to any one of its properties (or relations) any more 'intrinsically' than it is to any of its other properties or relations.

The problem that the believer in metaphysical realism (or 'transcendental realism' as Kant called it) has always faced involves the notion of 'correspondence'. There are many different ways of putting the signs of a language and the things in a set S in correspondence with one another, in fact infinitely many if the set S is infinite (and a very large finite number if S is a large finite set). Even if the 'correspondence' has to be a reference relation and we specify which *sentences* are to correspond to *states of affairs which actually obtain*, it follows from theorems of model theory that there are still infinitely many ways of *specifying* such a correspondence.[1] How can we pick out any *one* correspondence between our words (or thoughts) and the supposed mind-independent things *if we have no direct access to the mind-independent things?* (German philosophy almost always began with a particular answer to this question—the answer 'we can't'—after Kant.)

One thing is clear: an act of will (or intention) won't work. I can't simply *pick* one particular correspondence C and *will* (or stipulate) that C *is to be* the designated correspondence relation, because in order to do that I would need *already* to be able to *think about* the correspondence C—and C, being a relation to things which are external and mind-independent, is itself something outside the mind, something 'external'! In short, if the mind does not have the ability to grasp external things or forms directly, then no *mental* act can give it the ability to single out a correspondence (or anything else external, for that matter).

But if the denial of intrinsic properties is correct, then no external thing or event is connected to any one relation it may have to other things (including our thoughts) in a way which is special or essential or intrinsic. If the denial of intrinsic properties is right, then it is not more essential to a mental event that it stand in a relation C_1 to any object x than it is that it stands in any other relation C_2 to any other object y. Nor is it any more essential to a non-mental object that it stand in a relation C to any one of my thoughts than it is that it stand in any one of a myriad other relations to any one of my other thoughts. On such a view, no relation C is metaphysically singled out as *the* relation between thoughts and things; reference becomes an 'occult' phenomenon.

The tension or incompatibility between metaphysical realism and the denial of intrinsic properties has not gone unnoticed by modern materialists. And for this reason we now find many materialists employing a metaphysical vocabulary that smacks of the fourteenth century: materialists who talk of 'causal powers', of 'built-in' similarities and dissimilarities between things in nature, even materialists who speak unabashedly of *essences*. In this lecture I want to ask if this modern mixture of materialism and essentialism *is consistent*; and I shall argue that it *isn't*.

WHY I FOCUS ON MATERIALISM

The reason I am going to focus my attack on materialism is that materialism is the only *metaphysical* picture that has contemporary 'clout'. Metaphysics, or the enterprise of describing the 'furniture of the world', the 'things in themselves' apart from our conceptual imposition, has been rejected by many analytic philosophers (though *not*, as I remarked, by Russell), and by all the leading brands of continental philosophy. Today, apart from relics, it is virtually only materialists (or 'physicalists', as they like to call themselves) who continue the traditional enterprise.

It was not always thus. Between the tenth and twelfth centuries the metaphysical community which included the Arabic Averroes and Avicenna, the Jewish Maimonides, and the Angelic Doctor in Paris disagreed on many questions, creation in particular. It was regarded as a hard issue whether the world always existed obeying the same laws (the doctrine ascribed to Aristotle), or was created from pre-existing matter (the doctrine ascribed to Plato) or was created *ex nihilo* (the Scriptural doctrine). But the existence of a supersensible Cause of the contingent and moving sensible things was taken to be *demonstrable*. Speculative reason could *know* there was an Uncaused Cause.

When I was seven years old the question 'if God made the world, then who made God?' struck me one evening with vivid force. I remember pacing in circles around a little well for hours while the awful regress played itself out in my mind. If a medieval theologian had been handy, he would have told me that God was self-caused. He might have said God was the *ens necessarium*. I don't know if it would have helped; today philosophers would say that the doctrine of God's 'necessary' existence invokes a notion of 'necessity' which is incoherent or unintelligible.

The issue does, in a covert way, still trouble us. Wallace Matson (1967) ended a philosophic defense of atheism with the words, 'Still, why *is* there something rather than nothing?'. The doctrine that 'you take the universe you get' (a remark Steven Weinberg once made in a discussion) sounds close to saying it's some sort of metaphysical *chance* (we might just as well have *anything*). The idea of a supersensible Cause outside of the universe leads at once to the question that troubled me when I was seven. We don't even have the comfort of thinking of the universe as a kind of *ens necessarium: it* only came into existence a few billion years ago!

This situation was summed up by Kant: Kant held that the whole enterprise of trying to *demonstrate* the existence and nature of a supersensible world by speculation leads only to antinomies. (The universe *must* have a cause; but *that* cause would have to have a cause; but an infinite regress is no explanation and self-causation is impossible . . .) Today, as I remarked, only a few relics would challenge this conclusion, which put an end to rationalism as well as to the medieval synthesis of Greek philosophy with revealed religion.

This decline of medieval philosophy was a long process which overlapped the decline of medieval science (with its substantial forms). Here too Kant summed up the issue for our culture: the medievals (and the rationalists) thought the mind had an intellectual intuition (*intellektuelle Anschauung*), a sort of perception that would enable it to perceive essences, substantial forms, or whatever. But there is no such faculty. 'Nothing is in the mind that was not first in the senses *except the mind itself*', as Kant put it, quoting Leibnitz.

Again, no one but a few relics challenge *this* conclusion. But Kant drew a bold corollary, and this corollary is hotly disputed to the present day.

The corollary depends upon a claim that Kant made. The claim can be illustrated by a famous observation of Wittgenstein's. Referring to the 'duck-rabbit' illusion (the figure that can be seen as either a duck or a rabbit), Wittgenstein remarked that while the physical image is capable of being seen either way, no 'mental image' is capable of being seen either way: the 'mental image' is always unambiguously a duck image or a rabbit image (*Philosophical Investigations* II, xi, 194–6). It follows that 'mental images' are really very different from physical images such as line drawings and photographs. We might express this difference by saying the interpretation is *built in* to the 'mental image'; the mental image is a *construction.*

Kant made the same point with respect to *memory.* When I have a memory of an experience this is not, contrary to Hume, *just* an image which 'resembles' the earlier experience. To be a memory the interpretation has to be 'built in': the interpretation that this is a *past* experience of *mine.* Kant (1933, Transcendental Deduction) argues that the notion of the *past* involves causality and that causality involves laws and objects (so, according to Kant, does the assignment of all these experiences to *myself*). Past experiences are not directly available; saying we 'remember' them is saying we have succeeded in constructing a version with causal relations and a continuing self in which they are located.

The corollary Kant drew from all this is that even experiences are in part constructions of the mind: I know what experiences I have and have had partly because I know what *objects* I am seeing and touching and have seen and touched, and partly because I know what *laws* these objects obey. Kant may have been overambitious in thinking he could specify the *a priori* constraints on the construction process; but the idea that all experience involves mental construction, and the idea that the dependence of physical object concepts and experience concepts goes *both* ways, continue to be of great importance in contemporary philosophy (of many varieties).

Since sense data and physical objects are interdependent constructions, in Kant's view, the idea that 'all we know is sense data' is as silly as the idea that we can have knowledge of objects that goes beyond experience. Although Kant does not put it this way, I have suggested elsewhere (Putnam, 1981, ch. 3) that we can view him as rejecting the idea of truth as correspondence (to a mind-independent reality) and as saying that the only sort of truth we can have an idea of, or use for, is *assertibility* (by creatures with our rational natures) *under optimal conditions* (as determined by our sensible natures). Truth becomes a radically epistemic notion.

However, Kant remarks that the *desire* for speculative metaphysics, the desire for a theory of the furniture of the world, is deep in our nature. He thought we should abandon the enterprise of trying to have speculative knowledge of the 'things in themselves' and sublimate the metaphysical impulse in the moral project of trying to make a more perfect world; but he was surely right about the strength of the metaphysical urge.

Contemporary materialism and scientism are a reflection of this urge in two ways. On the one hand, the materialist claims that physics is an approximation to a sketch of the one true theory, the true and complete description of the furniture of the world. (Since he often leaves out quantum mechanics, his picture differs remarkably little from Democritus': it's all atoms swerving in the void.) On the other hand, he meets the epistemological argument against metaphysics by claiming that we don't *need* an intellectual intuition to do *his* sort of metaphysics: his metaphysics, he says, is as open ended, as infinitely revisable and fallible, as science itself. In fact, it *is* science itself! (interpreted as claiming absolute truth, or rather, claiming *convergence* to absolute truth). The appeal of materialism lies precisely in this, in its claim to be *natural* metaphysics, metaphysics within the bounds of science. That a doctrine which promises to gratify both our ambition (to know the noumena) and our caution (not to be unscientific) should have great appeal is hardly something to be wondered at.

This wide appeal would be reason

enough to justify a critique of metaphysical materialism. But a second reason is this: metaphysical materialism has replaced positivism and pragmatism as the dominant contemporary form of scientism. Since scientism is, in my opinion, one of the most dangerous contemporary intellectual tendencies, a critique of its most influential contemporary form is a duty for a philosopher who views his enterprise as more than a purely technical discipline.

CAUSATION

What makes the metaphysical realist a *metaphysical* realist is his belief that there is somewhere 'one true theory' (two theories which are true and complete descriptions of the world would be mere notational variants of each other). In company with a correspondence theory of truth, this belief in one true theory requires a *ready-made* world (an expression suggested in this connection by Nelson Goodman): the world itself has to have a 'built-in' structure since otherwise theories with different structures might correctly 'copy' the world (from different perspectives) and truth would lose its absolute (non-perspectival) character. Moreover, as I already remarked, 'correspondence' between our symbols and something which has no determinate structure is hardly a well-defined notion.

The materialist metaphysician often takes *causal relations* as an example of built-in structure. Events have causes; objects have 'causal powers'. And he proudly proclaims his realism about these, his faith that they are 'in' the world itself, in the metaphysical realist sense. Well, let us grant him that this is so, for the sake of argument: my question for the moment is not whether this sort of realism is justified, but whether it is really compatible with materialism. Is *causation* a physical relation?

In this discussion, I shall follow the materialist in ignoring quantum mechanics since it has *no* generally acceptable interpretation of the kind the realist advocates:[2] the standard (Copenhagen) interpretataion makes essential reference to *observers*, and the materialist wants to imagine a physics in which the observer is simply another part of the system, as seen from a God's eye view. Physics is then a theory whose fundamental magnitudes are defined at all points in space and time; a property or relation is physically definable if it is definable in terms of these.[3]

I shall also assume that the fundamental magnitudes are basically the usual ones: if no restraint at all is placed on what counts as a possible 'fundamental magnitude' in future physics, then *reference* or *soul* or *Good* could even be 'fundamental magnitudes' in future physics! I shall not allow the naturalist the escape hatch of letting 'future physics' mean we-know-not-what. Physicalism is only intelligible if 'future physics' is supposed to resemble what *we* call 'physics'. The possibility of natural metaphysics (metaphysics within the bounds of science) is, indeed, not conclusively refuted by showing that present-day materialism cannot be a correct sketch of the one true (metaphysical) theory: but present-day materialism is, as already remarked, the view with clout.

Now if '*A* causes *B*' simply meant 'whenever an *A*-type event happens, then a *B*-type event follows in time', 'causes' would be physically definable. Many attempts have been made to give such a definition of causation—one which would apply to genuine causal laws while not applying to sequences we would regard as coincidental or otherwise non-causal. Few philosophers believe today that this is possible.

But let us assume that 'causes' (in this sense) *is* somehow physically definable. A cause, in the sense this definition tries to capture, is a *sufficient* condition for its effect; whenever the cause occurs, the effect *must* follow (at least in a deterministic world). Following Mill, let us call such a cause a *total cause*. An example of a total cause at time t_0 of a physical event e occurring at a later time t_1, and a point x would be the entire distribution of values of the dynamical variables at time t_0 (inside a sphere S whose center is x and whose radius is sufficiently large so that events outside the sphere S could not influence events at x occurring at t_1 without having to send a signal to x faster than light, which I assume, on the basis of relativity, to be impossible).

Mill pointed out that in ordinary language 'cause' rarely (if ever) means 'total cause'. When I say 'failure to put out the campfire caused the forest fire', I do *not* mean that the campfire's remaining lit during a certain interval was the *total cause* of the forest fire. Many other things—the dryness of the leaves, their proximity to the campfire, the temperature of the day, even the presence of oxygen in the atmosphere—are part of the *total* cause of the forest fire. Mill's point is that we regard certain parts of the total cause as 'background', and refer only to the part of interest as 'the' cause.

Suppose a professor is found stark-naked in a girl's dormitory room at midnight. His being naked in the room at midnight $-\epsilon$, where ϵ is so small that he could neither get out of the room or put on his clothes between midnight $-\epsilon$ and midnight without moving faster than light, would be a 'total cause' of his being naked in the girl's room at midnight; but no one would refer to this as the 'cause' of his presence in the room in that state. On the other hand, when it is said that the presence of certain bodies of H_2O in our environment 'causes' us to use the word 'water' as we do, it is certainly *not* meant that the presence of H_2O is the 'total cause'. In its ordinary sense, 'cause' can often be paraphrased by a locution involving *explain*; the presence of H_2O in our environment, our dependence on H_2O for life, etc., are 'part of' the *explanation* of our having a word which we use as we use the word 'water'. The forest fire is *explained* (given background knowledge) by the campfire's not having been extinguished; but the professor's state at midnight $-\epsilon$ is not what we consider an *explanation* of the state of affairs at midnight.

When it is said that a word refers to x just in case the (use of the) word is connected to x by a 'causal chain of the appropriate type', the notion of 'causal chain' involved is that of an *explanatory* chain. Even if the notion of 'total cause' *were* physically definable, it would not be possible to *use* it either in daily

life or in philosophy; the notion the materialist really uses when he employs 'causal chain', etc., in his philosophical explications is the intuitive notion of an *explanation.*

But this notion is certainly not physically definable. To see that it isn't, observe, first, that 'explains' (and 'caused', when it has the force of 'explains why x happened') are abstract notions. Even when we imagine a possible world in which there are non-physical things or properties, we can conceive of these things and properties *causing* things to happen. A disembodied spirit would not have *mass* or *charge*, but (this is a conceptual question of course; I don't mean to suggest there *are* disembodied spirits) it could *cause* something (say, an emotional reaction in another spirit with which it communicated telepathically).

A definition of 'caused' (in this 'explanatory' sense) which was too 'first order', too tied to the particular magnitudes which are the 'fundamental magnitudes' of physics in *our* world, would make it *conceptually impossible* that a disembodied spirit (or an event involving magnitudes which are not 'physical' in *our* world) could be a cause. This is why the suggested Humean definition of *total* cause—A is the (total) cause of B if and only if an A-type event is always followed in time by a B-type event—contained no *specific* physical term (except 'time'): this definition *is* abstract enough to apply to possible worlds different from our own. (Although it fails even so.) Could there be an equally abstract (and more successful) definition of 'cause' in the explanatory sense?

Imagine that Venusians land on Earth and observe a forest fire. One of them says, 'I know what caused that—the atmosphere of the darned planet is saturated with oxygen.'

What this vignette illustrates is that one man's (or extraterrestrial's) 'background condition' can easily be another man's 'cause'. What is and what is not a 'cause' or an 'explanation' depends on background knowledge and our reason for asking the question.

No purely *formal* relation between events will be sensitive to this relativity of explanatory arguments to background knowledge and interests.

Nelson Goodman has shown that no purely formal criterion can distinguish arguments which are intuitively sound inductive arguments from unsound arguments: for every sound inductive argument there is an unsound one of the very same form. The actual predicates occurring in the argument make the difference, and the distinction between 'projectible' and 'non-projectible' predicates is not a formal one. It is not difficult to show that the same thing is true of *explanations.* If we think of explanation as relation in 'the world', then to define it one would need a predicate which could sort projectible from non-projectible properties; such a predicate could not be purely formal for then it would run afoul of Goodman's result, but it could not involve the particular fundamental magnitudes in *our* world in an essential way for then it would be open to counterexamples in other possible worlds.

'NON-HUMEAN' CAUSATION

Richard Boyd (1980) has suggested that the whole enterprise of *defining* causation was a mistake: physicalists should simply take the notion as a primitive one. He may only mean that to insist on a definition of 'causes' (or anything else) in the standard formalism for mathematics and physics (which contains *names* for only countably many real numbers, etc.) is unreasonable: if so, this would not be an argument against expecting every *physical* property and relation to be definable in an *infinitary extension* of physics, a language which allows *infinitely long* names and sentences. (Indeed, if a property or relation is *not* physically definable even in this liberal sense, what is meant by calling it 'physical'?) But he may have meant that one should literally take 'causes' as an irreducible notion, one whose failure to be physically definable is not due to syntactic accidents, such as the limit on the length of formulas. But can a philosopher who accepts the existence of an irreducible phenomenon of *causation* call himself a materialist?

'Causes', we have just seen, is often para-phrasable as 'explains'. It rarely or never means 'is the total cause of'. When Boyd, for example, says that a certain micro-structure is a 'causal power' (the micro-structure of sugar is a 'causal power' in Boyd's sense, because it *causally explains* why sugar dissolves in water) he does not mean that the micro-structure in question is the *total cause* of the explained events (sugar will not dissolve in water if the water is *frozen,* for example, or if the water is already saturated with sugar, or if the water-cum-sugar is in an exotic quantum mechanical state). 'Causal powers' are properties that *explain* something, given background conditions and given standards of salience and relevance.

A metaphysical view in which 'causation' and 'causal explanation' are built into the world itself is one in which explanation is wrenched out of what Professor Frederick Will (1974) has called 'the knowledge institution', the inherited tradition which defines for us what is a background condition and what a salient variable parameter, and projected into the structure of reality. Boyd would probably reply that the 'causal structure' of reality *explains* the success of the knowledge institution: our successful explanations simply copy the built-in causal structure.

Be that as it may, salience and relevance are attributes of thought and reasoning, not of nature. To project them into the realist's 'real world', into what Kant called the *noumenal* world, is to mix objective idealism (or, perhaps, medieval Aristoteleanism) and materialism in a totally incoherent way. To say 'materialism is *almost* true: the world is completely describable in the language of physics *plus* the one little added notion that some events intrinsically *explain* other events' would be ridiculous. This would not be a 'near miss' for materialism, but a total failure. If events *intrinsically* explain other events, if there are saliencies, relevancies, standards of what are 'normal' conditions, and so on, built into the world itself independently of minds, then the world is in many ways *like* a mind, or infused with something very much like reason. And if *that* is true, then materialism *cannot* be true.

One can try to revive the project of speculative metaphysics, if one wishes: but one should not pass *this* sort of metaphysics off as (future) *physics*.

COUNTERFACTUALS AND 'SIMILARITY'

Suppose I take a match from a new box of matches (in perfect condition), break it, and throw the pieces in the river. After all this, I remark, 'If I had struck that match (instead of breaking it, etc.) it would have lit'. Most of us would say, 'true', or 'probably true'. But what does the statement actually assert?

A first stab at an explication might go as follows: the statement is true if it follows from physical laws (assume these to be given by a list—otherwise there are further problems about 'laws') that if the match is struck (at an average (for me?) angle, with an average amount of force) against that striking surface, then it ignites. But this doesn't work: even if we describe the match down to the atomic level, and ditto for the striking surface and the angle and force involved, there are still many other relevant variables unmentioned. (Notice the similarity to the problem of 'cause' as 'total cause': the statement '*A* caused *B*', and the statement 'If *X* had happened, *Y* would have happened' have simple truth conditions when *all* the 'background conditions'—and all the 'laws'—are specified; but typically they *aren't* specified, and the speaker can't even conceive of *all* of them.) If no oxygen molecules happen to be near the top of the match, or if the entire match-cum-striking-surface-cum-atmosphere system is in a sufficiently strange quantum mechanical state, etc., then the match *won't* ignite (even if struck with that force, at that angle, etc.)

One is tempted to try: 'It follows from the physical laws that if the match is struck against that surface (at the specified force and angle) and everything is *normal* then the match ignites', but this brings the very strange predicate 'normal' into the story. Besides, maybe conditions *weren't* 'normal' (in

the sense of 'average') at the time. (In infinitely many respects, conditions are *always* 'abnormal': a truism from statistical theory). Or one is tempted to say: 'It follows from the laws that if the match is struck against that surface (with the specified force and at the specified angle), and *everything else is as it actually was at the time*, then the match must ignite.' But, as Nelson Goodman (1947) pointed out in a celebrated paper on this logical question, *everything* else *couldn't* be as it was at the time if the match were struck. The gravitational fields, the quantum mechanical state, the places where there were oxygen molecules in the air, and infinitely many other things *couldn't have been* 'as they actually were at the time' if the match had been struck.

The reason I mention this is that David Lewis (in 'Causation', *Journal of Philosophy* LXX, 1973) proposed to analyze 'causes' using precisely this sort of contrary-to-fact conditional. The idea is that '*A* caused *B*' can be analyzed as 'if *A* had not happened, *B* would not have happened'.

Actually, this doesn't seem right. (Even if *A* caused *B*, there are situations in which it just isn't true that if *A* hadn't happened, *B* wouldn't have happened.)[4] But suppose it were right, or that, if it isn't right, contrary-to-fact conditionals can at any rate be used to explicate the notions that we wanted to use the notion of causality to explicate. How are the truth conditions for contrary-to-fact conditionals *themselves* to be explicated?

One famous materialist, John Mackie (1974), thinks contrary-to-fact conditionals aren't true or false. He regards them as ways of indicating what inferences are allowable in one's knowledge situation, rather than as asserting something true or false in the realist sense, independently of one's knowledge situation. 'If I had struck that match it would have lit' indicates that my *knowledge situation* is such that (if I delete the information about what actually happened to the match) an inference from 'the match was struck' to 'the match ignited' would be *warranted*. The contrary-to-fact conditional signals the presence of what Wilfrid Sellars calls a 'material rule of inference'. It has *assertibility conditions*, rather than truth conditions in the sense of absolute truth semantics.

Mackie, who follows Lewis in using counterfactuals to analyze 'causes', concludes that *causation* (in the ordinary sense) is something *epistemic*, and not something in the world at all. But he believes there is another notion of causation, 'mechanical causation', which is in the world. (It has to do with energy flow; as Mackie describes it, it is hard to see either what it is, or that it could be spelled out without using counterfactuals,[5] which would be fatal to Mackie's project of having a non-epistemic notion of causation.)

But Lewis, following Professor Robert Stalnaker, chooses to give *truth conditions* for contrary-to-fact conditionals. He postulates that there actually exist 'other possible worlds' (as in science fiction), and that there is a 'similarity metric' which determines how 'near' or how 'similar' any two possible worlds are (Lewis, 1973). A contrary-to-fact conditional, 'If *X* had happened, then *Y* would have happened', is true just in case *Y* is *actually* true in all the *nearest* 'parallel worlds' to the actual world in which *X* is actually true.

To me this smacks more of science fiction than of philosophy. But one thing is clear: a theory which requires an ontology of parallel worlds and a built-in 'similarity metric' certainly does not have a *materialist* ontology. More important, it does not have a *coherent* ontology: not only is the actual existence of parallel worlds a dotty idea, but the idea of an *intrinsic* similarity metric, a metric highly sensitive to what we regard as relevant conditions, or normal conditions, one which gives weight to what sorts of features *we* count as similarities and dissimilarities between states of affairs, is one which once again implies that the world is like a mind, or imbued with something very much like reason. And if *this* is true, then it must have a (suitably metaphysical) *explanation*. Objective idealism can hardly be a *little bit* true. ('It's all physics, except that there's this similarity metric' just doesn't make *sense*.)

ESSENCES AND OBJECTS

In this philosophical culture, the denial of intrinsic or 'essential' properties began with examples like the example of the thing whose shape is an 'essential' property under *one* description ('that statue') but not under a different description ('that piece of clay'). One philosopher who thinks a wholly wrong moral was drawn from this example is Saul Kripke.

According to Kripke, the statue and the piece of clay are two objects, not one. The fact that the piece of clay has a modal property, namely the property 'being a thing which *could have been* spherical in shape', which the statue lacks (I assume this is not one of those contemporary statues) already proves the two objects cannot be identical, in Kripke's view.

Now, this sounds very strange at first hearing. If I put the statue on the scale, have I put *two objects* on the scale? If the piece of clay weighs 20 pounds and the statue weighs 20 pounds, why doesn't the scale read 40 and not 20 if both objects are on it right now? But what Kripke has in mind is not silly at all.

First of all, it also sounds strange to be told that a human being is not identical with the aggregation of the molecules in his body. Yet on a moment's reflection each of us is aware that he was not *that* aggregate of molecules a day ago. Seven years ago, precious few of those molecules were in my body. If after my death that exact set of molecules is assembled and placed in a chemical flask, it will be the same aggregation of molecules, but it won't be *me*. David Lewis (1976) has suggested that I and the aggregation of molecules are 'identical for a period of time' in somewhat the way that Highway 2 and Highway 16 can be 'identical for a stretch'; as he points out, 'identity for a time' is not strict logical identity. If *A* and *B* are identical in the strict sense, every property of *A* is a property of *B*; but it is not the case that every property of the aggregation of molecules is a property of *me*.

Just as we can recognize that I am not the

same object as the aggregation of molecules in my body without denying that I *consist* of those molecules right now (the difference between the object lies in the different statements that are true of them, not in their physical distinctness), so, one can agree with Kripke that the statue is not the same object as the piece of clay without denying that the piece of clay is the matter of the statue; once again the difference between the objects lies in the different statements that are true of them, not in their physical distinctness.

But now it begins to look as if objects, properly individuated, *do* have essences, do have *some* properties in a special way. Can Kripke's doctrine be of aid to materialism? (Kripke himself is quite averse to materialism, as is well known.)

A materialist whose ontology includes 'possible worlds' might introduce suitable intensional objects by identifying them with functions taking possible worlds as arguments and space-time regions in those worlds as values. Thus, the statue would be the function defined on each possible world Y in which the statue exists, whose value on Y is the space-time region occupied by the statue in Y. This would, indeed, make the 'statue' and the 'piece of clay' different 'objects' (different logical constructions) even if they occupy the same space-time region in the actual world, since there are other possible worlds in which they do not occupy the same space-time region.

But functions of this kind are standardly used in modern semantics to represent *concepts*. No one doubts that the *concept* 'that statue' is a different *concept* from the *concept* 'that piece of clay'; the question is whether there is some *individual* in the actual world to which one of these concepts *essentially* applies while the other only accidentally applies. The space-time region itself is *not* such an individual; and it is hard to see how a materialist is going to find one in *his* ontology.

Moreover, clever logical constructions are no answer to the philosophical difficulty. Doubtless one can come up with as many 'objects' as one wants given 'possible worlds' plus the resources of modern set theory; (the difficulty, indeed, is that one can come up with *too many*). Consider the metaphysical claim that my thoughts have some sort of intrinsic connection with external objects. If the events that take place in my brain are in a space-time region that has a set-theoretic connection with some abstract entity that involves certain external objects, then that same space-time region will have similar set-theoretic connections with some other abstract entities that involve some other external objects. To be sure, the materialist can say that my 'thoughts' *intrinsically* involve certain external objects by *identifying them* (the thoughts) with one abstract entity and not with another; but if this identification is supposed to be a feature of reality itself, then there must really *be* essences in the world in a sense which pure set theory can't hope to explicate.

The difficulty is that Kripke individuates objects *by their modal properties*, by what they (essentially) *could* and *could not* be. Kripke's ontology *presupposes* essentialism; it can not be used to ground it. And modal properties are not, on the face of it, part of the materialist's furniture of the world.

But, I will be reminded, I have myself spoken of 'essential properties' elsewhere (see Putnam, 1975). I have said that there are possible worlds (possible *states* of the world, that is, not parallel worlds à la Lewis) in which some liquid other than H_2O has the taste of water (we might have different taste buds, for example), fills the lakes and rivers, etc., but no possible world in which *water* isn't H_2O. Once we have discovered what water is in the actual world, we have discovered its *nature:* is this not essentialism?

It *is* a sort of essentialism, but not a sort which can help the materialist. For what I have said is that it has long been our *intention* that a liquid should *count* as 'water' only if it has the same composition as the paradigm examples of water (or as the majority of them). I claim that this was our intention even before we *knew* the ultimate composition of water. If I am right then, *given those referential intentions*, it was always impossible for a liquid other than H_2O to be water, even if it took empirical investigation to find it out. But the 'essence' of water in *this* sense is the product of our use of the word, the kinds of referential intentions we have: this sort of essence is not 'built into the world' in the way required by an *essentialist theory of reference itself* to get off the ground.

Similarly, Kripke has defended *his* essentialist theories by arguments which turn on speakers' referential intentions and practices; to date he has carefully refrained from trying to provide a metaphysical theory of reference (although he does seem to believe in mind-independent modal properties). I conclude that however one takes Kripke's theories (or mine); whether one takes them metaphysically, as theories of objective 'essences' which are somehow 'out there', or one takes them as theories of our referential practices and intentions, they are of no help to the materialist. On the metaphysical reading they are realist enough, but their realism is not of a materialist sort; on the purely semantical reading they *presuppose* the notion of reference, and cannot be used to support the metaphysical explanation of reference as intrinsic correspondence between thought and thing.

REFERENCE

Some metaphysical materialists might respond to what has been said by agreeing that '*A* causes *B*' does *not* describe a simple 'relation' between *A* and *B*. 'All you're saying is that causal statements *rest on* a distinction between background conditions and differentiating factors, and I agree that this distinction isn't built into the things themselves, but is a reflection of the way we think about the things', such a philosopher might say. But here he has used the words 'think about', i.e., he has appealed to the notion of *reference*.

The contemporary metaphysical materialist thinks about reference in the following way: the brain is a computer. Its computations involve *representations*. Some of these (perhaps all) are 'propositional': they resemble sentences in an internal *lingua mentis*.

(They have been called 'sentence-analogs'.) Some of them could be sentences in a public language, as when we engage in interior monolog. A person refers to something when, for example, the person thinks 'the cat is on the mat' (the sentence-analog is 'subvocalized') and the entire organism-cum-environment situation is such that the words 'the cat' in the particular sentence-analog stand in a physical relation R (the relation of *reference*) to some cat and the words 'the mat' stand in the relation R to some mat.

But what is this relation R? And what on earth could make anyone think it is a *physical* relation?

Well, there is *one* way in which *no one*, to my knowledge, would try to define R, and that is by giving a list of all possible reference situations. It is useful, however, to consider why not. Suppose someone proposed to define reference (for some set of languages, including '*lingua mentis*') thus:

X refers to Y if and only if X is a (token) word or word-analog and Y is an object or event and the entire situation (including the organism that produced X and the environment that contains Y) is S_1 or S_2 or S_3 or . . . (infinite—possibly non-denumerably infinite—list of situations, described at the level of physics).

There are (at least) three things wrong with this.

First, besides the fact that the list would have to be infinite, such a list would not tell us what the situations S_1, S_2, . . . *had in common*. To define a physical property or relation by *listing* the situations in which it is found is not to say what it *is*. In fact, the materialists themselves object to *Tarski's* definition of reference on just this ground: that Tarski defines primitive reference (for a fixed language), by a list of cases, and, as Hartry Field (1972, p. 363) writes,

Now, it would have been easy for a chemist, late in the last century, to have given a 'valence definition' of the following form:

(3)(E) (n) (E has valence $n \equiv E$ is potassium and n is $+ 1$, or . . . or E is sulphur and n is -2)

where in the blanks go a list of similar clauses, one for each element. But, though this is an extensionally correct definition of valence, it would not have been an acceptable reduction; and had it turned out that nothing else was possible—had all efforts to explain valence in terms of the structural properties of atoms proved futile—scientists would have eventually had to decide either (a) to give up valence theory, or else (b) to replace the hypothesis of physicalism by another hypothesis (chemicalism?). It is part of scientific methodology to resist doing (b); and I also think it is part of scientific methodology to resist doing (a) as long as the notion of valence is serving the purposes for which it was designed (i.e., as long as it is proving useful in helping us characterize chemical compounds in terms of their valences). But the methodology is not to resist (a) and (b) by giving lists like (3); the methodology is to look for a real reduction. This is a methodology that has proved extremely fruitful in science, and I think we'd be crazy to give it up in linguistics. And I think we are giving up this fruitful methodology, unless we realize that we need to add theories of primitive reference to T1 or T2 if we are to establish the notion of truth as a physicalistically acceptable notion.

Secondly, it would be philosophically naive to think that such a list could answer any *philosophical* question about reference. For example, one could hold Quine's view, that there are definite *true* and *false* sentences[6] in science, but *no* determinate reference relation (the true sentences have infinitely many models, and there is no such thing as *the* model, in Quine's view), and still accept the list. Quine would simply say that the terms used to describe the situations $S_1, S_2, \ldots$ *etc. refer to different events in different models; thus the list, while correct in each* admissible model, does not define a *determinate* reference relation (only a determinate reference relation *for each model*). Now Quine's view may be right, wrong, or meaningless; the question of the truth or falsity of metaphysical realism may be meaningful or meaningless (and if meaningful, may have a realist or a non-realist answer), but a list of cases (either this list or the one involved in the Tarskian truth definition referred to by Field), cannot speak to *this* issue. To think that it can is analogous to thinking (as G. E. Moore did) that one can refute Berkeley by holding up one's hand and saying 'This is a material object. Therefore matter exists.' This is, as Myles Burnyeat has put it, "to philosophize as if Kant had never existed". For better or worse, philosophy has gone second order.

Thirdly, the list is *too specific*. Reference is as 'abstract' as causation. In possible worlds which contain individual things or properties which are not physical (in the sense of 'physical₂':[7] not definable in terms of the fundamental magnitudes of the physics of the actual world), we could still *refer*: we could refer to disembodied minds, or to an emergent non-material property of Goodness, or to all sorts of things, in the appropriate worlds. But the relevant situations could not, by hypothesis, be completely described in terms of the fundamental magnitudes of the physics of *our* world. A definition of reference from which it followed that we could not refer to a non-physical magnitude if there were one is just *wrong*.

I know of only one realist who has sketched a way of defining reference which meets these difficulties, and that is David Lewis (1974). Lewis proposes to treat reference as a *functional* property of the organism-cum-environment-situation.

Typical examples of functional properties come from the world of computers. Having a particular program, for example, is a functional (or in computer jargon a 'software' property) as opposed to an ordinary first-order physical property (a 'hardware' property). Functional properties are typically defined in batches; the properties or 'states' in a typical batch (say, the properties that are involved in a given computer program) are characterized by a certain *pattern*. Each property has specified cause and effect relations to the other properties in the pattern and to certain non-functional properties (the 'inputs' and 'outputs' of the programs).

Lewis' suggestion is that *reference* is a member of such a batch of properties: not functional properties of the organism, but functional properties of the organism-environment system. If this could be shown, it would answer the question of what all the various situations in which something refers to something else 'have in common': what they would have in common is something as abstract as a program, a scheme or formal pattern of cause–effect relationships. And if this could be shown, it would characterize reference in a way that makes it sufficiently abstract; the definition would not require any particular set of magnitudes to be the fundamental ones any more than the abstract description of a computer program does. Whether the second difficulty I noted would be met, I shall not attempt to judge.

The crucial point is that functional properties are defined *using the notions of cause and effect*. This is no problem for Lewis; Lewis believes he can define cause and effect using counterfactuals, and, as already mentioned, he gives truth conditions for counterfactuals in terms of a primitive notion of 'similarity of possible worlds'. Since he has a non-physical primitive in his system, he does not have to show that any of the notions he uses is physically definable. But the notion of 'similarity of possible worlds' is not one to which the materialist is entitled; and neither is he entitled to counterfactuals or to the notion of 'functional organization'.

As Charles Fried remarked in his Tanner Lectures,[8] it is easy to *mistake* causality for a physical relation. *Act, smash, move,* etc. are causal verbs and describe events which are clearly physical. ('Smashed', for example, conveys two kinds of information: the information that *momentum* was transferred from one thing to another, which is purely physical information, and the information that the *breaking* of the second thing was *caused* by the momentum transfer.) As Fried points out, the causal judgment may be quite complicated in cases when both objects were in motion before the collision. Once one has made the error of taking causality to be a physical relation, it is easy to think that func-

tional properties are simply higher-order physical properties (an error I myself once committed), and then to think that reference (and just about anything else) may be a functional property and hence physical. But once one sees this is an error, there is no vestige of a reason that I know of to think reference is a physical relation.

If the materialist cannot *define* reference, he can, of course, just take it as *primitive.* But reference, like causality, is a flexible, interest-relative notion: what we count as *referring* to something depends on background knowledge and our willingness to be charitable in interpretation. To read a relation so deeply human and so pervasively intentional into the world and to call the resulting metaphysical picture satisfactory (never mind whether or not it is 'materialist') is absurd.

THE FAILURE OF NATURAL METAPHYSICS

As I've already pointed out, there are two traditional ways of attempting to overcome the obvious difficulties with a correspondence theory of truth. One way was to postulate a special mental power, an *intellektuelle Anschauung,* which gives the mind access to 'forms'. If the mind has direct access to the things in themselves, then there is no problem about how it can put them in correspondence with its 'signs'. The other way was to postulate a built-in structure of the world, a set of essences, and to say (what is certainly a dark saying) that this structure itself singles out *one* correspondence between signs and their objects. The two strategies were quite naturally related; if a philosopher believes in essences, he usually wants us to have epistemic access to them, and so he generally postulates an *intellektuelle Anschauung* to give us this access.

If all this is a failure, as Kant saw, where do we go from there? One direction, the only direction I myself see as making sense, might be a species of pragmatism (although the word 'pragmatism' has always been so ill-understood that one despairs of rescuing the term), 'internal' realism: a realism which recognizes a difference between '*p*' and 'I think that *p*' between being *right,* and merely thinking one is right without locating that objectivity in either transcendental correspondence or mere consensus. Nelson Goodman has done a wonderful job of 'selling' this point of view in *Ways of Worldmaking* (a book short enough to be read in an evening, and deep enough to be pondered for many). The other main direction—the one that does not make sense to me—is natural metaphysics, the tendency I have criticized here.

Goodman urges, shockingly, that we give up the notion of '*the* world'. Although he speaks of us as making *many* worlds, he does not mean that there are many worlds in the David Lewis (or science fiction) sense, but that rightness is relative to medium and message. We make many versions; the standards of rightness that determine what is right and what is wrong are corrigible, relative to task and technique, but not *subjective.* The question this tendency raises is whether a narrow path can indeed be found between the swamps of metaphysics and the quicksands of cultural relativism and historicism.

The approach to which I have devoted this paper is an approach which claims that there *is* a 'transcendental' reality in Kant's sense, one absolutely independent of our minds, that the regulative ideal of knowledge *is* to copy it or put our thoughts in 'correspondence' with it, *but* (and this is what makes it 'natural' metaphysics) we need no *intellektuelle Anschauung* to do this: the 'scientific method' will do the job for us. 'Metaphysics within the bounds of science alone' might be its slogan.

I can sympathize with the urge behind this view (I would not criticize it if I did not feel its attraction). I am not inclined to scoff at the idea of a noumenal ground behind the dualities of experience, even if all attempts to talk about it lead to antinomies. Analytic philosophers have always tried to dismiss the transcendental as nonsense, but it does have an eerie way of reappearing. (For one thing,

almost every philosopher makes statements which contradict his own explicit account of what can be justified or known; this even arises in formal logic, when one makes statements about 'all languages' which are barred by the prohibitions on self-reference. For another, almost everyone regards the statement that there is *no* mind-independent reality, that there are *just* the 'versions', or there is just the 'discourse', or whatever, as itself intensely paradoxical.) Because one cannot talk about the transcendent or even deny its existence without paradox, one's attitude to it must, perhaps, be the concern of religion rather than of rational philosophy.

The idea of a coherent theory of the noumena; consistent, systematic, and arrived at by 'the scientific method' seems to me to be chimerical. True, a metaphysician could say 'You have, perhaps, shown that *materialist* metaphysics is incoherent. If so, let us assume some primitive notions of an "intentional" kind, say "thinks about", or "explains", and construct a scientific theory of *these* relations.' But what reason is there to regard this as a reasonable program?

The whole history of science seems to accord badly with such dreams. Science as we know it has been anti-metaphysical from the seventeenth century on; and not just because of 'positivistic interpretations'. Newton was certainly no positivist; but he strongly rejected the idea that his theory of universal gravitation could or should be read as a description of metaphysically ultimate fact. ('*Hypotheses non fingo*' was a rejection of metaphysical 'hypotheses', not of scientific ones.)

And Newton was certainly right. Suppose we lived in a Newtonian world, and suppose we could say with confidence that Newton's theory of gravity and Maxwell's theory of electromagnetism (referred to a privileged 'ether frame') were perfectly accurate. Even then, these theories admit of a bewildering variety of empirically equivalent formulations; formulations which agree on the equations while disagreeing precisely on their metaphysical interpretation. There are action-at-a-distance versions of *both* electromagnetism and gravity; there are versions of both in which an extended physical agent, the field, mediates the interactions between distant bodies; there are even *space-time* versions of *Newtonian* gravitational theory. Philosophers today argue about which of these would be 'right' in such a case; but I know of not a single first-rate physicist who takes an interest in such speculations.

The physics that has replaced Newton's has the same property. A theorist will say he is doing 'field theory' while his fingers are drawing Feynman diagrams, diagrams in which field interactions are depicted as exchanges of *particles* (calling the particles 'virtual' is, perhaps, a ghost of empiricist metaphysics). Even the statement that 'the electron we measure is not the bare electron of the theory, but the bare electron surrounded by a cloud of virtual *particles*' counts as a statement of *field* theory, if you please! What used to be the metaphysical question of atom or vortex has become a question of the choice of a notation!

Worse still, from the metaphysician's point of view, the most successful and most accurate physical theory of all time, quantum mechanics, has *no* 'realistic interpretation' that is acceptable to physicists. It is understood as a description of the world as *experienced by observers*; it does not even pretend to the kind of 'absoluteness' the metaphysician aims at (which is not to say that, given time and ingenuity, one could not come up with any number of empirical equivalents which *did* pretend to be observer independent; it is just that physicists refuse to take such efforts seriously.)

There is, then, nothing in the history of science to suggest that it either aims at or should aim at one single *absolute* version of 'the world'. On the contrary, such an aim, which would require science itself to decide which of the empirically equivalent successful theories in any given context was 'really true', is contrary to the whole spirit of an enterprise whose strategy from the first has been to confine itself to claims with clear *empirical* significance. If metaphysics *is* ever revived as a culturally and humanly significant enterprise, it is far more likely to be along the

lines of a Kurt Gödel or, perhaps, Saul Kripke—i.e., along the lines of those who *do* think, in spite of the history I cited, that we *do* have an *intellektuelle Anschauung*—than along the lines of natural metaphysics. But a successful revival along either line seems to be overwhelmingly unlikely.

NOTES

[1]In Putnam (1981) this result is extended to intensional logic; it is shown that even if we specify which sentences are to be ture in each possible world, and not just in the actual world, the extensions of the extra-logical predicates are almost totally undetermined in almost all worlds.

[2]I ignore here my *own* past attempts at a realist interpretation of quantum mechanics (using non-standard logic) for two reasons: they have never found much acceptance, and (more importantly) I no longer think quantum logic enables one to reconcile quantum mechanics with realism.

[3]Strictly speaking, 'if it is definable in terms of these, using, if necessary, constants for all real numbers and functions, infinite conjunctions and disjunctions, etc.': there is no philosophical significance to the question of whether a physical magnitude can be defined by a formula of finite length (or one containing a constant for some undefinable real number) from a metaphysical materialist's point of view.

[4]These are situations in which *B* would have been produced by some other cause if *A* hadn't caused it. Another kind of counterexample: John and George are identical twins and have black hair. Is the following counterfactual true?

'If John hadn't had black hair, George wouldn't have had black hair either.' Everyone I've asked assures me it is. But then, on Lewis' theory it follows that 'John's having black hair *caused* George to have black hair too', which is absurd.

[5]If 'mechanical causation' is simply momentum transfer, for example, then my flicking a virtually frictionless switch is *not* the 'mechanical cause' of the light going on. Similarly, my putting my hand in front of a light is not the 'mechanical cause' of the shadow. Such a narrow notion might be physical, but would be of no use in explicating *reference*. If, on the other hand, the switching case *is* a case of 'mechanical causation', how does one characterize it without using the clause 'the current *would not have* travelled to the light if the switch *had not been* moved', or some such subjunctive clause?

[6]For Quine, this means true and false relative to our evolving doctrine; Quine rejects metaphysical realism and the idea of a unique 'correspondence' between our terms and things in themselves.

[7]Paul Meehl and Wilfrid Sellars introduced the terms 'physical$_1$' and 'physical$_2$'. 'Physical$_1$' properties are simply properties connected with space-time and with causal laws: thus a dualist could subscribe to the thesis 'all properties are physical$_1$'. 'Physical$_2$' properties are physical in the sense used here.

[8]'Is liberty possible?' *The Tanner Lectures on Human Values*, vol. 3, Cambridge 1982, pp. 89–135.

REFERENCES

Boyd, R., 1980. 'Materialism without reductionism: what physicalism does not entail', in N. Block (ed.) *Readings in the Philosophy of Psychology*, Cambridge, Mass., 67–106.

Field, H., 1972. 'Tarski's theory of truth', *Journal of Philosophy*, LXIX, 347–75.

Goodman, N., 1947. 'The problem of counterfactual conditionals'. *Journal of Philosophy*, XLIV, 113–28.

Kant, I., 1933. *The Critique of Pure Reason*, London.

Lewis, D., 1973. *Counterfactuals*, Oxford.
1974. 'Radical interpretation', *Synthese*, XXVII, 331–44.
1976. 'Survival and identity', in A. D. Rorty (ed.) *The Identity of Persons*, Berkeley, 17–40.

Mackie, J., 1974. *The Cement of the Universe*, Oxford.

Matson, W., 1967. *The Existence of God*, Ithaca, New York.

Putnam, H., 1975. 'The meaning of "meaning".' In Putnam, *Language, Mind, and Reality*, Cambridge.
1981. *Reason, Truth and History*, Cambridge.

Will, F. L., 1974. *Induction and Justification*, Ithaca, New York.

Wittgenstein, L. W., 1953. *Philosophical Investigations*, Oxford.

Realism vs. Anti-Realism*

Nicholas Wolterstorff

In our contemporary debate over metaphysical realism the anti-realists, in their attempt to dislodge us from our indigenous realism, give arguments—lots of them in fact. But arguments offered on important issues in philosophy generally prove indecisive; whether we find them cogent or not depends on the perspective from within which we consider them. So it is here. Behind the arguments of the anti-realist is "a way of seeing things" to which he is giving expression.

Consider this passage from Hilary Putnam, one of our leading anti-realists. "The current views of truth are alienated views," says Putnam in the Preface to his *Reason, Truth, and History,* speaking of the views of metaphysical realists; "they cause one to lose one part or another of one's self and the world, to see the world as simply consisting of elementary particles swerving in the void . . . , or to see the world as simply consisting of 'actual and possible sense-data . . . ,' or to deny that there is a world at all, as opposed to a bunch of stories that we make up for various (mainly unconscious) reasons." He adds that his own "purpose is to sketch the leading ideas of a non-alienated view."[1]

I suggest that here in this brief passage there comes to the surface what is perhaps the deepest issue in the dispute. At issue is whether or not we are at home in the world. The anti-realist sees metaphysical realism as an alienating perspective; it regards the world and even ourselves as something out there, over against us and alien to us with which we have to cope. The goal of the anti-realist is to show that this is mistaken; we are not thus alienated. His path toward that goal is making us see that we are the *makers* of our world. We are no more alien in the world than the artist is alien to his work which mirrors him back to himself as its maker.

But to regard ourselves as world-makers is to regard the world as an *expression* of ourselves. And so it is that one of the greatest anti-realists from earlier in our century, Ernst Cassirer, says in the course of attacking the mimetic view of art that:

Against this self-dissolution of the spirit there is only one remedy: to accept in all

*Reprinted by permission of the American Catholic Philosophical Association, from *Realism* (*Proceedings and Addresses of the American Catholic Philosophical Association, vol. 59*), ed. D. O. Dahlstrom, pp. 182–205. Washington, D.C.: The American Catholic Philosophical Association, 1984.

seriousness what Kant calls his 'Copernican revolution.' Instead of measuring the content, meaning, and truth of intellectual forms by something extraneous which is supposed to be reproduced in them, we must find in these forms themselves the measure and criterion for their truth and intrinsic meaning. Instead of taking them as mere copies of something else, we must see in each of these spiritual forms a spontaneous law of generation; an original way and tendency of expression which is more than a mere record of something initially given in fixed categories of real existence . . . In these realms the spirit exhibits itself in that inwardly determined dialectic by virtue of which alone there is any reality, any organized and definite Being at all. Thus the special symbolic forms are not imitations, but *organs* of reality . . ."[2]

The main point is clear: Language, art, science, myth, etc., are not ways of apprehending and recording a reality out there, structured independently of us; they are expressions of our own spirit, and "organs" of reality. We express ourselves by making a world, our instruments of world-making being our art, our science, our myths. The path toward seeing us at home in the world, says the anti-realist, is the path toward seeing our world as the product of our self-expression.

Cassirer makes explicit the fact that contemporary anti-realism stands in the lineage of Kant. But I suggest that if we want to understand the *spirit* as well as the *text* of contemporary anti-realism we would do even better to see it as standing in the lineage of Hegel and his romantic predecessors. Of course Hegel's own strategy for showing us that we are not aliens in the world was to urge us to see nature and society, along with us ourselves, as manifestations of *Geist*, of the divine, of God. Our contemporary anti-realists for the most part want no truck with God. For them, the reason we are not alienated from the world around us is just that we have made that world, not that God is making it *through* us.

But given this fundamental difference, surely one can hear in what I have already quoted from Putnam and Cassirer, loud echoes of such a passage as the following from Hegel:

The highest content which the subject can comprise in himself is what we can point-blank call *freedom*. Freedom is the highest destiny of the spirit. In the first place, on its purely formal side, it consists in this, that in what confronts the subject there is nothing alien and it is not a limitation or a barrier; on the contrary, the subject finds himself in it . . . The ignorant man is not free, because what confronts him is an alien world, something outside him and in the offing, on which he depends, without his having made this foreign world for himself and therefore without being at home in it by himself as in something his own. The impulse of curiosity, the pressure for knowledge, from the lowest level up to the highest rung of philosophical insight arises only from the struggle to cancel this situation of unfreedom and to make the world one's own in one's ideas and thought.[3]

Charles Taylor in his fine book *Hegel* argues that the central notion in the Romantic and Hegelian protest against both the Middle Ages and the Enlightenment was what he calls *expressivism:* the conviction that human activity and human life are to be seen as self-expression. "The realization of his essence is a subject's self-realization; so that what he defines himself in relation to is not an ideal order beyond, but rather something which unfolds from himself, is his own realization, and is first made determinate in that realization." This, says Taylor, "is one of the key ideas underlying the revolution of the late eighteenth century." He adds that "it is more than that; it is one of the foundational ideas of the civilization which has grown up since. In different forms, it is one of the major *idées-forces* which has shaped the contemporary world."[4] My suggestion is that one of the major manifestations of expressivism in the contemporary world is modern anti-realism. Expressivism vs. its alternatives—that is the deep issue before us.

But of course contemporary anti-realism is expressivism in a new guise; we must move on to describe that guise. Its most prominent feature, I would say, though not, I shall argue, its most fundamental, is a certain understanding of *truth.*

On a standard view of the workings of language, sometimes by uttering words we make assertions; we do the latter by doing the former. For example, I may assert that we had more snow than usual this past winter by uttering the sentence, "We had more snow than usual this past winter." Consider, then, an example of someone asserting something by uttering something. By virtue of what is the sentence in that use true or false?

The answer that comes at once to mind is that the sentence is true in that use because what was asserted to be the case by assertively uttering it is in fact the case. The sentence "P" is true when used to assert *that P* by virtue of its being a fact *that P.* This answer to the question is the heart of the correspondence theory of truth. More precisely, it is the heart of one version of that multifarious theory. Different versions adopt different understandings of the nature and interrelationships of sentences, assertions, propositions, facts, etc., from that which I shall presuppose; further, some versions treat the theory as involving more than the bare minimum of commitment which I have given to it here. For our purposes here, however, it will not be necessary to lay out the variants; we can raise the crucial issues by taking the correspondence theorist as holding that, in the use imagined, the sentence "We had more snow than usual this past winter" is true by virtue of its being a fact that we had more snow than usual this past winter.

Now part of what the metaphysical realist affirms is the correspondence theory of truth, in this or some other version. To this affirmation he then adds that, for the most part, the facts which make our sentences and assertions true are independent of any intellectual activity on the part of us human beings—independent of our conceptualiz-ing, of our asserting, etc. Whether there are ducks swimming on a pond somewhere—that is to say, whether it is *a fact that* there are ducks swimming on a pond somewhere—in no way depends on our intellectual activities. The history of our world might well have included ducks swimming on ponds even if human beings had never put in their appearance.

Central to the position of the *anti-*realist is the insistence that both parts of this perspective will have to go. "On this perspective," says Putnam, "the world consists of some fixed totality of mind-independent objects," and "Truth involves some sort of correspondence relation between words or thought-signs and external things and sets of things . . ."[5] In other words, "What the metaphysical realist holds is that we can think and talk about things as they are, independently of our minds, and that we can do this by virtue of a 'correspondence' relation between the terms in our language and some sorts of mind-independent entities."[6] But this is just unacceptable.

Notice, says Putnam, that when the realist states the truth-conditions for sentences-in-uses, he says nothing at all about *knowing* whether those conditions are satisfied. That is because, on the realist's way of thinking, our most warranted assertions and our best-confirmed theories might yet be false. "The most important consequence of metaphysical realism," says Putnam, "is that *truth* is supposed to be radically *non-epistemic* . . . 'Verified' (in any operational sense) does not imply 'true', on the metaphysical realist picture, even in the ideal limit."[7] But that's just a mistake. It is impossible that a sentence which we are ideally warranted in asserting might yet be false. Truth just is "some sort of (idealized) rational acceptability . . ."[8] It is at bottom an epistemic notion. Precisely *which* epistemic notion it is, will have to be uncovered in discussion. But that it cannot be a purely *non-*epistemic notion is evident. "The supposition that even an 'ideal' theory (from a pragmatic point of view) might *really* be false appears to collapse into *unintelligibility.*"[9]

A consequence, to which Michael

Dummett repeatedly calls attention, of this epistemizing of truth is that the law of excluded middle must be rejected. It may be that even in the best of circumstances we are neither warranted in accepting P nor warranted in accepting not-P. In that case, P is neither true nor false. P may fail to be true without being false, and may fail to be false without being true.

But why exactly is it thought to be unintelligible to suppose that our finest theories might nonetheless be false? At this point a large flurry of arguments has been thrown up by anti-realists—the very size of the flurry making one suspect that here we are touching a point deeper than argument. If the realist does not sense the strangeness, the weirdness, the absurdity of his view once he is forced to stare right at it, and if he is not repelled by the scepticism lurking within it—well, then it's hard to know what to say. It would be hopeless here to sample the arguments which have been offered.[10] Suffice it to mention what is perhaps the most challenging of them, one recently offered by Putnam. I cannot do better than give you David Lewis' summary:

Putnam's thesis is that, in virtue of considerations from the theory of reference, it makes no sense to suppose that an empirically ideal theory, as verified as can be, might nevertheless be false because the world is not the way the theory says it is. The reason given is, roughly, that there is no semantic glue to stick our words onto their referents, and so reference is very much up for grabs; but there is one force constraining reference, and that is our intention to refer in such a way that we come out right; and there is no countervailing force; and the world, no matter what it is like (almost) will afford *some* scheme of reference that makes us come out right; so how can we fail to come out right?[11]

We have been looking at the anti-realist's attack on the correspondence theory of truth. His attack on that, however, by no means completes his attack on realism. From there he moves on to attack at the point of the realist's adherence to mind-independent facts. Contemporary anti-realism incorporates not only a thesis about truth but a thesis about world-constitution.

Whatever be the sort of entity that we propose comparing to reality so as to determine truth, determining its truth requires judging whether certain concepts have application. If by uttering "We had more snow than usual this past winter" I assert that we had more snow than usual this past winter, then my determination of the truth of the sentence in that use requires applying, or judging the applicability of, such concepts as *snow* and *winter*. But there is no way, says the anti-realist, for us to judge the fit of concepts to mind-independent unconceptualized reality. For to reality unconceptualized we have no access. Let's be clear, says Putnam, that anti-realism "does not deny that there are experiential *inputs* to knowledge . . . ; but it does deny that there are any inputs *which are not themselves to some extent shaped by our concepts*, by the vocabulary we use to report and describe them, or any inputs *which admit of only one description, independent of all conceptual choices*. Even our description of our own sensations, so dear as a starting point for knowledge to generations of epistemologists, is heavily affected (as are the sensations themselves, for that matter) by a host of conceptual choices. The very inputs upon which our knowledge is based are conceptually contaminated . . ."[12] Thus ours is the Kantian or Quinean predicament "that there is a real world *but* we can only describe [and perceive] it in terms of our own conceptual systems . . ."[13] Accordingly, ". . . the notion of comparing our system of beliefs with unconceptualized reality to see if they match makes no sense . . ."[14] ". . . the notion of a transcendent match between our representation and the world is nonsense."[15]

The trouble, says the anti-realist, is not that we can never tell whether the conceptual structure we impose on reality fits the structure it has apart from us. Rather, it *has* no structure apart from us. " 'Objects' do not exist independently of conceptual schemes. *We* cut up the world into objects when we introduce one or another scheme of description."[16] Or to put the point in a somewhat more Kantian fashion: The very phenomenon of there being objects which we can experience again and which others can also experience is a consequence of our conceptualizing. Apart from our conceptualizing, the phenomena of *same thing again* and *different thing this time* do not occur.

In turn, *kinds* of objects do not exist independently of our conceptual schemes. " . . . 'of the same kind' makes no sense apart from a categoreal system which says what properties do and what properties do not count as similarities."[17] The fact that things come in kinds is the consequence of our performing the activity of distinguishing them into kinds. We impose the structure whereby two things are identified as both belonging to suchandsuch kind and whereby two other things are differentiated as one belonging to suchandsuch kind and the other not. Apart from our conceptualizing, the phenomena of *another thing of the same kind* and *a thing of a different kind* do not occur.

And now what must be added, says the contemporary anti-realist, is that it is always possible to carve up the world into objects and kinds of objects differently from how we actually do carve it up. A paradigm for how things go is that where you and I (purportedly) see only snow, the Eskimo is reported to distinguish a multitude of different kinds of snow.

It's worth remarking parenthetically here that though Kant would agree with his present day successors on this point concerning alternative modes of objectizing and sorting, his emphasis would be different. He would insist that whatever objectizings and sortings we may practice, they will always, deep down, exhibit a common ineluctable structure. On this matter our contemporary anti-realists tend either to be silent or to disagree with Kant.

Up to this point I have been using Putnam for my exposition of contemporary anti-realism. But this thesis, that the world's structure of objects and kinds is something we impose upon it, is so central and pivotal to the entire vision of the anti-realist that it may be well to let one or two others have their say here. Nelson Goodman, giving voice momentarily to an objection, asks "Shouldn't we stop speaking of right versions as if each were, or had, its own, world and recognize all as versions of one and the same neutral and underlying world?" His answer is firm: "The world thus regained . . . is a world without kinds or order or motion or rest or pattern—a world not worth fighting for or against."[18] And Ernst Cassirer, whom I have already cited, says that ". . . language and myth [are] spiritual functions which do not take their departure from a world of given objects, divided according to fixed and finished 'attributes,' but which actually first produce this organization of reality and make the positing of attributes possible."[19]

Of course the anti-realist does not regard our worlds as made up out of whole cloth. We should not, says Putnam, describe the view of the anti-realist as one "in which the mind *makes up* the world . . ." Rather, "If one must use metaphorical language, then let the metaphor be this: the mind and the world jointly make up the mind and the world."[20]

But if there are no recognizable objects and no objects of different sorts apart from our conceptualizing of reality, then too there are no facts apart from such activities of ours. Goodman chooses the phrase, "The Fabrication of Facts," as the title for one of the chapters in his *Ways of Worldmaking*, and then adds that this title has the virtue of "irritating those fundamentalists who know very well that facts are found not made, that facts constitute the one and only real world, and that knowledge consists of believing the facts."[21] The world is not constituted of a domain of facts waiting to be discovered and reported. Apart from our intellectual activities the world no more has a constitution of facts than of things and kinds. Only our various ways of taking the world have such a constitution; and it is we who constitute these various world versions.

But what then about ourselves and our version-constituting activity? Though the world has no constitution as such, do *we* nevertheless have one? To this Kant said "Yes," thereby postulating a self which transcends the world. It belongs to the *essence* of the self, he said, to constitute a spatio-temporal world version; but the self and its version-constituting activity is not itself something that the self constitutes. Our contemporary anti-realists, by contrast, have no taste for the transcendent, nor indeed for essences, not even for an essence of us, the world constituters. So Kant's way out—if that is what it is—is not available to them. The constituting self and its constituting activities are part of the world it constitutes. If the world as such has no constitution of things and kinds and facts, if whatever has a constitution has been constituted by us, then the self and its version-constituting activity are also part of the version it constitutes. Accordingly, it does not belong to the constitution of the world that there are human beings who constitute world versions. Neither, presumably, does it belong to the constitution of the world as such that it has no constitution. Rather, the facts that self and world have no constitution are themselves merely facets of how we constitute the world, facets of how we take the world—facets, it will be said, of *all* our versions of the world, but nonetheless, presumably, not *necessarily* such. The fact that the world has no constitution apart from us is not a fact about the world apart from us. It too is nothing more than a feature of our way of constituting the world; and presumably in this respect too we could have constituted the world differently.

These paradoxical results cry out for further reflection: Do they or do they not show that the position of the anti-realist is just incoherent? But rather than responding here to that cry, let me go on to call to your attention how different this contemporary dispute between realism and anti-realism is from the dispute in the Middle Ages which goes under the same rubric. To mark the difference, let me distinguish two different kinds of realism and anti-realism and name

them with words borrowed from Alvin Plantinga which he used for the same purpose. As preliminary, let us recognize that realism and anti-realism are always to be understood as *relative* to some domain of entities; one is a realist or anti-realist *with respect to* suchandsuch entities. Then what may be called *existential* anti-realism with respect to some entity or entities is the claim that that entity does not exist or those entities do not exist. By contrast, *creative* anti-realism with respect to some entity or entities is the claim that were it not for the intellectual activities of human beings, that entity would not exist or entities of that sort would not exist. Creative anti-realism is not the denial of the existence of entities but the affirmation of a subjunctive conditional to the effect that suchandsuch entities would not exist were it not for the practice of certain human intellectual activities.

Anti-realism in the Middle Ages was *existential* anti-realism, with respect to universals outside the mind. The contemporary anti-realism on which I have my eye in this discussion is *creative* anti-realism, with respect to everything whatsoever. With respect to everything whatsoever, and with respect to things of every kind whatsoever, the contemporary anti-realist says that there would not be that thing nor things of that kind were it not for the conceptualizing activities of human beings. Apart from us and our intellectual activities there are no ducks, no dens, no denizens of dens.

Nonetheless, though our present day dispute between realism and anti-realism is profoundly different from that which goes under the same name in the Middle Ages, there is, I suggest, a deep-lying continuity between the two. Fundamental to contemporary anti-realism is the affirmation of nominalism—that is, of existential anti-realism with respect to universals outside the mind. Radical creative anti-realism is the resolute spinning out of the implications of nominalism.

To see this, let us go back now and probe more deeply what our present day anti-realist says about truth. Correspondence theories of truth will have to go, he says, in favor of some epistemic theory of truth. The root thought is well expressed by Michael Dummett when he says that even the realist could, and indeed should, "agree to the following . . . principle: that a statement cannot be true unless it is in principle capable of being known to be true." From that principle, suggests Dummett, it is but a small step to this other principle: "that in virtue of which a statement is true is that by which the statement might be known to be true." Dummett then goes on to say that the fundamental difference between the realist and the anti-realist lies in this: "that, in the second principle, the anti-realist interprets 'capable of being known' to mean 'capable of being known *by us*', whereas the realist interprets it to mean 'capable of being known by some hypothetical being whose intellectual capacities and powers of observation may exceed our own'."[22]

I myself waffle back and forth as to whether there is even that connection between truth and knowledge which Dummett states in his first principle and which he says even the realist ought to acknowledge. The point to take from Dummett, though, is the realization that fundamental to anti-realism is the conviction that truth is connected to knowability, or less rigorously, to warranted assertibility: what makes a proposition true is connected with what makes us warranted in accepting and asserting it.

As Putnam remarks, however, we cannot simply "*identify* truth with rational acceptability. Truth cannot *be* rational acceptability for one fundamental reason; truth is supposed to be a property of a statement that cannot be lost, whereas justification can be lost."[23] Putnam's own suggestion, then, is that truth is to be identified with some *ideal* rational acceptability. Truth, he says, is "*assertibility* (by creatures with our rational natures) *under optimal conditions* (as determined by our sensible natures)."[24]

This suggestion raises a great many problems of interpretation. Rather than worrying those problems, however, let me move on to remind you of one of the important points made by Plantinga in his APA Presidential Address on this topic.[25] Plantinga

observed—let me put it now in my own terms—that, given the anti-realist's test-immanent concept of truth, the *thesis concerning truth* of the anti-realist entails the *thesis concerning world-constitution*. The argument in essence goes like this: The truth-theory of the anti-realist is that a sentence-in-a-use is true only if it satisfies our ideal tests or criteria for rational assertibility. So take a sentence like "There are some ducks," when used to assert that there are some ducks. Now if there are no criteria for ideal rational assertibility, then of course this sentence-in-this-use won't satisfy any such criteria. And if it doesn't satisfy any such criteria, then it won't, according to the anti-realist, be true. But if there were not human beings, there wouldn't be any such criteria. For criteria, as the radical anti-realist sees the matter, are laid down, established, ordained, by us. The world doesn't *just come* with criteria for rational acceptability of sentences. So if there were no human beings, it wouldn't be true that there are some ducks—from which it all too obviously follows that there wouldn't be any ducks. Hence, on this view, if there were no human beings, there would be no ducks—a conclusion which common sense and science join in telling us to pull back from.

This argument seems to me entirely cogent; and I judge it to be a reductio ad absurdum of the anti-realist's theory of truth. It is clear, however, that the anti-realist will not judge it so; he will not regard the consequence as absurd. For what the argument essentially shows, to repeat, is that the anti-realist's truth thesis entails his world-constitution thesis. But the anti-realist, so far from being repelled by this consequence, embraces it with fervor. Says Putnam, "the empirical world . . . depends upon our criteria of rational acceptability . . . we must have criteria of rational acceptability to even have an empirical world . . . I am saying that the 'real world' depends upon our values."[26]

What we shall have to do, then, is go beyond pointing out the connection of the truth-thesis of the anti-realist to his world-constitution thesis, and probe the former by itself. Here we might go in either of two directions. We might scrutinize the argument Putnam offers in favor of the conclusion that a non-epistemic concept of truth is unintelligible; or we might reflect on the intelligibility and consequences of the proposal as such. I judge that David Lewis, in the article referred to, and Alvin Plantinga, in the address referred to, have already adequately done the former; accordingly, I shall move on to the latter.

In my discussion up to this point I have tacitly assumed that the primary bearers of truth and falsehood are propositions, and that such acts as believing and asserting have propositions as their objects. Indeed, I would define a proposition as what can be asserted or believed. Thus a proposition is a Fregean *Gedanke;* only I depart from Frege in holding that propositions should not be identified with the sense of sentences. Here I accept the point, made for the first time, I believe, by Richard Cartwright in his article on propositions, that if, for example, you and I both assertively utter the English sentence, "I am in Milwaukee," we will have used the same sentence with the same meaning even though we will have asserted different propositions.

Now it is by doing such things as uttering sentences, that we *assert* propositions; given the right conditions, our utterance of the sentence *counts as* our asserting something. And if the something we assert, the proposition, is true, then we can also, derivatively, apply "true" to the sentence-in-that-use. As a convenient piece of terminology, let me say that the proposition asserted, in a given case of assertion, in a given case of assertion, is the *propositional content* of that belief or assertion—or more simply, is the *content* of it. And so too, let me say that the proposition asserted by someone's uttering of a sentence is the *propositional content* of that sentence-in-that-use. Furthermore, let us understand the *truth-condition* of a sentence-in-a-use to be that by virtue of which its content is true. In analogous fashion, we can understand the truth-condition of an act of asserting, or of a state of believing, to be that by virtue of which *its* content is true.

I am myself inclined to think that propositions are identical with states of affairs; and correspondingly, that the truth and falsehood of propositions is the same phenomenon as the holding or not holding of states of affairs. Further, I take states of affairs which are occurring to be the same as facts. Thus, on my view, there is not some sort of "representation" relation holding between, on the one hand, the propositional content of beliefs and assertions and sentences-in-uses, and on the other hand, states of affairs in the world. Rather, the content *is* a state of affairs—though of course it may not be a state of affairs which is holding, or occurring.

So suppose one asserts *that P* by uttering the sentence "P." Then the correspondence theory of truth says that the sentence "P" in that use is true by virtue of its being a fact *that P.* In other words, its truth-condition consists in its content's being true, or occurring, or being a fact. Its truth-condition does not consist in there being that proposition which is its content. Nor is that proposition itself its truth-condition. The truth-condition is this: *that proposition's occurring, that proposition's being true.* So too, the truth-condition of the *assertion that P* consists in its content's being true, or occurring, or being a fact; and similarly for the truth-condition of the *belief that P.* It follows that to *ascertain* whether "P" in some use is true I must ascertain whether its content holds, or is a fact, or is true, and so also, similarly, for beliefs and assertions. Of course, no one should suppose that in affirming all these things the correspondence theorist sees himself as *defining* "truth" or "is true."

Sometimes those who hold a correspondence theory maintain that there is some sort of isomorphism between sentences and facts; I have confined myself to the more basic thesis. And sometimes the correspondence theory is formulated as the thesis that an assertion is true by virtue of that to which one refers being as one says about it that it is. This assumes that whenever one asserts something, one refers to something and says something about it. Whether this assumption is correct is indeed an important issue; but I have put the thesis of the correspondence theorist in such a way that it also does not require commitment on this point.

To all this, the modern anti-realist says, Not so. The truth of "P" in some use does not consist in its content's holding but consists rather in the assertive utterance of the sentence on that occasion's satisfying ideal criteria for rational assertibility. Accordingly, to ascertain whether "P" is true I must ascertain whether my assertive utterance of "P" satisfies those criteria—I must ascertain, in short, whether it is *a fact* that my utterance satisfies the ideal criteria for rational assertibility. I don't try to ascertain whether the *content* of the sentence-in-that-use holds, but whether the state of affairs holds of my utterance's satisfying the ideal tests for rational assertibility.

It is of indispensable importance to realize here that the anti-realist of Putnam's stripe does not eliminate facts from the determination of truth, nor the ascertaining of facts from the process of ascertaining truth. Indeed, what else could ground something's being true than a fact—only facts can ground facts? Rather, the anti-realist claims that the facts grounding truth are exclusively facts about the satisfaction of ideal tests for rational assertibility and acceptability. Putnam himself embraces this point firmly. He says: That "there *are* better and worse epistemic conditions for most judgments, and a fact of the matter as to what the verdict would be if the conditions were sufficiently good, a verdict to which opinion would 'converge' if we were reasonable, is the heart of my own 'realism'." It *is*, he goes on, "a kind of realism, and I mean it to be a *human* kind of realism, a belief that there is a fact of the matter as to what is rightly assertible for us, as opposed to what is rightly assertible from the God's eye view so dear to the classical metaphysical realist."[27]

Reflection on this proposal will produce in most of us, I venture, a strange sense of dislocation, of always being out of phase. By uttering sentence "P" I assert *that P*. But "P" in that use is not true by virtue of its content's being a fact. Its truth-condition is not the factuality of its content. Rather, it is true by virtue of my assertive utterance of its being ideally ra-

tionally justified. Its truth-condition is the factuality of the satisfaction of its justification criteria. The *content* of the sentence in this use and its *truth-condition* are out of phase. Furthermore, Putnam does not deny that P may be a fact—for example, that it may be a fact that it snowed more than usual this past winter. He just denies that that fact makes true the sentence, "It snowed more than usual this past winter," even when I use that sentence to assert that it did snow more than usual this past winter.

But let us disregard these feelings of dislocation and press on yet deeper into the forest, trying now to articulate the vague intuition, which I suppose most of us have, that if the anti-realist were right, the ascertaining of the truth of anything whatsoever would be forever beyond our grasp.

Suppose I decide to ascertain whether "P" on the occasion in question satisfies the ideal tests for rational assertibility. Now one thing to say here at the start is that we don't know what those tests are; the notion of *ideal tests* is an eschatological concept. They are the tests which humanity will have adopted when it finally arrives at uncoerced consensus—or something like that. Already then we have the ironic development that, for the anti-realist, though truth may not be beyond our present grasp, it is beyond our present ascertaining. But let us not dwell on this point. Let us rather suppose that the anti-realist equates truth with the satisfaction of our best present tests for warranted assertibility—this of course having the consequence to which we saw Putnam pointing, that present truth may well not be future truth.

So let's start again: Suppose that I try to ascertain whether "P" on the occasion in question satisfies our *present* best tests for rational assertibility; and suppose now further that I come to the conclusion that, Yes indeed, the tests are satisfied. In other words, I come to *believe* that they are. What now determines the truth of my believing?

Well, the content of my belief is that the criteria for the rational assertibility of sentence "P" are satisfied on this occasion. But what determines its truth is not its content's being a fact. It may indeed *be* a fact; we have just heard Putnam saying that emphatically. But the truth-condition of a belief is not to be identified with its content's being a fact; what determines its truth is not the factuality of its content but the factuality of its rational assertibility. Accordingly, to *ascertain* whether my belief is true, my belief, viz., that the criteria for my rationally uttering sentence "P" are satisfied, I must try to ascertain, not whether it is a fact that *those* criteria are satisfied, but instead whether it is a fact that I am *warranted in believing* that those criteria are satisfied.

Suppose then that I investigate this new matter—not now the rationality of my utterance but the rationality of my belief about the rationality of my utterance—and come to a belief on *this* matter. What is it that determines the truth of this new belief about the rationality of my first belief? Once again, not whether the content of the believing is a fact but whether it is a fact that the conditions for rational acceptance of this new belief are satisfied.

Clearly we are off on a vicious regress of truth-ascertainings. What determines the truth of a belief is never its content's being a fact—though it may indeed be a fact—but whether the belief's being rationally held is a fact. Accordingly, to ascertain whether a belief is true we try to ascertain the facts not about its content but about its rational acceptability. Unless we remain undecided, we then form a new belief concerning the facts about the rational acceptability of the original belief. But to ascertain the truth of this new belief, we must again not try to ascertain whether its content is a fact—though again it may be—but whether it's a fact that *it* is rationally acceptable. And so on and on. What offends the anti-realist in the picture of the realist is that there can and may be facts whose truth can never be ascertained by us. His own counter-proposal ironically has the consequence that we can never ascertain the truth of anything. Take any belief: to ascertain whether it is true I must ascertain whether the belief next up in the hierarchy is true.

One can see, I think, how Putnam was

thinking: We can ascertain whether our tests for rational acceptability and assertibility are satisfied; the results of our tests are accessible to us. But how are we ever to ascertain the objective fact about how much it snowed this past winter? The contrast is an illusion, however. Surely it is often much easier to tell how much it snowed, than whether some belief is rationally acceptable or some sentence rationally assertible. The criteria for rationality are as much "out there" as the snow; or perhaps we should say that the snow is as much "in here" as the criteria.

How can this Putnam regress be avoided? Well, the obvious way to avoid it is to return to the correspondence theory with its test-transcendent concept of truth: The truth of a belief or assertion, and of a sentence-in-a-use, is determined by the holding of its content. What generates the Putnam regress is the discrepancy between the holding of its content and its truth-conditions. The correspondence theorist avoids that regress by avoiding that discrepancy.

But is it really true, someone may well protest at this juncture, that the anti-realist separates the truth-condition of a sentence-in-a-use from the holding of its content? Does he not rather join the realist in insisting that these are identical, departing only in his further insistence that the content of a sentence-in-a-use just consists of those conditions which determine its warranted assertibility?

Possibly this is the view expressed in some of the writings of Michael Dummett—though I say this hesitantly, since I find Dummett's views on this matter highly elusive. This would, though, fit the fact that Dummett describes the realist/anti-realist dispute as one about the *meaning* of certain statements and not (just) about the meaning of "truth." He says, "The dispute thus concerns the notion of truth appropriate for statements of the disputed class; and this means that it is a dispute concerning the kind of *meaning* which these statements have."[28]

It will be noted that Dummett speaks here about the meaning of *statements*, whereas I have spoken exclusively about the meaning of *sentences*. I am not at all confident that I know what Dummett has in mind by a statement. He does, though, equate statements with what he sometimes calls *assertoric utterances*. And that suggests that perhaps what he means by a statement, where that is understood as an act, is just what I would call an *act of asserting something by uttering something*. In any case, I fail to see what else he could mean. And if this is indeed what he means, then it seems likely that the *meaning* of a statement is just what I would call the propositional content of that act of asserting-by-uttering.

Consider, then, this sentence from Dummett: "For the anti-realist, an understanding of (a statement from a disputed class) consists in knowing what counts as evidence adequate for the assertion of the statement, and the truth of the statement can consist only in the existence of such evidence."[29] Upon reading this in the context of the entire essay in which it occurs, it appears to me that Dummett affirms or presupposes at least the following two theses here:

(1) The meaning of a statement consists of its truth-condition.

(2) A statement's truth-condition consists in its satisfying the criteria for its justified assertion.

But the combination of these two theses yields incoherence. Each of (1) and (2) by itself is intelligible enough. (1) just says that the content of an act of asserting-by-uttering is its truth-condition; and that seems to me true, if it is granted that a more precise formulation of the point is that the *holding* of its content is its truth-condition. (2), on the other hand, just affirms what I have been taking the anti-realist of the Putnam sort to say about truth. But someone who holds *both* (1) and (2) holds, in effect, that what we assert is never anything other than that we are warranted in making the assertion-by-utterance that we are making; whereas surely in all but a few unusual self-reflexive cases, this is not what we assert. One can indeed

claim that there is evidence for what one said; but it makes no sense to regard what one said in assertively uttering "P" as *that* there is evidence for what one said in assertively uttering "P." The anti-realist cannot identify the truth-conditions of sentences-in-uses with the holding of their content, when he regards the truth-conditions as conditions for warranted assertion, on pain of tumbling into incoherence. Such identification does not provide him with a way of avoiding the Putnam regress.

There is, though, a way of avoiding the Putnam regress other than that of returning home to the correspondence-theory—a way, however, which yields a form of anti-realism more radical than that embraced by Putnam. One might deny that there are any facts—and correspondingly, that beliefs and assertions and sentences-in-uses have any such thing as truth-conditions. For truth-conditions, remember, are always facts. Sentences, so it might be said, do indeed have correct and incorrect uses, just as for pieces in chess there are correct and incorrect moves. Specifically, declarative sentences have assertibility conditions. But the notion of truth-conditions must be discarded. Correctness of utterance is not determined by truth-conditions.

I am not inventing this view. It is, I judge, the view of the late Wittgenstein. Certainly it is the view which Saul Kripke *attributes* to the late Wittgenstein in his recent book, *Wittgenstein on Rules and Private Language*. Here, for example, is what Kripke says:

Wittgenstein replaces the question, "What must be the case for this sentence to be true?" by two others: first, "under what conditions may this form of words be appropriately asserted (or denied)?"; second, given an answer to the first question, "What is the role, and the utility, in our lives of our practice of asserting (or denying) the form of words under these conditions?"[30]

But the fact that this view, rejecting, as it does, the existence of facts and truth-conditions, does not generate the Putnam regress, is a virtue scarcely worth celebrating. For the Wittgenstein view generates its own peculiar regress, one just as vicious as the Putnam regress. Let us see how that happens.

Suppose I utter the sentence "P" and thereby assert *that P*. Though neither the sentence in this use nor my assertion has any truth-condition, nonetheless my uttering of the sentence is correct or incorrect—either in accord with the rules of the language or out of accord. It will be correct just in case the conditions of warranted assertibility which pertain to the sentence are satisfied on this occasion. Suppose then that I decide to ascertain whether my utterance of "P" was correct, when on this occasion I used it to assert *that P*. Now of course I do not try to ascertain whether it is a fact *that P*; that is, I do not try to ascertain whether the content of my assertion is a fact. For there are no facts. But also, and for the same reason, I do not try to ascertain whether it is a fact that the conditions of warranted assertibility for "P" are satisfied.

So what do I do then? Well, here it is important to keep in mind that picture which comes through so powerfully in late Wittgenstein of us as prisoners within our house of language. What I do is try to ascertain whether it would be correct assertively to utter the new sentence, "The conditions for the warranted assertibility of "P" were satisfied." Let us, in the manner of analytic philosophers, call this new sentence, "P*." So what now do I do to ascertain whether the conditions for warranted assertibility of "P*" are satisfied? Do I try to ascertain the fact of the matter? Not at all. There are no facts of the matter. Instead I try to ascertain whether it would be correct to utter this other sentence, call it "P**" . . . But you get the point. To ascertain whether it would be correct to utter one sentence I must ascertain whether it would be correct to utter another, and to ascertain whether it would be correct to utter that other I must ascertain whether it would be correct to utter yet another, and so forth. Wittgenstein's view yields a regress fully as vicious as

Putnam's—though a regress of correctness-ascertainings rather than of truth-ascertainings. For any sentence in the series, to ascertain whether it is correct to utter it assertively I must ascertain whether it is correct to utter assertively the next one higher up in the series.

The conclusion has to be that a correspondence theory of truth is inescapable. Twist and turn as we may, it cannot be avoided. At some point we have to break out of our prison of criterial facts or our prison of sentences and gratefully frolic among the richness of the world's facts.

But now for an important and generally overlooked point: From this it does not follow that the anti-realist is mistaken in his claim that the world as such has no constitution of objects, kinds and facts—that only the world as we constitute it has such a constitution. Earlier we saw that the truth-thesis of the anti-realist entails the world-constitution thesis. The connection does not hold in the reverse direction, however. The falsity of the truth-thesis does not entail the falsity of the world-constitution thesis. If the thesis that the world is inherently constitutionless is not itself contradictory, then no inconsistency is yielded by conjoining that thesis with the correspondence-theorist's claim that what makes the sentence true, "We had more snow than usual this past winter," when by uttering it I assert that we had more snow than usual this past winter, is its being a fact that we had more snow than usual this past winter. After all, the creative anti-realist (of the non-extreme sort) does not deny facts; rather, he holds that there would be no facts were it not for our activities of constituting world-versions. Putnam indeed thinks there is a connection in the direction where I am denying a connection. He says that "If the notion of comparing our system of beliefs with unconceptualized reality makes no sense, then the claim that science seeks to discover the truth can mean no more than that science seeks to construct a world picture which, in the ideal limit, satisfies certain criteria of rational acceptability."[31] But this, I suggest, is a non-sequitur. And since it is a non-sequitur, to dispose of the truth-thesis of the anti-realist is not to have disposed of anti-realism as a whole; it is not to have disposed of the world-constitution thesis. Indeed, my own interpretation of Kant is that he combined a correspondence theory of truth with the theory that we are the constitutors of our world. In conclusion, then, we must turn, all too briefly, to a consideration of the world-constitution thesis of the anti-realist.

Is it not absurd, says the creative anti-realist, to suppose that we can take our concepts in one hand and some segment of reality in the other and ask whether one of the concepts *fits* the reality? For we have no access to reality unconceptualized. I open my eyes and what do I see? A goose, perhaps. But *goose* is one of our concepts. Seeing is conceptual. I introspect and what do I notice? A feeling of vertigo, perhaps. But *feeling of vertigo* is one of our concepts. Introspecting is conceptual. There is no bare unconceptualized given. The given is always already conceptualized, always already divided up into geese and non-geese, feelings of vertigo and non-feelings-of-vertigo, or whatever. And it may be added that however a given person or group of persons divides up reality, it might always have been divided up differently. Though perhaps there are some deep-lying structural demands on all such possible dividings, reality's structure of things and kinds and facts is imparted to it by us in our application of concepts. Apart from us, it has no such structure.

This argument—or rather, this picture—has proved powerfully compelling for many people. But rather than just giving in and saying, "I too believe, help me in my unbelief," let us consider what might be said in response. The argument assumes that since *goose* is one of our concepts, reality apart from us does not come with geese in it. But why exactly is this thought to be so? Why can't it both be true that wholly apart from our conceptualizing activities, reality contains geese, and that some of us have the concept goose and find that it has application?

To answer this question, the anti-realist must tip his hand and reveal what he takes a concept to be; and it proves to be on this that the issue pivots. The anti-realist understands a concept to be a *rule*. Exactly what kind of rule is not so clear; perhaps we can let it go here by saying, a rule for ordering experience. In this he follows Kant. Kant took the immensely important and creative step of breaking with the practice of his "way of ideas" predecessors of construing concepts as a special kind of image, or perception. A concept, said Kant, is a rule for unifying the disparate manifold of intuitions—not itself an image or an intuition but a rule whereby a series of intuitions is unified as being "all of the same object," or alternatively, "all of objects of the same sort." It's because our concept of *goose* is a rule for the unification of the disparate protean stuff of reality that we cannot suppose that apart from us there are geese; there's only the disparate protean stuff of reality.

But now suppose that concepts, instead of being rules that we follow for introducing unities and divisions into reality, are graspings of properties; suppose, that is, that to have the concept *goose* is to grasp the property of being a goose. Putnam makes clear that he regards this as a thoroughly regressive proposal; only a "few relics," as he calls them,[32] still suppose that the mind can grasp properties. But let us stifle our horror over being out of step with the avant-garde and suppose for the moment that there are properties and that we can grasp them and that concepts are such graspings. Suppose, further, that some of the properties we grasp are instantiated; suppose, for example, that the property of being a goose is instantiated, as indeed it is, with the result that one of the kinds of things reality contains is geese. Then the resultant picture is very different, indeed, from that of the creative anti-realists. Then we don't *impart* to reality its structure of objects and kinds and facts but we *recognize* that structure.

But what about the snow, you ask. The Eskimo reputedly has over twenty snow-concepts whereas it is said that we have only one—though surely as a matter of fact we have at least two: heavy slushy snow and light fluffy snow. But why is this fact an embarrassment to the realist? There are indeed lots of kinds of snow—many more than twenty. The Eskimo recognizes some of these; we recognize others. His recognitions serve his purposes; ours serve ours. Why should it be supposed that unless we all recognize the same kinds of things in reality, there aren't any kinds of things in reality to recognize?

My suggestion, then, is that the fundamental issue in our contemporary debate between realists and anti-realists is the nature of concepts. Or better, the fundamental issue is whether there are properties which can be both grasped and instantiated. For if there are, then the suggestion that concepts are graspings of properties is obvious; whereas if there are no properties, then probably there is no better way of construing concepts than as rules of roughly the sort Kant suggests. If the anti-realist sticks to his convictions on truth, then his world-constitution thesis just follows. On the other hand, if he repents of his way with truth and once again embraces the correspondence theory, he can still hang onto his conviction that we are the constitutors of our world. It is for that reason that this is the fundamental issue in the debate. The fundamental issue is the tenability of the world-constitution thesis, not of the truth-thesis. And the resolution of that issue hinges on whether or not there are properties—and correlatively, on whether concepts are graspings of properties or whether they are rules for the unification of experience. The fundamental issue is still the old issue of nominalism versus existential realism concerning properties outside the mind. Modern creative anti-realism is, at bottom, the resolute spinning out of the radical implications of nominalism. The more things change, the more they stay the same.

But what, you ask, about alienation: Isn't the anti-realist right at least in observing that the perspective of the realist is an incurably alienating perspective? If nothing else, doesn't anti-realism have a spiritual attraction? Not at all. If the very properties I grasp are properties instantiated in the reality outside me, then surely, in a deep way, reality is not alien to me. It's true that its non-alienated character is not grounded in the fact that it reflects me back to myself; it's not grounded in the fact that its structure of objects and kinds and facts is a structure I have imparted to it. But is there not another mode of being at home with something than that of finding oneself mirrored back to oneself in something one has made? Is there not also the mode of being at home with something which consists of recognizing it, of grasping some of its character and hence no longer finding it strange, mysterious, alien? We are indeed at home in the world, at home because much of it we recognize—not recognize *ourselves* in it, but recognize it. The properties displayed, we grasp.

I close with what, for this audience, will be a rather provocative question: Aquinas, as you well know, held that though everything in the things is particular, natures nonetheless are universalized in the mind. Thus natures as grasped in the mind are fundamentally altered from how they are in the things. Is it fanciful to see there in Paris of the 1200's the beginnings of that alienation of self from world which the contemporary anti-realist goes to such extreme and, in my judgment, misguided lengths to undo?

NOTES

[1] Hilary Putnam, *Reason, Truth, and History* (Cambridge: Cambridge University Press, 1981), pp. xi–xii.

[2] Ernst Cassirer, *Language and Myth* (New York: Harper & Bros., 1946), pp. 6–8.

[3] G. W. F. Hegel, *Aesthetics*, tr. by T. M. Knox (Oxford: Oxford University Press, 1975), Vol. I, pp. 97–98.

[4] Charles Taylor, *Hegel* (Cambridge: Cambridge University Press, 1975), pp. 17–18.

[5] Putnam, *op. cit.*, p. 49.

[6] Hilary Putnam, *Realism and Reason* (Cambridge: Cambridge University Press, 1983), p. 205.

[7] Hilary Putnam, *Meaning and the Moral Sciences* (London: Routledge and Kegan Paul, 1978), p. 125.

[8] Putnam, *RT&H*, p. 49.

[9] Putnam, *M&MS*, p. 126.

[10] I have considered the most substantial argument that Nelson Goodman offers in my "Art in Realist Perspective," forthcoming in *Idealist Studies*.

[11] David Lewis, "Putnam's Paradox," in *Australasian Journal of Philosophy* (Vol. 62, No. 3; Sept. 1984), p. 221.

[12] Putnam, *RT&H*, p. 54.

[13] Putnam, *M&MS*, p. 32.

[14] Putnam, *RT&H*, p. 130.

[15] Putnam, *ibid.*, p. 134.

[16] Putnam, *ibid.*, p. 52.

[17] Putnam, *ibid.*, p. 53.

[18] Nelson Goodman, *Ways of Worldmaking* (Indianapolis: Hackett Publishing Co., 1978), p. 20.

[19] Cassirer, *op. cit.*, p. 66.

[20] Putnam, *RT&H*, p. xi.

[21] Goodman, *op. cit.*, p. 91.

[22] Michael Dummett, *Truth and Other Enigmas* (Cambridge: Harvard University Press, 1978), pp. 23–24.

[23] Putnam, *RT&H*, p. 55.

[24] Putnam, *R&R*, p. 210.

[25] Alvin Plantinga, "How to Be an Anti-Realist," Presidential Address delivered before the Eightieth Annual Western Division Meeting of the American Philosophical Association in Columbus, Ohio, April 29, 1982.

[26] Putnam, *RT&H*, pp. 134–35.

[27] Putnam, *R&R*, p. xviii.

[28] Dummett, *op. cit.*, p. 146.

[29] Dummett, *ibid.*, p. 155.

[30] Saul A. Kripke, *Wittgenstein on Rules and Private Language* (Cambridge: Harvard University Press, 1982), p. 73.

[31] Putnam, *RT&H*, p. 130.

[32] Putnam, *R&R*, p. 209.

On Scientific Realism

The Scope and Language of Science*

W. V. Quine

I

I am a physical object sitting in a physical world. Some of the forces of this physical world impinge on my surface. Light rays strike my retinas; molecules bombard my eardrums and fingertips. I strike back, emanating concentric air waves. These waves take the form of a torrent of discourse about tables, people, molecules, light rays, retinas, air waves, prime numbers, infinite classes, joy and sorrow, good and evil.

My ability to strike back in this elaborate way consists in my having assimilated a good part of the culture of my community, and perhaps modified and elaborated it a bit on my own account. All this training consisted in turn of an impinging of physical forces, largely other people's utterances, upon my surface, and of gradual changes in my own constitution consequent upon these physical forces. All I am or ever hope to be is due to irritations of my surface, together with such latent tendencies to response as may have been present in my original germ plasm. And all the lore of the ages is due to irritation of the surfaces of a succession of persons, together, again, with the internal initial conditions of the several individuals.

Now how is it that we know that our knowledge must depend thus solely on surface irritation and internal conditions? Only because we know in a general way what the world is like, with its light rays, molecules, men, retinas, and so on. It is thus our very understanding of the physical world, fragmentary though that understanding be, that enables us to see how limited the evidence is on which that understanding is predicated. It is our understanding, such as it is, of what lies beyond our surfaces, that shows our evidence for the understanding to be limited to our surfaces. But this reflection arouses certain logical misgivings: for is not our very talk of light rays, molecules, and men then only sound and fury, induced by irritation of our surfaces and signifying nothing? The world view which lent plausibility to this modest account of our knowledge is, according to this very account of our knowledge, a groundless fabrication.

To reason thus is, however, to fall into fallacy: a peculiarly philosophical fallacy, and one whereof philosophers are increasingly aware. We cannot significantly question the reality of the external world, or deny that there is evidence of external objects in the testimony of our senses; for, to do so is simply to dissociate the terms 'reality' and 'evidence' from the very applications which originally did most to invest those terms with whatever intelligibility they may have for us.

We imbibe an archaic natural philosophy with our mother's milk. In the fullness of time, what with catching up on current literature and making some supplementary observations of our own, we become clearer on things. But the process is one of growth and gradual change: we do not break with the past, nor do we attain to standards of evidence and reality different in kind from the vague standards of children and laymen. Science is not a substitute for common sense, but an extension of it. The quest for knowledge is properly an effort simply to broaden and deepen the knowledge which the man in the street already enjoys, in moderation, in relation to the commonplace things around him. To disavow the very core of common sense, to require evidence for that which both the physicist and the man in the street accept as platitudinous, is no laudable perfectionism; it is a pompous confusion, a failure to observe the nice distinction between the baby and the bath water.

Let us therefore accept physical reality, whether in the manner of unspoiled men in the street or with one or another degree of scientific sophistication. In so doing we constitute ourselves recipients and carriers of the evolving lore of the ages. Then, pursuing in detail our thus accepted theory of physical reality, we draw conclusions concerning, in particular, our own physical selves, and even concerning ourselves as lorebearers. One of these conclusions is that this very lore which we are engaged in has been induced in us by irritation of our physical surfaces and not otherwise. Here we have a little item of lore about lore. It does not, if rightly considered, tend to controvert the lore it is about. On the contrary, our initially uncritical hypothesis of a physical world gains pragmatic support from whatever it contributes towards a coherent account of lorebearing or other natural phenomena.

Once we have seen that in our knowledge of the external world we have nothing to go on but surface irritation, two questions obtrude themselves—a bad one and a good one. The bad one, lately dismissed, is the question whether there is really an external world after all. The good one is this: Whence the strength of our notion that there is an external world? Whence our persistence in representing discourse as somehow *about* a reality, and a reality beyond the irritation?

It is not as though the mere occurrence of speech itself were conceived somehow as *prima facie* evidence of there being a reality as subject matter. Much of what we say is recognized even by the man in the street as irreferential: 'Hello', 'Thank you', 'Ho hum', these make no claims upon reality. These are physical responses on a par, semantically, with the patellar reflex. Whence then the idea of scientific objectivity? Whence the idea that language is occasionally descriptive in a way that other quiverings of irritable protoplasm are not?

This is a question for the natural science of the external world: in particular, for the psychology of human animals. The question has two not quite separate parts: whence the insistence on a world of reference, set over against language? and whence the insistence on a world of external objects, set over against oneself? Actually we can proceed to answer this twofold question plausibly enough, in a general sort of way, without any very elaborate psychologizing.

II

Let us suppose that one of the early words acquired by a particular child is 'red'. How does he learn it? He is treated to utterances of the word simultaneously with red presentations; further, his own babbling is applauded when it approximates to 'red' in the presence of red. At length he acquires the art of applying the word neither too narrowly nor too broadly for his mother's tastes. This learning process is familiar to us under many names: association, conditioning, training, habit formation, reinforcement and extinction, induction.

Whatever our colleagues in the laboratory may discover of the inner mechanism of that process, we may be sure of this much: the very possibility of it depends on a prior tendency on the child's part to weight qualitative differences unequally. Logically, as long as a, b, and c are three and not one, there is exactly as much difference between a and b as between a and c; just as many classes, anyway, divide a from b (i.e., contain one and not the other) as a from c. For the child, on the other hand, some differences must count for more than others if the described process of learning 'red' is to go forward at all. Whether innately or as a result of pre-linguistic learning, the child must have more tendency to associate a red ball with a red ball than with a yellow one; more tendency to associate a red ball with a red ribbon than with a blue one; and more tendency to dissociate the ball from its surroundings than to dissociate its parts from one another. Otherwise no training could mold the child's usage of the word 'red', since no future occasion would be more strongly favored by past applications of the word than any other. A working appreciation of something like 'natural kinds', a tendency anyway to respond in different degrees to different differences, has to be there before the word 'red' can be learned.

At the very beginning of one's learning of language, thus, words are learned in relation to such likenesses and contrasts as are already appreciated without benefit of words. No wonder we attribute those likenesses and contrasts to real stuff, and think of language as a superimposed apparatus for talking *about* the real.

The likenesses and contrasts which underlie one's first learning of language must not only be pre-verbally appreciable; they must, in addition, be intersubjective. Sensitivity to redness will avail the child nothing, in learning 'red' from the mother, except insofar as the mother is in a position to appreciate that the child is confronted with something red. Hence, perhaps, our first glimmerings of an external world. The most primitive sense of externality may well be a sense of the mother's reinforcement of likenesses and contrasts in the first phases of word learning. The real is thus felt, first and foremost, as prior to language and external to oneself. It is the stuff that mother vouches for and calls by name.

This priority of the non-linguistic to the linguistic diminishes as learning proceeds. *Scholarship* sets in; i.e., the kind of learning which depends on prior learning of words. We learn 'mauve' at an advanced age, through a verbal formula of the form 'the color of' or 'a color midway between'. And the scholarly principle takes hold early; the child will not have acquired many words before his vocabulary comes to figure as a major agency in its own increase. By the time the child is able to sustain rudimentary conversation in his narrow community, his knowledge of language and his knowledge of the world are a unitary mass.

Nevertheless, we are so overwhelmingly impressed by the initial phase of our education that we continue to think of language generally as a secondary or superimposed apparatus for talking about real things. We tend not to appreciate that most of the things, and most of the supposed traits of the so-called world, are learned through language and believed in by a projection from language. Some uncritical persons arrive thus at a copy theory of language: they look upon elements of language as names of elements of reality, and true discourse as a map of reality. They project vagaries of language indiscriminately upon the world, stuffing the universe with ands and ors, singulars and plurals, definites and indefinites, facts and states of affairs, simply on the ground that there are parallel elements and distinctions on the linguistic side.

The general task which science sets itself is that of specifying how reality "really" is: the task of delineating the structure of reality as distinct from the structure of one or another traditional language (except, of course, when the science happens to be grammar itself). The notion of reality independent of language is carried over by the scientist from his earliest impressions, but the facile reification of linguistic features is avoided or minimized.

But how is it possible for scientists to be thus critical and discriminating about their reifications? If all discourse is mere response to surface irritation, then by what evidence may one man's projection of a world be said to be sounder than another's? If, as suggested earlier, the terms 'reality' and 'evidence' owe their intelligibility to their applications in archaic common sense, why may we not then brush aside the presumptions of science?

The reason we may not is that science is itself a continuation of common sense. The scientist is indistinguishable from the common man in his sense of evidence, except that the scientist is more careful. This increased care is not a revision of evidential standards, but only the more patient and systematic collection and use of what anyone would deem to be evidence. If the scientist sometimes overrules something which a superstitious layman might have called evidence, this may simply be because the scientist has other and contrary evidence which, if patiently presented to the layman bit by bit, would be conceded superior. Or it may be that the layman suffers from some careless chain of reasoning of his own whereby, long since, he came wrongly to reckon certain types of connection as evidential: wrongly in that a careful survey of his own ill-observed and long-forgotten steps would suffice to disabuse him. (A likely example is the "gambler's fallacy"—the notion that the oftener black pays the likelier red becomes.)

Not that the layman has an explicit standard of evidence—nor the scientist either. The scientist begins with the primitive sense of evidence which he possessed as layman, and uses it carefully and systematically. He still does not reduce it to rule, though he elaborates and uses sundry statistical methods in an effort to prevent it from getting out of hand in complex cases. By putting nature to the most embarrassing tests he can devise, the scientist makes the most of his lay flair for evidence; and at the same time he amplifies the flair itself, affixing an artificial proboscis of punch cards and quadrille paper.

Our latest question was, in brief, how science gets ahead of common sense; and the answer, in a word, is 'system'. The scientist introduces system into his quest and scrutiny of evidence. System, moreover, dictates the scientist's hypotheses themselves: those are most welcome which are seen to conduce most to simplicity in the overall theory. Predictions, once they have been deduced from hypotheses, are subject to the discipline of evidence in turn; but the hypotheses have, at the time of hypothesis, only the considerations of systematic simplicity to recommend them. Insofar, simplicity itself—in some sense of this difficult term—counts as a kind of evidence; and scientists have indeed long tended to look upon the simpler of the two hypotheses as not merely the more likeable, but the more likely. Let it not be supposed, however, that we have found at last a type of evidence that is acceptable to science and foreign to common sense. On the contrary, the favoring of the seemingly simpler hypothesis is a lay habit carried over by science. The quest of systematic simplicity seems peculiarly scientific in spirit only because science is what it issues in.

III

The notion of a reality independent of language is derived from earliest impressions, if the speculations in the foregoing pages are right, and is then carried over into science as a matter of course. The stress on externality is likewise carried over into science, and with a vengeance. For the sense of externality has its roots, if our speculations are right, in the intersubjectivity which is so essential to the learning of language; and intersubjectivity is vital not only to language but equally to the further enterprise, likewise a social one, of science. All men are to qualify as witnesses to the data of science, and the truths of science are to be true no matter who pronounces them. Thus it is that science has got on rather with masses and velocities than with likes and dislikes. And thus it is that when science does confront likes and dislikes it confronts them as behavior, intersubjectively observable. Language in general is robustly extravert, but science is more so.

It would be unwarranted rationalism to suppose that we can stake out the business of science in advance of pursuing science and arriving at a certain body of scientific theory. Thus consider, for the sake of analogy, the smaller task of staking out the business of chemistry. Having got on with chemistry, we can describe it *ex post facto* as the study of the combining of atoms in molecules. But no such clean-cut delimitation of the business of chemistry was possible until that business was already in large measure done. Now the situation is similar with science generally. To describe science as the domain of cognitive judgment avails us nothing, for the definiens here is in as urgent need of clarification as the definiendum. Taking advantage of existing scientific work, however, and not scrupling to identify ourselves with a substantive scientific position, we can then delineate the scientific objective, or the cognitive domain, to some degree. It is a commonplace predicament to be unable to formulate a task until half done with it.

Thought, if of any considerable complexity, is inseparable from language—in practice surely and in principle quite probably. Science, though it seeks traits of reality independent of language, can neither get on without language nor aspire to linguistic neutrality. To some degree, nevertheless, the scientist can enhance objectivity and diminish the interference of language, by his very choice of language. And we, concerned to distill the essence of scientific discourse, can profitably purify the language of science beyond what might reasonably be urged upon the practicing scientist. To such an operation we now turn.

In a spirit thus not of practical language reform but of philosophical schematism, we may begin by banishing what are known as *indicator words* (Goodman) or *egocentric particulars* (Russell): 'I', 'you', 'this', 'that', 'here', 'there', 'now', 'then', and the like. This we clearly must do if the truths of science are literally to be true independently of author and occasion of utterance. It is only thus, indeed, that we come to be able to speak of sentences, i.e., certain linguistic forms, as true and false. As long as the indicator words are retained, it is not the sentence but only the several events of its utterance that can be said to be true or false.

Besides indicator words, a frequent source of fluctuation in point of truth and falsity is ordinary ambiguity. One and the same sentence, qua linguistic form, may be true in one occurrence and false in another because the ambiguity of a word in it is differently resolved by attendant circumstances on the two occasions. The ambiguous sentence 'Your mothers bore you' is likely to be construed in one way when it follows on the heels of a sentence of the form 'x bore y', and in another when it follows on the heels of a sentence of the form 'x bores y'.

In Indo-European languages there is also yet a third conspicuous source of fluctuation in point of truth and falsity; viz., tense. Actually tense is just a variant of the phenomenon of indicator words; the tenses can be paraphrased in terms of tenseless verbs governed by the indicator word 'now', or by 'before now', etc.

How can we avoid indicator words? We can resort to personal names or descriptions in place of 'I' and 'you', to dates or equivalent descriptions in place of 'now', and to place names or equivalent descriptions in place of 'here'. It may indeed by protested that something tantamount to the use of indicator words is finally unavoidable, at least in the teaching of the terms which are to be made to supplant the indicator words. But this is no objection; all that matters is the *subsequent* avoidability of indicator words. All that matters is that it be possible in principle to couch science in a notation such that none of *its* sentences fluctuates between truth and falsity from utterance to utterance. Terms which are primitive or irreducible, from the point of view of that scientific notation, may still be intelligible to us only through explanations in an ordinary language rife with indicator words, tense, and ambiguity. Scientific language is in any event a splinter or ordinary language, not a substitute.

Granted then that we can rid science of indicator words, what would be the purpose? A kind of objectivity, to begin with, appropriate to the aims of science: truth becomes invariant with respect to speak and occasion. At the same time a technical purpose is served: that of simplifying and facilitating a basic department of science, viz., deductive logic. For, consider, e.g., the very elementary canons of deduction which lead from 'p and q' to 'p', and from 'p' to 'p or q', and from 'p and if p then q' to 'q'. The letter 'p', standing for any sentence, turns up twice in each of these rules; and clearly the rules are unsound if the sentence which we put for 'p' is capable of being true in one of its occurrences and false in the other. But to formulate logical laws in such a way as not to depend thus upon the assumption of fixed truth and falsity would be decidedly awkward and complicated, and wholly unrewarding.

In practice certainly one does not explicitly rid one's scientific work of indicator words, tense, and ambiguity, nor does one limit one's use of logic to sentences thus purified. In practice one merely *supposes* all such points of variation fixed for the space of one's logical argument; one does not need to resort to explicit paraphrase, except at points where local shifts of context *within* the logical argument itself threaten equivocation.

This practical procedure is often rationalized by positing abstract entities, 'propositions', endowed with all the requisite precision and fixity which is wanting in the sentences themselves; and then saying that it is with propositions, and not their coarse sentential embodiments, that the laws of logic really have to do. But this posit achieves only obscurity. There is less mystery in imagining an idealized form of scientific language in which sentences are so fashioned as never to vacillate between truth and falsity. It is significant that scientific discourse actually does tend toward this ideal, in proportion to the degree of development of the science. Ambiguities and local and epochal biases diminish. Tense, in particular, gives way to a four-dimensional treatment of space-time.

IV

A basic form for sentences of science may be represented as 'Fa', where 'a' stands in place of a singular term referring to some object, from among those which exist according to the scientific theory in question, and 'F' stands in place of a general term or predicate. The sentence 'Fa' is true if and only if the object fulfills the predicate. No tense is to be read into the predication 'Fa'; any relevant dating is to be integral rather to the terms represented by 'F' and 'a'.

Compound sentences are built up of such predications with help of familiar logical connectives and operators: 'and', 'not', the universal quantifier '(x)' ('each object x is such that'), and the existential quantifier '$(\exists x)$' ('at least one object x is such that'). An example is '(x) not (Fx and not Gx)', which says that no object x is such that Fx and not Gx; briefly, every F is a G.

A given singular term and a given general term or predicate will be said to *correspond* if the general term is true of just one object, viz., the object to which the singular term refers. A general term which thus corresponds to a singular term will of course be "of singular extension," i.e., true of exactly one object; but it belongs nevertheless to the grammatical category of general terms, represented by the 'F' rather than the 'a' of 'Fa'. Now the whole category of singular terms can, in the interests of economy, be swept away in favor of general terms, viz., the general terms which correspond to those singular terms. For let 'a' represent any singular term, 'F' any corresponding general term, and '. . . a . . .' any sentence we may have cared to affirm containing 'a'. Then we may instead dispense with 'a' and affirm '$(\exists x)$ (Fx

and . . . x. . .)'. Clearly this will be true if and only if '. . . a . . .' was true. If we want to go on explicitly to remark that the object fulfilling 'F' is unique, we can easily do that too, thus:

$$(x)(y) \text{ not } [Fx \text{ and } Fy \text{ and not } (x = y)]$$

provided that the identity sign '=' is in our vocabulary.

How, it may be asked, can we be sure there will be a general term corresponding to a given singular term? The matter can be viewed thus: we merely *reparse* what had been singular terms as general terms of singular extension, and what had been reference-to as truth-of, and what had been '. . . a . . .' as '($\exists x$) (Fx and . . . x . . .)'. If the old singular term was a proper name learned by ostension, then it is reparsed as a general term similarly learned.

The recent reference to '=' comes as a reminder that relative general terms, or polyadic predicates, must be allowed for along with the monadic ones; i.e., the atomic sentences of our regimented scientific language will comprise not only 'Fx', 'Fy', 'Gx', etc., but also 'Hxy', 'Hzx', 'Jyz', '$Kxyz$', and the like, for appropriately interpreted predicates 'F', 'G', 'H', 'J', 'K', etc. (whereof 'H' might in particular be interpreted as '='). The rest of the sentences are built from these atomic ones by 'and,' 'not,' '(x)', '(y)', etc. Singular terms 'a', 'b', etc., can, we have seen, be left out of account. So can the existential quantifiers '($\exists x$)', '($\exists y$)', etc., since '($\exists x$)' can be paraphrased 'not (x) not'.

Besides simple singular terms there are operators to reckon with, such as '+', which yield complex singular terms such as '$x + y$'. But it is not difficult to see how these can be got rid of in favor of corresponding polyadic predicates—e.g., a predicate 'Σ' such that 'Σzxy' means that z is $x + y$.

This pattern for a scientific language is evidently rather confining. There are no names of objects. Further, no sentences occur within sentences save in contexts of conjunction, negation, and quantification. Yet it suffices very generally as a medium for scientific theory. Most or all of what is likely to be wanted in a science can be fitted into this form, by dint of constructions of varying ingenuity which are familiar to logic students. To take only the most trivial and familiar example, consider the 'if-then' idiom; it can be managed by rendering 'if p then q' as 'not (p and not q)'.

It may be instructive to dwell on this example for a moment. Notoriously, 'not (p and not q)' is no translation of 'if p then q'; and it need not pretend to be. The point is merely that in the places where, at least in mathematics and other typical scientific work, we would ordinarily use the 'if-then' construction, we find we can get on perfectly well with the substitute form 'not (p and not q)', sometimes eked out with a universal quantifier. We do not ask whether our reformed idiom constitutes a genuine semantical analysis, somehow, of the old idiom; we simply find ourselves ceasing to depend on the old idiom in our technical work. Here we see, in paradigm, the contrast between linguistic analysis and theory construction.

V

The variables 'x', 'y', etc., adjuncts to the notation of quantification, bring about a widening of the notion of sentence. A sentence which contains a variable without its quantifier (e.g., 'Fx' or '(y)Fxy', lacking '(x)') is not a sentence in the ordinary true-or-false sense; it is true *for* some values of its free variables, perhaps, and false for others. Called an *open* sentence, it is akin rather to a predicate: instead of having a *truth value* (truth or falsity) it may be said to have an *extension,* this being conceived as the class of those evaluations of its free variables for which it is true. For convenience one speaks also of the extension of a closed sentence, but what is then meant is simply the truth value.

A compound sentence which contains a sentence as a component clause is called an *extensional* context of that component sentence if, whenever you supplant the component by any sentence with the same extension, the compound remains unchanged in point of its own extension. In the special case where the sentences concerned are closed sentences, then, contexts are extensional if all substitutions of truths for true components and falsehoods for false components leave true contexts true and false ones false. In the case of closed sentences, in short, extensional contexts are what are commonly known as truth functions.

It is well known, and easily seen, that the conspicuously limited means which we have lately allowed ourselves for compounding sentences—viz., 'and', 'not', and quantifiers—are capable of generating only extensional contexts. It turns out, on the other hand, that they confine us no more than that; the *only* ways of embedding sentences within sentences which ever obtrude themselves, and resist analysis by 'and', 'not', and quantifiers, prove to be contexts of other than extensional kind. It will be instructive to survey them.

Clearly *quotation* is, by our standards, non-extensional; we cannot freely put truths for truths and falsehoods for falsehoods within quotation, without affecting the truth value of a broader sentence whereof the quotation forms a part. Quotation, however, is always dispensable in favor of spelling. Instead, e.g., of:

Heraclitus said 'πάντα ῥεῖ',
'πάντα ῥεῖ' contains three syllables,

we can say (following Tarski):

Heraclitus said pi-alpha-nu-tau-alpha-space-rho-epsilon-iota,

and correspondingly for the other example, thus availing ourselves of names of letters together with a hyphen by way of concatenation sign. Now, whereas the quotational version showed a sentence (the Greek one) embedded within a sentence, the version based on spelling does not; here, therefore, the question of extensionality no longer arises.

Under either version, we are talking about a certain object—a linguistic form—with help, as usual, of a singular term which refers to that object. Quotation produces one singular term for the purpose; spelling another. Quotation is a kind of picture-writing, convenient in practice; but it is rather spelling that provides the proper analysis for purposes of the logical theory of signs.

We saw lately that singular terms are never finally needed. The singular terms involved in spelling, in particular, can of course finally be eliminated in favor of a notation of the sort envisaged in recent pages, in which there are just predicates, quantifiers, variables, 'and', and 'not'. The hyphen of concatenation then gives way to a triadic predicate analogous to the 'Σ' of §IV, and the singular terms 'pi', 'alpha', etc., give way to general terms which "correspond" to them in the sense of §IV.

A more seriously non-extensional context is indirect discourse: "Heraclitus said that all is flux." This is not, like the case of quotation, a sentence about a specific and namable linguistic form. Perhaps, contrary to the line pursued in the case of quotation, we must accept indirect discourse as involving an irreducibly non-extensional occurrence of one sentence in another. If so, then indirect discourse resists the schematism lately put forward for scientific language.

It is the more interesting, then, to reflect that indirect discourse is in any event at variance with the characteristic objectivity of science. It is a subjective idiom. Whereas quotation reports an external event of speech or writing by an objective description of the observable written shape or spoken sound, on the other hand indirect discourse reports the event in terms rather of a subjective projection of oneself into the imagined state of mind of the speaker or writer in question. Indirect discourse is quotation minus objectivity and precision. To marshal the evidence for indirect discourse is to revert to quotation.

It is significant that the latitude of paraphrase allowable in indirect discourse has never been fixed; and it is more significant that the need of fixing it is so rarely felt. To fix it would be a scientific move, and a scientifically unmotivated one in that indirect discourse tends away from the very objectivity which science seeks.

Indirect discourse, in the standard form 'says that', is the head of a family which includes also 'believes that', 'doubts that', 'is surprised that', 'wishes that', 'strives that', and the like. The subjectivity noted in the case of 'says that' is shared by these other idioms twice over; for what these describe in terms of a subjective projection of oneself is not even the protagonist's speech behavior, but his subjective state in turn.

Further cases of non-extensional idiom, outside the immediate family enumerated above, are 'because' and the closely related phenomenon of the contrary-to-fact conditional. Now it is an ironical but familiar fact that though the business of science is describable in unscientific language as the discovery of causes, the notion of cause itself has no firm place in science. The disappearance of causal terminology from the jargon of one branch of science and another has seemed to mark the progress in understanding of the branches concerned.

Apart from actual quotation, therefore, which we have seen how to deal with, the various familiar non-extensional idioms tend away from what best typifies the scientific spirit. Not that they should or could be generally avoided in everyday discourse, or even in science broadly so-called; but their use dwindles in proportion as the statements of science are made more explicit and objective. We begin to see how it is that the language form schematized in §IV might well, despite its narrow limitations, suffice for science at its purest.

VI

Insofar as we adhere to that idealized schematism, we think of a science as comprising those truths which are expressible in terms of 'and', 'not', quantifiers, variables, and certain predicates appropriate to the science in question. In this enumeration of materials we may seem to have an approxima-

tion to a possible standard of what counts as "purely cognitive." But the standard, for all its seeming strictness, is still far too flexible. To specify a science, within the described mold, we still have to say what the predicates are to be, and what the domain of objects is to be over which the variables of quantification range. Not all ways of settling these details will be congenial to scientific ideals.

Looking at actual science as a going concern, we can fix in a general way on the domain of objects. Physical objects, to begin with—denizens of space-time—clearly belong. This category embraces indiscriminately what would anciently have been distinguished as substances and as modes or states of substances. A man is a four-dimensional object, extending say eighty-three years in the time dimension. Each spatio-temporal part of the man counts as another and smaller four-dimensional object. A president-elect is one such, two months long. A fit of ague is another, if for ontological clarity we identify it, as we conveniently may, with its victim for the duration of the seizure.

Contrary to popular belief, such a physical ontology has a place also for states of mind. An inspiration or a hallucination can, like the fit of ague, be identified with its host for the duration. The feasibility of this artificial identification of any mental seizure, x, with the corresponding time slice x' of its physical host, may be seen by reflecting on the following simple maneuver. Where P is any predicate which we might want to apply to x, let us explain P' as true of x' if and only if P is true of x. Whatever may have been looked upon as evidence, cause, or consequence of P, as applied to x, counts now for P' as applied to x'. This parallelism, taken together with the extensionality of scientific language, enables us to drop the old P and x from our theory and get on with just P' and x', rechristened as P and x. Such, in effect, is the identification. It leaves our mentalistic idioms fairly intact, but reconciles them with a physical ontology.

This facile physicalization of states of mind rests in no way on a theory of parallelism between nerve impulses, say, or chemical concentrations, and the recurrence of pre-determined species of mental state. It might be, now and forever, that the only way of guessing whether a man is inspired, or depressed, or deluded, or in pain, is by asking him or by observing his gross behavior; not by examining his nervous workings, albeit with instruments of undreamed-of subtlety. Discovery of the suggested parallelism would be a splendid scientific achievement, but the physicalization here talked of does not require it.

This physicalization does not, indeed, suffice to make 'inspiration', 'hallucination', 'pain', and other mentalistic terms acceptable to science. Though these become concrete general terms applicable to physical objects, viz., time slices of persons, still they may, some or others of them, remain too vague for scientific utility. Disposition terms, and other predicates which do not lend themselves to immediate verification, are by no means unallowable as such; but there are better and worse among them. When a time slice of a person is to be classified under the head of inspiration or hallucination, and when not, may have been left too unsettled for any useful purpose. But what is then at stake is the acceptability of certain predicates, and not the acceptability of certain objects, values of variables of quantification.

Let us not leave the latter topic quite yet: ontology, or the values available to variables. As seen, we can go far with physical objects. They are not, however, known to suffice. Certainly, as just now argued, we do not need to add mental objects. But we do need to add *abstract* objects, if we are to accommodate science as currently constituted. Certain things we want to say in science may compel us to admit into the range of values of the variables of quantification not only physical objects but also classes and relations of them; also numbers, functions, and other objects of pure mathematics. For, mathematics—not uninterpreted mathematics, but genuine set theory, logic, number theory, algebra of real and complex numbers, differential and integral calculus, and so on—is best looked upon as an integral part of science, on a par with the physics,

economics, etc., in which mathematics is said to receive its applications.

Researches in the foundations of mathematics have made it clear that all of mathematics in the above sense can be got down to logic and set theory, and that the objects needed for mathematics in this sense can be got down to a single category, that of *classes*—including classes of classes, classes of classes of classes, and so one. Our tentative ontology for science, our tentative range of values for the variables of quantification, comes therefore to this: physical objects, classes of them, classes in turn of the elements of this combined domain, and so on up.

We have reached the present stage in our characterization of the scientific framework not by reasoning a priori from the nature of science qua science, but rather by seizing upon traits of the science of our day. Special traits thus exploited include the notion of physical object, the four-dimensional concept of space-time, the classial mold of modern classical mathematics, the true-false orientation of standard logic, and indeed extensionality itself. One or another of these traits might well change as science advances. Already the notion of a physical object, as an intrinsically determinate portion of the space-time continuum, squares dubiously with modern developments in quantum mechanics. Savants there are who even suggest that the findings of quantum mechanics might best be accommodated by a revision of the true-false dichotomy itself.

To the question, finally, of admissible predicates. In general we may be sure that a predicate will lend itself to the scientific enterprise only if it is relatively free from vagueness in certain crucial respects. If the predicate is one which is mainly to be used in application to the macroscopic objects of common sense, then there is obvious utility in there being a general tendency to agreement, among observers, concerning its application to those objects; for it is in such applications that the intersubjective verifiability of the data of science resides. In the case of a predicate which is mainly applicable to scientific objects remote from observation or common sense, on the other hand, what is required is that it be free merely from such vagueness as might blur its theoretical function. But to say these things is merely to say that the predicates appropriate to science are those which expedite the purposes of intersubjective confirmation and theoretical clarity and simplicity. These same purposes govern also the ontological decision—the determination of the range of quantification; for clearly the present tentative ontology of physical objects and classes will be abandoned forthwith when we find an alternative which serves those purposes better.

In science all is tentative, all admits of revision—right down, as we have noted, to the law of the excluded middle. But ontology is, pending revision, more clearly in hand than what may be called *ideology*—the question of admissible predicates. We have found a tentative ontology in physical objects and classes, but the lexicon of predicates remains decidedly open. That the ontology should be relatively definite, pending revision, is required by the mere presence of quantifiers in the language of science; for quantifiers may be said to have been interpreted and understood only insofar as we have settled the range of their variables. And that the fund of predicates should be forever subject to supplementation is implicit in a theorem of mathematics; for it is known that for any theory, however rich, there are classes which are not the extensions (cf. §V) of any of its sentences.

Arguments Concerning Scientific Realism*

Bas van Fraassen

The rigour of science requires that we distinguish well the undraped figure of nature itself from the gay-coloured vesture with which we clothe it at our pleasure.

Heinrich Hertz, quoted by Ludwig Boltzmann, letter to Nature, *28 February 1895*

In our century, the first dominant philosophy of science was developed as part of logical positivism. Even today, such an expression as 'the received view of theories' refers to the views developed by the logical positivists, although their heyday preceded the Second World War.

In this chapter I shall examine, and criticize, the main arguments that have been offered for scientific realism. These arguments occurred frequently as part of a critique of logical positivism. But it is surely fair to discuss them in isolation, for even if scientific realism is most easily understood as a reaction against positivism, it should be able to stand alone. The alternative view which I

*Reprinted by permission of Oxford University Press, from van Fraassen, *The Scientific Image,* pp. 6–25, 32–40. Oxford: Oxford University Press, 1980.

advocate—for lack of a traditional name I shall call it *constructive empiricism*—is equally at odds with positivist doctrine.

§1. SCIENTIFIC REALISM AND CONSTRUCTIVE EMPIRICISM

In philosophy of science, the term 'scientific realism' denotes a precise position on the question of how a scientific theory is to be understood, and what scientific activity really is. I shall attempt to define this position, and to canvass its possible alternatives. Then I shall indicate, roughly and briefly, the specific alternative which I shall advocate.

§1.1 Statement of Scientific Realism

What exactly is scientific realism? A naïve statement of the position would be this: the picture which science gives us of the world is a true one, faithful in its details, and the entities postulated in science really exist: the advances of science are discoveries, not in-

77

ventions. That statement is too naïve; it attributes to the scientific realist the belief that today's theories are correct. It would mean that the philosophical position of an earlier scientific realist such as C. S. Peirce had been refuted by empirical findings. I do not suppose that scientific realists wish to be committed, as such, even to the claim that science will arrive in due time at theories true in all respects—for the growth of science might be an endless self-correction; or worse, Armageddon might occur too soon.

But the naïve statement has the right flavour. It answers two main questions: it characterizes a scientific theory as a story about what there really is, and scientific activity as an enterprise of discovery, as opposed to invention. The two questions of what a scientific theory is, and what a scientific theory does, must be answered by any philosophy of science. The task we have at this point is to find a statement of scientific realism that shares these features with the naïve statement, but does not saddle the realists with unacceptably strong consequences. It is especially important to make the statement as weak as possible if we wish to argue against it, so as not to charge at windmills.

As clues I shall cite some passages most of which will also be examined below in the contexts of the authors' arguments. A statement of Wilfrid Sellars is this:

> to have good reason for holding a theory is *ipso facto* to have good reason for holding that the entities postulated by the theory exist.

This addresses a question of epistemology, but also throws some indirect light on what it is, in Sellars's opinion, to hold a theory. Brian Ellis, who calls himself a scientific entity realist rather than a scientific realist, appears to agree with that statement of Sellars, but gives the following formulation of a stronger view:

> I understand scientific realism to be the view that the theoretical statements of science are, or purport to be, true generalized descriptions of reality.[1]

This formulation has two advantages: It focuses on the understanding of the theories without reference to reasons for belief, and it avoids the suggestion that to be a realist you must believe current scientific theories to be true. But it gains the latter advantage by use of the word 'purport', which may generate its own puzzles.

Hilary Putnam gives a formulation which he says he learned from Michael Dummett:

> A realist (with respect to a given theory or discourse) holds that (1) the sentences of that theory are true or false; and (2) that what makes them true or false is something external—that is to say, it is not (in general) our sense data, actual or potential, or the structure of our minds, or our language, etc.

He follows this soon afterwards with a further formulation which he credits to Richard Boyd:

> That terms in mature scientific theories typically refer (this formulation is due to Richard Boyd), that the theories accepted in a mature science are typically approximately true, that the same term can refer to the same thing even when it occurs in different theories—these statements are viewed by the scientific realist . . . as part of any adequate scientific description of science and its relations to its objects.

None of these were intended as definitions. But they show I think that truth must play an important role in the formulation of the basic realist position. They also show that the formulation must incorporate an answer to the question what it is to *accept* or *hold* a theory. I shall now propose such a formulation, which seems to me to make sense of the above remarks, and also renders intelligible the reasoning by realists which I shall examine below—without burdening them with more than the minimum required for this.

Science aims to give us, in its theories, a literally true story of what the world is like; and acceptance of a scientific theory involves the belief that it is true. This is the correct statement of scientific realism.

Let me defend this formulation by showing that it is quite minimal, and can be agreed to by anyone who considers himself a scientific realist. The naïve statement said that science tells a true story; the correct statement says only that it is the aim of science to do so. The aim of science is of course not to be identified with individual scientists' motives. The aim of the game of chess is to checkmate your opponent; but the motive for playing may be fame, gold, and glory. What the aim is determines what counts as success in the enterprise as such; and this aim may be pursued for any number of reasons. Also, in calling something *the* aim, I do not deny that there are other subsidiary aims which may or may not be means to that end: everyone will readily agree that simplicity, informativeness, predictive power, explanation are (also) virtues. Perhaps my formulation can even be accepted by any philosopher who considers the most important aim of science to be something which only *requires* the finding of true theories—given that I wish to give the weakest formulation of the doctrine that is generally acceptable.

I have added 'literally' to rule out as realist such positions as imply that science is true if 'properly understood' but literally false or meaningless. For that would be consistent with conventionalism, logical positivism, and instrumentalism. I will say more about this below.

The second part of the statement touches on epistemology. But it only equates acceptance of a theory with belief in its truth.[2] It does not imply that anyone is ever rationally warranted in forming such a belief. We have to make room for the epistemological position, today the subject of considerable debate, that a rational person never assigns personal probability 1 to any propostion except a tautology. It would, I think, be rare for a scientific realist to take this stand in epistemology, but it is certainly possible.[3]

To understand qualified acceptance we must first understand acceptance *tout court.* If acceptance of a theory involves the belief that it is true, then tentative acceptance involves the tentative adoption of the belief that it is true. If belief comes in degrees, so does acceptance, and we may then speak of a degree of acceptance involving a certain degree of belief that the theory is true. This must of course be distinguished from belief that the theory is approximately true, which seems to mean belief that some member of a class centring on the mentioned theory is (exactly) true. In this way the proposed formulation of realism can be used regardless of one's epistemological persuasion.

§1.2 *Alternatives to Realism*

Scientific realism is the position that scientific theory construction aims to give us a literally true story of what the world is like, and that acceptance of a scientific theory involves the belief that it is true. Accordingly, anti-realism is a position according to which the aim of science can well be served without giving such a literally true story, and acceptance of a theory may properly involve something less (or other) than belief that it is true.

What does a scientist do then, according to these different positions? According to the realist, when someone proposes a theory, he is asserting it to be true. But according to the anti-realist, the proposer does not assert the theory; *he displays it,* and claims certain virtues for it. These virtues may fall short of truth: empirical adequacy, perhaps; comprehensiveness, acceptability for various purposes. This will have to be spelt out, for the details here are not determined by the denial of realism. For now we must concentrate on the key notions that allow the generic division.

The idea of a literally true account has two aspects: the language is to be literally construed; and so construed, the account is true. This divides the anti-realists into two sorts. The first sort holds that science is or aims to be true, properly (but not literally) construed. The second holds that the language of science should be literally construed, but its theories need not be true to be good. The anti-realism I shall advocate belongs to the second sort.

It is not so easy to say what is meant by a literal construal. The idea comes perhaps from theology, where fundamentalists construe the Bible literally, and liberals have a variety of allegorical, metaphorical, and analogical interpretations, which 'demythologize'. The problem of explicating 'literal construal' belongs to the philosophy of language. In Section 6 below, where I briefly examine some of Michael Dummett's views, I shall emphasize that 'literal' does not mean 'truth-valued'. The term 'literal' is well enough understood for general philosophical use, but if we try to explicate it we find ourselves in the midst of the problem of giving an adequate account of natural language. It would be bad tactics to link an inquiry into science to a commitment to some solution to that problem. The following remarks should fix the usage of 'literal' sufficiently for present purposes.

The decision to rule out all but literal construals of the language of science, rules out those forms of anti-realism known as *positivism* and *instrumentalism*. First, on a literal construal, the apparent statements of science really are statements, *capable of* being true or false. Secondly, although a literal construal can elaborate, it cannot change logical relationships. (It is possible to elaborate, for instance, by identifying what the terms designate. The 'reduction' of the language of phenomenological thermodynamics to that of statistical mechanics is like that: bodies of gas are identified as aggregates of molecules, temperature as mean kinetic energy, and so on.) On the positivists' interpretation of science, theoretical terms have meaning only through their connection with the observable. Hence they hold that two theories may in fact *say the same thing* although in form they contradict each other. (Perhaps the one says that all matter consists of atoms, while the other postulates instead a universal continuous medium; they will say the same thing nevertheless if they agree in their observable consequences, according to the positivists.) But two theories which contradict each other in such a way can 'really' be saying the same thing only if they are not literally construed. Most specifically, if a theory says that something exists, then a literal construal may elaborate on what that something is, but will not remove the implication of existence.

There have been many critiques of positivist intepretations of science, and there is no need to repeat them.

§1.3 Constructive Empiricism

To insist on a literal construal of the language of science is to rule out the construal of a theory as a metaphor or simile, or as intelligible only after it is 'demythologized' or subjected to some other sort of 'translation' that does not preserve logical form. If the theory's statements include 'There are electrons', then the theory says that there are electrons. If in addition they include 'Electrons are not planets', then the theory says, in part, that there are entities other than planets.

But this does not settle very much. It is often not at all obvious whether a theoretical term refers to a concrete entity or a mathematical entity. Perhaps one tenable interpretation of classical physics is that there are no concrete entities which are forces—that 'there are forces such that . . .' can always be understood as a mathematical statement asserting the existence of certain functions. That is debatable.

Not every philosophical position concerning science which insists on a literal construal of the language of science is a realist position. For this insistence relates not at all to our epistemic attitudes toward theories, nor to the aim we pursue in constructing theories, but only to the correct understanding of *what a theory says*. (The fundamentalist theist, the agnostic, and the atheist presumably agree with each other (though not with liberal theologians) in their understanding of the statement that God, or gods, or angels exist.) After deciding that the language of science must be literally understood, we can still say that there is no need to believe good theories to be true, nor to believe *ipso facto* that the entities they postulate are real.

Science aims to give us theories which are empirically adequate; and acceptance of a theory involves a belief only that it is empirically adequate. This is the statement of the anti-realist position I advocate; I shall call it *constructive empiricism.*

This formulation is subject to the same qualifying remarks as that of scientific realism in Section 1.1 above. In addition it requires an explication of 'empirically adequate'. For now, I shall leave that with the preliminary explication that a theory is empirically adequate exactly if what it says about the observable things and events in this world, is true—exactly if it 'saves the phenomena'. A little more precisely: such a theory has at least one model that all the actual phenomena fit inside. I must emphasize that this refers to *all* the phenomena; these are not exhausted by those actually observed, nor even by those observed at some time, whether past, present, or future. This term is intimately bound up with our conception of the structure of a scientific theory.

The distinction I have drawn between realism and anti-realism, in so far as it pertains to acceptance, concerns only how much belief is involved therein. Acceptance of theories (whether full, tentative, to a degree, etc.) is a phenomenon of scientific activity which clearly involves more than belief. One main reason for this is that we are never confronted with a complete theory. So if a scientist accepts a theory, he thereby involves himself in a certain sort of research programme. That programme could well be different from the one acceptance of another theory would have given him, even if those two (very incomplete) theories are equivalent to each other with respect to everything that is observable—in so far as they go.

Thus acceptance involves not only belief but a certain commitment. Even for those of us who are not working scientists, the acceptance involves a commitment to confront any future phenomena by means of the conceptual resources of this theory. It determines the terms in which we shall seek explanations. If the acceptance is at all strong, it is exhibited in the person's assumption of the role of explainer, in his willingness to answer questions *ex cathedra*. Even if you do not accept a theory, you can engage in discourse in a context in which language use is guided by that theory—but acceptance produces such contexts. There are similarities in all of this to ideological commitment. A commitment is of course not true or false: The confidence exhibited is that it will be *vindicated*.

This is a preliminary sketch of the *pragmatic* dimension of theory acceptance. Unlike the epistemic dimension, it does not figure overtly in the disagreement between realist and anti-realist. But because the amount of belief involved in acceptance is typically less according to anti-realists, they will tend to make more of the pragmatic aspects. It is as well to note here the important difference. Belief that a theory is true, or that it is empirically adequate, does not imply, and is not implied by, belief that full acceptance of the theory will be vindicated. To see this, you need only consider here a person who has quite definite beliefs about the future of the human race, or about the scientific community and the influences thereon and practical limitations we have. It might well be, for instance, that a theory which is empirically adequate will not combine easily with some other theories which we have accepted in fact, or that Armageddon will occur before we succeed. Whether belief that a theory is true, or that it is empirically adequate, can be equated with belief that acceptance of it would, under ideal research conditions, be vindicated in the long run, is another question. It seems to me an irrelevant question within philosophy of science, because an affirmative answer would not obliterate the distinction we have already established by the preceding remarks. (The question may also assume that counterfactual statements are objectively true or false, which I would deny.)

Although it seems to me that realists and anti-realists need not disagree about the pragmatic aspects of theory acceptance, I have mentioned it here because I think that typically they do. We shall find ourselves returning time and again, for example, to requests for explanation to which realists typically attach an objective validity which anti-realists cannot grant.

§2. *THE THEORY/OBSERVATION 'DICHOTOMY'*

For good reasons, logical positivism dominated the philosophy of science for thirty years. In 1960, the first volume of *Minnesota Studies in the Philosophy of Science* published Rudolf Carnap's "The Methodological Status of Theoretical Concepts', which is, in many ways, the culmination of the positivist programme. It interprets science by relating it to an observation language (a postulated part of natural language which is devoid of theoretical terms). Two years later this article was followed in the same series by Grover Maxwell's 'The Ontological Status of Theoretical Entities', in title and theme a direct counter to Carnap's. This is the *locus classicus* for the new realists' contention that the theory/observation distinction cannot be drawn.

I shall examine some of Maxwell's points directly, but first a general remark about the issue. Such expressions as 'theoretical entity' and 'observable-theoretical dichotomy' are, on the face of it, examples of category mistakes. Terms or concepts are theoretical (introduced or adapted for the purposes of theory construction); entities are observable or unobservable. This may seem a little point, but it separates the discussion into two issues. Can we divide our language into a theoretical and non-theoretical part? On the other hand, can we classify objects and events into observable and unobservable ones?

Maxwell answers both questions in the negative, while not distinguishing them too carefully. On the first, where he can draw on well-known supportive essays by Wilfrid Sellars and Paul Feyerabend, I am in total agreement. All our language is thoroughly theory-infected. If we could cleanse our language of theory-laden terms, begin-

ning with the recently introduced ones like 'VHF receiver', continuing through 'mass' and 'impulse' to 'element' and so on into the prehistory of language formation, we would end up with nothing useful. The way we talk, and scientists talk, is guided by the pictures provided by previously accepted theories. This is true also, as Duhem already emphasized, of experimental reports. Hygienic reconstructions of language such as the positivists envisaged are simply not on.

But does this mean that we must be scientific realists? We surely have more tolerance of ambiguity than that. The fact that we let our language be guided by a given picture, at some point, does not show how much we believe about that picture. When we speak of the sun coming up in the morning and setting at night, we are guided by a picture now explicitly disavowed. When Milton wrote *Paradise Lost* he deliberately let the old geocentric astronomy guide his poem, although various remarks in passing clearly reveal his interest in the new astronomical discoveries and speculations of his time. These are extreme examples, but show that no immediate conclusions can be drawn from the theory-ladenness of our language.

However, Maxwell's main arguments are directed against the observable-unobservable distinction. Let us first be clear on what this distinction was supposed to be. The term 'observable' classifies putative entities (entities which may or may not exist.) A flying horse is observable—that is why we are so sure that there aren't any—and the number seventeen is not. There is supposed to be a correlate classification of human acts: an unaided act of perception, for instance, is an observation. A calculation of the mass of a particle from the deflection of its trajectory in a known force field, is not an observation of that mass.

It is also important here not to confuse *observing* (an entity, such as a thing, event, or process) and *observing that* (something or other is the case). Suppose one of the Stone Age people recently found in the Philippines is shown a tennis ball or a car crash. From his behaviour, we see that he has noticed them; for example, he picks up the ball and throws it. But he has not seen *that* it is a tennis ball, or *that* some event is a car crash, for he does not even have those concepts. He cannot get that information through perception; he would first have to learn a great deal. To say that he does not see the same things and events as we do, however, is just silly; it is a pun which trades on the ambiguity between seeing and seeing that. (The truth-conditions for our statement '*x* observes *that A*' must be such that what concepts *x* has, presumably related to the language *x* speaks if he is human, enter as a variable into the correct truth definition, in some way. To say that *x* observed the tennis ball, therefore, does not imply at all that *x* observed that it was a tennis ball; that would require some conceptional awareness of the game of tennis.)

The arguments Maxwell gives about observability are of two sorts: one directed against the possibility of drawing such distinctions, the other against the importance that could attach to distinctions that can be drawn.

The first argument is from the continuum of cases that lie between direct observation and inference:

there is, in principle, a continuous series beginning with looking through a vacuum and containing these as members: looking through a windowpane, looking through glasses, looking through binoculars, looking through a low-power microscope, looking through a high-power microscope, etc., in the order given. The important consequence is that, so far, we are left without criteria which would enable us to draw a non-arbitrary line between 'observation' and 'theory'.[4]

This continuous series of supposed acts of observation does not correspond directly to a continuum in what is supposed observable. For if something can be seen through a window, it can also be seen with the window raised. Similarly, the moons of Jupiter can be seen through a telescope; but they can also be seen without a telescope if you are close enough. That something is observable does not automatically imply that the conditions are right for observing it now. The principle is:

X is observable if there are circumstances which are such that, if X is present to us under those circumstances, then we observe it.

This is not meant as a definition, but only as a rough guide to the avoidance of fallacies.

We may still be able to find a continuum in what is supposed detectable: perhaps some things can only be detected with the aid of an optical microscope, at least; perhaps some require an electron microscope, and so on. Maxwell's problem is: where shall we draw the line between what is observable and what is only detectable in some more roundabout way?

Granted that we cannot answer this question without arbitrariness, what follows? That 'observable' is a *vague predicate*. There are many puzzles about vague predicates, and many sophisms designed to show that, in the presence of vagueness, no distinction can be drawn at all. In Sextus Empiricus, we find the argument that incest is not immoral, for touching your mother's big toe with your little finger is not immoral, and all the rest differs only by degree. But predicates in natural language are almost all vague, and there is no problem in their use; only in formulating the logic that governs them.[5] A vague predicate is usable provided it has clear cases and clear counter-cases. Seeing with the unaided eye is a clear case of observation. Is Maxwell then perhaps challenging us to present a clear counter-case? Perhaps so, for he says 'I have been trying to support the thesis that any (non-logical) term is a *possible* candidate for an observation term.'

A look through a telescope at the moons of Jupiter seems to me a clear case of observation, since astronauts will no doubt be able to see them as well from close up. But the purported observation of micro-particles in a cloud chamber seems to me a clearly different case—if our theory about what happens there is right. The theory says that if a charged particle traverses a chamber filled with saturated vapour, some atoms in the neighborhood of its path are ionized. If this vapour is decompressed, and hence becomes super-saturated, it condenses in droplets on the ions, thus marking the path of the particle. The resulting silver-grey line is similar (physically as well as in appearance) to the vapour trail left in the sky when a jet passes. Suppose I point to such a trail and say: 'Look, there is a jet!'; might you not say: 'I see the vapour trail, but where is the jet?' Then I would answer: 'Look just a bit ahead of the trail . . . there! Do you see it?' Now, in the case of the cloud chamber this response is not possible. So while the particle is detected by means of the cloud chamber, and the detection is based on observation, it is clearly not a case of the article's being observed.

As second argument, Maxwell directs our attention to the 'can' in 'what is observable is what can be observed.' An object might of course be temporarily unobservable—in a rather different sense: it cannot be observed in the circumstances in which it actually is at the moment, but could be observed if the circumstances were more favourable. In just the same way, I might be temporarily invulnerable or invisible. So we should concentrate on 'observable' *tout court*, or on (as he prefers to say) 'unobservable in principle'. This Maxwell explains as meaning that the revelant scientific theory *entails* that the entities cannot be observed in any circumstances. But this never happens, he says, because the different circumstances could be ones in which we have different sense organs—electron–microscope eyes, for instance.

This strikes me as a trick, a change in the subject of discussion. I have a mortar and pestle made of copper and weighing about a kilo. Should I call it breakable because a giant could break it? Should I call the Empire State Building portable? Is there no distinction between a portable and a console record player? The human organism is, from the point of view of physics, a certain kind of measuring apparatus. As such it has certain inherent limitations—which will be described in detail in the final physics and biol-

ogy. It is these limitations to which the 'able' in 'observable' refers—our limitations, *qua* human beings.

As I mentioned however, Maxwell's article also contains a different sort of argument: even if there is a feasible observable/unobservable distinction, this distinction has no importance. The point at issue for the realist is, after all, the reality of the entities postulated in science. Suppose that these entities could be classified into observables and others; what relevance should that have to the question of their existence?

Logically, none. For the term 'observable' classifies putative entities, and has logically nothing to do with existence. But Maxwell must have more in mind when he says: 'I conclude that the drawing of the observational–theoretical line at any given point is an accident and a function of our physiological make-up, . . . and, therefore, that it has no ontological significance whatever.'[6] No ontological significance if the question is only whether 'observable' and 'exists' imply each other—for they do not; but significance for the question of scientific realism?

Recall that I defined scientific realism in terms of the aim of science, and epistemic attitudes. The question is what aim scientific activity has, and how much we shall believe when we accept a scientific theory. What is the proper form of acceptance: belief that the theory, as a whole, is true; or something else? To this question, what is observable by us seems eminently relevant. Indeed, we may attempt an answer at this point: to accept a theory is (for us) to believe that it is empirically adequate—that what the theory says *about what is observable* (by us) is true.

It will be objected at once that, on this proposal, what the anti-realist decides to believe about the world will depend in part on what he believes to be his, or rather the epistemic community's, accessible range of evidence. At present, we count the human race as the epistemic community to which we belong; but this race may mutate, or that community may be increased by adding other animals (terrestrial or extra-terrestrial) through relevant ideological or moral decisions ('to count them as persons'). Hence the anti-realist would, on my proposal, have to accept conditions of the form

If the epistemic community changes in fashion *Y*, then my beliefs about the world will change in manner *Z*.

To see this as an objection to anti-realism is to voice the requirement that our epistemic policies should give the same results independent of our beliefs about the range of evidence accessible to us. That requirement seems to me in no way rationally compelling; it could be honoured, I should think, only through a thorough-going scepticism or through a commitment to wholesale leaps of faith. But we cannot settle the major questions of epistemology *en passant* in philosophy of science; so I shall just conclude that it is, on the face of it, not irrational to commit oneself only to a search for theories that are empirically adequate, ones whose models fit the observable phenomena, while recognizing that what counts as an observable phenomenon is a function of what the epistemic community is (that *observable* is *observable-to-us*).

The notion of empirical adequacy in this answer will have to be spelt out very carefully if it is not to bite the dust among hackneyed objections. But the point stands: even if observability has nothing to do with existence (is, indeed, too anthropocentric for that), it may still have much to do with the proper epistemic attitude to science.

§3. INFERENCE TO THE BEST EXPLANATION

A view advanced in different ways by Wilfrid Sellars, J. J. C. Smart, and Gilbert Harman is that the canons of rational inference require scientific realism. If we are to follow the same patterns of inference with respect to this issue as we do in science itself, we shall find ourselves irrational unless we assert the truth of the scientific theories we accept. Thus Sellars says: 'As I see it, to

have good reason for holding a theory is *ipso facto* to have good reason for holding that the entities postulated by the theory exist.'[7]

The main rule of inference invoked in arguments of this sort is the rule of *inference to the best explanation*. The idea is perhaps to be credited to C. S. Peirce,[8] but the main recent attempts to explain this rule and its uses have been made by Gilbert Harman.[9] I shall only present a simplified version. Let us suppose that we have evidence *E*, and are considering several hypotheses, say *H* and *H'*. The rule then says that we should infer *H* rather than *H'* exactly if *H* is a better explanation of *E* than *H'* is. (Various qualifications are necessary to avoid inconsistency: we should always try to move to the best overall explanation of all available evidence.)

It is argued that we follow this rule in all 'ordinary' cases; and that if we follow it consistently everywhere, we shall be led to scientific realism, in the way Sellars's dictum suggests. And surely there are many telling 'ordinary' cases: I hear scratching in the wall, the patter of little feet at midnight, my cheese disappears—and I infer that a mouse has come to live with me. Not merely that these apparent signs of mousely presence will continue, not merely that all the observable phenomena will be as if there is a mouse; but that there really is a mouse.

Will this pattern of inference also lead us to belief in unobservable entities? Is the scientific realist simply someone who consistently follows the rules of inference that we all follow in more mundane contexts? I have two objections to the idea that this is so.

First of all, what is meant by saying that we all *follow* a certain rule of inference? One meaning might be that we deliberately and consciously 'apply' the rule, like a student doing a logic exercise. That meaning is much too literalistic and restrictive; surely all of mankind follows the rules of logic much of the time, while only a fraction can even formulate them. A second meaning is that we act in accordance with the rules in a sense that does not require conscious deliberation. That is not so easy to make precise, since each logical rule is a rule of permission (*modus ponens* allows you to infer *B* from *A* and (if *A* then *B*), but does not forbid you to infer (*B* or *A*) instead). However, we might say that a person behaved in accordance with a set of rules in that sense if every conclusion he drew could be reached from his premisses via those rules. But this meaning is much too loose; in this sense we always behave in accordance with the rule that any conclusion may be inferred from any premiss. So it seems that to be following a rule, I must be willing to believe all conclusions it allows, while definitely unwilling to believe conclusions at variance with the ones it allows—or else, change my willingness to believe the premisses in question.

Therefore the statement that we all follow a certain rule in certain cases, is a *psychological hypothesis* about what we are willing and unwilling to do. It is an empirical hypothesis, to be confronted with data, and with rival hypotheses. Here is a rival hypothesis: we are always willing to believe that the theory which best explains the evidence, is empirically adequate (that all the observable phenomena are as the theory says they are).

In this way I can certainly account for the many instances in which a scientist appears to argue for the acceptance of a theory or hypothesis, on the basis of its explanatory success. (A number of such instances are related by Thagard.) For, remember: I equate the acceptance of a scientific theory with the belief that it is empirically adequate. We have therefore two rival hypotheses concerning these instances of scientific inference, and the one is apt in a realist account, the other in an anti-realist account.

Cases like the mouse in the wainscoting cannot provide telling evidence between those rival hypotheses. For the mouse *is* an observable thing; therefore 'there is a mouse in the wainscoting' and 'All observable phenomena are as if there is a mouse in the wainscoting' are totally equivalent; each implies the other (given what we know about mice).

It will be countered that it is less interesting to know whether people do follow a rule of inference than whether they ought to follow it. Granted; but the premiss that we all follow the rule of inference to the best explanation when it comes to mice and other mundane matters—that premiss is shown wanting. It is not warranted by the evidence, because evidence is not telling *for* the premiss *as against* the alternative hypothesis I proposed, which is a relevant one in this context.

My second objection is that even if we were to grant the correctness (or worthiness) of the rule of inference to the best explanation, the realist needs some further premiss for his argument. For this rule is only one that dictates a choice when given a set of rival hypotheses. In other words, we need to be committed to belief in one of a range of hypotheses before the rule can be applied. Then, under favourable circumstances, it will tell us which of the hypotheses in that range to choose. The realist asks us to choose between different hypotheses that explain the regularities in certain ways; but his opponent always wishes to choose among hypotheses of the form 'theory T_i is empirically adequate.' So the realist will need his special extra premiss that every universal regularity in nature needs an explanation, before the rule will make realists of us all. And that is just the premiss that distinguishes the realist from his opponents.

The logically minded may think that the extra premiss can be bypassed by logical *léger-de-main*. For suppose the data are that all facts observed so far accord with theory T; then T is one possible explanation of those data. A rival is *not-T* (that T is false). This rival is a very poor explanation of the data. So we *always* have a set of rival hypotheses, and the rule of inference to the best explanation leads us unerringly to the conclusion that T is true. Surely I am committed to the view that T is true or T is false?

This sort of epistemological rope-trick does not work of course. To begin, I am committed to the view that T is true or T is false, but not thereby committed to an inferential move to one of the two! The rule operates only if I have decided not to remain neutral between these two possibilities.

Secondly, it is not at all likely that the rule will be applicable to such logically concocted rivals. Harman lists various criteria to apply to the evaluation of hypotheses *qua* explanations.[10] Some are rather vague, like simplicity (but is simplicity not a reason to use a theory whether you believe it or not?) The precise ones come from statistical theory which has lately proved of wonderful use to epistemology:

H is a better explanation than H' (*ceteris paribus*) of E, provided:
   (a) $P(H) > P(H')$—H has higher probability than H'
   (b) $P(E/H) > P(E/H')$—H bestows higher probability on E than H' does.

The use of 'initial' or *a priori* probabilities in (a)—the initial plausibility of the hypotheses themselves—is typical of the so-called *Bayesians*. More traditional statistical practice suggests only the use of (b). But even that supposes that H and H' bestow definite probabilities on E. If H' is simply the denial of H, that is not generally the case. (Imagine that H says that the probability of E equal ¾. The very most that *not-H* will entail is that the probability of E is some number other than ¾; and usually it will not even entail that much, since H will have other implications as well.)

Bayesians tend to cut through this 'unavailability of probabilities' problem by hypothesizing that everyone has a specific subjective probability (degree of belief) for every proposition he can formulate. In that case, no matter what E, H, H' are, all these probabilities really are (in principle) available. But they obtain this availability by making the probabilities thoroughly subjective. I do not think that scientific realists wish their conclusions to hinge on the subjectively established initial plausibility of there being unobservable entities, so I doubt that this sort of Bayesian move would help here. (This point will come up again in a more concrete form in connection with an argument by Hilary Putnam.)

I have kept this discussion quite abstract; but more concrete arguments by Sellars, Smart, and Putnam will be examined below. It should at least be clear that there is no open-and-shut argument from common sense to the unobservable. Merely following the ordinary patterns of inference in science

does not obviously and automatically make realists of us all.

§4. LIMITS OF THE DEMAND FOR EXPLANATION

In this section and the next I shall examine arguments for realism that point to explanatory power as a criterion for theory choice. That this is indeed a criterion I do not deny. But these arguments for realism succeed only if the demand for explanation is supreme—if the task of science is unfinished, *ipso facto*, as long as any pervasive regularity is left unexplained. I shall object to this line of argument, as found in the writings of Smart, Reichenbach, Salmon, and Sellars, by arguing that such an unlimited demand for explanation leads to a demand for hidden variables, which runs contrary to at least one major school of thought in twentieth-century physics. I do not think that even these philosophers themselves wish to saddle realism with logical links to such consequences: but realist yearnings were born among the mistaken ideals of traditional metaphysics.

In his book *Between Science and Philosophy*, Smart gives two main arguments for realism. One is that only realism can respect the important distinction between *correct* and *merely useful* theories. He calls 'instrumentalist' any view that locates the importance of theories in their use, which requires only empirical adequacy, and not truth. But how can the instrumentalist explain the usefulness of his theories?

Consider a man (in the sixteenth century) who is a realist about the Copernican hypothesis but instrumentalist about the Ptolemaic one. He can explain the instrumental usefulness of the Ptolemaic system of epicycles because he can prove that the Ptolemaic system can produce almost the same predictions about the apparent motions of the planets as does the Copernican hypothesis. Hence the assumption of the realist truth of the Copernican hypothesis explains the instrumental usefulness of the Ptolemaic one. Such an explanation of the instrumental usefulness of certain theories would not be possible if *all* theories were regarded as merely instrumental.[11]

What exactly is meant by 'such an explanation' in the last sentence? If no theory is assumed to be true, then no theory has its usefulness explained as following from the truth of another one—granted. But would we have less of an explanation of the usefulness of the Ptolemaic hypothesis if we began instead with the premiss that the Copernican gives implicitly a very accurate description of the motions of the planets as observed from earth? This would not assume the truth of Copernicus's heliocentric hypothesis, but would still entail that Ptolemy's simpler description was also a close approximation of those motions.

However, Smart would no doubt retort that such a response pushes the question only one step back: what explains the accuracy of predictions based on Copernicus's theory? If I say, the empirical adequacy of that theory, I have merely given a verbal explanation. For of course Smart does not mean to limit his question to actual predictions—it really concerns all actual and possible predictions and retrodictions. To put it quite concretely: what explains the fact that all observable planetary phenomena fit Copernicus's theory (if they do)? From the medieval debates, we recall the nominalist response that the basic regularities are merely brute regularities, and have no explanation. So here the anti-realist must similarly say: that the observable phenomena exhibit these regularities, because of which they fit the theory, is merely a brute fact, and may or may not have an explanation in terms of unobservable facts 'behind the phenomena'—it really does not matter to the goodness of the theory, not to our understanding of the world.

Smart's main line of argument is addressed to exactly this point. In the same chapter he argues as follows. Suppose that we have a theory *T* which postulates microstructure directly, and macro-structure indi-

rectly. The statistical and approximate laws about macroscopic phenomena are only partially spelt out perhaps, and in any case derive from the precise (deterministic or statistical) laws about the basic entities. We now consider theory *T'*, which is part of *T*, and says only what *T* says about the macroscopic phenomena. (How *T'* should be characterized I shall leave open, for that does not affect the argument here.) Then he continues:

> I would suggest that the realist could (say) . . . that the success of T' is explained by the fact that the original theory T is true of the things that it is ostensibly about: in other words by the fact that there really are electrons or whatever is postulated by the theory T. If there were no such things, and if T were not true in a realist way, would not the success of T' be quite inexplicable? One would have to suppose that there were innumerable lucky accidents about the behaviour mentioned in the observational vocabulary, so that they behaved miraculously *as if* they were brought about by the non-existent things ostensibly talked about in the theoretical vocabulary.[12]

In other passages, Smart speaks similarly of 'cosmic coincidences'. The regularities in the observable phenomena must be explained in terms of deeper structure, for otherwise we are left with a belief in lucky accidents and coincidences on a cosmic scale.

I submit that if the demand for explanation implicit in these passages were precisely formulated, it would at once lead to absurdity. For if the mere fact of postulating regularities, without explanation, makes *T'* a poor theory, *T* will do no better. If, on the other hand, there is some precise limitation on what sorts of regularities can be postulated as basic, the context of the argument provides no reason to think that *T'* must automatically fare worse than *T*.

In any case, it seems to me that it is illegitimate to equate being a lucky accident, or a coincidence, with having no explanation. It was by coincidence that I met my friend in the market—but I can explain why I was there, and he can explain why he came, so together we can explain how this meeting happened. We call it a coincidence, not because the occurrence was inexplicable, but because we did not severally go to the market in order to meet.[13] There cannot be a requirement upon science to provide a theoretical elimination of coincidences, or accidental correlations in general, for that does not even make sense. There is nothing here to motivate the demand for explanation, only a restatement in persuasive terms. . . . .

§5. *LIMITS TO EXPLANATION: A THOUGHT EXPERIMENT*

Wilfrid Sellars was one of the leaders of the return to realism in philosophy of science and has, in his writings of the past three decades, developed a systematic and coherent scientific realism. I have discussed a number of his views and arguments elsewhere; but will here concentrate on some aspects that are closely related to the arguments of Smart, Reichenbach, and Salmon just examined.[14] Let me begin by setting the stage in the way Sellars does.

There is a certain over-simplified picture of science, the 'levels picture', which pervades positivist writings and which Sellars successfully demolished.[15] In that picture, singular observable facts ('this crow is black') are scientifically explained by general observable regularities ('all crows are black') which in turn are explained by highly theoretical hypotheses not restricted in what they say to the observable. The three levels are commonly called those of *fact*, of *empirical law*, and of *theory*. But, as Sellars points out, theories do not explain, or even entail such empirical laws—they only show why observable things obey these so-called laws to the extent they do.[16] Indeed, perhaps we have no such empirical laws at all: all crows are black—except albinos; water boils at 100°C—provided atmospheric pressure is normal; a falling body accelerates—provided it is not intercepted, or attached to an aeroplane by a static line; and so forth. On the level of the observable we are liable to find only putative laws heavily subject to unwritten *ceteris paribus* qualifications.

This is, so far, only a methodological point. We do not really expect theories to 'save' our common everyday generalizations, for we ourselves have no confidence in their strict universality. But a theory which says that the micro-structure of things is subject to *some* exact, universal regularities, must imply the same for those things themselves. This, at least, is my reaction to the points so far. Sellars, however, sees an inherent inferiority in the description of the observable alone, an incompleteness which requires (*sub specie* the aims of science) an introduction of an unobservable reality behind the phenomena. This is brought out by an interesting 'thought-experiment'.

Imagine that at some early stage of chemistry it had been found that different samples of gold dissolve in *aqua regia* at different rates, although 'as far as can be observationally determined, the specimens and circumstances are identical'.[17] Imagine further that the response of chemistry to this problem was to postulate two distinct micro-structures for the different samples of gold. Observationally unpredictable variation in the rate of dissolution is explained by saying that the samples are mixtures (not compounds) of these two (observationally identical) substances, each of which has a fixed rate of dissolution.

In this case we have explanation through laws which have no observational counterparts that can play the same role. Indeed, no explanation seems possible unless we agree to find our physical variables outside the observable. But science aims to explain, must try to explain, and so must require a belief in this unobservable micro-structure. So Sellars contends.

There are at least three questions before us. Did this postulation of micro-structure really have no new consequences for the observable phenomena? Is there really such a demand upon science that it must explain—even if the means of explanation bring no gain in empirical predictions? And thirdly, could a *different* rationale exist for the use of a micro-structure picture in the development of a scientific theory in a case like this?

First, it seems to me that these hypothetical chemists did postulate new observable regularities as well. Suppose the two substances are A and B, with dissolving rates x and $x + y$ and that every gold sample is a mixture of these substances. Then it follows that every gold sample dissolves at a rate no lower than x and no higher than $x + y$; *and* that between these two any value may be found—to within the limits of accuracy of gold mixing. None of this is implied by the data that different samples of gold have dissolved at various rates between x and $x + y$. So Sellars's first contention is false.

We may assume, for the sake of Sellars's example, that there is still no way of predicting dissolving rates any further. Is there then a categorical demand upon science to explain this variation which does not depend on other observable factors? We have seen that a precise version of such a demand (Reichenbach's principle of the common sense) could result automatically in a demand for hidden variables, providing a 'classical' underpinning for indeterministic theories. Sellars recognized very well that a demand for hidden variables would run counter to the main opinions current in quantum physics. Accordingly he mentions '. . . . the familiar point that the irreducibly and lawfully statistical ensembles of quantum-mechanical theory are mathematically inconsistent with the assumption of hidden variables.'[18] Thus, he restricts the demand for explanation, in effect, to just those cases where it is *consistent* to add hidden variables to the theory. And consistency is surely a logical stopping-point.

This restriction unfortunately does not prevent the disaster. For while there are a number of proofs that hidden variables cannot be supplied so as to turn quantum mechanics into a classical sort of deterministic theory, those proofs are based on requirements much stronger than consistency. To give an example, one such assumption is that two distinct physical variables cannot have the same statistical distributions in measurement on all possible states.[19] Thus it is assumed that, if we cannot point to some possible difference in empirical predictions, then there is no real difference at all. If such requirements were lifted, and consistency alone were the criterion, hidden variables could indeed be introduced. I think we must conclude that science, in contrast to scientific realism does not place an overriding value on explanation in the absence of any gain for empirical results.

Thirdly, then, let us consider how an anti-realist could make sense of those hypothetical chemists' procedure. After pointing to the new empirical implications which I mentioned two paragraphs ago, he would point to methodological reasons. By imagining a certain sort of micro-structure for gold and other metals, say, we might arrive at a theory governing many observationally disparate substances; and this might then have implications for new, wider empirical regularities when such substances interact. This would only be a hope, of course; no hypothesis is guaranteed to be fruitful—but the point is that the true demand on science is not for explanation *as such*, but for imaginative pictures which have a hope of suggesting new statements of observable regularities and of correcting old ones. This point is exactly the same as that for the principle of the common cause.

§6. *DEMONS AND THE ULTIMATE ARGUMENT*

Hilary Putnam, in the course of his discussions of realism in logic and mathematics, advanced several arguments for scientific realism as well. In *Philosophy of Logic* he concentrates largely on indispensability arguments—concepts of mathematical entities are indispensable to non-elementary mathematics, theoretical concepts are indispensable to physics.[20] Then he confronts the philosophical position of Fictionalism, which he gleans from the writings of Vaihinger and Duhem:

(T)he fictionalist says, in substance, 'Yes, certain concepts . . . are indispensable, but no, that has no tendency to show that entities corresponding to those concepts actually exist. It only shows that those 'entities' are useful *fictions*'.[21]

Glossed in terms of theories: even if certain kinds of theories are indispensable for the advance of science, that does not show that those theories are true *in toto*, as well as empirically correct.

Putnam attacks this position in a roundabout way, first criticizing bad arguments against Fictionalism, and then garnering his reasons for rejecting Fictionalism from that discussion. The main bad reason he sees is that of Verificationism. The logical positivists adhered to the verificationist theory of meaning; which is roughly that the total cognitive content of an assertion, all that is meaningful in it, is a function of what empirical results would verify or refute it. Hence, they would say that there are no real differences between two hypotheses with the same empirical content. Consider two theories of what the world is like: Rutherford's atomic theory, and Vaihinger's hypothesis that, although perhaps there are no electrons and such, the observable world is nevertheless exactly as if Rutherford's theory were true. The Verificationist would say: these two theories, although Vaihinger's appears to be consistent with the denial of Rutherford's, amount to exactly the same thing.

Well, they don't, because the one says that there are electrons, and the other allows that they may not be. Even if the observable phenomena are as Rutherford says, the unobservable may be different. However, the positivists would say, if you argue that way, then you will automatically become a prey to scepticism. You will have to admit that there are possibilities you cannot prove or disprove by experiment, and so you will have to say that we just cannot know what the world is like. Worse; you will have no reason to reject any number of outlandish possibilities; demons, witchcraft, hidden powers collaborating to fantastic ends.

Putnam considers this argument for Verificationism to be mistaken, and his answer to it, strangely enough, will also yield an answer to the Fictionalism rejected by the verificationist. To dispel the bogey of scepticism, Putnam gives us a capsule introduction to contemporary (Bayesian) epistemology: Rationality requires that if two hypotheses have all the same testable consequences (consequences for evidence that could be gathered), then we should not accept the one which is *a priori the less plausible*. Where do we get our *a priori* plausibility orderings? These we supply ourselves, either individually or as communities: to accept a plausibility ordering is neither

> to make a judgment of empirical fact nor to state a theorem of deductive logic: it is to take a methodological stand. One can only say whether the demon hypothesis is 'crazy' or not if one has taken such a stand; I report the stand I have taken (and, speaking as one who has taken this stand, I add: and the stand all rational men take, implicitly or explicitly).[22]

On this view, the difference between Rutherford and Vaihinger, or between Putnam and Duhem, is that (although they presumably agree on the implausibility of demons) they disagree on the *a priori* plausibility of electrons. Does each simply report the stand he has taken, and add: this is, in my view, the stand of all rational men? How disappointing.

Actually, it does not quite go that way. Putnam has skilfully switched the discussion from electrons to demons, and asked us to consider how we could rule out their existence. As presented, however, Vaihinger's view differed from Rutherford's by being logically weaker—it only withheld assent to an existence assertion. It follows automatically that Vaihinger's view cannot be *a priori* less plausible than Rutherford's. Putnam's ideological manœuvre could at most be used to accuse an 'atheistic' anti-realist of irrationality (relative to Putnam's own stand, of course)—not one of the agnostic variety.

Putnam concludes this line of reasoning by asking what more could be wanted as evidence for the truth of a theory than what the realist considers sufficient: 'But then . . . what further reasons could one want before one regarded it as rational to *believe* a theory?'[23] The answer is: *none*—at least if he equates reasons here either with empirical evidence or with compelling arguments. (Inclining reasons are perhaps another matter, especially because Putnam uses the phrase 'rational to believe' rather than 'irrational not to believe'.) Since Putnam has just done us the service of refuting Verificationism, this answer 'none' cannot convict us of irrationality. He has himself just argued forcefully that theories could agree in empirical content and differ in truth-value. Hence, a realist will have to make a leap of faith. The decision to leap is subject to rational scrutiny, but not *dictated* by reason and evidence.

In a further paper, 'What is Mathematical Truth', Putnam continues the discussion of scientific realism, and gives what I shall call the *Ultimate Argument*. He begins with a formulation of realism which he says he learned from Michael Dummett:

> A realist (with respect to a given theory or discourse) holds that (1) the sentences of that theory are true or false; and (2) that what makes them true or false is something external—that is to say, it is not (in general) our sense data, actual or potential, or the structure or our minds, or our language, etc.[24]

This formulation is quite different from the one I have given even if we instantiate it to the case in which that theory or discourse is science or scientific discourse. Because the wide discussion of Dummett's views has given some currency to his usage of these terms, and because Putnam begins his discussion in this way, we need to look carefully at this formulation.

In my view, Dummett's usage is quite idiosyncratic. Putnam's statement, though very brief, is essentially accurate. In his 'Realism', Dummett begins by describing various sorts of realism in the traditional fashion, as disputes over whether there really exist entities of a particular type. But he says that in some cases he wishes to discuss, such as the reality of the past and intuitionism in mathematics, the central issues seem to him to be about other questions. For this reason he proposes a new usage: he will take such disputes

> as relating, not to a class of entities or a class of terms, but to a class of *statements* . . . Realism I characterize as the belief that statements of the disputed class possess an objective truth-value, independently of our means of knowing it: they are true or false in virtue of a reality existing independently of us. The anti-realist opposes to this the view that statements of the disputed class are to be understood only by reference to the sort of thing which we count as evidence for a statement of that class.[25]

Dummett himself notes at once that nominalists are realists in this sense.[26] If, for example, you say that abstract entities do not exist, and sets are abstract entities, hence sets do not exist, then you will certainly accord a truth-value to all statements of set theory. It might be objected that if you take this position then you have a decision procedure for determining the truth-values of these statements (*false* for existentially quantified ones, *true* for universal ones, apply truth tables for the rest). Does that not mean that, on your view, the truth-values are not independent of our knowledge? Not at all; for you clearly believe that if we had not existed, and *a fortiori* had had no knowledge, the state of affairs with respect to abstract entities would be the same.

Has Dummett perhaps only laid down a necessary condition for realism, in his definition, for the sake of generality? I do not think so. In discussions of quantum mechanics we come across the view that the particles of microphysics are real, and obey the principles of the theory, but at any time t when 'particle x has exact momentum p' is true then 'particle x has position q' is neither true nor false. In any traditional sense, this is a realist position with respect to quantum mechanics.

On Scientific Realism

We note also that Dummett has, at least in this passage, taken no care to exclude non-literal construals of the theory, as long as they are truth-valued. The two are not the same; when Strawson construed 'The king of France in 1905 is bald' as neither true nor false, he was not giving a non-literal construal of our language. On the other hand, people tend to fall back on non-literal construals typically in order to be able to say, 'properly construed, the theory is true.'[27]

Perhaps Dummett is right in his assertion that what is really at stake, in realist disputes of various sorts, is questions about language—or, if not really at stake, at least the only serious philosophical problems in those neighbourhoods. Certainly the arguments in which he engages are profound, serious, and worthy of our attention. But it seems to me that his terminology ill accords with the traditional one. Certainly I wish to define scientific realism so that it need not imply that all statements in the theoretical language are true or false (only that they are all capable of being true or false, that is, there are conditions for each under which it has a truth-value); to imply also that the aim at least is that the theories should be true. And the contrary position of constructive empiricism is not anti-realist in Dummett's sense, since it also assumes scientific statements to have truth-conditions entirely independent of human activity or knowledge. But then, I do not conceive the dispute as being about language at all.

In any case Putnam himself does not stick with this weak formulation of Dummett's. A little later in the paper he directs himself to scientific realism *per se*, and formulates it in terms borrowed, he says, from Richard Boyd. The new formulation comes in the course of a new argument for scientific realism, which I shall call the Ultimate Argument:

the positive argument for realism is that it is the only philosophy that doesn't make the success of science a miracle. That terms in mature scientific theories typically refer (this formulation is due to Rich-

ard Boyd), that the theories accepted in a mature science are typically approximately true, that the same term can refer to the same thing even when it occurs in different theories—these statements are viewed by the scientific realist not as necessary truths but as part of the only scientific explanation of the success of science, and hence as part of any adequate scientific description of science and its relations to its objects.[28]

Science, apparently, is required to explain its own success. There is this regularity in the world, that scientific predictions are regularly fulfilled; and this regularity, too, needs an explanation. Once *that* is supplied we may perhaps hope to have reached the *terminus de jure*?

The explanation provided is a very traditional one—*adequatio ad rem*, the 'adequacy' of the theory to its objects, a kind of mirroring of the structure of things by the structure of ideas—Aquinas would have felt quite at home with it.

Well, let us accept for now this demand for a scientific explanation of the success of science. Let us also resist construing it as merely a restatement of Smart's 'cosmic coincidence' argument, and view it instead as the question why we have successful scientific theories at all. Will this realist explanation with the Scholastic look be a scientifically acceptable answer? I would like to point out that science is a biological phenomenon, an activity by one kind of organism which facilitates its interaction with the environment. And this makes me think that a very different kind of scientific explanation is required.

I can best make the point by contrasting two accounts of the mouse who runs from its enemy, the cat. St. Augustine already remarked on this phenomenon, and provided an intensional explanation; the mouse *perceives that* the cat is its enemy, hence the mouse runs. What is postulated here is the 'adequacy' of the mouse's thought to the order of nature: the relation of enmity is correctly reflected in his mind. But the Darwinist says: Do not ask why the *mouse* runs from its enemy. Species which did not cope with their natural enemies no longer exist. That is why there are only ones who do.

In just the same way, I claim that the success of current scientific theories is no miracle. It is not even surprising to the scientific (Darwinist) mind. For any scientific theory is born into a life of fierce competition, a jungle red in tooth and claw. Only the successful theories survive—the ones which *in fact* latched on to actual regularities in nature.[29]

NOTES

[1]Brian Ellis, *Rational Belief Systems* (Oxford: Blackwell, 1979), p. 28.

[2]Hartry Field has suggested that 'acceptance of a scientific theory involves the belief that it is true' be replaced by 'any reason to think that any part of a theory is not, or might not be, true, is reason not to accept it.' The drawback of this alternative is that it leaves open what epistemic attitude acceptance of a theory does involve. This question must also be answered, and as long as we are talking about full acceptance—as opposed to tentative or partial or other qualified acceptance—I cannot see how a realist could do other than equate that attitude with full belief. (That theories believed to be false are used for practical problems, for example, classical mechanics for orbiting satellites, is of course a commonplace.) For if the aim is truth, and acceptance requires belief that the aim is served . . . I should also mention the statement of realism at the beginning of Richard Boyd, 'Realism, Underdetermination, and a Causal Theory of Evidence', *Noûs*, 7 (1973), 1–12. Except for some doubts about his use of the terms 'explanation' and 'causal relation' I intend my statement of realism to be entirely in accordance with his. Finally, see C. A. Hooker, 'Systematic Realism', *Synthese*, 26 (1974), 409–97; esp. pp. 409 and 426.

[3]More typical of realism, it seems to me, is the sort of epistemology found in Clark Glymour's book, *Theory and Evidence* (Princeton: Princeton University Press, 1980), except of course that there it is fully and carefully developed in one specific fashion. (See esp. his chapter 'Why I am not a Bayesian' for the present issue.) But I see no reason why a realist, as such, could not be a Bayesian of the type of Richard Jeffrey, even if the Bayesian position has in the past been linked with antirealist and even instrumentalist views in philosophy of science.

[4]G. Maxwell, 'The Ontological Status of Theoretical Entities', *Minnesota Studies in Philosophy of Science*, III (1962), p. 7

[5]There is a great deal of recent work on the logic of vague predicates; especially important, to my mind, is that of Kit Fine ('Vagueness, Truth, and Logic', *Synthese*, 30 (1975), 265–300) and Hans Kamp. The latter is currently working on a new theory of vagueness that does justice to the 'vagueness of vagueness' and the context-dependence of standards of applicability for predicates.

[6]Op. cit., p. 15. At this point I may be suspected of relying on modal distinctions which I criticize elsewhere. After all, I am making a distinction between human limitations and accidental factors. A certain apple was dropped into the sea in a bag of refuse, which sank; relative to that information it is necessary that no one ever observed the apple's core. That information, however, concerns an accident of history, and so it is not human limitations that rule out observation of the apple core. But unless I assert that some facts about humans are essential, or physically necessary, and others accidental, how can I make sense of this distinction? This question raises the difficulty of a philosophical retrenchment for modal language. This I believe to be possible through an ascent to pragmatics. In the present case, the answer would be, to speak very roughly, that the scientific theories we accept are a determining factor for the set of features of the human organism counted among the limitations to which we refer in using the term 'observable'.

[7]*Science, Perception and Reality* (New York: Humanities Press, 1962); cf. the footnote on p. 97. See also my review of his *Studies in Philosophy and its History*, in *Annals of Science*, January 1977.

[8]Cf. P. Thagard, doctoral dissertation, University of Toronto, 1977, and 'The Best Explanation: Criteria for Theory Choice', *Journal of Philosophy*, 75 (1978), 76–92.

[9]'The Inference to the Best Explanation', *Philosophical Review*, 74 (1965), 88–95 and 'Knowledge, Inference, and Explanation', *American Philosophical Quarterly*, 5 (1968), 164–73. Harman's views were further developed in subsequent publications (*Noûs*, 1967; *Journal of Philosophy*, 1968; in M. Swain (ed.), *Induction*, 1970; in H.-N. Castañeda (ed.), *Action, Thought, and Reality*, 1975; and in his book *Thought*, Ch. 10). I shall not consider these further developments here.

[10]See esp. 'Knowledge, Inference, and Explanation', p. 169.

[11]J. J. C. Smart, *Between Science and Philosophy* (New York: Random House, 1968), p. 151.

[12]Ibid., pp. 150f.

[13]This point is clearly made by Aristotle, *Physics*, II, Chs. 4–6 (see esp. 196[a] 1–20; 196[b] 20–197[a] 12).

[14]See my 'Wilfrid Sellars on Scientific Realism', *Dialogue*, 14 (1975), 606–16; W. Sellars, 'Is Scientific Realism Tenable?', pp. 307–34 in F. Suppe and P. Asquith (eds.), *PSA 1976* (East Lansing, Mich.: Philosophy of Science Association, 1977), vol. II, 307–34; and my 'On the Radical Incompleteness of the Manifest Image', ibid., 335–43; and see n. 7 above.

[15]W. Sellars, 'The Language of Theories', in his *Science, Perception, and Reality* (London: Routledge and Kegan Paul, 1963).

[16]Op. cit., p. 121.

[17]Ibid., p. 121.

[18]Ibid., p. 123.

[19]See my 'Semantic Analysis of Quantum Logic', in C. A. Hooker (ed.), *Contemporary Research in the Foundations and Philosophy of Quantum Theory* (Dordrecht: Reidel, 1973), Part III, Sects. 5 and 6.

[20]Hilary Putnam, *Philosophy of Logic* (New York: Harper and Row, 1971)—see also my review of this in *Canadian Journal of Philosophy*, 4 (1975), 731–43. Since Putnam's metaphysical views have changed drastically during the last few years, my remarks apply only to his views as they then appeared in his writings.

[21]Op. cit., p. 63.

[22]Ibid., p. 67.

[23]Ibid., p. 69.

[24]Hilary Putnam, *Mathematics, Matter and Method* (Cambridge: Cambridge University Press, 1975), vol. I, pp. 69f.

[25]Michael Dummett, *Truth and Other Enigmas* (Cambridge, Mass.: Harvard University Press, 1978), p. 146 (see also pp. 358–61).

[26]Dummett adds to the cited passage that he realizes that his characterization does not include all the disputes he had mentioned, and specifically excepts nominalism about abstract entities. However, he includes scientific realism as an example (op. cit., pp. 146f.).

[27]This is especially relevant here because the 'translation' that connects Putnam's two foundations of mathematics (existential and modal) as discussed in this essay, is not a literal construal: it is a mapping presumably preserving statementhood and theoremhood, but it does not preserve logical form.

[28] Putnam, op. cit., p. 73, n. 29. The argument is reportedly developed at greater length in Boyd's forthcoming book *Realism and Scientific Epistemology* (Cambridge University Press).

[29]Of course, we can ask specifically why the *mouse* is one of the surviving species, how *it* survives, and answer this, on the basis of whatever scientific theory we accept, in terms of its brain and environment. The analogous question for theories would be why, say, Balmer's formula for the line spectrum of hydrogen survives as a successful hypothesis. In that case too we explain, on the basis of the physics we accept now, why the spacing of those lines satisfies the formula. Both the question and the answer are very different from the global question of the success of science, and the global answer of realism. The realist may now make the *further* objection that the anti-realist cannot answer the question about the mouse specifically, nor the one about Balmer's formula, in this fashion, since the answer is in part an assertion that the scientific theory, used as basis of the explanation, is true. This is quite a different argument, which I shall take up elsewhere.

In his most recent publications and lectures Hilary Putnam has drawn a distinction between two doctrines, metaphysical realism and internal realism. He denies the former, and identifies his preceding scientific realism as the latter. While I have at present no commitment to either side of the metaphysical dispute, I am very much in sympathy with the critique of Platonism in philosophy of mathematics which forms part of Putnam's arguments. Our disagreement about scientific (internal) realism would remain of course, whenever we came down to earth after deciding to agree or disagree about metaphysical realism, or even about whether this distinction makes sense at all.

Scientific Realism vs. Constructive Empiricism: A Dialogue*

Gary Gutting

Note: *The following is a discussion between a scientific realist (SR) who has been strongly influenced by the work of Wilfrid Sellars and a constructive empiricist (CE) who has been equally influenced by the work of Bas van Fraassen. Indeed, the influence is so great that the interlocuters occasionally lapse into direct quotation of their masters. I do not, however, want anyone to* identify *the views of my two characters with those of Sellars and van Fraassen. What they say merely represents the dialectic of my own mind as I think through the issues raised by the debate between Sellars and van Fraassen on scientific realism.*

SR.: Realism is encapsulated in the claim that "to have good reason for holding a theory is *ipso facto* to have good reason for holding that the entities postulated by the theory exist."[1] For an appropriate scientific theory (say atomic theory), this claim allows us to argue as follows:

*Copyright © 1983 by *The Monist*, La Salle, IL 61301. Reprinted by permission, from *The Monist* 65 (1983), 336–49.

1. If we have good reason for holding atomic theory, we have good reasons for holding that atoms exist;

2. We do have good reason for holding atomic theory (it's highly confirmed, fruitful, simple, etc.);

3. Therefore, we have good reason for holding that atoms exist.

CE: Everything depends on what we mean by "holding a theory." If it means "believing that the theory is true," then premise (1) of your argument is obvious but premise (2) strikes me as false. There's a lot to be said for atomic theory but none of it constitutes a cogent case for its truth. At the most, the evidence shows that atomic theory is empirically adequate, by which I mean that there may be reason to think that all its *observable* consequences are true. But the evidence does not support the existence of the particular unobservable mechanisms and entities the theory postulates. On the other hand, if you take "holding a theory," as I do, to mean "believing it to be empirically adequate," then there's no problem with premise (2) but, for the reasons I've just been urging, there is no basis for premise (1).

SR: I'm willing to stand by the argument even if we take "holding a theory" to mean "believing it to be empirically adequate;" but we need to get clear on just what's involved in empirical adequacy. For example, it won't do to take empirical adequacy in the minimal sense of "accurately describing all the observable phenomena." With this sense of "empirically adequate" the argument will fall to the old problem of the underdetermination of theory by data. Specifically, with this meaning of "empirically adequate," premise (1) says: "If we have good reason for believing that atomic theory accurately describes all the observable phenomena, then we have good reason for believing that atoms exist." But this isn't so since, first, there are an infinity of other sorts of theoretical entities that would produce the same observable phenomena and, second, we could just as well believe only in the phenomena and forget about underlying entities.[2]

CE: Your second point is just my view. I'm not saying theoretical entities don't exist or that talk about them is meaningless. I don't even say there's anything wrong with believing in them if you want to. My point is simply that there's no evidence that makes it irrational to withhold judgment about their existence. I'm defending my right to be an agnostic on the issue. I suspect however that, just like theists who deny the rationality of religious agnosticism, you're going to invoke the explanatory power of your postulations to support their existence.

SR: Of course, though the case for scientific realism can avoid the pitfalls of "theological realism." The point is that the empirical adequacy of a scientific theory needs to be taken broadly enough to include the theory's explanatory power and, specifically, its explanatory superiority to the physical thing language used in the observation framework. Atomic theory and its associated ontology is needed precisely because of the explanatory failures of the observation framework. So, roughly, premise (1) needs to be understood as saying this: If we have good reasons to believe that atomic theory is needed to explain the observable data, then

we have good reason to believe that atoms exist.

CE: What I want to question is the move you're trying to make from an explanatory need for a theory to the existence of its entities. Consider, for example, Sellars's fictional case of observationally identical samples of gold that dissolve at different rates in *aqua regia*. I agree that available microtheory might explain the empirical fact of the different dissolution rates. "The microtheory of chemical reactions might admit of a simple modification to the effect that there are two structures of microentities each of which 'corresponds' to gold as an observational construct, but such that pure samples of one dissolve, under given conditions of pressure, temperature, etc., at a different rate from samples of the other. Such a modification of the theory would explain the observationally unpredicted variation in the rate of dissolution of gold by saying that samples of observational gold are mixtures of these two theoretical structures in various proportions, and have a rate of dissolution which varies with the proportion."[3] Of course, I'd expect the realist to admit in his turn that it might also be possible to sue the correspondence rules of our microtheory to "derive observational criteria for distinguishing between observational golds of differing theoretical compositions."[4] If so, we could formulate two empirical laws (in the observation framework), one for each variety of gold, that would explain the differing dissolution rates.

SR: But remember that it might also happen that a good theory does not allow the formulation of any such empirical generalizations. It might simply itself directly explain the singular observable fact of differing dissolution rates. In such a case, the theory would be necessary to give any explanation of the singular observed facts and so would have to be accepted as true if we were to have any explanation at all of these facts. And, of course, this is precisely my claim regarding postulational scientific theories that have actually been developed. If, for example, we do not accept the existence of atoms there are numerous singular empirical facts for which we simply have no explanation. This discussion lets me formulate more precisely premise (1) of the argument for realism. We should take it to say: If we have good reason to believe that atomic theory provides the only way of explaning some singular observed facts, then we have good reason to believe in the existence of atoms.

CE: Your more accurate formulation only serves to pinpoint the weakness of your position. Just what is the "explanatory failure" of the observation language? You agree that it can sustain inductive generalizations but insist that it cannot sustain "enough to explain all the singular facts that require explanation. In the case of the gold, one might have achieved a very precise statistical generalization: for each number r, the probability that a random sample of gold dissolves at rate r equal p(r). . . . But faced with the question why a given sample of gold dissolves at rate r, the physical thing language provides us with no property X such that we could say: this is an X-sample, and all X-samples dissolve at that rate."[5] You conclude from this that we need a theory to explain what the observation language cannot. But the claim is far too strong. On your principles, an exactly parallel argument could be made for the existence of hidden variables underlying quantum phenomena. As is well known, the laws of quantum mechanics are irreducibly statistical; that is, they can explain why certain events occur a certain percentage of times over a given period but they cannot explain why one particular event occurs rather than another. For example, quantum mechanics has no explanation of the fact that a particular radium atom decays at a particular time, though it can explain why, over a period of time, a given fraction of the atoms in a sample of radium will decay. Using your principles, a quantum physicist would have to accept the suggestion, made by some physicists, that there are "hidden" entities and processes, not taken account of by quantum theory, that are responsible for the occurrence of the singular facts that theory cannot explain. But this conclusion, generated by an a priori demand for explanation, conflicts

with the fact that the irreducibly statistical character of its laws does not, in the mind of the scientific community, constitute a case for the explanatory inadequacy of quantum theory and the need for the acceptance of hidden variables. So, just like the theist with his cosmological argument, you make your case by insisting on the need to explain something that there is no reason to think has to be explained. If the singular facts not explained by quantum theory don't need explanation, neither do the singular facts not explained by the observation framework.

SR: I entirely agree with you about quantum mechanics, and in arguing for realism I do not mean to "demand that all singular matters of fact be capable of explanation."[6] Perhaps the fictional gold example is misleading. The inadequacy of the observation framework does not consist in its inability to explain some singular empirical facts but in its inability to explain without relying on theoretical concepts. "It is not that the 'physical thing framework' doesn't sustain *enough* inductive generalizations, but rather that what inductive generalizations it *does* sustain, it sustains by a covert introduction of the framework of theory into the physical thing framework itself."[7]

CE: I take it, then, that you're revising even your most recent statement of premise (1) in your argument for realism. You now seem to be taking it to mean something like this: If we have reason to believe that all explanations of singular empirical facts (in a given empirical domain) must rely on the concepts of atomic theory, then we have good reason to believe in the existence of atoms.

SR: That's about what I have in mind.

CE: But then we need some clarification of what you mean by an explanation's "relying on the concepts of a theory." You're obviously assuming that explanation is at least partly a matter of subsuming singular empirical facts under generalizations. So one possible meaning of the claim that all of a set of observation-framework explanations "rely on the concepts of a theory" is that all the generalizations that accurately subsume the singular empirical facts must be expressed in theoretical terms. But taken this way the claim is clearly false. Even when theoretical corrections are provided for empirical generalizations, the results are typically expressible by a new empirical generalization in the observation language. For example, the correction of Boyle's Law by kinetic theory results in van der Waal's Law, which is still entirely observational.

SR: But my claim about the explanatory reliance of the observation framework on theory is not about the *content* of the generalizations used to explain singular empirical facts but about the way in which these generalizations are *inductively justified.* To a theoretical correction of an empirical generalization there will, I agree, typically correspond a revised empirical generalization. Further, this revised generalization will be compatible with the observational evidence. But, I claim, it will not typically be the law that would be accepted "on purely inductive grounds—i.e., in the absence of theoretical considerations."[8] Rather, lacking theoretical guidance, purely inductive reasoning in the observation framework alone would lead us to accept an empirical generalization that is shown by theoretical considerations to be false. So explanations of singular empirical facts rely on theory in the following sense: The empirical generalizations that explain these facts must be justified, ultimately, by theoretical considerations. This can be expressed by putting premise (1) in the following way: If we have good reason to believe that the empirical generalizations that explain singular empirical facts require an appeal to atomic theory for their justification, then we have good reason for believing in the existence of atoms.

CE: I have a number of reservations about your factual claim that the empirical data alone wouldn't lead us to the same law that theoretical considerations yield. We'd have to look at some examples to probe that thesis. But suppose I agree that theory plays the role you say it does, that it's essential for the development of adequate empirical generalizations. I still don't think there's any reason to accept such a theory as a true (or approximately true) description of the world. In

other words, I might be prepared to accept the antecedent of your last formulation of premise (1), but I'll still deny the consequent. Here my position is like Duhem's. He shared your conviction that "postulation of unobservable entities is indispensable to science." But since he also held that improved description of observable phenomena is the only basic role for theoretical postulation, he maintained that there is no need for us to accept the existence of postulated entities. "If that is how one sees it, then truth of the postulates becomes quite irrelevant. When a scientific theory plays [its] role well, we shall have reason to use the theory whether we do or do not believe it to be true; and we may do well to reserve judgment on the question of truth. The only thing we need to believe here is that the theory is empirically adequate, which means that in its round-about way it has latched on to actual regularities in the observable phenomena. Acceptance of the theory need involve no further beliefs."[9]

SR: Don't we at least need an explanation of why the theory is empirically adequate; that is, of why what we observe is just as it would be if the theory were true? And isn't the best explanation just that the theory is in fact true (or anyway near the truth)? Don't we ultimately need to invoke realism to explain the success of science?

CE: It seems to me that you're slipping back into the theological demand for explanation for its own sake. Why are you so sure that we need an explanation for science's success? But let me agree, at least for the moment, that we do need such an explanation. Even so, I think the appropriate explanation is quite different from the one you've proposed. After all, "science is a biological phenomenon, an activity by one kind of organism which facilitates its interaction with its environment."[10] Just as, from a Darwinian viewpoint, the only species that survive are those that are successful in coping with their environment, so too only successful scientific theories have survived. "Any scientific theory is born into a life of fierce competition, a jungle red in tooth and claw. Only the successful theories survive—the ones which in fact latched on to actual regularities in nature."[11] But this process of selection on the basis of empirical success need have nothing to do with the *truth* of the theories selected. Your argument is no different from that of an antievolutionist who holds that the survival of a species can be explained only by some design that has preadapted the species to its environment. But we don't need the hypothesis that theories are successful because truth has preadapted them to the world. We need only the hypothesis that theories that are not empirically successful have not survived.

SR: It seems to me you're ignoring the amazing *rate* at which empirically successful theories have emerged. Perhaps an extended process of trial and error would eventually lead to an empirically adequate scientific description of what we observe. But the use of theoretical postulations has led to success far more quickly than we could reasonably expect from mere trial and error selection. So even from your Darwinian viewpoint I think we need the realist hypothesis. But this is taking us off the track. The defense of realism that I'm interested in proposing need not be based on putting it forward as an explanation of science's success. Rather I have been arguing from the indispensable role of theoretical postulation in the formulation of empirically adequate laws. Think about it this way: Imagine that we are doing science initially only in the observation framework. We are aware of various singular observational facts and are trying to explain them by subsuming them under empirical generalizations—that is, under inductive generalizations that employ only the concepts of the observation framework.

CE: Excuse me a moment. Just how are you understanding the notion of *observation* when you speak of the observation framework? Some realists, you know, have maintained that anything—even electrons and other postulated submicroscopic entities—are in principle observable.

SR: I sympathize with some of the epistemological motives behind such claims. It is important to reject the idea that the realm of

entities and properties we in fact observe functions as an unchangable given. But in this context we must avoid trivializing the distinction between what is observable and what is not. When someone says that everything is observable, he is envisaging a situation in which concepts from the theoretical framework of science have ingressed into the observation framework. I'm speaking of the observation framework prior to any theoretical ingressions.

CE: All right. So what we observe are the ordinary objects of everyday life and their properties.

SR: Yes, but we need to distinguish two sorts of properties that we attribute to observable things. On the one hand, there are occurrent (nondispositional) properties that are, strictly speaking, *what we perceive of an object* that we perceive. There is, for example, "the occurrent sensuous redness of the facing side" of a brick.[12] On the other hand, there are dispositional or, more broadly, causal properties that correspond to *what we perceive an object as* (e.g., the brick seen as made of baked clay). Within the observation framework properties of the first sort are a constant factor. They correspond to the way that, for physiological reasons, we must perceive the world. The second sort of properties corresponds to our conceptual resources for classifying objects into kinds with distinctive causal features. These kinds are not constant but can change as "our classification of physical objects . . . becomes more complex and sophisticated."[13] An essential feature of scientific inquiry is its *revision* of the causal concepts of the observation framework in order to arrive at maximally accurate empirical generalizations. In many cases, these revisions take place entirely within the observation framework. In such cases, the causal properties are always built out of concepts expressing the occurrent properties of physical objects. We can imagine that science never required any conceptual revision other than this sort. In that case, the observation framework would be conceptually autonomous; that it, its conceptual resources would suffice for formulating and justifying entirely accurate empirical generalizations about singular observable facts. If this were the case, then the framework of postulational science would be "in principle otiose,"[14] and what Sellars calls the "manifest image" would provide a correct ontology for the world. But, as we have learned from the development of science, the observation framework is not autonomous. We cannot do the job of science using only its conceptual résources. Rather, we can arrive at justified empirical generalizations in the observation framework only by appealing to theories that employ concepts that cannot be built out of the conceptual resources of the observation framework.

CE: You seem to be missing the point of my antirealism. I'm willing to admit everything you've said about the *indispensability* of theories. But why should we also have to accept the *truth* of theories? As I see it, the highest virtue we need attribute to a theory needed for the successful practice of science is empirical adequacy. In other words, we need only agree that all of a successful theory's *observable consequences* are true. If we regard a theory as empirically adequate—and of course we are entitled to so regard highly successful theories—then from that alone we have sufficient justification for accepting the empirical generalizations that theory entails. The further assertion of the theory's truth is a gratuitous addition, entirely unnecessary for the fulfillment of science's fundamental aim; namely, an exact account of observable phenomena. The enterprise of science can be entirely successful without ever accepting the truth of its theories. Consider two scientists. One accepts atomic theory in the sense that he thinks it is empirically adequate: he knows that it fits all observations to date and expects that it will continue to fit all further observations. Accordingly, he thinks in terms of atomic theory and uses its conceptual resources to solve relevant scientific problems. However, he remains agnostic on the question of whether atoms really exist. A second scientist shares the first's views about the empirical adequacy of atomic theory, but he also holds that atoms really do exist. But what sort of work is done by this latter belief? It makes absolutely no difference for what the second scientist expects to observe or for

how he proceeds in his scientific work. His expectations and procedures are exactly the same as those of his agnostic colleague. So, while I agree with you that theories are not "otiose in principle," I do maintain that a realistic interpretation of theories is. There is nothing in the aims of scientific inquiry that is in the least affected by the acceptance or the rejection of the existence of theoretical entities.

SR: It seems to me that it's you who are missing the point of my realism. First of all, you misrepresent my view by taking it as a thesis about the aims of science. I am entirely content with the view that science aims only at empirical adequacy. Indeed, I agree that this aim might have (in some other possible world) been attained without the postulation of theoretical entities. My thesis is rather that empirical adequacy in fact requires theories that postulate unobservable entities and that this fact provides good reason for thinking such entities exist. My realism is not a thesis about the aim of science but rather a thesis about the philosophical (specifically, metaphysical) significance of the means that scientists have had to use in fulfilling this aim.

CE: I'm happy to accept this clarification of your views, but it does not affect the central point: that you haven't offered an argument from the indispensability of theories to the existence of the entities they postulate. Even Sellars, who develops the indispensability thesis much more cogently than you do, seems to ignore the need for such an argument. He seems just to assume that, once theories have been shown to be indispensable, the reality of the entities they postulate has been established. But in fact there is a gap that needs bridging. Sellars himself has emphasized this very point in parallel contexts. For example, he agrees that semantic concepts such as *meaning* and moral concepts such as *person* are indispensable, but nonetheless insists this doesn't entail that meanings and persons exist. Similarly, I think you should admit that the indispensability of theoretical language does not entail the existence of theoretical entities. Further, I submit that the only way of bridging the gap between indispensability and existence is by an act of faith that may be permissible for those who want to believe in atoms and similar things but is in no way required by the evidence.

SR: I agree that the gap needs to be bridged and I even agree that it cannot be bridged by a deductive argument. I admit that indispensability does not entail existence; theories could be indispensable and yet theoretical entities not exist. But I insist that there is a good *inductive* case for realism; reasons that make it highly probable that theoretical entities exist.

CE: I take it then that you're about to follow Putnam in presenting realism as a quasi-scientific hypothesis that is the best explanation of the success of science. I've already suggested my criticism of this sort of approach.

SR: On the contrary, I'm not entirely happy myself with this sort of "empirical" approach. Besides the difficulties you raised earlier about possible alternative hypotheses, it seems to me that realism lacks the fruitfulness we require of a good scientific hypothesis. From a purely scientific viewpoint, it looks a lot like an *ad hoc* explanation of one fact with no other explanatory significance. I rather see realism as a *philosophical* thesis based on an analysis of the nature of theoretical explanation in science. I have in mind the following strategy of argument: First find a generally valid type of argumentation from the explanatory power of a hypothesis to the reality of the entities the hypothesis refers to; then show that, in some specific cases, the results of theoretical science enable us to construct an argument of just this type for the existence of theoretical entities. Such a case is inductive because the argument type employed is inductive. But it's philosophical rather than scientific because it is not postulating an explanatory hypothesis but rather pointing out the essential similarity of two ways of arguing.

CE: I need to hear the type of argumentation you have in mind.

SR: The point is really quite simple. There's a standard way of arguing—in both everyday and scientific contexts—for the existence of unobserved entities. The mode of argument is this: from the ability of a hypothesis to (a) subsume all known facts and to (b) predict new and even unexpected facts, we infer the reality of the entities the hypothesis postulates. There's no doubt that we all accept this mode of argument in many cases that involve unobserved though observable entities. For example, this is just the way we proceed in arguing for the past existence of dinosaurs or for the present existence of stars, conceived as huge, tremendously hot, gaseous masses far distant from us. But the very same mode of argumentation used in these noncontroversial cases can be employed to argue for the existence of the unobserved entities postulated by microphysics. Just as we accepted the existence of dinosaurs because the hypothesis of their existence subsumed the known facts and successfully predicted new ones, so too we ought to accept the existence of electrons, neutrinos, etc. for precisely the same sort of reasons. The case for the existence of electrons and neutrinos is logically identical to the case for the existence of dinosaurs and stars. Since you can hardly reject the latter, I submit that you cannot consistently reject the former.

CE: You yourself have mentioned but ignored the crucial point: the nonobservability of the entities postulated by microphysics in contrast to the observability of stars and dinosaurs. This difference undermines your claim that the mode of argument for the two sorts of entities is the same. As I see it, the mode of inference at work in the examples you've given is not from a theory's explanatory power to its truth but from its explanatory power to its empirical adequacy. At any rate, the uncontroversial uses of the mode of argumentation—to the existence of stars and dinosaurs—cannot decide between the realist and the antirealist interpretations of it. For these are cases of inference to *observable* entities; and, for such cases, the claim that a postulation is empirically adequate is equivalent to the claim that it is true. For example, 'Stars (as described by modern astronomy) exist' is equivalent to 'All observable phenomena are as if stars exist', since the existence of stars is itself (in principle) observable. So I can accept the inference to stars and reject the inference to electrons, etc., on the grounds that, in both cases, we are only entitled to infer the empirical adequacy of a hypothesis from its explanatory and predictive success. In the case of stars, this is equivalent to inferring their existence; but in the case of electrons, which are not even in principle observable, it is not.

SR: This response keeps your position consistent but at the price of arbitrariness. By maintaining that explanatory and predictive success supports only the empirical adequacy of a theory, you are implicitly committing yourself to a sharp epistemic distinction between the observable and the unobservable. You say the explanatory success of a hypothesis is evidence of its truth only if the hypothesis is about observable entities. But why should observability matter in this context?

CE: The answer depends, of course, on what you mean by 'observable'. As we noted above, in one sense everything is observable: there might be some creature with sense organs appropriate for perceiving it. But, as we agreed when discussing this point, here a more restricted sense of 'observable' is appropriate. Specifically, observability must be taken as a function of certain empirical limitations of human beings. "The human organism is, from the point of view of physics, a certain kind of measuring apparatus. As such it has certain inherent limitations— which will be described in detail in the final physics and biology. It is these limitations to which the 'able' in 'observable' refers—our limitations, *qua* human beings."[15]

SR: I agree with this construal of 'observable'. But my question is, What does observability in this sense have to do with the existence or nonexistence of an entity? You're surely not so much of a positivist as to deny the possibility of the existence of what's unobservable?

CE: You're misconstruing my point. Of course observability in the sense we're taking it has nothing to do with the existence or the nonexistence of an entity. But it has a

great deal to do with what we have reason to believe exists. "The question is . . . how much we shall believe when we accept a scientific theory. What is the proper form of acceptance: belief that the theory, as a whole, is true; or something else? To this question, what is observable by us seems eminently relevant." And my answer to the question is this: "to accept a theory is (for us) to believe that it is empirically adequate—that what the theory says *about what is observable* (by us) is true."[16]

SR: Since you refer to what is observable "by us," I take it you make observability relative to an epistemic community, not to individuals?

CE: Of course. The dimmer component of the double star in the Big Dipper's handle is observable because some sharp-eyed people can see it, even if most of us can't.

SR: But then I have a problem. You surely must admit the possibility that our epistemic community might be enlarged, say by the inclusion of animals or extraterrestrials capable of observing things that we now can't observe. For example, we might encounter space travellers who, when we tell them our theories about electrons, say, "Of course, we see them all the time." If this happened, your principles would require that we then, for the first time, accept the existence of electrons. But this seems absurd. Why should the testimony of these aliens be decisive when the overwhelming evidence of our science was not? More generally, isn't it absurd to say that, just because our epistemic community has been enlarged in this way, our beliefs about what there is should change?

CE: Not at all. Your objection has weight only if we believe that "our epistemic policies should give the same results independent of our beliefs about the range of evidence accessible to us."[17] But I see absolutely no reason to believe this. On the contrary, it seems to me that to deny that what evidence is accessible is relevant to what we should believe is to open the door to scepticism or irrationalism.

SR: It seems to me you're equivocating on the expression "evidence accessible to us." Of course such evidence is relevant to our beliefs if it means "the evidence that we are in fact aware of." But this isn't what you mean here. Rather, you're saying that our beliefs ought to depend on the range of evidence that we *might* have even if we don't. Specifically, you're saying that believing that an entity exists ought to depend on whether or not there *could be* direct observations of its existence. Of course, actual observations of an entity are relevant to belief in its existence. And it's also true that, since evidence of actual observations of unobservable entities is not available, it's often harder to produce an adequate case for the existence of such things. But what reason could you have for thinking that the mere question of whether or not an entity could in principle be observed by us is decisive for the question of whether we ought to believe that it exists?

CE: What reason do you have for thinking this isn't the case?

SR: Well, consider an example. Suppose astronomical theory postulates the existence of a far distant star that has not been observed but which we have every reason to think we could observe if we were close enough. It might be, for example, that the star has been postulated as the much smaller double of a known star to explain certain anomalies in its motion. I suppose that if the evidence supporting this postulation is strong enough, you will agree that we have good reasons to believe in the existence of this star.

CE: Of course, since it is in principle observable.

SR: All right. But suppose further that, entirely independent of astronomical investigations, physiological studies subsequently show that there are previously unknown limits on human powers of observation that make the postulated star unobservable. We may, for example, have assumed that the star was observable because it emitted light in the visible spectrum and so could be seen if we got close enough to it. But physiologists might discover that the visible spectrum is not continuous, that there are small "holes" of invisibility corresponding to specific wave lengths, one of which is that emitted by the star. On your principles, such a physiological result would require us to abandon our conclusion that the star exists, even though all the empirical evidence that led us to postulate it remains the same. But surely such a move would be unreasonable; whether or not the star is observable does not alter the evidence in favor of its existence.

Notice that I'm not saying that observations we in fact have made are not relevant to our beliefs about what exists. But the mere fact that something is observable does not give us any reason to think that it ever has or will in fact be observed. The issue between us is whether mere observability—as distinct from actual observation—is relevant to our beliefs about what exists. I submit that it is not.

Another difficulty for your view derives from the fact that an observable entity may have unobservable properties. The sun, for example, is observable but the temperature of its interior is not. What then is your attitude toward the claim that the temperature at the sun's center is about 20 million degrees Centigrade? It would be odd not to accept it: After all, the claim is very well supported by a calculation based on observed facts (the average temperature of the earth, etc.) If these observed facts were appropriately different, the calculation would yield a temperature of the center of the sun that is observable (e.g., about 10 degrees Centigrade). Since you would accept the truth of the result of the calculation in the latter case, it's hard to see how you could coherently not accept its truth in the former case. But, if you accept the claim that the temperature of the sun's center is about 20 million degrees, then you've implicitly given up your principle that observability is relevant to the justification of existence claims.

CE: Not necessarily. The principle might distinguish between unobservable entities and unobservable properties of observable entities.

SR: Possibly. But then we'd need an explanation of why such a distinction is epistemically relevant.

CE: Of course, but you can see where this would lead. To respond to this objection— and your other one about the star that turns out to be unobservable—in a convincing way would require a very elaborate excursion into the theory of knowledge. "But we cannot settle the major questions of epistemology *en passant* in philosophy of science."[18] I'll just acknowledge the relevance of your objections but maintain that more careful epistemological analysis would disarm them. Furthermore, even if I can't answer your objections and your argument stands, remember that the argument is only inductive. This means that, even if I can't directly refute it, I might be able to blunt its force by pointing to overriding considerations that make realism implausible. There is, for example, the fact that, for any theory whose ontology you propose to accept, we can always formulate another theory with a different ontology that is just as well supported by the evidence as the theory you favor. Also, there's the strong historical evidence that scientific postulations are not converging to any single picture of what the unobservable world is like. Until you've dealt with these historical and logical objections to realism, you can't be content with your case for realism.

SR: I agree that the issue isn't fully settled, but your remarks strike me as a strategic retreat that, at least for the present, leaves me in control of the battlefield.

NOTES

[1] Wilfrid Sellars, *Science, Perception, and Reality* (New York: Humanities, 1963), p. 91.

[2] Cf. Bas van Fraassen, *The Scientific Image* (Oxford: The Clarendon Press, 1980), p. 12.

[3] Sellars, *Science, Perception, and Reality,* cited in n1, above, pp. 121–22.

[4] Ibid., p. 122.

[5] Bas van Fraassen, "Wilfrid Sellars and Scientific Realism," *Dialogue* 14 (1975): 611.

[6] Wilfrid Sellars, "Is Scientific Realism Tenable?," *PSA 1976,* ed. F. Suppe and P. Asquith (East Lansing, MI.: Philosophy of Science Association, 1977), p. 315.

[7] Ibid.

[8] Ibid., p. 319.

[9] Bas van Fraassen, "On the Radical Incompleteness of the Manifest Image," *PSA,* 1976, ed. F. Suppe and P. Asquith (East Lansing MI.: Philosophy of Science Association, 1977), p. 325.

[10] van Fraassen, *The Scientific Image,* p. 39, cited in n2, above.

[11] Ibid., p. 40.

[12] Sellars, "Is Scientific Realism Tenable?," cited in n6, above, p. 316.

[13] Ibid., p. 318.

[14] Sellars, *Science, Perception, and Reality,* p. 118, cited in n1, above.

[15] van Fraassen, *The Scientific Image,* p. 17.

[16] Ibid., p. 18.

[17] Ibid.

[18] Ibid., p. 19.

Recommended Readings on Realism

Churchland, Paul. *Scientific Realism and the Plasticity of Mind*. Cambridge: Cambridge University Press, 1979.

Churchland, Paul, and Clifford Hooker, eds. *Images of Science*. Chicago: University of Chicago Press, 1985.

Devitt, Michael. *Realism and Truth*. Princeton: Princeton University Press, 1984.

French, Peter, T. E. Uehling, and H. K. Wettstein, eds. *Midwest Studies in Philosophy, Vol. 12: Realism and Anti-Realism*. Minneapolis: University of Minnesota Press, 1988.

Goodman, Nelson. *Ways of Worldmaking*. Indianapolis: Hackett, 1978.

Harre, Rom. *Varieties of Realism*. Oxford: Basil Blackwell, 1987.

Leplin, Jarrett, ed. *Scientific Realism*. Berkeley: University of California Press, 1984.

Moser, Paul. *Knowledge and Evidence*. Cambridge: Cambridge University Press, 1989.

Putnam, Hilary. *Reason, Truth, and History*. Cambridge: Cambridge University Press, 1981.

———. *Realism and Reason*. Cambridge: Cambridge University Press, 1983.

———. *The Many Faces of Realism*. LaSalle, Ill.: Open Court, 1987.

Rescher, Nicholas. *Conceptual Idealism*. Oxford: Basil Blackwell, 1973.

———. *Scientific Realism*. Dordrecht: D. Reidel, 1987.

Trigg, Roger. *Reality at Risk: A Defense of Realism in Philosophy and the Sciences.* Brighton, Eng.: Harvester Press, 1980.

van Fraassen, Bas. *The Scientific Image.* Oxford: Clarendon Press, 1980.

Vision, Gerald. *Modern Anti-Realism and Manufactured Truth.* London: Routledge, 1988.

II

Space, Time, and Causation

This section consists of two subsections: *Space and Time* and *Causation*. The first subsection contains three essays on philosophical questions about the nature of space and time. Each of these essays focuses on the longstanding metaphysical issue of whether space or time has some sort of independent existence.

In "Space, Time and Space-Time," W. H. Newton-Smith begins with the claim that unless we clarify what we mean by the terms *space, time,* and *space-time,* we shall be unable to resolve certain fundamental debates in physics. Newton-Smith understands theories of space and time as general accounts that explain the relation between space and time, on the one hand, and the physical world, on the other. He uses the famous 18th-century exchange between Leibniz and Samuel Clarke to illustrate that debates about space and time involve philosophical as well as scientific issues.

Leibniz's view was *reductionistic.* It claimed that talk about time can be reduced to talk about events and relations between events, and that talk about space can be reduced to talk about bodies and relations between bodies. Leibniz's opponent was Newton as represented by Clarke. On the Newtonian view, space and time exist independently of what is in space and time. Newton-Smith calls this view *substantialism,* and he identifies some of the empirical and philosophical considerations that bear on the dispute between substantialism and reductionism. He also considers the contemporary view that our topic of concern should not be space and time considered as two separate items, but *space-time* (a system of points of space at a moment of time). Newton-Smith's proposal is that the contemporary theory of space-time (particularly the Special Theory of Relativity) is neutral in the debate between substantialism and reductionism.

In "Three Steps Toward Absolutism," J. L. Mackie begins with a systematic presentation of the issues involved in the dispute between absolutists and relativists concerning space, time, and space-time. On one key issue, the *absolutist* affirms that space and time each exist as independent entities, and the *relativist* denies this.

Mackie notes that relativism is often supported by the argument that we cannot observe space or time, by itself, apart from things or processes and, therefore, we should not affirm its existence as an independent entity. Mackie considers several principles that might lead one to deny the existence of whatever cannot be (directly) observed. He argues that each principle is incorrect, and thus that absolutism cannot be refuted by an appeal to unobservability.

This leads Mackie to ask whether there is any positive support for absolutism. He presents evidence, in turn, for *absolute acceleration, absolute duration,* and *absolute motion* and *rest.* One striking conclusion of Mackie's argument is that "the Special Theory of Relativity, as ordinarily understood, and as intended by Einstein, destroys itself, and collapses back into the Newtonian picture that includes absolute spatial positions and absolute motion."

In "The Meaning of Time," Adolf Grünbaum assesses, from the standpoint of current scientific theories, the view that the passage of time is the essence of the concept of time. Specifically, he asks whether *temporal becoming* has a mind-independent status. Grünbaum's thesis is: "Becoming is mind-dependent because it is not an attribute of physical events per se but requires the occurrence of certain *conceptualized conscious experiences* of the occurrence of physical events." Grünbaum focuses on the question of what characterizes a physical event as *now* (i.e., as belonging to the present). He claims that the *nowness* of an event at a time requires that there be a certain sort of *conceptualized experience* of the event or of another event simultaneous with it. Grünbaum defends his thesis of the mind-dependence of becoming against several likely objections. And he draws out the consequences of his thesis for the conflict between *determinism* and *indeterminism.*

The second subsection of Part II contains three essays on the nature of *causation.* These essays bear on the traditional metaphysical issue whether, and in what sense, causal relations are *necessary* connections.

In "Causality: Critique of Hume's Analysis," C. J. Ducasse summarizes David Hume's influential view of causation as follows:

To be is to be perceived; no [necessary] connection is ever perceived between a cause and its effect; therefore there is none.

According to Hume, "we may define a cause to be an object, followed
by another, and where all the objects similar to the first are followed
by objects similar to the second." Hume denies that such following of
one object upon another is necessary. However, Ducasse argues that
Hume's account of causation fails to fit the relevant facts. He argues
that there are cases where Hume's account is satisfied, but where we
judge the relevant events not to be causally related. He also argues
that there are cases where Hume's account is not satisfied, but where
we judge the relevant events to be causally related. If Ducasse is right,
causation is not just regular succession of events.

In "Causation and Recipes," Douglas Gasking rejects the
Humean view of causation as regular succession. He argues that "a
statement about the cause of something is very closely connected
with a recipe for producing it or for preventing it." Roughly formulated, this view claims that two events are causally related when we
have a "manipulative technique" for producing one of the events by
producing the other. For example: "A rise in the temperature of iron
causes it to glow" means "By applying to iron the general technique
for making things hot, you will also, in this case, make it glow."
Gasking's account is a variation on the view that our notion of causation is *anthropomorphic* (the view that this notion derives from the
ways *human* activity intervenes in the world).

In "Causation," Richard Taylor notes that in the ancient idea of
an efficient cause, we can find two related notions, namely, the
notion of power and the *notion of necessity*. The notion of power involves the idea that an efficient cause produces its effect by its own
power. The notion of necessity involves the idea that given a cause,
its effects cannot fail to occur. Taylor argues that the notions of
power and necessity are essential to the concept of causation. Thus,
he argues against the Humean view that causation is just regular
succession or mere constancy of conjunction. Taylor understands
causes as logically necessary and sufficient conditions of a certain
sort. His view is that the cause of an event is the set of conditions
that were, given all and only those other conditions that occurred,
individually necessary and jointly sufficient for the event. Taylor
also argues that "the causal conditions of an event cannot, in fact,
precede that event in time." This leads Taylor to a discussion of what
exactly distinguishes a cause from an effect.

Space and Time

Space, Time and Space-Time: A Philosopher's View*

W. H. Newton-Smith

To ask a philosopher to provide an account of something like space, time or space-time is perhaps a little unfair. For philosophers are better at asking difficult questions than in agreeing on the correctness of a particular philosophical account. Notoriously they are prone to agonize about questions of the form—what is *x*?—where '*x*' is replaced by, say, 'Truth', 'Beauty', 'Goodness'; or, in the case at hand by 'Space', 'Time' or 'Space-time'. These questions are curious. For in one sense we already know the answers. You have no problems in understanding me if I say that the *next time* a political figure is offered a chance to be proposed for an honorary degree, she will decline. Or to say that *every time* Professor Snerd lectures there is a lot of empty space in the lecture hall provokes no failure to understand what was meant. Our problem is that we cannot say what it is that we understand by words that we obviously do in one sense understand perfectly well. In this regard our predicament is rather like that of a

bicycle rider who can be in a position of skill but completely unable to say what it is he actually does to keep the bicycle upright. Indeed, focussing too much on this question while exercising the skill may interfere with the exercise of that skill.

To some this analogy will rather count against the philosophical enterprise. For one does not need an account of how it is that one rides a bicycle in order to get on with cycling. And that suggests that we simply get on with developing our scientific theories of space, time and space-time without bothering about saying what we mean by 'space', 'time' and 'space-time'. However, that is but a weakness in the analogy. For one conclusion which will emerge from this paper is that the resolution of certain debates in physics requires the resolution of certain philosophical issues that arise when we pursue these questions. Among those who thought that such philosophical questions needed answering was Isaac Barrow, whose thinking on these topics greatly influenced his student Isaac Newton.

But because Mathematicians frequently make use of Time, they ought to have a distinct Idea of the meaning of that Word,

*Copyright © 1986 by Basil Blackwell, Oxford, England. Reprinted by permission, from *The Nature of Time*, eds. Raymond Flood and Michael Lockwood, pp. 22–35. Oxford: Basil Blackwell, 1986.

otherwise they are Quacks. My Auditors may therefore, on this Occasion, very justly require an Answer from me, which I shall now give, and that in the plainest and least ambiguous Expressions, avoiding as much as possible all trifling and empty words. [From Barrow; see Further Reading.]

My theme is that Barrow is correct. Unless we have a philosophically adequate understanding of what we mean by these concepts we will be but quacks and will be prone to make mistakes in our physics as quacks make mistakes in medicine. Equally our philosophical understanding will be deficient if it does not take account of physical theory.

We can in fact learn something about space and time by first considering why it is difficult to say what we understand by 'space' and 'time'. And this will emerge if we compare the questions at hand with more tractable questions. Suppose, for example, I was asked what a cuttlefish is. Given a handy aquarium one natural way to proceed is to use ostension; that is, to provide an example of a cuttlefish. Such a procedure is not open to us in the case of space and time. We can neither point to space nor time nor to the points that make up space and time. Such items as locations in space or time are not items of our experience. If we try to think of a moment of time, for instance, the best we can do is to think of an event which happened at some moment. Like Hume's soul, the moment itself entirely eludes our grasp. We can express the problem here by saying that space, spatial items like locations, time and temporal items like moments or instants are *abstract*. For anyone with an empiricist orientation such items are bound to seem problematic for they cannot be displayed or studied in any direct fashion.

Another procedure which we might seek to use in the face of such questions is to give a verbal definition. If I am asked what we mean by a 'zemindar' I might well say that a zemindar was a revenue officer of the Mogul empire. This suggests that we might turn to the *Concise Oxford Dictionary* for enlightenment. If we look up the entry for 'time' it says: continued duration. But if we then turn to the entry for 'duration' we find it written that it is a part of time! Such a tight little circle of definitions is hardly enlightening. Aristotle's definition of 'time' as 'the number of motion' is equally circular, motion being defined itself by reference to change of location in space with regard to time. Not only have such neat verbal formulations tended sooner or later to be circular, they have also tended to explain the obscure notions of space and time in terms of equally if not more obscure notions. Other attempts to define time in terms of causation or consciousness manage to be both circular and obscure. This problem arises from the *promiscuous* character of the notions of space and time. These concepts are so intimately connected with such a wide range of fundamental ideas that the prospects of finding some unproblematic terms with which to define them are dim. If we turn our attention to the concept of space-time the prospects of gaining any easy insight are even more remote. For while the concepts of space and time are in some sense familiar, the concept of space-time, as we shall see, depends on highly technical theory and involves strange and counter-intuitive elements. What then is to be done? Augustine in a frequently quoted passage said that he understood what time was so long as no one asked him. But if asked what he understood by time he did not know. This reduced him to praying for enlightenment. In a more secular age the way forward is to consider what I will call theories of space and time. By theories I mean general accounts of space and time that are meant to cover *some* aspects of these notions through an account of the relation between space and time on the one hand and the physical world on the other.

Caroline, Princess of Wales, provided an important introduction to this approach when in the early eighteenth century she acted as an intermediary between Leibniz and the Reverend Samuel Clarke. Leibniz wrote to her lamenting the decay in England of natural religion, a phenomenon for which he held Newton responsible. Caroline passed the letters to Clarke who answered on Newton's behalf. In the ensuing exchange of letters a major controversy about space and time emerged which is as open and lively today as it was in the days when Princesses of Wales took an interest in such matters. And this provides a convenient starting point for us. For the debate takes place in the context of classical physics and enables us to get a sense of the issue without bringing in the more demanding contemporary physical theories. A brief historical reconstruction of that debate will display the importance of an interplay of philosophy and physics in discussions of space and time. With that in the background we will be able to see that the same issue arises with regard to space-time and that the contemporary debate similarly involves both philosophical and physical issues.

To characterize the Leibnizian position we need to distinguish between *things in time* such as events and *temporal items* such as moments and instants. In the case of space we similarly distinguish between things in space such as bodies and the spatial items such as locations. Initially, we can think of time as a system of temporal items such as instants and space as a system of spatial items such as locations. Leibniz's fundamental claim was that time is nothing over and above an ordered system of events and that space was nothing over and above a system of bodies. We can describe Leibniz's approach as *reductionistic*. Focussing on time for the moment. Leibniz thought that all talk about time or temporal items could be translated without loss of meaning into talk about events and various relations between events.

An analogy will be helpful in bringing out the content of a reductionist approach. It may well be true to say that the average reader of this book has 2.2 children. If I search through the readers eager to meet the average one with his or her 2.2 children I will be disappointed. And if I cling to the view that there is such a person that person will come to seem most mysterious being

invisible and intangible. My mistake, reminiscent of Lewis Carroll, arose from taking 'the average reader' on a par with 'the youngest reader'. In fact there is no such person as the average reader over and above the actual readers of this paper. The original truth is to be construed as saying that the total number of children divided by the total number of readers yields the result 2.2.

The Leibnizian approach is to treat such assertions as 'Time had a beginning' or 'The *moment* I began to lecture you yawned' as requiring a translation into assertions which make reference only to events and to temporal relations between events. The former would be construed as the claim that there was an event with no events before it and the latter would be construed as saying that the set of all events simultaneous with my beginning to lecture contained your yawning. Thus, for Leibniz there is nothing to time or temporal items over and above the events and processes that we would normally say occurred in time. And, similarly, all assertions about space or about spatial locations would be translated into assertions about bodies and spatial relations between bodies. Talk of space, spatial items, time and temporal items is a mere *façon de parler* which it is convenient to use in the same way that the phrase 'the average reader' serves to give economy of expression.

Since all talk of space and time is to be construed as talk about events and objects, the investigation of space and time becomes an empirical matter. Whether time had a beginning is something to be settled by reference to the cosmological question as to whether there was a first event in the history of the universe. And the question of the structure of space, whether it is Euclidean or not, will require a physical investigation into the contents of space. Such an approach to space and time is attractive for at least two reasons. First, it is ontologically parsimonious. We do not need to admit the existence of space and time as items over and above events and bodies. Secondly, it is demystifying. We do not have instants of time and points of space as mysterious items not given in experience. Events and bodies are types of items of which we can have experience and we can restrict attention to them and to items constructed out of them.

Such a reductionist approach, however, has immediate and controversial consequences. In the case of time it follows that there can be no time without change. If we seek to treat a period of time as a collection of events, we could not have a temporal vacuum. It would be a contradiction to speak of an interval containing no events if an interval is just a certain collection of events. And in the case of space there could be no motion that was not the motion of bodies in relation to other bodies. Suppose, for example, that we try to entertain the idea that the entire universe is moving to the left. Before and after such a putative motion all bodies would have the same spatial relation to one another. But if locations are to be defined in terms of relations between bodies we cannot have a difference in location without a difference in the relations between bodies. If all bodies keep the same relations to one another it would be a contradiction to speak of them as nonetheless moving. We will return to consider the significance of these consequences after considering the Newtonian alternative to this Leibnizian reductionism.

This alternative might well be called the Cambridge theory—not because Cambridge is the home of lost causes and this is a lost cause, but because the most important articulation of the position was given by the Cambridge neo-Platonists who taught it to Newton. On this view space and time are taken to have an existence independently of the contents of space and time. To put it in theological terms, if it had not pleased God to create the physical world, space and time would nonetheless have existed as the containers into which God could have put events and bodies. Having an existence independent of the existence of events and bodies, the structure of space and time would not depend on the properties of such items. This absolutist or substantialist conception has resulted in the thought that the properties of space and time are to be discovered not by investigations of the physical world but by *a priori* philosophical reflection.

The strains of such a conception are to be found in Newton's writings. This Newton, who I will call *Bad Newton*, held that space and time are aspects of God. They had to be aspects of God because otherwise we would have other infinite things besides God and that would detract from his glory. And since God existed necessarily, these aspects of him had to similarly have necessary existence. Necessarily existing they would have what properties they had prior to his creation of the physical world. Consequently, we do not need telescopes to investigate space and time but the ample armchairs of philosophy and theology.

There can be discerned in Newton's writings a significantly more plausible version of this substantialist view which is not at all a lost cause. To make it clear that this is more suggested than explicitly stated by Newton I will attribute it to a fictional character to be called *Good Newton*. *Good Newton* argues that reductionism has failed to give satisfactory translations of all assertions about space, spatial items, time and temporal items into assertions referring only to bodies and events. *Good Newton* argues that space and time are systems of spatial and temporal items, respectively, which cannot be treated reductionistically. In order to deal with the events and objects which we experience we posit the existence of space and time each with a certain structure. Just which structures to posit is to be determined by considering which gives us the best description and explanation of the contents of space and time. We do not directly observe the properties of space and time but infer them in the course of developing physical theories. *Good Newton* sees the reductionist as operating with too restricted a version of empiricism. He will draw attention to the fact that in physics we frequently infer the existence of unobservables. For instance, without believing in the possibility of observing free quarks we may nonetheless posit their existence on the grounds that this is required if we are to explain the phenomena of hadronic jets.

This form of substantialism, the substantialism of *Good Newton*, might be called *empirical substantialism* in contrast to the *theological substantialism* of *Bad Newton*. To see how empirical considerations could be deployed in arguing for such a position, it will be instructive to elaborate the thought experiment used by Newton in the *Scholium* to the *Definitions* in his *Principia*. (See Thayer in Further Reading.) To this end imagine that we live in a universe consisting *solely* of two spheres each rather like the earth but joined by a cord. We who live on one of the spheres have discovered Newtonian mechanics and have found that it works well when applied to objects on the surface of our sphere. One day we discover that there is a tension in the cord connecting the spheres and ask for an explanation. Given Newtonian mechanics we know that if two bodies joined by a cord rotate, there will be a tension in the cord due to the effects of centrifugal force. But in the case of the spheres there is no motion with respect to any physical body. For everything except small objects on the surface of our sphere keeps a fixed spatial relation to everything else. Thus, if the spheres are rotating with respect to something, it can only be with respect to absolute space. Since rotation would explain the tension we assume rotation and thereby posit the existence of a substantial space.

The above argument draws attention to circumstances in which it would be entirely respectable from the scientific point of view to posit the existence of a substantial space, a space which cannot be treated reductionistically. That is not to say that our world is such a world. Newton thought it was and if he was mistaken it was an entirely respectable mistake. It is to be noted that the argument even in the circumstances sketched is not compelling. There will no doubt be some counterpart of Mach in our imaginary world seeking to explain the tension by reference to repulsive forces acting between the spheres thereby avoiding a substantial space. But such a move is *ad hoc*. For if we

have found that Newtonian mechanics works on the surface of a sphere and have no experience of repulsive forces between massive bodies it would be more reasonable to posit rotation, an application of a familiar idea, rather than posit a new repulsive force for the sole reason of avoiding substantial space.

Newton held that we do live in a substantial space. As we know, this assumption leads to embarrassing consequences. For it turned out that there is no possibility of distinguishing between rest and uniform motion with respect to such a substantial space. In classical physics we can at best detect accelerations with respect to substantial space. Newton was thus led to posit something, substantial space, which gives rise to unanswerable questions; namely, is such and such a body at rest or in uniform motion with respect to that space? Some philosophers of a positivistic orientation have held that to the extent to which a theory gives rise to utterly unanswerable questions it is meaningless. However, we do not need to make such a controversial assumption in order to feel uncomfortable with this substantialist conception of space in the context of classical physics. For it is certainly methodologically undesirable to adopt theories giving rise to unanswerable questions.

We have seen how empirical consideration can be deployed in certain contexts which would favour the empirical substantialism of *Good Newton*. Philosophical considerations concerning meaning have also played a role in this debate which will be illustrated with regard to time. It was noted that the reductionist was committed to the view that there can be no time without change. For the substantialist of either a theological or an empirical kind empty time is a possibility. And this seems to the reductionist to be just nonsense. In the first place he will draw attention to the fact that we cannot imagine empty time. If by 'imagine' he means 'imagine what it would be like to experience' this is certainly so. We cannot be in the position of noticing that everything has stopped, thinking to ourselves 'Is this ever boring! Absolutely nothing is happening.' For in imagining ourselves thinking this we have to imagine change; namely, change in our mental states. But that something cannot be imagined in this sense does not mean that it will not happen. I cannot, for example, imagine in this sense my own death which nonetheless is highly likely to occur one day.

In addition, a reductionist of a positivistic orientation will claim that one could not have evidence for the existence of a temporal vacuum as a prelude to denying the meaningfulness of any theory involving such a notion. If this means that we could not have direct evidence in the sense of actually experiencing it we can agree but reply that much of physics depends on reference to items of which we cannot have direct experience—photons, fields, quarks and so on. We can reject temporal vacua on these grounds only at the cost of rejecting much of theoretical physics. It is standard practice to argue for hypotheses that cannot be directly tested on the grounds of their explanatory power. To show that the idea of empty time is at least no worse off than much of physics, we can sketch an account of circumstances in which an hypothesis employing that idea would be reasonable on the normal criteria used in adopting scientific hypotheses. In this I follow Newton's strategy by offering a thought experiment. An adequate argument to this effect is the subject for an entire chapter and in the present context I can only indicate how it might begin. For reasons of space I borrow a story from Sydney Shoemaker (see Further Reading).

Suppose we lived in a universe having three regions—A, B and C. We, the As, notice by our clocks that all change ceases in the B region for a year every three years. The Bs and everything else in their region are 'frozen' throughout every third year during which time we cannot enter the region. We notice that the same thing happens to the Cs every four years. Thus far we do not have time without change. We have only made reference to periods of time during which there is no change in certain regions of the universe. During a time when no region is frozen representatives of all regions

meet to discuss the situation. Initially the Bs and the Cs decline to accept the idea that they are periodically frozen. For being totally 'frozen' they are conscious of these periods. However, they come to accept this on the grounds that they notice the other regions to be subject to local 'freezes' and that it would explain something otherwise puzzling. This is that every so often it appears to them as if the other regions of the universe undergo a discontinuous change, a change of the sort that would normally take a year to come about. The Bs and Cs draw our attention to the fact that we are the victims of a local freeze every five years.

Once the inhabitants come to agree that they are subject to periodic local freezes they agree to advance their calendars by a year when prompted by the inhabitants of the other regions. At the meeting someone draws attention to the fact that every sixty years the local 'freezes' will match up giving a year in which there is absolutely no change anywhere in the universe. If this begins at midnight on New Year's Eve we will be able to lift our glasses and drink a toast to the year that went past unnoticed between the time we picked the glasses up and set them down.

As in the case of the Newtonian thought experiment this argument is more persuasive than compelling. For it would be possible to insist that we should adopt more complicated hypotheses concerning the local freezes. For example, we could say that the A region freezes every five years except one year in sixty in which it skips a freeze. We could similarly complicate the hypotheses governing the B and C regions. But why should we insist on the more complicated hypotheses unless we are begging the question at hand by assuming that there simply could not be empty time? Obviously much more would need to be said to make this argument for the respectability in certain contexts of empty time itself respectable. Enough has been said, however, to show that from the philosophical point of view the reductionist has a case to answer.

Against the background of classical physics it seems that the container view of space and time of *Good Newton* has more to commend it than the contents view of Leibniz in certain contexts. For we have seen that the substantialist's space would explain certain observations better than a reductionist's could and we have seen that the reductionist's assumption that empty time is nonsense is dubious. It is often claimed that this conclusion holds at best in the context of classical physics. The positivists, for example, claimed that Einstein's *Special Theory of Relativity* was a victory for the Leibnizian approach over the Newtonian approach. However, attention to some of the basic features of the Special Theory of Relativity shows that this conclusion is not warranted.

Newton's container view encourages the idea that any event E_1 is either simultaneous with any other event E_2 or it is not. For the location in the time container of E_1 is either the same location as the location of E_2 or it is not. The discovery that there is an upper maximum to the speed with which information can be transmitted, the speed of light, means that we cannot find out which event at our present location really is simultaneous with some distant event. In fig. 3.1 a light signal is represented as leaving our location at time t_1 to arrive at the occurrence of the distant event E_2 and is reflected to return to our location at time t_2. The event E_1 occurring at our location which is simultaneous with E_2 could be anywhere between t_1 and t_2. If we insist that there is some event which is *really* simultaneous with E_2 we have the embarrassment of allowing questions which do not admit of answers. Einstein proposed dropping the notion of absolute simultaneity to avoid this consequence. Instead we should talk of simultaneity relative to a particular frame of reference. Assuming we adopt the convention of fixing the time of E_1 as midway between t_1 and t_2 we find according to the Special Theory that in other frames of reference in motion relative to ours E_1 and E_2 are not counted as simultaneous. In general different frames of reference in relative motion will assign different values to the time and the spatial distance between the same pair of events. While these quantities vary from frame to frame there is in the Special Theory a quantity that does not vary. This is space-time distance between a pair of events defined by the following expression: $(x - x')^2 + (y - y')^2 + (z - z')^2 - c^2 (t - t')^2$, where c is the speed of light and the events occur at times t and t' and at spatial locations $(x,y,z,)$ and (x',y',z'). In a different frame of reference the spatial and the temporal separation between these events will be different but these will vary so as to give the same space-time separation. The fact that while spatial and temporal separation taken separately vary, and space-time separation does not, suggested to Minkowski that the fundamental item of concern should not be space and time treated separately but space-time:

> The views of space and time which I wish to lay before you have sprung from the soil of experimental physics, and therein lies their strength. They are radical. Henceforth space by itself, and time by itself, are doomed to fade away into mere shadows, and only a kind of union of the two will preserve an independent reality (see Further Reading).

In explicating the notion of space-time it will be convenient to use 'container' terminology. Space-time is a system of space-time points in which events are located. A point of space-time is a point of space at a moment

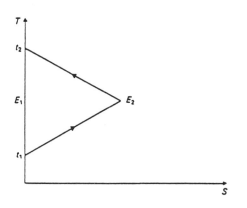

FIGURE 3.1

of time. The full-stop ending the preceding sentence is at a different location in space-time at each different moment of time. The full-stop's history would be represented as a line of space-time, a space-time having four dimensions, three spatial and one temporal. It is, however, important to note that the spatial and temporal dimensions of this space-time are treated as being very different, a difference which is signalled by the fact that there is a different sign before the temporal component in the expression for space-time separation.

When Minkowski put space and time together this was not like putting a knife and fork together on a table, it was more akin to putting an acid and base together. Space and time put together in the context of the Special Theory of Relativity gives us something with new properties, something that does not simply come apart into space and time as traditionally conceived. In classical physics spatial and temporal separation taken on their own were invariant in the sense of being the same in all frames of reference. As was noted above, in the Special Theory this is no longer the case. The invariant is instead space-time separation. And what lies behind Minkowski's claim that space and time must fade away in favour of space-time is a philosophical principle according to which what is really real is what is invariant.

What would Newton and Leibniz make of this move to space-time? Let us imagine that the current Princess of Wales having read Minkowski finds herself travelling back to 1715 thanks to Dr Who's Tardis. She inquires of Newton whether Mr Leibniz was not after all nearer the truth. Newton, I imagine, would reply:

'Not at all. Einstein and Minkowski have vindicated what I always thought. Of course I was wrong about the details. I thought I could treat space and time *separately* and that is why I advanced substantialist characterizations of each. Now I see that it is physically more reasonable to admit but one container, one substantial item, space-time. This Minkowskian space-time exists independently of its contents.'

Crossing the Channel the Princess puts to Leibniz the thought that the use of space-time in twentieth-century physics is more in keeping with the substantialist position of Newton. Not at all, Leibniz could reply:

'Things have worked out as I thought they would. True. I got the details wrong. I assumed that I could *separately* reduce all talk about space to talk about bodies and all talk about time to talk about events. The incomparable Mr Einstein shows that we must use space-time rather than space and time. So I will have to reduce all talk about that to talk about, say, point-events. Of course I must confess to a temporary problem: empty space-times. But that is nothing new and does not arise because of any special features of twentieth-century physics. My critics used to worry me about it in the context of classical physics. I very much doubt that such nonsense will be a permanent feature of gravitational theories. What is more, certain contemporary philosophers of language are advancing verificationist theories of meaning which should help to establish the nonsensical character of talk about empty space-time.'

My suggestion is then that the Special Theory of Relativity is neutral in the debate between the substantialist and the reductionist. That being so the question arises as to whether the General Theory of Relativity provides a resolution. This is a complex and controversial matter which can only be touched on within the confines of this chapter. For some this brings definitive victory to Newton. Solutions of the field equations of the theory give descriptions of the structure of a space-time. And these can be solved even when it is assumed that there is no matter or radiation whatsoever. But if space-time could not exist in the absence of matter as Leibniz would have us suppose we should expect something to go wrong when we attempt to find out what an empty space-time would be like. Such is not the case. The theory admits of the possibility of the existence of different well-behaved, entirely empty space-times. Those of a reductionist orientation have only been momentarily silenced by this result. Drawing attention to the fact that, in general, mathematical equations may have some solutions which are physically sensible and some that are not, the reductionist argues that they are extraneous roots which should be cast out. Rather than establishing the possibility of empty space-time they show a deficiency in the General Theory. And other reductionists have sought to modify the field equations so as to block vacuum solutions.

Whether the General Theory of Relativity favours reductionism or substantialism or is neutral between them is an open question. The only conclusion that can be drawn with confidence is that there will be no purely philosophical nor a purely physical resolution of this controversy. In the exchanges between Leibniz and Newton against the background of classical physics such considerations intermingle. Reference is made to the more scientific question of which theory will provide the better explanation and reference is made to the more philosophical question of the meaningfulness of, for example, rotation relative to absolute space. Then as now, these conflicting orientations to space-time must be tested by reference to both physical theories about gravitation and philosophical theories about meaning. Thus far it remains an open issue.

In seeking to relieve our perplexity about what we mean by 'space' and 'time' we considered theories about the relation between the physical world and space and time. These theories offered conflicting elucidations of *an* aspect of our conceptions of space and time. In seeking to adjudicate between them we have seen that reference must be made to physical theories. This suggests that no satisfactory philosophical understanding of the nature of space, time or space-time can be achieved by remaining at the purely semantical level. Our question about meaning took us to physics and certain results in physics take us back to meaning. We have not said in plain words what we mean by 'space', 'time' or 'space-time' and remain, in Barrow's eyes, but 'Quacks'. Still, to have an appreciation of an issue that needs resolving may be progress of a sort.

FURTHER READING

Barrow, I., *Lectiones Geometricae,* quoted from translation given in *Concepts of Space and Time: their Structure and their Development,* ed. M. Capek (Reidel, Dordrecht, 1975), pp. 203–4.

Leibniz, G. W., *The Leibniz-Clarke Correspondence,* tr. H. G. Alexander (Manchester University Press, Manchester, 1956).

Minkowski, H., 'Space and Time', in *The Principle of Relativity,* ed. W. Peerrett and G. B. Jeffrey (Dover, New York, 1923).

Nerlich, G., *The Shape of Space* (Cambridge University Press, Cambridge, 1976).

Newton-Smith, W. H., *The Structure of Time* (Routledge and Kegan Paul, London, 1980).

Shoemaker, S., 'Time without Change', *Journal of Philosophy,* 66 (1969), pp. 363–81. There are difficulties in Shoemaker's story which I have tried to rectify in my book, *The Structure of Time* (see above).

Sklar, L., *Space, Time and Spacetime* (University of California Press, Berkeley, 1974).

Swinburne, R., *Space and Time* (Macmillan, London, 1968).

Thayer, H. S., (ed.), *Newton's Philosophy of Nature* (Hafner, London, 1953).

Van Frassen, B. C., *An Introduction to the Philosophy of Time and Space* (Random House, New York, 1970).

Three Steps Towards Absolutism*

J. L. Mackie

1. INTRODUCTION: ISSUES AND GENERAL ARGUMENTS

Quite a number of philosophers of science have argued, in recent years, for at least some kind of absolutism about space or time or space-time; but most philosophers who do not specialize in this area seem to take a relativist view, and indeed a fairly extreme form of relativism, to be simply obvious, or to be established beyond the need for controversy. This paper is addressed primarily to such general philosophers, and its purpose is at least to disturb their complacency.

There are many issues, not just one, that come under the heading of 'absolutism *versus* relativism about space and time', and the first task is to distinguish them. One question is whether space and time are entities, existing independently of things and processes, whether they are proper objects of reference, or whether we should speak only of spatial and temporal features—qualities

and relations—of things and processes. This is the issue about absolute or relative existence. But we might decide that space and time are not altogether distinct from one another, that we have rather space-time which can be sorted out into spatial and temporal dimensions only relatively to some arbitrarily chosen frame of reference; even so, there will still be an issue about the absolute or relative existence of space-time, the question whether it is a proper object of reference, whether it exists independently or only as a collection of features of things and processes. Distinct from these issues of existence is the issue about position: are there absolute positions in space and dates in time (or, again, points in space-time), or does one thing or event have a position or a date or a space-time location only relatively to some other thing(s) or event(s)? Again, is there an absolute difference between motion and rest, or can one thing move or not move only in relation to another? Similarly, is there an absolute difference between acceleration—change of motion, including rotation—and non-acceleration, or is there change or non-change of motion only relatively to some arbitrarily chosen frame of reference? There are further issues about metrical features. One kind of absolutism will say that things have intrinsic spatial lengths, or that there are intrinsic metrical relations of distance between spatial positions—whether such positions themselves are absolute or merely relative—and similarly that processes have intrinsic temporal lengths or durations, or that there are intrinsic metrical relations of time-interval between occurrences—whether these occurrences in themselves have absolute or merely relative dates, positions in time. The relativism opposed to this kind of absolutism will say that all such metrical features are merely relative, that the most we have is that one thing or process or interval is equal or unequal in spatial or temporal length to another. But this kind of relativism still leaves room for a more limited kind of absolutism, namely the thesis that there are absolute equalities and inequalities of spatial length and distance and of temporal interval and duration. Opposed to this kind of absolutism is the relativism which holds that even these metrical relations are themselves relative to some arbitrarily chosen metrical system or method of measurement, or to some 'observer'—for example, that equalities or inequalities of temporal duration hold only in relation to some chosen clock or set of clocks. And even this does not exhaust the range of questions. For it can be at least plausibly argued that even if the measures of space and time separately, the equalities of length or distance on its own and the equalities of duration on its own, are thus relative to clocks or space-measuring procedures and instruments, yet there are intrinsic equalities and inequalities of time-like length and space-like length along space-time paths, so that, as we may put it, space-time has an intrinsic metric even if space and time separately do not: this would be a further kind of absolutism, while the denial of any such intrinsic space-time metric would be a yet more radical relativism. In fact, when we set them out systematically we find that there are at least fourteen distinct issues, fourteen possible absolutist theses (as shown in Table I), with a relativist thesis as the denial of each of these.

But of course these issues are not wholly independent of one another. Roughly speaking, as we go down the table we come to progressively weaker absolutist theses—and by contrast to stronger and stronger or more and more radical relativist theses. Equally, the conjunction of the separate theses about space and time on any one line will entail the corresponding thesis about space-time on the same line, but neither of those separate theses will be entailed by the corresponding space-time thesis. For example, absolutism about spatial positions and dates requires, but it is not required by, absolutism about motion, and absolutism about motion requires but is not required by absolutism about acceleration; if space-time paths have intrinsic lengths, then there will be absolute equalities and inequalities between them, but there might be such absolute equalities and inequalities even if they had no intrinsic lengths. If space and time

---

TABLE I. **Varieties of Absolutism and Relativism.**

There may be absolutisms and contrasting relativisms about:

1.1. the *existence* of space	1.2. of time	1.3. of space-time
2.1. *position* in space	2.2. in time	2.3. in space-time
	3. *motion/rest*	
	4. *acceleration/non-acceleration*	
5.1. *length/distance* in space	5.2. *duration/interval* in time	5.3. *time-like and space-like lengths* of paths in space-time
6.1. *equality/inequality of length/ distance* in space	6.2. *equality/inequality of duration/interval* in time	6.3. *equality/inequality* of *time-like and space-like lengths* of paths in space-time

---

each exist as independent entities, we should at least expect this fact to carry with it all the other absolutisms—though they *might* perhaps be amorphous entities, with no metrical features or even with no distinguishable parts—but the various absolutisms lower down the table might hold without such absolute existence; and the same applies to absolutism about the existence of space-time and the various absolutisms below this in the right-hand column.

There is a connection of another kind between these issues. In each case the relativist view is commonly supported by the same general line of argument. We cannot observe space or time by itself apart from things or processes, so we have no right to assert its existence as an independent entity. We cannot fix a thing's position except in relation to other things. There would be no detectable difference if everything in the universe were a mile further north than it is, so this form of words fails to specify any real difference. We cannot tell whether one thing is moving or not on its own, but only whether it is moving in relation to other things or to ourselves. There would be no way of detecting whether the whole universe was moving together. And so on. The relativist typically argues that whatever the particular absolutism which he is opposing asserts is unobservable, or at any rate not directly observable, and therefore cannot be real.

But how does the alleged unobservability bear upon the issue in each case? The relativist must be relying not on the unobservability alone but also on some philosophical principle which authorizes him to deny or reject or dismiss whatever cannot be (directly) observed. In fact, several such principles have been put forward.

One of these is Leibniz's principle of sufficient reason: nothing happens without a sufficient reason, and in particular God does nothing without a sufficient reason. But, Leibniz argues, there could be no sufficient reason why everything in the universe should be where it is rather than all together being a mile further north; so there can be no real difference between these alternatives, as

absolutism about spatial position holds that there is. If there were absolute positions in time, God would have been faced with the choice whether to create the world at one time or, say, twenty-four hours later, letting it run on in just the same way. But since the difference between these would be utterly undetectable for anyone within the universe, and neither course of events could be better than the other in any way, he could not have had a sufficient reason for preferring one to the other. But if there are no absolute temporal positions, God is spared the embarrassment of such an unresolvable choice. In this way the principle of sufficient reason would support various relativisms. However, there is no sufficient reason why we should accept this principle.

Another suitable principle is the verificationist theory of meaning. If the meaning of every statement is constituted by the method(s) by which it would be verified, a supposed statement which was utterly cut off from the possibility of verification would lack meaning, and so would not really be a statement after all. So if absolute motion, for example, is undetectable, the statement that something is moving absolutely, or that it is absolutely at rest, must after all say nothing.

Even if this principle is accepted, it seems to leave room for a defence of at least some varieties of absolutism. For example, it has been argued, by Newton and by others following him, that although absolute acceleration is not directly observable, it is indirectly observable and indeed measurable, by way of its dynamic causes and effects. For example, if there were two equal metal spheres joined by a spring, then if we knew the masses of the spheres and the elastic characteristics of the spring we could determine whether, and if so at what angular velocity, this little system was rotating absolutely merely by seeing whether, and if so how much, the spring was extended.

But the verificationist-relativist will reply that if absolute acceleration is never directly observed, we cannot infer it from such effects—or, likewise, from any causes. We cannot establish or even confirm the causal law on which such an inference must rely unless we directly observe, sometimes at least, each of the terms that the law connects. And in default of such an inference, if we claim that, for example, the extension of the spring is a measure of absolute rotation, we must simply be introducing the name 'absolute rotation' as a name for such a directly observed change: 'The system is rotating absolutely with such and such an angular velocity' can only mean 'The spring is extended so far'. And in general instead of being able thus to introduce indirectly observed items, we succeed only in introducing what are likely to be misleading names for the features which are directly observed, and which the absolutist was trying to use as evidence for something else.

However, I shall show (in Section 2) that this reply cannot be sustained. The criticism of it there will bring out the weakness of the verificationist theory of meaning; but this theory has in any case some very unpalatable cosequences in both scientific and commonsense contexts, and it can, I believe, be decisively refuted.[1]

Another principle on which the appeal to unobservability may rely is that of economy of postulation, Ockham's razor. An entity, or a quality, or a relation, that is never directly observed is one that we are not forced to admit, and therefore one that we could do without. However, there is more than one kind of economy, and I shall show (in Section 3) that is may be more economical in an important sense to postulate at least some of the items favoured by absolutism than to do without them as the relativist would prefer.

A fourth principle is the operationalist one, that science should use only operationally defined terms. But this would at most exclude absolutist terms and theses from science: it would not settle any philosophical issues about the existence or non-existence of absolute space or time or space-time, or about the absolute or relative status of the various other features. In any case operationalism derives whatever plausibility it has as a programme for science either from a verificationist theory of meaning or from some principle of the economy of postulation. If these fail, it has no independent appeal.

I maintain, therefore, that there is no cogent general argument for the different varieties of spatio-temporal relativisms, based on the impossibility of observing directly each of the controversial absolute entities or features. Rather, the specific issues have to be examined one by one, to see whether, in each case, the absolutist has good grounds for postulating the item(s) in question. *That is, absolutisms cannot be systematically ruled out: nevertheless each particular absolutism will need to have a case developed for it before it can be ruled in.*

Obviously, I cannot hope to deal with all these issues in one paper; instead, in the three following sections, I shall discuss a few of them, but I hope in doing this, to illustrate some general principles which should guide us in this area as a whole.

2. ABSOLUTE ACCELERATION

I shall treat the problem of absolute acceleration fairly summarily, because it has been thoroughly discussed by (for example) Newton, Mach, Reichenbach, and Swinburne, and most of what needs to be said about it emerges directly from their discussions.[2]

As everyone knows, Newton argued that since, if we rotate a bucket of water, we find that the surface becomes concave—and the more concave the more rapidly it rotates—we have here an indication of absolute acceleration: the 'centrifugal force' which seems to push the water outwards so that it builds up at the sides of the bucket is really a symptom of the fact that the water is constantly being forced to accelerate towards the centre of the bucket. Similarly, with the two spheres joined by a spring, the tension of the spring is needed to exert on each sphere the force which makes it accelerate towards the centre as the system rotates. The result of the bucket experiment can be checked by anyone in his back garden; observations that are practically equivalent to the two-sphere experiment can be made on planetary and satellite systems and double stars. So far, these results favour Newton: there is independent evidence for the presence of forces which are just the ones that we should expect to find if there were absolute rotations and therefore absolute accelerations involved in them. Moreover, these rotations are not in general rotations relative to some nearby body. The bucket's rotation is indeed relative to the earth, but there is nothing corresponding to this in the other cases. But, as Mach points out, the rotations that are doing the work need not be interpreted as absolute rotations. For they are, obviously, rotations relative to 'the great masses of the universe', the fixed stars and beyond them the galaxies. However, Mach erred in arguing *a priori* that it must be this relative rotation that is doing the work. As Reichenbach points out, it is an empirical question whether this is so. Suppose that we find centrifugal phenomena on an earth E_1 which is rotating relatively to a surrounding shell of fixed stars F_1; then if there were, far away, another earth E_2 stationary relative to F_1, but with a shell of stars surrounding it, F_2, which is stationary relative to E_1, then E_1 and E_2 will each have the same rotation relative to its own surrounding shell. But it is an empirical question whether the same centrifugal phenomena are in fact found on both. If they are, this will confirm Mach's hypothesis: since the effects are correlated with the relative rotations between each earth and its own star shell, it is these relative rotations that are doing the work. But if the centrifugal phenomena are found in E_1 but not in E_2, Mach's hypothesis is disconfirmed. We may be tempted to say that in this case Newton's interpretation, that it is an absolute rotation of E_1 that is producing these effects, is confirmed; but Reichenbach argues that this would be too hasty a conclusion. *Some* absolute rotation, he concedes, is responsible; but it might be either an absolute rotation of E_1 or an absolute rotation of its surrounding shell F_1. And Reichenbach thinks that we shall be unable to decide which it is. But, as Swinburne says, this is not so: some further additions to the possible observations could decide this. If we have other earths, E_3 and E_4 and so on, with various different rotations relatively to E_1

but within the same star shell F_1, we shall be able to decide, by seeing what centrifugal effects, if any, they exhibit, whether these effects are correlated with what would have to be the different absolute rotations of each earth or with the rotation of the common surrounding star shell F_1. The whole discussion is a straightforward application of the methods of eliminative induction that are known as Mill's Methods. With a sufficient range of partly similar and partly different situations, we could show that various proposed factors in turn are not causally responsible for the 'centrifugal effects'; and the elimination of enough rival hypotheses could in the end powerfully confirm Newton's view that these effects are being produced by an absolute rotation of the body in which these effects appear, and hence by an absolute acceleration of its parts. Of course, the empirical outcome of such a range of observations could go the other way, and confirm, say, Mach's relativist interpretation. All I am insisting on at present is that it is an empirical question; I am protesting against the tendency of many relativists to suppose that the relativist account is the only possible one, that is can be established on some general philosophical grounds without waiting for the empirical evidence.

But now we have a puzzle on our hands. How does this manage to survive as an empirical question? How does it escape the general argument sketched in Section 1 against the possibility of introducing items which are never directly observed, for which we have at best indirect evidence? Specifically, how can we first give meaning to a statement of the form 'X has such-and-such an absolute rotation' and secondly confirm it? If the very notion of rotation is first introduced in connection with the observed rotation of one thing in relation to another, how can we even frame, without internal contradiction, the concept of a rotation that is not relative to anything?

Well, we can first introduce, quite arbitrarily, the notion of a purely abstract standard or frame of reference. There is a frame of reference, for example, with respect to which this book is rotating clockwise as seen from above about an axis perpendicular to its cover through its centre of gravity at sixty revolutions a minute; and there is another frame of reference with respect to which the same book is rotating about the same axis in the opposite direction at twice that angular velocity. Abstract frames of reference are cheap: you can have as many of them as you like at no cost at all; and as such they have no physical significance. But suppose that there is some one abstract frame of reference such that certain dynamic causes and effects are systematically associated with rotations (which vary in magnitude, in their axes of rotation, and in direction) relative to it. Suppose, that is, that there is one 'preferred' frame of reference rotations relative to which do, as it turns out, have physical significance. Next, we may have either of two alternatives. Perhaps there is no physical object at all, and no set of objects, which are associated with this preferred frame (by being, say, at rest in it, or having their motions with respect to it somehow complementary). Or perhaps, as in the Reichenbach-Swinburne worlds, there *is* a set of objects thus associated with the preferred frame, but other observations or experiments show, by Millian methods of eliminative induction, that these objects are *not* causally involved in the cause-effect relationships which pick this out as the one preferred frame. Then we must conclude that what is doing the work is rotations relative simply to this preferred abstract frame of reference itself. Briefly, experiments and observations can show that there are causally significant rotations, but that, as causally significant, they are rotations relative to no *thing* at all. That, I suggest, is what we mean by 'absolute rotation', and the possible observations I have sketched show how we might confirm its reality. It is, of course, a trivial and merely technical task to extend this account from rotations to accelerations of all sorts.

This account shows how, on thoroughly empiricist principles, meaning can be given to such a term as 'absolute rotation'. This is what Locke or Hume, for example, would call a complex idea, and empiricists generally have had no difficulty in constructing new complex ideas, provided that the materials out of which they are constructed are found within the content of our experience. It is only a 'simple idea' that has to be copied from a preceding 'impression'. Essentially the same principle is expressed in Russell's dictum, "Every proposition which we can understand must be composed wholly of constituents with which we are acquainted".[3] This general empiricism is much more plausible than the verificationist thesis that each form of sentence or statement as a whole must be given meaning by a method by which it could be verified, or, equivalently, that each meaningful term, however complex, must be correlated with some direct observation. That more extreme form of empiricism would preclude the constructing of complex ideas or meanings out of simpler empirical components, and there is no good reason for accepting any such restriction. In the particular case we have been studying, there is a set of possible observations which, interpreted by the ordinary (roughly Millian) canons of causal investigation, would show that it is *rotations* that are at work, and further possible observations which would show that what is causally relevant is rotations relative to no *thing*. These are the constituents out of which the required complex concept of absolute rotation (or, more generally, of absolute acceleration) are put together. (In effect, I am here rejecting what Swinburne calls 'verificationism proper', but, like Swinburne, I am accepting what he calls 'word-verificationism', and using it to show how the term 'absolute acceleration' has meaning.)

By analogy with absolute acceleration we can readily explain how meaning can be given to the term 'absolute motion', and how it is at least conceivable that observations and experiments should confirm its reality. If there were some one preferred frame of reference such that even uniform motions (rather than rest) relative to it systematically required causes and had effects, without any *things* associated with that frame being causally relevant to these processes, then we could call motion or rest relative to that one preferred frame absolute motion or rest. To say in general that there is absolute motion would therefore be to say that there is some one such preferred frame; and this might conceivably be confirmed by the discovery of such systematically causally relevant motions without any *things* that could account for their relevance. However, while both 'absolute acceleration' and 'absolute motion' are meaningful, there is dynamic evidence that supports the view that the former term has application, but there is no such dynamic evidence to show that there is absolute motion. A different kind of argument for absolute motion will be put forward in Section 4 below.

3. ABSOLUTE DURATION

Another topic with which I want to deal fairly summarily is that of absolute duration. This has not been discussed so widely as that of absolute acceleration, but I have myself written and read (though not published) papers about it on a number of occasions, and while the conclusion I shall reach in this section is not uncontroversial, it may be not too difficult for unprejudiced people to accept.

Let us consider initially how in a single frame of reference—to which our situation on earth and in the neighbouring solar system is a close enough approximation—we decide whether two time intervals $A–B$ and $C–D$, marked out by four near-instantaneous events A, B, C, and D, are equal or not. We use, of course, various sorts of 'clocks', where the term 'clock' can include not only manufactured devices of many kinds but also the rotations and revolutions of planets and satellites, the decay of radioactive materials, and so on. All such clocks are probably inaccurate to some extent, because of causally relevant variations in the circumstances in which they go through their characteristic performances; but we can identify the causes of inconstancy by seeing how similar clocks running side by side may diverge from one another, and once we have found these

causes we can either correct the deviant clocks or allow for their inconstancies. For example, we find that of two otherwise similar pendulums swinging side by side, the longer swings more slowly. We can use this knowledge, along with the discovery that pendulum number two is longer during $C–D$ than it was in $A–B$, while pendulum number one has remained the same length, to explain why pendulum number two says that $C–D$ is shorter than $A–B$ while pendulum number one says that these two intervals are equal—that is, swings the same number of times in the two intervals. That is, we can 'correct' pendulum number two on the ground that it, and not pendulum number one, has suffered a causally relevant change. Let us speak of a 'corrected clock' when we are referring to the set of readings given by a clock after allowance has been made for all thus discoverable causes of inconstancy. We can then ask what happens when we apply to our two intervals $A–B$ and $C–D$ a large battery of corrected clocks. (The only question we are asking of them is whether they measure these two intervals as equal or not: the obviously arbitrary and trivial choice of units does not come into the matter.) Any one of three things might happen. They might all agree with one another in saying that these two intervals were equal, or, say, that $A–B$ was longer than $C–D$; or they might all disagree in a chaotic way; or they might fall into two or more distinct families, with all the corrected clocks of one family agreeing with one another, but systematically disagreeing with the corrected clocks of another family. It is a thoroughly synthetic, empirical, question which of these three results emerges: I can show that the natural procedure for the causal correction of clocks does *not* prejudice this issue by counting as corrected clocks only ones which all agree with one another. Moreover, we can ask what happens when we apply our large battery of corrected clocks not just to a single pair of intervals $A–B$ and $C–D$, but to a large number of such pairs of intervals. Now it seems to be an empirical fact that for clocks in this solar system the first of our three possibilities is realised: corrected clocks systematically agree with one another within the limits of observational accuracy in saying, for example, that A–B and C–D are equal, that of some other pair of intervals the first is greater than the second, and so on.

Now how is this empirical fact to be explained? How does it come about that so many and such different clocks keep on giving agreed answers to a long series of questions of this form? As I said, this result has not been faked up by 'correcting' the clocks in an *ad hoc* way to yield this result. Nor is there any sort of interaction between the various clocks by which they could, so to speak, keep in step with one another. But it is implausible to say that it is a mere coincidence—or rather a whole series of coincidences—that corrected clocks keep on agreeing with one another about the equality or inequality of each pair of intervals. The only plausible explanatory hypothesis is that there is some intrinsic equality between A–B and C–D, some intrinsic inequality between another pair of intervals, and so on. There are intrinsic metrical relations between such intervals, and that is why each separate clock (once any caused inconstancies have been eliminated) performs the same number of its characteristic performances, whatever they are, in A–B as in C–D, but systematically different numbers of these performances in other intervals, and so on. This is, in a new sense, the more economical hypothesis.

On these grounds there seems to be a strong case for the absolutist view about the issue numbered 6.2. But we can then go further. Once it is admitted that there are absolute relations of equality or inequality of time intervals, it is an easy further step to the conclusion that these absolute relations are themselves to be explained by the hypothesis that each interval on its own has an intrinsic metrical feature that we can call 'time-length' or 'duration', something that, as we may put it, interacts with the intrinsic features of each clock to determine just what performances it will go through in that interval. In other words, we can regard as well confirmed also the absolutist view on the issue numbered 5.2.

However, this triumph may be premature. This case collapses, this line of argument fails, when we relax our initial restriction and consider 'clocks' which are not all (approximately) in the same inertial frame of reference. When we consider particles, or clocks on space-ships, which are moving, relatively to the solar system, at speeds that are a fair proportion of the speed of light, we have to recognize and allow for the Fitzgerald-Lorentz 'retardation'. The Special Theory of Relativity seems to be empirically well confirmed, and it entails that corrected clocks will conform not to the first but to the third of the possibilities distinguished above. While all clocks which are roughly stationary with respect to the solar system form one family, clocks that are all moving together in a different frame of reference, even another inertial one—say clocks of many different sorts on a rapidly receding space-ship—form another family, and so on. This is dramatically illustrated by the Clock Paradox, for example that the interval which is measured by all corrected earth-related clocks as a hundred years will be measured as only sixty years by clocks on a pair of space-ships which have passed the earth, and one another, as in Figure 1, with four-fifths of the speed of light relatively to the earth. This result is a firm and unavoidable consequence of the Special Theory, and within that theory it has nothing to do with accelerations or decelerations: it depends purely on relative velocities.

The Clock Paradox is, however, very easily solved. We have merely to recognize that

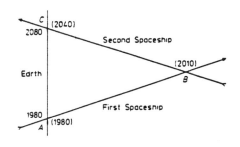

FIGURE 1

clocks do not measure time. What they measure is something else, 'proper time', or the 'time-like length' of particular space-time paths—the path followed by each particular clock. Whereas our old-fashioned concept is of time as a single dimension, so that there is only one unique time interval between two specified events, such as *A* and *C* in Figure 1, the first space-ship's passing earth and the second space-ship's passing earth, once we introduce this new concept of proper time we can see that there can be one proper time interval along the earth's path from *A* to *C*, but a different—and, as it turns out, shorter—proper time interval along the joint path of the two space-ships *A-B-C*.

Once we have thus introduced proper time, we can see that the whole of the above argument for absolutism can be transferred to it. What explains the agreements about equality and inequality of intervals among all corrected earth-related clocks? Surely a real, objective, equality or inequality of each pair of slices of proper time along the earth's path. What explains the agreements among themselves of all the corrected clocks of another family, say those on one space-ship? Likewise a real, objective equality or inequality of each pair of slices of proper time along the space-ship's path. And these various equalities and inequalities are themselves explained in turn by the hypothesis that each slice of proper time on its own, each interval along a space-time path or 'world line', has an intrinsic metrical feature of time-like length. That is, we here abandon the absolutist answers to issues 6.2 and 5.2, but accept instead the corresponding absolutist answers to issues 6.3 and 5.3.

It would be only a technical exercise to construct a closely analogous argument with regard to spatial length, first arguing for intrinsic equalities and inequalities of lengths, that is, for the absolutist answer to issue 6.1, then using this to support the absolutist answer to issue 5.1, that there are intrinsic metrical features of length or distance for each spatial stretch on its own, but then abandoning these conclusions in the face of the success of the Special Theory of Relativity, but falling back on another part of

the absolutist answer to issues 6.3 and 5.3, that space-like lines in space-time have intrinsic equalities and inequalities, and that each on its own has an intrinsic space-like length. I shall not waste time or space on this technical exercise.

We cannot, of course, appeal to our present *concept* of time as a single universal dimension against the recognition of an indefinite multiplicity of equally real proper times. That concept is exactly what we could have been expected to develop through being acquainted with one and only one proper time, that of things practically stationary with respect to the earth, and through having no experience until very recently of things moving at high speeds in relation to this frame.

The conclusion of this discussion, which I have given in only a condensed form, is that there is indeed an intrinsic metric of space-time. Though the choice of units is of course arbitrary, there are intrinsic absolute quantitative features that have the general character of lengths or distances, though what they are lengths of or distances along are something other than the purely temporal or purely spatial dimensions of Newtonian theory. And it is worth noting that this conclusion rests upon and accommodates and incorporates all the characteristic doctrines of what is called the Special Theory of Relativity. This name is misleading: the doctrines themselves are very far from constituting a pure relativism about space and time.

4. ABSOLUTE MOTION AND REST

In this final section I shall put forward an argument that is much more radical than those of Sections 2 and 3. Whereas 2 and 3 were directed only against loose thinking in some philosophical views about scientific matters, Section 4 will challenge what has been an orthodox view for about seventy years within science itself. I shall argue that the Special Theory of Relativity, as ordinarily understood, and as intended by Einstein, destroys itself, and collapses back into the Newtonian picture that includes absolute spatial positions and absolute motion. I have little doubt that my argument in this section is correct. On the other hand, I am not optimistic enough to hope that so heretical a thesis will win widespread acceptance in the foreseeable future. Though, like Hume with respect to religion, I am endeavouring to open the eyes of the public, and look forward to the ultimate downfall of a prevailing system of superstition, I am as reconciled as he was to the reflection that this will not happen in my lifetime, though I need not assume, as he did, that the superstition would last 'these many hundred years'.[4] So I would stress that while the arguments of Sections 2 and 3 may prepare people's minds for that of Section 4, they in no way depend upon the acceptance of the latter. *The conclusions of Sections 2 and 3 will stand, as will the general argument in Section 1 against attempts to settle all the issues together in favour of relativism, even if the more extreme speculations of Section 4 are not cogent.*

I shall restrict my discussion to a type of situation which seems to be adequately represented by the Special Theory of Relativity, not bringing in the complications of the General Theory: that is, situations which are to all intents and purposes free from 'gravitational' forces. My argument starts from the above-mentioned fact, that the Special Theory of Relativity is ill-named, since it is itself far from being a pure space-time relativism. This comes out strikingly in the fact that light paths in space-time, the 'world lines' of light and other electromagnetic radiations, are physically determinate: *light does not overtake light*. These paths are independent of the source of the radiation. They are equally independent of any observers, and of any choice of frame of reference. If, for simplicity of representation, we neglect two of the three spatial dimensions and picture space-time as a two-dimensional manifold of spatiotemporal points (or possible point-events), possible light paths constitute a rigid grid as in Figure 2. That is, there are two physically determinate families of parallel light paths. (Of course, there are really infinitely

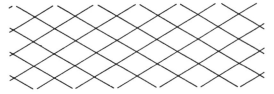

FIGURE 2

FIGURE 3

many such paths in the two sets of parallels.) This is a very different grid from that presupposed in Newtonian mechanics, shown in Figure 3, where the horizontal lines represent simultaneity at different places, and the vertical lines represent sameness of position at different times. But the Einsteinian grid is no less rigid than the Newtonian one, and it has the advantage of being experimentally detectable, which even Newton did not claim for his. We can tell directly whether two point-events lie on the same light path or not, by seeing whether light emitted at one reaches the other.

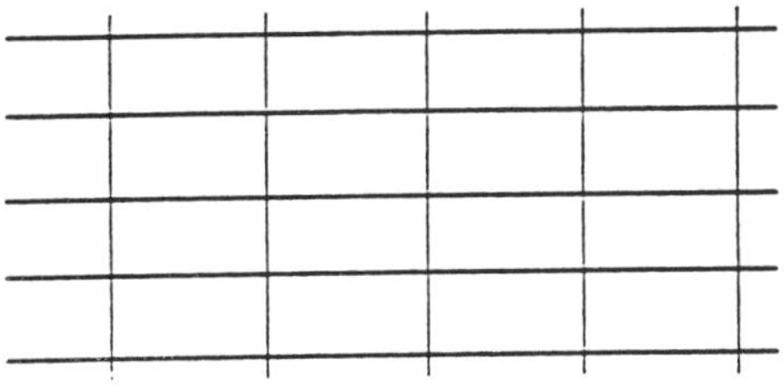

Now consider a single point-event 0, where a burst of radiation is sent out in all directions. Again, for simplicity, let us represent merely the light sent out in two diametrically opposite directions, represented as to the left and to the right in Figure 4. An equal group of photons, say, goes in each direction. Then the world lines of these two groups of photons are the determinate light paths in space-time $0A$ and $0B$. Along such a light path there is neither a time-like length nor a space-like length other than zero. If, *per impossibile*, a set of clocks were to travel with the photons, they would all agree in measuring the proper time along any stretch of this path as zero, whether from 0 to C, say, or from 0 to A. Yet in the going of the photons from 0 through C to A, there is undoubtedly a causal process. If the radiation had not been emitted at 0, it would not have been received at A. Equally, if something had intercepted it at C, it would not have been received at A. The photons' being at C is causally intermediate between their being at 0 and their being at A. Also, the causal process represented by the line 0A is exactly like that represented by the line 0B in all respects other than the diametrically opposite directions in which the light travels. It follows that if we arbitrarily select a particular space-time point C on 0A, there is a unique corresponding space-time point— call it D—on 0B. That is, there is a part 0D of the 0B process which is, apart from direction, just like the 0C part of the 0A process. (See Figure 4.)

Here someone might object, asking 'How can you determine this corresponding point?' He might go on: 'Since anything that you could use to measure the "length" of 0C would yield the answer "zero", and anything you used to measure the "lengths" of 0E, 0D, 0F, and so on along 0B would also measure *each* of these as zero, you could not pick out *which* of 0E, 0D, and 0F, for example, corresponds exactly to 0C, and hence you could not decide that D, say, rather than E or F, corresponds to C'. I fully concede this. I do not claim that there is any way of *determining* the point that corresponds to C; I say that *there is* one. And nothing but the sort of extreme verificationism which I mentioned, but set aside, in Section 1 would rule out this claim as meaningless. Verificationism apart, there may well *be* things which *we*

cannot discover or identify; I persist, therefore, in the assertion that there is, on 0B, some point that corresponds, in the sense indicated, to C.

Now suppose that radiation is sent to the right from C just as the original group of photons reaches C, and to the left from D just as the original group of photons reaches D. (A mirror at each of these two space-time locations would do the trick.) Then these two new lots of radiation (or reflected photons) will also follow determinate space-time paths, as in Figure 4, and these paths will intersect at a unique, determinate, space-time point, which we can call G. The symmetry of the situation shows that, in the single spatial dimension represented in our diagrams, G is symmetrically placed with respect to 0A and 0B. If we were to repeat the procedure, selecting a series of points C_1, C_2, . . . , C_n, . . . on 0A, and identifying the corresponding points D_1, D_2, . . . , D_n, . . . on 0B, and hence deriving a series of intersections G_1, G_2, . . . , G_n, . . . , then the line 0G_1G_2, . . . , G_n . . . would be the one and only one world line in this plane which was thus symmetrically related to the physically determinate world lines, the light paths, 0A and 0B. That is, 0G_1G_2, . . . , G_n . . . represents absolute rest, so far as this one spatial dimension is concerned. Similar constructions yield lines of absolute rest with respect to any two other spatial axes at right angles to this one, and putting them together we have a unique line of absolute rest through 0.

The same point can be made in a slightly different but equivalent way. If a single burst of radiation is sent out in all directions from a space-time point 0, and a space-time point C is arbitrarily chosen on one of the rays, then there is a sphere constituted by the corresponding points on all the other rays—in the sense of 'corresponding' indicated above. Secondary (or reflected) radiation from all over that sphere, coming inwards, will meet at a unique space-time point G; then the line 0G will be a line of absolute rest.

This conclusion can be related to what was said about the meaning and determina-

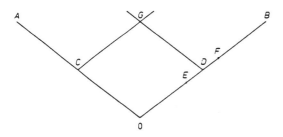

FIGURE 4

tion of absolute motion at the end of Section 2. Our present argument shows that *there is* a preferred frame of reference which is the only one to which all the causal processes constituted by the paths taken by radiation (with no 'gravitational' disturbance) are symmetrically related, though there is no *dynamically* preferred frame of reference there is a frame preferred on these other grounds.

This conclusion will, no doubt, seem shocking to anyone with even a slight acquaintance with Relativity Theory. A very natural reaction will be to object that the proposed construction is somehow circular, that the selection of the point D as that corresponding to C must be made from the point of view of some particular observer, or some particular frame of reference, who, or which, has already implicitly taken $0G$ as a line of rest in that frame. But I reply that the light paths $0A$ and $0B$ are observer-independent and frame-independent. They, above all else, are physically real and determinate. I concede that it is only from the point of view of a particular frame or observer that we can *specify* a point on $0B$ which we take to correspond to C, a point D' such that $0D'$ *looks* to this observer exactly like $0C$. But I maintain that as a frame-independent and observer-independent fact there must *be* some point D which really corresponds to C, which may well not be the D' which from some particular point of view seems to correspond to C, and I support this claim by an appeal to the concrete reality of the similar causal processes represented by $0A$ and $0B$.

How can this conclusion be reconciled with the empirical success of the the Special Theory? Very easily. All that success involves is that there is no physical procedure that will pick out a uniquely preferred frame of reference from the set of inertial frames. My argument does not pretend to supply any such physical procedure. It is an abstract, philosophical, argument to show that there really is such a uniquely preferred frame, although we cannot identify it. In a sense my argument makes no difference to physics as a practical concern, as an applied theory. It would not matter at all to someone whose interest in science was purely techno-logical or utilitarian. But it should matter to someone who is interested in the truth, in the question about what is the case.

Though shocking to those familiar with the scientific orthodoxy of the twentieth century, my conclusion should not really be surprising to anyone who reflects upon the way in which, as I said, possible light paths constitute a physically determinate space-time grid. We are simply using the admitted rigidity and symmetry of that grid to show that there must be a further, though concealed, symmetry, in fact to show that there is, though we cannot discover it, the Newtonian grid of Figure 3.

However, there is *something* surprising here. Why, and how, does it come about that although there really is such a thing as absolute rest, we cannot identify it? There must be something odd about the laws of nature that enables them to constitute such a conspiracy of silence. In effect, this means that although there is a unique line of absolute rest through 0 with respect to which the light paths $0A$ and $0B$ are symmetrically placed, they appear, to each observer, to be symmetrically placed with respect to the line of rest in the inertial frame, whichever it is, with which he is moving. But this is simply the fact that the *measured* velocity of light in both directions (along $0A$ and $0B$) is equal in each inertial frame, when that velocity is measured by the means which it is natural for an observer at rest in that frame to use. In effect, we shall have to take the Fitzgerald-Lorentz 'contractions' and 'retardations' literally, as real effects of high-speed absolute movement, that is, as Fitzgerald and Lorentz themselves interpreted them. But this is only a hint; a rather long story would be needed to explain in detail how mere motion could have such effects. And I agree that until such an explanation is given, this conspiracy of silence will provide the best available evidence for the existence and activity of Descartes's *malin genie*—though I would, for this purpose, translate '*malin*' not as 'malignant' but merely as 'mischievous'.

When we thus take the 'contractions' and 'retardations' literally, as effects of absolute motion, we are explicitly satisfying the definition of 'absolute motion' that was offered at the end of Section 2, at least to the extent that we are saying that there is a preferred frame of reference such that even uniform motions relative to it have systematic effects, quite independently of there being any things associated with that frame.

If the argument of this section is sound, and there is such a thing as absolute rest (and therefore also absolute spatial position), this not only settles the issues numbered 3 and 2.1 in favour of absolutism, it also reacts upon the decisions we reached at the end of Section 3. At that point I said that the belief in absolute durations—lengths of time rather than proper time—could be rejected as resulting from the fact that our experience, until recently, has been confined to the proper time of one particular inertial frame, which we have therefore mistaken for a single universally applicable dimension. But it now appears that out of all the different proper times there will be a unique one with a special status, namely the proper time of things at absolute rest. This we can now call 'time' *simpliciter*, and we can call the determinate lengths of this time 'absolute durations'. Other proper time intervals will still be intrinsic features of the space-time paths, but as resultants of their spatial and temporal components, and their significance as measurements will be a consequence of the odd behaviour of clocks systematically affected by Fitzgerald-Lorentz retardation. These clocks can therefore be corrected (as in the early part of Section 3) for these causal disturbances to yield measurements of *time*, and then *all* corrected clocks will, after all, come into line with one another. However, this unification of all families of clocks is purely theoretical: we can make no practical use of absolute time. In particular, we have no right to assume (at least without some further argument) that the proper time of our solar system is time *simpliciter*. Though our old-fashioned belief in a unique time dimension will turn out to have been true, it will still have been, as I said at the end of Section 3, unjustified.

To conclude, then, there is a case for absolutisms about each of the issues numbered 2.1, 3, 5.1, 5.2, 5.3, 6.1, 6.2, and 6.3. About that numbered 4, my specific conclusion in Section 2 was only that it is an empirical question whether there is absolute acceleration or not, but if Section 4 shows that there is absolute motion, this will carry absolute acceleration with it. I have said nothing specifically about issue 2.2, or about any of the issues concerning absolute or relative existence.

However, I am at least as much concerned about the methods used in this discussion as about the conslusions reached on particular issues. My general thesis is that items that are not directly observable, and terms and statements to which meaning cannot be given directly by methods of verification, can be legitimately introduced. To justify such introductions, we require only familiar methods for the sorting out of causally relevant factors, together with the principle that a hypothesis which would compel us to accept certain observed agreements as no more than a massive coincidence can be rejected in favour of a hypothesis which explains that apparent coincidence by resolving the agreements into consequences of some unitary state of affairs.

NOTES

[1]See, for example, my 'Truth and Knowability', *Analysis* 40 (1980), 90–92.

[2]I. Newton, *Principia*, Scholium following Definition viii; E. Mach, *The Science of Mechanics*, LaSalle, Illinois, 1960, Chapter 2; H. Reichenbach, *The Philosophy of Space and Time*, New York, 1957, Chapter III, §34; R. Swinburne, *Space and Time*, London, 1981, Chapter 3.

[3]B. Russell, *The Problems of Philosophy*, London, 1912, Chapter 5.

[4]Letter from Adam Smith to William Strahan dated November 9, 1776, in *Hume's Dialogues concerning Natural Religion*, ed. by Norman Kemp Smith, London, 1947, pp. 243–8.

The Meaning of Time*

Adolf Grünbaum

I. INTRODUCTION

Studies of time by scientists have often been concerned with the multifaceted problems of measuring time intervals in atomic, geophysical, biological and astronomical contexts. It has been claimed that in addition to exhibiting measurable intervals, time is characterized by a *transiency* of the present, which has often been called 'flux' or 'passage'.

Indeed, it has been maintained that '*the passage of time . . .* is the very essence of the concept'.[1] I therefore wish to focus my concern with the meaning of time on the credentials which this transiency of the present can claim from the point of view of current physical theories.

In the common-sense view of the world, it is of the very essence of time that events occur now, or are past, or future. Furthermore, events are held to change with respect to belonging to the future or the pres-

*Reprinted by permission of The Open Court Publishing Company, La Salle, IL 61301, from *Basic Issues in the Philosophy of Time*, eds. Eugene Freeman and Wilfrid Sellars, pp. 195–228. La Salle, Ill: Open Court, 1971.

ent. Our commonplace use of tenses codifies our experience that any particular present is superseded by another whose event-content thereby 'comes into being'. It is this occurring *now* or coming into being of previously future events and their subsequent belonging to the past which is called 'becoming' or 'passage'. Thus, by involving reference to *present* occurrence, becoming involves more than mere occurrence at various serially ordered clock times. The past and the future can be characterized as respectively before and after the present. Hence I shall center my account of becoming on the status of the present or now as an attribute of events which is encountered in *perceptual* awareness.

II. THE ISSUE OF THE MIND-DEPENDENCE OF BECOMING

Granted that becoming is a prominent feature of our temporal awareness, I ask: *must* becoming therefore also be a feature of the order of physical events *independently* of our awareness of them, as the common-sense view supposes it to be? And if not, is there anything within physical theory *per se* to warrant this common-sense conclusion?

It is apparent that the becoming of physical events in our temporal awareness does not itself guarantee that becoming has a mind-independent physical status. Common-sense color attributes, for example, surely *appear* to be properties of physical objects independently of our awareness of them and are held to be such by common sense. And yet scientific theory tells us that they are mind-dependent qualities like sweet and sour are. Of course, if physical theory claims that, contrary to common sense, becoming is not a feature of the temporal order of physical events with respect to earlier and later, then a more comprehensive scientific and philosophical theory must take suitable cognizance of becoming as a conspicuous characteristic of our *temporal awareness* of both physical and mental events.

In this lecture, I aim to clarify the status of temporal becoming by dealing with each of the questions I posed. Clearly, an account of becoming which provides answers to these questions is *not* an analyis of what the common-sense man actually *means* when he says that a physical event belongs to the present, past, or future; instead, such an account sets forth how these ascriptions ought to be construed within the framework of a theory which would supplant the scientifically untutored view of common sense. That the common-sense view is indeed scientifically untutored is evident from the fact that *at a time t*, both of the following physical events qualify as occurring 'now' or 'belonging to the present' according to that view: (i) a stellar explosion that occurred several million years before time *t* but which is first seen on earth at time *t*, (ii) a lightning flash originating only a fraction of a second before *t* and observed at time *t*. If it be objected that present-day common-sense beliefs have *begun* to allow for the finitude of the speed of light, then I reply that they err at least to the extent of associating absolute simultaneity with the now.

The temporal relations of earlier (before) and later (after) can obtain between two physical events independently of the transient now and of any minds. On the other hand, the classification of events into past, present, and future, which is inherent to becoming, requires reference to the adverbial attribute now as well as to the relations of earlier and later. Hence the issue of the mind-dependence of becoming turns on the status of the adverbial attribute now. And to assert in this context that becoming is mind-dependent is *not* to assert that the obtaining of the relation of temporal precedence among physical events is mind-dependent. Nor is it to assert that the mere occurrence of events at various serially-ordered clock times is mind-dependent.

With these explicit understandings, I can state my thesis as follows: Becoming is mind-dependent because it is not an attribute of physical events per se but requires the occurrence of certain *conceptualized conscious experiences* of the occurrence of physical events. The doctrine that becoming is mind-dependent has been misnamed 'the theory of the block universe'. I shall therefore wish to dissociate the tenets of this doctrine both from serious misunderstandings by its critics and from the very misleading suggestions of the metaphors used by some of its exponents. Besides stating my positive reasons for asserting the mind-dependence of becoming, I shall defend this claim against the major objections which have been raised against it.

III. THE DISTINCTION BETWEEN TEMPORAL BECOMING AND THE ANISOTROPY OF TIME

In order to treat these various issues without risking serious confusions, we must sharply distinguish the following two questions: (i) do physical events *become* independently of any conceptualized awareness of their occurrence, and (ii) are there any kinds of physical or biological processes which are *irreversible* on the strength of the laws of nature and/or of *de facto* prevailing boundary conditions? I shall first state how these two questions have come to be identified and will then explain why it is indeed an error of consequence to identify them. The second of these questions, which pertains to irreversibility, is often formulated by asking whether the time of physics and biology has an 'arrow'. But this formulation of question (ii) can mislead by inviting misidentification of (ii) with (i). For the existence of an arrow is then misleadingly spoken of as constituting a 'one-way forward flow of time', but so also is becoming on the strength of being conceived as the forward 'movement' of the present. And this misidentification is then used to buttress the false belief that an affirmative answer to the question about irreversibility entails an affirmative answer to the question about becoming. To see why I claim that there is indeed a weighty misidentification here, let us first specify what is involved logically when we inquire into the existence of kinds of processes in nature which are irreversible.

If the system of world lines, each of which represents the career of a physical object, is to exhibit a one-dimensional temporal order, relations of simultaneity between spatially separated events are required to define world states. For our purposes, it will suffice to use the simultaneity criterion of some one local inertial frame of the special theory of relativity instead of resorting to the cosmic time of some cosmological model.

Assume now that the events belonging to *each* world-line are invariantly ordered with respect to all inertial systems by a *betweenness* relation having the following *formal* property of the spatial betweenness of the points on an Euclidean straight line: of any three elements, only one can be between the other two. This betweenness of the events is clearly temporal rather than spatial, since it *invariantly* relates the events belonging to each *individual world line* with respect to all inertial systems, while no such *spatial* betweenness obtains invariantly.[2] So long as the temporal betweenness of the world lines is formally Euclidean in the specified sense, any two events on one of them or any two world states can serve to define two time senses which are *ordinally*

opposite to each other with respect to the assumed temporal betweenness relations.[3] And the members of the simultaneity-classes of events constituting one of these two opposite senses can then bear lower real number coordinates while those of the other sense can bear the higher coordinates. It is immaterial at this stage which of the two opposite senses is assigned the higher real numbers. All we require is that the real number coordinatization reflect the temporal betweenness relations among the events as follows: events which are temporally between two given events E and E' must bear real number coordinates which are numerically between the time coordinates of E and E'. Employing some one time coordinatization meeting this minimal requirement, we can use the locutions 'initial state', 'final state', 'before', and 'after' on the basis of the magnitudes of the real number coordinates, entirely without prejudice to whether there are irreversible kinds of processes.[4] By an 'irreversible process' (à la Planck) we understand a process such that no counter-process is capable of restoring the original *kind* of state of the system at another time. Note that the temporal vocabulary used in this definition of what is *meant* by an irreversible kind of process does *not* assume tacitly that there *are* irreversible processes: as used here, the terms 'original state', 'restore', and 'counter-process' presuppose only the coordinatization based on the assumed betweenness.

It has been charged that one is guilty of an illicit spatialization of time if one speaks of temporal betweenness while still leaving it *open* whether there are irreversible kinds of processes. But this charge overlooks that the *formal* property of the betweenness on the Euclidean line which I invoked is abstract and, as such, neither spatial nor temporal. And the meaningful attribution of this formal property to the betweenness relation among the events belonging to each world line without any assumption of irreversibility is therefore *not* any kind of illicit spatialization of time. As well say that since temporal betweenness does have this abstract property, the ascription of the latter to the betweenness among the points on a line of space is a temporalization of space![5]

Thus the assumption that the events belonging to each world line are invariantly ordered by an abstractly Euclidean relation of temporal betweenness does not entail the existence of irreversible kinds of processes, but allows every kind of process to be reversible.[6] If there are irreversible processes, then the two ordinally opposite time senses are indeed *further* distinguished structurally as follows: there are certain kinds of sequences of states of systems specified in the order of increasing time coordinates such that these same kinds of sequences do *not* likewise exist in the order of decreasing time coordinates. Or, equivalently, the existence of irreversible processes *structurally* distinguishes the two opposite time senses as follows: there are certain kinds of sequences of states of systems specified in the order of *decreasing* time coordinates such that these same kinds of sequences do *not* likewise obtain in the order of increasing time coordinates. Accordingly, if there are irreversible kinds of processes, then time is *anisotropic*.[7] When physicists say with Eddington that time has an 'arrow', it is this anisotropy to which they are referring metaphorically. Specifically, the spatial opposition between the head and the tail of the arrow represents the structural anisotropy of time.

Note that we were able to characterize a process as irreversible and time as anisotropic without any explicit or tacit reliance on the transient now or on tenses of past, present, and future.[8] By the same token, we are able to assert metaphorically that time has an 'arrow' without any covert or outright reference to events as occurring *now,* happening at present, or coming into being. Nonetheless, the anisotropy of time symbolized by the arrow has been falsely equated in the literature with the transiency of the now or becoming of events via the following steps of reasoning: (1) the becoming of events is described by the kinematic metaphor 'the flow of time' and is conceived as a *shifting* of the now which *singles out the future direction of time* as the sense of its 'advance', and (2) although the physicist's arrow does

not involve the transient now, his assertion that there is an arrow of time is taken to be equivalent to the claim that there is a *flow* of time in the direction of the future; this is done by attending to the head of the arrow *to the neglect of its tail* and identifying the former with the direction of 'advance' of the now. The physicist's assertion that time has an 'arrow' discerningly codifies the empirical fact that the two ordinally opposite time senses are *structurally different* in specified respects. But in thus codifying this empirical fact, the physicist does *not* invoke the transient now to single out one of the two time senses as preferred over the other. By contrast, the claim that the present or now shifts in the direction of the future does invoke the transient now to single out one of the two time senses and—as we are about to see—is a mere truism like 'All bachelors are males'. Specifically, the terms 'shift' or 'flow' are used in their literal kinematic senses in such a way that the *spatial* direction of a shift or flow is specified by where the shifting object is at *later* times. Hence when we speak metaphorically of the now as 'shifting' temporally in a particular *temporal* direction, it is then simply a matter of definition that the now shifts or advances in the direction of the future. For this declaration tells us no more than that the nows corresponding to later times are later than those corresponding to earlier ones, which is just as uninformative as the truism that the earlier nows precede the later ones.[9]

It is now apparent that to assert the existence of irreversible processes in the sense of physical theory by means of the metaphor of the arrow does not entail at all that there is a mind-independent becoming of physical events as such. Hence those wishing to assert that becoming is independent of mind cannot rest this claim on the anisotropy of physical time.

Being only a tautology, the kinematic metaphor of time flowing in the direction of the future does not itself render any empirical fact about the time of our experience. But the role played by the present in becoming is a feature of the experienced world codified by common-sense time in the following informative sense: to each of a great diversity of events which are ordered with respect to earlier and later by physical clocks, there corresponds one or more particular experiences of the event as occurring *now*. Hence we shall say that our experience exhibits a *diversity of 'now-contents'* of awareness which are temporally ordered with respect to each of the relations earlier and later. Thus, it is a significant feature of the experienced world codified by common-sense time that there is a sheer diversity of nows, and in that sheer diversity the role of the future is no greater than that of the past. In this *directionally-neutral* sense, therefore, it is informative to say that there is a *transiency* of the now or a coming-into-being of different events. And, of course, in the context of the respective relations of earlier and later, this flux of the present makes for events being past and future.

In order to deal with the issue of the mind-dependence of becoming, I wish to forestall misunderstandings that can arise from uses of the terms 'become', and 'come into being' in senses which are *tenseless*. These senses do not involve belonging to the present or occurring now as understood in tensed discourse, and I must emphasize strongly that my thesis of the mind-dependence of becoming pertains only to the *tensed* variety of becoming. Examples of tenseless uses of the terms 'come into being', 'become', and 'now' are the following: (1) A child *comes into being* as a legal entity the moment it is conceived biologically. What is meant by this possibly false assertion is that for legal purposes, the career of a child *begins* (tenselessly) at the moment at which the ovum is (tenselessly) fertilized. (2) If gunpower is suitably ignited at any particular time *t*, an explosion *comes into being* at that time *t*. The species of coming into being meant here involves a common-sense event which is here asserted to *occur tenselessly at time t*. (3). When heated to a suitable temperature, a piece of iron *becomes* red. Clearly, this sentence asserts that after a piece of iron is or has been (tenselessly) suitably heated, it is (tenselessly) red for an unspecified time interval. (4) In Minkowski's two-dimensional spatial representation of the space-time of special relativity, the event shown by the origin-point is called the 'Here-NOW', and correlatively certain event classes in the diagram are respectively called 'Absolute PAST' and 'Absolute FUTURE'; But Minkowski's 'Here-NOW' denotes an arbitrarily chosen event of reference which can be chosen *once and for all* and continues to qualify as 'now' at various times independently of when the diagram is used. Hence there is no transiency of the now in the relativistic scheme depicted by Minkowski, and his absolute past and absolute future are simply absolutely earlier and absolutely later than the arbitrarily chosen fixed reference event called 'Here-NOW'.[10] Accordingly, we must be mindful that there are tenseless senses of the words 'becoming' and 'now'.

But conversely, we must realize that some important *seemingly* tenseless uses of the terms 'to exist', 'to occur', 'to be actual', and 'to have being or reality' are in fact laden with the present tense. Specifically, all of these terms are often used in the sense of to occur NOW. And by tacitly making the *nowness* of an event a necessary condition for its occurrence, existence, or reality, philosophers have argued fallaciously as follows. They first assert that the universe can be held to exist only to the extent that there are present events. Note that this either asserts that only present events exist now (which is trivial) or it is false. They then invoke the correct premiss that the existence of the physical universe is not mind-dependent and conclude (from the first assertion) that being present, occurring now, or becoming is *independent* of mind or awareness. Thus, Thomas Hobbes wrote: 'The present only has a being in nature; things past have a being in the memory only, but things to come have no being at all, the future being but a fiction of the mind. . . .'[11] When declaring here that only present events or present memories of past events 'have being', Hobbes *appears* to be appealing to a sense of 'to have being' or of 'to exist' which is *logically independent* of the concept of existing-NOW. But his claim depends for its plausibility on the tacit invocation of *present* occurrence as a logically necessary condition for having being or existing. Once this fact is recognized, his claim that 'the present only has a being in nature' is seen to be the mere tautology that 'only what exists now does indeed exist now'. And by his covert appeal to the irresistible conviction carried by this triviality, he makes plausible the utterly unfounded conclusion that nature can be held to exist only to the extent that there are *present* events and *present* memories of past events. Clearly the fact that an event does not occur now does not justify the conclusion that it does not occur at some time or other.

IV. THE MIND-DEPENDENCE OF BECOMING

Being cognizant of these logical pitfalls, we can turn to the following important question: if a physical event occurs *now* (at present, in the present), what attribute or relation of its occurrence can warrantedly be held to qualify it as such?

In asking this question, I am being mindful of the following fact: if at a given clock time t_0 it is true to say of a particular event E that it is occurring now or happening at present, then this claim could not also be truly made at all other clock times $t \neq t_0$. And hence we must distinguish the tensed assertion of *present* occurrence from the tenseless assertion that the event E occurs at the time t_0: namely, the latter tenseless assertion, if true at all, can truly be made at all times t other than t_0 no less than at the time t_0. By the same token we must guard against identifying the tensed assertion, made at some particular time t_0, that the event E happens *at present* with the tenseless assertion made at *any* time t, that the event E occurs or 'is present' at time t_0. And similarly for the distinction between the tensed senses of being past or being future, on the one hand, and the tenseless senses of being *past at time t_0* or being future at time t_0, on the other. To be future at time t_0 just means to be later than t_0, which is a tenseless relation. Thus our question is: what *over and above its otherwise*

tenseless occurrence at a certain clock time t, in fact at a time t characterizes a physical event as *now* or as belonging to the present? It will be well remembered from the *Introduction* why my construal of this question does *not* call for an analysis of the common-sense meaning of 'now' or of 'belonging to the present' but for a critical assessment of the status which common sense attributes to the present.[12] Given this construal of the question, my reply to it is: what qualifies a physical event at a time t as belonging to the present or as now is *not* some physical attribute of the event or some relation it sustains to other *purely physical* events. Instead what is *necessary* so to qualify the event is that at the time t at least one human or other *mind-possessing* organism M is conceptually aware of experiencing at that time either the event itself or another event simultaneous with it in M's reference frame.[13] And that awareness does not, in general, comprise information concerning the date and numerical clock time of the occurrence of the event. What then is the content of M's conceptual awareness at time t that he *is experiencing* a certain event *at that time*? M's experience of the event at time t is coupled with an awareness of the temporal coincidence of his experience of the event with a state of *knowing* that he has that experience at all. In other words, M experiences the event at t *and* knows that he is experiencing it. Thus, presentness or nowness of an event requires conceptual awareness of the presentational immediacy of either the experience of the event or, if the event is itself *un*perceived, of the *experience* of another event simultaneous with it. For example, if I just hear a noise at a time t, then the noise does not qualify at t as *now* unless at t I am judgmentally aware of the fact of my hearing it at all and of the temporal coincidence of the hearing with that awareness.[14] If the event at the time t is itself a mental event (e.g., a pain), then there is no distinction between the event and our experience of it. With this understanding, I claim that the nowness at a time t of either a physical or a mental event requires that there be an *experience* of the event or of another event simultaneous with it which satisfies the specified requirements. And by satisfying these requirements, the *experience* of a physical event qualifies at the time *t* as occurring *now*. Thus, the fulfillment of the stated requirements by the *experience* of an event at time *t* is also *sufficient* for the nowness of that *experience* at the time *t*. But the mere fact that the experience of a physical event qualifies as now at a clock time *t* allows that in point of physical fact the physical event itself occurred millions of years before *t*, as in the case of now seeing an explosion of a star millions of light years away. Hence, the mere presentness of the experience of a physical event at a time *t* does *not* warrant the conclusion that the clock time of the event is *t* or some *particular* time before *t*. Indeed, the occurrence of an external physical event *E* can never be simultaneous in any inertial system with the direct perceptual registration of *E* by a conceptualizing organism. Hence if *E* is presently experienced as happening at some particular clock time *t*, then there is no inertial system in which *E* occurs at the *same* clock time *t*. Of course, for *some* practical purposes of daily life, a nearby terrestrial flash in the sky can be held to be simultaneous with someone's experience of it with impunity, whereas the remote stellar explosion of a supernova or an eclipse of the sun, for example, may not. But this kind of practical impunity of common-sense perceptual judgments of the presentness of physical events cannot detract from their scientific falsity. And hence I do not regard it as incumbent upon myself to furnish a philosophical account of the status of nowness which is compatible with the now-verdicts of common sense. In particular, I would scarcely countenance making the nowness of the *experience* of a physical event *sufficient* for the nowness of the event, and even informed common sense might balk at this in cases such as a stellar explosion. But all that is essential to my thesis of mind-dependence is that the nowness of the *experience* of at least one member of the simultaneity class to which an event *E* belongs is *necessary* for the nowness of the event *E* itself. And hence my thesis would allow a compromise with common sense to the following extent: allowing ascriptions of nowness to those physical events which have the very vague relational property of occurring only 'slightly earlier' than someone's appropriate experience of them.

Note several crucial commentaries on my characterization of the now:

1. My characterization of *present* happening or occurring *now* is intended to *deny* that belonging to the present is a physical attribute of a physical event *E* which is *independent* of any *judgmental awareness* of the occurrence of either *E* itself or of another event simultaneous with it. But I am *not* offering any kind of *definition* of the adverbial attribute now, which belongs to the conceptual framework of tensed discourse, solely in terms of attributes and relations drawn from the tenseless (Minkowskian) framework of temporal discourse familiar from physics. In particular, I avowedly invoked the present tense when I made the nowness of an event *E* at time *t* dependent on someone's knowing at *t* that he *is experiencing E*. And this is tantamount to someone's judging at *t*: I am experiencing *E now*. But this formulation is *non*viciously circular. For it serves to articulate the mind-dependence of nowness, *not* to claim erroneously that nowness has been eliminated by explicit definition in favor of tenseless temporal attributes or relations. In fact, I am very much less concerned with the adequacy of the specifics of my characterization than with its thesis of mind-dependence.

2. It makes the nowness of an event at time *t* depend on the existence of conceptualized awareness that an experience of the event or of an event simultaneous with it is being had at *t*, and points out the insufficiency of the mere having of the experience. Suppose that at time *t* I express such conceptualized awareness in a linguistic

utterance, the utterance being quasi-simultaneous with the experience of the event. Then the utterance satisfies the condition necessary for the *present* occurrence of the experienced event.[15]

3. *In the first instance,* it is only an experience (i.e., a mental event) which can ever qualify as occurring now, and moreover a mental event (e.g., a pain) must meet the specified awareness requirements in order to qualify. A *physical* event like an explosion can qualify as now at some time *t* only *derivatively* in one of the following two ways:
   (a) it is necessary that someone's *experience* of the physical event does so qualify, or
   (b) if unperceived, the physical event must be simultaneous with another physical event that does so qualify in the derivative sense indicated under (a). For the sake of brevity, I shall refer to this complex state of affairs by saying that physical events belonging to regions of space-time wholly devoid of conceptualizing percipients at no time qualify as occurring now and hence as such do not become.

4. My characterization of the now is narrow enough to exclude past and future events: It is to be understood here that the *reliving* or anticipation of an event, however vivid it may be, is *not* to be misleadingly called 'having an experience' of the event when my characterization of the now is applied to an experience.

My claim that nowness is mind-dependent does not assert at all that the nowness of an event is arbitrary. On the contrary, it follows from my account that it is not at all arbitrary what event or events qualify as being *now* at any given time *t*: to this extent, my account accords with common sense. But I repudiate much of what common sense conceives to be the status of the now. Thus, when I wonder in thought (which I *may* con-

vey by means of an interrogative verbal utterance) whether it is 3 P.M. Eastern Standard Time now, I am asking myself the following: Is the particular percept of which I am now aware when asking this question a member of the simultaneity class of events which qualify as occurring at 3 P.M., E.S.T. on this particular day? And when I wonder in thought about what is happening now, I am asking the question: What events of which I am not aware are simultaneous with the particular now-percept of which I *am* aware upon asking this question?

That the nowness attribute of an occurrence, when ascribed nonarbitrarily to an event, is inherently mind-dependent seems to me to emerge from a consideration of the kind of information which the judgment 'It is 3 P.M., E.S.T. now' can be warrantedly held to convey. Clearly such a judgment is informative, unlike the judgment 'All bachelors are males'. But if the word 'now' in the informative temporal judgment does not involve reference to a particular content of conceptualized awareness or to the linguistic utterance which renders it at the time, then there would seem to be nothing left for it to designate other than either the time of the events already identified as occurring at 3 P.M., E.S.T. or the time identified as occurring at some other time. In the former case, the initially informative temporal judgment 'It is 3 P.M., E.S.T. now' turns into the utter triviality that the events of 3 P.M., E.S.T. occur at 3 P.M., E.S.T.! And in the latter case, the initially informative judgment, if false in point of fact, becomes self-contradictory like 'No bachelors are males'.

What of the retort to this objection that independently of being perceived physical events themselves possess an unanalyzable property of nowness (i.e., presentness) at their respective times of occurrence over and above merely occurring at these clock times? I find this retort wholly unavailing for several reasons as follows: (1) It must construe the assertion 'It is 3 P.M., E.S.T. now' as claiming *non-trivially* that when the clock strikes 3 P.M. on the day in question, this clock event and all of the events simultaneous with it intrinsically have the unanalyzable property of nowness or presentness. But I am totally at a loss to see that anything non-trivial can possibly be asserted by the claim that at 3 P.M. nowness (presentness) inheres in the events of 3 P.M. For all I am able to discern here is that the events of 3 P.M. are indeed those of 3 P.M. on the day in question! (2) It seems to me of decisive significance that nowness, in the sense associated with becoming, plays no role as a property of physical events themselves in any of the extant theories of physics. There have been allegations in the literature (most recently in H. A. C. Dobbs, 'The "Present" in Physics', *British Journal for the Philosophy of Science* 19 (1968–1969), 317–24) that such branches of statistical physics as meteorology and inde-terministic quantum mechanics implicitly assert the existence of a physical counterpart to the human sense of the present. But both below (§V) and elsewhere (in my Reply to Dobbs in the *British Journal for the Philosophy of Science*, 20 (1969), 145–53), I argue that these allegations are mistaken. Hence I maintain that if nowness were a mind-*independent* property of physical events themselves, it would be very strange indeed that it could be omitted *as such* from all extant physical theories *without detriment to their explanatory success.* And I hold with Reichen-bach[16] that 'if there is Becoming [independently of awareness] the physicist must know it'. (3) As we shall have occasion to note near the end of Section V, the thesis that nowness is *not* mind-dependent poses a serious perplexity pointed out by J. J. C. Smart, and the defenders of the thesis have not even been able to hint how they might resolve that perplexity without utterly trivializing their thesis.

The claim that an event can be now (present) only upon either being experienced or being simultaneous with a suitably experienced event accords fully, of course, with the common-sense view that there is no more than one time at which a particular event is present and that this time cannot be chosen arbitrarily. But if an event is ever experienced at all such that there is simultanecus awareness of the fact of that experience, then there exists a time at which the event does qualify as being now provided that the event occurs only 'slightly earlier' than the experience of it.

The relation of the conception of becoming espoused here to that of common sense may be likened to the relation of relativity physics to Newtonian physics. My account of nowness as mind-dependent disavows rather than vindicates the common-sense view of its status. Similarly, relativity physics entails the falsity of the results of its predecessor. Though Newtonian physics thus cannot be reduced to relativity physics (in the technical sense of reducing one theory to another), the latter enables us to see why the former works as well as it does in the domain of low velocities: relativity theory shows (via a comparison of the Lorentz and Galilean transformations) that the observational results of the Newtonian theory in that domain are sufficiently correct numerically for some practical purposes. In an analogous manner, my account of nowness enables us to see why the common-sense concept of becoming can function as it does in serving the pragmatic needs of daily life.

A *now-content* of awareness can compromise awareness that one event is later than or succeeds another, as in the following examples: (1) When I perceive the 'tick-tock' of a clock, the 'tick' is not yet part of my past when I hear the 'tock'.[17] As William James and Hans Driesch have noted, melody awareness is another such case of quasi-instantaneous awareness of succession.[18] (2) Memory states are contained in now-contents when we have awareness of other events as being earlier than the event of our awareness of them. (3) A now-content can comprise an envisionment of an event as being later than its ideational anticipation.

V. CRITIQUE OF OBJECTIONS TO THE MIND-DEPENDENCE OF BECOMING

Before dealing with some interesting objections to the thesis of the mind-dependence of becoming, I wish to dispose of some of the caricatures of that thesis with which the literature has been rife under the misnomer of 'the theory of the block universe'. The worst of these is the allegation that the thesis asserts the timelessness of the universe and espouses, in M. Capek's words, the 'preposterous view . . . that . . . time is merely a huge and chronic [sic!] hallucination of the human mind'.[19] But even the most misleading of the spatial metaphors that have been used by the defenders of the mind-dependence thesis do not warrant the inference that the thesis denies the objectivity of the so-called 'time-like separation' of events known from the theory of relativity. To assert that nowness, and thereby, pastness and futurity are mind-dependent is surely *not* to assert that the earlier-later relations between the events of a world line are mind-dependent, let alone hallucinatory.

The mind-dependence thesis does deny that physical events themselves happen in the tensed sense of coming into being apart from anyone's awareness of them. But this thesis clearly avows that physical events do happen independently of any mind in the tenseless sense of merely occurring at certain clock times in the context of objective relations of earlier and later. Thus it is a travesty to equate the objective *becominglessness* of physical events asserted by the thesis with a claim of timelessness. In this way the thesis of mind-dependence is misrepresented as entailing that all events happen simultaneously or form a '*totum simul*'.[20] But it is an egregious blunder to think that if the time of physics lacks *passage* in the sense of there not being a transient now, then physical events cannot be temporally separated but must all be simultaneous.

A typical example of such a misconstrual of Weyl's and Einstein's denial of physical passage is given by supposing them to have claimed 'that the world is like a film strip: the photographs *are already there* and are merely being exhibited to us'.[21] But when photographs of a film strip 'are already there', they all exist now and hence *simultaneously*. Therefore it is wrong to identify Weyl's denial of physical becoming with the pseudo-image of the 'block universe' and then to charge his denial with entailing the absurdity that all events are simultaneous. Thus Whitrow says erroneously: 'the theory of "the block universe" . . . implies that past (and future) events co-exist with those that are present'.[22] We shall see in Section VI that a corresponding error vitiates the allegation that determinism entails the absurd contemporaneity of all events. And it simply begs the question to declare in this context that 'the *passage of time* . . . is the very essence of the concept'.[23] For the undeniable fact that passage in the sense of transiency of the now is integral to the common-sense concept of time may show only that, in this respect, this concept is anthropocentric.

The becomingless physical world of the Minkowski representation is viewed *sub specie aeternitatis* in that representation in the sense that the relativistic account of time represented by it makes no reference to the particular times of anyone's *now*-perspectives. And, as J. J. C. Smart observed, 'the tenseless way of talking does not therefore imply that physical things or events are eternal in the way in which the number 7 is'.[24] We must therefore reject Whitrow's odd claim that according to the relativistic conception of Minkowski, 'external events *permanently* exist and we merely come across them'.[25] According to Minkowski's conception, an event qualifies as a *becomingless* occurrence by occurring in a network of relations of earlier and later and thus can be said to occur 'at a certain time *t*'. Hence to assert tenselessly that an event exists (occurs) is to claim that there is a time or clock reading *t* with which it coincides. But surely this assertion does not entail the absurdity that the event exists (occurs) at *all* clock times or 'permanently'. To occur tenselessly at some time *t* or other is not at all the same as to exist 'permanently'.

Whitrow himself acknowledges Minkowski's earlier-later relations when he says correctly that 'the relativistic picture of the world recognizes only a difference between earlier and later and not between past, present, and future'.[26] But he goes on to query: 'if no events *happen*, except our observations, we might well ask—why are the latter exceptional?'[27] I reply first of all: But Minkowski asserts that events happen tenselessly in the sense of occurring at certain clock times. And as for the exceptional status of the events which we register in observational awareness, I make the following obvious but only partial retort: being registered in awareness, these events are *eo ipso* exceptional.

I say that this retort is only partial because behind Whitrow's question there lurks a more fundamental query. This query must be answered by those of us who claim with Russell that 'past, present, and future arise from time-relations of subject and object, while earlier and later arise from time-relations of object and object'.[28] That query is: Whence the becoming in the case of mental events that become and are causally dependent on physical events, given that physical events themselves do not become independently of being perceived but occur tenselessly? More specifically, the question is: if our *experiences* of (extra and/or intradermal) physical events are causally dependent upon these events, how is it that the former *mental* events can properly qualify as being 'now', whereas the eliciting physical events *themselves* do not so qualify, and yet both kinds of events are (severally and collectively) alike related by quasi-serial relations of earlier and later?[29]

But, as I see it, this question does not point to refuting evidence against the mind-dependence of becoming. Instead, its force is to demand (a) the recognition that the complex mental states of judgmental awareness as such have distinctive features of their own, and (b) that the articulation of these features as part of a theoretical account of 'the place of mind in nature' acknowledges *what may be peculiar to the time of awareness.* That the existence of features peculiar to the time of awareness does not pose perplexities militating against the mind-dependence of becoming seems to me to emerge from the following three counter questions, which I now address to the critics:

1. Why is the mind-dependence of becoming more perplexing than the mind-dependence of common-sense color attributes? That is, why is the former more puzzling than that physical events like the reflection of certain kinds of photons from a surface causally induce mental events like seeing blue which are qualitatively fundamentally different in some respects? In asking this question, I am *not* assuming that nowness is a *sensory quality* like red or sweet, but only that nowness and sensory qualities alike depend on awareness.

2. Likewise assuming the causal dependence of mental on physical events, why is the mind-dependence of becoming more puzzling than the fact that the raw feel components of mental events, such as a particular event of seeing green, are not members of the *spatial* order of physical events?[30] Yet mental events and the raw feels ingredient in them are part of a time system of relations of earlier and later that comprises physical events as well.[31]

3. Mental events must differ from physical ones in some respect qua being mental, as illustrated by their not being members of the same system of spatial order. Why then should it be puzzling that on the strength of the *distinctive* nature of conceptualized awareness and self-awareness, mental events differ further from physical ones with respect to becoming, while both kinds of events sustain temporal relations of simultaneity and precedence?

What is the reasoning underlying the critics' belief that their question has the capability of pointing to the refutation of the mind-dependence of becoming? Their reasoning seems to me reminiscent of Descartes' misinvocation of the principle that there must be nothing more in the effect than is in the cause *à propos* of one of his arguments for the existence of God: the more perfect, he argued, cannot proceed from the less perfect as its efficient and total cause. The more perfect, i.e., temporal relations involving becoming, critics argue, cannot proceed from the less perfect, i.e., becomingless physical time, as its efficient cause. By contrast, I reason that nowness (and thereby pastness and futurity) are features of events *as experienced* conceptually, *not* because becoming is likewise a feature of the physical events which causally elicit our awareness of them, but because these elicited states are indeed specified states of *awareness*. Once we recognize the role of awareness here, then the diversity and order of the events of which we have awareness in the form of now-contents gives rise to the transiency of the now as explained in Section III above, due cautions being exercised, as I emphasized there, that this transiency not be construed tautologically.

In asserting the mind-dependence of becoming, I allow fully that the kind of neurophysiological brain state which underlies our mere awareness of an event as simply occurring now differs in specifiable ways from the ones underlying tick-tock or melody awareness, memory-awareness, anticipation-awareness, and dream-free sleep. But I cannot see why the states of awareness which make for becoming must have physical event-counterparts which isomorphically become in their own right. Hence I believe to have coped with Whitrow's question as to why only perceived events become. Indeed, it seems to me that the thesis of mind-dependence is altogether free from an important perplexity which besets the opposing claim that physical events are inherently past, present, and future. This perplexity was stated by Smart as follows: 'If past, present, and future were real properties of events [i.e., properties possessed by physical events independently of being perceived], then it would require [non-trivial] explanation that an event which becomes present [i.e., qualifies as occurring *now*] in 1965 becomes present [now] at that date and not at some other (and this would have to be an explanation over and above the explanation of why an event of this sort occurred in 1965)'.[32] It would, of course, be a complete trivialization of the thesis of the mind-*in*dependence of becoming to reply that *by*

definition an event occurring at a certain clock time *t* has the unanalyzable attribute of nowness at time *t*.

Thus to the question 'Whence the becoming in the case of mental events that become and are causally dependent on physical events which do not themselves become?' I reply: 'Becoming can characterize mental events qua their being both bits of *awareness* and sustaining relations of temporal order'.

The awareness which each of several human percipients has of a given physical event can be such that all of them are alike prompted to give the same tensed description of the external event. Thus, suppose that the effects of a given physical event are simultaneously registered in the awareness of several percipients such that they each perceive the event as occurring at essentially the time of their first awareness of it. Then they may each think at that time that the event belongs to the present. The parity of access to events issuing in this sort of intersubjectivity of tense has prompted the common-sense belief that the nowness of a physical event is an intrinsic, albeit transient attribute of the event. But this kind of intersubjectivity does not discredit the mind-dependence of becoming; instead, it serves to show that the becoming present of an event, though mind-dependent no less than a pain, need not be *private* as a pain is. Some specific person's particular pain is private in the sense that this person has privileged access to its raw feel component.[33] The mind-dependence of becoming is no more refuted by such intersubjectivity as obtains in regard to tense than the mind-dependence of common-sense color attributes is in the least disproven by agreement among several percipients as to the color of some chair.

VI. BECOMING AND THE CONFLICT BETWEEN DETERMINISM AND INDETERMINISM

If the doctrine of mind-dependence of becoming is correct, a very important consequence follows, which seems to have been previously overlooked: Let us recall that the nowness of events is generated by (our) conceptualized *awareness* of them. Therefore, *nowness is made possible by processes sufficiently macro-deterministic (causal) to assure the requisitely high correlation between the occurrence of an event and someone's being made suitably aware of it.* Indeed, the very concept of experiencing an external event rests on such macro-determinism, and so does the possibility of empirical knowledge. In short, insofar as there is a transient present, it is made possible by the existence of the requisite degree of macro-determinism in the physical world. And clearly, therefore, the transiency of the present can obtain in a completely deterministic physical universe, be it relativistic or Newtonian.

The theory of relativity has repudiated the uniqueness of the simultaneity slices within the class of physical events which the Newtonian theory had affirmed. Hence Einstein's theory certainly precludes the conception of 'the present' which some defenders of the objectivity of becoming have linked to the Newtonian theory. But it must be pointed out that the doctrine of the mind-dependence of becoming, being entirely compatible with the Newtonian theory as well, does not depend for its validity on the espousal of Einstein's theory as against Newton's.

Our conclusion that there can be a transient now in a completely deterministic physical universe is altogether at variance with the contention of a number of distinguished thinkers that the indeterminacy of the laws of physics is both a necessary and sufficient condition for becoming. And therefore I now turn to the examination of their contention.

According to such noted writers as A. S. Eddington, Henri Bergson, Hans Reichenbach, H. Bondi, and G. J. Whitrow, it is a distinctive feature of an *indeterministic* universe, as constrasted with a deterministic one, that physical events belong to the present, occur *now,* or come into being over and above merely becoming present in *awareness.* I shall examine the argument given by Bondi, although he no longer defends it, as well as Reichenbach's argument. And I shall wish to show the following: insofar as

events do become, the indeterminacy of physical laws is neither sufficient nor necessary for conferring nowness or presentness on the occurrences of events, an attribute whereby the events come into being. And thus my analysis of their arguments will uphold my previous conclusion that far from depending on the indeterminacy of the laws of physics, becoming requires a considerable degree of macro-determinism *and* can obtain in a completely deterministic world. Indeed, I shall go on to point out that not only the becoming of any kind of event but the temporal order of earlier and later among physical events depends on the at least quasi-deterministic character of the macrocosm. And it will then become apparent in what way the charge that a deterministic universe must be completely *timeless* rests on a serious misconstrual of determinism.

Reichenbach contends: 'When we speak about the progress of time [from earlier to later] . . . , we intend to make a synthetic [i.e., factual] assertion which refers both to an immediate experience and to physical reality'.[34] And he thinks that this assertion about events coming *into* being independently of mind—as distinct from merely occurring tenselessly at a certain clock time—can be justified in regard to physical reality on the basis of indeterministic quantum mechanics by the following argument:[35] In classical deterministic physics, both the past and the future were determined in relation to the present by one-to-one functions even though they differed in that there could be direct observational records of the past and only predictive inferences concerning the future. On the other hand, while the results of past measurements on a quantum mechanical system are *determined* in relation to the present *records* of these measurements, a present measurement of one of two conjugate quantities does *not* uniquely determine in any way the result of a *future* measurement of the other conjugate quantity. Hence, Reichenbach concludes:

The concept of "becoming" acquires significance in physics: the present, which separates the future from the past, is the moment at which that which was undetermined becomes determined, and "becoming" has the same meaning as "becoming determined." . . . it is with respect to "now" that the past is determined and that the future is not.[36]

I join Hugo Bergmann[37] in rejecting this argument for the following reasons. In the indeterminstic quantum world, the relations between the sets of measurable values of the state variables characterizing a physical system at different times are, in principle, *not* the one-to-one relations linking the states of classically behaving closed systems. But I can assert correctly in 1966 that this holds for a given state of a physical system and its absolute future quite independently of whether that state occurs at midnight on December 31, 1800 or at noon on March 1, 1984. Indeed, if we consider *any one* of the temporally successive regions of space-time, we can veridically assert the following at *any* time: the events belonging to that particular region's absolute past could be (more or less) uniquely specified in records which are a part of that region, whereas its particular absolute future is thence quantum mechanically unpredictable. Accordingly, *every* event, be it that of Plato's birth or the birth of a person born in the year 2000 A.D., *at all times* constitutes a divide in Reichenbach's sense between its own recordable past and its unpredictable future, *thereby satisfying Reichenbach's definition of the 'present' or 'now' at any and all times!* And if Reichenbach were to reply that the indeterminacies of the events of the year of Plato's birth have already been transformed into a determinacy, whereas those of 2000 A.D. have not, then the rejoinder would be: this tensed conjunction holds for any state between sometime in 428 B.C. and 2000 A.D. that qualifies as now during that interval on grounds other than Reichenbach's asymmetry of determinedness; but the second conjunct of this conjunction does not hold for any state after 2000 A.D. which qualifies as now after that date. Accordingly, contrary to Reichenbach, the

now of conceptualized awareness must be invoked tacitly at time *t*, if the instant *t* is to be nontrivially and nonarbitrarily singled out as present or now by Reichenbach's criterion, i.e., if the instant *t* is to be uniquely singled out at time *t* as being 'now' in virtue of being the threshold of the transition from indeterminacy to determinacy.

Turning to Bondi, we find him writing:

. . . the flow of time has no significance in the logically fixed pattern demanded by deterministic theory, time being a mere coordinate. In a theory with indeterminacy, however, the passage of time transforms statistical expectations into real events.[38]

If Bondi intended this statement to assert that the indeterminacy makes for our human inability to know in advance of their actual occurrence what particular kinds of events will in fact materialize, then, of course, there can be no objection. For in an indeterministic world, the attributes of specified kinds of events are indeed not uniquely fixed by the properties of earlier events and are therefore correspondingly unpredictable. But I take him to affirm beyond this the following traditional philosophical doctrine; in an indeterministic world, events come *into* being by becoming present with time, whereas in a deterministic world the status of events is one of merely occurring tenselessly at certain times. And my objections to his appeal to the transformation of statistical expectations into real events by the passage of time fall into several groups as follows.

1. Let us ask: what is the character and import of the difference between a (micro-physically) indeterministic and a deterministic physical world in regard to the attributes of future events? The difference concerns only the type of functional connection linking the attributes of future events to those of present or past events. Thus, *in relation to the states existing at other times*, an

indeterministic universe allows alternatives as to the attributes of an event that occurs at some given time, whereas a deterministic universe provides no corresponding latitude. But this difference does *not* enable (micro-physical) indeterminism—as contrasted with determinism—to make for a difference in the *occurrence-status* of future events by enabling them to come *into* being. Hence in an indeterministic world, physical events no more *become* real (i.e., present) and are no more precipitated into existence, as it were, than in a deterministic one. In either a deterministic or indeterministic universe, events can be held to come into being or to become 'actual' by becoming *present in (our) awareness;* but becoming actual in virtue of occurring *now* in that way no more makes for a mind-independent coming into existence in an indeterministic world than it does in a determinstic one.

2. Nor does indeterminacy as constrasted with determinacy make for any difference whatever at any time in regard to the *intrinsic attribute-specificity* of the future events themselves, i.e., to their being (tenselessly) what they are. For in either kind of universe, it is a fact of logic that what will be, will be, no less than what is present or past is indeed present or past![39] The result of a future quantum mechanical measurement may not be definite prior to its occurrence in relation to earlier states, and thus our prior knowledge of it correspondingly cannot be definite. But a quantum mechanical event has a tenseless occurrence status at a certain time which is fully compatible with its intrinsic attribute-definiteness just as a measurement made in a deterministic world does. Contrary to a widespread view, this statement holds also for those events which are constituted by energy states of quantum mechanical systems, since energy *can* be measured in an arbitrarily short time in that theory.[40]

Let me remark parenthetically that the quantum theory of measurement has been claimed to show that the *consciousness* of the human observer is essential to the definite-ness of a quantum mechanical event. I am not able to enter into the technical details of the argument for this conclusion, but I hope that I shall be pardoned for nonetheless rais-ing the following question in regard to it. Can the quantum theory account for the rele-vant physical events which presumably oc-curred on the surface of the earth *before* man and his consciousness had evolved? If so, then these physical events cannot depend on human consciousness for their specific-ity. On the other hand, if the quantum theory cannot in principle deal with *pre-*evolutionary physical events, then one won-ders whether this fact does not impugn its adequacy in a fundamental way.

In an indeterministic world, there is a lack of attribute-specificity of events *in rela-tion to events at other times.* But this *relational* lack of attribute-specificity cannot alter the fact of logic that an event is intrinsically attribute-specific in the sense of tenselessly being what it is at a certain clock time *t.*[41]

It is therefore a far-reaching mistake to suppose that unless and until an event of an indeterministic world belongs to the present or past, the event must be *intrinsically* attribute-*in*definite. This error is illustrated by Capek's statement that in the case of an event 'it is only its presentness [i.e., nowness] which creates its specificity . . . by eliminating all other possible features in-compatible with it'.[42] Like Bondi, Capek overlooks that it is only with respect to some now or other that an event can be future at all to begin with and that the lack of attribute-specificity or 'ambiguity' of a fu-ture event is not intrinsic but relative to the events of the prior now-perspectives.[43] In an indeterministic world, an event is intrinsi-cally attribute-determinate by being (tense-lessly) what it is (tenselessly), regardless of whether the time of its occurrence be now (the present) or not. What makes for the coming into being of a future event at a later time *t* is *not* that its attributes are indeter-ministic with respect to prior times but only that it is registered in the now-content of awareness at the subsequent time t.

3. Two quite different things also seem to be confused when it is inferred that in an indeterministic quantum world, future physical events themselves distinctly come into being with the passage of time over and above merely occurring and becoming present to awareness, whereas in a deterministic universe they do not come into being:
   (a) the epistemic precipitation of the *de facto* event-properties of future events out of the wider matrix of the possible properties allowed in advance by the quantum-mechanical probabilities, a precipitation or becoming definite which is constituted by our getting to *know* these *de facto* properties at the later times, and
   (b) a mind-independent coming into being over and above merely occurring and becoming present to awareness at the later time. The *epistemic* precipitation is indeed effected by the passage of time through the transformation of a merely statistical expectation into a definite piece of available information. But this does *not* show that in an indeterministic world there obtains any kind of becoming present ('real') with the passage of time that does not also obtain in a deterministic one. And in either kind of world, becoming as distinct from mere occurrence at a clock time requires conceptualized awareness.

We see then that the physical events of the indeterministic quantum world as such do not come into being anymore than those of the classical deterministic world but alike occur tenselessly. And my earlier contention that the transient now is mind-dependent and irrelevant to physical events as such therefore stands.

Proponents of indeterminism as a physical basis of objective becoming have charged that a deterministic world is timeless. Thus, Capek writes:

. . . the future in the deterministic framework . . . becomes something *actually* existing, a sort of disguised and hidden present which remains hidden only from our limited knowledge, just as distant regions of space are hidden from our sight. "Future" is merely a label given by us to the unknown part of the *present* reality, which exists in the same degree as scenery hidden from our eyes. As this hidden portion of the present is *contemporary* with the portion accessible to us, the temporal relation between the present and the future is eliminated; the future loses its status of "futurity" because instead of succeeding the present it *coexists* with it.[44]

In the same vein, G. J. Whitrow declares:

There is indeed a profound connection between the reality of time and the existence of an incalculable element in the universe. Strict causality would mean that the consequences pre-exist in the premises. But, if the future history of the universe pre-exists logically in the present, why is it not already present? If, for the strict determinist, the future is merely "the hidden present," whence comes the illusion of temporal succession?[45]

But I submit that there is a clear and vast difference between the relation of one-to-one functional connection between two temporally-separated states, on the one hand, and the relation of temporal coexistence or simultaneity on the other. How, one must ask, does the fact that a future state is uniquely specified by a present state detract in the least from its being later and entail that it paradoxically exists at present? It is not plain that Capek trades on an ambiguous use of the terms 'actually existing' and 'coexists' to confuse the time sequential relation of being *determined* by the present with the simultaneity relation of contemporaneity with the present? In this way, he fallaciously saddles determinism with entailing that future events exist now just because they are determined by the state which exists now. When he tells us that according to determinism's view of the future, 'we are already dead without realizing it now',[46] he makes fallacious use of the correct premiss that according to determinism, the present state uniquely specifies at what later time any one of us shall be dead. For he refers to the determinedness of our subsequent deaths misleadingly as our 'already' being dead and hence concludes that determinism entails that absurdity that we are dead *now!* Without this ambiguous construal of the term 'already', no absurdity is deducible.

When Whitrow asks us why, given determinism, the future is not already present even though it 'pre-exists logically in the present', the reply is: precisely because existing at the present time is radically different in the relevant temporal respect from what he calls 'logical pre-existence in the present'. Whitrow ignores the fact that states hardly need to be simultaneous just because they are related by one-to-one functions. And he is able to claim that determinism entails the illusoriness of temporal succession (i.e., of the earlier-later relations) only because he use the term 'hidden present' just as ambiguously as Capek uses the term 'coexists'. But, more fundamentally, we have learned from the theory of relativity that events sustain time-like separations to one another *because* of their *causal* connectibility or deterministic relatedness, *not* despite that deterministic relatedness. And nothing in the relativistic account of the temporal order depends on the existence of an indeterministic microphysical substratum! Indeed, in the absence of the causality assumed in the theory in the form of causal (signal) connectibility, it is altogether unclear how the system of relations between events would possess the kind of *structure* that we call the 'time' of physics.[47]

VII. SUMMARY

In this lecture, I have presented my reasons for denying that nowness and temporal becoming are entitled to a place within physical theory, be it deterministic or indeterministic. On the other hand, the temporal relations of earlier than, later than, and of simul-taneity do, of course, obtain among physical events in their own right in the sense familiar from the theory of relativity. Hence, if the 'meaning' of time is held to comprise becoming or passage, then one of the features of time is mind-dependent. But in characterizing becoming as mind-dependent, I allow fully that the mental events on which it depends themselves require a biochemical physical base or possibly a physical basis involving cybernetic hardware.

NOTES

[1]G. J. Whitrow, *The Natural Philosophy of Time* (London: Thomas Nelson & Sons, Ltd., 1961), p. 88.

[2]For example, consider the events in the careers of human beings or of animals who *return* to a spatially fixed terrestrial habitat every so often. These events occur at space points on the earth which certainly do *not* exhibit the betweenness of the points on a Euclidean straight line.

[3]For details, cf. A. Grünbaum, "Space, Time and Falsifiability," Part I, *Philosophy of Science*, 37 (1970), 485–86 and 584–85. This treatment supersedes the earlier one in A. Grünbaum, *Philosophical Problems of Space and Time* (New York: Alfred A. Knopf, Inc., 1964), pp. 214–16, hereinafter cited as PPST.

[4]This noncommittal character of the term 'initial state' seems to have been recognized by O. Costa de Beauregard in one part of his paper entitled 'Irreversibility Problems', *Logic, Methodology and Philosophy of Science*, Proceedings of the 1964 International Congress. Y. Bar-Hillel, ed. (Amsterdam: North-Holland Publishing Co., 1965), p. 327. But when discussing my criticism of Hans Reichenbach's account of irreversibility (PPST, pp. 261–63), Costa de Beauregard (*ibid.*, p. 331) overlooks that my criticism invokes initial states in only the noncommittal sense set forth above.

[5]Thus, it is erroneous to maintain, as Milic Capek does, that the distinction between temporal betweenness and irreversibility is 'fallacious' in virtue of being 'based on the superficial and deceptive analogy of "the course of time" with a geometrical line', *The Philosophical Impact of Contemporary Physics* (Princeton: D. Van Nostrand Co., Inc., 1961), p. 349; see also pp. 347 and 355. If Capek's condemnation of this distinction were correct, the following fundamental question of theoretical physics could not even be intelligibly and legitimately asked: Are the *prime facie* irreversible processes known to us indeed irreversible, and, if so, on the strength of what laws and/or boundary conditions are they so? For this

question is predicated on the very distinction which Capek rejects as 'fallacious'. By the same token, Capek errs (*ibid.*, p. 355) in saying that when Reichenbach characterizes entropically counterdirected epochs as 'succeeding each other', then irreversibility 'creeps in' along with the asymmetrical relations of before and after. For all that he needs to assume here to speak of 'before' and 'after' is a time coordinatization which reflects the assumed kind of betweenness and simultaneity.

[6]On the basis of a highly equivocal use of the term 'irreversible', M. Capek *ibid.*, pp. 166–67 and 344–45 has claimed incorrectly that the account of the space-time properties of world lines given by the special theory of relativity entails the irreversibility of physical processes represented by world lines. He writes: 'The world lines, which by definition are constituted by a succession of isotopic events, are *irreversible* in all systems of reference' (*ibid.*, p. 167) and 'the relativistic universe is dynamically constituted by the network of causal lines *each of which is irreversible; . . .* this irreversibility is a topological invariant' (*ibid.*, pp. 344–345). But Capek fails to distinguish between (1) the *non-inversion or invariance of time-order as between different Galilean frames* which the Lorentz-transformation equations assert in the case of causally connectible events, and (2) the irreversibility of processes represented by world lines in the standard sense of the *nonrestorability* of the same kind of state in any frame. Having applied the term 'irreversibility' to (1) no less than to (2) after failing to distinguish them, Capek feels entitled to infer that the Lorentz transformations attribute irreversibility within any one frame to processes depicted by world lines, just because these transformations assert the invariance of time order on the world lines as between different frames. That the Lorentz equations do not disallow the reversibility of physical processes becomes clear upon making each of the *two* replacements $t' \rightarrow -t$ and $t \rightarrow -t'$ in them: these replacements issue in the same set of equations except for the sign of the velocity term in each of the numerators, i.e., they merely reverse the direction of the motion. Therefore, these two replacements do *not* involve any violation of the theory's time-order invariance as between different frames S and S'. By contrast, different equations exhibiting a violation of time-order invariance on the world lines would be obtained by replacing *only* one of the two variables t and t' by its negative counterpart in the Lorentz equations.

Furthermore, the transformation $t \leftrightarrow -t$ is a topological one, but it clearly does not preserve the time sequence relations on a time-like world line. Hence it is unsound for Capek to characterize the time-order invariance on time-like world lines as "topological."

[7]For a discussion of the various kinds of irreversible processes which make for the anisotropy of time and furnish specified criteria for the relations of temporal

precedence and succession, see Costa de Beauregard, *op. cit.*, p. 327; and A. Grünbaum, PPST, Ch. 8, and 'The Anisotropy of Time', in *The Nature of Time* (ed. by D. L. Schumacher and T. Gold) (Ithaca: Cornell University Press, 1967), pp. 149–86.

[8]Some have questioned the possibility of stating what specific physical events do occur in point of fact at particular clock times without covert appeal to the transient now. Cf. Hermann Weyl, *Philosophy of Mathematics and Natural Science* (Princeton: Princeton University Press, 1949), p. 75. In their view, any physical description will employ a time coordinatization, and any such coordinatization must ostensively invoke the now to designate at least one state as, say, the origin of the time coordinates. But I do not see a genuine difficulty here for three reasons. Firstly, it is not clear that the designation of the birth of Jesus, for example, as the origin of time coordinates tacitly makes logically indispensable use of the now or of tenses in virtue of making use of a proper name. Secondly, in some cosmological models of the universe, an origin of time coordinates can clearly be designated non-ostensively: in the 'big bang' model, the big bang itself can be designated uniquely and *non*-ostensively as the one state having no temporal predecessor. And thirdly, any two descriptions of the world which differ only in the choice of the origin of time coordinates while employing the same time metric and time topology are equivalent with respect to their factual *physical* content. Thus such descriptions differ only in regard to the way in which they numerically name or label particular simultaneity classes of events. Hence, let us grant for argument's sake that tacit use of the now or of tenses is logically indispensable to designating the origin of any one particular time coordinatization. Even if this is granted, it does *not* follow that past, present, and future have a mind-independent status in the temporal structure of the physical world.

[9]The claim that the now advances in the direction of the future is a truism as regards both the correspondence between nows and *physically* later clock times and their correspondence with psychologically (introspectively) later contents of awareness. What is *not* a truism, however, is that the *introspectively* later nows are *temporally correlated* with states of our physical environment that are later as per criteria furnished by irreversible physical processes. This latter correlation depends for its obtaining on the laws governing the physical and neural processes necessary for the *mental* accumulation of memories and for the registry of information *in awareness*. (For an account of some of the relevant laws, see A. Grünbaum, PPST, Ch. 9, Secs. A and B.) Having exhibited the aforementioned truisms as such and having noted the role of the empirical laws just mentioned, I believe to have answered Costa de Beauregard's complaint (in 'Irreversibility Problems', *op. cit.*, p. 337) that

'stressing that the arrows of entropy and information increase are parallel to each other is *not* proving that the flow of subjectivistic time has to follow the arrows!'

[10]A very illuminating account of the logical relations of Minkowski's language to tensed discourse is given by Wilfrid Sellars in 'Time and the World Order', *Minnesota Studies in the Philosophy of Science*, Vol. III (ed. by H. Feigl and G. Maxwell) (Minneapolis: University of Minnesota Press, 1962), p. 571.

[11]Quoted from G. J. Whitrow, *op. cit.*, pp. 129–30.

[12]For a searching treatment of the ramifications of the contrast pertinent here, see Wilfrid Sellars, 'Philosophy and the Scientific Image of Man', *Frontiers of Science and Philosophy* (ed. by Robert G. Colodny) (Pittsburgh: University of Pittsburgh Press, 1962), pp. 35–78

[13]It will be noted that I speak here of the dependence of nowness on an organism *M* which is mind-possessing in the sense of having conceptualized or judgmental awareness, as contrasted with mere sentiency. Since biological organisms other than man (e.g., extra-terrestrial ones) may be mind-possessing in this sense, it would be unwarrantedly restrictive to speak of the mind-dependence of nowness as its 'anthropocentricity'. Indeed, it might be that conceptualized awareness turns out not to require a *biochemical* substratum but can also inhere in a suitably complex 'hardware' computer. That a physcial substratum of some kind is required would seem to be abundantly supported by the known dependence of the content and very existence of consciousness in man on the adequate functioning of the human body.

[14]The distinction pertinent here between the *mere* hearing of something and judgmental awareness that it is being heard is well stated by Roderick Chisholm as follows: 'We may say of a man simply that he observes a cat on the roof. Or we may say of him that he observes *that* a cat is on the roof. In the second case, the verb "observe" takes a "that"-clause, a propositional clause as its grammatical object. We may distinguish, therefore, between a "propositional" and a "nonpropositional" use of the term "observe", and we may make an analogous distinction for "perceive", "see", "hear", and "feel".

'If we take the verb "observe" propositionally, saying of the man that he observes that a cat is on the roof, or that he observes a cat to be on the roof, then we may also say of him that he *knows* that a cat is on the roof; for in the propositional sense of "observe", observation may be said to imply knowledge. But if we take the verb non-propositionally, saying of the man only that he observes a cat which is on the roof, then what we say will not imply that he knows that there is a cat on the roof. For a man may be said to observe a cat, to see a cat, or hear a cat, in the nonpropositional sense of these terms, without his knowing that a cat is what he

is observing, or seeing, or hearing. "It was not until the following day that I found out that what I saw was only a cat" '. *Theory of Knowledge* (Englewood Cliffs, New Jersey: Prentice-Hall, 1966), p. 10. I am indebted to Richard Gale for this reference.

[15]The judgmental awareness which I claim to be essential to an event's qualifying as now may, of course, be expressed by a linguistic utterance, but it clearly need not be so expressed. I therefore consider an account of nowness which is *confined* to utterances as inadequate. Such an overly restrictive account is given in J. J. C. Smart's otherwise illuminating defense of the anthropocentricity of tense, *Philosophy and Scientific Realism* (London: Routledge & Kegan Paul, 1963), Chapter VII. But this undue restrictiveness is quite inessential to his thesis of the anthropocentricity of nowness. And the non-restrictive treatment which I am advocating in its stead would obviate his having to rest his case on (1) denying that 'this utterance' can be analyzed as 'the utterance which is *now*', and (2) insisting that 'now' must be elucidated in terms of 'this utterance' (*ibid.*, pp. 139–40).

[16]Hans Reichenbach, *The Direction of Time* (Berkeley: University of California Press, 1956), p. 16.

[17]Paul Fraisse, *The Psychology of Time* (London: Eyre & Spottiswoode, 1964), p. 73.

[18]A. Grünbaum, PPST, p. 325.

[19]M. Capek, *op. cit.*, p. 337.

[20]On the basis of such a misunderstanding, M. Capek incorrectly charges the thesis with a 'spatialization of time' in which 'successive moments already *coexist*' (*ibid.*, pp. 160–63) and in which 'the universe with its whole history is conceived as a single huge and timeless bloc, given at once' (*ibid.*, p. 163). See also p. 355.

[21]G. J. Whitrow, *op. cit.*, p. 228 (my italics). For a criticism of another such misconstrual, see A. Grünbaum, PPST, pp. 327–28.

[22]G. J. Whitrow, *ibid.*, p. 88.

[23]*Ibid.*, pp. 227–28.

[24]J. J. C. Smart, *op. cit.*, p. 139.

[25]G. J. Whitrow, *op cit.*, p. 88, n. 2 (my italics).

[26]*Ibid.*, p. 293.

[27]*Ibid.*, p. 88, n. 2.

[28]Bertrand Russell, 'On the Experience of Time', *The Monist*, 25 (1915), 212.

[29]The need to deal with this question has been pointed out independently by Donald C. Williams and Richard Gale.

[30]Mental events, as distinct from the neurophysiological counterpart states which they require for their occurrence, are *not* in our heads in the way in which,

say, a biochemical event in the cortex or medulla oblongata is.

[31]Thus a conscious state of elation induced in me by the receipt of good news from a telephone call C_1 could be *temporally between* the physical chain C_1 and another such chain C_2 consisting of my telephonic transmission of the good news to someone else.

[32]J. J. C. Smart, *op. cit.*, p. 135.

[33]I am indebted to Richard Gale for pointing out to me that since the term 'psychological' is usefully reserved for mind-dependent attributes which are private, as specified, it would be quite misleading to assert the mind-dependence of tense by saying that tense is 'psychological'. In order to allow for the required kind of intersubjectivity, I have therefore simply used the term 'mind-dependent'.

[34]Hans Reichenbach, *The Philosophy of Space and Time* (New York: Dover Publications, Inc., 1958), pp. 138–39.

[35]Hans Reichenbach, 'Les Fondements Logiques de la Mécanique des Quanta', *Annales de l'Institut Poincaré,* 13 (1953), 154–57.

[36]*Ibid.*

[37]Cf. H. Bergmann, *Der Kampf um das Kausalgesetz in der jüngsten Physik* (Braunschweig: Vieweg & Sohn, 1929), pp. 27–28.

[38]H. Bondi, 'Relativity and Indeterminacy', *Nature,* 169 (1952), 660.

[39]I am indebted to Professor Wilfrid Sellars for having made clarifying remarks to me in 1956 which relate to this point. And Costa de Beauregard has reminded me of the pertinent French dictum *Ce qui sera, sera.* There is also the well-known (Italian) song *Che Sera, Sera.*

[40]Yakir Aharonov and David Bohm have noted that time does not appear in Schrödinger's equation as an operator but only as a parameter and have pointed out the following: (1) The time of an energy state is a dynamical variable belonging to the measuring apparatus and therefore *commutes* with the energy of the observed system. (2) Hence the energy state and the time at which it exists do *not* reciprocally limit each other's well-defined status in the manner of the noncommuting conjugate quantities of the Heisenberg Uncertainty Relations. (3) Analysis of illustrations of energy measurement (e.g., by collision) which seemed to

indicate the contrary shows that the experimental arrangements involved in these examples did not exhaust the measuring possibilities countenanced by the theory. Cf. their two papers on 'Time in the Quantum Theory and the Uncertainty Relation for Time and Energy', *Physical Review,* 122 (1961), 1649, and *Physical Review,* 134 (1964), B1417. I am indebted to Professor A. Janis for this reference.

[41]A helpful account of the difference relevant here between being *determinate* (i.e., intrinsically attribute-specific) and being *determined* (in the relational sense of causally necessitated or informationally ascertained), is given by Donald C. Williams in *Principles of Empirical Realism* (Springfield, Ill.: Charles C. Thomas, 1966), pp 274 ff.

[42]Capek, *op. cit.*, p. 340.

[43]Capek writes further: 'As long as the ambiguity of the future is a mere appearance due to the limitation of our knowledge, the temporal character of the world remains necessarily illusory', and 'the principle of indeterminacy . . . means the *reinstatement of becoming in the physical world*' [*ibid.*, p. 334]. But granted that the indeterminacy of quantum theory is ontological rather than merely epistemological, this indeterminacy is nonetheless relational and hence unavailing as a basis for Capek's conclusions.

[44]*Ibid.*, pp. 334–35, cf. also p. 164.

[45]G. J. Whitrow, *op. cit.*, p. 295.

[46]M. Capek, *op. cit.*, p. 165.

[47]Accordingly, we must qualify the following statement by J. J. C. Smart, *op. cit.*, pp. 141–42: 'We can now see also that the view of the world as a space-time manifold no more implies determinism than it does the fatalistic view that the future "is already laid up". It is compatible both with determinism and with indeterminism, i.e., both with the view that earlier time slices of the universe are determinately related by laws of nature to later time slices and with the view that they are not so related'. This statement needs to be qualified importantly, since it would not hold if 'indeterminism' here meant a macro-indeterminism such that macroscopic causal chains would not exist.

For a discussion of other facets of the issues here treated by Smart, see A. Grünbaum, "Free Will and Laws of Human Behavior," *The American Philosophical Quarterly,* October 1971.

Causation

Causality: Critique of Hume's Analysis*

C. J. Ducasse

A variety of opinions are current today as to the nature and the role of the causal relation. One finds accounts of what science now means by causal connection, but also statements that the notion of cause is not employed in science at its maturity, but only appears at the crude, early stages of its development. Again, many philosophers are dissatisfied with Hume's analysis of causality, upon which Mill's failed to improve. Yet, in default of some definite and more acceptable positive analysis, Hume's probably remains still the most influential. I shall now set forth the reasons I see for rejecting his account.

1. HUME'S SKEPTICISM

Hume's famous skepticism is not, like that of some of the ancients, a doctrine he propounds, but rather the acknowledgment by him of "a malady, which can never be radically cur'd, but must return upon us every

*Reprinted from Ducasse, *Nature, Mind and Death* (La Salle: Open Court, 1951), pp. 91–100, by permission of The Open Court Publishing Company, La Salle, IL 61301.

moment, however we may chase it away, and sometimes may seem entirely free from it."[1] This malady, as Hume observes it in himself, consists in the fact that although reflection shows certain ones and certain others of our beliefs to be mutually incompatible, yet we cannot give up either the ones or the others. The self-stultification which is noticeable at so many points in Hume's writings, and which so baffles the reader who would extract from them a consistent doctrine, is rooted in that malady. Again and again, especially in the *Treatise*, Hume disregards at one place conclusions he had reached earlier, and he could not without doing so proceed to say what he next wants to say. The *Treatise*, I believe, is thus to be regarded not as an attempt to set forth one consistent doctrine, but much rather only as an account of the philosophical sights to be seen from the road one travels under the guidance of certain principles which Hume accepts from the outset— one of the chief of these being that nothing exists or is known to us except "perceptions." Hume simply follows these principles remorselessly wherever they seem to him to lead; and when the conclusions to which they bring him are mutually incompatible or incompatible with firm natural beliefs, he just admits the fact as he would admit having gout or a cold in the head and similarly calls it a malady. His great service to philosophy thus is not that he solved, but much rather that he raised, important philosophical problems. There is perhaps no philosophical book more intellectually irritating—nor therefore more thought-provoking—than his *Treatise*. This is true in particular of what he has to say in it concerning causation.

2. HUME'S ANALYSIS OF CAUSALITY

Hume's "official" view on this subject may perhaps be summarized as follows: To be is to be perceived. No connection is ever perceived between a cause and its effect. Therefore there is none. An "object" of kind *A* is called the cause of one of kind *B* if, in our experience, objects of kind *A* have always been followed each by an object of kind *B*. But such following of one object upon a certain other is not "necessary." In logic and mathematics, that is necessary the contradictory of which is self-contradictory. But no self-contradiction is ever involved in supposing an object we call a cause to exist without its effect following, or one we call an effect to exist without having been preceded by one such as we call its cause. Where objects are concerned, "necessity" is the name not of a relation among them, but only of the felt "propensity, which custom produces, to pass from an object to the idea of its usual attendant." Necessity, then, is "but an internal impression of the mind"; it is a relation between certain ideas, something "that exists in the mind, not in objects." Hume accordingly offers two definitions of cause. According to one, formulated in purely objective terms, "we may define a cause to be *an object, followed by another, and where all the objects similar to the first are followed by objects similar to the second.*" According to the other we may say, in subjective terms, that a cause is *"an object followed by another and whose appearance always conveys the thought to that other."*[2] The first of these is the basic one, since unless we had experi-

ence of causation as there described, the "conveying of the thought," in terms of which the second definition is worded, would not occur.

3. HUME'S ANALYSIS FAILS TO FIT SOME OF THE FACTS

As stated at the outset, I believe that this account of the nature of causation—simply as succession *de facto* regular—represents an incorrect analysis of the ordinary notion of cause—of the notion, that is to say, in the light of which our ordinary judgments of causation actually are made. To make evident the incorrectness of that analysis it will be sufficient to show, on the one hand, that there are cases which conform to Hume's definition but where we judge the events concerned not to be related as cause to effect; and on the other hand, that there are cases which do not conform to Hume's definition but which we nevertheless judge to be cases of causation.

As to the first, if a man were so situated as always to have heard two clocks striking the hours, one of which always struck immediately before the other, he would according to Hume's definition of cause have to say that the strokes of the first cause the strokes of the second; whereas in fact they do not. Of course, the relation he observes between the strokes of the two clocks is the effect of a common remote cause of the strokes of the two clocks. But although this is true, it is irrelevant; for to say that *B* is caused by *A* is one thing, and to say that both *B* and *A* are caused by *C* is quite another thing. The example thus shows that Hume's definition of the relation of cause and effect fits some cases where the relation between the two events concerned is in fact not that of cause to effect but a different one.

Other examples of sequences which are regular, and yet the terms of which are not related as cause to effect, are not hard to find. Thomas Reid mentioned the succession of day and night; and we may add to the list the fact, for instance, that in infants the growth of hair is regularly followed by the growth of teeth; or that in human beings birth regularly follows the tenth return of the moon since conception.[3]

In connection with such cases, it should be noted that what observation of *de facto* regular succession or correlation of two events does is not to *answer* the question whether one of the two events causes the other, but much rather to *raise* the question as to whether one causes the other, or whether some antecedent third causes both, or whether the conjunction of the two is simply accidental. For although causation of *B* by *A* entails constancy of their conjunction (*i.e.*, recurrence of *B* as often as *A* recurs), the converse does not hold: constancy of conjunction, far from itself being the relation of cause to effect, is not sure evidence even of indirect or of as yet hidden causal connection between the events concerned.

To show now, on the other hand, that there are cases which do not conform to Hume's definition, but which we nevertheless judge to be cases of causation, I shall mention a simple experiment I have sometimes performed with students. I bring into the room and place on the desk a paper-covered parcel tied with string in the ordinary way, and ask the students to observe closely what occurs. Then, proceeding slowly so that observation may be easy, I put my hand on the parcel. The end of the parcel the students face then at once glows. I then ask them what caused it to glow at that moment, and they naturally answer that the glowing was caused by what I did to the parcel immediately before.

In this case it is clear that what the spectators observed, and what they based their judgment of causation upon, was not repetition of a certain act of mine followed each time by the glow, but *one single case* of sequence of the latter upon the former. The case, that is to say, does not conform to Hume's definition of causation as constant conjunction but is nevertheless judged by unprejudiced observers to be a case of causation.

If I then further ask: What makes you think that my having done what I did caused the parcel to glow? they answer: Be-

cause nothing else happened to the parcel at the time. Thus, by the *cause* of the observed glowing they do not mean some event having repeatedly preceded it. They mean *the only change introduced into the situation immediately before the glowing occurred.*

It may be said truly, of course, that the change they observed was perhaps not the only change which actually occurred in that situation, and that their judgment as to the cause of the observed glowing was thus perhaps mistaken. To urge this, however, is to question not their conception of the meaning of "causation," but their claim that what they observed was a true case of what they meant and still mean by that word. For what indicates what they meant when they called what I did the cause of the observed glowing is not whether what I did *really* was the only change that occurred in the situation immediately before, but whether they *believed* it to have been the only change. So long as they do believe it to have been the only change, they continue to describe it as having been the cause of that glowing—even if a glowing should never again occur on repetition of my act.

4. HUME ON ASCERTAINMENT OF CAUSATION BY A SINGLE EXPERIMENT

In this connection, it is interesting to note that Hume himself asserts that "we may attain the knowledge of a particular cause merely by one experiment, provided it be made with judgment, and after a careful removal of all foreign and superfluous circumstances." But how a *single* experiment, in which a case of *B* was observed to have followed a case of *A*, can assure us that *every* case of *A* is followed by a case of *B* is anything but obvious. One would expect, rather, that, once causation has been defined merely as *de facto* constant conjunction, the only way to observe its presence or absence would be to observe *many* cases of *A* and note whether or not a case of *B* follows constantly, *i.e.*, each time.

Hume perceives this difficulty, or rather

the difficulty corresponding to it when his second definition of causation is the one considered—the difficulty, namely, how the customary expectation of B upon the occurrence of A, which he has stated before is the result of having *repeatedly* observed B following after A, can be present when the sequence, A,B has been observed not repeatedly but only once. He attempts to meet this difficulty by saying that even then we have had millions of experiments "to convince us of this principle, *that like objects placed in like circumstances, will always produce like effects*," and that this principle then "bestows an evidence and firmness on any opinion, to which it can be applied."[4]

By itself, however, this principle would support equally the generalizing of *any* sequence observed—of one which is accidental as well as of one which turns out to be causal. The possibility of its being useful therefore rests on the stipulated preliminary "careful removal of all foreign and superfluous circumstances." But the principle does not tell us how to discover by one experiment which these are; for obviously the "foreign and superfluous circumstances" are those which are not the cause, *i.e.*, on his view, those which are not *constantly* followed by B. Preliminary removal of the circumstances which are "foreign and superfluous" therefore amounts to preliminary discovery of the circumstance which *is* the cause! Thus, the principle is good not for discovering the cause in a single experiment, but *only for generalizing it* if we have already managed somehow to discover it by a single experiment. If, however, causation can be ascertained by a single experiment, then causation does not consist in constancy of conjunction even if it entails such constancy.

5. HUME'S "RULES BY WHICH TO JUDGE OF CAUSES AND EFFECTS"

Hume appears to have been obscurely conscious of this. For one thing, he introduces the two definitions of cause quoted above by the remark: "So imperfect are the ideas which we form concerning [the rela-

tion of cause and effect] that it is impossible to give any just definition of cause, except what is drawn from something extraneous and foreign to it." And, after the second definition, he repeats that both definitions are "drawn from circumstances foreign to the cause." Again, in his "Rules by which to judge of causes and effects," which are rules for discovering a cause by a single experiment and therefore, as pointed out above, really concern causation in a sense other than that of empirically constant conjunction, Hume at first refers to causation as "that constant conjunction, on which the relation of cause and effect *totally* depends"; but in the third rule, he no longer says "totally" but instead "chiefly"; and in the fourth rule he describes "constant repetition" only as that "from which the *first* idea of [the causal relation] is derived."[5]

Of the rules given by Hume for discovering a cause by single experiment, the fifth, sixth, and seventh are the clearest statements not only up to Hume's time, but until the appearance of Herschel's *Discourse* nearly a hundred years later, of what Mill afterwards called the experimental methods of Agreement, Difference, and Concomitant Variations. Hume's fourth, fifth, and sixth rules, which are the most important theoretically, are as follows:

4. The same cause always produces the same effect, and the same effect never arises but from the same cause. This principle we derive from experience, and is the source of most of our philosophical reasonings. For when by any clear experiment we have discovered the causes or effects of any phenomenon, we immediately extend our observation to every phenomenon of the same kind, without waiting for that constant repetition, from which the first idea of this relation is derived.

5. There is another principle, which hangs upon this, *viz.* that where several different objects produce the same effect, it must be by means of some quality, which we discover to be common amongst them. For as like

effects imply like causes, we must always ascribe the causation to the circumstance, wherein we discover the resemblance.

6. . . . The difference in the effects of two resembling objects must proceed from that particular, in which they differ. For as like causes always produce like effects, when in any instance we find our expectation to be disappointed, we must conclude that this irregularity proceeds from some difference in the causes.

It will be noticed that in the fourth rule the principle mentioned earlier (same cause, same effect) is supplemented by its converse (same effect, same cause), but is now presented explicitly as a principle not for discovering causal relations but only for generalizing them once we have managed to discover them somehow in a single case by a "clear experiment." But the fifth and sixth rules might be thought to give us just what we need for such discovery, *viz.*, the criteria by which to decide which circumstances are "foreign and superfluous" to the cause.

Scrutiny of them, however, reveals that they do not do this, for they are presented by Hume as corollaries of the principle mentioned in the fourth rule (*viz.*, same cause, same effect; same effect, same cause), and this principle is not as he there asserts derived from experience, nor is it derivable from it. As he himself has shown earlier with admirable clearness,[6] neither reason nor experience gives us anything which would warrant us in assuming (as the principle in his fourth rule does assume and has to assume if the fifth and sixth rules are to be corollaries of it) that those instances, of which we have had as yet no experience, resemble those of which we have had experience. A principle, which experience might conceivably have yielded, would be that like antecedents placed in like circumstances *have always been observed to have had*

like sequents, and that like sequents have always been observed to have had like antecedents. But this principle not only does not yield his fifth and sixth rules as corollaries, but indeed is itself *invalidated by every situation to which Hume would apply these two rules.* For (to quote from rule 5) "where several different objects produce the same effect" what obviously follows is that, as a strict matter of experience, an *exception* to the principle "same effect, same cause" is then confronting us and the principle is thereby invalidated. Just this is what follows, and not, as Hume asserts, that these different objects must have some hidden common quality; for either such a common quality is itself observed, and then the objects are experienced as alike rather than, as supposed, different; or else a common quality is not observed, and then, to know that it exists nonetheless we should need to know that the same effect has the same cause in all cases, future as well as past; and, as recalled above, Hume himself has shown that neither experience nor reason can give us this knowledge.

NOTES

[1]Hume, *A Treatise of Human Nature,* Selby-Bigge ed., p. 218.

[2]Hume, *An Enquiry Concerning Human Understanding,* Open Court ed., p. 79.

[3]A striking instance, in the case of which the relation between the events concerned is patently neither that of cause to effect nor that of joint effects of a common cause, is quoted by Morris Cohen (*Reason and Nature,* p. 92) from an unpublished study by George Marshall at the Brookings Institute. It is that, for a number of years, the membership in the International Association of Machinists shows a very high correlation (86%) with the death rate in an Indian state of Hyderabad.

[4]Hume, *Treatise,* pp. 104–5.

[5]Hume, *Treatise,* pp. 173 ff. (Italics mine.)

[6]Hume, *Treatise,* pp. 87 ff.

Causation and Recipes*

Douglas Gasking

We sometimes speak of one thing, or of one sort of thing, causing another—of the second as being the result of or due to the former. In what circumstances do we do so?

If we start with some typical statements of causal connection—"The train-smash was due to a buckled rail"; "Vitamin B deficiency causes beri-beri"—two things are likely to strike us. First, the effect is something that comes into being after the cause, and secondly, we suppose that anyone fully conversant with the circumstances and the relevant causal laws could, from a knowledge of the cause, predict the effect. So it is very natural to suggest, as an answer to our question: We say that A causes B whenever a person with the requisite empirical information could infer from the occurrence of A to the subsequent occurrence of B. Or we might put it: We say that A causes B whenever B regularly follows A.

But this "regular succession" notion will not do. For there are cases where we would speak of A causing B where it is not the case that from the occurrence of A we may infer the subsequent occurrence of B.

An example to illustrate this: Iron begins to glow when its temperature reaches a certain point. I do not know what that temperature is: for the sake of the illustration I will suppose it to be 1,000°C., and will assume that iron never glows except at or above this temperature. Now, if someone saw a bar of iron glowing and, being quite ignorant of the physical facts, asked: "What makes that iron glow? What causes it to glow?" we should answer: "It is glowing because it is at a temperature of 1,000°C. or more." The glowing, B, is caused by the high temperature, A. And here the B that is caused is not an event subsequent to the cause A. Iron reaches 1,000°C. and begins glowing at the same instant. Another example: current from a battery is flowing through a variable resistance, and we have a voltmeter connected to the two poles of the battery to measure the potential difference. Its reading is steady. We now turn the knob of our variable resistance and immediately the voltmeter shows that the potential difference has increased. If someone now asks: What caused this increase?, we reply: "the increase of the resistance in the circuit". But here again the effect was not something subsequent to the cause, but simultaneous.

*Reprinted by permission of Oxford University Press, from *Mind* 64 (1955), 479–87.

So perhaps our account should be emended so as to read: We speak of A as causing B when the occurrence of B may be inferred from the occurrence of A and the occurrence of B is either subsequent to or simultaneous with the occurrence of A.

But this will not do either. For there are, first of all, cases where from the occurrence of A we may infer the subsequent occurrence of B, yet would not speak of A as causing B. And secondly there are cases where from the occurrence of A we may infer the simultaneous occurrence of B, yet would not speak of A as causing B.

Here is an example of the first case. Given (A) that at t_1 a body freely falling *in vacuo* is moving at a speed of 32 feet per second we can infer (B) that at t_2, one second later, it will be moving at 64 feet per second. We might be prepared to say that this inference was in some sense or other a causal inference. But it would be a most unnatural and 'strained' use of the word 'cause' to say that the body's movement at 64 feet per second at t_2 was caused by its moving at 32 feet per second at t_1. It would be even more unnatural, to take a famous example, to say that the day that will be here in twelve hours' time is caused by the fact that it is now night. Yet from the present fact we can certainly infer that in twelve hours' time it will be day.

An example to illustrate the second point. From the fact that a bar of iron is now glowing we can certainly infer (and it will be a causal inference) that it is now at a temperature of 1,000°C. or over. Yet we should not say that its high temperature was caused by the glowing: we say that the high temperature causes the glowing, not *vice-versa*. Another example: watching the voltmeter and battery in the electrical circuit previously described we see that the needle suddenly jumps, showing that the potential difference has suddenly increased. From this we infer that the electrical resistance of the circuit has, at that moment, increased. But we should not say that the rise in potential difference caused the increase in resistance: rather that the rise in resistance caused a rise in the potential difference. Or again, knowing the

properties of a certain sort of wax, we infer from the fact that the wax has melted that, at that very moment, it reached such and such a temperature. Yet we should not say that the wax's melting caused it to reach the critical temperature: rather that its reaching that temperature caused it to melt. Why do we speak of 'cause' in some cases in which we can infer from A to B, but not in others?

The reason is not always of the same sort. Sometimes in such a case it would be nonsense to speak of A causing B, sometimes it would merely be false. Our very last example is a rather trivial instance of the first sort of reason. It is nonsense to speak of the melting of the wax causing the high temperature of the wax because "x melts" means "high temperature causes x to become liquid". So "the melting of the wax caused the high-temperature of the wax" is equivalent to the absurdity "The high temperature of the wax's causing of the wax to become liquid caused the high temperature of the wax".

But it is not for this sort of reason that we do not say that the glowing of the iron causes the high temperature of the iron. "Melting" is by definition an effect and not a cause of an increase in temperature, but the same is not true of "glowing". It is not logically absurd to say that the glowing of a piece of iron causes its high temperature; it is merely untrue. It is possible to imagine and to describe a world in which it would have been true. Here is an account of such an imaginary world.

"Our early ancestors many millennia ago discovered that you could make a large range of substances (wood, water, leaves, etc.) glow first blue, then purple, then red by a process of alternately covering them so as to exclude light, then rapidly letting light fall on them, then quickly covering them again, and so on. Wood, for instance, starts glowing after about six minutes of this treatment, and reaches the red stage in about ten minutes. If it is then left in constant daylight or in constant darkness it gradually fades through purple to blue and then ceases glowing. A number of other substances behave similarly, though the time needed to produce the glowing effect differs somewhat from substance to substance. None of the things that early man thus learnt to make glow, however, suffered any change of temperature in the process. Then, about 1000 B.C. men got hold of samples of fairly pure iron, for the first time. They tried the covering-uncovering technique on it to see if it too, like wood and water, but unlike certain sorts of rock, would glow if manipulated in this way. They found that it would, but that, unlike other substances, iron began to get hot when it started glowing, got hotter still at the purple stage, and when glowing red was very hot indeed. Precise measurements in modern times showed that on reaching the red stage the temperature of iron was 1,000°C. In other respects this imaginary world is just like our world, except that when you put a poker or other non-combustible object in a fire it does not begin to glow, however hot it gets."

Who can doubt that in this imaginary world we should have said that the glowing of the iron caused its temperature to rise, and not *vice-versa*? What, then, are the essential differences between this world and ours, which would lead us to say one thing in one world and another in another?

Human beings can make bodily movements. They do not move their arms, fingers, mouths and so on by doing anything else; they just move them. By making bodily movements men can manipulate things: can lift them, hold them in certain positions, squeeze them, pull them, rub them against each other, and so on. Men discovered that whenever they manipulated certain things in certain ways in certain conditions certain things happened. When you hold a stone in your hand and make certain complex movements of arm and fingers the stone sails through the air approximately in a parabola. When you manipulate two bits of wood and some dry grass for a long time in a certain way the grass catches fire. When you squeeze an egg, it breaks. When you put a stone in the fire it gets hot. Thus men found out how to produce certain effects by manipulating things in certain ways: how to make an egg break, how to make a stone hot, how to make dry grass catch fire, and so on.

We have a general manipulative technique for making anything hot: we put it on a fire. We find that when we manipulate certain things in this way, such as water in a vessel, it gets hot but does not begin to glow. But we find, too, that certain other things, such as bars of iron, when manipulated in this way do not only get hot, they also, after a while, start to glow. And we have no general manipulative technique for making things glow: the only way to make iron glow is to apply to it the general technique for making things hot. We speak of making iron glow by making it hot, *i.e.* by applying to it the usual manipulative technique for making things hot, namely, putting on a fire, which in this special case, also makes it glow. We do not speak of making iron hot by making it glow, for we have no general manipulative technique for making things glow. And we say that the high temperature causes the glowing, not *vice-versa.*

In our imaginary world there is a general manipulative technique for making things glow—namely, rapidly alternating exposure to light and shielding from light. There is no other way of making them glow. In general, things manipulated in this way glow, but do not get hot. Iron, however, glows and gets hot. In this world we speak of making iron hot by making it glow, *i.e.* by applying to it the usual manipulative technique for making things glow which, in this special case, also makes it hot. We do not speak of making iron glow by making it hot, for the general manipulative technique of putting things on fires, which makes them hot, does not, in this world, also make things glow. And in this world, we should say that the glowing causes the high temperature, not *vice-versa.*

What this example shows is the following: When we have a general manipulative technique which results in a certain sort of event A, we speak of producing A by this technique. (Heating things by putting them on a fire.) When in certain cases application of the general technique for producing A also results in B we speak of producing B by producing A. (Making iron glow by heating it.) And in such a case we speak of A causing B, but not *vice-versa*. Thus the notion of causation is essentially connected with our manipulative techniques for producing results. Roughly speaking: "A rise in the temperature of iron causes it to glow" means "By applying to iron the general technique for making things hot you will also, in this case, make it glow". And "The glowing of iron causes its temperature to rise" means "By applying to iron the general technique for making things glow you will also, in this case, make it hot". This latter statement is, as it happens, false, for there is no general technique for making things glow, let alone one which, applied to iron, also makes it hot.

Thus a statement about the cause of something is very closely connected with a recipe for producing it or for preventing it. It is not exactly the same, however. One often makes a remark of the form "A causes B" with the practical aim of telling someone how to produce or prevent B, but not always. Sometimes one wishes to make a theoretical point. And one can sometimes properly say of some particular happening, A, that it caused some other particular event, B, even when no-one could have produced A, by manipulation, as a means of producing B. For example, one may say that the rise in mean sea-level at a certain geological epoch was due to the melting of the Polar ice-cap. But when one can properly say this sort of thing it is always the case that people can produce events of the first sort as a means to producing events of the second sort. For example, one can melt ice in order to raise the level of water in a certain area. We could come rather closer to the meaning of "A causes B" if we said: "Events of the B sort can be produced by means of producing events of the A sort."

This account fits in with the principle that an event, A, at time t_2 cannot be the cause of an event B at an earlier time, t_1. It is a logical truth that one cannot alter the past. One cannot, therefore, by manipulations at t_2 which produce A at t_2 also produce B retrospectively at t_1.

Let us turn now to the cases where, although from a state of affairs A we can infer a later state of affairs B, we nevertheless would not say that A causes B; *e.g.* to the case where from the speed of a freely falling body at t_1 we can infer its speed at t_2, or infer coming darkness from present daylight. These are cases where a process is taking place whose law we know, so that we can infer from one stage in the process a later stage. Our inference presupposes that nothing happens to interfere with the process; the falling body will not encounter an obstruction, the earth's spinning will not be stopped by, say, our sun becoming a super-nova. The difference between the earth's spinning and the body's falling is that in the latter case we can set the process going and arrange that nothing shall thereafter interfere with it for a certain time; in the former case we cannot. It is the same sort of difference as there is between melting ice in a bucket and the water-level rising in the bucket and melting Polar ice-caps and sea-level rising. We cannot set the earth spinning, but we can set a top spinning.

Imagine a world in which there is an exact correlation between the colour and the temperature of everything. Anything at a certain low temperature is a certain shade of, say, blue. If an object becomes warmer its colour changes to purple, then red, then orange, then yellow and finally to white. Cold (or blue) objects can be made hot (or red) by putting them in a fire; after a long time in a very big fire they become very hot (yellow). In such a world we should very probably not have had two sets of words: "cold", "warm", "hot", "very hot" and also "blue", "purple", "red", "yellow"—but only one set—say the words "blue", "purple", "red", and so on. We should have spoken of things "looking purple", or "being purple to the eyes" and of their "feeling purple" or "being purple to the touch". (In our actual world we talk of things being round or square whether we apprehend their shapes by the eye or by the touch: we do not have a special word meaning "round to the eye" and another quite different word meaning "round to the touch", since there is a correlation between these.)

In such a world we should speak of making purple things red by putting them on a fire, but should not normally speak of making something "red to the eye" (*i.e.* what we mean by "red") by putting it on a fire; nor of making something "red to the touch" (*i.e.* what we mean by "hot") by this method. Still less should we speak of making something "red to the eye" by making it "red to the touch", or of making it "red to the touch" by making it "red to the eye". (In our actual world we do not speak of making things "visibly round" by making them "tangibly round", nor *vice versa*.) When a single manipulation on our part invariably produces two effects A and B, we do not speak of producing one by producing the other, nor do we speak of one as a cause of the other. (The visible roundness is neither cause nor effect of the tangible roundness of a penny.) It is only when we have a technique for producing A which in some circumstances but not in all also produces B that we speak of producing B by producing A, and speak of A as causing B.

When we set a process going—drop a stone from a tower, set a top spinning—we set the stage, see that nothing shall interfere (for a certain time at least) with the process we are about to start, and then set things going. After that, things take their own course without further intervention on our part—the stone gathers speed, the top loses it. There are successive stages in the process. At stage A at t_1 the stone is moving fairly fast, at a later stage B at t_2 the stone is going very fast. But, on the presupposition that the process continues undisturbed, the very same initial stage-setting and send-off, C, which will produce fairly fast motion at t_1 (A), will always produce very fast motion at t_2 (B), and the initial stage-setting and send-off C which will produce very fast motion at t_2 (B) will always produce fairly fast motion at t_1 (A). That is, the process being undisturbed, an initial send-off C will always produce both A and B: there is not a general technique for producing A which in some circumstances also produces B. Hence we

do not speak of producing B by producing A. There is not a general technique for bringing it about that, one second after the start, a stone is falling at 32 feet per second, which in some circumstances can also be used to bring it about that two seconds after the start it is falling at 64 feet per second. Hence we do not speak of achieving the latter by means of the former, and do not speak of the former as causing the latter.

Of course one could, by attaching a rocket to the falling body, which fires one second after the start, secure that a body which is moving at 32 feet per second one second after departure is one second later travelling much faster than 64 feet per second. But this would contradict our presupposition that the process, after being started, was left uninterfered with. It is on this presupposition only that C always produces both A and B.

I have made two points:

First: that one says "A causes B" in cases where one could produce an event or state of the A sort as a means to producing one of the B sort. I have, that is, explained the "cause-effect" relation in terms of the "producing-by-means-of" relation.

Second: I have tried to give a general account of the producing-by-means-of relation itself: what it is to produce B by producing A. We learn by experience that whenever in certain conditions we manipulate objects in a certain way a certain change, A, occurs. Performing this manipulation is then called: "producing A". We learn also that in certain special cases, or when certain additional conditions are also present, the manipulation in question also results in another sort of change, B. In these cases the manipulation is also called "producing B", and since it is in general the manipulation of producing A, in this case it is called "producing B by producing A". For example, one makes iron glow by heating it. And I discussed two sorts of case where one does not speak of "producing B by producing A". (1) Where the manipulation for producing A is the general technique for producing B, so that one cannot speak of "producing B by producing A" but only *vice-versa*. (2) Where the given manipulation invariably produces both A and B, so that the manipulation for producing B is not a special case only of that for producing A.

The notion of "cause" here elucidated is the fundamental or primitive one. It is not the property of scientists; except for those whose work most directly bears on such things as engineering, agriculture or medicine, and who are naturally interested in helping their practical colleagues, scientists hardly ever make use of the notion. A statement about causes in the sense here outlined comes very near to being a recipe for producing or preventing certain effects. It is not simply an inference-licence. Professional scientists, when they are carefully stating their findings, mostly express themselves in functional laws, which are pure inference-licences, with nothing of the recipe about them (explicitly at least). Thus the

formula $1 = \frac{E}{R}$ tells you how to infer the current in a given circuit, knowing the electromotive force and the resistance; it tells you how to infer the electro-motive force, knowing the resistance and current; and how to infer the resistance from current and electromotive force. All these three things it tells you; and no one of them any more specially than any other—it works all ways, as in inference-licence. But while one might say a current of 3 amps. was caused by an e.m.f. of 6 volts across a resistance of 2 ohms, one would hardly say that a resistance of 2 ohms in the circuit was caused by an e.m.f. of 6 volts and a current of 3 amps. Why not? Given an e.m.f. of 6 volts one could make 3 amps. flow by making the resistance equal to 2 ohms. But one could not, given an e.m.f. of 6 volts, make the resistance of the circuit equal to 2 ohms by making a current of 3 amps. flow.

From one point of view the progress of natural science can be viewed as resulting from the substitution of pure inference-licences for recipes.

There is, however, what might be called a "popular science" use of "cause" which may not exactly fit the account given—a use of the word by laymen who know some science and by some scientists in their less strictly professional moments. I have in mind such a locution as "Gravity causes unsupported bodies to fall". Such a statement is not quite on a par, logically, with "Great heat causes steel to melt". It would be fair to say, I think, that the use of the word "cause" here is a sophisticated extension from its more primitive and fundamental meaning. It is the root notion that I have been concerned with.

In accounts of causation given by philosophers in the past a specially fundamental role was often played by the motion of bodies. Every kind of change and every kind of natural law was often supposed to be "ultimately reducible to" or to be explicable in terms of it. In this account, too, though in a rather different way, the motion of bodies occupies a special position. Central to this account is the notion of a manipulation to produce A and thereby to produce B. When we manipulate things we control the motion of bodies, *e.g.* by rubbing sticks together (motion of bodies) men made them hot and thereby caused them to ignite. At least all those causal chains that are initiated by human beings go back to manipulations, that is, to matter in motion.

Causation*

Richard Taylor

Metaphysicians, theologians and philosophers generally once thought of an efficient cause as something that *produces* something. That which was produced, according to this ancient idea, was a new being. In the case the new being was a substance—a soul, for example, or matter, or any substance at all— then the causation of that being was considered an act of creation. It is in this sense that God was quite naturally thought of as the creator of the world, and also, as its efficient cause. If, on the other hand, the new being was simply a modification of an existing substance, then there was no creation, in the strict sense, but only what Aristotle called generation. When a sculptor, for instance, fabricates a statue, he does not create anything, but simply imposes changes upon what already exists. Still, he does produce a new being—namely, a statue—even though this new being is only the modification of a substance that already existed. This is the the way Plato, in contrast to later Christian theologians, thought of God's relation to the world. God, or the demiurge, according to

*Copyright © 1963 by *The Monist*, La Salle, IL 61301. Reprinted by permission, from *The Monist* 47 (1963), 287–313.

this idea, was the cause of the world only in the sense that he converted chaos into a universe. He did not create the chaos with which he began.

Now this original idea of an efficient cause had no necessary connection with the ideas of uniformity, constancy or law. It was always supposed that, given the cause, the effect must follow; but this was not usually understood to mean that, given the same cause, the same effect must always follow. A particular sculptor, for example, was considered the efficient cause of a particular statue, but it was not supposed that this sculptor could do nothing but make statues. The necessity of an effect, given its cause, was thought to be a consequence of the *power* of the cause to produce it, and not of any invariance between that cause and that effect. Thus, if a sculptor has the power to make a statue, and exercises that power upon marble, then the marble cannot help but become a statue; the effect must follow, given its cause. Thus arose the idea, so clear to our predecessors but so obscure and implausible to us, that a cause must be as great or greater than its effect; the greater cannot be produced by the lesser. It is also this idea of the power of a cause to produce its effect which gave rise to the common distinction between acting and being acted upon, and the kindred distinctions between agent and patient, activity and passivity. A sculptor *acts* in creating, or causing, a statue, but the marble upon which he acts, or exercises his power, does not act; it is a purely passive recipient of changes imposed by an active cause.

We thus find in this ancient idea of an efficient cause two closely related concepts, that of *power* or *efficacy,* and that of *necessity* or *compulsion,* both of which concepts modern philosophers have been eager to eschew if they can. The idea of efficacy is, of course, part of the very etymology of "efficient cause."

Power. An efficient cause was thought to produce its effect by virtue of its power to do so. Berkeley considered this so obvious that he used it as an important argument to prove that our ideas cannot be caused by other ideas, but must be produced by an active being. Ideas, he said, are altogether inert or passive things, without the power to cause anything. God, of course, has always been thought of by theologians and philosophers as a being of such power that he can produce a world. This is essentially what was meant by calling God a "first cause"—namely, that everything ultimately depends for its existence upon his power, whereas he depends upon the power of nothing except himself. It was in the same way that statues, temples and other human artifacts were considered the expression of human power. The very movements of men and animals were thought to be the expression of the power of such creatures over their own bodies, leading Aristotle to describe animals as self-moved. When philosophers eventually came to analyze this idea of power within the presuppositions of empiricism they became involved, of course, in enormous difficulties. The longest part of Locke's *Essay* is devoted to a tortuous and inconclusive discussion of it. Thomas Reid finally affirmed that the idea of the active power of a cause—as exemplified, for instance, in the power of a man over his own voluntary movements—cannot be analyzed or defined at all, though it seemed to him perfectly clear and intelligible.

This is but an intimation of the importance that the idea of causal power once had in philosophy and metaphysics. It is seldom any longer referred to, being now assumed to be, at best, a derivative concept, with the result that much traditional metaphysics is simply incomprehensible to modern students.

There is, however, one element in this notion of causal power or efficacy that has never been doubted, and is even still a part of everyone's conception of causation; namely, that the power of an efficient cause never extends to things past. This priority of efficient causes to their effects is not, moreover, a mere convention of speech, but a metaphysical necessity. The power of a cause to produce an effect has a fixed temporal direction that results, not from the connotation of words, but from its very nature as an efficient cause. Nothing past is within the power of anything, either to do or undo. Aristotelians might express this by saying that the past contains no potentialities or real possibilities; everything past can only be what it actually is. Things present, on the other hand, are capable of becoming a variety of things, depending on what they are converted to by the causes that act upon them. It is in this sense, according to this way of looking at things, that the future, unlike the past, contains alternative and mutually incompatible possibilities, and is thus within the power of men and other efficient causes and movers to determine in this way and that.

Necessity. The second concept involved in this original idea of an efficient cause, it was noted, is that of *necessity* or *compulsion.* The efficient cause, it was always thought, *makes* its effect happen, the relation between cause and effect being such that, given the former, the latter cannot fail to occur. There was never thought to be any necessitation or compulsion in the reverse direction, however; that is, an effect was never thought of as compelling the occurrence of its cause, despite the fact that the cause could be as certainly inferred from the effect as the effect from the cause. Thus, a man vanquishes his foe by making him die; that is, by doing something which renders it impossible for him to live. But despite the fact that one can infallibly infer a cause from such an effect, it was never thought that the effect compelled the occurence of the cause. Similarly, a man, in raising his arm, makes it move upwards, the arm being the passive recipient of changes wrought by an active cause. Or, to take an example from inanimate nature, the sun warms a stone, or makes it become warmer, in a manner in which it cannot be said that the stone, in becoming warmer, makes the sun shine upon it.

A return to the metaphysics of causation.

This ancient idea of an efficient cause that I have very loosely sketched is generally considered by contemporary philosophers to be metaphysical and obscure, and quite plainly erroneous. We have, it is generally thought, long since gotten rid of such esoteric concepts as power and compulsion, reducing causation to simple, empirically discoverable relationships such as succession and uniformity. I believe, on the contrary, that while this older metaphysical idea of an efficient cause is not an easy one to grasp, it is nonetheless superior and far closer to the truth of things than the conceptions of causation that are now usually taken for granted.

It is the aim of this discussion to defend this claim. I shall do so by showing that the attempts of modern philosophy to expurgate the ideas of necessity and power from the concept of causation, and to reduce causation to constancy of sequence, have failed, and that the ideas of power and necessity are essential to that concept. Many philosophers are now apparently agreed that causation cannot be described without in one way or another introducing modal concepts, which amounts to re-establishing the necessity which Hume was once thought to have gotten rid of, but hardly anyone, apparently, has noticed that we need also the idea of power or efficacy. If, as I believe, both of these ideas are indispensable, then it will be found that the advance of contemporary philosophy over the metaphysics of our predecessors is much less impressive than we had supposed.

Necessity vs. invariable sequence.

Let the letters A, B, C . . . etc., designate events, states of affairs, conditions, or substances which, we assume, *have* existed. These symbols, in other words, shall designate anything we please that was ever real. This stipulation excludes from our consideration not only things future, but also things that might have but in fact did not exist, as well as impossible things, kinds or classes of things as distinguished from things themselves, and so on. Now we want to consider true assertions of the form "A was the cause of B," wherein we assume that A was in fact, as asserted, the cause of B.

Let A, for example, be the beheading of Anne Boleyn, and B her subsequent death, and assume that the former was the cause of the latter. What, then, is asserted by that statement? Does it mean that A and B are constantly conjoined, B following upon A? Plainly not, for the event A, like B, occurred only once in the history of the universe. The assertion that A and B are constantly conjoined—that the one never occurs without the other—is therefore true, but not significant. Each is also constantly conjoined with every other event that has occurred only once. Nor do we avoid this obvious difficulty by saying that B must follow immediately upon A in order to be the effect of A; for there were numberless things that followed immediately upon A. At the moment of Anne's death, for instance, numberless persons were being born here and there, others were dying, and, let us suppose, some bird was producing a novel combination of notes from a certain twig, any of which events we may assume not to have happened before or since. Yet the beheading of that queen had nothing to do with these. Mere constancy of conjunction, then, even with temporal contiguity, does not constitute causation.

Here there is an enormous temptation to introduce classes or kinds, and to say, after the fashion familiar to all students of philosophy, that A was the cause of B, provided A was immediately followed by B, and that things similar to A are always in similar circumstances followed by things similar to B. This, however, only allows us to avoid speaking of necessary connections by exploiting the vagueness in the notion of similarity. When confronted with counter examples, one can always say that the requisite similarity was lacking, and thus avoid having to say that the necessary connection was lacking. What does "similar" mean in this context? If we construe it to mean *exactly* similar, then the class of things similar to A and the class of things similar to B have each only one member, namely, A and B, and we are back where we started. The only thing exactly similar to the beheading of Anne Boleyn, for instance, is the beheading of Anne Boleyn, and the only thing exactly similar to her death is her death. Other things are only more or less similar to these—similar, that is, in some respects, and dissimilar in others. If, however, we allow the similarity to be one of degree, then the statement that things similar to A are always followed by things similar to B is not true. A stage dramatization of the beheading of Anne Boleyn is similar—perhaps very similar—to the beheading of Anne Boleyn, but it is not followed by anything very similar to her death. Here it is tempting to introduce the idea of relevance, and say that things similar to A in all relevant respects are followed by things similar to B in all relevant respects; but this just gives the whole thing away. "Relevant respects," it soon turns out, are nothing but those features of the situation that have some causal connection with each other. Or consider another example. Suppose we have two pairs of matches. The first pair are similar to each other in all respects, let us suppose, except only that one is red and the other blue. The other pair are likewise similar in all respects, except only that one is wet and the other dry. Now the degree of similarity between the members of each pair is the same. One of the differences, however, is "relevant" to the question of what happens when the matches are rubbed, while the other is not. Whether the match is red or blue is irrelevant, but whether it is wet or dry is not. But all this means, obviously, is that the dryness of a match is causally connected to its igniting, while its color is not.

Laws. Sometimes difficulties of the kind suggested have been countered by introducing the idea of a *law* into the description of casual connections. For instance, it is sometimes suggested that a given A was the cause of a given B, provided there is a law to the effect that whenever A occurs in certain circumstances, it is followed by B. This appears, however, to involve the same problems of uniqueness and similarity that we have just considered. There can be no law connecting just two things. It can be no law, for example, that if Anne Boleyn is beheaded, *she* dies, or whenever a particular match is rubbed, *it* ignites.

One could, perhaps, overcome these difficulties by embodying in the statement of the law precisely those respects in which things must be similar in order to behave similarly under certain specified conditions, all other similarities and differences being disregarded as irrelevant. For example, there could be a law to the effect that whenever *any* match of such and such precisely stated chemical composition is treated in a certain specified way, under certain specified conditions, then it ignites. Any match of that description would, of course, be similar to any other fitting the same description, and any other similarities and differences between such matches, however conspicuous, would be "irrelevant," i.e., not mentioned in the law.

That overcomes the difficulty of specifying how similar two causes must be in order to have similar effects. They must, according to this suggestion, be exactly similar in certain respects only, and can be as dissimilar as one pleases in other respects. But here we shall find that, by introducing the idea of a law, we have tacitly re-introduced the idea of a necessary connection between cause and effect—precisely the thing we were trying to avoid. A general statement counts as a *law* only if we can use it to infer, not only what does happen, but what would happen if something else were to happen, and this we can never do from a statement that is merely a true general statement.

To make this clear, assume that there is a true statement to the effect that any match having a certain set of properties ignites when rubbed in a certain manner under certain conditions. Such a statement, though true, need not be a law. We could easily take a handful (or a car full) of matches, and give all of them some set of properties that distinguished them from all other matches that ever have existed or ever will exist. For example, we could put the same unique combination of marks on the sticks. Having done so, we could then rub each in a certain way and, if all of them in fact ignited, it would then be *true* that *any* match that has those properties ignites when rubbed in that fashion. But this, though a true statement, would be no law, simply because there is no necessary connection between a match's having those properties and behaving as it does when rubbed. If, contrary to fact, another match were to have those properties, but lacked, say, the property of dryness, it might not ignite. For a true general statement of this kind to count as a law, then, we must be able to use it to infer what would happen if something else, which does not happen, were to happen; for instance, that a certain match which lacks some property would ignite if only it had that property. This, however, expresses some necessary, and not merely *de facto*, connection between properties and events. There is some connection between a match's being dry and igniting when rubbed. There is not the same connection between its being decorated in a certain way and igniting when rubbed— even though it may be true that every match so decorated does ignite when rubbed. But this only means that the decoration on its stick does not have anything to do—has no necessary connection—with a match's igniting when rubbed, while its being dry does.[1]

Causes as necessary and sufficient conditions. In the light of the foregoing we can now set forth our problem more clearly in the following way.

Every event occurs under innumerable and infinitely complex conditions. Some of these are relevant to the occurrence of the event in question, while others have nothing to do with it. This means, that some of the conditions under which a given event occurs are such that it would not have occurred, had those conditions been absent, while others are such that their presence or absence makes no difference.

Suppose, for instance, that a given match has ignited, and assume that this was caused by something. Now it would be impossible to set forth all the conditions under which this occurred, for they are numberless. A description of them would be incomplete if it were not a description of the entire universe at that moment. But among those conditions there were, let us suppose, those consisting of (a) the match's being dry (b) its being rubbed in a certain way, (c) its being of such and such chemical composition, (d) the rubbing surface being of such and such roughness, (e) the presence of dust motes in the air nearby, (f) the sun shining, (g) the presence of an observer named Smith, and so on. Now some of these conditions— namely, (a) through (d), and others as well—had something to do with the match igniting, while others—such as (e), for instance—had no causal connection with it. This we have learned from experience. Our problem, then, is not to state how we *know* which were the causal conditions of its igniting and which were not. The answer to this is obvious—we know by experience and induction. Our problem is, rather, to state just what relationship those causal conditions had to the match igniting, but which the numberless irrelevant conditions had not; to state, for example, what connection the match's being rubbed had to its igniting, but which the presence of dust motes had not.

The most natural way of expressing this connection is to say that had the match not been rubbed, then it would not have ignited, given all the other conditions that occurred, but only those that occurred, whereas, given those other conditions that occurred, including the match's being rubbed as it was, it would still have ignited, even had the dust motes been absent. This appears to be exactly what one has in mind in saying that the friction on the match head had something to do with its igniting, while the presence of the dust motes did not—the latter condition was not at all necessary for the igniting of the match, whereas the former was. This, however, is simply a way of saying that the friction was a *necessary condition* of the match igniting, given the other conditions that occurred but no others, whereas the presence of dust motes was not.

If this is correct, then we can simply assert that the cause, A, of an event, B, is that totality of conditions, from among all those, but only those, that occurred, each of which was necessary for the occurrence of B. Now if this set of conditions, A, is thus understood, as it should be, to include *every* condition, out of that totality that occurred, that was necessary for the occurrence of B, then we can say that the set of conditions, A, is also *sufficient* for B, since no other condition was necessary. We can, accordingly, understand the relationship between any set of conditions A, and any set B, expressed in the statement that A was the cause of B, to be simply described in this fashion: That A was the set, from among all those conditions that occurred, each of which was necessary, and the totality of which was sufficient, for the occurrence of B. This appears to be exactly what distinguishes the causal conditions of any event from all those that occurred but which were not causally connected with the event in question.

It is now evident that this reintroduces the concept of necessity which Hume was once so widely believed to have gotten rid of. For to say of any condition that a certain event would not have occurred if that condition had been absent is exactly equivalent to saying that this condition was necessary for its occurrence, or, that it was such that the event in question would not have occurred without it, given only those other conditions that occurred. There seems, however, as we have seen, to be no other way of distinguishing the causal conditions of any

event from those infinitely numerous and complex other conditions under which any given event occurs. We cannot distinguish them by introducing the concept of a law, unless we understand the law to be, not merely a statement of what does happen, but what must happen; for we can find true statements of what does happen, and happens invariably, which are not laws. The conjunction of properties and events can be as constant as we please, with no exception whatever, without there being any causal connections between them. It is not until we can say what would have happened, had something else happened which did not happen, that we leave the realm of mere constancy of conjunction and find ourselves speaking of a causal connection; and as soon as we speak in this fashion, we are speaking of necessary connections.

Now to say of a given event that it would not have occurred without the occurrence of another is the same as saying that the occurrence of the one without the other was causally, though not logically, impossible; or, that in a non-logical sense, the one without the other could not have occurred. We can accordingly define the concepts of necessity and sufficiency in the following way.

To say of any condition or set of conditions, x, that it was *necessary* for the occurrence of some event, E, means that, within the totality of other conditions that occurred, but only those, the occurrence of E without x was impossible, or could not obtain. Similarly, to say of any condition or set of conditions, x, that it was *sufficient* for some event, E, means that, within the totality of other conditions that occurred, but only those, the occurrence of x without E was impossible, or could not obtain. The expression "was impossible" in these definitions has, of course, the same sense as "could not have occurred" in the discussion preceding and not the sense of *logical* impossibility. There are, we can grant at once, no logically necessary connections between causes and effects. In terms of our earlier example, we can say that Anne Boleyn could not live long after being beheaded, or that it was impossible for her to do so, without maintaining that this was logically impossible.

The concepts of necessity and sufficiency, as thus defined, are of course the converses of each other, such that if any condition or set of conditions is necessary for another, that other is sufficient for it, and vice versa. The statement, that x is necessary for E, is logically equivalent to saying the E is sufficient for x, and similarly, the statement that x is sufficient for E is logically equivalent to saying that E is necessary for x. This fact enables us now to introduce a very convenient notation, as follows. If we let x and E represent any conditions, events or sets of these, we can symbolize the expression, "x is sufficient for E," with an arrow in this way:

$$x \longrightarrow E.$$

Similarly, we can symbolize the expression "x is necessary for E" with a reverse arrow, in this way:

$$x \longleftarrow E.$$

Since, moreover, the expression "x is sufficient for E" is exactly equivalent to "E is necessary for x," we can regard as exactly equivalent the following representations of this relationship:

$$x \longrightarrow E.$$
$$E \longleftarrow x,$$

since the first of these means that the occurence of x without E is impossible, and the second means exactly the same thing. It should be noted, however, that the arrows symbolize no temporal relations whatever.

With this clear and convenient way of symbolizing these relationships, we can now represent the conception of causation at which we have arrived in the following way.

Consider again a particular event that has occurred at a particular time and place, such as the igniting of a particular match, and call this E. Now E, we can be sure, occurred under a numerous set of conditions, which

we can represent as $a, b, c \ldots n$. Let a, for instance, be the condition consisting of the match's being dry, b its being rubbed, c its being of such and such chemical composition, d the rubbing surface being of such and such roughness, e the presence of dust motes in the air, f the sun shining, and so on, *ad infinitum*. Now some of these conditions—namely, a, b, c, and d—were presumably necessary for E, in the sense that E would not have occurred in the absence of any of them, given only the other conditions that occurred, whereas others, such as e and f, had nothing to do with E. If, furthermore, as we can assume for illustration, a, b, c and d were jointly sufficient for E, the relations thus described can be symbolized as follows:

$$a \longleftarrow E$$
$$b \longleftarrow E$$
$$c \longleftarrow E$$
$$d \longleftarrow E$$
$$e$$
$$f$$
$$abcd \longrightarrow E$$

And since a, b, c and d are each individually necessary for E, it follows that E is sufficient for all of them, and we can accordingly symbolize this:

$$abcd \longleftarrow E.$$

And this permits us to express the causal relation, in this example, with the utmost simplicity as follows:

$$abcd \leftrightarrows E,$$

which means, simply, that the cause of E was that set of conditions, within the totality, only, of those that actually occurred, that was necessary and sufficient for E.

It is at this point that our metaphysical difficulties really begin, but before turning to those, two points of clarification must be made.

The first point is, that this analysis does not exactly express the "ordinary use" of the word "cause," and does not purport to. The reason for this is not that the analysis itself is unprecise, but rather that ordinary usage is, in such cases. Most persons, for example, are content to call "the cause" of any event some one condition that is conspicuous or, more commonly, whatever part of the causal conditions that is novel. In the example we have been using, for example, the rubbing of the match would normally be regarded as "the cause" of its igniting, without regard to its dryness, its chemical composition, and so on. But the reason for this, quite obviously, is that these other conditions are taken for granted. They are not mentioned, not because they are thought to have nothing to do with the match igniting, but rather, because they are presupposed. Philosophically, it makes no difference at all whether we say that, given the other conditions necessary for the match's igniting, it was then caused to ignite by being rubbed, or whether we say that its being rubbed was, together with these other conditions, the cause of its igniting. Its being rubbed has neither more nor less to do with its igniting than does, say, its being dry. The only difference is that it was, presumably, dry all the while and, in that state, was rubbed. It might just as well have been rubbed all the while and, in that state, suddenly rendered dry, in which case we could say that it was ignited by suddenly becoming dry.

The second point is, that there is a perfectly natural point of view from which perhaps no condition is ever really necessary for the occurrence of any event, nor any set of conditions sufficient for it, from which one could derive the absurd result that, on the analysis suggested, events do not have any causes. We said, for instance, that the match's being rubbed was a necessary condition for its igniting. But, it might at first seem, that is not a necessary condition at all, since there are other ways of igniting matches—touching them to hot surfaces, for instance. Similarly, we said that rubbing the match was, together with certain other conditions, sufficient for its igniting. But this might seem false, since it would be possible to prevent it from igniting, even under these conditions—by applying a fire extinguisher, for instance.

This objection overlooks an essential qualification in the analysis, however. We said that the cause of an event E is that set of conditions that were, within the totality of those other conditions, only, that in fact occurred, individually necessary and jointly sufficient for E. If, in terms of our example, that totality of other conditions that in fact occurred did not, in fact, include some such condition as the match's being in contact with a hot surface, nor the application of any fire extinguisher, etc., then, within the totality of conditions that did occur, its being rubbed *was* necessary for its igniting, and was also, together with certain other conditions that occurred, sufficient for its igniting.

Time and efficacy. Our analysis of the causal relationship, as it now stands, has one strange consequence that is immediately obvious; namely, that it does not enable us to draw any distinction between cause and effect. We have suggested that the cause of an event is that set of conditions, among all those that occur, which is necessary and sufficient for that event, from which it of course follows that if any condition or set of conditions, A, is the cause of another, B, then B is automatically also the cause of A. For concerning any A and any B, if A is necessary and sufficient for B, and therefore, on our analysis, the cause of B, then it logically follows that B is necessary and sufficient for A, and therefore the cause of A. This is quite plainly absurd. One cannot possibly say that a match's igniting is the cause of its being rubbed, that a stone's being warm is the cause of the sun's shining upon it, or that a man's being intoxicated is the cause of his having alcohol in his blood, despite the fact that the relationships of necessity and sufficiency between cause and effect are the same in both directions.

Earlier metaphysicians took it for granted that the difference between cause and effect was one of power or efficacy or, what amounts to the same thing, that the cause of anything was always something active, and its effect some change in something that is passive. Thus, the sun has the power to warm a stone, but the stone has no power to make the sun shine; it is simply the passive recipient of a change wrought by the sun. Similarly, alcohol in the blood has the power to produce feelings of intoxication, but a man cannot by having such feelings, produce alcohol in his blood.

Modern philosophers, on the contrary, have almost universally supposed that the difference between cause and effect is not to be found in anything so esoteric as power or efficacy, but is simply a temporal difference, nothing more. The cause of an event, it is now almost universally supposed, is some condition or set of conditions that precedes some other, its effect, in time. Thus, if our analysis of the causal relationship is otherwise correct, then it should, according to this prevalent view, have some qualification added about time, such as to require that the cause should occur before its effect.

I believe this to be the profoundest error in modern philosophy, and the source of more misconceptions than any other. By this simple expedient of introducing considerations of time, philosophers imagine that they no longer need to talk metaphysically of causal power or efficacy. In fact, of course, philosophers, like everyone else, do still speak freely of power and efficacy—of the power of various substances to corrode, to dissolve, to cause intoxication, to cause death, and so on. But in their philosophies, they imagine that such terms express only ideas of *time*, and that they can be omitted from any exact description of causal connections, just by the simple device of introducing temporal qualifications.

I intend to prove that this is an error, by showing, first, that in many perfectly clear instances of causation, causes do not precede their effects in time, but are entirely contemporaneous with them, and second, that the causal conditions of an event cannot, in fact, precede that event in time.

Before doing this, however, let us consider a question that is meant to give some intimation that what I have called a profound error is an error indeed.

Let us suppose, for now, that there is a temporal interval between a cause and its effect, such that it is true to say that one occurs *before* the other. Now if the relationships between the two are otherwise identical—namely, are simply the relationships of necessity and sufficiency set forth above, or, for that matter, any other relationships whatever—the question can be asked, *why* it should be thought so important to regard only the prior condition or set of conditions as the cause of the subsequent one, and never the subsequent one as the cause of the prior one. There is, certainly, an absurdity in saying that a man's dying is the cause of his being shot, or that a man's being intoxicated is the cause of his having imbibed alcohol, rather than the other way around; but what *kind* of absurdity is it? Is it merely a verbal error, a wrong choice of vocabulary, or is it a metaphysical absurdity? Compare it with the following simple example. If one were to point out that a son cannot exist before his father, he would probably not be *merely* calling attention to a point of vocabulary. He would be stating an obvious truth of biology. If, on the other hand, one were to say that one's brother's sons cannot be his nieces, but must be his nephews, he would obviously be making only a point about language, about the use of certain words. Now then, when one says that a cause cannot come after its effect, which kind of point is he making? Is he *merely* calling attention to a matter of vocabulary, or is he saying something metaphysically significant about causes and their effects?

It seems fairly clear that there is something metaphysically absurd, and not merely an inept choice of words, in supposing that efficient causes might work backwards. There is surely some reason why nothing can produce an effect in the past, and the reason cannot just be, that if it did, we would not then *call* it a cause.

Consider the following illustration.[2] There is a variety of ways in which one might ensure that a certain man—say, some political rival—is dead on a certain day. One way would be to shoot him the day before. We can assume that this, together with all the other conditions prevailing, is sufficient for his being dead the next day, and further, that in case conditions are such that he would not have died had he not been shot, then it is also necessary for his being dead then. But another, equally good way of ensuring that he is dead on that day would be to attend his funeral later on. This would surely be sufficient for his prior death and, in case conditions are such that his being dead is sufficient for someone's attending his funeral, then it is also a necessary condition of his prior death. Suppose, then, that one man shoots him, and another attends his funeral, and that both of these acts are related to that man's death in exactly the same way, except only for the difference in time; that is, that each act is, given only those other conditions that occur, both necessary and sufficient for his being dead on the day in question. Why should one man be blamed more than the other, or held any more responsible for the death? Each man, equally with the other, did something necessary and sufficient for that man's death. Either act guarantees the death as well as the other. The thing to note is, that this question is *not* answered by merely observing that one of these acts occurred before the death, and the other after; that is already quite obvious. Nor is it answered by noting that we do not, as it happens, *call* the subsequent event the cause. That is obvious and irrelevant; the word "cause" was not even used in the example. We do not hold a man responsible for any event, unless something he does is a necessary and sufficient *prior* condition of it. That is granted. But merely stating that fact does not answer the question, Why not? It cannot be a mere question of vocabulary whether, for example, a certain man should be hanged for what he has done.

The correct answer to this question, I believe, is that no cause exerts any power over the past. The same idea is expressed, more metaphysically, by saying that all past things are actual, and never at some later time potentially what they are not then actually, whereas a present thing can be actually one thing but potentially another. This would be expressed in terms of our example by saying that a man who shoots another acts upon him, or does something to him, or

is an agent, whereas the man who is thus killed does not, in dying, act upon his assassin, but is the passive recipient, or patient, of the other's causal activity. The man who merely attends the funeral, on the other hand, does not act upon him who is already dead. He is merely the passive observer of what has already been done.

This metaphysical way of conceiving these relationships seems, moreover, to be the way all men do think of causes and effects, and it explains the enormous absurdity in the supposition that causes might act so as to alter things already past. For anything to be a cause it must act upon something and, as a matter of fact—indeed, of metaphysical necessity—nothing past can be acted upon by anything. The profound error of modern philosophy has been to suppose that, in making that point, one is making only a point about language.

Contemporaneous causes and effects. If we can cite clear examples of causal connections, wherein those conditions that constitute the cause and those that constitute the effect are entirely contemporaneous, neither occurring before the other, then it will have been proved that the difference between a cause and its effect cannot be a temporal one, but must consist of something else.

In fact, such examples are not at all hard to find. Consider, for instance, a locomotive that is pulling a caboose, and to make it simple, suppose this is all it is pulling. Now here the motion of the locomotive is sufficient for the motion of the caboose, the two being connected in such a way that the former cannot move without the latter moving with it. But so also, the motion of the caboose is sufficient for the motion of the locomotive, for, given that the two are connected as they are, it would be impossible for the caboose to be moving without the locomotive moving with it. From this it logically follows that, conditions being such as they are—viz., both objects being in motion, there being no other movers present, no obstructions to motion, and so on—the motion of each object is also necessary for the motion of the other. But is there any temporal gap between the motion of one and the motion of the other? Clearly, there is not. They move together, and in no sense is the motion of one followed by the motion of the other.

Here it is tempting to say that the locomotive must *start* moving before the caboose can start moving, but this is both irrelevant and false. It is irrelevant, because the effect we are considering is not the caboose's *beginning* to move, but its moving. And it is false because we can suppose the two to be securely connected, such that as soon as either begins to move the other must move too. Even if we do not make this supposition, and suppose, instead, that the locomotive does begin moving first, and moves some short distance before overcoming the looseness of its connection with the caboose, still, it is no cause of the motion of the caboose until that looseness is overcome. When that happens, and not until then, the locomotive imparts its motion to the caboose. Cause and effect are, then, perfectly contemporaneous.

Again, consider the relationships between one's hand and a pencil he is holding while writing. We can ignore here the difficult question of what causes the *hand* to move. It is surely true, in any case, that the motion of the pencil is caused by the motion of the hand. This means, first, that conditions are such that the motion of the hand is sufficient for the motion of the pencil. Given precisely those conditions, however, the motion of the pencil is sufficient for the motion of the hand; neither can move, under the conditions assumed—that the fingers are grasping the pencil, etc.—without the other moving with it. It follows, then, that under these conditions the motion of either is also necessary for the motion of the other. And, quite obviously, both motions are contemporaneous; the motion of neither is *followed* by the motion of the other.

Or again, consider a leaf that is being fluttered by the wind. Here it would be quite clearly erroneous to say that the wind currents impinge upon the leaf, and then, some time later, the leaf flutters in response. There is no gap in time at all. One might want to say that the leaf, however light, does offer some resistance to the wind, and that the wind must overcome this slight resistance before any fluttering occurs. But then we need only add, that the wind is no cause of the leaf's motion until that resistance is overcome. Cause and effect are again, then, contemporaneous.

What, then, distinguishes cause and effect in the foregoing examples? It is not the time of occurrence, for both occur strictly together. It is not any difference in the relations of necessity and sufficiency, for these are identical both ways. But there is one thing which, in all these cases, appears to distinguish the cause from the effect; namely, that the cause acts upon something else to produce some change. The locomotive pulls the caboose, but the caboose does not push the locomotive; it just follows passively along. The hand pushes the pencil, and imparts motion to it, while the pencil is just passively moved. The wind acts upon the leaf, to move it; but it is no explanation of the wind's blowing to say that the leaf is moving. In all these cases, to be sure, what has been distinguished as the cause is itself moved by something else—the locomotive by steam in its cylinders, the hand by a man, the wind by things more complex and obscure; but that only calls attention to the fact that causes can themselves be the effects of other causes. Whether all causes must be such, or whether, on the contrary, something can be a "first cause" or a "prime mover" is something that need not concern us here. One can, in any case, see why it has seemed plausible, and even necessary, to some thinkers.

The examples just considered suggest our final point; namely, that there not only is no temporal gap between cause and effect in certain examples that come readily to mind, but that there is in fact never any such gap in any example that one carefully considers.[3] This will be seen, I think, if we consider a clear example of causation wherein the cause seems, at first, to precede its effect, and then find that, even in such a case, there is no such temporal priority at all.

Consider, then, the case of a window

breaking as a result of a stone being thrown against it. Here it is tempting to say that the stone is first thrown, and then the window breaks, implying that the cause occurs before the effect. But that is not a good description of what happens. It is not enough that the stone should be thrown; it must hit the window. Even then, it must overcome the resistance of the window. Only then does the window break; cause and effect are simultaneous. Nor does one avoid this conclusion by the familiar device of conceiving of both cause and effect as events, both having duration in time, and being such that the effect begins to occur as soon as the cause ceases. It is, at best, simply arbitrary how one divides any process up into events. But even if one does permit himself to do this, and regards a cause, for instance, as a change occurring over a length of time, it is obvious that not all that change can be counted as the cause of some other change following it in time. In the example we are considering, for instance, it is the impact of the stone against the glass that causes the shattering; it is not what the stone was doing before then. Had the stone behaved exactly as it did up to that moment, but then made no contact with the glass, or had it then struck the glass with a force insufficient to break it, the glass would not have shattered. The behavior of the stone up to that moment was, accordingly, not sufficient for the effect in question. Similarly, had the stone behaved entirely differently up to that moment, but then somehow, at that moment, exerted upon the glass the pressure that it did exert, the glass would have broken as it did anyway. The behavior of the stone up to that moment was, accordingly, neither necessary nor sufficient for the effect in question. What *was* necessary and sufficient, on the other hand, was that the stone should at that moment only have exerted the pressure it did; and, given that condi-

tion, then the window breaks—not a day or two later, and not a second or two later, but at that very moment. The shattering of the glass can also, of course, be conceived as a process that takes time; but here we need only note that the only part of that shattering that is caused by the impact of the stone is that part that occurs at the moment of impact. The subsequent behavior of the glass is the effect of what happens after the glass has been struck.

Here again, then—and, I believe, in any example one closely considers—cause and effect are contemporaneous. It is therefore no priority in time that distinguishes the cause from the effect, nor is it, again, any difference in the relations of necessity and sufficiency, these being, as always, identical either way. What does seem to distinguish cause from effect is that the former is something that acts upon the glass to produce its shattered condition. Of course the glass acts upon the stone, too, to produce, for example, its retarded velocity, but that is a different effect, and a different cause, and these are also contemporaneous. To point this out is only, in any case, to call attention to the fact that causes, in acting, can sometimes be acted upon. Whether this is always so is a question, important to theology and to the problem of free will, that need not concern us.

NOTES

[1]This point was suggested by R. M. Chisholm's "Law Statements and Counterfactual Inference," *Analysis*, 15 (1955), pp. 97–105.

[2]This example was suggested by R. M. Chisholm.

[3]A similar point is made by Bertrand Russell, "On the Notion of Cause," in *Mysticism and Logic* (London: Allen and Unwin, 1950).

Recommended Readings on Space, Time, and Causation

Beauchamp, T. L., and A. Rosenberg. *Hume and the Problem of Causation.* Oxford: Oxford University Press, 1981.

Brand, Myles, ed. *The Nature of Causation.* Urbana: University of Illinois Press, 1976.

Bunge, Mario. *Causality.* Cambridge, Mass.: Harvard University Press, 1959.

Ducasse, C. J. *Causation and the Types of Necessity.* New York: Dover, 1969.

Earman, J. S., C. N. Glymour, and J. J. Stachel, eds. *Foundations of Space-Time Theories: Minnesota Studies in the Philosophy of Science, Vol. 8.* Minneapolis: University of Minnesota Press, 1977.

Einstein, Albert. *Relativity: The Special and the General Theory.* New York: Crown, 1961.

Field, Hartry. *Science Without Numbers: A Defence of Nominalism.* Princeton: Princeton University Press, 1980.

Fisk, Milton. *Nature and Necessity.* Bloomington: Indiana University Press, 1973.

Freeman, Eugene, and Wilfrid Sellars, eds. *Basic Issues in the Philosophy of Time.* LaSalle, Ill.: Open Court, 1971.

French, Peter, T. E. Uehling, and H. K. Wettstein, eds. *Midwest Studies in Philosophy, Vol. 9: Causation and Causal Theories*. Minneapolis: University of Minnesota Press, 1984.

Gale, Richard, ed. *The Philosophy of Time*. Garden City, N.Y.: Doubleday, 1967.

Goodman, Nelson. *Fact, Fiction, and Forecast*, 3d ed. Indianapolis: Hackett, 1979.

Grünbaum, Adolf. *Philosophical Problems of Space and Time*, 2d ed. Dordrecht: D. Reidel, 1973.

Mackie, J. L. *The Cement of the Universe—A Study of Causation*. Oxford: Clarendon Press, 1974.

Mellor, D. H. *Real Time*. Cambridge: Cambridge University Press, 1981.

Nerlich, Graham. *The Shape of Space*. Cambridge: Cambridge University Press, 1976.

Newton-Smith, W. H. *The Structure of Time*. London: Routledge and Kegan Paul, 1980.

Reichenbach, Hans. *The Philosophy of Space and Time*. New York: Dover, 1957.

———. *The Direction of Time*. Berkeley: University of California Press, 1956.

Rucker, Rudolf. *Geometry, Relativity, and the Fourth Dimension*. New York: Dover, 1977.

Salmon, Wesley. *Scientific Explanation and the Causal Structure of the World*. Princeton: Princeton University Press, 1984.

Sklar, Lawrence. *Space, Time, and Space-Time*. Berkeley: University of California Press, 1974.

Smart, J. J. C., ed. *Problems of Space and Time*. New York: Macmillan, 1964.

Sosa, Ernest, ed. *Causation and Conditionals*. Oxford: Oxford University Press, 1975.

Swinburne, Richard. *Space and Time*. London: Macmillan, 1968.

Swinburne, Richard, ed. *Space, Time, and Causality*. Dordrecht: D. Reidel, 1983.

Tooley, Michael. *Causation*. Oxford: Oxford University Press, 1988.

van Fraassen, Bas. *An Introduction to the Philosophy of Time and Space*, 2d ed. New York: Columbia University Press, 1985.

von Wright, G. H. *Causality and Determinism*. New York: Columbia University Press, 1974.

III

Persons, Minds, and Free Will

This section, like Parts I and II, consists of two subsections. The first subsection is *Persons and Minds;* the second is *Persons and Free Will.* Both subsections bear directly on our notion of a person. The essays in the first subsection deal with the traditional *mind-body problem.* Basically, this is the problem of explaining how one's mind is related to one's body, or at least how one's mental features are related to one's bodily features. This problem originated with the beginning of western philosophy in ancient Greece and persists in contemporary philosophy. The essays in the first subsection take opposing views on the perennial mind-body problem.

In "The Traditional Problem of Body and Mind," C. D. Broad defends *two-sided interaction,* or what philosophers now call *dualistic interactionism.* This is the view that (a) there are mental phenomena (e.g., thoughts, feelings, and sensations) distinct from (i.e., irreducible to) physical features of the human body, and (b) mental and physical phenomena causally interact in the sense that some physical events cause some mental events, and some mental events cause some physical events.

Broad replies to prominent philosophical and scientific arguments against dualistic interactionism. For instance, on the philosophical side, he opposes the familiar claim that mental states are so different from bodily states that they could not be causally connected. Broad suggests that with voluntary action we have a fairly clear case of the mind's acting on the body. On the scientific side, Broad opposes the common view that the principle of the conservation of energy precludes dualistic interaction. If mental volitions cause bodily movements, energy flows from a mind to a body, causing bodily energy to increase; but it is doubtful that energy does, in fact, increase in this way. In reply, Broad argues that causal relations between the mental and the physical need not violate the principle of conservation. (See the subsequent essay by Cornman for relevant discussion.)

In "Materialism," J. J. C. Smart endorses *materialism* (the theory that there is nothing in the world over and above those entities postulated by physics). On Smart's materialism, there are no non-physical items, and so there is no dualistic causal interaction between the mental and the physical.

Smart argues that our reports of immediate experiences (e.g., "I have an aching pain") are *topic-neutral* in the sense that they do not commit us either to materialism or to dualism. He claims that such reports are quite compatible with his thesis that sensations and other subjective experiences are just brain processes.

Smart also opposes behaviorism on the ground that "what is essential to a pain is what goes on in the brain, not what goes on in the arms or legs or larynx or mouth." Smart's materialist philosophy of mind is motivated by this rhetorical question: "How could a non-physical property or entity suddenly arise in the course of animal evolution?" Smart proposes that we should "vastly simplify our cosmological outlook" by endorsing a version of materialism that reduces sensations to brain processes.

In "A Nonreductive Identity Thesis about Mind and Body," James Cornman begins with a survey of the main problems facing *dualistic interactionism* (of Broad's sort), *epiphenomenalism* (one-sided action of the body on the mind), and *reductive materialism* (of Smart's sort). He opposes reductive materialism on the ground that pains can be "intense," "stabbing," and "throbbing," and that if pains have such properties, "then it is false that all mental phenomena are nothing but physical phenomena."

Cornman's alternative theory is the *neutral identity theory*. This theory stems from Spinoza's view that the mind and the body are one and the same thing conceived in different ways: at one time as something with mental properties, and at another time as something with physical properties. On Cornman's view, every mental phenomenon is identical with some physical item (such as a brain process), but also has certain *psychological* properties in addition to the physical properties of the physical items with which it is identical. So, Cornman's mental phenomena are neither purely physical nor purely mental.

In "Mind-Body Identity, Privacy, and Categories," Richard Rorty

Persons, Minds, and Free Will

supports the materialist view that the mind and the body are identical. Specifically, he supports a "disappearance" version of this identity relation. On this version, "the relation in question is not strict identity, but rather the sort of relation which obtains between . . . existent entities and non-existent entities when reference to the latter once served (some of) the purposes presently served by reference to the former— the sort of relation that holds, e.g., between "quantity of caloric fluid" and "mean kinetic energy of molecules."

Rorty's *disappearance theory,* in contrast to Smart's reductive materialism, does not require that our talk of sensations be translated into *topic-neutral language*. Rather, the disappearance theory claims that talk of sensations is talk that will disappear with the advance of science. On this view, sensations will be to future science what demons are to current science: non-existent entities reference to which once served, but no longer serves, a legitimate purpose. Rorty also claims that the distinction between observation terms and nonobservation terms is relative to alterable linguistic practices. On this ground, he claims that brain-processes can be the subject-matter of noninferential reports. He also claims that the philosophical distinction between *private* and *public* subject matters is similarly relative to alterable linguistic practices. This claim underlies Rorty's reply to the objection that privacy is essential to mental events, and that any theory that makes mental events public is confused.

In "The Mind-Body Problem," Jerry Fodor presents a view of the mind-body relation called *functionalism*. This view implies that things as diverse as humans, computers, and disembodied spirits could all have mental states. According to functionalism, "the psychology of a system depends not on the stuff it is made of (living cells, metal, or spiritual energy), but on how the stuff is put together." Functionalism is "a relational account of mental properties that abstracts them from the physical structure of their bearers."

Specifically, functionalism claims that the *causal* role of a mental particular in an organism's life determines the psychological type to which the particular belongs. On this view, a mental state is defined by its causal relations to other mental states. But Fodor notes that functionalism allows that mental particulars can be physical and that functionalism is compatible with a materialist view of the mind-body relation. Fodor clarifies the notion of a mental process by relating it to the class of computers called *Turing machines*. He also discusses the question of how functionalism can accommodate what some philosophers call *qualitative psychological content,* such as the color component of an experience.

The second subsection of Part III contains four essays on the longstanding topic of persons and free will. *Determinism* states that all events, including human actions, are causally determined. *Indeterminism* states that some events are not causally determined. Typically the indeterminist claims that human actions are not causally determined.

Soft determinism states that determinism is true, and that determinism is compatible with free will and moral responsibility. (The view that determinism is logically compatible with free will is now called *compatibilism*.) Soft determinists often understand freedom simply as one's being able to do what one chooses to do. *Hard determinism* states that determinism is true, and that determinism is logically *in*compatible with free will and moral responsibility. The philosophical problem of free will is basically the problem of deciding between indeterminism, hard determinism, and soft determinism, and of working out the details of the preferred option.

In "Free Will and Psychoanalysis," John Hospers endorses hard determinism. We often think that one is free to do something so long as one *can* do it *if* one wants to do it. But Hospers claims that one's wanting is itself "caught up in the stream of determinism," on the ground that unconscious forces drive one into the wanting or the not wanting to do the thing in question. Hospers appeals to psychoanalysis to support this claim. His view states that "the analogy of the puppet whose motions are manipulated from behind by invisible wires, or better still, by springs inside, is a telling one at almost every point." On the basis of his determinism, Hospers denies that humans have free will and moral responsibility.

In "Freedom and Determinism," Richard Taylor defends a version of indeterminism called *the theory of agency*. Taylor begins with two data: the belief that we sometimes deliberate, and the belief that it is sometimes up to us what we do. Taylor argues that neither determinism nor standard versions of indeterminism can accommodate these data. Taylor's theory of agency states that we are sometimes *self-determining* beings, for instance, when we are the causes of our own behavior. A free action "must be such that it is caused by the agent who performs it, but such that no antecedent conditions were sufficient for his performing just that action." On Taylor's view, *persons*, in contrast to mere events, have causal powers that generate actions. Taylor acknowledges that his conception of such powers "is strange indeed, if not positively mysterious."

In "Acting Freely," Gerald Dworkin defends a version of *compatibilism*. On his version, one acts freely if and only if one performs an action for reasons that one does not mind acting from. So long as one does not find acting from certain reasons painful or disagreeable, one's acting from those reasons qualifies as one's acting freely. On this view, one can do something freely even if one is causally determined to do it. Acting freely is a matter of one's attitudes toward one's reasons; such acting does not require that indeterminism be true.

In "Freedom of the Will and the Concept of a Person," Harry Frankfurt takes free will to be the capacity to form *second-order volitions*, i.e., desires that some particular desire be one's will (or, prompt one to act). In fact, Frankfurt takes this capacity also to be a necessary condition of personhood. Frankfurt uses the term *wanton* for creatures that do not have second-order volitions. Such creatures do not care about their will; they do not prefer to be moved to act by certain desires. Frankfurt denies that wantons are capable of having free will. On his view, "the statement that a person enjoys freedom of the will means . . . that he is free to will what he wants to will, or to have the will he wants." Frankfurt construes his conception of freedom to be neutral on the question whether determinism is true. In that respect, Frankfurt's account is compatibilist.

Persons and Minds

The Traditional Problem of Body and Mind*

C. D. Broad

There is a question which has been argued about for some centuries now under the name of "Interaction"; this is the question whether minds really do act on the organisms which they animate, and whether organisms really do act on the minds which animate them. (I must point out at once that I imply no particular theory of mind or body by the word "to animate". I use it as a perfectly neutral name to express the fact that a certain mind is connected in some peculiarly intimate way with a certain body, and, under normal conditions with no other body. This is a fact even on a purely behaviouristic theory of mind; on such a view to say that the mind M animates the body B would mean that the body B, in so far as it behaves in certain ways, *is* the mind M. A body which did not act in these ways would be said not to be animated by a mind. And a different Body B', which acted in the same general way as B, would be said to be animated by a different mind M'.)

The problem of Interaction is generally discussed at the level of enlightened common-

sense; where it is assumed that we know pretty well what we mean by "mind", by "matter" and by "causation". Obviously no solution which is reached at that level can claim to be ultimate. If what we call "matter" should turn out to be a collection of spirits of low intelligence, as Leibniz thought, the argument that mind and body are so unlike that their interaction is impossible would become irrelevant. Again, if causation be nothing but regular sequence and concomitance, as some philosophers have held, it is ridiculous to regard psychoneural parallelism and interaction as mutually exclusive alternatives. For interaction will mean no more than parallelism, and parallelism will mean no less than interaction. Nevertheless I am going to discuss the arguments here at the common-sense level, because they are so incredibly bad and yet have imposed upon so many learned men.

We start then by assuming a developed mind and a developed organism as two distinct things, and by admitting that the two are now intimately connected in some way or other which I express by saying that "this mind *animates* this organism". We assume that bodies are very much as enlightened common-sense believes them to be; and

*Reprinted by permission, from Broad, *The Mind and Its Place in Nature*, pp. 95–121. London: Routledge and Kegan Paul, 1925.

that, even if we cannot define "causation", we have some means of recognising when it is present and when it is absent. The question then is: "Does a mind ever act on the body which it animates, and does a body ever act on the mind which animates it?" The answer which common-sense would give to both questions is: "Yes, certainly." On the face of it my body acts on my mind whenever a pin is stuck into the former and a painful sensation thereupon arises in the latter. And, on the face of it, my mind acts on my body whenever a desire to move my arm arises in the former and is followed by this movement in the latter. Let us call this common-sense view "Two-sided Interaction". Although it seems so obvious it has been denied by probably a majority of philosophers and a majority of physiologists. So the question is: "Why should so many distinguished men, who have studied the subject, have denied the apparently obvious fact of Two-sided Interaction?"

The arguments against Two-sided Interaction fall into two sets:—Philosophical and Scientific. We will take the philosophical arguments first; for we shall find that the professedly scientific arguments come back in the end to the principles or prejudices which are made explicit in the philosophical arguments.

Philosophical Arguments against Two-sided Interaction

No one can deny that there is a close correlation between certain bodily events and certain mental events, and conversely. Therefore anyone who denies that there is action of mind on body and of body on mind must presumably hold (a) that concomitant variation is not an adequate criterion of causal connexion, and (b) that the other feature which is essential for causal connexion is absent in the case of body and mind. Now the common philosophical argument is that minds and mental states are so extremely unlike bodies and bodily states that it is inconceivable that the two should be causally connected. It is certainly true

that, if minds and mental events are just what they seem to be to introspection and nothing more, and if bodies and bodily events are just what enlightened common-sense thinks them to be and nothing more, the two *are* extremely unlike. And this fact is supposed to show that, however closely correlated certain pairs of events in mind and body respectively may be, they cannot be causally connected.

Evidently the assumption at the back of this argument is that concomitant variation, together with a high enough degree of likeness, is an adequate test for causation; but that no amount of concomitant variation can establish causation in the absence of a high enough degree of likeness. Now I am inclined to admit part of this assumption. I think it is practically certain that causation does not simply *mean* concomitant variation. (And, if it did, *cadit quaestio*.) Hence the existence of the latter is not *ipso facto* a proof of the presence of the former. Again, I think it is almost certain that concomitant variation between A and B is not in fact a sufficient sign of the presence of a *direct* causal relation between the two. (I think it may perhaps be a sufficient sign of *either* a direct causal relation between A and B *or* of several causal relations which indirectly unite A and B through the medium of other terms C, D, etc.) So far I agree with the assumptions of the argument. But I cannot see the least reason to think that the other characteristic, which must be added to concomitant variation before we can be sure that A and B are causally connected, is a high degree of likeness between the two. One would like to know just how unlike two events may be before it becomes impossible to admit the existence of a causal relation between them. No one hesitates to hold that draughts and colds in the head are causally connected, although the two are extremely unlike each other. If the unlikeness of draughts and colds in the head does not prevent one from admitting a causal connexion between the two, why should the unlikeness of volitions and voluntary movements prevent one from holding that they are causally connected? To sum up. I am willing to admit that an adequate criterion of causal connexion needs some other relation between a pair of events beside concomitant variation; but I do not believe for a moment that this other relation is that of qualitative likeness.

This brings us to a rather more refined form of the argument against Interaction. It is said that, whenever we admit the existence of a causal relation between two events, these two events (to put it crudely) must also form parts of a single substantial whole. *E.g.*, all physical events are spatially related and form one great extended whole. And the mental events which would commonly be admitted to be causally connected are always events in a single mind. A mind is a substantial whole of a peculiar kind too. Now it is said that between bodily events and mental events there are no relations such as those which unite physical events in different parts of the same space or mental events in the history of the same mind. In the absence of such relations, binding mind and body into a single substantial whole, we cannot admit that bodily and mental events can be causally connected with each other, no matter how closely correlated their variations may be.

This is a much better argument than the argument about qualitative likeness and unlikeness. If we accept the premise that causal relations can subsist only between terms which form parts of a single substantial whole must we deny that mental and bodily events can be causally connected? I do not think that we must. (i) It is of course perfectly true that an organism and the mind which animates it do not form a physical whole, and that they do not form a mental whole; and these, no doubt, are the two kinds of substantial whole with which we are most familiar. But it does not follow that a mind and its organism do not form a substantial whole of *some* kind. There, plainly, is the extraordinary intimate union between the two which I have called "animation" of one by the other. Even if the mind be just what it seems to introspection, and the body be just what it seems to perception aided by the more precise methods of science, this seems to me to be enough to make a mind and its body a substantial whole. Even so extreme a dualist about Mind and Matter as Descartes occasionally suggests that a mind and its body together form a quasi-substance; and, although we may quarrel with the language of the very numerous philosophers who have said that the mind is "the form" of its body, we must admit that such language would never have seemed plausible unless a mind and its body together had formed something very much like a single substantial whole.

(ii) We must, moreover, admit the possibility that minds and mental events have properties and relations which do not reveal themselves to introspection, and that bodies and bodily events may have properties and relations which do not reveal themselves to perception or to physical and chemical experiment. In virtue of these properties and relations the two together may well form a single substantial whole of the kind which is alleged to be needed for causal interaction. Thus, if we accept the premise of the argument, we have no right to assert that mind and body *cannot* interact; but only the much more modest proposition that introspection and perception do not suffice to assure us that mind and body are so interrelated that they *can* interact.

(iii) We must further remember that the Two-sided Interactionist is under no obligation to hold that the *complete* conditions of any mental event are bodily or that the complete conditions of any bodily event are mental. He needs only to assert that some mental events include certain bodily events among their necessary conditions, and that some bodily events include certain mental events among their necessary conditions. If I am paralysed my volition may not move my arm; and, if I am hypnotised or intensely interested or frightened, a wound may not produce a painful sensation. Now, if the complete cause and the complete effect in all interaction include both a bodily and a mental factor, the two wholes will be related by the fact that the mental constituents belong to a single mind, that the bodily constituents belong to a single body, and that this mind animates this body. This amount of connexion should surely be enough to allow of causal interaction.

This will be the most appropriate place to deal with the contention that, in voluntary action, and there only, we are immediately acquainted with an instance of causal connexion. If this be true the controversy is of course settled at once in favour of the Inter-actionist. It is generally supposed that this view was refuted once and for all by Mr. Hume in his *Enquiry concerning Human Understanding* (Sect. VII, Part I). I should not care to assert that the doctrine in question is true; but I do think that it is plausible, and I am quite sure that Mr Hume's arguments do not refute it. Mr Hume uses three closely connected arguments. (1) The connexion between a successful volition and the resulting bodily movement is as mysterious and as little self-evident as the connexion between any other event and its effect. (2) We have to learn from experience which of our volitions will be effective and which will not. *E.g.*, we do not know, until we have tried, that we can voluntarily move our arms and cannot voluntarily move our livers. And again, if a man were suddenly paralysed, he would still expect to be able to move his arm voluntarily, and would be surprised when he found that it kept still in spite of his volition. (3) We have discovered that the immediate consequence of a volition is a change in our nerves and muscles, which most people know nothing about; and is not the movement of a limb, which most people believe to be its immediate and necessary consequence.

The second and third arguments are valid only against the contention that we know immediately that a volition to make a certain movement is the *sufficient* condition for the happening of that movement. They are quite irrelevant to the contention that we know immediately that the volition is a *necessary* condition for the happening of just that movement at just that time. No doubt many other conditions are also necessary, *e.g.*, that our nerves and muscles shall be in the right state; and these other necessary conditions can be discovered only by special investigation. Since our volitions to move our limbs are in fact followed in the vast majority of cases by the willed movement, and since the other necessary conditions are not very obvious, it is natural enough that we should think that we know immediately that our volition is the *sufficient* condition of the movement of our limbs. If we think so, we are certainly wrong; and Mr Hume's arguments prove that we are. But they prove nothing else. It does not follow that we are wrong in thinking that we know, without having to wait for the result, that the volition is a *necessary* condition of the movement.

It remains to consider the first argument. Is the connexion between cause and effect as mysterious and as little self-evident in the case of the voluntary production of bodily movement as in all other cases? If so, we must hold that the first time a baby wills to move its hand it is just as much surprised to find its hand moving as it would be to find its leg moving or its nurse bursting into flames. I do not profess to know anything about the infant mind; but it seems to me that this is a wildly paradoxical consequence, for which there is no evidence or likelihood. But there is no need to leave the matter there. It is perfectly plain that, in the case of volition and voluntary movement, there *is* a connexion between the cause and the effect which is not present in other cases of causation, and which does make it plausible to hold that in this one case the nature of the effect can be foreseen by merely reflecting on the nature of the cause. The peculiarity of a volition as a cause-factor is that it involves as an essential part of it the idea of the effect. To say that a person has a volition to move his arm involves saying that he has an idea of his arm (and not of his leg or his liver) and an idea of the position in which he wants his arm to be. It is simply silly in view of this fact to say that there is no closer connexion between the desire to move my arm and the movement of my arm than there is between this desire and the movement of my leg or my liver. We cannot detect any analogous connexion between cause and effect in causal transactions which we view wholly from outside, such as the movement of a billiard-ball by a cue. It is therefore by no means unreasonable to suggest that, in the one case of our own voluntary movements, we can see without waiting for the result that such and such a volition is a necessary condition of such and such a bodily movement.

It seems to me then that Mr Hume's arguments on this point are absolutely irrelevant, and that it may very well be true that in volition we positively know that our desire for such and such a bodily movement is a necessary (though not a sufficient) condition of the happening of just that movement at just that time. On the whole then I conclude that the philosophical arguments certainly do not disprove Two-sided Interaction, and that they do not even raise any strong presumption against it. And, while I am not prepared definitely to commit myself to the view that, in voluntary movement, we positively *know* that the mind acts on the body, I do think that this opinion is quite plausible when properly stated and that the arguments which have been brought against it are worthless. I pass therefore to the scientific arguments.

Scientific Arguments against Two-sided Interaction.

There are, so far as I know, two of these. One is supposed to be based on the physical principle of the Conservation of Energy, and on certain experiments which have been made on human bodies. The other is based on the close analogy which is said to exist between the structures of the physiological mechanism of reflex action and that of voluntary action. I will take them in turn.

(1) The Argument from Energy.
It will first be needful to state clearly what is asserted by the principle of the Conservation of Energy. It is found that, if we take certain material systems, *e.g.* a gun, a cartridge, and a bullet, there is a certain magnitude which keeps approximately constant throughout all their changes. This is called "Energy". When the gun has not been fired it and the bullet have no motion, but the explosive in the cartridge has great chemical energy. When it has been fired the bullet is moving very fast and has great energy of movement. The gun, though not moving fast in its recoil, has also great energy of movement because it is very massive. The gases produced by the explosion have some energy of movement and some heat-energy, but much less chemical energy than the unexploded charge had. These various kinds of energy can be measured in common units according to certain conventions. To an innocent mind there seems to be a good deal of "cooking" at this stage, *i.e.*, the conventions seem to be chosen and various kinds and amounts of concealed energy seem to be postulated in order to make the principle come out right at the end.

I do not propose to go into this in detail, for two reasons. In the first place, I think that the conventions adopted and the postulates made, though somewhat suggestive of the fraudulent company-promoter, can be justified by their coherence with certain experimental facts, and that they are not simply made *ad hoc*. Secondly, I shall show that the Conservation of Energy is absolutely irrelevant to the question at issue, so that it would be waste of time to treat it too seriously in the present connexion. Now it is found that the total energy of all kinds in this system, when measured according to these conventions, is approximately the same in amount though very differently distributed after the explosion and before it. If we had confined our attention to a part of this system and *its* energy this would not have been true. The bullet, *e.g.*, had no energy at all before the explosion and a great deal afterwards. A system like the bullet, the gun, and the charge, is called a "Conservative System"; the bullet alone, or the gun and the charge, would be called "Nonconservative Systems". A conservative system might therefore be defined as one whose total energy is redistributed, but not altered in amount, by changes that happen within it. Of course a given system might be conservative for some kinds of change and not for others.

So far we have merely defined a "Conservative System", and admitted that there are systems which, for some kinds of change at any rate, answer approximately to our definition. We can now state the Principle of the Conservation of Energy in terms of the conceptions just defined. The principle asserts that every material system is either itself conservative, or, if not, is part of a larger material system which is conservative. We may take it that there is good inductive evidence for this proposition.

The next thing to consider is the experiments on the human body. These tend to prove that a living body, with the air that it breathes and the food that it eats, forms a conservative system to a high degree of approximation. We can measure the chemical energy of the food given to a man, and that which enters his body in the form of Oxygen breathed in. We can also, with suitable apparatus, collect, measure and analyse the air breathed out, and thus find its chemical energy. Similarly, we can find the energy given out in bodily movement, in heat, and in excretion. It is alleged that, on the average, whatever the man may do, the energy of his bodily movements is exactly accounted for by the energy given to him in the form of food and of Oxygen. If you take the energy put in in food and Oxygen, and subtract the energy given out in waste-products, the balance is almost exactly equal to the energy put out in bodily movements. Such slight differences as are found are as often on one side as on the other, and are therefore probably due to unavoidable experimental errors. I do not propose to criticise the interpretation of these experiments in detail, because, as I shall show soon, they are completely irrelevant to the problem of whether mind and body interact. But there is just one point that I will make before passing on. It is perfectly clear that such experiments can tell us only what happens on the average over a long time. To know whether the balance was accurately kept at every moment we should have to kill the patient at each moment and analyse his body so as to find out the energy present then in the form of stored-up products. Obviously we cannot keep on killing the patient in order to analyse him, and then reviving him in order to go on with the experi-

ment. Thus it would seem that the results of the experiment are perfectly compatible with the presence of quite large excesses or defects in the total bodily energy at certain moments, provided that these average out over longer periods. However, I do not want to press this criticism; I am quite ready to accept for our present purpose the traditional interpretation which has been put on the experiments.

We now understand the physical principle and the experimental facts. The two together are generally supposed to prove that mind and body cannot interact. What precisely is the argument, and is it valid? I imagine that the argument, when fully stated, would run somewhat as follows: "I will to move my arm, and it moves. If the volition has anything to do with causing the movement we might expect energy to flow from my mind to my body. Thus the energy of my body ought to receive a measurable increase, not accounted for by the food that I eat and the Oxygen that I breathe. But no such physically unaccountable increases of bodily energy are found. Again, I tread on a tin-tack, and a painful sensation arises in my mind. If treading on the tack has anything to do with causing the sensation we might expect energy to flow from my body to my mind. Such energy would cease to be measurable. Thus there ought to be a noticeable decrease in my bodily energy, not balanced by increases anywhere in the physical system. But such unbalanced decreases of bodily energy are not found." So it is concluded that the volition has nothing to do with causing my arm to move, and that treading on the tack has nothing to do with causing the painful sensation.

Is this argument valid? In the first place it is important to notice that the conclusion does not follow from the Conservation of Energy and the experimental facts alone. The real premise is a tacitly assumed proposition about causation; viz., that, if a change in A has anything to do with causing a change in B, energy must leave A and flow into B. This is neither asserted nor entailed by the Conservation of Energy. What it says is that, if energy leaves A, it must appear in something else, say B; so that A and B together form a conservative system. Since the Conservation of Energy is not itself the premise for the argument against Interaction, and since it does not entail that premise, the evidence for the Conservation of Energy is not evidence against Interaction. Is there any independent evidence for the premise? We may admit that it *is* true of many, though not of all, transactions within the physical realm. But there are cases where it is not true even of purely physical transactions; and, even if it were always true in the physical realm, it would not follow that it must also be true of trans-physical causation. Take the case of a weight swinging at the end of a string hung from a fixed point. The total energy of the weight is the same at all positions in its course. It is thus a conservative system. But at every moment the direction and velocity of the weight's motion are different, and the proportion between its kinetic and its potential energy is constantly changing. These changes are caused by the pull of the string, which acts in a different direction at each different moment. The string makes no difference to the total energy of the weight; but it makes all the difference in the world to the particular way in which the weight moves and the particular way in which the energy is distributed between the potential and the kinetic forms. This is evident when we remember that the weight would begin to move in an utterly different course if at any moment the string were cut.

Here, then, we have a clear case even in the physical realm where a system is conservative but is continually acted on by something which affects its movement and the distribution of its total energy. Why should not the mind act on the body in this way? If you say that you can see how a string can affect the movement of a weight, but cannot see how a volition could affect the movement of a material particle, you have deserted the scientific argument and have gone back to one of the philosophical arguments. Your real difficulty is either that volitions are so very unlike movements, or that the volition is in your mind whilst the movement belongs to the physical realm. And we

have seen how little weight can be attached to these objections.

The fact is that, even in purely physical systems, the Conservation of Energy does not explain what changes will happen or when they will happen. It merely imposes a very general limiting condition on the changes that are possible. The fact that the system composed of bullet, charge, and gun, in our earlier example, is conservative does not tell us that the gun ever will be fired, or when it will be fired if at all, or what will cause it to go off, or what forms of energy will appear if and when it does go off. The change in this case is determined by pulling the trigger. Likewise the mere fact that the human body and its neighbourhood form a conservative system does not explain any particular bodily movement; it does not explain why I ever move at all, or why I sometimes write, sometimes walk, and sometimes swim. To explain the happening of these particular movements at certain times it seems to be essential to take into account the volitions which happen from time to time in my mind; just as it is essential to take the string into account to explain the particular behaviour of the weight, and to take the trigger into account to explain the going off of the gun at a certain moment. The difference between the gun-system and the body-system is that a little energy does flow into the former when the trigger is pulled, whilst it is alleged that none does so when a volition starts a bodily movement. But there is not even this amount of difference between the body-system and the swinging weight.

Thus the argument from energy has no tendency to disprove Two-sided Interaction. It has gained a spurious authority from the august name of the Conservation of Energy. But this impressive principle proves to have nothing to do with the case. And the real premise of the argument is not self-evident, and is not universally true even in purely intra-physical transactions. In the end this scientific argument has to lean on the old philosophic arguments; and we have seen that these are but bruised reeds. Nevertheless, the facts brought forward by the argument from energy do throw some light on the *nature* of the interaction between mind and body, assuming this to happen. They do suggest that all the energy of our bodily actions comes out of and goes back into the physical world, and that minds neither add energy to nor abstract it from the latter. What they do, if they do anything, is to determine that at a given moment so much energy shall change from the chemical form to the form of bodily movement; and they determine this, so far as we can see, without altering the total amount of energy in the physical world.

(2) The Argument from the Structure of the Nervous System.

There are purely reflex actions, like sneezing and blinking, in which there is no reason to suppose that the mind plays any essential part. Now we know the nervous structure which is used in such acts as these. A stimulus is given to the outer end of an afferent nerve; some change or other runs up this nerve, crosses a synapsis between this and an afferent nerve, travels down the latter to a muscle, causes the muscle to contract, and so produces a bodily movement. There seems no reason to believe that the mind plays any essential part in this process. The process may be irreducibly vital, and not merely physico-chemical; but there seems no need to assume anything more than this. Now it is said that the whole nervous system is simply an immense complication of interconnected nervous arcs. The result is that a change which travels inwards has an immense number of alternative paths by which it may travel outwards. Thus the reaction to a given stimulus is no longer one definite movement, as in the simple reflex. Almost any movement may follow any stimulus according to the path which the afferent disturbance happens to take. This path will depend on the relative resistance of the various synapses at the time. Now a variable response to the same stimulus is characteristic of deliberate as opposed to reflex action.

These are the facts. The argument based on them runs as follows. It is admitted that the mind has nothing to do with the causation of purely reflex actions. But the nervous structure and the nervous processes involved in deliberate action do not differ in kind from those involved in reflex action; they differ only in degree of complexity. The variability which characterises deliberate action is fully explained by the variety of alternative paths and the variable resistances of the synapses. So it is unreasonable to suppose that the mind has any more to do with causing deliberate actions than it has to do with causing reflex actions.

I think that this argument is invalid. In the first place I am pretty sure that the persons who use it have before their imagination a kind of picture of how mind and body must interact if they interact at all. They find that the facts do not answer to this picture, and so they conclude that there is no interaction. The picture is of the following kind. They think of the mind as sitting somewhere in a hole in the brain, surrounded by telephones. And they think of the afferent disturbance as coming to an end at one of these telephones and there affecting the mind. The mind is then supposed to respond by sending an afferent impulse down another of these telephones. As no such hole, with afferent nerves stopping at its walls and afferent nerves starting from them, can be found, they conclude that the mind can play no part in the transaction. But another alternative is that this picture of how the mind must act if it acts at all is wrong. To put it shortly, the mistake is to confuse a gap in an explanation with a spatio-temporal gap, and to argue from the absence of the latter to the absence of the former.

The Interactionist's contention is simply that there is a gap in any purely physiological explanation of deliberate action; *i.e.,* that all such explanations fail to account completely for the facts because they leave out one necessary condition. It does not follow in the least that there must be a spatio-temporal breach of continuity in the physiological conditions, and that the missing condition must fill this gap in the way in which the movement of a wire fills the spatio-temporal interval between the pulling of a bell-handle and the ringing of a distant bell. To assume this is to make the mind a kind of physical object, and to make its action a kind of mechanical action. Really, the mind and its actions are not literally in space at all, and the time which is occupied by the mental even is no doubt *also* occupied by some part of the physiological process. Thus I am inclined to think that much of the force which this argument actually exercises on many people is simply due to the presupposition about the *modus operandi* of interaction, and that it is greatly weakened when this presupposition is shown to be a mere prejudice due to our limited power of envisaging unfamiliar alternative possibilities.

We can, however, make more detailed objections to the argument than this. There is a clear introspective difference between the mental accompaniment of voluntary action and that of reflex action. What goes on in our minds when we decide with difficulty to get out of a hot bath on a cold morning is obviously extremely different from what goes on in our minds when we sniff pepper and sneeze. And the difference is qualitative; it is not a mere difference of complexity. This difference has to be explained somehow; and the theory under discussion gives no plausible explanation of it. The ordinary view that, in the latter case, the mind is not acting on the body at all; whilst, in the former, it is acting on the body in a specific way, does at least make the introspective difference between the two intelligible.

Again, whilst it is true that deliberate action differs from reflex action in its greater variability of response to the same stimulus, this is certainly not the whole or the most important part of the difference between them. The really important difference is that, in deliberate action, the response is varied *appropriately* to meet the special circumstances which are supposed to exist at the time or are expected to arise later; whilst reflex action is not varied in this way, but is blind and almost mechanical. The complexity of the nervous system explains the *possi-bility* of variation; it does not in the least explain why the alternative which actually takes place should as a rule be appropriate and not merely haphazard. And so again it seems as if some factor were in operation in deliberate action which is not present in reflex action; and it is reasonable to suppose that this factor is the volition in the mind.

It seems to me that this second scientific argument has no tendency to disprove interaction; but that the facts which it brings forward do tend to suggest the particular form which interaction probably takes if it happens at all. They suggest that what the mind does to the body in voluntary action, if it does anything, is to lower the resistance of certain synapses and to raise that of others. The result is that the nervous current follows such a course as to produce the particular movement which the mind judges to be appropriate at the time. On such a view the difference between reflex, habitual, and deliberate actions for the present purpose becomes fairly plain. In pure reflexes the mind cannot voluntarily affect the resistance of the synapses concerned, and so the action takes place in spite of it. In habitual action it deliberately refrains from interfering with the resistance of the synapses, and so the action goes on like a complicated reflex. But it *can* affect these resistances if it wishes, though often only with difficulty; and it is ready to do so if it judges this to be expedient. Finally, it may lose the power altogether. This would be what happens when a person becomes a slave to some habit, such as drug-taking.

I conclude that, at the level of enlightened common-sense at which the ordinary discussion of Interaction moves, no good reason has been produced for doubting that the mind acts on the body in volition, and that the body acts on the mind in sensation. The philosophic arguments are quite inconclusive; and the scientific arguments, when properly understood, are quite compatible with Two-sided Interaction. At most they suggest certain conclusions as to the form which interaction probably takes if it happens at all.

The Traditional Problem of Body and Mind

Difficulties in the Denial of Interaction

I propose now to consider some of the difficulties which would attend the denial of Interaction, still keeping the discussion at the same common-sense level. If a man denies the action of body on mind he is at once in trouble over the causation of new sensations. Suppose that I suddenly tread on an unsuspected tin-tack. A new sensation suddenly comes into my mind. This is an event, and presumably it has some cause. Now, however carefully I introspect and retrospect, I can find no other mental event which is adequate to account for the fact that just that sensation has arisen at just that moment. If I reject the common-sense view that treading on the tack is an essential part of the cause of the sensation, I must suppose either that it is uncaused, or that it is caused by other events in my mind which I cannot discover by introspection or retrospection, or that it is caused telepathically by other finite minds or by God. Now enquiry of my neighbours would show that it is not caused telepathically by any event in their minds which they can introspect or remember. Thus anyone who denies the action of body on mind, and admits that sensations have causes, must postulate either (a) immense numbers of unobservable states in his own mind; or (b) as many unobservable states in his neighbours' minds, together with telepathic action; or (c) some non-human spirit together with telepathic action. I must confess that the difficulties which have been alleged against the action of body on mind seem to be mild compared with those of the alternative hypotheses which are involved in the denial of such action.

The difficulties which are involved in the denial of the action of mind on body are at first sight equally great; but I do not think that they turn out to be so serious as those which are involved in denying the action of body on mind. The *prima facie* difficulty is this. The world contains many obviously artificial objects, such as books, bridges, clothes, etc. We know that, if we go far

enough back in the history of their production, we always do in fact come on the actions of some human body. And the minds connected with these bodies did design the objects in question, did will to produce them, and did believe that they were initiating and guiding the physical process by means of these designs and volitions. If it be true that the mind does not act on the body, it follows that the designs and volitions in the agents' minds did not in fact play any part in the production of books, bridges, clothes, etc. This appears highly paradoxical. And it is an easy step from it to say that anyone who denies the action of mind on body must admit that books, bridges, and other such objects *could* have been produced even though there had been no minds, no thought of these objects and no desire for them. This consequence seems manifestly absurd to common-sense, and it might be argued that it reflects its absurdity back on the theory which entails it.

The man who denies that mind can act on body might deal with this difficulty in two ways: (1) He might deny that the conclusion *is* intrinsically absurd. He might say that human bodies are extraordinarily complex physical objects, which probably obey irreducible laws of their own, and that we really do not know enough about them to set limits to what their unaided powers could accomplish. This is the line which Spinoza took. The conclusion, it would be argued, *seems* absurd only because the state of affairs which it contemplates is so very unfamiliar. We find it difficult to imagine a body like ours without a mind like ours; but, if we could get over this defect in our powers of imagination, we might have no difficulty in admitting that such a body could do all the things which our bodies do. I think it must be admitted that the difficulty is not so great as that which is involved in denying the action of body on mind. There we had to postulate *ad hoc* utterly unfamiliar entities and modes of action; here it is not certain that we should have to do this.

(2) The other line of argument would be to say that the alleged consequence does not necessarily follow from denying the action

of mind on body. I assume that both parties admit that causation is something more than mere *de facto* regularity of sequence and concomitance. If they do not, of course the whole controversy between them becomes futile; for there will certainly be causation between mind and body and between body and mind, in the only sense in which there is causation anywhere. This being presupposed, the following kind of answer is logically possible. When I say that B could not have happened unless A had happened, there are two alternative possibilities. (*a*) A may itself be an indispensable link in any chain of causes which ends up with B. (*b*) A may not itself be a link in any chain of causation which ends up with B. But there may be an indispensable link α in any such chain of causation, and A may be a necessary accompaniment or sequent of α. These two possibilities may be illustrated by diagrams. (*a*) is represented by the figure below:—

$$A_0 \quad A \quad A_1 \quad A_2 \quad B$$
$$. \longrightarrow . \longrightarrow . \longrightarrow . \longrightarrow .$$

The two forms of (*b*) are represented by the two figures below:—

$$\begin{array}{ccccc} & A & & & \\ A_0 & \uparrow & A_1 & A_2 & B \\ . \longrightarrow & . \longrightarrow & . \longrightarrow & . \longrightarrow & . \\ & \alpha & & & \end{array}$$

$$\text{and} \quad \begin{array}{ccccc} & .A & & & \\ A_0 & \nearrow A_1 & A_2 & B \\ . \longrightarrow . \longrightarrow & . \longrightarrow & . \longrightarrow & . \\ & \alpha & & & \end{array}$$

Evidently, if B cannot happen unless α precedes, and if α cannot happen without A accompanying or immediately following it, B will not be able to happen unless A precedes it. And yet A will have had no part in causing B. It will be noticed that, on this view, α has a complex effect AA_1, of which a certain part, viz., A_1 is sufficient by itself to produce A_2 and ultimately B. Let us apply this abstract possibility to our present position. Suppose that B is some artificial object, like a book or a bridge. If we admit that this could not have come into existence unless a certain design and volition had existed in a certain mind, we could interpret the facts in two ways. (*a*) We could hold that the design and volition are themselves an indispensable link in the chain of causation which ends in the production of a bridge or a book. This is the common view, and it requires us to admit the action of mind on body. (*b*) We might hold that the design and the volition are not themselves a link in the chain of causation which ends in the production of the artificial object; but that they are a necessary accompaniment or sequent of something which *is* an indispensable link in this chain of causation. On this view the chain consists wholly of physical events; but one of these physical events (viz., some event in the brain) has a complex consequent. One part of this consequent is purely physical, and leads by purely physical causation to the ultimate production of a bridge or a book. The other is purely mental, and consists of a certain design and volition in the mind which animates the human body concerned. If this has any consequences they are purely mental. Each part of this complex consequent follows with equal necessity; this particular brain-state could no more have existed without such and such a mental state accompanying or following it than it could have existed without such and such a bodily movement following it. If we are willing to take some such view as this, we can admit that certain objects could not have existed unless there had been designs of them and desires for them; and yet we could consistently deny that these desires and designs have any effect on the movements of our bodies.

It seems to me then that the doctrine which I will call "One-sided Action of Body on Mind" is logically possible; *i.e.*, a theory which accepts the action of body on mind but denies the action of mind on body. But I do not see the least reason to accept it, since I see no reason to deny that mind acts on body in volition. One-sided Action has, I think, generally been held in the special form called "Epiphenomenalism." I take this doctrine to consist of the following four propositions: (1) Certain bodily events cause certain mental events. (2) No mental event plays any part in the causation of any bodily event. (3) No mental event plays any part in the causation of any other mental event. Consequently (4) all mental events are caused by bodily events and by them only. Thus Epiphenomenalism is just One-sided Action of Body on Mind, together with a special theory about the nature and structure of mind. This special theory does not call for discussion here, where I am dealing only with the relations between minds and bodies, and am not concerned with a detailed analysis of mind.

Arguments in Favour of Interaction

The only arguments *for* One-sided Action of Body on Mind or for Parallelism are the arguments *against* Two-sided Interaction; and these, as we have seen, are worthless. Are there any arguments in favour of Two-sided Interaction? I have incidentally given two which seem to me to have considerable weight. In favour of the action of mind on body is the fact that we seem to be immediately aware of a causal relation when we voluntarily try to produce a bodily movement, and that the arguments to show that this cannot be true are invalid. In favour of the action of body on mind are the insuperable difficulties which I have pointed out in accounting for the happening of new sensations on any other hypothesis. There are, however, two other arguments which have often been thought to prove the action of mind on body. These are (1) an evolutionary argument, first used, I believe, by William James; and (2) the famous "telegram argument." They both seem to me to be quite obviously invalid.

(1) The evolutionary argument runs as follows: It is a fact, which is admitted by persons who deny Two-sided Interaction, that minds increase in complexity and power with the growth in complexity of the brain and nervous system. Now, if the mind makes no difference to the actions of the body, this development on the mental side is quite unintelligible from the point of view

of natural selection. Let us imagine two animals whose brains and nervous systems were of the same degree of complexity; and suppose, if possible, that one had a mind and the other had none. If the mind makes no difference to the behavior of the body the chance of survival and of leaving descendants will clearly be the same for the two animals. Therefore natural selection will have no tendency to favour the evolution of mind which has actually taken place. I do not think that there is anything in this argument. Natural selection is a purely negative process; it simply tends to eliminate individuals and species which have variations unfavourable to survival. Now, by hypothesis, the possession of a mind is not *unfavourable* to survival; it simply makes no difference. Now it may be that the existence of a mind of such and such a kind is an inevitable consequence of the existence of a brain and nervous system of such and such a degree of complexity. Indeed we have seen that some such view is essential if the opponent of Two-sided Interaction is to answer the common-sense objection that artificial objects could not have existed unless there had been a mind which designed and desired them. On this hypothesis there is no need to invoke natural selection twice over, once to explain the evolution of the brain and nervous system, and once to explain the evolution of the mind. If natural selection will account for the evolution of the brain and nervous system, the evolution of the mind will follow inevitably, even though it adds nothing to the survival-value of the organism. The plain fact is that natural selection does not account for the origin or for the growth in complexity of anything whatever; and therefore it is no objection to any particular theory of the relations of mind and body that, if it were true, natural selection would not explain the origin and development of mind.

(2) The "telegram argument" is as follows: Suppose there were two telegrams, one saying "Our son has been killed", and the other saying: "Your son has been killed". And suppose that one or other of them was delivered to a parent whose son

was away from home. As physical stimuli they are obviously extremely alike, since they differ only in the fact that the letter "Y" is present in one and absent in the other. Yet we know that the reaction of the person who received the telegram might be very different according to which one he received. This is supposed to show that the reactions of the body cannot be wholly accounted for by bodily causes, and that the mind must intervene causally in some cases. Now I have very little doubt that the mind does play a part in determining the action of the recipient of the telegram; but I do not see why this argument should prove it to a person who doubted or denied it. If two very similar stimuli are followed by two very different results, we are no doubt justified in concluding that these stimuli are not the complete causes of the reactions which follow them. But of course it would be admitted by every one that the receipt of the telegram is not the complete cause of the recipient's reaction. We all know that his brain and nervous system play an essential part in any reaction that he may make to the stimulus. The question then is whether the minute structure of his brain and nervous system, including in this the supposed traces left by past stimuli and past reactions, is not enough to account for the great difference in his behaviour on receiving two very similar stimuli. Two keys may be very much alike, but one may fit a certain lock and the other may not. And, if the lock be connected with the trigger of a loaded gun, the results of "stimulating" the system with one or other of the two keys will be extremely different. We know that the brain and nervous system are very complex, and we commonly suppose that they contain more or less permanent traces and linkages due to past stimuli and reactions. If this be granted, it is obvious that two very similar stimuli may produce very different results, simply because one fits in with the internal structure of the brain and nervous system whilst the other does not. And I do not see how we can be sure that anything more is needed to account for the mere difference of reaction adduced by the "telegram argument."

Materialism*

J. J. C. Smart

First of all let me try to explain what I mean by "materialism." I shall then go on to try to defend the doctrine.[1] By "materialism" I mean the theory that there is nothing in the world over and above those entities which are postulated by physics (or, of course, those entities which will be postulated by future and more adequate physical theories). Thus I do not hold materialism to be wedded to the billiard-ball physics of the nineteenth century. The less visualizable particles of modern physics count as matter. Note that energy counts as matter for my purposes: indeed in modern physics energy and matter are not sharply distinguishable. Nor do I hold that materialism implies determinism. If physics is indeterministic on the micro-level, so must be the materialist's theory. I regard materialism as compatible with a wide range of conceptions of the nature of matter and energy. For example, if matter and energy consist of regions of special curvature of an absolute space-time, with "worm holes" and what not,[2] this is still compatible with materialism: we can still argue that in the last resort the world is made up entirely of the ultimate entities of physics, namely space-time points.

It will be seen that my conception of materialism is wider than that of Bertrand Russell in his Introduction to Lange's *History of Materialism*.[3] But my definition will in some respects be narrower than those of some who have called themselves "materialists." I wish to lay down that it is incompatible with materialism that there should be any irreducibly "emergent" laws or properties, say in biology or psychology. According to the view I propose to defend, there are no irreducible laws or properties in biology, any more than there are in electronics. Given the "natural history" of a superheterodyne (its wiring diagram), a physicist is able to explain, using only laws of physics, its mode of behavior and its properties (for example, the property of being able to receive such and such a radio station which broadcasts on 25 megacycles). Just as electronics gives the physical explanation of the workings of superheterodynes, etc., so biology gives (or approximates to giving) physical and chemical explanations of the workings of organisms or parts of organisms. The biologist needs natural history just as the engineer needs wiring diagrams, but neither needs nonphysical laws.[4]

It will now become clear why I define materialism in the way I have done above. I am concerned to deny that in the world there are nonphysical entities and nonphysical laws. In particular I wish to deny the doctrine of psychophysical dualism.[5] (I also want to deny any theory of "emergent properties," since irreducibly nonphysical properties are just about as repugnant to me as are irreducibly nonphysical entities.)

Popular theologians sometimes argue against materialism by saying that "you can't put love in a test tube." Well you can't put a gravitational field in a test tube (except in some rather strained sense of these words), but there is nothing incompatible with materialism, as I have defined it, in the notion of a gravitational field.

Similarly, even though love may elude test tubes, it does not elude materialistic metaphysics, since it can be analyzed as a pattern of bodily behavior or, perhaps better, as the internal state of the human organism that accounts for this behavior. (A dualist who analyzes love as an internal state will perhaps say that it is a soul state, whereas the materialist will say that it is a brain state. It seems to me that much of our ordinary language about the mental is neither dualistic nor materialistic but is neutral between the two. Thus, to say that a locution is not materialistic is not to say that it is immaterialistic.)

But what about consciousness? Can we interpret the having of an after-image or of a painful sensation as something material, namely, a brain state or brain process? We seem to be immediately aware of pains and after-images, and we seem to be immediately aware of them as something different from a neurophysiological state or process. For example, the after-image may be green speckled with red, whereas the neurophysiologist looking into our brains would be unlikely to see something green speckled with red. However, if we object to materialism in this way we are victims of a confusion which U. T. Place has called "the phenomenological fallacy."[6] To say that an image or

sense datum is green is not to say that the conscious experience of having the image or sense datum is green. It is to say that it is the sort of experience we have when in normal conditions we look at a green apple, for example. Apples and unripe bananas can be green, but not the experiences of seeing them. An image or a sense datum can be green in a derivative sense, but this need not cause any worry, because, on the view I am defending, images and sense data are not constituents of the world, though the processes of having an image or a sense datum are actual processes in the world. The experience of having a green sense datum is not itself green; it is a process occurring in grey matter. The world contains plumbers, but does not contain the average plumber; it also contains the having of a sense datum, but does not contain the sense datum.

It may be objected that, in admitting that apples and unripe bananas can be green, I have admitted colors as emergent properties, not reducible within a physicalist scheme of thought. For a reply to this objection I must, for lack of space, refer to my article "Colours," *Philosophy*, 36 (1961): 128–142. Here colors are elucidated in terms of the discriminatory reactions of normal percipients, and the notion of a normal color percipient is defined without recourse to the notion of color. Color classifications are elucidated as classifications in terms of the highly idiosyncratic discriminatory reactions of a complex neurophysiological mechanism. It is no wonder that these classifications do not correspond to anything simple in physics. (There is no one-one correlation between color and wave length, since infinitely many different mixtures of wave lengths correspond to the same color, *i.e.*, produce the same discriminatory reaction in a normal percipient.)

When we report that a lemon is yellow we are reacting to the lemon. But when we report that the lemon looks yellow we are reacting to our own internal state. When I say, "it looks to me that there is a yellow lemon" I am saying, roughly, that what is going on in me is like what goes on in me when there really is a yellow lemon in front of me, my eyes are open, the light is daylight, and so on. That is, our talk of immediate experience is derivative from our talk about the external world. Furthermore, since our talk of immediate experience is in terms of a typical stimulus situation (and in the case of some words for aches and pains and the like it may, as we shall see, be in terms of some typical *response* situation) we can see that our talk of immediate experience is itself neutral between materialism and dualism. It reports our internal goings on as like or unlike what internally goes on in typical situations, but the dualist would construe these goings on as goings on in an immaterial substance, whereas the materialist would construe these goings on as taking place inside our skulls.

Our talk about immediate experiences is derivative from our language of physical objects. This is so even with much of our language of bodily sensations and aches and pains. A stabbing pain is the sort of going on which is like what goes on when a pin is stuck into you. (Trivially, you also have a stabbing pain when a pin is in fact stuck into you, for in this essay I am using 'like' in a sense in which a thing is like itself. That I am using 'like' in this sense can be seen by reflecting on what the analysis of the last paragraph would imply in the case of having a veridical sense datum of a yellow lemon.) However, some of our sensation words do not seem to work like 'stabbing pain.' Consider 'ache'. Perhaps here the reference to a typical stimulus situation should be replaced by a reference to a typical response situation. Instead of "what is going on in me is like what goes on in me when a yellow lemon is before me" we could have some such thing as "what is going on in me is like what goes on in me when I groan, yelp, etc." In any case it is not inconsistent with the present view to suppose that, when children have got the idea of referring to their own internal goings on as like or unlike what goes on in some typical situation, they can then in some cases go on simply to classify them as like or unlike one another. (All the aches are more like one another than any of them are to any of the itches, for example.) In other words, they may be able to report some of their internal goings on as like or unlike one another, and thus to report these goings on, even when their language is not tied closely to stimulus or response situations. Notice that I am still denying that we introspect any nonphysical property such as *achiness*. To say that a process is an ache is simply to classify it with other processes that are felt to be like it, and this class of processes constitutes the aches.

An important objection is now sure to be made. It will be said that anything is like anything else in *some* respect or other. So how can our sensation reports be classifications in terms of likenesses and unlikenesses alone? And if you say that they are likenesses or unlikenesses in virtue of properties that are or are not held in common, will these properties not have to be properties (e.g., *achiness*) that are beyond the conceptual resources of a physicalist theory?

Looked at in the abstract this argument appears impressive, but it becomes less persuasive when we think out, in terms of bits of cybernetic hardware, what it is to recognize likenesses and unlikenesses. Thus, consider a machine for recognizing likenesses and unlikenesses between members of a set of round discs, square discs, and triangular discs. It would probably be easier to construct a machine that just told us (on a tape, say) "like" or "unlike" than it would be to construct a machine that told us wherein the likenesses consisted, whether in roundness, squareness, or triangularity. Moreover, we may agree that everything is like everything else and still say that some things are much liker than others. Consider the notion of following a rule, which plays so important a part in Wittgenstein's philosophy.[7] Suppose that one man continues the sequence 0, 1, 2, 3, . . . up to 1000 and then continues 1001, 1002, 1003, 1004, ... Here we certainly feel like saying that he goes on doing the same thing after 1000 as he did before 1000. Now suppose that a second man goes 0, 1, 2, 3, . . . 1000, 1002, 1004, . . . , and a third man goes 0, 1, 2, 3, . . . 1000, 1001, 1002, 1003, 1005, 1007, 1013, ... According to Wittgenstein's account, it would seem that the second and third men also could say that they were doing the same thing after 1000 as they did up to 1000. Indeed there are rules to cover these cases too, for example, "add one up to 1000 and then add twos until 2000, threes until 3000, and so on" and "add ones up to 1001 and then go up by prime numbers." These rules are more complicated than the original one; moreover, like even the first rule, they could be divergently interpreted. We can concede Wittgenstein all this. Nevertheless, it does not follow that there is no sense in which some sequences are objectively more like one another than are others. It will not do to say that the continuations of the sequence 0, 1, 2, 3, . . . that go 1002, 1004, 1006, . . . or 1001, 1002, 1003, 1005, 1007, 1013, . . . are as like what goes before 1000 as is the continuation 1001, 1002, 1003,. . . . This can be seen if we reflect that a machine built to churn out the symbols of the sequence 0, 1, 2, 3, . . . 1001, 1002, 1003, 1004, . . . could be a simpler machine (i.e., could contain fewer parts) than one built to churn out either of the other two sequences. This indicates that absolute likeness and unlikeness is something objective, even though it is also a matter of degree.

I conclude, therefore, that it is by no means empty to say that some of our internal processes are like or unlike one another, even though we do not indicate in what respect they are like. This makes our reports of immediate experience quite open or "topic neutral," to use a phrase of Ryle's. They do not commit us either to materialism or to dualism, but they are quite *compatible* with the hypothesis which I wish to assert: that the internal goings on in question are brain processes.[8]

It may be said: But on your view you can have no criterion of correctness when you report a sensation simply as *like* one you had before (cf. Wittgenstein, *Investigations*, §258). But must I have such a criterion? On my view my internal mechanism is just built so that I react in the way I do. And I may *in fact* react correctly, though I have no criterion for saying that my reaction is correct. That is, when I report my internal processes as alike, it may always, or at least

mostly, be the case that they *are* alike. Indeed, on the basis of common-sense psychology, scientific psychology, or perhaps (in the future) electroencephalography, we may gain indirect evidence that our reactions are correct in reporting likenesses of internal processes. A slot machine that puts out a bar of chocolate only when a shilling (or a coin indistinguishable in size and shape from a shilling) is inserted into it certainly has no criterion for the size and shape. But its reactions are veridical: it will not give you a bar of chocolate if you put a sixpence into it.

It is important to realize that, if the view that I wish to defend is correct, conscious experiences must be processes involving millions of neurons, and so their important likenesses and unlikenesses to one another may well be statistical in nature. As P. K. Feyerabend[9] has pointed out, this shows how a sensation (or a brain process) can possess such properties as of being clear or confused (well-defined or ill-defined), as well as why a sensation seems to be a simple entity in a way in which the details of a brain process are not simple. Brain processes can well have statistical properties that cannot even meaningfully be asserted of individual neurons, still less of individual molecules or atoms. Feyerabend compares this case with that of the density of a fluid, the notion of which can be meaningfully applied only to a large statistically homogenous ensemble of particles and which has no application in the case of a single particle or small group of particles. Notice also that the materialist hypothesis does not imply that there is anything like consciousness in a single atom, or even in a single neuron for that matter. A conscious experience is a very complex process involving vast numbers of neurons. It is a process, not a stuff. The materialist does not need to accept Vogt's crude and preposterous idea that the brain secretes thought much as the liver secretes bile.[10] We can certainly agree with Wittgenstein thus far: that thought is not a *stuff*. Indeed this side of Wittgenstein's thought is particularly attractive: his elucidation of mental concepts in terms of bodily behavior would, if it were adequate, be perfectly compatible with the sort of physicalist world view which, for reasons of scientific plausibility, it seems to me necessary to defend. (I differ from Wittgenstein since I wish to elucidate thought as inner process and to keep my hypothesis compatible with a physicalist viewpoint by identifying such inner processes with brain processes.) The trouble with Wittgenstein is that he is too operationalistic.[11]

This can perhaps be brought out by considering something Wittgenstein says in §293 of his *Philosophical Investigations*. He there argues against the tendency to construe "the grammar of the expression of sensation on the model of 'object and name'." He says that if we try to do so "the object drops out of consideration as irrelevant." I imagine that he would argue equally strongly against the model (more relevant to the present issue) of *process* and name. I am not sure how seriously we are to take the word 'name' here. Surely all we need are predicates, e.g., ". . . is a pain." (Wittgenstein is considering the case of someone who says "here is a pain" or "this is a pain.") Indeed, in a Quinean language there would be no names at all. Suppose, therefore, that we construe the word 'name' rather more widely, so that we can say, for example, that 'electron' is a name of electrons. (More properly we should say that ". . . is an electron" is a predicate true of anything which is an electron.) Now let us apply Wittgenstein's argument of "the beetle in the box" to electrons (*Investigations*, §293). A person can see only the beetle in his own box (just as, on the view Wittgenstein is attacking, my pain is something of which only I can be acquainted), but the case with electrons is even worse, since no one at all can literally see an electron. We know of electrons only through their observable effects on macroscopic bodies. Thus Wittgenstein's reasons for saying that pains are not objects would be even stronger reasons for saying that electrons are not objects either.[12]

I have no doubt that Wittgenstein would have been unmoved by this last consideration. For I think he would have been likely to say that electrons are grammatical fictions and that electrons must be understood in terms of galvanometers, etc., just as pains are to be understood in terms of groans, etc. In reply to the question, "Are you not really a behaviourist in disguise? Aren't you at bottom really saying that everything except human behavior is a fiction?", he replies: "If I do speak of a fiction it is of a *grammatical fiction*" (§307). Certainly, if a philosopher says that pains are grammatical fictions, he is not denying that there are pains. Nevertheless he is denying that pains are anything (to use John Wisdom's useful expression) "over and above" pain behavior. Such a philosopher is not a crude behaviorist who denies that there are pains, but surely he can well be said to be a behaviorist of a more sophisticated sort. Why should he be shy of admitting it? Now the very same reasons which lead Wittgenstein to go behaviorist about pains would surely lead him to go instrumentalist (in an analogously sophisticated way) about electrons.

This is not the place to contest instrumentalism about the theoretical entities of physics. But I wish to put forward one consideration which will be followed by an analogous one in the case of sensations. Can we conceive of a universe consisting only of a swarm of electrons, protons, neutrons, etc., that have never and never will come together as constituents of macroscopic objects? It would seem that we can, even though the supposition might be inconsistent with certain cosmological theories, and it might become inconsistent with physics itself, if physics one day becomes united with cosmology in a unified theory. On this supposition, then, there could be electrons, protons, etc., but no macroscopic objects.[13] On the other hand, there could not be the average plumber without plumbers, or nations without nationals. (In arguing thus I am indebted to C. B. Martin.) It is therefore not clear in what sense electrons and protons could be said to be grammatical fictions. Now let us ask analogously in what sense Wittgenstein could allow that pain experiences are grammatical fictions. It is not evident that there is any clear sense.

Consider this example.[14] In some future

state of physiological technology we might be able to keep a human brain alive *in vitro*. Leaving the question of the morality of such an experiment to one side, let us suppose that the experiment is done. By suitable electrodes inserted into appropriate parts of this brain we get it to have the illusion of perceiving things and also to have pains, and feelings of moving its nonexistent limbs, and so on. (This brain might even be able to think verbally, for it might have learned a language before it was put *in vitro*, or else, by suitable signals from our electrodes, we might even give it the illusion of learning a language in the normal way.) Here we have the analogue to the case of the world of electrons, etc., but with no macroscopic objects. In the present case we have mental experiences, but no behaviour. This brings out vividly that what is important in psychology is what goes on in the central nervous system, not what goes on in the face, larynx, and limbs. It can of course be agreed that what goes on in the face, larynx, and limbs provides observational data whereby the psychologist can postulate what goes on in the central nervous system. If experiences are postulated on the basis of behavior, instead of being grammatical fictions out of behavior, then we can deal with the case of the brain *in vitro*. For whereas grammatical fictions are nothing over and above what they are fictions out of, entities such as are postulated in an hypothesis could still exist even if there had been no possible evidence for them. There could be electrons even if there were no macroscopic bodies, and there could be processes in the central nervous system even if there were no attached body and, hence, no bodily behavior. Of course I do not wish to deny that in the case of the brain *in vitro* we could have evidence other than that of bodily behavior: electroencephalographic evidence, for example.[15]

It is true that Wittgenstein is arguing against someone who says that he knows what pain is only from his own case. I am not such a person. I want to say that sensations are postulated processes in other people and *also* processes which, when they occur in ourselves, we can report as like or unlike one another. If we cannot look at the beetle in another person's box, that does not matter; no one can look into any box at all when in the simile the beetle is taken to be not a pain but an electron. We have very good indirect evidence for asserting that all electrons are like one another and unlike, say, protons.

I have suggested that, in spite of his own disclaimer, Wittgenstein is in fact a sort of behaviorist. I have also suggested that such a behaviorism is no more tenable than is an analogous instrumentalism about the theoretical entities of physics. Nevertheless, Wittgenstein's philosophy of mind, if it could be accepted, would be very attractive. For, like the analysis that I am advocating, it would be compatible with materialism: it would not land us with emergent properties or nonphysical entities. But even a disguised or Wittgensteinian behaviorism falls down because, as I have argued, it cannot account for the overriding importance of the central nervous system: the example of the brain *in vitro* shows that what is essential to a pain is what goes on in the brain, not what goes on in the arms or legs or larynx or mouth. Furthermore, it is hard to accept the view that so-called "reports" of inner experience are to be construed as surrogates for behavior, as if a report of a pain were a wince-substitute. To say that these behavior surrogates are properly called "reports" in ordinary language does little to mitigate the paradoxical nature of the theory.

It may be asked why I should demand of a tenable philosophy of mind that it should be compatible with materialism, in the sense in which I have defined it. One reason is as follows. How could a nonphysical property or entity suddenly arise in the course of animal evolution? A change in a gene is a change in a complex molecule which causes a change in the biochemistry of the cell. This may lead to changes in the shape or organization of the developing embryo. But what sort of chemical process could lead to the springing into existence of something nonphysical? No enzyme can catalyze the production of a spook! Perhaps it will be said that the nonphysical comes into existence as a by-product: that whenever there is a certain complex physical structure, then, by an irreducible extraphysical law, there is also a nonphysical entity. Such laws would be quite outside normal scientific conceptions and quite inexplicable: they would be, in Herbert Feigl's phrase, "nomological danglers."[16] To say the very least, we can vastly simplify our cosmological outlook if we can defend a materialistic philosophy of mind.

In defending materialism I have tried to argue that a materialist and yet nonbehaviorist account of sensations is perfectly consistent with our ordinary language of sensation reports. (Though I have had space to consider only a selection of the arguments commonly put forward against materialism; for example, I have not considered the argument from the alleged incorrigibility of reports of inner experience. Elsewhere I have argued that, even if such incorrigibility were a fact, it would provide as much of a puzzle to the dualist as it does to the materialist.)[17]

Nevertheless there is also in ordinary language a dualistic overtone: to some extent it enshrines the plain man's metaphysics, which is a dualism of body and soul. We cannot therefore hope (even if we wished) to reconcile *all* of ordinary language with a materialist metaphysics. Or, to put it otherwise, it is hard to decide just where to draw the line between nonmetaphysical ordinary language and the plain man's metaphysics. Nevertheless, I think that the attempt to reconcile the hard core of ordinary language with materialism is worth while. For one thing, some features of ordinary language will probably remain constant for a very long time. This is because much of our perception of macroscopic objects depends on innate mechanisms, not on mechanisms that have developed through learning processes. For example, consider our perception of objects as three-dimensional. Again, we shall probably continue indefinitely to need a color language, anthropocentric though it is. The color classifications we make depend on the peculiarities of the human visual apparatus, and, so long as we retain our present physiological characteristics, we shall retain our present color language. With these reservations, however, I am also attracted to P. K. Feyerabend's contention that in defending materialism we do not need to show its consistency with ordinary language, any more than in defending the general theory of relativity we need to show its consistency with Newtonian theory.[18] (Newtonian theory and general relativity are indeed inconsistent with one another: for example, the advance of the perihelion of Mercury is inconsistent with Newtonian theory, but follows from general relativity.) Feyerabend is perhaps therefore right in arguing that the scientific concept of pain does not need to be (and indeed should not be) even extensionally equivalent to the concept of pain in ordinary language. (The concept of a planetary orbit in general relativity does not quite coincide extensionally with that in Newtonian theory, since the orbit of Mercury fits the former but not the latter.) Perhaps, therefore, even if it should be shown that materialism is incompatible with the core of our ordinary language, it could still be defended on the basis of Feyerabend's position. Nevertheless, just as J. K. Galbraith in his book *The Affluent Society* prefers where possible to argue against what he calls "the conventional wisdom" on its own ground, so I think that it is worth while trying to meet some of my philosophical friends as far as possible on their own ground, which is the analysis of ordinary language. Indeed it seems probable that the ordinary language of perception and of inner experience has more to recommend it than has the conventional wisdom of the last generation of economists: we are not confronted with a rapidly changing universe or with a rapidly changing human physiology in the way in which the economist is faced with a rapidly changing human environment.

NOTES

[1] I wish to thank Dr. C. B. Martin and Mr. M. C. Bradley, who have commented on an earlier version of this paper. I have made some slight changes, but space

prevents me from taking up some of their fundamental objections.

[2]See J. A. Wheeler, "Curved Empty Space-Time as the Building Material of the Physical World: An Assessment," in E. Nagel, P. Suppes, and A. Tarski, eds., *Logic, Methodology and Philosophy of Science* (Stanford University Press, 1962).

[3]F. A. Lange, *The History of Materialism*, translated by E. C. Thomas, 3d ed., with an Introduction by Bertrand Russell (New York: Harcourt Brace, 1925).

[4]For a fuller discussion see my paper "Can Biology Be an Exact Science?", *Synthèse*, 11 (1959): 359–368.

[5]In recent years essentially dualistic theories have been propounded in rather sophisticated forms, for example, by P. F. Strawson, *Individuals*, (London: Methuen, 1959). That Strawson's view is essentially dualistic can be seen from the fact that he admits that disembodied existence is logically compatible with it.

[6]U. T. Place, "Is Consciousness a Brain Process?", *British Journal of Psychology*, 47 (1956): 44–50.

[7]*Philosophical Investigations*, translated by G. E. M. Anscombe (Oxford: Blackwell, 1953) §§185 ff.

[8]Jerome Shaffer, in his interesting article "Mental Events and the Brain," this JOURNAL, 60, 6 (Mar. 14, 1963): 160–166, thinks (pp. 163–164) that it is implausible that what we notice in inner experience are brain processes. If my view is correct, we do notice brain processes, though only in a "topic-neutral" way: we do not notice *that* they are brain processes. I do not find this implausible—not as implausible as nonphysical entities or properties, anyway.

[9]In an unpublished paper, 1963.

[10]See Lange, *op. cit.*, vol. II, p. 312.

[11]In coming to this conclusion I have been very much influenced by my colleague C. B. Martin. See also H. Putnam, "Dreaming and 'Depth Grammar'," in R. J. Butler, ed., *Analytical Philosophy* (Oxford: Blackwell, 1962).

[12]See the excellent article by Helen Hervey, "The Private Language Problem," *Philosophical Quarterly*, 7 (1957): 63–79, especially p. 67.

[13]An analogous argument, based on a gaseous universe, is used by B. A. O. Williams, "Mr. Strawson on Individuals," *Philosophy*, 36 (1961): 309–332; see pp. 321–322.

[14]I gather that D. M. Armstrong has also been using this example to make the same point.

[15]H. Reichenbach in his *Experience and Prediction* (Univ. of Chicago Press, 1938), in one of the best defenses of physicalism in the literature, has put forward a similar account of experiences as postulated things; see §§19 and 26.

[16]See his paper "The 'Mental' and the 'Physical'," in *Minnesota Studies in the Philosophy of Science*, vol. 2 (1958), pp. 370–497.

[17]See my note, "Brain Processes and Incorrigibility," *Australasian Journal of Philosophy*, 40 (1962): 68–70.

[18]And Wilfrid Sellars has argued that what he calls "the scientific image" should be sharply separated off from "the manifest image," and would probably say that in the present paper I am wrongly importing elements of the manifest image into the scientific image.

A Nonreductive Identity Thesis about Mind and Body*

James W. Cornman

In his paper, "The Traditional Problem of Mind and Body," C. D. Broad discusses and defends the dualistic thesis derived from René Descartes that is known as dualistic interactionism, or as Broad calls it, "two-sided interactionism."[1] It consists of two theses. First, there are mental phenomena (such as sensations of pain, feelings of pleasure, thoughts, desires, and hopes) over and above the physical parts and processes of the human body (such as the brain, brain processes, nerve fibers, nerve impulses, molecules, and molecular motion). Thus the view is dualistic because it proposes two distinct kinds of entities—mental and physical. Second, these two sorts of entities causally interact in the sense that some physical events (for example, a pin pricking a finger) cause mental events (for example, a feeling of pain), and some mental events (a feeling of pain) cause physical events (a scream). Thus the theory proposes "two-sided" causation. And it is because of this that many people have rejected the theory. One of Broad's cen-

tral concerns in his paper is to show that this rejection is not justified. My present aim is to show that Broad fails in his attempt and to argue that a quite different mind-body thesis should be accepted instead.

DUALISTIC INTERACTIONISM

Broad clearly and carefully delineates the main strengths and weaknesses of dualistic interactionism. He examines several arguments for and several others against the thesis, including two against the thesis that are derived from facts of science. Although he successfully rebuts many of these arguments, my claim is that his reply to what he calls "the argument from energy" is inadequate, and that a version of that argument casts serious doubt on dualistic interactionism.[2]

MENTAL CAUSATION AND THE CONSERVATION OF ENERGY AND MOMENTUM

If a mental event, such as a feeling of pain, or what Broad calls a volition or an act of will, causally affects something that is physical, it is generally accepted that it would directly affect the brain in some way. The main problem facing dualistic interactionism is that the two most plausible sorts of ways this might occur violate either the principle of the conservation of mass-energy or the principle of the conservation of linear-momentum. Thus, because these principles are well justified, the interaction theory becomes implausible and should be rejected.

One way that brain processes are causally affected is by stimulation of neurons or nerve fibers in the brain so that the neurons fire and cause series of nerve impulses to move through the brain. Might a feeling of pain or a volition affect the brain in this way? If either one did this, then the total energy of the affected neurons would be increased without any corresponding decrease in energy of the cause, which, because it is mental, has no mass and therefore no energy. But it seems quite reasonable, as Broad notes, that each human body is a conservative system. In other words, it is a physical system, as Broad says, "whose total energy is redistributed, but not altered in amount, by changes that happen within it," that is, by changes within it that are not the result of external physical causes.[3] But, it seems, no human body would be a conservative system if affected by this first sort of mental cause.

It might be replied, however, that we need not accept this conclusion. Perhaps bodies affected by these mental causes remain conservative, because each of the many times that neurons in a human brain are stimulated to fire by mental phenomena, each of the corresponding human bodies loses a compensating amount of energy to its physical environment. However, not only does it seem implausible that all these many equalizing losses of energy occur, but such a thesis would also seem to violate the principle of mass-energy conservation. As Broad puts it, the principle states that "every material system is either itself conservative, or, if not, is part of a larger material system which is conservative."[4] So, given this principle, the total physical universe is conservative. But if the preceding reply

were correct, then the physical universe would not be conservative, because its total energy would be increased without a corresponding loss to some other physical system. The same problem would be created by another reply which denies that each human body is a conservative system so that its total energy can increase without corresponding loss by any other physical system. Since each of these bodies is part of the physical universe, the total energy of the universe would also increase from within, contrary to the conservation of mass-energy.

So far, nothing said would disturb Broad's reply to this objection of dualistic interactionism. This is because he suggests that the mind affects the brain in a different way, a way that involves no change of energy and thus avoids any conflict with the conservation of mass-energy. We can begin to understand his suggestion by considering his example:

Take the case of a weight swinging at the end of a string hung from a fixed point. The total energy of the weight is the same at all positions in its course. It is thus a conservative system. But at every moment the direction and velocity of the weight's motion are different, and the proportion between its kinetic and its potential energy is constantly changing. These changes are caused by the pull of the string, which acts in a different direction at each different moment. The string makes no difference to the total energy of the weight; but it makes all the difference in the world to the particular way in which the energy is distributed between the potential and the kinetic forms. . . .

Here, then, we have a clear case even in the physical realm where a system is conservative but is continually acted on by something which affects its movement and the distribution of its total energy. Why should not the mind act on the body in this way?[5]

Broad's example is helpful in two ways. First, it shows how a system can be causally affected by something without the total energy of the system being affected. Second, it helps us see how a system can have different effects itself, without its own cause affecting its total energy. Just imagine that a swinging weight activates different machines by hitting different buttons at the top of its arc. Also imagine that at certain times the length of the string is changed. Then the radius and position of the arc are changed, so the weight hits a different button and starts a different machine. Yet the total energy of the weight remains unchanged.

Is it reasonable that mental phenomena affect brains in some way like the way the string affects the weight? Again we can turn to Broad for what I believe to be the most plausible suggestion. He says that certain facts

> suggest that what the mind does to the body in voluntary action, if it does anything, is to lower the resistance of certain synapses and to raise that of others. The result is that the nervous current follows such a course as to produce the particular movement which the mind judges to be appropriate at the time.[6]

The point is that the route that a nerve current takes through a brain depends on which neurons are "excited," that is, which are caused by other neurons to be stimulated to have electrical impulses. And whether a neuron is excited by another depends on what Broad calls the "resistance" at the synapse or junction connecting the two neurons. As Broad puts it, if the resistance is high at the synapse joining two neurons, n_1 and n_2, then, even when there is a nerve impulse in n_1, the other neuron, n_2, is not excited because of the high resistance. As a result, one series of nerve impulses is stopped, and so one route of nerve current through the brain is blocked. But if the resistance at this synapse is low, then when neuron n_1 is excited, it causes n_2 to become excited and that particular series of nerve impulses continues through the brain. But because different nerve currents, or series of brain impulses, in a brain cause different bodily behavior, changes in the amounts of resistance at certain synapses result in different bodily behavior. Broad's suggestion is that mental phenomena, such as volitions, affect a brain, and thereby bodily behavior, by changing the distribution of resistance among a certain group of synapses without affecting the total resistance of this group of synapses. As a result, mental phenomena affect bodily behavior without changing the total energy of the brain.

Broad's proposal shows how mental phenomena might affect bodily behavior without violating the conservation of energy principle. But this does not solve all problems for his thesis, because if it is correct, mental phenomena would seem to change the total linear-momentum within the brain by changing the resistances of synapses. The linear-momentum of something equals its mass times its velocity, where velocity is a vector quantity. That is, it is specified not only by a magnitude but also by a direction. Thus momentum is also a vector quantity. Now, each nerve impulse traveling through a neuron is caused by movements of charged particles, or ions, across a membrane in the neuron. Consequently, because each series of nerve impulses involves different neurons, it seems clear that the linear-momentum of the ions involved in each series differs from that for every other one, even if, implausibly, the total mass of the ions moving into and out of the neurons, and the magnitude of their velocities should be identical for each series. Given this, then if, by changing the resistance at certain synapses, a volition stopped one series of nerve impulses but allowed another one to continue instead, the resultant total linear-momentum of the brain would be different from what it would have been if this volition had not affected the synapses. But, by the principle of the conservation of linear-momentum, any change of a system's total linear-momentum requires that some net external physical force affect the system. The only appropriate physical forces are gravitational, which require mass, and electromagnetic, which require electrical charge. But, for a dualist, no mental phenomenon has either one. So it surely seems that no brain is subject to any force from a volition. We can conclude, then, that this conservation principle requires that no volition affects any brain in the way that Broad has proposed.

The preceding discussion shows it is reasonable that two of the most plausible ways a mental phenomenon might affect a brain violate either the principle of mass-energy conservation or the principle of linear-momentum conservation. Consequently, although Broad was correct to claim that mental causation of physical events does not require the violation of the mass-energy conservation principle, he overlooked another conservation principle which his suggested hypothesis seems to violate. It is reasonable, therefore, to conclude that dualistic interactionism violates one or the other of these well-established conservation principles and should be rejected for some other mind-body theory that avoids such a violation.

EPIPHENOMENALISM

Broad briefly mentions a dualistic theory that avoids the preceding crucial objection to two-sided interactionism. This is epiphenomenalism, which is one species of the theory of "one-sided action of body on mind."[7] Thomas Huxley, who championed this theory, stated it as follows:

> All states of consciousness, in us, as in [brutes], are immediately caused by molecular changes of the brain-substance. It seems to me that in men, as in brutes, there is no proof that any state of consciousness is the cause of change in the motion of the matter of the organism. If these positions are well based, it follows that our mental conditions are simply the symbols in consciousness of the changes which take place automatically in the organism; and that, to take an extreme illustration, the feeling we call volition is not the cause of a voluntary act, but the symbol of that state of the brain which is the immediate cause of that act. We are conscious automata. . .[8]

Huxley's claim is that we human beings, and also some brute animals, are conscious automata in the sense that, although we have mental phenomena, such as volitions and pains, that are distinct from anything physical, all these mental entities are merely epiphenomena, that is, by-products, of ongoing physical processes. In other words, mental events are effects of physical processes, such as nerve impulses in the brain, but no mental event causally affects anything else at all—whether mental or physical. Thus, contrary to the two-sided interaction theory, none of my desires, hopes, fears, or feelings of pain or pleasure ever affect my bodily behavior. Instead, it is always some brain event that produces each mental phenomenon, such as a pain, and also causes the eventual bodily behavior, such as a scream.

Epiphenomenalism has appealed to scientists for several reasons. These include one that attracted Huxley, namely, that it is well-suited to the Darwinian theory of evolution. As more and more complex physical systems evolved, it seems quite natural that certain by-products would also result. Why should not one of these be a conscious mental life? Another attractive feature for scientists is that if epiphenomenalism is correct, then it seems that the physical sciences would be able to explain the behavior of human beings in the same ways they explain the behavior of nonliving physical objects. A third advantage, which is most important for our purposes, is that a one-sided action theory avoids the preceding objection to interaction theories. There is no mental causation of physical events to violate conservation laws for physical systems.

Should we, then, adopt epiphenomenalism? It seems appealing and it does avoid a serious objection. But we must first pause to do two things. We should consider whether this theory faces any objections uniquely its own, and then attempt to discover whether any of its rivals prove to be more reasonable than it is. Regarding the first task, it is important to see that the way in which epiphenomenalism avoids the crucial objection to interactionism results in two undesirable features which detract from the appeal and reasonableness of the theory.

TWO OBJECTIONS TO EPIPHENOMENALISM: THE MENTAL AS A MERE BY-PRODUCT

Broad points out the first undesirable feature when he says, "In favour of the action of mind on body is the fact that we seem to be immediately aware of a causal relation when we voluntarily try to produce a bodily movement."[9] That is, it seems intuitively obvious to us that often, for example, when we will or choose to raise our arm, it goes up *because of* our choosing. And it seems clear to us that, all too often, a feeling of pain will cause us to scream and writhe and squirm. Consequently, any theory like epiphenomenalism that denies such effects of the mental is quite counterintuitive and its reasonableness is decreased accordingly. Nevertheless, an epiphenomenalist could counter this objection and lessen its force somewhat by postulating that the almost constant correlation of mental choosings to do something (for example, my choosing to raise my arm) with the ensuing bodily movement (my arm going up) misleads us into the mistaken belief that the choosing causes the movement. Instead, both these choosings and these bodily movements have the same physical causes in the brain. That is why they regularly accompany each other and why we mistake one effect of the common cause for the cause of the other effect.

Nevertheless, as Broad stresses, we do seem to be aware of the effect of our choices on our own bodily movements. Surely, if all else should prove equal, a theory that accommodates what is so hard for us to deny is preferable to epiphenomenalism, which denies it.

The second weakness that the denial of mental causation creates for epiphenomenalism is less telling than the first, but it is well worth noting. It is stated by the contemporary philosopher, Herbert Feigl:

[Epiphenomenalism] accepts two fundamentally different sorts of laws—the usual causal laws and laws of psychophysiological correspondence. The physical (causal) laws connect the events in the physical world in the manner of a complex network, while the correspondence laws involve relations of physical events with purely mental "danglers." These correspondence laws are peculiar in that they may be said to postulate "effects" (mental states as dependent variables) which by themselves do not function, or at least do not seem to be needed, as "causes" (independent variables) for any observable behavior.[10]

Feigl's point is that, unlike its main rivals, epiphenomenalism is forced to assume that there are two distinct sorts of causal laws, and this is scientifically unsatisfactory. According to Feigl, mental entities would be "nomological danglers" if epiphenomenalism were true. These entities are mentioned in psychophysical laws (that is, scientific laws linking mental and physical phenomena), but neither they nor these laws would have any function in the scientific explanation and prediction of human behavior. In this sense, mental phenomena would "dangle" uselessly. But physical phenomena and physical laws are quite different. Both are crucial to the explanation and prediction of the behavior of both animate and inanimate objects, as, ideally, all scientifically respectable entities and laws should be.

As before, I believe we can agree that if all else should prove equal, a theory that avoids this consequence would be more reasonable than epiphenomenalism. Yet if this were the only objection to epiphenomenalism, it is not at all clear that it would be unreasonable to adopt the theory. After all, although it may violate an ideal of scientific theory, it requires no change whatsoever in the procedures of observation, experimentation, and theory development that scientists actually use.

REDUCTIVE MATERIALISM

Epiphenomenalism is flawed, but not overwhelmingly so. Nevertheless, we should consider whether there is a preferable alternative to it. For many people, reductive materialism is just such a theory. Consider the version attributed to Thomas Hobbes. He held that sense experience is the source of all man's thoughts, dreams, imaginings, and rememberings, "for there is no conception in a man's mind, which hath not at first, totally or by parts, been begotten upon the organs of sense. The rest are derived from that original."[11] Given this, we can see why Hobbes has been interpreted as a materialist because of his claim that sense experience is "some internal motion in the sentient, generated by some internal motion, of the parts of the object, and propagated through all the media to the innermost part of the organ."[12] It seems, then, that Hobbes might well hold the view that everything, whether living or not, is a purely physical object which is itself, and whose internal parts are, either in motion or at rest. It is true that some of these physical bodies that have sense organs also have sense experience, thoughts, dreams, and the like. But all of these mental phenomena are nothing but physical motion within these bodies, caused there originally by the effects of physical stimuli on the physical sense organs of the body. This is surely reductive materialism, because all mental phenomena are claimed to be reduced to—that is, nothing but—certain motions (perhaps, certain nerve currents) within the human body.

But it is worth noting that Hobbes may not be a reductive materialist, as another passage indicates. He says that "sense, in all cases, is nothing else but original fancy, caused, as I have said, by the pressure, that is by the motion, of external things upon our eyes, ears, and other organs there unto ordained."[13] Here Hobbes seems to be saying that sense experience is "fancy" which is caused by motion, rather than being identical with motion. Indeed, he holds that fancy is merely the appearance of motion.[14] But appearances— seemingly, mental images such as dream images—are quite different from physical bodies or motion. It may be we should consider Hobbes to be a mind-body dualist who is an epiphenomenalist.

Our main task here, however, is not to uncover the best construal of Hobbes' views. It is likely he was confused and did not hold one clear, consistent thesis. Nevertheless, his confusion is a clue to us. We should clearly delineate the principal mind-body theories before we critically compare them and adopt one as the most reasonable. We can do this for reductive materialism by first stating and then explaining its central thesis:

> RM Each mental phenomenon is nothing but (that is, reduced to) some physical phenomenon (presumably, a brain part or process).

That is, a human being is nothing but a physical body. In this respect, the theory is monistic rather than dualistic. For dualistic theories, each volition, thought, or feeling is something distinct from everything physical, including the brain and its processes. For reductive materialism, each mental phenomenon is identical with something physical, such as some part of the brain. So, although we may be conscious automata as Huxley claimed, consciousness is reduced to brain activity rather than being its nonphysical by-product. This is one central difference between epiphenomenalism and reductive materialism. An important similarity, which distinguishes both from dualistic interactionism, is their thesis that all causes are physical.

CONCERNING THE MENTAL BEING "NOTHING BUT" THE PHYSICAL

The crucial phrase in thesis *RM* is 'nothing but.' What is it for *A* to be nothing but *B*? For one thing, if *A* is nothing but *B*, then *A* is identical with *B*. Thus reductive materialism implies that each mental phenomenon (for example, a pain I feel) is identical with a physical phenomenon (for example, stimulated nerve fibers in my brain). But this raises the question of what is required for A to be identical with B. Following what is known as Leibniz's Principle of the Identity of Indiscernibles, we can say, somewhat roughly, that A is identical with B *if* A and B have exactly the same properties; and A is *not* identical with B *if* one of them has a property the other one lacks. For example, the president of the United States who resigned is identical with Richard M. Nixon, because that president and Nixon have exactly the same properties. But Nixon is not identical with the president who was impeached because, among other things, Nixon has the property of living in the 20th century, but the impeached president lacked that property.

If A is nothing but B, then A is identical with B. But the converse is false. A can be identical with B, yet not be nothing but B. Identity is a symmetrical relationship. Thus, if A is identical with B, then B is identical with A. But it is false that if A is nothing but B, then B is nothing but A. The latter relationship is nonsymmetrical. Consequently, mere identity is not sufficient for the reduction that "nothing but" implies. It is, however, very hard to uncover just what more is needed. Perhaps some examples will help clarify the difference between the two. Consider the following sentences:

1. The object that frightened you in the cemetery last night *is identical with* the gnarled tree behind Jones' grave.
2. The gnarled tree behind Jones' grave *is identical with* the object that frightened you in the cemetery last night.
3. The object that frightened you last night *is nothing but* the gnarled tree behind Jones' grave.
4. The gnarled tree behind Jones' grave *is nothing but* the object that frightened you last night.

We can easily conceive of situations in which (1), (2), and (3) are true, but (4) sounds quite odd, indeed, false even when (1), (2), and (3) are true. How can a tree be nothing more than something that frightens someone? It has properties, such as having bark, branches, and leaves, that are over and above the properties something has in virtue of it being something that frightens you. That is, a tree is not reducible to a frightening object. But, as (3) states, a frightening object which last night seemed to you to have ghostly properties, turns out to be nothing but an ordinary tree. That is, it is reduced to a tree, which is an object that, aside from its effect on you, has only those properties it has because it is a tree. Thus because (4) is false when (3) is true, 'nothing but' is a nonsymmetrical relationship.

How does this help clarify reductive materialism? Considering pains again, we can now understand better the claim of a reductive materialist that all pains are nothing but stimulated nerve fibers in brains. No pains have properties that are different from those they have because they are stimulated nerve fibers, and so they have no psychological properties.[15] In this sense, then, pains and other mental phenomena are, according to reductive materialism, reduced to something physical. In other words, each mental entity is identical with something physical, contrary to all dualistic theories; each has physical properties; but none has psychological or mental properties that are distinct from physical properties.

Reductive materialism has much appeal. It has all those features that attract many scientists to epiphenomenalism, including its avoidance of the central objection to dualistic interactionism. But, helpfully, materialism avoids this objection in a way that also allows it to bypass the two objections to epiphenomenalism. If each mental phenomenon, such as a volition or a choosing, is identical with something in the brain, as a reductive materialist would claim, then no causal activity by something mental violates any physical conservation law because that same causal activity is activity by something physical. Thus even if volitions cause brain activity either by initiating nerve impulses within the brain or by redistributing the resistance at synapses in the brain, this would violate no conservation principles. All volitions would be physical brain occurrences, and so they would be capable of changes in energy or momentum that counterbalance any changes they bring about in other brain activity.

Notice how neatly reductive materialism avoids the two objections to epiphenomenalism. Being a monistic rather than a dualistic theory, materialism requires no nomological danglers and allows all mental events to be causes as well as effects, as we can easily see. If each mental event is identical with a brain event, and each brain event is a link in an ongoing causal process in which each link is caused by a preceding one and then causes a subsequent one, then each mental event is both an effect and a cause. And, also, psychophysical laws, which relate mental to physical phenomena, would relate entities that are identical with brain phenomena to certain physical entities, all of which would function in some way or other to explain and predict human behavior.

AN OBJECTION TO REDUCTIVE MATERIALISM: THE ACHINESS OF PAINS

So far, reductive materialism seems clearly superior to the two dualistic theories previously discussed. Unfortunately, however, it faces one fatal objection, uniquely its own. Recall some of the pains you have had, and consider those properties you were sure that they had. Probably you have often been convinced that many pains you felt were intense, stabbing, throbbing, and ached unbearably. Such properties with which pains all too often seem to confront us are not the same as those physical properties that physiologists or physicists discover or ascribe to physical phenomena such as nerve impulses and molecular activity. They are mental or psychological properties which are quite distinct from the physical properties of brain parts and processes. Consequently, if, as surely is undeniable to someone when he experiences pain, pains have these properties, then it is false that all mental phenomena are nothing but physical phenomena. That is, it is false that they have only those properties

they have because they are physical entities, such as stimulated nerve fibers in human brains. And this is also true of other mental phenomena, such as itching, tickling, or tingling sensations, and feelings of pleasure, fear, or anxiety. Thus, each person's own experiences of his own bodily sensations, feelings, and emotions provide him with compelling reason to reject reductive materialism, in spite of its many attractive features.

INTERIM CONCLUSION: ALL THE PRECEDING THEORIES ARE DEFICIENT

Where has our investigation led us? Must we reject all mind-body theories? Perhaps not, because, although defective, epiphenomenalism seems not to be severely damaged. Yet I would hope we can do better. Indeed, I think we can. Recall which feature of reductive materialism allows it to retain the strengths of epiphenomenalism while avoiding its weaknesses. It is its monistic claim that each mental phenomenon is identical with something physical, presumably a brain entity. This identity claim is all that is required to avoid the objection to dualistic interactionism that it violates some conservation principle, and the objections to epiphenomenalism about its nomological danglers and its denial of the causal efficacy of anything mental. Again, no more than the identity of the mental with something physical is needed to maintain what many scientists find appealing about epiphenomenalism, namely, its being well suited to the theory of evolution and its allowing for the explanation of all human bodily behavior by the physical sciences. Might we then devise a mind-body identity theory which has all these advantages yet avoids what devastates reductive materialism?

We have seen that identity is a symmetrical relationship, but reduction is not. Furthermore, identity of A and B requires only that A and B have exactly the same properties. That is, unlike the claim that A is nothing but (reduced to) B, the claim that A is identical with B puts no restrictions on the sorts of properties that *A* has. Consequently, a pain can be identical with certain stimulated nerve fibers, and still have its psychological properties of being intense, throbbing, stabbing, aching, and the like. And, of course, mere identity would also allow such a pain to have the physical and physiological properties of that brain entity with which it is identical. That is, one and the same entity might have both psychological properties and physical properties.

THE NEUTRAL IDENTITY THEORY

A view that proposes such nonreductive, monistic identities was adumbrated in the writings of Benedict Spinoza, who said, "the mind and the body are one and the same thing conceived at one time under the attribute of thought [that is, when understood as something with mental properties], and at another under the attribute of extension [that is, when understood as something with physical properties.]"[16] Because this one entity has both of these aspects according to Spinoza, his theory is often called, "the double aspect theory." I believe, however, that a more accurate title for the theory we shall discuss is "the neutral identity theory." The entities proposed by such a theory are neither purely physical nor purely mental. They are some third sort of neutral entity, because they have psychological properties which nothing purely physical has, and they have physical properties which nothing purely mental has.

We can state this nonreductive, neutral, monistic theory more precisely in terms of the following thesis:

NI For each existing mental phenomenon, *m:* (a) *m* is identical with some physical phenomena (presumably, a brain entity), and (b) *m* has both certain psychological properties and the physical properties of the physical phenomenon with which it is identical.

It is, as previously mentioned, clause (a) of *NI* that affords the neutral identity theory

the advantages and appeal of epiphenomenalism and reductive materialism without the deficiencies of epiphenomenalism. It is clause (b) that provides the means for this neutral theory to avoid the fatal objection to reductive materialism, because it allows mental phenomena, such as our pains, to have whatever psychological properties we find so hard to deny them when we experience them. The neutral identity theory, then, seems clearly superior to the other theories we have examined. But, of course, once again we must search for its flaws before drawing any conclusion about its reasonableness.

FOUR OBJECTIONS TO THE NEUTRAL IDENTITY THEORY

What objections might there be to the neutral identity theory? I confess I find it hard to uncover any that have much force at all. Nevertheless, let me suggest four that seem to be either the most plausible or the most appealing of those I have considered.

First Objection: The Neutral Theory Implies Something Meaningless. The first objection is one type of argument that is quite popular among contemporary linguistic philosophers. It is an attempt to argue from statements about language to conclusions about non-linguistic facts, such as claims about identity. In this particular case, the objection argues from the oddity of certain sentences that the neutral theory seems to imply to their meaninglessness and the rejection of the theory. If the neutral theory is true, and, for example, each pain is identical with a group of stimulated nerve fibers, then the sentences 'Some of my nerve fibers are aching and throbbing' and 'My present pain is constituted of a group of molecules' are both true. But according to this first objection, neither is true. Indeed, both seem to be linguistically odd and even meaningless, much like 'Next Saturday is in bed.' And nothing meaningless is true. So the neutral theory is not true.

I find it clearly debatable whether the oddity of 'My present pain is constituted of molecules' and 'Some of my nerve fibers are aching and throbbing' should be classified with the seemingly clear meaninglessness of 'Next Saturday is in bed.' After all, it seems absurd to assign some spatial location, such as being in bed, to a duration of time. But it is not clear it is equally absurd to attribute these properties to pains and nerve fibers. It may sound odd and most unusual, but that is not always a sign of meaninglessness. Consider, for example, how odd and unusual it must have sounded when someone first proposed that each motionless, clear, liquid pool of water is identical with a swarm of discrete particles each of which is constantly in motion. Nevertheless, by now we have become used to such statements and would never claim they are meaningless.

Let us, however, assume for present purposes that the two preceding sentences about pains and nerve fibers are meaningless. Would that refute the neutral identity theory? It would if the following deductively valid argument is successful:

1. If clause (a) of *NI* is true, then my present pain is identical with (let us assume) stimulated nerve fibers.
2. If clause (b) of *NI* is true and each pain is identical with stimulated nerve fibers, then it is true that each pain has the physical properties of stimulated nerve fibers.
3. All nerve fibers are constituted of molecules.
4. The property of being constituted of molecules is a physical property.
Therefore
5. If *NI* is true, then it is true that my present pain is constituted of molecules.
6. But it is meaningless (and so not true) that my present pain is constituted of molecules.
Therefore
7. *NI* is not true (and so should be rejected).

The only way that a neutral identity theorist who accepts (6) can rebut this objection is by attacking premises (1) and (2). All the other premises are clearly true. One way to launch an attack is by arguing that anyone who accepts *NI* and also (6) should replace the word 'pain' in premises (1) and (2) to avoid committing his theory to the meaningless consequences that (1) and (2) require of it. I suggest that he might devise new technical terms, such as 'fibain' which can be defined as follows:

> *x* is a fibain = df. *x* is an entity that has the properties all pains have, and the properties all stimulated nerve fibers have.

Then a neutral theorist could replace premise (1) by:

1'. If clause (a) of *NI* is true, then the aching entity that I am now experiencing is not a pain but rather a fibain.

And he could replace (2) by:

2'. If clause (b) of *NI* is true and each aching entity is not a pain but rather a fibain, then it is true that each aching entity has the physical properties of fibains.

Now the four premises no longer yield conclusion (5), but rather:

5'. If *NI* is true, then it is true that the fibain I am now experiencing is constituted of molecules.

And, now, not only is (6) irrelevant to the argument, but its replacement that would yield (7) is false:

6'. It is meaningless that the fibain I am now experiencing is constituted of molecules.

The main point emphasized by this reply is that an objection that is aimed at a nonlinguistic ontological thesis but which is based on claims solely about language is often easy to circumvent by avoiding the language that seems to raise the problem. In the present case we assumed a debatable claim about certain sentences being meaningless. The crucial question then becomes whether this claim about language established anything about a mind-body identity thesis. The answer seems clearly to be that it merely required an identity theorist to avoid certain language in stating the consequences of his theory. Thus this first objection fails, even granting the claim about meaninglessness. Of course, the objection does not even arise if, as is not unreasonable, we should reject that claim rather than grant it.

Second Objection: The Implausibility of Only Brains with Psychological Properties.

The second objection I wish to consider is, like the first, based on the view that the neutral theory has odd consequences. But the oddity ascribed to the theory by the second objection is not a linguistic one implying meaninglessness; it is rather a nonlinguistic one implying implausibility. The objection is based on two premises. First, if the neutral identity theory is true, then only certain groups of molecules in only certain brains of only certain animals have psychological properties. All other groups have only their usual physical properties. But, second, this consequence of the theory is odd or unusual enough to be implausible. Therefore, the theory itself is implausible.

The problem with this objection is that neither of its premises is reasonable. Indeed, the first one is clearly false. The neutral identity theory does not require that only certain groups of molecules have psychological properties. The theory is mute about any properties of all other groups of molecules. Indeed, it is clearly consistent with the panpsychism with which Spinoza combines his double aspect theory. That is, it is consistent with the thesis that every object with physical properties also has psychological properties, whether or not we can discover them. Panpsychism, however, is quite implausible in its ascription of some undiscoverable low-level mental life even to inanimate objects such as rocks. I would propose, then, that a neutral identity theorist should adopt the view, in addition to his basic theory, that only certain very special groups of molecules have psychological properties. This does make these groups of molecules unique and unusual, but I disagree with the second premise of the present objection which states that any theory that requires there to be such unique and unusual groups of molecules is implausible.

Regardless of whether groups of molecules in the human brain have psychological properties, it must be admitted that this brain is unique and unusual in the complexity of its structure and constitutents. Consequently, it is not implausible to think that it would have some very unusual properties. Indeed, I find it plausible to consider psychological properties to be what are called "emergent" properties that emerge in the development of the universe only when a group of molecules is of a certain complex sort— perhaps only when it constitutes a certain complex system of interconnected nerve fibers. There are other sorts of emergent properties, that is, properties that certain groups of atomic and subatomic particles have which none of the individual constituents of the group have.[17] Why should we not construe psychological properties this way also?

Consider, for example, that certain systems of *NaCl* molecules have the properties of salt—they are white, crystalline, and soluble in water. But neither sodium and chlorine ions, nor their constituents—protons, neutrons, and electrons—have any of these properties individually. Or take *DNA* molecules. Only when their many constituents form together the required double helix is there something that has the unique, unusual, but not implausible biological properties of a living cell. When these constituents are not united in this way none of these emergent properties of a cell result. Likewise, I suggest, when and only when certain sorts of molecules form certain very complex systems, as in the brains of humans and some other living things, do the unique, unusual, but not implausible emergent psychological properties arise. Furthermore, this view of the emergence of psychological properties fits quite nicely with the Darwinian theory of evolution. We can, then, I find, reject this second objection to the neutral theory on the ground that it has failed to show that what would be unique and unusual about certain brains would also be implausible.

Third Objection: Extrasensory Perception and Minds Distinct from Bodies.

The third objection is quite different from the first two. I find it considerably even less plausible than they are, but it may be quite appealing to some. It is based on the claim that no acceptable theory about the relationship between mind and body should require the rejection of any thesis, no matter how odd or unusual, for which there is at least some scientific evidence. And, according to this objection, more and more evidence is accumulating in favor of the hypothesis that some human beings have extrasensory perception. In particular, the evidence is mounting that there is mental telepathy and communication among human beings without reliance on any sense organs. But any means of communication which involves no sense organs requires some sort of mental contact between people, and that is impossible unless there are mental phenomena quite distinct from what is merely physical. So we should reject identity theories for some sort of dualism.

There are two claims made in this objection which we can accept. First, what little evidence there is favors the view that some sort of communication among people occurs without the use of sense organs. The evidence, however, is far from conclusive. Nevertheless, there is enough to justify considerably more research and investigation. Second, any philosophical thesis that presupposes an answer to justified scientific research whose results are far from determined, faces a significant objection. However, whether it is serious enough to require the rejection of the thesis depends on how damaging the problems are that face the competing theories which avoid this particular objection. For example, although dualistic interactionism seems particularly well suited to accommodate extrasensory perception, the objection that it violates some conservation law seems too serious to resurrect it because of this one advantage.

Fortunately, however, we are not forced to choose between a theory that violates some conservation law and a theory that precludes extrasensory perception. This is because, in addition to the two preceding claims which are plausible, the objection rests on two others which are quite dubious. The first is that communication between human beings that does not involve sense organs requires there to be some sort of nonphysical, mental means of communication. But it has not been established that there are no purely physical processes by which one person's brain can affect another person's brain without affecting any one of his sense organs. Until, if ever, there comes a time when extrasensory communication is shown to be plausible, and such nonsensory *physical* communication between brains is shown to be implausible, extrasensory perception is not even an objection to a theory which rejects causation by entities with psychological properties. Thus, at present, it is not even an objection to epiphenomenalism and reductive materialism. And it is even less of a threat to the neutral identity theory which allows causation by entities with both physical and psychological properties.

The second claim is more dubious than the first. It is the claim that mental communication and telepathy require mental causes that are distinct from anything physical. That is, it requires dualistic interactionism. It is true that if there should be *mental* telepathy, then epiphenomenalism and reductive materialism would be false. But the neutral theory would be quite compatible with it. It may be that one nonphysical, mental, emergent property of certain very complex physical systems is an ability to send and receive nonphysical signals that require no physical medium whatsoever. Admittedly, such communication seems very mysterious, given our present level of knowledge. And, insofar as it affects the brain of the person who receives it, it seems to violate some conservation law. But it is no more mysterious or less plausible than communication between minds which are distinct from bodies, although causally related to them. Thus, for two reasons, this third objection to the neutral theory fails.

Fourth Objection: Communication with the Dead and Disembodied Minds.

It may be protested at this point that the preceding refutation of the third objection depends on the dubious thesis that all extrasensory communication consists in some living human being receiving extrasensory information from another living human being. But surely communication with the dead requires the existence of mental activity after death, and this is incompatible with the neutral theory, as well as with epiphenomenalism and reductive materialism. So, according to this fourth objection, we should reject all three of these theories for dualistic interactionism which is compatible with messages from the dead, and with disembodied life in the hereafter.

For many people, this may be the most appealing and persuasive objection of the four. It is indeed true that if the neutral theory is correct, then, when that brain activity with which a mental phenomenon is identical ceases, the mental phenomenon also ceases to exist. And when death occurs, all such brain activity ceases. Thus, if the neutral theory is true, there is no life after death and also no communication from anyone who is dead. Of course, this is also a consequence of reductive materialism with its reduction of the mental to brain activity, and of epiphenomenalism for which the mental is merely a by-product of that brain activity. But does this provide reason to reject these three theories? It does, only if it is reasonable to think there is such communication.

I believe that a neutral theorist should admit that psychical research has uncovered many reports of experiences that provide some evidence for the thesis of communication from the dead. For example, C. J. Ducasse mentions a case "of a father whose apparition some time after death revealed to one of his sons the existence and location of an unsuspected second will, benefiting him, which was then found as indicated."[18]

Ducasse also notes phenomena of a different sort: "Sometimes the same mark of identity of a dead person, or the same message from him, or complementary parts of one message, are obtained independently from two mediums in different parts of the world."[19] These many reports cannot be ignored, and even if the great majority are fraudulent, it is still true, as Ducasse says, that "they cannot all just be laughed off; for to accept the hypothesis of fraud or malobservation would often require more credulity than to accept the facts reported."[20]

It seems reasonable, then, that some of these strange experiences occur. That is, sometimes people are caused to have these apparitions, and sometimes mediums are caused to believe they are receiving messages. But, as Ducasse points out, the crucial question is how these phenomena are to be explained. If we follow Ducasse here, then we would agree that only two explanatory hypotheses are even remotely plausible, namely, communication from the dead, and, where a medium is involved, unconscious, extrasensory communication from living persons, often far away from the medium and unknown by him. I think, however, that, in spite of what Ducasse says, we should also consider the hypothesis that each of these experiences is a case of "malobservation" or hallucination—especially when "apparitions" are experienced. At present, none of these three hypotheses is clearly more reasonable than the other two. And no fourth explanation seems to be any more reasonable than these three. This fact provides a neutral theorist with what he needs to justify the rejection of this objection. Both extrasensory communication and hallucination are compatible with the neutral theory and also with the conservation laws of physics. But communication from the dead would seem to violate some conservation law, because it would seem to require that nonphysical causes affect the brains and bodily behavior of the mediums and the persons having apparitions. Therefore, because, at the present time, communication from the dead is not clearly a better explanation of these phenomena than its two chief rivals, and, of the three, only it seems to violate a conservation law, we should, at least for now, reject the explanation that the phenomena result from communication from the dead.

CONCLUSION: THE NEUTRAL IDENTITY THEORY SHOULD BE ACCEPTED

We have examined the four objections to the neutral identity theory that I have found most plausible or most appealing. I have argued that we have reason to reject all of these objections. If I am right, then, the neutral theory not only avoids all the unrefuted objections to its chief rivals, namely, dualistic interactionism, epiphenomenalism, and reductive materialism, but it also faces none of its own. On that basis, I conclude, the neutral identity theory is not only more reasonable than the other theories about the relationship between mind and body, but is also reasonable enough to be clearly acceptable. It is, consequently, the hypothesis we should adopt—at least until, if ever, new evidence arises that forces its reevaluation.

NOTES

[1]C. D. Broad, "The Traditional Problem of Body and Mind," in this anthology, p. 187.

[2]*Ibid.*, pp. 191–93.

[3]*Ibid.*, p. 191.

[4]*Ibid.*, p. 192.

[5]*Ibid.*, p. 193.

[6]*Ibid.*, p. 195.

[7]ibid., p. 197.

[8]T. H. Huxley, "Animals and Human Beings as Conscious Automata."

[9]Broad, p. 197.

[10]H. Feigl, "Mind-Body, *Not* a Pseudoproblem," in S. Hook, ed., *Dimensions of Mind* (New York: Collier Books, 1961), p. 37.

[11]T. Hobbes, *Hobbes Selections*, edited by F. J. E. Woodbridge (New York: Scribner's, 1930), p. 139.

[12]*Ibid.*, p. 107

[13]*Ibid.*, p. 140.

[14]*Ibid.*, pp. 139–40.

[15]For a more detailed discussion and definition of materialism, see my *Materialism and Sensations* (New Haven: Yale University Press, 1971), pp. 1–19. In this book I claim that, strictly speaking, materialism requires no more than that each "instance" of a psychological property (e.g., the particular aching of my present pain) be identical with some "instance" of a physical property. This allows each psychological property (e.g., achiness) to be distinct from all physical properties. Nevertheless, I argue in *Perception, Common Sense, and Science* (New Haven: Yale University Press, 1975), Appendix, that, contrary to materialism, some instances of psychological properties are not identical with any instance of a physical property.

[16]B. Spinoza, *Spinoza Selections*, edited by J. Wild (New York: Scribner's, 1930), p. 209.

[17]For a more detailed discussion of emergent properties, see my *Materialism and Sensations*, pp. 249–251.

[18]C. J. Ducasse, *Is Life after Death Possible?* U. Cal. Press, 1947.

[19]*Ibid.*

[20]*Ibid.*

Mind-Body Identity, Privacy, and Categories*

Richard Rorty

1. INTRODUCTORY

Current controversies about the Mind-Body Identity Theory form a case-study for the investigation of the methods practiced by linguistic philosophers. Recent criticisms of these methods question that philosophers can discern lines of demarcation between "categories" of entities, and thereby diagnose "conceptual confusions" in "reductionist" philosophical theories. Such doubts arise once we see that it is very difficult, and perhaps impossible, to draw a firm line between the "conceptual" and the "empirical," and thus to differentiate between a statement embodying a conceptual confusion and one that expresses a surprising empirical result. The proponent of the Identity Theory (by which I mean one who thinks it sensible to assert that empirical inquiry will discover that *sensations* (not thoughts) are identical with certain brain-processes[1]) holds that his opponents' arguments to the effect that empirical inquiry *could* not identify brain-processes and sensations are admirable illustrations of this diffi-

culty. For, he argues, the classifications of linguistic expressions that are the ground of his opponents' criticism are classifications of a language which is as it is because it is the language spoken at a given stage of empirical inquiry. But the sort of empirical results that would show brain processes and sensations to be identical would also bring about changes in our ways of speaking. These changes would make these classifications out of date. To argue against the Identity Theory on the basis of the way we talk now is like arguing against an assertion that supernatural phenomena are identical with certain natural phenomena on the basis of the way in which superstitious people talk. There is simply no such thing as a method of classifying linguistic expressions that has results guaranteed to remain intact despite the results of future empirical inquiry. Thus in this area (and perhaps in all areas) there is no method which will have the sort of magisterial neutrality of which linguistic philosophers fondly dream.

In this paper I wish to support this general line of argument. I shall begin by pressing the claims of the analogy between mental events and supernatural events. Then I shall try to rebut the objection which seems

*Originally published in *The Review of Metaphysics*, Volume 19, Number 1 (September 1965), 24–54. Reprinted with permission of the Editor.

generally regarded as fatal to the claims of the Identity Theory—the objection that "privacy" is of the essence of mental events, and thus that a theory which holds that mental events might *not* be "private" is *ipso facto* confused. I shall conclude with some brief remarks on the implications of my arguments for the more general metaphysical issues at stake.

2. THE TWO FORMS OF THE IDENTITY THEORY

The obvious objection to the Identity Theory is that "identical" either means a relation such that

$$(x)(y)[(x = y) \supset (F)(Fx \equiv Fy)]$$

(the relation of "strict identity") or it does not. If it does, then we find ourselves forced into

saying truthfully that physical processes such as brain processes are dim or fading or nagging or false, and that mental phenomena such as after-images are publicly observable or physical or spatially located or swift,[2]

and thus using meaningless expressions, for

we may say that the above expressions are meaningless in the sense that they commit a category mistake; i.e., in forming these expressions we have predicated predicates, appropriate to one logical category, of expressions that belong to a different logical category. This is surely a conceptual mistake.[3]

But if by "identical" the Identity Theory does *not* mean a relation of strict identity, then what relation *is* intended? How does it differ from the mere relation of "correlation" which, it is admitted on all sides, might without confusion be said to hold between sensations and brain-processes?

Given this dilemma, two forms of the identity theory may be distinguished. The first, which I shall call the *translation* form, grasps the first horn, and attempts to show that the odd-sounding expressions mentioned above do not involve category-mistakes, and that this can be shown by suitable translations into "topic neutral" language of the sentences in which these terms are originally used.[4] The second, which I shall call the *disappearance* form, grasps the second horn, and holds that the relation in question is not strict identity, but rather the sort of relation which obtains between, to put it crudely, existent entities and non-existent entities when reference to the latter once served (some of) the purposes presently served by reference to the former—the sort of relation that holds, e.g., between "quantity of caloric fluid" and "mean kinetic energy of molecules." There is an obvious sense of "same" in which what used to be called "a quantity of caloric fluid" is *the same thing* as what is now called a certain mean kinetic energy of molecules, but there is no reason to think that all features truly predicated of the one may be sensibly predicated of the other.[5] The translation term of the theory holds that if we really understood what we were saying when we said things like "I am having a stabbing pain" we should see that since we are talking about "topic-neutral" matters, we might, for all we know, be talking about brain processes. The disappearance form holds that it is unnecessary to show that suitable translations (into "topic-neutral" language) of our talk about sensations can be given—as unnecessary to show that statements about quantities of caloric fluid, when properly understood, may be seen to be topic-neutral statements.[6]

From the point of view of this second form of the theory, it is a mistake to assume that "X's are nothing but Y's" entails "All attributes meaningfully predicable of X's are meaningfully predicated of Y's," for this assumption would forbid us ever to express the results of scientific inquiry in terms of (in Cornman's useful phrase) "cross-category identity."[7] It would seem that the verb in such statements as "Zeus's thunderbolts are discharges of static electricity" and "Demoniacal possession is a form of hallucinatory psychosis" is the "is" of identity, yet it can hardly express *strict* identity. The disappearance form of the Identity Theory suggests that we view such statements as elliptical for e.g., "What people used to call 'demoniacal possession' is a form of hallucinatory psychosis," where the relation in question *is* strict identity. Since there is no reason why "what people call 'X' " should be in the same "category" (in the Rylean sense) as "X," there is no need to claim, as the translation form of the theory must, that topic-neutral translations of statements using "X" are possible.

In what follows, I shall confine myself to a discussion and defense of the disappearance form of the theory. My first reason for this is that I believe that the analysis of "Sensations are identical with certain brain-processes" proposed by the disappearance form (viz., "What people now call 'sensations' are identical with certain brain-processes") accomplishes the same end as the translation form's program of topic-neutral translation —namely, avoiding the charge of "category-mistake," while preserving the full force of the traditional materialist position. My second reason is that I believe that an attempt to defend the translation form will inevitably get bogged down in controversy about the adequacy of proposed topic-neutral translations of statements about sensations. There is obviously a sense of "adequate translation" in which the topic-neutrality of the purported translations *ipso facto* makes them inadequate. So the proponent of the translation form of the theory will have to fall back on a weaker sense of "adequate translation." But the weaker this sense becomes, the less impressive is the claim being made, and the less difference between the Identity Theory and the non-controversial thesis that certain brain-processes may be constantly correlated with certain sensations.

3.   THE ANALOGY BETWEEN DEMONS AND SENSATIONS

At first glance, there seems to be a fatal weakness in the disappearance form of the Identity Theory. For normally when we say "What people call 'X's' are nothing but Y's" we are prepared to add that "There are no X's." Thus when, e.g., we say that "What people call 'caloric fluid' is nothing but the motion of molecules" or "What people call 'witches' are nothing but psychotic women" we are prepared to say that there are no witches, and no such thing as caloric fluid. But it seems absurd to say that there might turn out to be no such things as sensations.

To see that this disanalogy is not fatal to the Identity Theory, let us consider the following situation. A certain primitive tribe holds the view that illnesses are caused by demons—a different demon for each sort of illness. When asked what more is known about these demons than that they cause illness, they reply that certain members of the tribe—the witch-doctors—can see, after a meal of sacred mushrooms, various (intangible) humanoid forms on or near the bodies of patients. The witch-doctors have noted, for example, that a blue demon with a long nose accompanies epileptics, a fat red one accompanies sufferers from pneumonia, etc., etc. They know such further facts as that the fat red demon dislikes a certain sort of mold which the witch-doctors give people who have pneumonia. (There are various competing theories about what demons do when not causing diseases, but serious witch-doctors regard such speculations as unverifiable and profitless.)

If we encountered such a tribe, we would be inclined to tell them that there are no demons. We would tell them that diseases were caused by germs, viruses, and the like. We would add that the witch-doctors were not seeing demons, but merely having hallucinations. We would be quite right, but would we be right on *empirical* grounds? What empirical criteria, built into the demon-talk of the tribe, go unsatisfied? What predictions which the tribesmen make fail to come true? If there are none, a sophisticated witch-doctor may reply that all modern science can do is to show (1) that the presence of demons is constantly correlated with that of germs, viruses, and the like, and (2) that eating certain mushrooms sometimes makes people think they see things that aren't really there. This is hardly sufficient to show that there are no demons. At best, it shows that if we forget about demons, then (a) a simpler account of the cause and cure of disease and (b) a simpler account of why people make the perceptual reports they do, may be given.

What do we reply to such a sophisticated witch-doctor? I think that all that we would have left to say is that the simplicity of the accounts which can be offered if we forget about demons *is* an excellent reason for saying that there are no demons. Demon-discourse is one way of describing and predicting phenomena, but there are better ways. We *could* (as the witch-doctor urges) tack demon-discourse on to modern science by saying, first, that diseases are caused by the co-presence of demons and germs (each being a necessary, but neither a sufficient, condition) and, second, that the witch-doctors (unlike drunkards and psychotics) really do see intangible things (about whom, alas, nothing is known save their visual appearances). If we did so, we would retain all the predictive and explanatory advantages of modern science. We would know as much about the cause and cure of disease, and about hallucinations, as we did before. We would, however, be burdened with problems which we did not have before: the problem of why demons are visible only to witch-doctors, and the problem of why germs cannot cause diseases all by themselves. We avoid both problems by saying that demons do not exist. The witch-doctor may remark that this use of Occam's Razor has the same advantage as that of theft over honest toil. To such a remark, the only reply could be an account of the practical advantages gained by the use of the Razor in the past.

Now the Identity Theorist's claim is that sensations may be to the future progress of psycho-physiology as demons are to modern science. Just as we now want to deny that there are demons, future science may want to deny that there are sensations. The only obstacle to replacing sensation-discourse with brain-discourse seems to be that sensation-statements have a reporting as well as an explanatory function. But the demon case makes clear that the discovery of a new way of explaining the phenomena previously explained by reference to a certain sort of entity, *combined with a new account of what is being reported by observation-statements about that sort of entity,* may give good reason for saying that there are no entities of that sort. The absurdity of saying "Nobody has ever felt a pain" is no greater than that of saying "Nobody has ever seen a demon," *if* we have a suitable answer to the question, "What *was* I reporting when I said I felt a pain?" To this question, the science of the future may reply, "You were reporting the occurrence of a certain brain-process, and it would make life simpler for us if you would, in the future, *say*, 'My C-fibers are firing' instead of saying 'I'm in pain'." In so saying, he has as good a prima facie case as the scientist who answers the witch-doctor's question, "What *was* I reporting when I reported a demon?" by saying "You were reporting the content of your hallucination, and it would make life simpler if, in the future, you would describe your experiences in those terms."

Given this prima facie analogy between demons and sensations, we can now attend to some disanalogies. We may note, first, that there is no simple way of filling in the blank in "What people call 'demons' are nothing but——." For neither "hallucinatory contents" nor "germs" will do. The observational and the explanatory roles of "demon" must be distinguished. We need to say something like "What people who reported seeing demons were reporting was simply the content of their hallucinations," and *also* something like "What people explained by reference to demons can be explained better by reference to germs, viruses, etc." Because of the need for a relatively complex account of how we are going to get along without reference to demons, we cannot *identify* "What we called 'demons' " with anything. So, instead, we simply deny their existence. In the case of sensations, however, we can give a relatively simple account of how to get along in the future. Both the explanatory *and* the reporting functions of statements about sensations can be taken over by statements about brain-processes. Therefore we are prepared to identify "What we called 'sensations' " with brain-processes, and to say "What we called 'sensations' turn out to be nothing but brain-processes."

Thus this disanalogy does not have the importance which it appears to have at first. In both the demon case and the sensation case, the proposed reduction has the same pragmatic consequences: namely, that we should stop asking questions about the causal and/or spatio-temporal relationships holding between the "reduced" entities (demons, sensations) and the rest of the universe, and replace these with questions about the relationship holding between certain other entities (germs, hallucinatory experiences, brain-processes) and the rest of the universe. It happens, for the reasons just sketched, that the proposed reduction is put in the form of a denial of existence in one case, and of an identification in another case. But "There are no demons" and "What people call 'sensations' are nothing but brain processes" can both equally well be paraphrased as "Elimination of the referring use of the expression in question ('demon,' 'sensation') from our language would leave our ability to describe and predict undiminished."

Nevertheless, the claim that there might turn out to be no such thing as a "sensation" seems scandalous. The fact that a witch-doctor might be scandalized by a similar claim about demons does not, in itself, do much to diminish our sense of shock. In what follows, I wish to account for this intuitive implausibility. I shall argue that it rests *solely* upon the fact that elimination of the referring use of "sensation" from our language would be in the highest degree *impractical*. If this can be shown, then I think that the Identity Theorist will be cleared of the charge of "conceptual confusion" usually leveled against him. Rather than proceeding directly to this argument, however, I shall first consider a line of argument which has often been used to show that he *is* guilty of this charge. Examining this line of argument will permit me to sketch in greater detail what the Identity Theorist is and is not saying.

4. THE ELIMINABILITY OF OBSERVATION TERMS

The usual move made by the opponents of the Identity Theory is to compare suggested reduction of sensations to brain-processes to certain other cases in which we say that "X's turn out to be nothing but Y's." There are two significantly different classes of cases and it might seem that the Identity Theorist confuses them. First, there is the sort of case in which both "X" and "Y" are used to refer to observable entities, and the claim that "What people called 'X's' are nothing but Y's" backed up by pointing out that the statement that "This is an X" commits one to an empirically false proposition. For example, we say that "What people called 'unicorn horns' are nothing but narwhal horns," and urge that we cease to respond to a perceptual situation with "This is a unicorn horn." We do this because "This is a unicorn horn" commits one to the existence of unicorns, and there are, it turns out, no unicorns. Let us call this sort of case *identification of observables with other observables*. Second, there is the sort of case in which "X" is used to refer to an observable entity and "Y" is used to refer to an unobservable entity. Here we do not (typically) back up the claim that "What people called 'X's' are nothing but Y's" by citing an empirically false proposition presupposed by "This is an X." For example, the statement that "What people call 'tables' are nothing but clouds of molecules" does not suggest, or require as a ground, that people who say "This is a table" hold false beliefs. Rather, we are suggesting that something *more* has been found out about the sort of situation reported by "This is a table." Let us call this second sort of case *identification of observables with theoretical entities*.

It seems that we cannot assimilate the identification of sensations with brain-processes to either of these cases. For, unlike the typical case of identification of observables with other observables, we do not wish to say that people who have reported sensations in the past have (necessarily) any empirically disconfirmed beliefs. People are not wrong about sensations in the way in which they were wrong about "unicorn horns." Again, unlike the typical case of the identification of observables with theoretical entities, we do not want to say that brain-processes are "theoretical" or unobservable. Furthermore, in cases in which we identify an observable X with an unobservable Y, we are usually willing to accept the remark that "That does not show that there are no X's." The existence of tables is not (it would seem) impugned by their identification with clouds of electrons, as the existence of unicorn horns is impugned by their identification with narwhal horns. But a defender of the disappearance form of the Identity Theory *does* want to impugn the existence of sensations.

Because the claim that "What people call 'sensations' may turn out to be nothing but brain-processes" cannot be assimilated to either of these cases, it has been attacked as trivial or incoherent. The following dilemma is posed by those who attack it: either the Identity Theorist claims that talk about sensations presupposes some empirically disconfirmed belief (and what could it be?) or the "identity" which he has in mind is the uninteresting sort of identity which holds between tables and clouds of molecules (mere "theoretical replacability").

The point at which the Identity Theorist should attack this dilemma is the premiss invoked in stating the second horn—the premiss that the identification of tables with clouds of molecules does not permit us to infer to the non-existence of tables. This premiss is true, but *why* is it true? That there is room for reflection here is apparent when we place the case of tables side-by-side with the case of demons. If there is any point to saying that tables are nothing but clouds of molecules it is presumably to say that, in principle, we could stop making a referring use of "table," and of any extensionally equivalent term, and still leave our ability to describe and predict undiminished. But this would seem just the point of (and the justification for) saying that there are no demons. Why does the realization that nothing would be lost by the dropping of "table" from our vocabulary still leave us with the conviction that there are tables, whereas the same realization about demons leave us with the conviction that there are no demons? I suggest that the only answer to this question which will stand examination is that although we could *in principle* drop "table," it would be monstrously inconvenient to do so, whereas it is both possible in principle and convenient in practice to drop "demon." The reason "But there are still tables" sounds so plausible that nobody would dream of suggesting that we stop reporting our experiences in table-talk and start reporting them in molecule-talk. The reason "There are no demons" sounds so plausible that we are quite willing to suggest that the witch-doctors stop reporting their experiences in demon-talk and start reporting them in hallucination-talk.

A conclusive argument that this practical difference is the *only* relevant difference would, obviously, canvass all the other differences which might be noted. I shall not attempt this. Instead, I shall try to make my claim plausible by sketching a general theory of the conditions under which a term may cease to have a referring use without those who made such a use being convicted of having held false beliefs.

Given the same sorts of correlations between X's and Y's, we are more likely to say "X's are nothing but Y's" when reference to X's is habitually made in non-inferential reports, and more likely to say "There are no X's" when such reference is never or rarely made. (By "non-inferential report" I mean a statement in response to which questions like "How did you know?" "On what evidence do you say . . . ?" and "What leads you to think . . . ?" are normally considered misplaced and unanswerable, but which is nonetheless capable of empirical confirmation.) Thus we do not say that the identification of temperature with the kinetic energy of molecules shows that there is no such thing as temperature, since "temperature" originally (i.e., before the invention of thermometers) stood for something which was always reported non-inferentially, and still is frequently so reported. Similarly for all identifications of familiar macro-objects with unfamiliar micro-objects. But since in our culture-circle we do not *habitually* report non-inferentially the presence of caloric fluid, demons, etc., we do not feel unhappy at the bald suggestion that there are no such things.

Roughly speaking, then, the more accustomed we are to "X" serving as an observation-term (by which I mean a term habitually used in non-inferential reports) the more we prefer, when inquiry shows the possibility of accounting for the phenomena explained by reference to X's without such reference, to "identify" X's with some sort of Y's, rather than to deny existence to X's *tout court. But the more grounds we have for such identification, the more chance there is that we shall stop using "X" in non-inferential reports,* and thus the greater chance of our eventually coming to accept the claim that "there are no X's" with equanimity. This is why we find borderline cases, and gradual shifts from assimilations of X's to Y's to an assertion that X's do not exist. For example, most people do not report the presence of pink rats non-inferentially (nor inferentially, for that matter), but some do. The recognition that they are in the minority helps those who do so to admit that there are no pink rats. But suppose that the vast majority of us had always seen (intangible and uncatchable) pink rats; would it not then be likely that we should resist the bald assertion that there are no pink rats and insist on something of the form "pink rats are nothing but . . ."? It might be a very long time before we came to drop the habit of reporting pink rats and began reporting hallucinations instead.

The typical case-history of an observation-term ceasing to have a referring use runs the following course: (1) X's are the subjects of both inferential and non-inferential reports;[8] (2) empirical discoveries are made which enable us to subsume X-laws under Y-laws and to produce new X-laws by studying Y's; (3) inferential reports of X's cease to be made; (4) non-inferential reports of X's are reinterpreted either (4a) as reports of Y's, *or* (4b) as reports of mental entities (thoughts that one

is seeing an X, hallucinatory images, etc.); (5) non-inferential reports of X's cease to be made (because their place is taken by non-inferential reports either of Y's or of thoughts, hallucinatory images, etc.); (6) we conclude that there simply are no such things as X's.

This breakdown of stages lets us pick out two crucial conditions that must be satisfied if we are to move from "X's are nothing but Y's" (stage 2) to "there are no X's" (stage 6). These conditions are:

(A) The Y-laws must be *better* at explaining the kinds of phenomena explained by the X-laws (not just equally good). Indeed, they must be sufficiently better so that *the inconvenience of changing one's linguistic habits by ceasing to make reports about X's is less than the inconvenience of going through the routine of translating one's X-reports into Y-reports in order to get satisfactory explanations of the phenomena in question.* If this condition is not satisifed, the move from stage (2) to stage (3) will not be made, and thus no later move will be made.

(B) Either Y-reports may themselves be made non-inferentially, or X-reports may be treated as reports of mental entities. For we must be able to have some answer to the question "What *am* I reporting when I non-inferentially report about an X?," and the only answers available are "you're reporting on a Y" or "you're reporting on some merely mental entity." If neither answer is available, we can move neither to (4a) nor to (4b), nor, therefore, on to (5) and (6).

Now the reason we move from stage (2) to stage (3) in the case of demons is that (A) is obviously satisifed. The phenomena which we explained by reference to the activity of demons are so much better explained in other ways that it is simpler to stop inferring to the existence of demons altogether than to continue making such inferences, and then turning to laws about germs and the like for an explanation of the behavior of the demons. The reason why we do *not* move from (2) to (3)—much less to (6)—in the case of temperature or tables is that explanations formulated in terms of temperatures are so good, on the ground which they were originally intended to cover, that we feel no temptation to stop talking about temperatures and tables merely because we can, in some cases, get more precise predictions by going up a level to laws about molecules. The reason why we move on from (3) to (4) in the case of demons is that the alternative labeled (4b) is readily available—we can easily consign experiences of demons to that great dumping-ground of out-dated entities, the Mind. There were no experiences of demons, we say, but only experiences of mental images.

Now it seems obvious that, in the case of sensations, (A) will not be satisfied. The inconvenience of ceasing to talk about sensations would be so great that only a fanatical materialist would think it worth the trouble to cease referring to sensations. If the Identity Theorist is taken to be predicting that some day "sensation," "pain," "mental image," and the like will drop out of our vocabulary, he is almost certainly wrong. But if he is saying simply that, at no greater cost than an inconvenient linguistic reform, we *could* drop such terms, he is entirely justified. And I take this latter claim to be all that traditional materialism has ever desired.

Before leaving the analogy between demons and sensations, I wish to note one further disanalogy which an opponent of the Identity Theory might pounce upon. Even if we set aside the fact that (A) would not be satisfied in the case of sensations, such an opponent might say, we should note the difficulty in satisfying (B). It would seem that there is no satisfactory answer to the question "What *was* I non-inferentially reporting when I reported on my sensations?" For neither (4a) nor (4b) seems an available option. The first does not seem to be available because it is counter-intuitive to think of, e.g., "I am having my C-fibers stimulated," as capable of being used to make a non-inferential report. The second alternative is simply silly—there is no point in saying that when we report a sensation we are reporting some "merely mental" event. For sensations are *already* mental events. The last point is important for an understanding of the prima facie absurdity of the disappearance form of the Identity Theory. The reason why most statements of the form "there might turn out to be no X's at all" can be accepted with more or less equanimity in the context of forecasts of scientific results is that we are confident we shall always be able to "save the phenomena" by answering the question "But what about all those X's we've been accustomed to observe?" with some reference to thoughts-of-X's, images-of-X's, and the like. Reference to mental entities provides non-inferential reports of X's with something to have been about. But when we want to say "There might turn out to be no mental entities at all," we cannot use this device. This result makes clear that if the analogy between the past disappearance of supernatural beings and the possible future disappearance of sensations is to be pressed, we must claim that alternative (4a) is, appearances to the contrary, still open. That is, we must hold that the question, "What *was* I non-inferentially reporting when I non-inferentially reported a stabbing pain?" can be sensibly answered "You were reporting a stimulation of your C-fibers."

Now why should this *not* be a sensible answer? Let us begin by getting a bad objection to it out of the way. One can imagine someone arguing that this answer can only be given if a stimulation of C-fibers is strictly identical with a stabbing pain, and that such strict identification involves category-mistakes. But this objection presupposes that "A report of an X is a report of a Y" entails that "X's are Y's." If we grant this presupposition we shall not be able to say that the question "What was I reporting when I reported a demon?" is properly answered by "You were reporting the content of an hallucination which you were having." However, if we ask why this objection is plausible, we can see the grain of truth which it embodies and conceals. We are usually unwilling to accept "You were reporting a Y" as an answer to the question "What *was* I non-inferentially reporting when I non-inferentially reported an X?" unless (a) Y's are themselves the kind of thing we habitually report on non-inferentially, and (b) there does not exist already an habitual practice of reporting Y's non-inferentially. Thus we accept "the content of an hallucination" as a sensible answer because we know that such contents, being "mental images," are just the sort of thing which does get non-inferentially reported (once it is recognized for what it is) and because we are not accustomed to making non-inferential reports in the form "I am having a hallucinatory image of. . . ."[9] To take an example of answers to this sort of question that are *not* sensible, we reject the claim that when we report on a table we are reporting on a mass of whirling particles, for either we think we know under what circumstances we should make such a report, and know that these circumstances do not obtain, or we believe that the presence of such particles can only be inferred and never observed.

The oddity of saying that when I think I am reporting on a stabbing pain I am actually reporting on a stimulation of my C-fibers is similar to these last two cases. We either imagine a situation in which we can envisage ourselves non-inferentially reporting such stimulation (periscope hitched up to microscope so as to give us a view of our trepanned skull, overlying fibers folded out of the way, stimulation evident by change in color, etc., etc.), or else we regard "stimulation of C-fibers" as not the sort of thing which *could* be the subject of a non-inferential report (but inherently a "theoretical" state of affairs whose existence can only be inferred, and not observed). In either case, the assertion that we have been non-inferentially reporting on a brain-process all our lives seems absurd. So the proponent of the disappearance form of the Identity Theory must show that reports of brain-processes are neither incapable of being non-inferential nor, if non-inferential, necessarily made in the same way just imagined (with the periscope-microscope gadget) or

in some other peculiar way. But now we must ask who bears the burden of proof. Why, after all, should we think that brain-processes are *not* a fit subject-matter for non-inferential reports? And why should it not be the case that the circumstances in which we make non-inferential reports about brain-processes are just those circumstances in which we make non-inferential reports about sensations? For this will in fact be the case if, when we were trained to say, e.g., "I'm in pain" we were in fact being trained to respond to the occurrence within ourselves of a stimulation of C-fibers. If this is the case, the situation will be perfectly parallel to the case of demons and hallucinations. We *will*, indeed, have been making non-inferential reports about brain-processes all our lives *sans le savoir*.

This latter suggestion can hardly be rejected a priori, unless we hold that we can only be taught to respond to the occurrence of A's with the utterance "A!" if we were able, prior to this teaching, to be aware, when an A was present, that it was present. But this latter claim is plausible only if we assume that there is an activity which can reasonably be called "awareness" prior to the learning of language. I do not wish to fight again the battle which has been fought by Wittgenstein and many of his followers against such a notion of awareness. I wish rather to take it as having been won, and to take for granted that there is no a priori reason why a brain-process is inherently unsuited to be the subject of a non-inferential report. The distinction between observation terms and non-observation terms is relative to linguistic practices (practices which may change as inquiry progresses), rather than capable of being marked out once and for all by distinguishing between the "found" and the "made" elements in our experience. I think that the recognition of this relativity is the first of the steps necessary for a proper appreciation of the claims of the Identity Theory. In what follows, I want to show that this first step leads naturally to a second: the recognition that the distinction between *private* and *public* subject-matters is as relative as that between items signified by observation-terms and items not so signified.

The importance of this second step is clear. For even if we grant that reports of brain-processes may be non-inferential, we still need to get around the facts that reports of sensations have an epistemological peculiarity that leads us to call them reports of *private entities*, and that brain-processes are intrinsically *public* entities. Unless we can overcome our intuitive conviction that a report of a private matter (with its attendant infallibilty) cannot be identified with a report of a public matter (with its attendant fallibility), we shall not be able to take seriously the claim of the proponents of the disappearance form of the Identity Theory that alternative (4a) is open, and hence that nothing prevents sensations from disappearing from discourse in the same manner, and for the same reasons, as supernatural beings have disappeared from discourse. So far in this paper I have deliberately avoided the problem of the "privacy" of sensations, because I wished to show that if this problem *can* be surmounted, the Identity Theorist may fairly throw the burden of proof onto his opponent by asking whether a criterion can be produced which would show that the identification of sensations and brain-processes involves a conceptual confusion, while absolving the claim that demons do not exist because of such a confusion. Since I doubt that such a criterion *can* be produced, I am inclined to say that if the problem about "privacy" is overcome, then the Identity Theorist has made out his case.

5. *THE "PRIVACY" OBJECTION*

The problem that the privacy of first-person sensation reports presents for the Identity Theory has recently been formulated in considerable detail by Baier.[10] In this section, I shall confine myself to a discussion of his criticism of Smart's initial reply to this argument. Smart holds that the fact that "the language of introspective reports has a different logic from the logic of material processes" is no objection to the Identity Theory, since we may expect that empirical inquiry can and will change this logic:

It is obvious that until the brain-process theory is much improved and widely accepted there will be no *criteria* for saying 'Smith has an experience of such-and-such a sort' except Smith's introspective reports. So we have adopted a rule of language that (normally) what Smith says goes.[11]

Baier thinks that this reply "is simply a confusion of the privacy of the subject-matter and the availability of external evidence."[12] Baier's intuition is that the difference between a language-stratum in which the fact that a report is sincerely made is sufficient warrant for its truth, and one in which this situation does not obtain, seems so great as to call for an explanation—and that the only explanation is that the two strata concern different subject-matters. Indeed Baier is content to let the mental-physical distinction stand or fall with the distinction between "private" subject-matters and "public" subject-matters, and he therefore assumes that to show that "introspective reports are necessarily about something private, and that being about something private is *incompatible with being* about something public"[13] is to show, once and for all, that the Identity Theory involves a conceptual confusion. Baier, in short, is undertaking to show that "once private, always private."

He argues for his view as follows:

To say that one day our physiological knowledge will increase to such an extent that we shall be able to make absolutely reliable encephalograph-based claims about people's experiences, is only to say that, if carefully checked, our encephalograph-based claims about 'experiences' will always be *correct*, i.e. will make the *same claims* as a *truthful* introspective reports. If correct encephalograph-based claims about Smith's experiences contradict Smith's introspective reports, we shall be entitled to infer that he is *lying*. In that sense, what Smith says will no longer go. But we cannot of course infer that he is making a mistake, for that is nonsense. . . . *However good the evidence may be, such a physiological theory can never be used to show to the sufferer that he was mistaken in thinking that he had a pain, for such a mistake is inconceivable.* The sufferer's epistemological authority must therefore be better than the best physiological theory can ever be. Physiology can therefore never provide a person with more than *evidence* that someone else is having an experience of one sort or another. It can never lay down *criteria* for saying that someone is having an experience of a certain sort. Talk about brain processes therefore must be about something other than talk about experiences. Hence, introspective reports and brain-process talk cannot be merely different ways of talking about the same thing.[14]

Smart's own reply to this line of argument is to admit that

> No physiological evidence, say from a gadget attached to my skull, could make me withdraw the statement that I have a pain when as a matter of fact I feel a pain. For example, the gadget might show no suitable similarities of cerebral processes on the various occasions on which I felt a pain. . . . I must, I think, agree with Baier that if the sort of situation which we have just envisaged did in fact come about, then I should have to reject the brain process thesis, and would perhaps espouse dualism.[15]

But this is not the interesting case. The interesting case is the one in which suitable similarities are in fact found to occur—the same similarities in all subjects—until one day (long after all empirical generalizations about sensations *qua* sensations have been subsumed under physiological laws, and long after direct manipulation of the brain has become the exclusive method of relieving pain)

somebody (call him Jones) thinks he has no pain, but the encephalograph says that the brain-process correlated with pain did occur. (Let us imagine that Jones himself is observing the gadget, and that the problem about whether he might have made a mistake is a problem for Jones; this eliminates the possibility of lying.) Now in most cases in which one's observation throws doubt on a correlation which is so central to current scientific explanations, one tries to eliminate the possibility of observational error. But in Baier's view it would be absurd for Jones to do this, for "a mistake is inconceivable." Actually, however, it is fairly clear what Jones' first move would be—he will begin to suspect that he does not know what pain is—i.e., that he is not using the word "pain" in the way in which his fellows use it.[16]

So now Jones looks about for independent verification of the hypothesis that he does not use "I am in pain" incorrectly. But here he runs up against the familiar difficulty about the vocabulary used in making introspective reports—the difficulty of distinguishing between "misuse of language" and "mistake in judgment", between (a) recognizing the state of affairs which obtains for what it is, but describing it wrongly because the words used in the description are not the right words, and (b) being able to describe it rightly once it is recognized for what it is, but not in fact recognizing it for what it is (in the way in which one deceived by an illusion does not recognize the situation for what it is). If we do not have a way of determining which of these situations obtains, we do not have a genuine contrast between misnaming and misjudging. To see that there is no genuine contrast in this case, suppose that Jones was not burned prior to the time that he hitches on the encephalograph, but now he is. When he is, the encephalograph says that the brain-process constantly correlated with pain-reports occurs in Jones' brain. However, although he exhibits pain-behavior, Jones thinks that he does not feel pain. (But, now as in the past, he both exhibits pain-behavior and thinks that he feels pain when he is frozen, stuck, struck, racked, etc.) Now is it that he does not know that *pain* covers what you feel when you are burned as well as what you feel when you are stuck, struck, etc.? Or is it that he really does not feel pain when he is burned? Suppose we tell Jones that what he feels when he is burned is *also* called "pain." Suppose he then admits that he does feel *something*, but insists that what he feels is quite *different* from what he feels when he is stuck, struck, etc. Where does Jones go from here? Has he failed to learn the language properly, or is he correctly (indeed infallibly) reporting that he has different sensations than those normally had in the situation in question? (Compare the parallel question in the case of a man who uses "blue" in all the usual ways except that he refuses to grant that blue is a color—on the ground that it is so different from red, yellow, orange, violet, etc.)

The only device which would decide this question would be to establish a convention that anyone who sincerely denied that he felt a pain while exhibiting pain-behavior and being burned ipso facto did not understand how to use "pain." This denial would *prove* that he lacked such an understanding. But this would be a dangerous path to follow. For not to understand when to use the word "pain" in non-inferential reports is presumably to be unable to know which of one's sensations to call a "pain." And the denial that one felt pain in the circumstances mentioned would only prove such inability if one indeed *had* the sensation normally called a pain. So now we would have a public criterion, satisfaction of which would count as showing that the subject had such a sensation—i.e., that he felt a pain even though he did not think that he did. But if such a criterion exists, its application overrides any contradictory report that he may make—for such a report will be automatically disallowed by the fact that it constitutes a demonstration that he does not know what he is talking about. The dilemma is that either a report about one's sensations which violates a certain public criterion is a sufficient condition for saying that the reporter does not know

how to use "pain" in the correct way, or there is no such criterion. If there is, the fact that one cannot be mistaken about pains does not entail that sincere reports of pain cannot be over-ridden. If there is not, then there is no way to answer the question formulated at the end of the last paragraph, and hence no way to eliminate the possibility that Jones may not know what pain is. Now since the a priori probability that he does not is a good deal higher than the a priori probability that the psycho-physiological theory of Jones' era is mistaken, this theory has little to fear from Jones. (Although it would have a great deal to fear from a sizable accumulation of cases like Jones'.)

To sum up this point, we may look back at the italicized sentence in the above quotation from Baier. We now see that the claim that "such a mistake is inconceivable" is an ellipsis for the claim that a mistake, made *by one who knows what pain is*, is inconceivable, for only this expanded form will entail that when Jones and the encephalograph disagree, Jones is always right. But when formulated in this way our infallibility about our pains can be seen to be empty. Being infallible about something would be useful only if we could draw the usual distinction between misnaming and misjudging, and, having ascertained that we were not misnaming, know that we were not misjudging. But where there are no criteria for misjudging (or to put it more accurately, where in the crucial cases the criteria for misjudging turn out to be the same as the criteria for misnaming) than to say that we are infallible is to pay ourselves an empty compliment. Our neighbors will not hesitate to ride roughshod over our reports of our sensations unless they are assured that we know our way around among them, and we cannot satisfy them on this point unless, up to a certain point, we tell the same sort of story about them as they do. The limits of permissible stories are flexible enough for us to be able to convince them occasionally that we have odd sensations, but not flexible enough for us to use these surprising sensations to break down, at one blow, well-confirmed scientific theories. As in the case of other infallible pronouncements, the price of retaining one's epistemological authority is a decent respect for the opinions of mankind.

Thus the common-sense remark that first-person reports always will be a better source of information about the occurrence of pains than any other source borrows its plausibility from the fact that we normally do not raise questions about a man's ability to use the word "pain" correctly. Once we *do* raise such questions seriously (as in the case of Jones), we realize that the question (1) "Does he know which sensations are called 'pains'?" and (2) "Is he a good judge of whether he is in pain or not?" are simply two ways of asking the same question: viz., "Can we fit his pain-reports into our scheme for explaining and predicting pains?" or, more bluntly, "Shall we disregard his pain-reports or not?" And once we see this we realize that if "always be a better source of information" means "will never be over-ridden on the sort of grounds on which presumed observational errors are over-ridden elsewhere in science," then our common-sensical remark is probably false. If "always be a better source of information" means merely "can only be over-ridden on the basis of a charge of misnaming, and never on the basis of a charge of misjudging," then our common-sensical remark turns out to depend upon a distinction that is not there.

This Wittgensteinian point that sensation-reports must conform to public criteria or else be disallowed may also be brought out in the following way. We determine whether to take a surprising first-person report of pain or its absence seriously (that is, whether to say that the sensation reported is something that science must try to explain) by seeing whether the reporter's overall pattern of pain-reporting is, by the usual behavioral and environmental criteria, normal. Now suppose that these public criteria (for "knowing how to use 'pain' ") change as physiology and technology progress. Suppose, in particular, that we find it convenient to speed up the learning of contrasting observa-

tion predicates (such as "painful," "tickling," etc.) by supplying children with portable encephalographs-cum-teaching-machines which, whenever the appropriate brain-process occurs, murmur the appropriate term in their ears. Now "appropriate brain-process" will start out by meaning "brain-process constantly correlated with sincere utterances of 'I'm in pain' by people taught the use of 'pain' in the old rough-and-ready way." But soon it will come to mean, "the brain-process which we have always programmed the machine to respond to with a murmur of 'pain.' " (A meter is [now, but was not always] what matches the Standard Meter; intelligence is [now, but was not always] what intelligence tests test; pains will be [but are not now] what the Standard "Pain"-Training Program calls "pain.") Given this situation, it would make sense to say things like "You say you are in pain, and I'm sure you are sincere, but you can see for yourself that your brain is not in the state in which you were trained to respond to with "Pain," so apparently the training did not work, and you do not yet understand what pain is." In such a situation, our "inability to be mistaken" about our pains would remain, but our "final epistemological authority" on the subject would be gone, for there would be a standard procedure for overriding our reports. Our inability to be mistaken is, after all, no more than our ability to have such hypothetical statements as "If you admit that I'm sincere and that I know the language, you have to accept what I say" accepted by our fellows. But this asset can only be converted into final epistemological authority if we can secure both admissions. Where a clear-cut public criterion *does* exist for "knowing the language," inability to be mistaken does not entail inability to be over-ridden.

Now Baier might say that if such criteria did exist, then we should no longer be talking about what we presently mean by "pains." I do not think that this needs to be conceded,[17] but suppose that it is. Would this mean that there was now a subject-matter which was not being discussed—viz., the private subject-matter the existence of which Baier's argument was intended to demonstrate? That we once had contact with such a subject-matter, but lost it? These rhetorical questions are meant to suggest that Baier's explanation of the final epistemological authority of first-person reports of pains by the fact that this "logic" is "a function of this type of subject-matter" rather than, as Smart thinks, a convention—is an explanation of the obscure by the more obscure. More precisely, it will not be an explanation of the epistemological authority in question—but only an unenlightening redescription of it—unless Baier can give a meaning to the term "private subject-matter" other than "kind of thing which is reported in reports which cannot be over-ridden." These considerations show the need for stepping back from Baier's argument and considering the criteria which he is using to demarcate distinct subject-matters.

6. "PRIVACY" AS A CRITERION OF CATEGOREAL DEMARCATION

The closest Baier comes to giving a definition of "private subject-matter" is to say that

We must say that 'I have a pain' is about 'something private,' because in making this remark we report something which is (1) *necessarily owned* . . . (2) *necessarily exclusive and unsharable* . . . (3) *necessarily imperceptible by the senses* . . . (4) *necessarily asymmetrical*, for whereas it makes no sense to say 'I could see (or hear) that I had a pain,' it makes quite good sense to say 'I could see (or hear) that *he* had a pain'; (5) something about the possession of which the person who claims to possess it could not possibly examine, consider, or weigh any evidence, although other people could . . . and lastly (6) it is something about which the person whose private state it is has final epistemological authority, for it does not make sense to say 'I have a pain unless I am mistaken.'[18]

Now this definition of "something private" entails that nothing could be private except a state of a person, and is constructed to delimit all and only those states of a person which we call his "mental" states. To say that mental states are private is to say simply that mental states are described in the way in which mental states are described. But it is not hard to take *any* Rylean category of terms (call it C), list all the types of sentence-frames which do and do not make sense when their gaps are filled with terms belonging to this category, and say that "something C" is distinguished by the fact that it is "necessarily X," "necessarily Y," etc. where "X" and "Y" are labels for the fact that certain sentence-frames will or will not receive these terms as gap-fillers. For example, consider the thesis that:

We must say that 'The devil is in that corner' is about 'something supernatural' because in making this report we report something which is *necessarily intangible*, since it makes no sense to ask about the texture of his skin, not *necessarily simply-located*, since it does not follow from the fact that a supernatural being is in the corner that the same supernatural being is not simultaneously at the other side of the globe, *necessarily immortal*, since it does not make sense to say that a supernatural being has died, *necessarily perceptible to exorcists*, since it would not make sense to say that a man was an exorcist and did not perceive the devil when he was present. . . .

Are devils hallucinations? No, because when one reports a hallucination one reports something which, though intangible, is simply-located, is neither mortal nor immortal, and is not always perceptible to exorcists. Are reports of devils reports of hallucinations? No, because reports of devils are reports of something supernatural and reports of hallucinations are reports of something private. It is simply because we lack further information about devils that we take exorcists' sincere reports as the best possible reports about them? No, for this suggestion confuses the supernatural character of the subject-matter with the availability of external evidence. Those without the supernatural powers with which the exorcist is gifted may find ways of gathering *evidence* for the presence of supernatural beings, but they can never formulate an overriding and independent *criterion* for saying that such a being is present. Their theories might become so good that we might sometimes say that a given exorcist was *lying*, but we could never say that he was *mistaken*.

If this pastiche of Baier's argument seems beside the point, it is presumably either (1) because the language-game I have described is not in fact played, or else (2) because "necessarily intangible, not necessarily simply-located, necessarily immortal, and necessarily perceptible to exorcists" it does not delimit a subject-matter in the way in which "necessarily owned, exclusive, imperceptible by the senses, asymmetrical, etc., etc." does. In (1) one has to ask "what if it *had* been played?" After all, if the technique of detecting distinct subject-matters which Baier uses is a generally applicable technique, and not just constructed *ad hoc* to suit our Cartesian intuitions, then it ought to work on imaginary as well as real language games. But if it is, we ought to be able to formulate rules for applying it which would tell us *why* (2) is the case. For if we cannot, and if the language-game described once was played, then Baier's objection to the Identity Theory is an objection to the theory that reports of visible supernatural beings are reports of hallucinations.

Baier gives no more help in seeing what these rules would be. But I think that the root of Baier's conviction that "something private" is a suitable candidate for being a "distinct subject matter" is the thesis that certain terms are *intrinsically* observation predicates, and signify, so to speak, "natural explananda." When in quest of such predicates we look to the "foundations" of empirical knowledge, we tend to rapidly identify "observation predicate" with "predicate occurring in report having final epistemological authority" with "predicate occurring in report about something pri-

vate." This chain of identifications leaves us with the suspicion that if there were no longer a private subject-matter to be infallible about, the whole fabric of empirical inquiry about public matters would be left up in the air, unsupported by any absolute epistemological authority. The suggestion that the distinction between items reportable in infallible reports and items not so reportable is "ultimate," or "irreducible," or "categorical," owes its intuitive force to the difficulty of imagining a stage in the progress of inquiry in which there was not *some* situation in which absolute epistemological authority about *something* would be granted to *somebody*.

There probably could *not* be such a stage, for inquiry cannot proceed if everything is to be doubted at once, and if inquiry is even to get off the ground we need to get straight about what is to be questioned and what not. These practical dictates show the kernel of truth in the notion that inquiry cannot proceed without a foundation. Where we slide from truth into error is in assuming that certain items are *naturally* reportable in infallible reports, and thus assume that the items presently so reportable always were and always will be reportable (and conversely for items not presently so reportable). A pain looks like a paradigm of such an item, with the situation described by "seems to me as if I were seeing something red" almost as well-qualified. But in both cases, we can imagine situations in which we should feel justified in overriding sincere reports using these predicates. More important, we see that the device which we should use to justify ourselves in such situations—viz., "The reporter may not know how to use the word . . ."—is one which can apply in *all* proposed cases. Because this escape-hatch is always available, and because the question of whether the reporter does know how to use the word or not is probably not in itself a question which could ever be settled by recourse to any absolute epistemological authority, the situation envisaged by Baier—namely, the body of current scientific theory foundering upon the rock of a single over-riding report—can probably never arise. Baier sees a difference in kind between the weight of evidence produced by such a theory and the single, authoritative, *criterion* provided by such a report. But since there can be no over-riding report until the ability of the speaker to use the words used in the report is established, and since this is to be established only by the weight of the evidence and not by recourse to any single criterion, this difference in kind (even though it may indeed be "firmly embedded in the way we talk" for millennia) is always capable of being softened into a difference of degree by further empirical inquiry.

7. *REDUCTIONIST PHILOSOPHICAL THEORIES AND CATEGOREAL DISTINCTIONS*

In the preceding sections of this paper I have constantly invoked the fact that language changes as empirical discoveries are made, in order to argue that the thesis that "What people now call 'sensations' might be discovered to be brain-processes" is sensible and unconfused. The "deviance" of a statement of this thesis should not, I have been urging, blind us to the facts that (a) entities referred to by expressions in one Rylean category may also be referred to by expressions in another, (b) expressions in the first category may drop out of the language once this identity of reference is realized, and (c) the thesis in question is a natural way of expressing the result of this realization in the case of "sensation" and "brain-process." Now a critic might object that this strategy is subject to a *reductio ad absurdum*. For the same fact about linguistic change would seem to justify the claim that *any* statement of the form (S) "What people call 'X's' may be discovered to be Y's" is *always* sensible and unconfused. Yet this seems paradoxical, for consider the result of substituting, say "neutrino" for "X" and "mushroom" for "Y." If the resulting statement is not conceptually confused, what statement is?

In answer to this objection, I should argue that it is a mistake to attribute "conceptual confusions" to *statements*. No statement can be known to express a conceptual confusion simply by virtue of an acquaintance with the meanings of its component terms. Confusion is a property of people. Deviance is a property of utterances. Deviant utterances made by using sentences of the form (S) *may* betoken confusion on the part of the speaker about the meanings of words, but it may simply indicate a vivid (but unconfused) imagination, or perhaps (as in the neutrino-mushroom case) merely idle fancy. Although the making of such statements may be prima facie evidence of conceptual confusion—i.e., of the fact that the speaker is insufficiently familiar with the language to find a non-deviant way of making his point—this evidence is only prima facie, and questioning may bring out evidence pointing the other way. Such questioning may show that the speaker actually has some detailed suggestions about possible empirical results which would point to the discovery in question, or that he has no such suggestions, but is nevertheless not inclined to use the relevant words in any *other* deviant utterances, and to cheerfully admit the deviance of his original utterance. The possibility of such evidence, pointing to imagination or fancy rather than to confusion, shows that from the fact that certain questions are typically asked, and certain statements typically made, by victims of conceptual confusion, it does not follow that all those who use the sentences used to ask these questions or to make these statements are thus victimized.

This confusion about confusion is due to the fact that philosophers who propound "reductionist" theories (such as "There is no insensate matter," "There are no minds," "There are no physical objects," etc.) often *have* been conceptually confused. Such theories are often advocated as solutions to pseudo-problems whose very formulation involves deviant uses of words—uses which in fact result from a confusion between the uses of two or more senses of the same term, or between two or more related terms (e.g., "name" and "word") or between the kind of questions appropriately asked of entities referred to by one set of terms and the kind appropriately asked of entities referred to by another. (That these deviant uses *are* the result of such confusion, it should be noticed, is only capable of being determined by questioning of those who use them—and we only feel *completely* safe in making this diagnosis when the original user has, in the light of the linguistic facts drawn to his attention, admitted that his putative "problem" has been dissolved.) Because reductionist theories may often be choked off at the source by an examination of uses of language, anti-reductionist philosophers have lately become prone to use "conceptual confusion" or "category-mistake" as an all-purpose diagnosis for any deviant utterance in the mouth of a philosopher. But this is a mistake. Predictions of the sort illustrated by (S) may be turned to confused purposes, and they may be made by confused people. But we could only infer with certainty the deviance of the utterance of a sentence of the form (S) to the conceptual confusion of the speaker if we had a map of the categories which are exhibited in all possible languages, and were thus in a position to say that the cross-category identification envisaged by the statement was eternally impossible. In other words, we should only be in a position to make this inference with certainty if we knew that empirical inquiry could *never* bring about the sort of linguistic change which permits the non-deviant use of "There are no X's" in the case of the "X's" to which the statement in question refers. But philosophers are in no position to say that such change is impossible. The hunt for categorical confusions at the source of reductionist philosophical theories is an extremely valuable enterprise. But their successes in this enterprise should not lead linguistic philosophers to think that they can do better what metaphysicians did badly—namely, prove the irreducibility of entities. Traditional materialism embodied many confusions, but at its heart was the unconfused prediction about future empirical inquiry which is the Identity Theory. The confusions may be

eradicated without affecting the plausibility or interest of the prediction.[19]

NOTES

[1]A proponent of the Identity Theory is usually thought of as one who predicts that empirical inquiry *will* reach this result—but few philosophers in fact stick their necks out in this way. The issue is not the truth of the prediction, but whether such a prediction makes sense. Consequently, by "Identity Theory" I shall mean the assertion that it does make sense.

I include only sensations within the scope of the theory because inclusion of thoughts would raise a host of separate problems (about the reducibility of intentional and semantic discourse to statements about linguistic behavior), and because the form of the Identity Theory which has been most discussed in the recent literature restricts itself to a consideration of sensations.

[2]James Cornman, "The Identity of Mind and Body," *Journal of Philosophy*, 59 (1962), p. 490.

[3]Cornman, p. 491.

[4]Cf. J. J. C. Smart, "Sensations and Brain Processes," reprinted in *The Philosophy of Mind*," ed. by V. C. Chappell (Englewood Cliffs, 1962), pp. 160–172, esp. pp. 166–68, and especially the claim that "When a person says 'I see a yellowish-orange after-image' he is saying something like this: 'There is something going on which is like what is going on when I have my eyes open, am awake, and there is an orange illuminated in good light in front of me, that is, when I really see an orange' " (p. 167). For criticisms of Smart's program of translation, see Cornman, op. cit.; Jerome Shaffer, "Could Mental States Be Brain Processes?," *Journal of Philosophy*, 58 (1961), pp. 812–822; Shaffer, "Mental Events and the Brain," *Journal of Philosophy* 60 (1963), pp. 160–166. See also the articles cited in the first footnote to Smart's own article.

[5]No statement of the disappearance form of the theory with which I am acquainted is as clear and explicit as Smart's statement of the translation form. See, however, Feyerabend, "Mental Events and the Brain," *Journal of Philosophy*, 60 (1963), pp. 295–296, and "Materialism and the Mind-Body Problem," *The Review of Metaphysics*, 17 (1963), pp. 49–67. See also Wilfrid Sellars, "The Identity Approach to the Mind-Body Problem," *ibid.*, 18 (1965). My indebtedness to this and other writings of Sellars will be obvious in what follows.

[6]Both forms agree, however, on the requirements which would have to be satisfied if we are to claim that the empirical discovery in question has been made. Roughly, they are (1) that one-one or one-many correlations could be established between every type of sensa-

tion and some clearly demarcated kind(s) of brain-processes; (2) that every known law which refers to sensations would be subsumed under laws about brain-processes; (3) that new laws about sensations be discovered by deduction from laws about brain-processes.

[7]Cornman, p. 492.

[8]Note that if X's are *only* referred to in inferential reports—as in the case of "neutrons" and "epicycles," no philosophically interesting reduction takes place. For in such cases there is no hope of getting rid of an explanandum; all we get rid of is a putative explanation.

[9]Note that people who *become* accustomed to making the latter sort of reports may no longer accept explanations of their erroneous non-inferential reports by reference to hallucinations. For they know what mental images are like, and they know that *this* pink rat was not an hallucinatory content. The more frequent case, fortunately, is that they just cease to report pink rats and begin reporting hallucinations, for their hallucinations no longer deceive them.

[10]Kurt Baier, "Smart on Sensations," *Australasian Journal of Philosophy*, 40 (1962), pp. 57–68.

[11]Smart, "Sensations and Brain Processes," p. 169.

[12]Baier, p. 63.

[13]Baier, p. 59.

[14]Baier, pp. 64–5; italics added.

[15]Smart, "Brain Processes and Incorrigibility—a Reply to Professor Baier," *Australasian Journal of Philosophy*, 40 (1962), p. 68.

[16]This problem will remain, of course, even if Jones merely *thinks* about whether he is in pain, but does not say anything.

[17]My reasons for thinking this concession unnecessary are the same as those presented in some recent articles by Hilary Putnam: cf. "Minds and Machines," *Dimensions of Mind*, ed. by S. Hook (New York, 1961), pp. 138–161, esp. pp. 153–160; "The Analytic and the Synthetic," *Minnesota Studies in the Philosophy of Science*, III, pp. 358–397; "Brains and Behavior," in *Analytic Philosophy*, II, ed. by R. J. Butler (Oxford, 1965).

[18]Baier, "Smart on Sensations," p. 60; the numbers in parentheses have been added.

[19]I have been greatly helped in preparing this paper by the comments of Richard Bernstein, Keith Gunderson, Amélie Rorty, and Richard Schmitt.

The Mind-Body Problem*

Jerry Fodor

Modern philosophy of science has been devoted largely to the formal and systematic description of the successful practices of working scientists. The philosopher does not try to dictate how scientific inquiry and argument ought to be conducted. Instead he tries to enumerate the principles and practices that have contributed to good science. The philosopher has devoted the most attention to analyzing the methodological peculiarities of the physical sciences. The analysis has helped to clarify the nature of confirmation, the logical structure of scientific theories, the formal properties of statements that express laws and the question of whether theoretical entities actually exist.

It is only rather recently that philosophers have become seriously interested in the methodological tenets of psychology. Psychological explanations of behavior refer liberally to the mind and to states, operations and processes of the mind. The philosophical difficulty comes in stating in unambiguous language what such references imply.

Traditional philosophies of mind can be divided into two broad categories: dualist theories and materialist theories. In the dualist approach the mind is a nonphysical substance. In materialist theories the mental is not distinct from the physical; indeed, all mental states, properties, processes and operations are in principle identical with physical states, properties, processes and operations. Some materialists, known as behaviorists, maintain that all talk of mental causes can be eliminated from the language of psychology in favor of talk of environmental stimuli and behavioral responses. Other materialists, the identity theorists, contend that there are mental causes and that they are identical with neurophysiological events in the brain.

In the past 15 years a philosophy of mind called functionalism that is neither dualist nor materialist has emerged from philosophical reflection on developments in artificial intelligence, computational theory, linguistics, cybernetics and psychology. All these fields, which are collectively known as the cognitive sciences, have in common a certain level of abstraction and a concern with systems that process information. Functionalism, which seeks to provide a philosophical account of this level of abstraction, recognizes the possibility that systems as diverse as human beings, calculating machines and disembodied spirits could all have mental states. In the functionalist view the psychology of a system depends not on the stuff it is made of (living cells, metal or spiritual energy) but on how the stuff is put together. Functionalism is a difficult concept, and one way of coming to grips with it is to review the deficiencies of the dualist and materialist philosophies of mind it aims to displace.

The chief drawback of dualism is its failure to account adequately for mental causation. If the mind is nonphysical, it has no position in physical space. How, then, can a mental cause give rise to a behavioral effect that has a position in space? To put it another way, how can the nonphysical give rise to the physical without violating the laws of the conservation of mass, of energy and of momentum?

The dualist might respond that the problem of how the immaterial substance can cause physical events is not much obscurer than the problem of how one physical event can cause another. Yet there is an important difference: there are many clear cases of physical causation but not one clear case of nonphysical causation. Physical interaction is something philosophers, like all other people, have to live with. Nonphysical interaction, however, may be no more than an artifact of the immaterialist construal of the mental. Most philosophers now agree that no argument has successfully demonstrated why mind-body causation should not be regarded as a species of physical causation.

Dualism is also incompatible with the practices of working psychologists. The psychologist frequently applies the experimental methods of the physical sciences to the study of the mind. If mental processes were different in kind from physical processes, there would be no reason to expect these methods to work in the realm of the mental. In order to justify their experimental methods many psychologists urgently sought an alternative to dualism.

In the 1920's John B. Watson at Johns Hopkins University made the radical suggestion that behavior does not have mental causes. He regarded the behavior of an organism as its observable responses to stimuli, which he took to be the causes of its behavior. Over the next 30 years psychologists such as B. F. Skinner of Harvard University developed Watson's ideas into an elaborate world view in which the role of psychology was to catalogue the laws that determine causal relations between stimuli and responses. In this "radical behaviorist" view the problem of explaining the nature of the mind-body interaction vanishes; there is no such interaction.

Radical behaviorism has always worn an air of paradox. For better or worse, the idea of mental causation is deeply ingrained in our everyday language and in our ways of understanding our fellow men and ourselves. For example, people commonly attribute behavior to beliefs, to knowledge and to expectations. Brown puts gas in his tank because he believes the car will not run without it. Jones writes not "acheive" but "achieve" because he knows the rule about putting *i* before *e*. Even when a behavioral response is closely tied to an environmental stimulus, mental processes often intervene. Smith carries an umbrella because the sky is cloudy, but the weather is only part of the story. There are apparently also mental links in the causal chain: observation and expectation. The clouds affect Smith's behavior only because he observes them and because they induce in him an expectation of rain.

The radical behaviorist is unmoved by appeals to such cases. He is prepared to dismiss references to mental causes, however plausible they may seem, as the residue of outworn creeds. The radical behaviorist predicts that as psychologists come to understand more about the relations between stimuli and responses they will find it increasingly possible to explain behavior without postulating mental causes.

The strongest argument against behaviorism is that psychology has not turned out this way; the opposite has happened. As psychology has matured, the framework of mental states and processes that is apparently needed to account for experimental observations has grown all the more elaborate. Particularly in the case of human behavior psychological theories satisfying the methodological tenets of radical behaviorism have proved largely sterile, as would be expected if the postulated mental processes are real and causally effective.

Nevertheless, many philosophers were initially drawn to radical behaviorism because, paradoxes and all, it seemed better than dualism. Since a psychology committed to immaterial substances was unacceptable, philosophers turned to radical behaviorism because it seemed to be the only alternative materialist philosophy of mind. The choice, as they saw it, was between radical behaviorism and ghosts.

By the early 1960's philosophers began to have doubts that dualism and radical behaviorism exhausted the possible approaches to the philosophy of mind. Since the two theories seemed unattractive, the right strategy might be to develop a materialist philosophy of mind that nonetheless allowed for mental causes. Two such philosophies emerged, one called logical behaviorism and the other called the central-state identity theory.

Logical behaviorism is a semantic theory about what mental terms mean. The basic idea is that attributing a mental state (say thirst) to an organism is the same as saying that the organism is disposed to behave in a particular way (for example to drink if there is water available). On this view every mental ascription is equivalent in meaning to an if-then statement (called a behavioral hypothetical) that expresses a behavioral disposition. For example, "Smith is thirsty" might be taken to be equivalent to the dispositional statement "If there were water available, then Smith would drink some." By definition a behavioral hypothetical includes no mental terms. The if-clause of the hypothetical speaks only of stimuli and the then-clause speaks only of behavioral responses. Since stimuli and responses are physical events, logical behaviorism is a species of materialism.

The strength of logical behaviorism is that by translating mental language into the language of stimuli and responses it provides an interpretation of psychological explanations in which behavioral effects are attributed to mental causes. Mental causation is simply the manifestation of a behavioral disposition. More precisely, mental causation is what happens when an organism has a behavioral disposition and the if-clause of the behavioral hypothetical expressing the disposition happens to be true. For example, the causal statement "Smith drank some water because he was thirsty" might be taken to mean "if there were water available, then Smith would drink some, and there was water available."

I have somewhat oversimplified logical behaviorism by assuming that each mental ascription can be translated by a unique behavioral hypothetical. Actually the logical behaviorist often maintains that it takes an open-ended set (perhaps an infinite set) of behavioral hypotheticals to spell out the behavioral disposition expressed by a mental term.

The mental ascription "Smith is thirsty" might also be satisfied by the hypothetical "If there were orange juice available, then Smith would drink some" and by a host of other hypotheticals. In any event the logical behaviorist does not usually maintain he can actually enumerate all the hypotheticals that correspond to a behavioral disposition expressing a given mental term. He only insists that in principle the meaning of any mental term can be conveyed by behavioral hypotheticals.

The way the logical behaviorist has interpreted a mental term such as *thirsty* is modeled after the way many philosophers have interpreted a physical disposition such as fragility. The physical disposition "The glass is fragile" is often taken to mean something like "If the glass were struck, then it would break." By the same token the logical behaviorist's analysis of mental causation is similar to the received analysis of one kind of physical causation. The causal statement "The glass broke because it was fragile" is taken to mean something like "If the glass were struck, then it would break, and the glass was struck."

By equating mental terms with behavioral

dispositions the logical behaviorist has put mental terms on a par with the nonbehavioral dispositions of the physical sciences. That is a promising move, because the analysis of nonbehavioral dispositions is on relatively solid philosophical ground. An explanation attributing the breaking of a glass to its fragility is surely something even the staunchest materialist can accept. By arguing that mental terms are synonymous with dispositional terms, the logical behaviorist has provided something the radical behaviorist could not: a materialist account of mental causation.

Nevertheless, the analogy between mental causation as construed by the logical behaviorist and physical causation goes only so far. The logical behaviorist treats the manifestation of a disposition as the sole form of mental causation, whereas the physical sciences recognize additional kinds of causation. There is the kind of causation where one physical event causes another, as when the breaking of a glass is attributed to its having been struck. In fact, explanations that involve event-event causation are presumably more basic than dispositional explanations, because the manifestation of a disposition (the breaking of a fragile glass) always involves event-event causation and not vice versa. In the realm of the mental many examples of event-event causation involve one mental state's causing another, and for this kind of causation logical behaviorism provides no analysis. As a result the logical behaviorist is committed to the tacit and implausible assumption that psychology requires a less robust notion of causation than the physical sciences require.

Event-event causation actually seems to be quite common in the realm of the mental. Mental causes typically give rise to behavioral effects by virtue of their interaction with other mental causes. For example, having a headache causes a disposition to take aspirin only if one also has the desire to get rid of the headache, the belief that aspirin exists, the belief that taking aspirin reduces headaches and so on. Since mental states interact in generating behavior, it will be necessary to find a construal of psychological explanations that posits mental processes: causal sequences of mental events. It is this construal that logical behaviorism fails to provide.

Such considerations bring out a fundamental way in which logical behaviorism is quite similar to radical behaviorism. It is true that the logical behaviorist, unlike the radical behaviorist, acknowledges the existence of mental states. Yet since the underlying tenet of logical behaviorism is that references to mental states can be translated out of psychological explanations by employing behavioral hypotheticals, all talk of mental states is in a sense heuristic. The only facts to which the behaviorist is actually committed are facts about relations between stimuli and responses. In this respect logical behaviorism is just radical behaviorism in a semantic form. Although the former theory offers a construal of mental causation, the construal is Pickwickian. What does not really exist cannot cause anything, and the logical behaviorist, like the radical behaviorist, believes deep down that mental causes do not exist.

An alternative materialist theory of the mind to logical behaviorism is the central-state identity theory. According to this theory, mental events, states and processes are identical with neurophysiological events in the brain, and the property of being in a certain mental state (such as having a headache or believing it will rain) is identical with the property of being in a certain neurophysiological state. On this basis it is easy to make sense of the idea that a behavioral effect might sometimes have a chain of mental causes; that will be the case whenever a behavioral effect is contingent on the appropriate sequence of neurophysiological events.

The central-state identity theory acknowledges that it is possible for mental causes to interact causally without ever giving rise to any behavioral effect, as when a person thinks for a while about what he ought to do and then decides to do nothing. If mental processes are neurophysiological, they must have the causal properties of neurophysiological processes. Since neurophysiological processes are presumably physical processes, the central-state identity theory ensures that the concept of mental causation is as rich as the concept of physical causation.

The central-state identity theory provides a satisfactory account of what the mental terms in psychological explanations refer to, and so it is favored by psychologists who are dissatisfied with behaviorism. The behaviorist maintains that mental terms refer to nothing or that they refer to the parameters of stimulus-response relations. Either way the existence of mental entities is only illusory. The identity theorist, on the other hand, argues that mental terms refer to neurophysiological states. Thus he can take seriously the project of explaining behavior by appealing to its mental causes.

The chief advantage of the identity theory is that it takes the explanatory constructs of psychology at face value, which is surely something a philosophy of mind ought to do if it can. The identity theory shows how the mentalistic explanations of psychology could not be mere heuristics but literal accounts of the causal history of behavior. Moreover, since the identity theory is not a semantic thesis, it is immune to many arguments that cast in doubt logical behaviorism. A drawback of logical behaviorism is that the observation "John has a headache" does not seem to mean the same thing as a statement of the form "John is disposed to behave in such and such a way." The identity theorist, however, can live with the fact that "John has a headache" and "John is in such and such a brain state" are not synonymous. The assertion of the identity theorist is not that these sentences mean the same thing but only that they are rendered true (or false) by the same neurophysiological phenomena.

The identity theory can be held either as a doctrine about mental particulars (John's current pain or Bill's fear of animals) or as a doctrine about mental universals, or properties (having a pain or being afraid of animals). The two doctrines, called respectively token physicalism and type physicalism, differ in strength and plausibility. Token physicalism maintains only that all mental particulars that happen to exist are neurophysiological, whereas type physicalism makes the more sweeping assertion that all the mental particulars there could possibly be are neurophysiological. Token physicalism does not rule out the logical possibility of machines and disembodied spirits having mental properties. Type physicalism dismisses the possibility because neither machines nor disembodied spirits have neurons.

Type physicalism is not a plausible doctrine about mental properties even if token physicalism is right about mental particulars. The problem with type physicalism is that the psychological constitution of a system seems to depend not on its hardware, or physical composition, but on its software, or program. Why should the philosopher dismiss the possibility that silicon-based Martians have pains, assuming that the silicon is properly organized? And why should the philosopher rule out the possibility of machines having beliefs, assuming that the machines are correctly programmed? If it is logically possible that Martians and machines could have mental properties, then mental properties and neurophysiological processes cannot be identical, however much they may prove to be coextensive.

What it all comes down to is that there seems to be a level of abstraction at which the generalizations of psychology are most naturally pitched. This level of abstraction cuts across differences in the physical composition of the systems to which psychological generalizations apply. In the cognitive sciences, at least, the natural domain for psychological theorizing seems to be all systems that process information. The problem with type physicalism is that there are possible information-processing systems with the same psychological constitution as human beings but not the same physical organization. In principle all kinds of physically different things could have human software.

This situation calls for a relational account of mental properties that abstracts them from the physical structure of their bearers. In spite of the objections to logical behaviorism that I presented above, logical behaviorism was at least on the right track in offering a relational interpretation of mental properties: to have a headache is to be disposed to exhibit a certain pattern of relations between the stimuli one encounters and the responses one exhibits. If that is what having a headache is, however, there is no reason in principle why only heads that are physically similar to ours can ache. Indeed, according to logical behaviorism, it is a necessary truth that any system that has our stimulus-response contingencies also has our headaches.

All of this emerged 10 or 15 years ago as a nasty dilemma for the materialist program in the philosophy of mind. On the one hand the identity theorist (and not the logical behaviorist) had got right the causal character of the interactions of mind and body. On the other the logical behaviorist (and not the identity theorist) had got right the relational character of mental properties. Functionalism has apparently been able to resolve the dilemma. By stressing the distinction computer science draws between hardware and software the functionalist can make sense of both the causal and the relational character of the mental.

The intuition underlying functionalism is that what determines the psychological type to which a mental particular belongs is the causal role of the particular in the mental life of the organism. Functional individualism is differentiated with respect to causal role. A headache, for example, is identified with the type of mental state that among other things causes a disposition for taking aspirin in people who believe that aspirin relieves a headache, causes a desire to rid oneself of the pain one is feeling, often causes someone who speaks English to say such things as "I have a headache" and is brought on by overwork, eyestrain and tension. This list is presumably not complete. More will be known about the nature of a headache as psychological and physiological research discovers more about its causal role.

Functionalism construes the concept of causal role in such a way that a mental state can be defined by its causal relations to other mental states. In this respect functionalism is completely different from logical behaviorism. Another major difference is that functionalism is not a reductionist thesis. It does not foresee, even in principle, the elimination of mentalistic concepts from the explanatory apparatus of psychological theories.

The difference between functionalism and logical behaviorism is brought out by the fact that functionalism is fully compatible with token physicalism. The functionalist would not be disturbed if brain events turn out to be the only things with the functional properties that define mental states. Indeed, most functionalists fully expect it will turn out that way.

Since functionalism recognizes that mental particulars may be physical, it is compatible with the idea that mental causation is a species of physical causation. In other words, functionalism tolerates the materialist solution to the mind-body problem provided by the central-state identity theory. It is possible for the functionalist to assert both that mental states are typically defined in terms of their relations and that interactions of mind and body are typically causal in however robust a notion of causality is required by psychological explanations. The logical behaviorist can endorse only the first assertion and the type physicalist only the second. As a result functionalism seems to capture the best features of the materialist alternatives to dualism. It is no wonder that functionalism has become increasingly popular.

Machines provide good examples of two concepts that are central to functionlism: the concept that mental states are interdefined and the concept that they can be realized by many systems. The illustration on the next page contrasts a behavioristic Coke machine with a mentalistic one. Both machines dispense a Coke for 10 cents. (The price has not been affected by inflation.) The states of the machines are defined by reference to their causal roles, but only the machine on the left would satisfy the behaviorist. Its single state ($S0$) is completely specified in terms of stimuli and responses. $S0$ is the state a machine is in if, and only if, given a dime as the input, it dispenses a Coke as the output.

The machine on the right in the illustra-

TWO COKE MACHINES bring out the difference between behaviorism (the doctrine that there are no mental causes) and mentalism (the doctrine that there are mental causes). Both machines dispense a Coke for 10 cents and have states that are defined by reference to their causal role. The machine at the left is a behavioristic one: its single state (*S0*) is defined solely in terms of the input and the output. The machine at the right is a mentalistic one: its two states (*S1, S2*) must be defined not only in terms of the input and the output but also in terms of each other. To put it another way, the output of the Coke machine depends on the state the machine is in as well as on the input. The functionalist philosopher maintains that mental states are interdefined, like the internal states of the mentalistic Coke machine.

	STATE S0
DIME INPUT	DISPENSES A COKE

	STATE S1	STATE S2
NICKEL INPUT	GIVES NO OUTPUT AND GOES TO S2	DISPENSES A COKE AND GOES TO S1
DIME INPUT	DISPENSES A COKE AND STAYS IN S1	DISPENSES A COKE AND A NICKEL AND GOES TO S1

tion has interdefined states (*S1* and *S2*), which are characteristic of functionalism. *S1* is the state a machine is in if and only if, (1) given a nickel, it dispenses nothing and proceeds to *S2*, and (2) given a dime, it dispenses a Coke and stays in *S1*. *S2* is the state a machine is in if, and only if, (1) given a nickel, it dispenses a Coke and proceeds to *S1*, and (2) given a dime, it dispenses a Coke and a nickel and proceeds to *S1*. What *S1* and *S2* jointly amount to is the machine's dispensing a Coke if it is given a dime, dispensing a Coke and a nickel if it is given a dime and a nickel and waiting to be given a second nickel if it has been given a first one.

Since *S1* and *S2* are each defined by hypothetical statements, they can be viewed as dispositions. Nevertheless, they are not behavioral dispositions because the consequences an input has for a machine in *S1* or *S2* are not specified solely in terms of the output of the machine. Rather, the consequences also involve the machine's internal states.

Nothing about the way I have described the behavioristic and mentalistic Coke machines puts constraints on what they could be made of. Any system whose states bore the proper relations to inputs, outputs and other states could be one of these machines. No doubt it is reasonable to expect such a system to be constructed out of such things as wheels, levers and diodes (token physicalism for Coke machines). Similarly, it is reasonable to expect that our minds may prove to be neurophysiological (token physicalism for human beings).

Nevertheless, the software description of a Coke machine does not logically require wheels, levers and diodes for its concrete realization. By the same token, the software description of the mind does not logically require neurons. As far as functionalism is concerned a Coke machine with states *S1* and *S2* could be made of ectoplasm, if there is such stuff and if its states have the right causal properties. Functionalism allows for the possibility of disembodied Coke machines in exactly the same way and to the same extent that it allows for the possibility of disembodied minds.

To say that *S1* and *S2* are interdefined and realizable by different kinds of hardware is not, of course, to say that a Coke machine has a mind. Although interdefinition and functional specification are typical features of mental states, they are clearly not sufficient for mentality. What more is required is a question to which I shall return below.

Some philosophers are suspicious of functionalism because it seems too easy. Since functionalism licenses the individuation of states by reference to their causal role, it appears to allow a trivial explanation of any observed event *E*, that is, it appears to postulate an *E*-causer. For example, what makes the valves in a machine open? Why, the operation of a valve opener. And what is a valve opener? Why, anything that has the functionally defined property of causing valves to open.

In psychology this kind of question-begging often takes the form of theories that in effect postulate homunculi with the selfsame intellectual capacities the theorist set out to explain. Such is the case when visual perception is explained by simply postulating psychological mechanisms that process visual information. The behaviorist has often charged the mentalist, sometimes justifiably, of mongering this kind of question-begging pseudo explanation. The charge will have to be met if functionally defined mental states are to have a serious role in psychological theories.

The burden of the accusation is not untruth but triviality. There can be no doubt that it is a valve opener that opens valves, and it is likely that visual perception is mediated by the processing of visual information. The charge is that such putative functional explanations are mere platitudes. The functionalist can meet this objection by allowing functionally defined theoretical constructs only where mechanisms exist that can carry out the function and only where he has some notion of what such mechanisms might be like. One way of imposing this requirement is to identify the mental processes that psychology postulates with the operations of the restricted class of possible computers called Turing machines.

A Turing machine can be informally characterized as a mechanism with a finite number of program states. The inputs and outputs of the machine are written on a tape that is divided into squares each of which includes a symbol from a finite alphabet. The machine scans the tape one square at a time. It can erase the symbol on a scanned square and print a new one in its place. The machine can execute only the elementary mechanical operations of scanning, erasing, printing, moving the tape and changing state.

The program states of the Turing machine are defined solely in terms of the input symbols on the tape, the output symbols on the tape, the elementary operations and the other states of the program. Each program state is therefore functionally defined by the part it plays in the overall operation of the machine. Since the functional role of a state depends on the relation of the state to other states as well as to inputs and outputs, the relational character of the mental is captured by the Turing-machine version of functionalism. Since the definition of a program state never refers to the physical structure of the system running the program, the Turing-machine version of functionalism also captures the idea that the character of a mental state is independent of its physical realization. A human being, a roomful of people, a computer and a disembodied spirit would all be a Turing machine if they operated according to a Turing-machine program.

The proposal is to restrict the functional definition of psychological states to those that can be expressed in terms of the program states of Turing machines. If this restriction can be enforced, it provides a guarantee that psychological theories will be compatible with the demands of mechanisms. Since Turing machines are very simple devices, they are in principle quite easy to build. Consequently by formulating a psychological explanation as a Turing-machine program the psychologist ensures that the explanation is mechanistic, even though the hardware realizing the mechanism is left open.

There are many kinds of computational mechanisms other than Turing machines, and so the formulation of a functionalist psychological theory in Turing-machine notation provides only a sufficient condition for the theory's being mechanically realizable. What makes the condition interesting, however, is that the simple Turing machine can perform many complex tasks. Although the elementary operations of the Turing machine are restricted, iterations of the operations enable the machine to carry out any well-defined computation on discrete symbols.

An important tendency in the cognitive sciences is to treat the mind chiefly as a device that manipulates symbols. If a mental process can be functionally defined as an operation on symbols, there is a Turing machine capable of carrying out the computation and a variety of mechanisms for realizing the Turing machine. Where the manipulation of symbols is important the Turing machine provides a connection between functional explanation and mechanistic explanation.

The reduction of a psychological theory to a program for a Turing machine is a way of exorcising the homunculi. The reduction ensures that no operations have been postulated except those that could be performed by a familiar mechanism. Of course, the working psychologist usually cannot specify the reduction for each functionally individuated process in every theory he is prepared to take seriously. In practice the argument usually goes in the opposite direction; if the postulation of a mental operation is essential to some cherished psychological explanation, the theorist tends to assume that there must be a program for a Turing machine that will carry out that operation.

The "black boxes" that are common in flow charts drawn by psychologists often serve to indicate postulated mental processes for which Turing reductions are wanting. Even so, the possibility in principle of such reductions serves as a methodological constraint on psychological theorizing by determining what functional definitions are to be allowed and what it would be like to know that everything has been explained that could possibly need explanation.

Such is the origin, the provenance and

the promise of contemporary functionalism. How much has it actually paid off? This question is not easy to answer because much of what is now happening in the philosophy of mind and the cognitive sciences is directed at exploring the scope and limits of the functionalist explanations of behavior. I shall, however, give a brief overview.

An obvious objection to functionalism as a theory of the mind is that the functionalist definition is not limited to mental states and processes. Catalysts, Coke machines, valve openers, pencil sharpeners, mousetraps and ministers of finance are all in one way or another concepts that are functionally defined, but none is a mental concept such as pain, belief and desire. What, then, characterizes the mental? And can it be captured in a functionalist framework?

The traditional view in the philosophy of mind has it that mental states are distinguished by their having what are called either qualitative content or intentional content. I shall discuss qualitative content first.

It is not easy to say what qualitative content is; indeed, according to some theories, it is not even possible to say what it is because it can be known not by description but only by direct experience. I shall nonetheless attempt to describe it. Try to imagine looking at a blank wall through a red filter. Now change the filter to a green one and leave everything else exactly the way it was. Something about the character of your experience changes when the filter does, and it is this kind of thing that philosophers call qualitative content. I am not entirely comfortable about introducing qualitative content in this way, but it is a subject with which many philosophers are not comfortable.

The reason qualitative content is a problem for functionalism is straightforward. Functionalism is committed to defining mental states in terms of their causes and effects. It seems, however, as if two mental states could have all the same causal relations and yet could differ in their qualitative content. Let me illustrate this with the classic puzzle of the inverted spectrum.

It seems possible to imagine two observers who are alike in all relevant psychological respects except that experiences having the qualitative content of red for one observer would have the qualitative content of green for the other. Nothing about their behavior need reveal the difference because both of them see ripe tomatoes and flaming sunsets as being similar in color and both of them call that color "red." Moreover, the causal connection between their (qualitatively distinct) experiences and their other mental states could also be identical. Perhaps they both think of Little Red Riding Hood when they see ripe tomatoes, feel depressed when they see the color green and so on. It seems as if anything that could be packed into the notion of of the causal role of their experiences could be shared by them, and yet the qualitative content of the experiences could be as different as you like. If this is possible, then the functionalist account does not work for mental states that have qualitative content. If one person is having a green experience while another person is having a red one, then surely they must be in different mental states.

The example of the inverted spectrum is more than a verbal puzzle. Having qualitative content is supposed to be a chief factor in what makes a mental state conscious. Many psychologists who are inclined to accept the functionalist framework are nonetheless worried about the failure of functionalism to reveal much about the nature of consciousness. Functionalists have made a few ingenious attempts to talk themselves and their colleagues out of this worry, but they have not, in my view, done so with much success. (For example, perhaps one is wrong in thinking one can imagine what an inverted spectrum would be like.) As matters stand, the problem of qualitative content poses a serious threat to the assertion that functionalism can provide a general theory of the mental.

Functionalism has fared much better with the intentional content of mental states. Indeed, it is here that the major achievements of recent cognitive science are found. To say that a mental state has intentional content is to say that it has certain semantic properties. For example, for Enrico to believe Galileo was Italian apparently involves a three-way relation between Enrico, a belief and a proposition that is the content of the belief (namely the proposition that Galileo was Italian). In particular it is an essential property of Enrico's belief that it is about Galileo (and not about, say, Newton) and that it is true if, and only if, Galileo was indeed Italian. Philosophers are divided on how these considerations fit together, but it is widely agreed that beliefs involve semantic properties such as expressing a proposition, being true or false and being about one thing rather than another.

It is important to understand the semantic properties of beliefs because theories in the cognitive sciences are largely about the beliefs organisms have. Theories of learning and perception, for example, are chiefly accounts of how the host of beliefs an organism has are determined by the character of its experiences and its genetic endowment. The functionalist account of mental states does not by itself provide the required insights. Mousetraps are functionally defined, yet mousetraps do not express propositions and they are not true or false.

There is at least one kind of thing other than a mental state that has intentional content: a symbol. Like thoughts, symbols seem to be about things. If someone says "Galileo was Italian," his utterance, like Enrico's belief, expresses a proposition about Galileo that is true or false depending on Galileo's homeland. This parallel between the symbolic and the mental underlies the traditional quest for a unified treatment of language and mind. Cognitive science is now trying to provide such a treatment.

The basic concept is simple but striking. Assume that there are such things as mental symbols (mental representations) and that mental symbols have semantic properties. On this view having a belief involves being related to a mental symbol, and the belief inherits its semantic properties from the mental symbol that figures in the relation. Mental processes (thinking, perceiving, learning and so on) involve causal interactions among relational states such as having a belief. The

semantic properties of the words and sentences we utter are in turn inherited from the semantic properties of the mental states that language expresses.

Associating the semantic properties of mental states with those of mental symbols is fully compatible with the computer metaphor, because it is natural to think of the computer as a mechanism that manipulates symbols. A computation is a causal chain of computer states and the links in the chain are operations on semantically interpreted formulas in a machine code. To think of a system (such as the nervous system) as a computer is to raise questions about the nature of the code in which it computes and the semantic properties of the symbols in the code. In fact, the analogy between minds and computers actually implies the postulation of mental symbols. There is no computation without representation.

The representational account of the mind, however, predates considerably the invention of the computing machine. It is a throwback to classical epistemology, which is a tradition that includes philosophers as diverse as John Locke, David Hume, George Berkeley, René Descartes, Immanuel Kant, John Stuart Mill and William James.

Hume, for one, developed a representational theory of the mind that included five points. First, there exist "Ideas," which are a species of mental symbol. Second, having a belief involves entertaining an Idea. Third, mental processes are causal associations of Ideas. Fourth, Ideas are like pictures. And fifth, Ideas have their semantic properties by virtue of what they resemble: the Idea of John is about John because it looks like him.

Contemporary cognitive psychologists do not accept the details of Hume's theory, although they endorse much of its spirit. Theories of computation provide a far richer account of mental processes than the mere association of Ideas. And only a few psychologists still think that imagery is the chief vehicle of mental representation. Nevertheless, the most significant break with Hume's theory lies in the abandoning of resemblance as an explanation of the semantic properties of mental representations.

Many philosophers, starting with Berkeley, have argued that there is something seriously wrong with the suggestion that the semantic relation between a thought and what the thought is about could be one of resemblance. Consider the thought that John is tall. Clearly the thought is true only of the state of affairs consisting of John's being tall. A theory of the semantic properties of a thought should therefore explain how this particular thought is related to this particular state of affairs. According to the resemblance theory, entertaining the thought involves having a mental image that shows John to be tall. To put it another way, the relation between the thought that John is tall and his being tall is like the relation between a tall man and his portrait.

The difficulty with the resemblance theory is that any portrait showing John to be tall must also show him to be many other things: clothed or naked, lying, standing or sitting, having a head or not having one, and so on. A portrait of a tall man who is sitting down resembles a man's being seated as much as it resembles a man's being tall. On the resemblance theory it is not clear what distinguishes thoughts about John's height from thoughts about his posture.

The resemblance theory turns out to encounter paradoxes at every turn. The possibility of construing beliefs as involving relations to semantically interpreted mental representations clearly depends on having an acceptable account of where the semantic properties of the mental representations come from. If resemblance will not provide this account, what will?

The current idea is that the semantic properties of a mental representation are determined by aspects of its functional role. In other words, a sufficient condition can be specified in causal terms. This is the connection between functionalism and the representational theory of the mind. Modern cognitive psychology rests largely on the hope that these two doctrines can be made to support each other.

No philosopher is now prepared to say exactly how the functional role of mental representation determines its semantic properties. Nevertheless, the functionalist recognizes three types of causal relation among psychological states involving mental representations, and they might serve to fix the semantic properties of mental representations. The three types are causal relations among mental states and stimuli, mental states and responses and some mental states and other ones.

Consider the belief that John is tall. Presumably the following facts, which correspond respectively to the three types of causal relation, are relevant to determining the semantic properties of the mental representation involved in the belief. First, the belief is a normal effect of certain stimulations, such as seeing John in circumstances that reveal his height. Second, the belief is the normal cause of certain behavioral effects, such as uttering "John is tall." Third, the belief is a normal cause of certain other beliefs and a normal effect of certain other beliefs. For example, anyone who believes John is tall is very likely also to believe someone is tall. Having the first belief is normally causally sufficient for having the second belief. And anyone who believes everyone in the room is tall and also believes John is in the room will very likely believe John is tall. The third belief is a normal effect of the first two. In short, the functionalist maintains that the proposition expressed by a given mental representation depends on the causal properties of the mental states in which that mental representation figures.

The concept that the semantic properties of mental representations are determined by aspects of their functional role is at the center of current work in the cognitive sciences. Nevertheless, the concept may not be true. Many philosophers who are unsympathetic to the cognitive turn in modern psychology doubt its truth, and many psychologists would probably reject it in the bald and unelaborated way that I have sketched it. Yet even in its skeletal form, there is this much to be said in its favor: It legitimizes the notion of mental representation, which has become increasingly important to theorizing in every branch of the cognitive sciences. Recent advances in formulating and testing hypotheses about the character of mental representations in fields ranging from phonetics to computer vision suggest that the concept of mental representation is fundamental to empirical theories of the mind.

The behaviorist has rejected the appeal to mental representation because it runs counter to his view of the explanatory mechanisms that can figure in psychological theories. Nevertheless, the science of mental representation is now flourishing. The history of science reveals that when a successful theory comes into conflict with a methodological scruple, it is generally the scruple that gives way. Accordingly the functionalist has relaxed the behaviorist constraints on psychological explanations. There is probably no better way to decide what is methodologically permissible in science than by investigating what successful science requires.

Persons and Free Will

Free Will and Psychoanalysis*

John Hospers

O Thou who didst with pitfall and with gin Beset the Road I was to wander in,
  Thou wilt not with Predestined Evil round Enmesh, and then impute my Fall to Sin!

Edward FitzGerald,
The Rubaiyat of Omar Khayyam

It is extremely common for nonprofessional philosophers and iconoclasts to deny that human freedom exists, but at the same time to have no clear idea of what it is that they are denying to exist. The first thing that needs to be said about the free-will issue is that any meaningful term must have a meaningful opposite: if it is meaningful to assert that people are not free, it must be equally meaningful to assert that people *are* free, whether this latter assertion is in fact true or not. Whether it is true, of course, will depend on the meaning that is given the weasel-word "free." For example, if

freedom is made dependent on indeterminism, it may well be that human freedom is nonexistent. But there seem to be no good grounds for asserting such a dependence, especially since lack of causation is the furthest thing from people's minds when they call an act free. Doubtless there are other senses that can be given to the word "free"—such as "able to do anything we want to do"—in which no human beings are free. But the first essential point about which the denier of freedom must be clear is *what* it is that he is denying. If one knows what it is like for people not to be free, one must know what it *would* be like for them to *be* free.

Philosophers have advanced numerous senses of "free" in which countless acts performed by human beings can truly be called free acts. The most common conception of a free act is that according to which an act is free if and only if it is a *voluntary* act. But the word "voluntary" does not always carry the same meaning. Sometimes to call an act voluntary means that we can do the act *if* we choose to do it: in other words, that it is physically and psychologically possible for us to do it, so that the occurrence of the act follows upon the decision to do it. (One's decision to raise his arm is in fact followed by the actual raising of his arm, unless he is a paralytic; one's decision to pluck the moon from the sky is not followed by the actual event.) Sometimes a voluntary act is conceived (as by G. E. Moore[1]) as an act which would not have occurred if, just beforehand, the agent had chosen not to perform it. But these senses are different from the sense in which a voluntary act is an act resulting from *deliberation,* or perhaps merely from *choice.* For example, there are many acts which we could have avoided, if we had chosen to do so, but which we nevertheless did not *choose* to perform, much less *deliberate* about them. The act of raising one's leg in the process of taking a step while out for a walk, is one which a person could have avoided by choosing to, but which, after one has learned to walk, takes place automatically or semi-automatically through habit, and thus is not the result of choice. (One may have chosen to take the walk, but not to take this or that step while walking.) Such acts are free in Moore's sense but are not free in the sense of being deliberate. Moreover, there are classes of acts of the same general character which are not even covered by Moore's sense: sudden outbursts of feeling, in some cases at least, could not have been avoided by an immediately preceding volition, so that if these are to be included under the heading of voluntary acts, the proviso that the act could have been avoided by an immediately preceding volition must be amended to read "could have been avoided by a volition or series of volitions by the agent *at some time in the past*"—such as the adoption of a different set of habits in the agent's earlier and more formative years.

(Sometimes we call *persons,* rather than their acts, free. S. Stebbing, for example, declares that one should never call acts free, but only the doers of the acts.[2] But the two do not seem irreconcilable: can we not speak of a *person* as free *with respect to a certain act* (never just free in general) if that *act* is free—whatever we may then go on to mean by saying that an act is free? Any statement about a free act can then be translated into a statement about the doer of the act.)

Now, no matter in which of the above ways we may come to define "voluntary," there are still acts which are voluntary *but which we would be very unlikely to think of as free.* Thus, when a person submits to the command of an armed bandit, he may do so voluntarily in every one of the above senses: He may do so as a result of choice, even of deliberation, and he could have avoided doing it by willing not to—he could, instead, have refused and been shot. The man who reveals a state secret under torture does the same: he could have refused and endured more torture. Yet such acts, and persons in respect of such acts, are not generally called free. We say that they were performed *under compulsion,* and if an act is performed under compulsion we do not call it free. We say, "He wasn't free because he was forced to do as he did," though of course his act was voluntary.

This much departure from the identification of free acts with voluntary acts almost everyone would admit. Sometimes, however, it would be added that this is all the departure that can be admitted. According to Moritz Schlick, for example,

> Freedom means the opposite of compulsion; a man *is free* if he does not act under *compulsion,* and he is compelled or unfree when he is hindered from without in the realization of his natural desires. Hence he is unfree when he is locked up, or chained, or when someone forces him at the point of a gun to do what otherwise he would not do. This is quite clear, and everyone will admit that the everyday or legal notion of the lack of freedom is thus correctly interpreted, and that a man will be considered quite free . . . if no such external compulsion is exerted upon him.[3]

Schlick adds that the entire vexed freewill controversy in philosophy is so much wasted ink and paper, because compulsion has been confused with causality and necessity with uniformity. If the question is asked whether every event is caused, the answer is doubtless yes; but if it is whether every event is compelled, the answer is clearly no. Free acts are uncompelled acts, not un-caused acts. Again, when it is said that some state of affairs (such as water flowing downhill) is necessary, if "necessary" means "compelled," the answer is no; if it means merely that it always happens that way, the answer is yes: universality of application is confused with compulsion. And this, accord-ing to Schlick, is the end of the matter.

Schlick's analysis is indeed clarifying and helpful to those who have fallen victim to the confusion he exposes—and this proba-bly includes most persons in their philo-sophical growing-pains. But *is* this the end of the matter? Is it true that all acts, though caused, are free as long as they are not com-pelled in the sense which he specifies? May it not be that, while the identification of "free" with "uncompelled" is acceptable, the area of compelled acts is vastly greater than he or most other philosophers have ever suspected? (Moore is more cautious in this respect than Schlick; while for Moore an act is free if it is voluntary in the sense specified above, he thinks there may be an-other sense in which human beings, and human acts, are not free at all.[4]) We remem-ber statements about human beings being pawns of their early environment, victims of conditions beyond their control, the re-sult of causal influences stemming from their parents, and the like, and we ponder and ask, "Still, are we really free?" Is there not something in what generations of sages have said about man being fettered? Is there not perhaps something too facile, too sleight-of-hand, in Schlick's cutting of the Gordian knot? For example, when a metro-politan newspaper headlines an article with the words "Boy Killer is Doomed Long be-fore He Is Born,"[5] and then goes on to de-scribe how a twelve-year-old boy has been sentenced to prison for the murder of a girl, and how his parental background in-cludes records of drunkenness, divorce, so-cial maladjustment, and paresis, are we still to say that his act, though voluntary and assuredly *not* done at the point of a gun, is free? The boy has early displayed a ten-dency toward sadistic activity to hide an underlying masochism and "prove that he's a man"; being coddled by his mother only worsens this tendency, until, spurned by a girl in his attempt on her, he kills her—not simply in a fit of anger, but calcu-latingly, deliberately. Is he free in respect of his criminal act, or for that matter in most of the acts of his life? Surely to ask this question is to answer it in the negative. Per-haps I have taken an extreme case; but it is only to show the superficiality of the Schlick analysis more clearly. Though not everyone has criminotic tendencies, every-one has been molded by influences which in large measure at least determine his pres-ent behavior; he is literally the product of these influences, stemming from periods prior to his "years of discretion," giving him a host of character traits that he cannot change now even if he would. So obviously does what a man is depend upon how a man comes to be, that it is small wonder that philosophers and sages have consid-ered man far indeed from being the master of his fate. It is not as if man's will were standing high and serene above the flux of events that have molded him; it is itself caught up in this flux, itself carried along on the current. An act is free when it is determined by the man's character, say moralists; but what if the most decisive as-pects of his character were already irrevoca-bly acquired before he could do anything to mold them? What if even the degree of will power available to him in shaping his hab-its and disciplining himself now to over-come the influence of his early environ-ment is a factor over which he has no con-trol? What are we to say of this kind of "freedom"? Is it not rather like the freedom of the machine to stamp labels on cans when it has been devised for just that pur-pose? Some machines can do so more effi-ciently than others, but only because they have been better constructed.

It is not my purpose here to establish this thesis in general, but only in one specific respect which has received comparatively lit-tle attention, namely, the field referred to by psychiatrists as that of unconscious motivation. In what follows I shall restrict my attention to it because it illustrates as clearly as anything the points I wish to make.

Let me try to summarize very briefly the psychoanalytic doctrine on this point.[6] The conscious life of the human being, including the conscious decisions and volitions, is merely a mouthpiece for the unconscious—not directly for the enactment of unconscious drives, but of the compromise between unconscious drives and unconscious reproaches. There is a Big Three behind the scenes which the automaton called the conscious personality carries out: the id, and "eternal gimme," presents its wish and demands its immediate satisfaction; the super-ego says no to the wish immediately upon presentation, and the unconscious ego, the mediator between the two, tries to keep peace by means of compromise.[7]

To go into examples of the functioning of these three "bosses" would be endless; psychoanalytic case books supply hundreds of them. The important point for us to see in the present context is that *it is the unconscious that determines what the conscious impulse and the conscious action shall be.* Hamlet, for example, had a strong Oedipus wish, which was violently counteracted by super-ego reproaches; these early wishes were vividly revived in an unusual adult situation in which his uncle usurped the coveted position from Hamlet's father and won his mother besides. This situation evoked strong strictures on the part of Hamlet's super-ego, and it was this that was responsible for his notorious delay in killing his uncle. A dozen times Hamlet could have killed Claudius easily; but every time Hamlet "decided" not to: a free choice, moralists would say—but no, listen to the super-ego: "What you feel such hatred toward your uncle for, what you are plotting to kill him for, is precisely the crime which you yourself desire to commit: to kill your father and replace him in the affections of your mother. Your fate and your uncle's are bound up together." This paralyzes Hamlet into inaction. Consciously all he knows is that he is unable to act; this conscious inability he rationalizes, giving a different ex-

cuse each time.[8] We have always been conscious of the fact that we are not masters of our fate in every respect—that there are many things which we cannot do, that nature is more powerful than we are, that we cannot disobey laws without danger of reprisals, etc. We have become "officially" conscious, too, though in our private lives we must long have been aware of it, that we are not free with respect to the emotions that we feel—whom we love or hate, what types we admire, and the like. More lately still we have been reminded that there are unconscious motivations for our basic attractions and repulsions, our compulsive actions or inabilities to act. But what is not welcome news is that our very acts of volition, and the entire train of deliberations leading up to them, are but façades for the expression of unconscious wishes, or rather, unconscious compromises and defenses.

A man is faced by a choice: shall he kill another person or not? Moralists would say, here is a free choice—the result of deliberation, an action consciously entered into. And yet, though the agent himself does not know it, and has no awareness of the forces that are at work within him, his choice is already determined for him: his conscious will is only an instrument, a slave, in the hands of a deep unconscious motivation which determines his action. If he has a great deal of what analysts call "free-floating guilt," he will not; but if the guilt is such as to demand immediate absorption in the form of self-damaging behavior, this accumulated guilt will have to be discharged in some criminal action. The man himself does not know what the inner clockwork is; he is like the hands on the clock, thinking they move freely over the face of the clock.

A woman has married and divorced several husbands. Now she is faced with a choice for the next marriage: shall she marry Mr. A, or Mr. B, or nobody at all? She may take considerable time to "decide" this question, and her decision may appear as a final triumph of her free will. Let us assume that A is a normal, well-adjusted, kind, and generous man, while B is a leech, an imposter, one who will become entangled constantly in quarrels with her. If she belongs to a certain classifiable psychological type, she will inevitably choose B, and she will do so even if her previous husbands have resembled B, so that one would think that she "had learned from experience." Consciously, she will of course "give the matter due consideration," etc., etc. To the psychoanalyst this is all irrelevant chaff in the wind—only a camouflage for the inner workings about which she knows nothing consciously. If she is of a certain kind of masochistic strain, as exhibited in her previous set of symptoms, she *must* choose B: her super-ego, always out to maximize the torment in the situation, seeing what dazzling possibilities for self-damaging behavior are promised by the choice of B, compels her to make the choice she does, and even to conceal the real basis of the choice behind an elaborate façade of rationalizations.

A man is addicted to gambling. In the service of his addiction he loses all his money, spends what belongs to his wife, even sells his property and neglects his children. For a time perhaps he stops; then, inevitably, he takes it up again. The man does not know that he is a victim rather than an agent; or, if he sometimes senses that he is in the throes of something-he-knows-not-what, he will have no inkling of its character and will soon relapse into the illusion that he (his conscious self) is freely deciding the course of his own actions. What he does not know, of course, is that he is still taking out on his mother the original lesion to his infantile narcissism, getting back at her for her fancied refusal of his infantile wishes—and this by rejecting everything identified with her, namely education, discipline, logic, common sense, training. At the roulette wheel, almost alone among adult activities, chance—the opposite of all these things—rules supreme; and his addiction represents his continued and emphatic reiteration of his rejection of Mother and all she represents to his unconscious.

This pseudo-aggression of his is of course masochistic in its effects. In the long run he always loses; he can never quit while he is winning. And far from playing in order to win, rather one can say that his losing is a *sine qua non* of his psychic equilibrium (as it was for example with Dostoyevsky): guilt demands punishment, and in the ego's "deal" with the super-ego the super-ego has granted satisfaction of infantile wishes in return for the self-damaging conditions obtaining. Winning would upset the neurotic equilibrium.[9]

A man has wash-compulsion. He must be constantly washing his hands—he uses up perhaps 400 towels a day. Asked why he does this, he says, "I need to, my hands are dirty"; and if it is pointed out to him that they are not really dirty, he says, "They feel dirty anyway; I feel better when I wash them." So once again he washes them. He "freely decides" every time; he feels that he must wash them, he deliberates for a moment perhaps, but always ends by washing them. What he does not see, of course, are the invisible wires inside pulling him inevitably to do the things he does: the infantile id-wish concerns preoccupation with dirt, the super-ego charges him with this, and the terrified ego must respond, "No, I don't like dirt, see how clean I like to be, look how I wash my hands!"

Let us see what further "free acts" the same patient engages in (this is an actual case history): he is taken to a concentration camp, and given the worst of treatment by the Nazi guards. In the camp he no longer chooses to be clean; does not even try to be—on the contrary, his choice is now to wallow in filth as much as he can. All he is aware of now is a disinclination to be clean, and every time he must choose he chooses not to be. Behind the scenes, however, is another drama being enacted: the super-ego, perceiving that enough torment is being administered from the outside, can afford to cease pressing its charges in this quarter—the outside world is doing the torturing now, so the super-ego is relieved of the responsibility. Thus the ego is relieved of the agony of constantly making terrified replies in the form of washing to prove that the super-ego is wrong. The defense no longer being needed, the person slides back into what is his natural predilection anyway, for filth. This becomes too much even for the Nazi guards: they take hold of him one day, saying "We'll teach you how to be clean!", drag him into the snow, and pour bucket after bucket of icy water over him until he freezes to death. Such is the end-result of an original id-wish, caught in the machinations of a destroying super-ego.

Let us take, finally, a less colorful, more everyday example. A student at a university, possessing wealth, charm, and all that is usually considered essential to popularity, begins to develop the following personality-pattern: although well taught in the graces of social conversation, he always makes a *faux pas* somewhere, and always in the worst possible situation; to his friends he makes cutting remarks which hurt deeply—and always apparently aimed in such a way as to hurt the most: a remark that would not hurt A but would hurt B he invariably makes to B rather than to A, and so on. None of this is conscious. Ordinarily he is considerate of people, but he contrives always (unconsciously) to impose on just those friends who would resent it most, and at just the times when he should know that he should not impose: at 3 o'clock in the morning, without forewarning, he phones a friend in a near-by city demanding to stay at his apartment for the weekend; naturally the friend is offended, but the person himself is not aware that he has provoked the grievance ("common sense" suffers a temporary eclipse when the neurotic pattern sets in, and one's intelligence, far from being of help in such a situation, is used in the interest of the neurosis), and when the friend is cool to him the next time they meet, he wonders why and feels unjustly treated. Aggressive behavior on his part invites resentment and aggression in turn, but all that he consciously sees is others' behavior towards him—and he considers himself the innocent victim of an unjustified "persecution."

Each of these acts is, from the moralist's point of view, free: he chose to phone his friend at 3 A.M., he chose to make the cutting remark that he did, etc. What he does not know is that an ineradicable masochistic pattern has set in. His unconscious is far more shrewd and clever than is his conscious intellect; it sees with uncanny accuracy just what behavior will damage him most, and unerringly forces him into that behavior. Consciously, the student "doesn't know why he did it"—he gives different "reasons" at different times, but they are all, once again, rationalizations cloaking the unconscious mechanism which propels him willy-nilly into actions that his "common sense" eschews.

The more of this sort of thing one observes, the more he can see what the psychoanalyst means when he talks about *the illusion of freedom*. And the more of a psychiatrist one becomes, the more he is overcome with a sense of what an illusion this free will can be. In some kinds of cases most of us can see it already: it takes no psychiatrist to look at the epileptic and sigh with sadness at the thought that soon this person before you will be as one possessed, not the same thoughtful intelligent person you know. But people are not aware of this in other contexts, for example when they express surprise at how a person whom they have been so good to could treat them so badly. Let us suppose that you help a person financially or morally or in some other way, so that he is in your debt; suppose further that he is one of the many neurotics who unconsciously identify kindness with weakness and aggression with strength, then he will unconsciously take your kindness to him as weakness and use it as the occasion for enacting some aggression against you. He can't help it, he may regret it himself later; still, he will be driven to do it. If we gain a little knowledge of psychiatry, we can look at him with pity, that a person otherwise so worthy should be so unreliable—but we will exercise realism too, and be aware that there are some types of people that you cannot be good to. In "free" acts of their conscious volition, they will use your own goodness against you.

Sometimes the persons themselves will become dimly aware that "something behind the scenes" is determining their behavior. The divorcee will sometimes view herself with detachment, as if she were some machine (and indeed the psychoanalyst does call her a "repeating-machine"): "I know I'm caught in a net, that I'll fall in love with this guy and marry him and the whole ridiculous merry-go-round will start all over again."

We talk about free will, and we say, for example, the person is free to do so-and-so if he *can* do so *if* he wants to—and we forget that his wanting to is itself caught up in the stream of determinism, that unconscious forces drive him into the wanting or not wanting to do the thing in question. The analogy of the puppet whose motions are manipulated from behind by invisible wires, or better still, by springs inside, is a telling one at almost every point.

And the glaring fact is that it all started so early, before we knew what was happening. The personality-structure is inelastic after the age of five, and comparatively so in most cases after the age of three. Whether one acquires a neurosis or not is determined by that age—and just as involuntarily as if it had been a curse of God. If, for example, a masochistic pattern was set up, under pressure of hyper-narcissism combined with real or fancied infantile deprivation, then the masochistic snowball was on its course downhill long before we or anybody else knew what was happening, and long before anyone could do anything about it. To speak of human beings as "puppets" in such a context is no idle metaphor; but a stark rendering of a literal fact: only the psychiatrist knows what puppets people really are; and it is no wonder that the protestations of philosophers that "the act which is the result of a volition, a deliberation, a conscious decision, is free" leave these persons, to speak mildly, somewhat cold.

But, one may object, all the states thus far described have been abnormal, neurotic ones. The well-adjusted (normal) person at least is free.

Leaving aside the question of how clearly and on what grounds one can distinguish the neurotic from the normal, let me use an illustration of a proclivity that everyone would call normal, namely, the decision of a man to support his wife and possibly a family, and consider briefly its genesis, according to psychoanalytic accounts.[10]

Every baby comes into the world with a full-fledged case of megalomania—interested only in himself, acting as if believing that he is the center of the universe and that others are present only to fulfill his wishes, and furious when his own wants are not satisfied immediately no matter for what reason. Gratitude, even for all the time and worry and care expended on him by the mother, is an emotion entirely foreign to the infant, and as he grows older it is inculcated in him only with the greatest difficulty; his natural tendency is to assume that everything that happens to him is due to himself, except for denials and frustrations, which are due to the "cruel, denying" outer world, in particular the mother; and that he owes nothing to anyone, is dependent on no one. This omnipotence-complex, or illusion of non-dependence, has been called the "autarchic fiction." Such a conception of the world is actually fostered in the child by the conduct of adults, who automatically attempt to fulfill the infant's every wish concerning nourishment, sleep, and attention. The child misconceives causality and sees in these wish-fulfillments not the results of maternal kindness and love, but simply the result of his own omnipotence.

This fiction of omnipotence is gradually destroyed by experience, and its destruction is probably the deepest disappointment of the early years of life. First of all, the infant discovers that he is the victim of organic urges and necessities: hunger, defecation, urination. More important, he discovers that the maternal breast, which he has not previously distinguished from his own body (he has not needed to, since it was available when he needed it), is not a part of himself after all, but of another creature upon whom he is dependent. He is forced to recognize this, e.g., when he wants nourishment and it is at the moment not present; even a small delay is most damaging to the "autarchic fiction." Most painful of all is the experience of weaning, probably the greatest tragedy in every baby's life, when his dependence is most cruelly emphasized; it is a frustrating experience because what he wants is no longer there at all; and if he has been able to some extent to preserve the illusion of non-dependence heretofore, he is not able to do so now—it is plain that the source of his nourishment is not dependent on him, but he on it. The shattering of the autarchic fiction is a great disillusionment to every child, a tremendous blow to his ego which he will, in one way or another, spend the rest of his life trying to repair. How does he do this?

First of all, his reaction to frustration is anger and fury; and he responds by kicking, biting, etc., the only ways he knows. But he is motorically helpless, and these measures are ineffective, and only serve to emphasize his dependence the more. Moreover, against such responses of the child the parental reaction is one of prohibition, often involving deprivation of attention and affection. Generally the child soon learns that this form of rebellion is profitless, and brings him more harm than good. He wants to respond to frustration with violent aggression, and at the same time he learns that he will be punished for such aggression, and that in any case the latter is ineffectual. What face-saving solution does he find? Since he must "face facts," since he must in any case "conform" if he is to have any peace at all, he tries to make it seem as if he himself is the source of the commands and prohibitions: the *external* prohibitive force is *internalized*—and here we have the origin of conscience. By making the prohibitive agency seem to come from within himself, the child can "save face"—as if saying, "The prohibition comes from within me, not from outside, so I'm not subservient to external rule, I'm only obeying rules I've set up myself," thus to some extent saving the autarchic fiction, and at the same time avoiding unpleasant consequences directed against himself by complying with parental commands.

Moreover, the boy[11] has unconsciously never forgiven the mother for his dependence on her in early life, for nourishment

and all other things. It has upset his illusion of non-dependence. These feelings have been repressed and are not remembered; but they are acted out in later life in many ways—e.g., in the constant deprecation man has for woman's duties such as cooking and housework of all sorts ("All she does is stay home and get together a few meals and she calls that work"), and especially in the man's identification with the mother in his sex experiences with women. By identifying with someone one cancels out in effect the person with whom he identifies—replacing that person, unconsciously denying his existence, and the man, identifying with his early mother, playing the active role in "giving" to his wife as his mother has "given" to him, is in effect the denial of his mother's existence, a fact which is narcissistically embarrassing to his ego because it is chiefly responsible for shattering his autarchic fiction. In supporting his wife, he can unconsciously deny that his mother gave to him, and that he was dependent on her giving. Why is it that the husband plays the provider, and wants his wife to be dependent on no one else, although twenty years before he was nothing but a parasitic baby? This is a face-saving device on his part: he can act out the reasoning, "See, I'm not the parasitic baby; on the contrary I'm the provider, the giver." His playing the provider is a constant face-saving device, to deny his early dependence which is so embarrassing to his ego. It is no wonder that men generally dislike to be reminded of their babyhood, when they were dependent on women.

Thus we have here a perfectly normal adult reaction which is unconsciously motivated. The man "chooses" to support a family—and his choice is as unconsciously motivated as anything could be. (I have described here only the "normal" state of affairs, uncomplicated by the well-nigh infinite number of variations that occur in actual practice.)

Now what of the notion of responsibility? What happens to it on our analysis?

Let us begin with an example, not a fictitious one. A woman and her two-year-old baby are riding on a train to Montreal in mid-winter. The child is ill. The woman wants badly to get to her destination. She is, unknown to herself, the victim of a neurotic conflict whose nature is irrelevant here except for the fact that it forces her to behave aggressively toward the child, partly to spite her husband whom she despises and who loves the child, but chiefly to ward off super-ego charges of masochistic attachment. Consciously she loves the child, and when she says this she says it sincerely, but she must behave aggressively toward it nevertheless, just as many children love their mothers but are nasty to them most of the time in neurotic pseudo-aggression. The child becomes more ill as the train approaches Montreal; the heating system of the train is not working, and the conductor pleads with the woman to get off the train at the next town and get the child to a hospital at once. The woman refuses. Soon after, the child's condition worsens, and the mother does all she can to keep it alive, without, however, leaving the train, for she declares that it is absolutely necessary that she reach her destination. But before she gets there the child is dead. After that, of course, the mother grieves, blames herself, weeps hysterically, and joins the church to gain surcease from the guilt that constantly overwhelms her when she thinks of how her aggressive behavior has killed her child.

Was she responsible for her deed? In ordinary life, after making a mistake, we say, "Chalk it up to experience." Here we should say, "Chalk it up to the neurosis." She could not help it if her neurosis forced her to act this way—she didn't even know what was going on behind the scenes, her conscious self merely acted out its assigned part. This is far more true than is generally realized: criminal actions in general are not actions for which their agents are responsible; the agents are passive, not active—they are victims of a neurotic conflict. Their very hyperactivity is unconsciously determined.

To say this is, of course, not to say that we should not punish criminals. Clearly, for our own protection, we must remove them from

our midst so that they can no longer molest and endanger organized society. And, of course, if we use the word "responsible" in such a way that justly to hold someone responsible for a deed is by definition identical with being justified in punishing him, then we can and do hold people responsible. But this is like the sense of "free" in which free acts are voluntary ones. It does not go deep enough. In a deeper sense we cannot hold the person responsible: we can hold his neurosis responsible, but *he is not responsible for his neurosis,* particularly since the age in which its onset was inevitable was an age before he could even speak.

The neurosis is responsible—but isn't the neurosis a part of *him?* We have been speaking all the time as if the person and his unconscious were two separate beings; but isn't he one personality, including conscious and unconscious departments together?

I do not wish to deny this. But it hardly helps us here; for what people want when they talk about freedom, and what they hold to when they champion it, is the idea that the *conscious* will is the master of their destiny. "I am the master of my fate, I am the captain of my soul"—and they surely mean their conscious selves, the self that they can recognize and search and introspect. Between an unconscious that willy-nilly determines your actions, and an external force which pushes you, there is little if anything to choose. The unconscious is just *as if* it were an outside force; and indeed, psychiatrists will assert that the inner Hitler (your super-ego) can torment you far more than any external Hitler can. Thus the kind of freedom that people want, the only kind they will settle for, is precisely the kind that psychiatry says they cannot have.

Heretofore it was pretty generally thought that, while we could not rightly blame a person for the color of his eyes or the morality of his parents, or even for what he did at the age of three, or to a large extent what impulses he had and whom he fell in love with, one *could* do so for other of his adult activities, particularly the acts he performed voluntarily and with premeditation. Later this attitude was

Persons and Free Will

shaken. Many voluntary acts came to be recognized, at least in some circles, as compelled by the unconscious. Some philosophers recognized this too—Ayer[12] talks about the kleptomaniac being unfree, and about a person being unfree when another person exerts a habitual ascendancy over his personality. But this is as far as he goes. The usual examples, such as the kleptomaniac and the schizophrenic, apparently satisfy most philosophers, and with these exceptions removed, the rest of mankind is permitted to wander in the vast and alluring fields of freedom and responsibility. So far, the inroads upon freedom left the vast majority of humanity untouched; they began to hit home when psychiatrists began to realize, though philosophers did not, that the domination of the conscious by the unconscious extended, not merely to a few exceptional individuals, but to all human beings, that the "big three behind the scenes" are not respecters of persons, and dominate us all, even including that *sanctum sanctorum* of freedom, our conscious will. To be sure, the domination by the unconscious in the case of "normal" individuals is somewhat more benevolent than the tyranny and despotism exercised in neurotic cases, and therefore the former have evoked less comment; but the principle remains in all cases the same: the unconscious is the master of every fate and the captain of every soul.

We speak of a machine turning out good products most of the time but every once in a while it turns out a "lemon." We do not, of course, hold the product responsible for this, but the machine, and via the machine, its maker. Is it silly to extend to inanimate objects the idea of responsibility? Of course. But is it any less so to employ the notion in speaking of human creatures? Are not the two kinds of cases analogous in countless important ways? Occasionally a child turns out badly too, even when his environment and training are the same as that of his brothers and sisters who turn out "all right." He is the "bad penny." His acts of rebellion against parental discipline in adult life (such as the case of the gambler, already cited) are

traceable to early experiences of real or fancied denial of infantile wishes. Sometimes the denial has been real, though many denials are absolutely necessary if the child is to grow up to observe the common decencies of civilized life; sometimes, if the child has an unusual quantity of narcissism, every event that occurs is interpreted by him as a denial of his wishes, and nothing a parent could do, even granting every humanly possible wish, would help. In any event, the later neurosis can be attributed to this. Can the person himself be held responsible? Hardly. If he engages in activities which are a menace to society, he must be put into prison, of course, but responsibility is another matter. The time when the events occurred which rendered his neurotic behavior inevitable was a time long before he was capable of thought and decision. As an adult, he is a victim of a world he never made—only this world is inside him.

What about the children who turn out "all right"? All we can say is that "it's just lucky for them" that what happened to their unfortunate brother didn't happen to them; *through no virtue of their own* they are not doomed to the life of unconscious guilt, expiation, conscious depression, terrified ego-gestures for the appeasement of a tyrannical super-ego, that he is. The machine turned them out with a minimum of damage. But if the brother cannot be blamed for his evils, neither can they be praised for their good; unless, of course, we should blame people for what is not their fault, and praise them for lucky accidents.

We all agree that machines turn out "lemons," we all agree that nature turns out misfits in the realm of biology—the blind, the crippled, the diseased; but we hesitate to include the realm of the personality, for here, it seems, is the last retreat of our dignity as human beings. Our ego can endure anything but this; this island at least must remain above the encroaching flood. But may not precisely the same analysis be made here also? Nature turns out psychological "lemons" too, in far greater quantities than any other kind; and indeed all of us are "lemons" in some respect or other, the difference being one of degree. Some of us are lucky enough not to have a gambling-neurosis or criminotic tendencies or masochistic mother-attachment or overdimensional repetition-compulsion to make our lives miserable, but most of our actions, those usually considered the most important, are unconsciously dominated just the same. And, if a neurosis may be likened to a curse of God, let those of us, the elect, who are enabled to enjoy a measure of life's happiness without the hell-fire of neurotic guilt, take this, not as our own achievement, but simply for what it is—a gift of God.

Let us, however, quit metaphysics and put the situation schematically in the form of a deductive argument.

1. An occurrence over which we had no control is something we cannot be held responsible for.
2. Events E, occurring during our babyhood, were events over which we had no control.
3. Therefore events E were events which we cannot be held responsible for.
4. But if there is something we cannot be held responsible for, neither can we be held responsible for something that inevitably results from it.
5. Events E have as inevitable consequence Neurosis N, which in turn has inevitable consequence Behavior B.
6. Since N is the inevitable consequence of E and B is the inevitable consequence of N, B is the inevitable consequence of E.
7. Hence, not being responsible for E, we cannot be responsible for B.

In Samuel Butler's Utopian satire *Erewhon* there occurs the following passage, in which a judge is passing sentence on a prisoner:

> It is all very well for you to say that you came of unhealthy parents, and had a severe accident in your childhood which permanently undermined your constitution; excuses such as these are the ordinary refuge of the criminal; but they cannot for one moment be listened to by the ear of justice. I am not here to enter upon curious metaphysical questions as to the origin of this or that—questions to which there would be no end were their introduction once tolerated, and which would result in throwing the only guilt on the tissues of the primordial cell, or on the elementary gases. There is no question of how you came to be wicked, but only this—namely, are you wicked or not? This has been decided in the affirmative, neither can I hesitate for a single moment to say that it has been decided justly. You are a bad and dangerous person, and stand branded in the eyes of your fellow countrymen with one of the most heinous known offenses.[13]

As moralists read this passage, they may perhaps nod with approval. But the joke is on them. The sting comes when we realize what the crime is for which the prisoner is being sentenced: namely, consumption. The defendant is reminded that during the previous year he was sentenced for aggravated bronchitis, and is warned that he should profit from experience in the future. Butler is employing here his familiar method of presenting some human tendency (in this case, holding people responsible for what isn't their fault) to a ridiculous extreme and thereby reducing it to absurdity.

Assuming the main conclusions of this paper to be true, is there any room left for freedom?

This, of course, all depends on what we mean by "freedom." In the senses suggested at the beginning of this paper, there are countless free acts, and unfree ones as well. When "free" means "uncompelled," and only external compulsion is admitted, again there are countless free acts. But now we have extended the notion of compulsion to include determination by unconscious forces. With this sense in mind, our question is, "With the concept of compulsion thus extended, and in the light of present psychoanalytic knowledge, is there any freedom left in human behavior?"

Persons and Free Will

If practicing psychoanalysts were asked this question, there is little doubt that their answer would be along the following lines: they would say that they were not accustomed to using the term "free" at all, but that if they had to suggest a criterion for distinguishing the free from the unfree, they would say that a person's freedom is present *in inverse proportion to his neuroticism;* in other words, the more his acts are determined by a *malevolent* unconscious, the less free he is. Thus they would speak of *degrees* of freedom. They would say that as a person is cured of his neurosis, he becomes more free—free to realize capabilities that were blocked by the neurotic affliction. The psychologically well-adjusted individual is in this sense comparatively the most free. Indeed, those who are cured of mental disorders are sometimes said to have *regained their freedom:* they are freed from the tyranny of a malevolent unconscious which formerly exerted as much of a domination over them as if they had been abject slaves of a cruel dictator.

But suppose one says that a person is free only to the extent that his acts are *not unconsciously determined at all*, be they unconsciously benevolent *or* malevolent? If this is the criterion, psychoanalysts would say, most human behavior cannot be called free at all; our impulses and volitions having to do with our basic attitudes toward life, whether we are optimists or pessimists, tough-minded or tender-minded, whether our tempers are quick or slow, whether we are "naturally self-seeking" or "naturally benevolent" (and *all the acts consequent upon these things*), what things annoy us, whether we take to blondes or brunettes, old or young, whether we become philosophers or artists or businessmen—all this has its basis in the unconscious. If people generally call most acts free, it is not because they believe that compelled acts should be called free, it is rather through not knowing how large a proportion of our acts actually are compelled. Only the comparatively "vanilla-flavored" aspects of our lives—such as our behavior toward people who don't really matter to us—are exempted from this rule.

These, I think, are the two principal criteria for distinguishing freedom from the lack of it which we might set up on the basis of psychoanalytic knowledge. Conceivably we might set up others. In every case, of course, it remains trivially true that "it all depends on how we choose to use the word." The facts are what they are, regardless of what words we choose for labeling them. But if we choose to label them in a way which is not in accord with what human beings, however vaguely, have long had in mind in applying these labels, as we would be doing if we labeled as "free" many acts which we know as much about as we now do through modern psychoanalytic methods, then we shall only be manipulating words to mislead our fellow creatures.

NOTES

[1] *Ethics,* pp. 15–16.

[2] *Philosophy and the Physicists,* p. 212.

[3] *The Problems of Ethics,* Rynin translation, p. 150.

[4] *Ethics,* Chapter 6, pp. 217ff.

[5] *New York Post,* Tuesday, May 18, 1948, p. 4.

[6] I am aware that the theory presented below is not accepted by all practicing psychoanalysts. Many non-Freudians would disagree with the conclusions presented below. But I do not believe that this fact affects my argument, as long as the concept of unconscious motivation is accepted. I am aware, too, that much of the language employed in the following descriptions is animistic and metaphorical; but as long as I am presenting a view I would prefer to "go the whole hog" and present it in its most dramatic form. The theory can in any case be made clearest by the use of such language, just as atomic theory can often be made clearest to students with the use of models.

[7] This view is very clearly developed in Edmund Bergler, *Divorce Won't Help,* especially Chapter 1.

[8] See *The Basic Writings of Sigmund Freud,* Modern Library Edition, p. 310. (In *The Interpretation of Dreams.*) Cf. also the essay by Ernest Jones, "A Psycho-analytical Study of Hamlet."

[9] See Edmund Bergler's article on the pathological gambler in *Diseases of the Nervous System* (1943). Also "Suppositions about the Mechanism of Criminosis," *Journal of Criminal Psychopathology* (1944) and "Clinical Contributions to the Psychogenesis of Alcohol Addiction," *Quarterly Journal of Studies on Alcohol,* 5:434 (1944).

[10]E.g., Edmund Bergler, *The Battle of the Conscience*, Chapter 1.

[11]The girl's development after this point is somewhat different. Society demands more aggressiveness of the adult male, hence there are more super-ego strictures on tendencies toward passivity in the male; accordingly his defenses must be stronger.

[12]A. J. Ayer, "Freedom and Necessity," *Polemic* (September–October 1946), pp. 40–43.

[13]Samuel Butler, *Erewhon* (Modern Library edition), p. 107.

Persons and Free Will

Freedom and Determinism*

Richard Taylor

If I consider the world or any part of it at any particular moment, it seems certain that it is perfectly determinate in every detail. There is no vagueness, looseness, or ambiguity. There is, indeed, vagueness, and even error, in my conceptions of reality, but not in reality itself. A lilac bush, which surely has a certain exact number of blossoms, appears to me only to have many blossoms, and I do not know how many. Things seen in the distance appear of indefinite form, and often of a color and size which in fact they have not. Things near the border of my visual field seem to me vague and amorphous, and I can never even say exactly where that border itself is, it is so indefinite and vague. But all such indeterminateness resides solely in my conceptions and ideas; the world itself shares none of it. The sea, at any exact time and place, has exactly a certain salinity and temperature, and every grain of sand on its shore is exactly disposed with respect to all the others. The wind at any point in space has at any moment a certain direction and

*Richard Taylor, *Metaphysics*, 2/E, 1974, pp. 39–47. Reprinted by permission of Prentice-Hall, Inc., Englewood Cliffs, NJ.

force, not more nor less. It matters not whether these properties and relations are known to anyone. A field of wheat at any moment contains just an exact number of ripening grains, each having reached just the ripeness it exhibits, each presenting a determinate color and shade, an exact shape and mass. A man, too, at any given point in his life, is perfectly determinate to the minutest cells of his body. My own brain, nerves—even my thoughts, intentions, and feelings—are at any moment just what they then specifically are. These thoughts might, to be sure, be vague and even false as representations, but as thoughts they are not, and even a false idea is no less an exact and determinate idea than a true one.

Nothing seems more obvious. But if I now ask *why* the world and all its larger or smaller parts are this moment just what they are, the answer comes to mind: Because the world, the moment before, was precisely what it then was. Given exactly what went before, the world, it seems, could now be none other than it is. And what it was a moment before, in all its larger and minuter parts, was the consequence of what had gone just before then, and so on, back to the very beginning of the world, if it had a beginning, or through an infinite past time, in case it had not. In any case, the world as it now is, and every part of it, and every detail of every part, would seem to be the only world that now could be, given just what it has been.

DETERMINISM

Reflections such as these suggest that, in the case of everything that exists, there are antecedent conditions, known or unknown, given which that thing could not be other than it is. That is an exact statement of the metaphysical thesis of determinism. More loosely, it says that everything, including every cause, is the effect of some cause or causes; or that everything is not only determinate but causally determined. The statement, moreover, makes no allowance for time, for past, or for future. Hence, if true, it holds not only for all things that have existed but for all things that do or ever will exist.

Of course men rarely think of such a principle, and hardly one in a thousand will ever formulate it to himself in words. Yet all men do seem to assume it in their daily affairs, so much so that some philosophers have declared it an a priori principle of the understanding, that is, something that is known independently of experience, while others have deemed it to be at least a part of the common sense of mankind. Thus, when I hear a noise I look up to see where it came from. I never suppose that it was just a noise that came from nowhere and had no cause. All men do the same—even animals, though they have never once thought about metaphysics or the principle of universal determinism. Men believe, or at least act as though they believed, that things have causes, without exception. When a child or animal touches a hot stove for the first time, it unhesitatingly believes that the pain then felt was caused by that stove, and so firm and immediate is that belief that hot stoves are avoided ever after. We all use our metaphysical principles,

whether we think of them or not, or are even capable of thinking about them. If I have a bodily or other disorder—a rash, for instance, or a fever or a phobia—I consult a physician for a diagnosis and explanation, in the hope that the cause of it might be found and removed or moderated. I am never tempted to suppose that such things just have no causes, arising from nowhere, else I would take no steps to remove the causes. The principle of determinism is here, as in everything else, simply assumed, without being thought about.

Determinism and Human Behavior

I am a part of the world. So is each of the cells and minute parts of which I am composed. The principle of determinism, then, in case it is true, applies to me and to each of those minute parts, no less than to the sand, wheat, winds, and waters of which we have spoken. There is no particular difficulty in thinking so, as long as I consider only what are sometimes called the "purely physiological" changes of my body, like growth, the pulse, glandular secretions, and the like. But what of my thoughts and ideas? And what of my behavior that is supposed to be deliberate, purposeful, and perhaps morally significant? These are all changes of my own being, changes that I undergo, and if these are all but the consequences of the conditions under which they occur, and these conditions are the only ones that could have obtained, given the state of the world just before and when they arose, what now becomes of my responsibility for my behavior and of the control over my conduct that I fancy myself to possess? What am I but a helpless product of nature, destined by her to do whatever I do and to become whatever I become?

There is no moral blame nor merit in any man who cannot help what he does. It matters not whether the explanation for his behavior is found within him or without, whether it is expressed in terms of ordinary physical causes or allegedly "mental" ones, or whether the causes be proximate or remote. I am not responsible for being a man rather than a woman, nor for having the temperament, desires, purposes, and ideals characteristic of that sex. I was never asked whether these should be given to me. The kleptomaniac, similarly, steals from compulsion, the chronic alcoholic drinks from compulsion, and sometimes even the hero dies from compulsive courage. Though these causes are within them, they compel no less for that, and their victims never chose to have them inflicted upon themselves. To say they are compulsions is to say only that they compel. But to say they compel is only to say that they cause; for the cause of a thing being given, the effect cannot fail to follow. By the thesis of determinism, however, everything whatever is caused, and not one single thing could ever be other than exactly what it is. Perhaps one thinks that the kleptomaniac and the drunkard did not have to become what they are, that they could have done better at another time and thereby ended up better than they are now, or that the hero could have done worse and then ended up a coward. But this shows only an unwillingness to understand what made them become as they are. Having found that their behavior is caused from within them, we can hardly avoid asking what caused these inner springs of action, and then asking what were the causes of these causes, and so on through the infinite past. We shall not, certainly, with our small understanding and our fragmentary knowledge of the past ever know why the world should at just this time and place have produced just this thief, this drunkard, and this hero, but the vagueness and smattered nature of our knowledge should not tempt us to imagine a similar vagueness in nature itself. Everything in nature is and always has been determinate, with no loose edges at all, and she was forever destined to bring forth just what she has produced, however slight may be our understanding of the origins of these works. Ultimate responsibility for anything that exists, and hence for any man and his deeds, can thus only rest with the first cause of all things, if there is such a cause, or nowhere at all, in case there is not. Such at least seems to be the unavoidable implication of determinism.

Determinism and Morals

Some philosophers, faced with all this, which seems quite clear to the ordinary understanding, have tried to cling to determinism while modifying traditional conceptions of morals. They continue to *use* such words as "merit," "blame," "praise," and "desert," but they so divest them of their meanings as to finish by talking about things entirely different, sometimes without themselves realizing that they are no longer on the subject. An ordinary man will hardly understand that anyone can possess merit or vice and be deserving of moral praise or blame, as a result of traits that he has or of behavior arising from those traits, once it is well understood that he could never have avoided being just what he is and doing just what he does.

We are happily spared going into all this, however, for the question whether determinism is true of human nature is not a question of ethics at all but of metaphysics. There is accordingly no hope of answering it within the context of ethics. One can, to be sure, simply *assume* an answer to it—assume that determinism is true, for instance—and then see what are the implications of this answer for ethics; but that does not answer the question. Or one can *assume* some theory or other of ethics—assume some version of "the great happiness" principle, for instance—and then see whether that theory is consistent with determinism. But such confrontations of theories with theories likewise makes us no wiser, so far as any fundamental question is concerned. We can suppose at once that determinism is consistent with some conceptions of morals, and inconsistent with others, and that the same holds for indeterminism. We shall still not know what theories are true; we shall only know which are consistent with each other.

We shall, then, eschew all considerations of ethics, as having no real bearing on our problem. We want to learn, if we can, whether determinism is true, and this is a question of metaphysics. It can, like all good questions of philosophy, be answered only on the basis of certain data; that is, by seeing whether or not it squares with certain things which every man knows, or believes himself to know, or things of which every man is at least more sure than the answer to the question at issue.

Now I could, of course, simply affirm that I am a morally responsible being, in the sense in which my responsibility for my behavior implies that I could have avoided that behavior. But this would take us into the nebulous realm of ethics, and it is, in fact, far from obvious that I am responsible in that sense. Many have doubted that they are responsible in that sense, and it is in any case not difficult to doubt it, however strongly one might feel about it.

There are, however, two things about myself of which I feel quite certain and which have no necessary connection with morals. The first is that I sometimes deliberate, with the view to making a decision; a decision, namely, to do this thing or that. And the second is that whether or not I deliberate about what to do, it is sometimes up to me what I do. This might all be an illusion, of course; but so also any philosophical theory, such as the theory of determinism, might be false. The point remains that it is far more difficult for me to doubt that I sometimes deliberate, and that it is sometimes up to me what to do, than to doubt any philosophical theory whatever, including the theory of determinism. We must, accordingly, if we ever hope to be wiser, adjust our theories to our data and not try to adjust our data to our theories.

Let us, then, get these two data quite clearly before us so we can see what they are, what they presuppose, and what they do and do not entail.

DELIBERATION

Deliberation is an activity, or at least a kind of experience, that cannot be defined, or even described without metaphors. We speak of weighing this and that in our minds, of trying to anticipate consequences of various possible courses of action, and so on, but such descriptions do not convey to us what deliberation is unless we already know.

Whenever I deliberate, however, I find that I make certain presuppositions, whether I actually think of them or not. That is, I assume that certain things are true, certain things which are such that, if I thought they were not true, it would be impossible for me to deliberate at all. Some of these can be listed as follows.

First, I find that I can deliberate only about my own behavior and never about the behavior of another. I can try to guess, speculate, or figure out what another person is going to do; I can read certain signs and sometimes infer what he will do; but I cannot deliberate about it. When I deliberate I try to decide something, to make up my mind, and this is as remote as anything could be from speculating, trying to guess, or to infer from signs. Sometimes one *does* speculate on what he is going to do, by trying to draw conclusions from certain signs or omens—he might infer that he is going to sneeze, for instance, or speculate that he is going to become a grandfather—but he is not then deliberating whether to do these things or not. One does, to be sure, sometimes deliberate about whether another person will do a certain act, when that other person is subject to his command or otherwise under his control; but then he is not really deliberating about another person's acts at all, but about his own—namely, whether or not to have that other person carry out the order.

Second, I find that I can deliberate only about future things, never things past or present. I may not know what I did at a certain time in the past, in case I have forgotten, but I can no longer deliberate whether or not to do it then or not. I can, again, only speculate, guess, try to infer, or perhaps try to remember. Similarly, I cannot deliberate whether or not to be doing something now; I can only ascertain whether or not I am in fact doing it. If I am sitting I cannot deliberate about whether or not to be sitting. I can only deliberate about whether to remain sitting—and this has to do with the future.

Third, I cannot deliberate about what I shall do, in case I already know what I am going to do. If I were to say, for example, "I know that I am going to be married tomorrow and in the meantime I am going to deliberate about whether to get married," I would contradict myself. There are only two ways that I could know now what I am going to do tomorrow; namely, either by inferring this from certain signs and omens or by having already decided what I am going to do. But if I have inferred from signs and omens what I am going to do, I cannot deliberate about it—there is just nothing for me to decide; and similarly, if I have already decided. If, on the other hand, I can still deliberate about what I am going to do, to that extent I must regard the signs and omens as unreliable, and the inference uncertain, and I therefore do not know what I am going to do after all.

And finally, I cannot deliberate about what to do, even though I may not know what I am going to do, unless I believe that it is up to me what I am going to do. If I am within the power of another person, or at the mercy of circumstances over which I have no control, then, although I may have no idea what I am going to do, I cannot deliberate about it. I can only wait and see. If, for instance, I am a conscript, and regulations regarding uniforms are posted each day by my commanding officer and are strictly enforced by him, then I shall not know what uniforms I shall be wearing from time to time, but I cannot deliberate about it. I can only wait and see what regulations are posted; it is not up to me. Similarly, a woman who is about to give birth to a child cannot deliberate about whether to have a boy or a girl, even though she may not know. She can only wait and see; it is not up to her. Such examples can be generalized to cover any case wherein one does not know what he is going to do, but believes that it is not up to him, and hence no matter for his decision and hence none for his deliberation.

"IT IS UP TO ME"

I sometimes feel certain that it is, at least to some extent, up to me what I am going to do; indeed, I must believe this if I am to deliberate about what to do. But what does this mean? It is, again, hard to say, but the idea can be illustrated, and we can fairly easily see what it does *not* mean.

Let us consider the simplest possible sort of situation in which this belief might be involved. At this moment, for instance, it seems quite certain to me that, holding my finger before me, I can move it either to the left or to the right, that each of these motions is possible for me. This does not mean merely that my finger can move either way, although it entails that, for this would be true in case nothing obstructed it, even if I had no control over it at all. I can say of a distant, fluttering leaf that it can move either way, but not that I can move it, since I have no control over it. How it moves is not up to me. Nor does it mean merely that my finger can be moved either way, although it entails this too. If the motions of my finger are under the control of some other person or of some machine, then it might be true that the finger can be moved either way, by that person or machine, though false that I can move it at all.

If I say, then, that it is up to me how I move my finger, I mean that I can move it in this way and I can move it in that way, and not merely that it can move or be moved in this way and that. I mean that the motion of my finger is within my direct control. If someone were to ask me to move it to the right, I could do that, and if he were to ask me to move it to the left, I could do that too. Further, I could do these simple acts without being asked at all, and, having been asked, I could move it in a manner the exact opposite of what was requested, since I can ignore the request. There are, to be sure, some motions of my finger that I cannot make, so it is not *entirely* up to me how it moves. I cannot bend it backward, for instance, or bend it into a knot, for these motions are obstructed by the very anatomical construction of the finger itself; and to say that I can move my finger at all means at least that nothing obstructs such a motion, though it does not mean merely this. There is, however, at this moment, no obstruction, anatomical or otherwise, to my moving it to the right, and none to my moving it to the left.

This datum, it should be noted, is properly expressed as a conjunction and not as a disjunction. That is, my belief is that I can move my finger in one way, *and* that I can also move it another way; and it does not do justice to this belief to say that I can move it one way *or* the other. It is fairly easy to see the truth of this, for the latter claim, that I can move it one way *or* the other, would be satisfied in case there were only one way I could move it, and *that* is not what I believe. Suppose, for instance, my hand were strapped to a device in such a fashion that I could move my finger to the right but not to the left. Then it would still be entirely true that I could move it either to the left *or* to the right—since it would be true that I could move it to the right. But that is not what I now believe. My finger is not strapped to anything, and nothing obstructs its motion in either direction. And what I believe, in this situation, is that I can move it to the right *and* I can move it to the left.

We must note further that the belief expressed in our datum is not a belief in what is logically impossible. It is the belief that I now *can* move my finger in different ways but not that I can move it in different ways at once. What I believe is that I am now able to move my finger and that I am now equally able to move it another way, but I do not claim to be able now or any other time to move it both ways simultaneously. The situation here is analogous to one in which I might, for instance, be offered a choice of either of two apples but forbidden to take both. Each apple is such that I may select it, but neither is such that I may select it together with the other.

Now are these two data—the belief that I do sometimes deliberate, and the belief that it is sometimes up to me what I do—consistent with the metaphysical theory of determinism? We do not know yet. We intend to find out. It is fairly clear, however, that they are going to present difficulties to that theory. But let us not, in any case, try to avoid those difficulties by just denying the data themselves. If we eventually deny the data, we shall do so for better reasons than this. Virtually all men are convinced that beliefs such as are expressed in our data are sometimes true. They cannot be simply dismissed as false just because they might appear to conflict with a metaphysical theory that hardly any men have ever really thought much about at all. Almost any man, unless his fingers are paralyzed, bound, or otherwise incapable of movement, believes sometimes that the motions of his fingers are within his control, in exactly the sense expressed by our data. If consequences of considerable importance to him depend on how he moves his fingers, he sometimes deliberates before moving them, or at least, he is convinced that he does, or that he can. Philosophers might have different notions of just what things are implied by such data, but there is in any case no more, and in fact considerably less, reason for denying the data than for denying some philosophical theory.

CAUSAL VS. LOGICAL NECESSITY

Philosophers have long since pointed out that causal connections involve no logical necessity, that the denial of a particular causal connection is never self-contradictory, and this is undoubtedly true. But neither does the assertion or the denial of determinism involve any concept of what is and what is not logically necessary. If determinism is true, then anything that happens is, given the conditions under which it occurs, the only thing possible, the thing that is necessitated by those conditions. But it is not the only thing that is logically possible, nor do those conditions logically necessitate it. Similarly, if one denies the thesis of determinism, by asserting, for instance, that each of two bodily motions is possible for him under identical conditions, he is asserting much more than that each is logically possible, for that would be a trivial claim.

This distinction, between logical necessity and the sort of necessity involved in determinism, can be illustrated with examples. If, for instance, a man is beheaded, we can surely say that it is impossible for him to go on living, that his being beheaded necessitates his death, and so on; but there are no logical necessities or impossibilities involved here. It is not logically impossible for a man to live without his head. Yet no one will deny that a man cannot live under conditions that include his being headless, that such a state of affairs is in a perfectly clear sense impossible. Similarly, if my finger is in a tight and fairly strong cast, then it is impossible for me to move it in any way at all, though this is not logically impossible. It is logically possible that I should be vastly stronger than I am, and that I should move it and, in doing so, break the cast, though this would ordinarily not be possible in the sense that concerns us. Again, it is not logically impossible that I should bend my finger backward, or into a knot, though it is, in fact, impossible for me to do either or, what means the same thing, necessary that I should do neither. Certain conditions prohibit my doing such things, though they impose no logical barrier. And finally, if someone—a physician, for example—should ask me whether I can move my finger, and I should reply that truly I can, I would not merely be telling him that it is logically possible for me to move it, for this he already knows. I would be telling him that I am able to move it, that it is within my power to do so, that there are no conditions, such as paralysis or whatnot, that prevent my moving it.

It follows that not all necessity is logical necessity, nor all impossibility logical impossibility, and that to say that something is possible is sometimes to say much more than that it is logically possible. The kind of necessity involved in the thesis of determinism is quite obviously the nonlogical kind, as is also the kind of possibility involved in its denial. If we needed a *name* for these nonlogical modalities, we could call them *causal* necessity, impossibility, and possibility, but the concepts are clear enough without making a great deal of the name.

FREEDOM

To say that it is, in a given instance, up to me what I do, is to say that I am in that instance *free* with respect to what I then do. Thus, I am sometimes free to move my finger this way and that, but not, certainly, to bend it backward or into a knot. But what does this mean?

It means, first, that there is no *obstacle* or *impediment* to my activity. Thus, there is sometimes no obstacle to my moving my finger this way and that, though there are obvious obstacles to my moving it far backward or into a knot. Those things, accordingly, that pose obstacles to my motions limit my freedom. If my hand were strapped in such a way as to permit only a leftward motion of my finger, I would not then be free to move it to the right. If it were encased in a tight cast that permitted no motion, I would not be free to move it at all. Freedom of motion, then, is limited by obstacles.

Further, to say that it is, in a given instance, up to me what I do, means that nothing *constrains* or *forces* me to do one thing rather than another. Constraints are like obstacles, except that while the latter prevent, the former enforce. Thus, if my finger is being forcibly bent to the left—by a machine, for instance, or by another person, or by any force that I cannot overcome—then I am not free to move it this way and that. I cannot, in fact, move it at all; I can only watch to see how it is moved, and perhaps vainly resist: its motions are not up to me, or within my control, but in the control of some other thing or person.

Obstacles and constraints, then, both obviously limit my freedom. To say I am free to perform some action thus means at least that there is no obstacle to my doing it, and that nothing constrains me to do otherwise.

Now if we rest content with this observation, as many have, and construe free activity simply as activity that is unimpeded and unconstrained, there is evidently no inconsistency between affirming both the thesis of determinism and the claim that I am sometimes free. For to say that some action of mine is neither impeded nor constrained does not by itself imply that it is not causally determined. The absence of obstacles and constraints are mere negative conditions, and do not by themselves rule out the presence of positive causes. It might seem, then, that we can say of some of my actions that there are conditions antecedent to their performance so that no other actions were possible, and also that these actions were unobstructed and unconstrained. And to say that would logically entail that such actions were both causally determined, and free.

SOFT DETERMINISM

It is this kind of consideration that has led many philosophers to embrace what is sometimes called "soft determinism." All versions of this theory have in common three claims, by means of which, it is naïvely supposed, a reconciliation is achieved between determinism and freedom. Freedom being, furthermore, a condition of moral responsibility and the only condition that metaphysics seriously questions, it is supposed by the partisans of this view that determinism is perfectly compatible with such responsibility. This, no doubt, accounts for its great appeal and wide acceptance, even by some men of considerable learning.

The three claims of soft determinism are (1) that the thesis of determinism is true, and that accordingly all human behavior, voluntary or other, like the behavior of all other things, arises from antecedent conditions, given which no other behavior is possible—in short, that all human behavior is caused and determined; (2) that voluntary behavior is nonetheless free to the extent that it is not externally constrained or impeded; and (3) that, in the absence of such obstacles and constraints, the causes of voluntary behavior are certain states, events, or conditions within the agent himself; namely, his own acts of

will or volitions, choices, decisions, desires, and so on.

Thus, on this view, I am free, and therefore sometimes responsible for what I do, provided nothing prevents me from acting according to my own choice, desire, or volition, or constrains me to act otherwise. There may, to be sure, be other conditions for my responsibility—such as, for example, an understanding of the probable consequences of my behavior, and that sort of thing—but absence of constraint or impediment is, at least, one such condition. And, it is claimed, it is a condition that is compatible with the supposition that my behavior is caused—for it is, by hypothesis, caused by my own inner choices, desires, and volitions.

The Refutation of This

The theory of soft determinism looks good at first—so good that it has for generations been solemnly taught from numberless philosophical chairs and implanted in the minds of students as sound philosophy—but no great acumen is needed to discover that far from solving any problem, it only camouflages it.

My free actions are those unimpeded and unconstrained motions that arise from my own inner desires, choices, and volitions; let us grant this provisionally. But now, whence arise those inner states that determine what my body shall do? Are they within my control or not? Having made my choice or decision and acted upon it, could I have chosen otherwise or not?

Here the determinist, hoping to surrender nothing and yet to avoid the problem implied in that question, bids us not to ask it; the question itself, he announces, is without meaning. For to say that I could have done otherwise, he says, means that I *would* have done otherwise *if* those inner states that determined my action had been different; if, that is, I had decided or chosen differently. To ask, accordingly, whether I could have chosen differently is only to ask whether had I decided differently or chosen to choose differently, or willed to will differently, I would have decided or chosen or willed differently. And this, of course, *is* unintelligible nonsense.

But it is not nonsense to ask whether the causes of my actions—my own inner choices, decisions, and desires—are themselves caused. And of course they are, if determinism is true, for on that thesis everything is caused and determined. And if they are, then we cannot avoid concluding that, given the causal conditions of those inner states, I could not have decided, willed, chosen, or desired otherwise than I in fact did, for this is a logical consequence of the very definition of determinism. Of course we can still say that, *if* the causes of those inner states, whatever they were, had been different, then their effects, those inner states themselves, would have been different, and that in this hypothetical sense I could have decided, chosen, willed, or desired differently—but that only pushes our problem back still another step. For we will then want to know whether the causes of those inner states were within my control; and so on, *ad infinitum*. We are, at each step, permitted to say "could have been otherwise" only in a provisional sense—provided, that is, something else had been different—but must then retract it and replace it with "could not have been otherwise" as soon as we discover, as we must at each step, that whatever would have to have been different could not have been different.

Examples

Such is the dialectic of the problem. The easiest way to see the shadowy quality of soft determinism, however, is by means of examples.

Let us suppose that my body is moving in various ways, that these motions are not externally constrained or impeded, and that they are all exactly in accordance with my own desires, choices, or acts of will and what not. When I will that my arm should move in a certain way, I find it moving in that way, unobstructed and unconstrained. When I will to speak, my lips and tongue

move, unobstructed and unconstrained, in a manner suitable to the formation of the words I choose to utter. Now given that this is a correct description of my behavior, namely, that it consists of the unconstrained and unimpeded motions of my body in response to my own volitions, then it follows that my behavior is free, on the soft determinist's definition of "free." It follows further that I am responsible for that behavior; or at least, that if I am not, it is not from any lack of freedom on my part.

But if the fulfillment of these conditions renders my behavior free—that is to say, if my behavior satisfies the conditions of free action set forth in the theory of soft determinism—then my behavior will be no less free if we assume further conditions that are perfectly consistent with those already satisfied.

We suppose further, accordingly, that while my behavior is entirely in accordance with my own volitions, and thus "free" in terms of the conception of freedom we are examining, my volitions themselves are caused. To make this graphic, we can suppose that an ingenious physiologist can induce in me any volition he pleases, simply by pushing various buttons on an instrument to which, let us suppose, I am attached by numerous wires. All the volitions I have in that situation are, accordingly, precisely the ones he gives me. By pushing one button, he evokes in me the volition to raise my hand; and my hand, being unimpeded, rises in response to that volition. By pushing another, he induces the volition in me to kick, and my foot, being unimpeded, kicks in response to that volition. We can even suppose that the physiologist puts a rifle in my hands, aims it at some passer-by, and then, by pushing the proper button, evokes in me the volition to squeeze my finger against the trigger, whereupon the passer-by falls dead of a bullet wound.

This is the description of a man who is acting in accordance with his inner volitions, a man whose body is unimpeded and unconstrained in its motions, these motions being the effects of those inner states. It is hardly the description of a free and responsible agent. It is the perfect description of a puppet. To render a man your puppet, it is not necessary forcibly to constrain the motions of his limbs, after the fashion that real puppets are moved. A subtler but no less effective means of making a man your puppet would be to gain complete control of his inner states, and ensuring, as the theory of soft determinism does ensure, that his body will move in accordance with them.

The example is somewhat unusual, but it is no worse for that. It is perfectly intelligible, and it does appear to refute the soft determinist's conception of freedom. One might think that, in such a case, the agent should not have allowed himself to be so rigged in the first place, but this is irrelevant; we can suppose that he was not aware that he was, and was hence unaware of the source of those inner states that prompted his bodily motions. The example can, moreover, be modified in perfectly realistic ways, so as to coincide with actual and familiar cases. One can, for instance, be given a compulsive desire for certain drugs, simply by having them administered to him over a course of time. Suppose, then, that I do, with neither my knowledge nor consent, thus become a victim of such a desire and act upon it. Do I act freely, merely by virtue of the fact that I am unimpeded in my quest for drugs? In a sense I do, surely, but I am hardly free with respect to whether or not I shall use drugs. I never chose to have the desire for them inflicted upon me.

Nor does it, of course, matter whether the inner states which allegedly prompt all my "free" activity are evoked in me by another agent or by perfectly impersonal forces. Whether a desire which causes my body to behave in a certain way is inflicted upon me by another person, for instance, or derived from hereditary factors, or indeed from anything at all, matters not the least. In any case, if it is in fact the cause of my bodily behavior, I cannot but act in accordance with it. Wherever it came from, whether from personal or impersonal origins, it was entirely caused or determined, and not within my control. Indeed, if determinism is true, as the theory of soft determinism holds it to be, all those inner states which cause my body to behave in whatever ways it behaves must arise from circumstances that existed before I was born; for the chain of causes and effects is infinite, and none could have been the least different, given those that preceded.

SIMPLE INDETERMINISM

We might at first now seem warranted in simply denying determinism, and saying that, insofar as they are free, my actions are not caused; or that, if they are caused by my own inner states—my own desires, impulses, choices, volitions, and whatnot—then these, in any case, are not caused. This is a perfectly clear sense in which a man's action, assuming that it was free, could have been otherwise. If it was uncaused, then, even given the conditions under which it occurred and all that preceded, some other act was nonetheless possible, and he did not have to do what he did. Or if his action was the inevitable consequence of his own inner states, and could not have been otherwise given these, we can nevertheless say that these inner states, being uncaused, could have been otherwise, and could thereby have produced different actions.

Only the slightest consideration will show, however, that this simple denial of determinism has not the slightest plausibility. For let us suppose it is true, and that some of my bodily motions—namely, those that I regard as my free acts—are not caused at all or, if caused by my own inner states, that these are not caused. We shall thereby avoid picturing a puppet, to be sure—but only by substituting something even less like a man; for the conception that now emerges is not that of a free man, but of an erratic and jerking phantom, without any rhyme or reason at all.

Suppose that my right arm is free, according to this conception; that is, that its motions are uncaused. It moves this way and that from time to time, but nothing causes these motions. Sometimes it moves forth vigorously, sometimes up, sometimes down, sometimes it just drifts vaguely about—these motions all being wholly free and uncaused. Manifestly I have nothing to do with them at all; they just happen, and neither I nor anyone can ever tell what this arm will be doing next. It might seize a club and lay it on the head of the nearest bystander, no less to my astonishment than his. There will never be any point in asking why these motions occur, or in seeking any explanation of them, for under the conditions assumed there is no explanation. They just happen, from no causes at all.

This is no description of free, voluntary, or responsible behavior. Indeed, so far as the motions of my body or its parts are entirely uncaused, such motions cannot even be ascribed to me as my behavior in the first place, since I have nothing to do with them. The behavior of my arm is just the random motion of a foreign object. Behavior that is mine must be behavior that is within my control, but motions that occur from no causes are without the control of anyone. I can have no more to do with, and no more control over, the uncaused motions of my limbs than a gambler has over the motions of an honest roulette wheel. I can only, like him, idly wait to see what happens.

Nor does it improve things to suppose that my bodily motions are caused by my own inner states, so long as we suppose these to be wholly uncaused. The result will be the same as before. My arm, for example, will move this way and that, sometimes up and sometime down, sometimes vigorously and sometimes just drifting about, always in response to certain inner states, to be sure. But since these are supposed to be wholly uncaused, it follows that I have no control over them and hence none over their effects. If my hand lays a club forcefully on the nearest bystander, we can indeed say that this motion resulted from an inner club-wielding desire of mine; but we must add that I had nothing to do with that desire, and that it arose, to be followed by its inevitable effect, no less to my astonishment than to his. Things like this do, alas, sometimes happen. We are all sometimes seized by compulsive impulses that arise we know not whence and we do sometimes act upon these. But because they are far from being examples of free, voluntary, and responsible behavior, we need only to learn that behavior was of this sort to conclude that it was not free, voluntary, or responsible. It was erratic, impulsive, and irresponsible.

DETERMINISM AND SIMPLE INDETERMINISM AS THEORIES

Both determinism and simple indeterminism are loaded with difficulties, and no one who has thought much on them can affirm either of them without some embarrassment. Simple indeterminism has nothing whatever to be said for it, except that it appears to remove the grossest difficulties of determinism, only, however, to imply perfect absurdities of its own. Determinism, on the other hand, is at least initially plausible. Men seem to have a natural inclination to believe in it; it is, indeed, almost required for the very exercise of practical intelligence. And beyond this, our experience appears always to confirm it, so long as we are dealing with everyday facts of common experience, as distinguished from the esoteric researches of theoretical physics. But determinism, as applied to human behavior, has implications which few men can casually accept, and they appear to be implications which no modification of the theory can efface.

Both theories, moreover, appear logically irreconcilable to the two items of data that we set forth at the outset; namely, (1) that my behavior is sometimes the outcome of my deliberation, and (2) that in these and other cases it is sometimes up to me what I do. Because these were our data, it is important to see, as must already be quite clear, that these theories cannot be reconciled to them.

I can deliberate only about my own future actions, and then only if I do not already know what I am going to do. If a certain nasal tickle warns me that I am about to sneeze, for instance, then I cannot deliberate whether to sneeze or not; I can only prepare for the impending convulsion. But if determinism is true, then there are always conditions existing antecedently to everything I do, sufficient for my doing just that, and such as to render it inevitable. If I can know what those conditions are and what behavior they are sufficient to produce, then I can in every such case know what I am going to do and cannot then deliberate about it.

By itself this only shows, of course, that I can deliberate only in ignorance of the causal conditions of my behavior; it does not show that such conditions cannot exist. It is odd, however, to suppose that deliberation should be a mere substitute for clear knowledge. Ignorance is a condition of speculation, inference, and guesswork, which have nothing whatever to do with deliberation. A prisoner awaiting execution may not know when he is going to die, and he may even entertain the hope of reprieve, but he cannot deliberate about this. He can only speculate, guess—and wait.

Worse yet, however, it now becomes clear that I cannot deliberate about what I am going to do, if it is even possible for me to find out in advance, whether I do in fact find out in advance or not. I can deliberate only with the view to deciding what to do, to making up my mind; and this is impossible if I believe that it could be inferred what I am going to do, from conditions already existing, even though I have not made that inference myself. If I believe that what I am going to do has been rendered inevitable by conditions already existing, and could be inferred by anyone having the requisite sagacity, then I cannot try to decide whether to do it or not, for there is simply nothing left to decide. I can at best only guess or try to figure it out myself, or, all prognostics failing, I can wait and see; but I cannot deliberate. I deliberate in order to *decide* what *to* do, not to *discover* what it is that I am *going* to do. But if determinism is true, then there are always antecedent conditions sufficient for everything that I do, and this can always be inferred by anyone having the requisite sagacity; that is, by anyone having a knowledge of what those conditions are and what behavior they are sufficient to produce.

This suggests what in fact seems quite clear, that determinism cannot be reconciled with our second datum either, to the effect that it is sometimes up to me what I am going to do. For if it is ever really up to me whether to do this thing or that, then, as we have seen, each alternative course of action must be such that I can do it; not that I can do it in some abstruse or hypothetical sense of "can"; not that I could do it if only something were true that is not true; but in the sense that it is then and there within my power to do it. But this is never so, if determinism is true, for on the very formulation of that theory whatever happens at any time is the only thing that can happen, given all that precedes it. It is simply a logical consequence of this that whatever I do at any time is the only thing I can then do, given the conditions that precede my doing it. Nor does it help in the least to interpose, among the causal antecedents of my behavior, my own inner states, such as my desires, choices, acts of will, and so on. For even supposing these to be always involved in voluntary behavior—which is highly doubtful in itself—it is a consequence of determinism that these, whatever they are at any time, can never be other than what they then are. Every chain of causes and effects, if determinism is true, is infinite. This is why it is not now up to me whether I shall a moment hence be male or female. The conditions determining my sex have existed throughout my whole life, and even prior to my life. But if determinism is true, the same holds of anything that I ever am, ever become, or ever do. It matters not whether we are speaking of the most patent facts of my being, such as my sex; or the most subtle, such as my feelings, thoughts, desires, or choices. Nothing could be other than it is, given what it was; and while we may indeed say, quite idly, that something—some inner state of mind, for instance—*could* have been different, had only something *else* been different, any consolation of this thought evaporates as soon as we add that whatever would have to have been different could not have been different.

It is even more obvious that our data cannot be reconciled to the theory of simple indeterminism. I can deliberate only about my own actions; this is obvious. But the random, uncaused motion of any body whatever, whether it be a part of my body or not, is no action of mine and nothing that is within my power. I might try to guess what these motions will be, just as I might try to guess how a roulette wheel will behave, but I cannot deliberate about them or try to decide what they shall be, simply because these things are not up to me. Whatever is not caused by anything is not caused by me, and nothing could be more plainly inconsistent with saying that it is nevertheless up to me what it shall be.

THE THEORY OF AGENCY

The only conception of action that accords with our data is one according to which men—and perhaps some other things too—are sometimes, but of course not always, self-determining beings; that is, beings which are sometimes the causes of their own behavior. In the case of an action that is free, it must be such that it is caused by the agent who performs it, but such that no antecedent conditions were sufficient for his performing just that action. In the case of an action that is both free and rational, it must be such that the agent who performed it did so for some reason, but this reason cannot have been the cause of it.

Now this conception fits what men take themselves to be; namely, beings who act, or who are agents, rather than things that are merely acted upon, and whose behavior is simply the causal consequence of conditions which they have not wrought. When I believe that I have done something, I do believe that it was I who caused it to be done, I who made something happen, and not merely something within me, such as one of my own subjective states, which is not identical with myself. If I believe that something not identical with myself was the cause of my behavior—some event wholly external to myself, for instance, or even one internal to myself, such as a nerve

impulse, volition, or whatnot—then I cannot regard that behavior as being an act of mine, unless I further believe that I was the cause of that external or internal event. My pulse, for example, is caused and regulated by certain conditions existing within me, and not by myself. I do not, accordingly, regard this activity of my body as my action, and would be no more tempted to do so if I became suddenly conscious within myself of those conditions or impulses that produce it. This is behavior with which I have nothing to do, behavior that is not within my immediate control, behavior that is not only not free activity, but not even the activity of an agent to begin with; it is nothing but a mechanical reflex. Had I never learned that my very life depends on this pulse beat, I would regard it with complete indifference, as something foreign to me, like the oscillations of a clock pendulum that I idly contemplate.

Now this conception of activity, and of an agent who is the cause of it, involves two rather strange metaphysical notions that are never applied elsewhere in nature. The first is that of a *self* or *person*—for example, a man—who is not merely a collection of things or events, but a substance and a self-moving being. For on this view it is a man himself, and not merely some part of him or something within him, that is the cause of his own activity. Now we certainly do not know that a man is anything more than an assemblage of physical things and processes, which act in accordance with those laws that describe the behavior of all other physical things and processes. Even though a man is a living being, of enormous complexity, there is nothing, apart from the requirements of this theory, to suggest that his behavior is so radically different in its origin from that of other physical objects, or that an understanding of it must be sought in some metaphysical realm wholly different from that appropriate to the understanding of nonliving things.

Second, this conception of activity involves an extraordinary conception of causation, according to which an agent, which is a substance and not an event, can nevertheless be the cause of an event. Indeed, if he is a free agent then he can, on this conception, cause an event to occur—namely, some act of his own—without anything else causing him to do so. This means that an agent is sometimes a cause, without being an antecedent sufficient condition; for if I affirm that I am the cause of some act of mine, then I am plainly not saying that my very existence is sufficient for its occurrence, which would be absurd. If I say that my hand causes my pencil to move, then I am saying that the motion of my hand is, under the other conditions then prevailing, sufficient for the motion of the pencil. But if I then say that I cause my hand to move, I am not saying anything remotely like this, and surely not that the motion of my self is sufficient for the motion of my arm and hand, since these are the only things about me that are moving.

This conception of the causation of events by beings or substances that are not events is, in fact, so different from the usual philosophical conception of a cause that it should not even bear the same name, for "being a cause" ordinarily just means "being an antecedent sufficient condition or set of conditions." Instead, then, of speaking of agents as *causing* their own acts, it would perhaps be better to use another word entirely, and say, for instance, that they *originate* them, *initiate* them, or simply that they *perform* them.

Now this is on the face of it a dubious conception of what a man is. Yet it is consistent with our data, reflecting the presuppositions of deliberation, and appears to be the only conception that is consistent with them, as determinism and simple indeterminism are not. The theory of agency avoids the absurdities of simple indeterminism by conceding that human behavior is caused, while at the same time avoiding the difficulties of determinism by denying that every chain of causes and effects is infinite. Some such causal chains, on this view, have beginnings, and they begin with agents themselves. Moreover, if we are to suppose that it is sometimes up to me what I do, and understand this in a sense which

is not consistent with determinism, we must suppose that I am an agent or a being who initiates his own actions, sometimes under conditions which do not determine what action he shall perform. Deliberation becomes, on this view, something that is not only possible but quite rational, for it does make sense to deliberate about activity that is truly my own and that depends in its outcome upon me as its author, and not merely upon something more or less esoteric that is supposed to be intimately associated with me, such as my thoughts, volitions, choices, or whatnot.

One can hardly affirm such a theory of agency with complete comfort, however, and wholly without embarrassment, for the conception of men and their powers which is involved in it is strange indeed, if not positively mysterious. In fact, one can hardly be blamed here for simply denying our data outright, rather than embracing this theory to which they do most certainly point. Our data—to the effect that men do sometimes deliberate before acting, and that when they do, they presuppose among other things that it is up to them what they are going to do—rest upon nothing more than fairly common consent. These data might simply be illusions. It might in fact be that no man ever deliberates, but only imagines that he does, that from pure conceit he supposes himself to be the master of his behavior and the author of his acts. Spinoza has suggested that if a stone, having been thrown into the air, were suddenly to become conscious, it would suppose itself to be the source of its own motion, being then conscious of what it was doing but not aware of the real cause of its behavior. Certainly men are *sometimes* mistaken in believing that they are behaving as a result of choice deliberately arrived at. A man might, for example, easily imagine that his embarking upon matrimony is the result of the most careful and rational deliberation, when in fact the causes, perfectly sufficient for that behavior, might be of an entirely physiological, unconscious origin. If it is sometimes false that we deliberate and then act as the result of a decision deliberately arrived at, even when we suppose it to be true, it might always be false. No one seems able, as we have noted, to describe deliberation without metaphors, and the conception of a thing's being "within one's power" or "up to him" seems to defy analysis or definition altogether, if taken in a sense which the theory of agency appears to require.

These are, then, dubitable conceptions, despite their being so well implanted in the common sense of mankind. Indeed, when we turn to the theory of fatalism, we shall find formidable metaphysical consider-ations which appear to rule them out alto-gether. Perhaps here, as elsewhere in meta-physics, we should be content with discov-ering difficulties, with seeing what is and what is not consistent with such convic-tions as we happen to have, and then draw-ing such satisfaction as we can from the realization that, no matter where we begin, the world is mysterious and the men who try to understand it are even more so. This realization can, with some justification, make one feel wise, even in the full realiza-tion of his ignorance.

Acting Freely*

Gerald Dworkin

And those who act under compulsion and unwillingly act with pain.

> Aristotle
> *Nichomachean Ethics*

Whenever coercion takes place one will is subordinated to another. The coerced is no longer a completely independent agent. If my will is overborne by yours I serve your ends and not mine. I am motivated by your interests and not mine. I do what you want, not what I want.

The domain of human motivation is always haunted by a tautology hovering overhead. The strongest motive always prevails; the dominant desire determines action; we always do what we want to do. Since coercion designates a process in which a particular class of reasons for acting is singled out it might be predicted that, sooner or later, these truisms would make their appearance. And following close behind, as usual, we find paradox.

I

The following is surely a plausible explication of what it is for a man to be free.

> I am free when my conduct is under my control, and I act under constraint when my conduct is controlled by someone else. My conduct is under my own control when it is determined by my own desires, motives, and intentions, and not under my control when it is determined by the desires, motives, and intentions of someone else. [11], p. 599.

Against this view Oppenheim [8], p. 36, argues that

> Whenever I act my conduct is 'determined by my own desires, motives, and intentions.' This follows from the very definitions of 'action'.

Plamenatz [10], p. 110, takes a similar position.

> It is, of course, quite clear that all action is necessarily voluntary, since it is never pos-

sible for a man to do what he does not wish. Indeed, to do what one wishes is the same thing as to act, for an action which has no motive is inconceivable.

This remark occurs in the context of a discussion of freedom and Plamenatz illustrates his comment with a typical example of coercion.

If, for instance, A threatens to shoot B unless he raises his hand above his head, then B's motive for doing what is required, although it consists in the fear of what will happen to him if he does not (or rather in the effect of this fear, which is the desire to do what may ensure its not happening to him) is as much his motive as any other motive would be.

But if it is true that we always do what we wish, that we always act in accordance with our own desires, then how is the distinction between acting freely and acting under constraint to be drawn? What happens to Mill's definition of liberty as "doing what one desires"? What sense is to be attached to the idea of making or forcing someone to do what he doesn't want to do? How is coercion possible?

Another way of putting the problem is in terms of the kinds of explanation we give of human action. If asked to explain why Jones acts in a certain way we may make reference to certain goals he is pursuing, certain intentions or desires, and/or particular beliefs he has about his condition and environment. If we have specified correctly his beliefs and his goals and have ascertained further that the proper connection exists between them, we have given an explanation of his behavior (assuming it is an action which is to be explained, for we may give the same kind of explanation to explain why someone desires something). If a reference to beliefs and desires is possible in every case of explanation of motivated behavior, there will necessarily be a reference to something the agent wants or desires. Hence, so this argument goes, it is always true that an agent does something that he wants to do. This form of the argu-

ment is presented by Daveney [2], p. 139, in an article on "Wanting."

It may be stated of every intentional action that I perform that in some sense I *want* to do it; because if I didn't want to do it I wouldn't do it. If anyone wishes to deny this, let him explain how it is possible for every action to be explained in terms of some "want" statement.

What for Oppenheim and Plamenatz is a necessary connection between the concepts of action and desire is for Daveney a consequence of the kinds of explanation that are available for understanding human action. In both cases the conclusion is that we always do as we wish or want.

II

Obviously those who hold this view can find ways of drawing a distinction between actions done under compulsion and those done freely, just as, in another philosophical tradition, the egoist can argue that he can distinguish altruism from selfishness. The enlightened egoist having read his Butler and Bradley agrees that a man's laying down his life for his country is, in many respects, quite different from a man's betraying his country for monetary gains. All the egoist insists upon is that both men act to satisfy some desire of theirs. Similarly one can argue that to act under compulsion is to act as one wants but there are important differences which depend on the source of our wants. There are desires which a man has naturally and spontaneously and those which are imposed upon him by force. There are wants which come from inside and those which come from outside. This view assimilates desires to possessions, some of which a man comes with, some of which he borrows or acquires, and some of which are thrust upon him—still they are all "his." Even with property, however, not every mode of acquisition entitles us to say that something belongs to a man, is his. With the "inner" world, whether it be the realm of the will or the understanding, "mine" and "thine" are immensely complicated notions. I propose in this essay to follow out some of the alternative ways of conceptualizing this relation and to examine the consequences of adopting various alternatives.

III

It is essential to clarify the relationship between the identification of a desire as belonging to a man, as being his desire, and the mode of acquisition of the desire. With property we can consider both possession and ownership, what a man has and what belongs to him. The concepts are independent for something may belong to a man although he does not possess it, e.g., it is stolen from him, and he may possess something that doesn't belong to him. Sometimes determining what belongs to someone will be, in part, tracing how the object came into his possession. Did he buy it? Was it given to him? Did he take it without permission? Did he make a mistake and take the wrong object? The criteria for either posession or ownership are very complicated and may only be defined by considering appropriate conventions and the purposes they serve.

Can a similar distinction be drawn with respect to our desires? We might begin by considering another "inner state", that of "belief." We identify a belief p as belonging to X i.e., that X believes p, if his behavior is such that it can be explained on the assumption that he does so believe. Others, or indeed X himself, may know that he acquired the belief in some unusual manner, say, through conditioning or manipulation or the injection of a drug, and this may make a difference in their appraisal of his actions but this does not affect the fact that X believes p, i.e., that the belief belongs to X. The assertion "He (X) doesn't believe p; he was brainwashed" is a *non sequitur.* The latter part has no logical bearing on the former. Nor will it help to bring in a "really" to save the situation. "He doesn't really believe it" applies to someone who pretends to believe p, or, per-

haps to someone who deceives (pretends to) himself about p. There is no question in any of these situations of acting in accordance with the beliefs of another, of one's action being determined not by one's own beliefs but by those of someone else. The normal, rational paths to belief may have been circumvented but then there are no necessary (essential) paths that one must tread before the belief can be ascribed to one.

In view of this it seems plausible to say much the same kind of thing in the case of desire. Don't we identify a desire as belonging to someone in terms of the role played by the desire in explaining the actions of the individual? Shouldn't there be this parallel since beliefs and wants enter explanation in a symmetric fashion? Action can only be explained in terms of a belief given knowledge, perhaps assumed, about the wants of the agent. If I explain X's crossing the street by saying that he believes the drugstore is open, it is in a context that assumes X must want something that is in some way connected with the drugstore being open. Aren't there, then, exactly parallel cases to the ones I gave in connection with belief? A man may desire to eat toothpaste because of a post-hypnotic suggestion. Someone may want to commit suicide given the choice between that and public disgrace. The father of a kidnapped child may want to give money to the kidnapper. In each case we identify the desire as belonging to the agent in terms of what is needed to adequately explain his behavior. I am going to argue that cases like the last example are significantly different from the others and that bringing out the difference will show that the basis for ascribing desires to individuals is more complicated than that for ascribing beliefs.

IV

When we speak of what a man wants to do we may be referring to his intentions or to his desires, to what he is prepared to do or to what he is pleased to do. When we focus on the former we are interested in what he is aiming at, what the point of his doings is.

When we examine the latter we are concerned with what satisfies, with that which brings action to a (temporary) stop. In many instances the two notions go together as we prepare to do what we wish to do and so it is easy to pass from "he did it" to "he intended to do it" to "he wanted to do it." In general we can form two lists, the first containing notions such as intention, decision, choice, will, the second containing desire, want, wish. The terms of these two lists are related in non-contingent ways—no special explanation is required to account for the fact that we intend to do what we want to do. When I have decided what I want to do then I have decided what I intend to do if the circumstances are favorable and there is no countervailing consideration. But our wishes and our intentions may spring apart due to such varied factors as obligations, natural necessities, conventional pressures, coercion, etc. Though these all differ from one another they all represent constraints on our inclinations, obstacles to the normal satisfaction of our desires.

Consider the victim of a highwayman. Why do we say that he doesn't do what he wants? Is it that he is doing something that he doesn't want to do? That depends on how what he is doing is described. If it is described as handing over money to another then he may or may not mind doing that sort of thing; it depends on the circumstances. A man might want to hand over some money to another because he is asked by a relative, or because he is feeling charitable, or because he has desires to rid himself of worldly things. What he doesn't want to do when faced with the highwayman is to hand money over in these circumstances, for these reasons. Suppose it is claimed that handing the money over in these circumstances is a way of preserving his life and that this *is* something that he wants to do. This is presumably the kind of thing Daveney has in mind when he says it is 'possible for every action to be explained in terms of some 'want' statement." I don't know whether the general form of this thesis is correct or not. It could be stated this way. Given any action of an agent he either

wants to perform the action for its own sake *or* there is something the agent wants which is such that he believes that performing this action is a condition (necessary or sufficient) for obtaining what he wants. I am inclined to think that this isn't so, that one may perform an action for reasons that have nothing to do with one's wants and that the only way to establish the thesis would be to invent "pseudo-wants." But even accepting the general thesis doesn't commit one to accepting the view that we always do what we want to do unless we accept the inference from 'X wants A' and 'B is a necessary condition for obtaining A' to 'X wants B'; a form of inference which is clearly invalid in view of any number of counter-examples. "He who wills the end, wills the necessary means to it" is only true if by 'willing' is understood 'intending' and not 'wanting.' There are very good grounds for supposing that a man doesn't intend to go on living when we find out that he doesn't intend to go on breathing. On the other hand finding out that a man doesn't want to go to the dentist doesn't supply very good grounds for supposing that he doesn't want to get rid of his toothache.

It might be argued that we can describe what the man is doing as "preserving his life" instead of doing x as a means of preserving his life just as we can describe what a person does as "turning on the light" instead of "flipping the switch in order to turn on the light." Under this description isn't the man doing what he wants to do? More generally won't it always be possible to redescribe the action in terms of some more general desire whose object is promoted by the action as described more narrowly? Thus the man who hands money over to a kidnapper is "saving the life of his child"! the man who accedes to the demands of a blackmailer is "preserving his reputation", etc.[1] And since it is admitted that *these* are genuine desires of the agent it follows that the agent is doing what he wants.

Normally the difficulty with this type of argument is that statements of desire are cases of indirect discourse so that it is not safe to take inferences for granted. From

"Kennedy wanted to become the 37th President of the United States" we cannot infer that "Kennedy wanted to be the only President assassinated in Dallas" although, in fact, the two descriptions refer to the same man. The usual explanation for this is that a man may want something under a certain description and not be aware that another description is also true of the object of his desire. This explanation cannot account for the kinds of situations we are considering for there is no ignorance present in these cases. If it is proper to redescribe the act of handing money over to the kidnapper as "saving the child's life" one cannot avoid the conclusion that the man is doing what he wants by claiming that he is not aware of both descriptions. His reason for handing over the money *is* to save the child's life. This is not something he might discover later as a man might discover that the 37th President will be assassinated.

This argument relies on two premises neither of which can be taken for granted. The first assumes the legitimacy of redescribing the specific action that takes place (handing over the money, keeping silent) as "saving his child" or "preserving his life." The second premise asserts that a certain form of inference is valid; that from "X wants A" and "X knows that A is B (doing A is doing B)" we can infer that "X wants B." Let us consider each of these assumptions.

The first assumption concerns the conditions under which we may replace one description of an action by some other description. It is a claim that one and the same action may be referred to by different descriptions. Unfortunately we know very little about the modes of individuating actions and the criteria for the identity of actions. All that we have are some pre-systematic data about when we are inclined to say that doing one thing is the same as doing another and when we feel reluctant to make such claims. Anscombe [1], p. 40, gives an example of a man pumping water (which is poisoned) into a cistern which supplies water to a house in which a number of party chiefs are living. She points out that we may ask the man why he is x'ing (moving his arm) and get an an-

swer that is either of the form "to y" (to operate the pump) or "I'm y'ing" (I'm pumping the water"). This can go on for a while but at some point there is a break such that while one can ask "Why are you x'ing?" the answer can only be of the form "to y" not of the form "I'm y'ing." To the question "Why are you poisoning the inhabitants?" the answer "to save the Jews" does not allow the further description of what the man is doing as "saving the Jews." Unfortunately Anscombe gives us no tests for determining when such a break occurs. There are obvious hypotheses which suggest themselves. For example that it is a necessary condition for redescribing x as y (where one does x in order to bring about y) that x and y be sufficiently close together in time and that there be reasonable grounds for supposing that x will be followed by y. Thus A's stabbing B in order that B shall die may be redescribed as A's killing B (provided that 1) B dies, and 2) does so within a reasonably short period of time). But A's making a speech in order to be elected President will not be redescribed as A's being elected President. However, both these conditions are met by the example of the man who hands over his money to a kidnapper. He has grounds for supposing this will save his child and this will presumably happen within a short span of time.

The general thesis that we can always replace "doing x in order to do y" by "doing x, in these circumstances, is doing y" is false. If I am practicing parking in order to pass my driver's test then it just is not the case that practicing parking, in those circumstances, *is* passing my driver's test. The specific thesis that when a man hands money to a kidnapper we can identify "what he does" as saving his life seems to me to be wrong and to arise from a confusion between an *action* which is discrete, particular, done or performed, and an *end* which is general, occupies no definite stretch in time, is accomplished or succeeded in. One can succeed in an end (acquiring money) without doing anything at all. On the other hand one can succeed in an end (preserving one's life) by performing very different kinds of actions (eating a steak dinner, running from the battlefield). To fully substantiate this point one would have to have a fully developed theory about how we individuate and typify actions. All I have hoped to accomplish here is throw doubt on the first premise of the argument.

The second premise states that the following inference is always valid: "X wants (to do) A", "X knows that (doing) A is (doing) B", hence "X wants (to do) B." One can think of a number of counter-examples. X wants to marry A, knows that A is the woman with the worst temper in the world, but it is not the case that X wants to marry the woman with the worst temper in the world. X wants to push the switch (to see if his hand still functions after an accident), knows that pushing the switch turns on the lights, yet X doesn't want to turn on the lights. X wants to sleep with A, knows that sleeping with A is committing adultery, but it is not the case that X wants to commit adultery. As in the case with many such arguments about intensional contexts one may deny the plausibility of the counter-example and insist in each case upon the validity of the inference. It is possible to say that "in a sense" X wants B in all these cases, but the sense is specified by repeating the conditions of the example. One can also insist, to refer to more familiar problems, that if Smith believes that Jones is next door, and Jones is the murderer of Robinson, then "in a sense" Smith believes that the murderer of Robinson is next door, where again the sense is specified by the belief condition and the identity condition. Such victories are hollow because if anything significant depended upon them we would ultimately rely on our prior recognition of the meaning of the key terms; a meaning which is usually less problematic than the inferences.

Although I think that the thesis that we always do what we want to is false it does bring to our attention a significant point about motivating conduct by creating reasons for action. When we speak of providing a motive for someone to act this may be taken in two ways. It may mean that we have created or stimulated a new type of motivation (curiosity, exercise of skill) or that we have harnessed a pre-existing motivation of the agent by creating a situation in which he now has a reason for acting which he lacked previously, i.e., he can satisfy an antecedently existing basic drive. Coercion always involves this latter process, utilizing basic drives which almost everyone shares—self-preservation, avoidance of pain, embarrassment, concern for the welfare of those close to us. It is a mistake, however, to jump from the fact that there must be some pre-existing desire of the agent to be exploited to claiming that when the agent acts to satisfy those desires he does what he wants.

Two patterns of action should be kept distinct although they may both be schematized as follows: X wants to do A, some factor intervenes, X does B. Sometimes when the intervening factor is of the proper kind, e.g., incentives, new information, re-examination of the consequences of doing A, X no longer wants to do A and doing B is a result of this transformation, of his changing his mind. Sometimes, however, we do not think of X's desires as changing but of being frustrated or thwarted. To return to the earlier discussion of the mode of acquisition of desires I am suggesting that it is a mistake to think of someone as acquiring a new "want" or "desire to do something" as a result of coercion. What a person may acquire as a result of such intervention is a new intention, a new disposition to act. But wants are not to be equated with mere dispositions to act. We must be able to distinguish between those actions which we perform because we want to and those we perform because we have to.

V

Granted that sometimes we do things for other reasons than our wanting to do them there still remains the problem of why acting on some of these reasons, but not others, is not acting freely. What I want to do now is account for the fact that only certain reasons are considered coercive and restrictive of liberty; why, *contra* Hobbes, we regard fear and not covetousness as cancelling liberty.[2] It is obvious that the mere presence of external intervention, that is the creating of reasons for action by others is not enough to explain why acting on some of these reasons, but not others, is acting unfreely.[3] If I had not been told of a book sale or been given a ticket to the opera I would have done something else this evening. Given the new situation I no longer do what I wanted to do formerly but that is because I now want to do something else. But the notions of "doing what I want" and "acting freely" cannot be identified. It does not follow that if I do what I do not want to do I act unfreely. Consider the following situation in which another person creates a reason for my doing something which I would not choose to do had the reason not been created. A dull and boring acquaintance invites me to his home for dinner knowing that I accept some principle of reciprocity or gratitude. I now have a reason for extending him an invitation to my house—something I do not want to do. Yet my invitation is issued freely, albeit reluctantly. My liberty has not been infringed upon. What differentiates this kind of situation from that of the kidnapper or blackmailer? I suggest it is the attitude a man takes toward the reasons for which he acts, whether or not he identifies himself with these reasons, assimilates them to himself, which is crucial for determining whether or not he acts freely. Men resent acting for certain reasons; they would not choose to be motivated in certain ways. They mind acting simply in order to preserve a present level of welfare against diminution by another. They resent acting simply in order to avoid unpleasant consequences with no attendant promotion of their own interests and welfare. On the other hand although I may not want to perform the particular act of issuing a dinner invitation to a boring acquaintance I do not mind acting for reasons which fall under the heading of reciprocity. Such examples are interesting because there are many parallels in the vocabulary used to talk about obligations and that used to talk about compulsion. We speak of "having to do it, having no choice." There is present in both a contrast between what one does reluctantly and what one does willingly. In his *Lectures on Ethics* Kant [6], p. 27, has a category called "moral compulsion" which is defined as "a determination to the unwilling performance of an action" and I am morally compelled to act by another if he "forces me by moral motives to do an action which I do reluctantly." The Japanese have a species of moral obligation called Giri and they talk of being "forced with giri" or of someone "concerning me with giri" meaning that someone has argued the speaker into an act he did not want to perform by raising some issue of *on* (moral indebtedness). Many of these situations involve calling someone's attention to reasons which already exist for doing something rather than creating reasons for acting and therefore fall under the heading of moral persuasion—but the dividing line is not sharp. The weight of advice is often due as much to the stature of the adviser—*his* saying it is a new reason for acting—as to the cogency of the reasons to which attention is directed. I am chiefly interested in what Fried [3], p. 1261, calls "moral causation"; moving another to action by "bringing about circumstances such that the desired action is one which in the circumstance is required by an acknowledged moral principle." Like coercion this provides reasons for acting which depend for their efficacy on pre-established motivations. One might say that the difference between moral persuasion and moral causation is the difference between blowing on existing coals to make them glow (or burn) and providing new fuel.

Why don't we consider moral causation an infringement on the liberty of the agent? The agent doesn't do what he wants to do and he only acts in this way because a reason has been provided by another agent. I suggest that it is the agent's attitude toward acting for that kind of reason which makes the difference. Since moral causation can only succeed if the person accepts certain principles of morality and accepting such principles is accepting new reasons for acting the agent has already accepted the legitimacy of certain motivations. Whether this acceptance is due to the fact that such principles are ultimately self-imposed limitations (Kant) or whether some reference must be made to prudential gains that accrue from such acceptance (Hobbes) need not be settled at this juncture. All that is essential is that most of us do not resent acting for reasons of morality.

This factor, the attitude of the agent toward the reasons and desires which motivate his conduct, makes it difficult, at times, for us to assess correctly whether or not someone acts freely. The kleptomaniac who regards his impulses to steal as, in some sense, an alien feature of his personality and resents being driven to act as he does, is a case in point. It is highly questionable whether such people literally could not act otherwise, that it is beyond their powers to offer resistance to their anti-social impulses. It is more plausible to suppose that it is just very difficult for them to refrain, that they act in this fashion not in order to satisfy some rationally recognized need but rather to avoid some danger to their psychic economy the details of which may be spelled out by psychologists. They are, therefore, similar in important ways to victims of external coercion. Any theory of internal, psychological freedom has to have notions which correspond to those psychoanalysts refer to as "ego-alien." There must be part of the human personality which takes up an "attitude" toward the reasons, desires, and motives which determine the conduct of the agent.

Let me put my thesis in another way. Aristotle observes that "those who act under compulsion and unwillingly act with pain." I am arguing that this is a necessary fact. We only consider ourselves as being interfered with, as no longer acting on our own free will, when we find acting for certain reasons painful. To put the thesis epigrammatically; we do not find it painful to act because we are compelled; we consider ourselves compelled because we find it painful to act for these reasons.

VI

I shall conclude by discussing some objections that can be raised to my theory and some applications of it. First some objections. Consider a kleptomaniac who knows that what he does is wrong, who cannot stop himself by his own conscious efforts, but does know that constant surveillance with its attendant threats of detection and punishment is effective in preventing him from stealing. It could be said of him that he welcomes the motivation provided by threat of punishment yet isn't it true that he is interfered with, deprived of liberty, as much as any other person would be? It is important to bear in mind the distinction between what a man is free to do and what he does freely. The kleptomaniac is not free to take other people's property in a society which has a legal apparatus which forbids such acts. A man is not free to do something if he is either prevented from doing it or if his doing it would result in severe deprivation to him. All this is true independently of the wants of a particular person. That I have never contemplated kidnapping anyone, nor have any desire to do so, doesn't negate the fact that I am not free to do so. Nevertheless it may be the case that at some point I want to kidnap somebody and yet refrain from doing so and it can now be asked whether I did so of my own free will. The answer to *that* question will depend on my reasons. It will make a difference whether I refrained out of fear of being punished or because I decided it would be wrong to act on my desire or because an easier way of making money occurred to me. To give another example, I may pay my taxes freely (because, say, I accept some principle of fairness which requires all to make an equal sacrifice in return for benefits which all share in), although I am not free not to pay my taxes. Even if I didn't want to pay my taxes I would be forced to.

There are a number of distinct locutions that include the word "free" and which deserve some systematic analysis. The only one who has attempted this, as far as I know, is

Oppenheim [8]. In addition to "acting freely" and "being free to do x" there are the notions of "feeling free," "being free," and something we might call "being free with respect to x." I am free to pay my taxes because nobody prevents me from doing so or threatens me with harm if I do so. Oppenheim says I am not free to pay my taxes because I am not free to refrain from doing so, but this is a mistake. What he should say, and what he does sometimes slip into saying, is that I am not free with respect to paying my taxes, e.g., it is not open to me to refrain. Thus some sample definitions would run: (I use "iff" to mean "if and only if".)

1. A is unfree to do X, iff either A is prevented from doing X or it is made punishable for A to do X.
2. A is free to do X, iff it is not the case that A is unfree to do X.
3. A is free with respect to doing X, iff A is free to do X and A is free to refrain from doing X.[4]

How the notions of "feeling free" and "being free" are related is very obscure. The following observation seems quite wrong as it stands, although it is reasonable if "being free" were replaced by "feeling free":

> . . . an individual may be free even when subject to restrictions (and compulsions) if those restrictions facilitate the achievement of his purposes, and provided that he willingly accepts these restrictions in principle. Pennock [9], p. 59.

If one accepts the statement as it stands then one is led to the paradox of the free slave, the individual who accepts the fetters that bind him. But fetters are fetters even if they are accepted fetters. Nevertheless, as opposed to those like Oppenheim who dismiss the notion of "feeling free" as somehow "subjective" and not a worthy candidate for "scientific treatment" of the question of human freedom, I think that this idea is a very important one, that ultimately we care about being free because there are occasions on which we want to feel free. We think that

it is significant to the slave that he is not free because we believe, given certain plausible assumptions about human nature, that there will come a time when he will desire to do something (which he doesn't at this moment of time) and will then resent the restrictions that have always been present. He will mind not being free to do certain things which hitherto he has not wanted to do.

As for "acting freely", which is what I have been concerned about, I am suggesting that it be defined as follows:

> A does X freely iff A does X for reasons which he doesn't mind acting from.

This definition implies that A may do something freely though he is neither free to do it nor free with respect to doing it.

To return to the kleptomaniac, normally people who refrain from stealing because of fear of punishment are said not to be acting freely but I would argue that given the case as it is described this man does act freely. For since he welcomes the motivation provided by the fear of punishment we can take this as an indication that what he really wants to do is to be stopped from acting as it appears he wants to act. In so far as the threat enables him to do what he really wants to do he cannot regard it as an obstacle to acting freely but merely as an additional and necessary motivation for doing what he wants to do. To understand what a man wants to do is at least partly to understand which intervention he regards as obstacles and which he regards as either aids to present desires or considerations for changing desires.

Still it might be objected that there may be aberrant individuals who don't mind acting for reasons which most of us do mind acting for, and conversely do mind acting for reasons that most of us are indifferent to or welcome. Thus Mr. X doesn't mind being motivated by fear of loss. Are we to say that he acts freely when he hands his money over to the robber? It is difficult to know what to say here for we are faced with a breakdown of normal connections which are not quite strong enough to be necessary bonds but are not so loose that their severance does not create difficulties for our understanding of what is occurring. We are asked to imagine a man who having the normal attitudes toward his goods does not resent giving them up when confronted with a "money or your life" situation. What will this man do when faced with a choice between two paths: one of which he knows to be free of robbers and the other of which he believes to be lined with them? Consider the following dialogue.

A: "He will take the robber-free path."

B: "Why?"

A: "Because he wants to retain his goods."

B: "Not in all circumstances. Otherwise one would make the prediction that if faced with two paths one of which is lined with people selling food and the other not, X would choose the path free of vendors."

A: "That's true. But in the case of buying food he is willing to give up some of his goods. In the case of the robbers he is not."

B: "Why not? By hypothesis, once in a coercive situation he doesn't mind giving up his goods, so what reasons does he have for avoiding getting into such situations?"

It begins to look as if Mr. X cannot have the normal attitude toward his possessions for it is part of *that* attitude that one tries to avoid getting into situations in which one gives up valued things without getting something in return. This is too crude for it sounds as if I am ruling out the possibility of altruistic or charitable acts. What I want to say is that we can only understand Mr. X if we interpret his actions as being altruistic ("Poor man, he needs the money more than I do.") or motivated by some need to atone or stemming from a re-evaluation of the worth of possessions, etc. Given our normal attitudes toward valued objects a man must resent having them taken from him by force.

None of this denies that human beings vary with respect to what they mind being motivated by. There are undoubtedly those

like Thrasymachus who view morality as a subtle scheme enabling the powerful to enforce their rule. Such persons when they act for reasons of "morality" resent having to conform to the demands of others. But I am willing to say of such people that they do not act freely. They do not identify themselves with the reasons for which they act. They do regard such considerations as alien to their personality. I don't regard it as a weakness of my view that acting for certain reasons will be acting unfreely for some persons but not for others. In fact the theory will be confirmed by explaining such differences which are found on the pre-analytic level.

What I have tried to do in this essay is give an account of why we pick out a certain class of reasons for acting and say that acting for such reasons but not others is not acting freely, why we consider some interventions of others as creating obstacles to our desires and others not, why coercion is thought of as a way of getting someone to do what he doesn't want to do rather than a way of getting someone to want to do something else. My explanation was in terms of the resentment or aversion men have to acting for certain reasons. If we could conceive of a creature so devoid of inner resources, so docile and submissive that he never minded acting in a way different from his original intentions, who saw every action of his as arising from a new desire, then we would also have a being whose liberty we could not infringe. Just as one cannot force open a door that swings freely on its hinges one cannot force a man whose will swings willingly in any direction.[5]

NOTES

[1] It is interesting in this connection to read discussions by the Scholastics concerning the binding force of coerced oaths. St. Bonaventure in his *Commentary on the Book of Sentences* argued that a forced oath was not binding in the ecclesiastical forum since "the Church presumes that one who is forced to swear does not swear with the intention of fulfilling the oath, but rather of avoiding the danger." McCoy [7], p. 42. While the argument itself is not very cogent, for it is not the mere absence of intention to carry out one's promises that

excuses one from being obliged to carry them out—or else all insincere promises would be excused—it is a move similar to the one I am discussing.

²"For there appeareth no reason why that which we do upon fear, should be less firm than that which we do for covetousness. For both the one and the other make the action voluntary." Hobbes [5], p. 286.

³Cf. "What we say of a man when we say that he has not acted of his own free will is that the action of some other person has caused him to be confronted with an object of desire or aversion but for which he would not have acted as he did." Hardie [4], p. 22.

⁴As one of the referees for this paper points out there is a purely normative sense of being free with respect to doing an action which is roughly equivalent to being permitted to do or not to do the action in question. Thus if I promise to come to your dinner party I have limited my freedom of action. There is also a sense of punishable which involves making an assessment of responsibility and is thus also normative in character. As I am using the term I am only referring to the use of threats in order to deter. My definitions, therefore, should be understood as normatively neutral.

⁵A shorter version of this paper was read at the Pacific Division meetings of the American Philosophical Association, September, 1968. I am much indebted to Professor Robert Nozick for many helpful suggestions.

REFERENCES

[1] Anscombe, G. E. M. *Intention* (Ithaca: Cornell University Press, 1957).

[2] Daveney, T. V. "Wanting" *Philosophical Quarterly*, Vol. 11, No. 43, April, 1961.

[3] Fried, Charles. "Moral Causation", *Harvard Law Review* (April, 1964).

[4] Hardie, W. F. R. "My Own Free Will", *Philosophy*, January, 1957.

[5] Hobbes, T. "De Corpore Politico", in *Body, Man and Citizen*, ed. R. S. Peters (New York: Crowell-Collier, 1962).

[6] Kant, I. *Lectures on Ethics* (New York: Harper & Row, 1963).

[7] McCoy, A. E. *Force and Fear in Relation to Delictual Imputability and Penal Responsibility* (Washington: Catholic University of America Press, 1944).

[8] Oppenheim, F. *Dimensions of Freedom* (New York: St. Martin's Press, 1961).

[9] Pennock, J. R. *Liberal Democracy* (New York: Rinehart, 1950).

[10] Plamenatz, J. P. *Consent, Freedom and Political Obligation* (London: Oxford University Press, 1938).

[11] University of California Associates, "The Freedom of the Will", reprinted in Feigl and Sellars, *Readings in Philosophical Analysis* (New York: Appleton-Century-Crofts, 1949).

Freedom of the Will and The Concept of A Person*

Harry G. Frankfurt

WHAT philosophers have lately come to accept as analysis of the concept of a person is not actually analysis of *that* concept at all. Strawson, whose usage represents the current standard, identifies the concept of a person as 'the concept of a type of entity such that *both* predicates ascribing states of consciousness *and* predicates ascribing corporeal characteristics . . . are equally applicable to a single individual of that single type.'[1] But there are many entities besides persons that have both mental and physical properties. As it happens—though it seems extraordinary that this should be so—there is no common English word for the type of entity Strawson has in mind, a type that includes not only human beings but animals of various lesser species as well. Still, this hardly justifies the misappropriation of a valuable philosophical term.

Whether the members of some animal species are persons is surely not to be settled merely be determining whether it is correct to apply to them, in addition to predicates ascribing corporeal characteristics,

predicates that ascribe states of consciousness. It does violence to our language to endorse the application of the term 'person' to those numerous creatures which do have both psychological and material properties but which are manifestly not persons in any normal sense of the word. This misuse of language is doubtless innocent of any theoretical error. But although the offence is 'merely verbal', it does significant harm. For it gratuitously diminishes our philosophical vocabulary, and it increases the likelihood that we will overlook the important area of inquiry with which the term 'person' is most naturally associated. It might have been expected that no problem would be of more central and persistent concern to philosophers than that of understanding what we ourselves essentially are. Yet this problem is so generally neglected that it has been possible to make off with its very name almost without being noticed and, evidently, without evoking any widespread feeling of loss.

There is a sense in which the word 'person' is merely the singular form of 'people' and in which both terms connote no more than membership in a certain biological species. In those senses of the word which are of greater philosophical interest, however,

*Copyright © 1971 *The Journal of Philosophy.* Reprinted by permission, from *The Journal of Philosophy* 68 (January 1971), 5–20.

the criteria for being a person do not serve primarily to distinguish the members of our own species from the members of other species. Rather, they are designed to capture those attributes which are the subject of our most humane concern with ourselves and the source of what we regard as most important and most problematical in our lives. Now these attributes would be of equal significance to us even if they were not in fact peculiar and common to the members of our own species. What interests us most in the human condition would not interest us less if it were also a feature of the condition of other creatures as well.

Our concept of ourselves as persons is not to be understood, therefore, as a concept of attributes that are necessarily species-specific. It is conceptually possible that members of novel or even of familiar non-human species should be persons; and it is also conceptually possible that some members of the human species are not persons. We do in fact assume, on the other hand, that no member of another species is a person. Accordingly, there is a presumption that what is essential to persons is a set of characteristics that we generally suppose—whether rightly or wrongly—to be uniquely human.

It is my view that one essential difference between persons and other creatures is to be found in the structure of a person's will. Human beings are not alone in having desires and motives, or in making choices. They share these things with the members of certain other species, some of whom even appear to engage in deliberation and to make decisions based upon prior thought. It seems to be peculiarly characteristic of humans, however, that they are able to form what I shall call 'second-order desires' or 'desires of the second order.'

Besides wanting and choosing and being moved *to do* this or that, men may also want to have (or not to have) certain desires and motives. They are capable of wanting to be different, in their preferences and purposes, from what they are. Many animals appear to have the capacity for what I shall call 'first-order desires' or 'desires of

the first order', which are simply desires to do or not to do one thing or another. No animal other than man, however, appears to have the capacity for reflective self-evaluation that is manifested in the formation of second-order desires.[2]

I

The concept designated by the verb 'to want' is extraordinarily elusive. A statement of the form 'A wants to X'—taken by itself, apart from a context that serves to amplify or to specify its meaning—conveys remarkably little information. Such a statement may be consistent, for example, with each of the following statements: (a) the prospect of doing X elicits no sensation or introspectible emotional response in A; (b) A is unaware that he wants to X; (c) A believes that he does not want to X; (d) A wants to refrain from X-ing; (e) A wants to Y and believes that it is impossible for him both to Y and to X; (f) A does not 'really' want to X; (g) A *would rather die than X*; and so on. It is therefore hardly sufficient to formulate the distinction between first-order and second-order desires, as I have done, by suggesting merely that someone has a first-order desire when he wants to do or not to do such-and-such, and that he has a second-order desire when he wants to have or not to have a certain desire of the first order.

As I shall understand them, statements of the form 'A wants to X' cover a rather broad range of possibilities.[3] They may be true even when statements like (a) through (g) are true: when A is unaware of any feelings concerning X-ing, when he is unaware that he wants to X, when he deceives himself about what he wants and believes falsely that he does not want to X, when he also has other desires that conflict with his desire to X, or when he is ambivalent. The desires in question may be conscious or unconscious, they need not be univocal, and A may be mistaken about them. There is a further source of uncertainty with regard to statements that identify someone's desires, however, and here it is important for my purposes to be less permissive.

Consider first those statements of the form '*A* wants to *X*' which identify first-order desires—that is, statements in which the term 'to *X*' refers to an action. A statement of this kind does not, by itself, indicate the relative strength of *A*'s desire to *X*. It does not make it clear whether this desire is at all likely to play a decisive role in what *A* actually does or tries to do. For it may correctly be said that *A* wants to *X* even when his desire to *X* is only one among his desires and when it is far from being paramount among them. Thus, it may be true that *A* wants to *X* when he strongly prefers to do something else instead; and it may be true that he wants to *X* despite the fact that, when he acts, it is not the desire to *X* that motivates him to do what he does. On the other hand, someone who states that *A* wants to *X* may mean to convey that it is this desire that is motivating or moving *A* to do what he is actually doing or that *A* will in fact be moved by his desire (unless he changes his mind) when he acts.

It is only when it is used in the second of these ways that, given the special usage of 'will' that I propose to adopt, the statement identifies *A*'s will. To identify an agent's will is either to identify the desire (or desires) by which he is motivated in some action he performs or to identify the desire (or desires) by which he will or would be motivated when or if he acts. An agent's will, then, is identical with one or more of his first-order desires. But the notion of the will, as I am employing it, is not coextensive with the notion of first-order desires. It is not the notion of something that merely inclines an agent in some degree to act in a certain way. Rather, it is the notion of an *effective* desire—one that moves (or will or would move) a person all the way to action. Thus the notion of the will is not coextensive with the notion of what an agent intends to do. For even though someone may have a settled intention to do *X*, he may none the less do something else instead of doing *X* because, despite his intention, his desire to do *X* proves to be weaker or less effective than some conflicting desire.

Now consider those statements of the form '*A* wants to *x*' which identify second-order desires—that is, statements in which the term 'to *X*' refers to a desire of the first order. There are also two kinds of situation in which it may be true that *A* wants to want to *X*. In the first place, it might be true of *A* that he wants to have a desire to *X* despite the fact that he has a univocal desire, altogether free of conflict and ambivalence, to refrain from *x*-ing. Someone might want to have a certain desire, in other words, but univocally want that desire to be unsatisfied.

Suppose that a physician engaged in psychotherapy with narcotics addicts believes that his ability to help his patients would be enhanced if he understood better what it is like for them to desire the drug to which they are addicted. Suppose that he is led in this way to want to have a desire for the drug. If it is a genuine desire that he wants, then what he wants is not merely to feel the sensations that addicts characteristically feel when they are gripped by their desires for the drug. What the physician wants, in so far as he wants to have a desire, is to be inclined or moved to some extent to take the drug.

It is entirely possible, however, that, although he wants to be moved by a desire to take the drug, he does not want this desire to be effective. He may not want it to move him all the way to action. He need not be interested in finding out what it is like to take the drug. And in so far as he now wants only to *want* to take it, and not to *take* it, there is nothing in what he now wants that would be satisfied by the drug itself. He may now have, in fact, an altogether univocal desire *not* to take the drug; and he may prudently arrange to make it impossible for him to satisfy the desire he would have if his desire to want the drug should in time be satisfied.

It would thus be incorrect to infer, from the fact that the physician now wants to desire to take the drug, that he already does desire to take it. His second-order desire to be moved to take the drug does not entail that he has a first-order desire to take it. If the drug were now to be administered to him, this might satisfy no desire that is implicit in his desire to want to take it. While he wants to want to take the drug, he may have *no* desire to take it; it may be that *all* he wants is to taste the desire for it. That is, his desire to have a certain desire that he does not have may not be a desire that his will should be at all different than it is.

Someone who wants only in this truncated way to want to X stands at the margin of preciosity, and the fact that he wants to want to X is not pertinent to the identification of his will. There is, however, a second kind of situation that may be described by 'A wants to X'; and when the statement is used to describe a situation of this second kind, then it does pertain to what A wants his will to be. In such cases the statement means that A wants the desire to X to be the desire that moves him effectively to act. It is not merely that he wants the desire to X to be among the desires by which, to one degree or another, he is moved or inclined to act. He wants this desire to be effective—that is, to provide the motive in what he actually does. Now when the statement that A wants to want to X is used in this way, it does entail that A already has a desire to X. It could not be true both that A wants the desire to X to move him into action and that he does not want to X. It is only if he does want to X that he can coherently want the desire to X not merely to be one of his desires but, more decisively, to be his will.[4]

Suppose a man wants to be motivated in what he does by the desire to concentrate on his work. It is necessarily true, if this supposition is correct, that he already wants to concentrate on his work. This desire is now among his desires. But the question of whether or not his second-order desire is fulfilled does not turn merely on whether the desire he wants is one of his desires. It turns on whether this desire is, as he wants it to be, his effective desire or will. If, when the chips are down, it is his desire to concentrate on his work that moves him to do what he does, then what he wants at that time is indeed (in the relevant sense) what he wants to want. If it is some other desire that actually moves him when he acts, on the other hand, then what he wants at that time is not (in the relevant sense) what he wants to want. This will be so despite the fact that the desire to concentrate on his work continues to be among his desires.

II

Someone has a desire of the second order either when he wants simply to have a certain desire or when he wants a certain desire to be his will. In situations of the latter kind, I shall call his second-order desires 'second-order volitions' or 'volitions of the second order'. Now it is having second-order volitions, and not having second order desires generally, that I regard as essential to being a person. It is logically possible, however unlikely, that there should be an agent with second-order desires but with no volitions of the second order. Such a creature, in my view, would not be a person. I shall use the term 'wanton' to refer to agents who have first-order desires but who are not persons because, whether or not they have desires of the second order, they have no second-order volitions.[5]

The essential characteristic of a wanton is that he does not care about his will. His desires move him to do certain things, without its being true of him either that he wants to be moved by those desires or that he prefers to be moved by other desires. The class of wantons includes all non-human animals that have desires and all very young children. Perhaps it also includes some adult human beings as well. In any case, adult humans may be more or less wanton; they may act wantonly, in response to first-order desires concerning which they have no volitions of the second order, more or less frequently.

The fact that a wanton has no second-order volitions does not mean that each of his first-order desires is translated heedlessly and at once into action. He may have no opportunity to act in accordance with some of his desires. Moreover, the translation of his desires into action may be delayed or precluded either by conflicting desires of the first order or by the intervention of deliberation. For a wanton may possess and employ rational faculties of a high order. Nothing in the concept of a wanton implies that he cannot reason or that he cannot deliberate concerning how to do what he wants to do. What distinguishes the rational wanton from other rational agents is that he is not concerned with the desirability of his desires themselves. He ignores the question of what his will is to be. Not only does he pursue whatever course of action he is most strongly inclined to pursue, but he does not care which of his inclinations is the strongest.

Thus a rational creature, who reflects upon the suitability to his desires of one course of action or another, may none the less be a wanton. In maintaining that the essence of being a person lies not in reason but in will, I am far from suggesting that a creature without reason may be a person. For it is only in virtue of his rational capacities that a person is capable of becoming critically aware of his own will and of forming volitions of the second order. The structure of a person's will presupposes, accordingly, that he is a rational being.

The distinction between a person and a wanton may be illustrated by the difference between two narcotics addicts. Let us suppose that the physiological condition accounting for the addiction is the same in both men, and that both succumb inevitably to their periodic desires for the drug to which they are addicted. One of the addicts hates his addiction and always struggles desperately, although to no avail, against its thrust. He tries everything that he thinks might enable him to overcome his desires for the drug. But these desires are too powerful for him to withstand, and invariably, in the end, they conquer him. He is an unwilling addict, helplessly violated by his own desires.

The unwilling addict has conflicting first-order desires: he wants to take the drug, and he also wants to refrain from taking it. In addition to these first-order desires, however, he has a volition of the second order. He is not a neutral with regard to the conflict between his desire to take the drug and

his desire to refrain from taking it. It is the latter desire, and not the former, that he wants to constitute his will; it is the latter desire, rather than the former, that he wants to be effective and to provide the purpose that he will seek to realize in what he actually does.

The other addict is a wanton. His actions reflect the economy of his first-order desires, without his being concerned whether the desires that move him to act are desires by which he wants to be moved to act. If he encounters problems in obtaining the drug or in administering it to himself, his responses to his urges to take it may involve deliberation. But it never occurs to him to consider whether he wants the relation among his desires to result in his having the will he has. The wanton addict may be an animal, and thus incapable of being concerned about his will. In any event he is, in respect of his wanton lack of concern, no different from an animal.

The second of these addicts may suffer a first-order conflict similar to the first-order conflict suffered by the first. Whether he is human or not, the wanton may (perhaps due to conditioning) both want to take the drug and want to refrain from taking it. Unlike the unwilling addict, however, he does not prefer that one of his conflicting desires should be paramount over the other; he does not prefer that one first-order desire rather than the other should constitute his will. It would be misleading to say that he is neutral as to the conflict between his desires, since this would suggest that he regards them as equally acceptable. Since he has no identity apart from his first-order desires, it is true neither that he prefers one to the other nor that he prefers not to take sides.

It makes a difference to the unwilling addict, who is a person, which of his conflicting first-order desires wins out. Both desires are his, to be sure; and whether he finally takes the drug or finally succeeds in refraining from taking it, he acts to satisfy what is in a literal sense his own desire. In either case he does something he himself wants to do, and he does it not because of some external influence whose aim happens to coincide with his own but because of his desire to do it. The unwilling addict identifies himself, however, through the formation of a second-order volition, with one rather than with the other of his conflicting first-order desires. He makes one of them more truly his own and, in so doing, he withdraws himself from the other. It is in virtue of this identification and withdrawal, accomplished through the formation of a second-order volition, that the unwilling addict may meaningfully make the analytically puzzling statements that the force moving him to take the drug is a force other than his own, and that it is not of his own free will but rather against his will that this force moves him to take it.

The wanton addict cannot or does not care which of his conflicting first-order desires wins out. His lack of concern is not due to his inability to find a convincing basis for preference. It is due either to his lack of the capacity for reflection or to his mindless indifference to the enterprise of evaluating his own desires and motives[6] There is only one issue in the struggle to which his first-order conflict may lead: whether the one or the other of his conflicting desires is the stronger. Since he is moved by both desires, he will not be altogether satisfied by what he does no matter which of them is effective. But it makes no difference *to him* whether his craving or his aversion gets the upper hand. He has no stake in the conflict between them and so, unlike the unwilling addict, he can neither win nor lose the struggle in which he is engaged. When a *person* acts, the desire by which he is moved is either the will he wants or a will he wants to be without. When a *wanton* acts, it is neither.

III

There is a very close relationship between the capacity for forming second-order volitions and another capacity that is essential to persons—one that has often been considered a distinguishing mark of the human condition. It is only because a person has volitions of the second order that he is capable both of enjoying and of lacking freedom

of the will. The concept of a person is not only, then, the concept of a type of entity that has both first-order desires and volitions of the second order. It can also be construed as the concept of a type of entity for whom the freedom of its will may be a problem. This concept excludes all wantons, both infrahuman and human, since they fail to satisfy an essential condition for the enjoyment of freedom of the will. And it excludes those suprahuman beings, if any, whose wills are necessarily free.

Just what kind of freedom is the freedom of the will? This question calls for an identification of the special area of human experience to which the concept of freedom of the will, as distinct from the concepts of other sorts of freedom, is particularly germane. In dealing with it, my aim will be primarily to locate the problem with which a person is most immediately concerned when he is concerned with the freedom of his will.

According to one familiar philosophical tradition, being free is fundamentally a matter of doing what one wants to do. Now the notion of an agent who does what he wants to do is by no means an altogether clear one: both the doing and the wanting, and the appropriate relation between them as well, require elucidation. But although its focus needs to be sharpened and its formulation refined, I believe that this notion does capture at least part of what is implicit in the idea of an agent who *acts* freely. It misses entirely, however, the peculiar content of the quite different idea of an agent whose *will* is free.

We do not suppose that animals enjoy freedom of the will, although we recognize that an animal may be free to run in whatever direction it wants. Thus, having the freedom to do what one wants to do is not a sufficient condition of having a free will. It is not a necessary condition either. For to deprive someone of his freedom of action is not necessarily to undermine the freedom of his will. When an agent is aware that there are certain things he is not free to do, this doubtless affects his desires and limits the range of choices he can make. But suppose that someone, without being aware of it, has in fact lost or been deprived of his freedom of action. Even though he is no longer free to do what he wants to do, his will may remain as free as it was before. Despite the fact that he is not free to translate his desires into actions or to act according to the determinations of his will, he may still form those desires and make those determinations as freely as if his freedom of action had not been impaired.

When we ask whether a person's will is free we are not asking whether he is in a position to translate his first-order desires into actions. That is the question of whether he is free to do as he pleases. The question of the freedom of his will does not concern the relation between what he does and what he wants to do. Rather, it concerns his desires themselves. But what question about them is it?

It seems to me both natural and useful to construe the question of whether a person's will is free in close analogy to the question of whether an agent enjoys freedom of action. Now freedom of action is (roughly, at least) the freedom to do what one wants to do. Analogously, then, the statement that a person enjoys freedom of the will means (also roughly) that he is free to want what he wants to want. More precisely, it means that he is free to will what he wants to will, or to have the will he wants. Just as the question about the freedom of an agent's action had to do with whether it is the action he wants to perform, so the question about the freedom of his will has to do with whether it is the will he wants to have.

It is in securing the conformity of his will to his second-order volitions, then, that a person exercises freedom of the will. And it is in the discrepancy between his will and his second-order volitions, or in his awareness that their coincidence is not his own doing but only a happy chance, that a person who does not have this freedom feels its lack. The unwilling addict's will is not free. This is shown by the fact that it is not the will he wants. It is also true, though in a different way, that the will of the wanton addict is not free. The wanton addict neither has the will he wants nor has a will that differs from the will he wants. Since he has no volitions of the second order, the free-

dom of his will cannot be a problem for him. He lacks it, so to speak, by default.

People are generally far more complicated than my sketchy account of the structure of a person's will may suggest. There is as much opportunity for ambivalence, conflict, and self-deception with regard to desires of the second order, for example, as there is with regard to first-order desires. If there is an unresolved conflict among someone's second-order desires, then he is in danger of having no second-order volition; for unless this conflict is resolved, he has no preference concerning which of his first-order desires is to be his will. This condition, if it is so severe that it prevents him from identifying himself in a sufficiently decisive way with *any* of his conflicting first-order desires, destroys him as a person. For it either tends to paralyse his will and to keep him from acting at all, or it tends to remove him from his will so that his will operates without his participation. In both cases he becomes, like the unwilling addict though in a different way, a helpless bystander to the forces that move him.

Another complexity is that a person may have, especially if his second-order desires are in conflict, desires and volitions of a higher order than the second. There is no theoretical limit to the length of the series of desires of higher and higher orders; nothing except common sense and, perhaps, a saving fatigue prevents an individual from obsessively refusing to identify himself with any of his desires until he forms a desire of the next higher order. The tendency to generate such a series of acts of forming desires, which would be a case of humanization run wild, also leads toward the destruction of a person.

It is possible, however, to terminate such a series of acts without cutting it off arbitrarily. When a person identifies himself *decisively* with one of his first-order desires, this commitment 'resounds' throughout the potentially endless array of higher orders. Consider a person who, without reservation or conflict, wants to be motivated by the desire to concentrate on his work. The fact that his second-order volition to be moved by his desire is a decisive one means that there is no room for questions concerning the pertinence of desires or volitions of higher orders. Suppose the person is asked whether he wants to want to concentrate on his work. He can properly insist that the question concerning a third-order desire does not arise. It would be a mistake to claim that, because he has not considered whether he wants the second-order volition he has formed, he is indifferent to the question of whether it is with this volition or with some other that he wants his will to accord. The decisiveness of the commitment he has made means that he has decided that no further question about his second-order volition, at any higher order, remains to be asked. It is relatively unimportant whether we explain this by saying that this commitment implicitly generates an endless series of confirming desires of higher orders, or by saying that the commitment is tantamount to a dissolution of the pointedness of all questions concerning higher order of desire.

Examples such as the one concerning the unwilling addict may suggest that volitions of the second order, or of higher orders, must be formed deliberately and that a person characteristically struggles to ensure that they are satisfied. But the conformity of a person's will to his higher-order volitions may be far more thoughtless and spontaneous than this. Some people are naturally moved by kindness when they want to be kind, and by nastiness when they want to be nasty, without any explicit forethought and without any need for energetic self-control. Others are moved by nastiness when they want to be kind and by kindness when they intend to be nasty, equally without forethought and without active resistance to these violations of their higher-order desires. The enjoyment of freedom comes easily to some. Others must struggle to achieve it.

IV

My theory concerning the freedom of the will accounts easily for our disinclination to allow that this freedom is enjoyed by the members of any species inferior to our own. It also satisfies another condition that must be met by any such theory, by making it apparent why the freedom of the will should be regarded as desirable. The enjoyment of a free will means the satisfaction of certain desires—desires of the second or of higher orders—whereas its absence means their frustration. The satisfactions at stake are those which accrue to a person of whom it may be said that his will is his own. The corresponding frustrations are those suffered by a person of whom it may be said that he is estranged from himself, or that he finds himself a helpless or a passive bystander to the forces that move him.

A person who is free to do what he wants to do may yet not be in a position to have the will he wants. Suppose, however, that he enjoys both freedom of action and freedom of the will. Then he is not only free to do what he wants to do; he is also free to want what he wants to want. It seems to me that he has, in that case, all the freedom it is possible to desire or to conceive. There are other good things in life, and he may not possess some of them. But there is nothing in the way of freedom that he lacks.

It is far from clear that certain other theories of the freedom of the will meet these elementary but essential conditions: that it be understandable why we desire this freedom and why we refuse to ascribe it to animals. Consider, for example, Roderick Chisholm's quaint version of the doctrine that human freedom entails an absence of causal determination.[7] Whenever a person performs a free action, according to Chisholm, it's a miracle. The motion of a person's hand, when the person moves it, is the outcome of a series of physical causes; but some event in this series, 'and presumably one of those that took place within the brain, was caused by the agent and not by any other events' (18). A free agent has, therefore, 'a prerogative which some would attribute only to God: each of us, when we act, is a prime mover unmoved' (23).

This account fails to provide any basis for doubting that animals of subhuman species enjoy the freedom it defines. Chisholm says nothing that makes it seem less likely that a rabbit performs a miracle when it moves its leg than that a man does so when he moves his hand. But why, in any case, should anyone *care* whether he can interrupt the natural order of causes in the way Chisholm describes? Chisholm offers no reason for believing that there is a discernible difference between the experience of a man who miraculously initiates a series of causes when he moves his hand and a man who moves his hand without any such breach of the normal causal sequence. There appears to be no concrete basis for preferring to be involved in the one state of affairs rather than in the other.[8]

It is generally supposed that, in addition to satisfying the two conditions I have mentioned, a satisfactory theory of the freedom of the will necessarily provides an analysis of one of the conditions of moral responsibility. The most common recent approach to the problem of understanding the freedom of the will has been, indeed, to inquire what is entailed by the assumption that someone is morally responsible for what he has done. In my view, however, the relation between moral responsibility and the freedom of the will has been very widely misunderstood. It is not true that a person is morally responsible for what he has done only if his will was free when he did it. He may be morally responsible for having done it even though his will was not free at all.

A person's will is free only if he is free to have the will he wants. This means that, with regard to any of his first-order desires, he is free either to make the desire his will or to make some other first-order desire his will instead. Whatever his will, then, the will of the person whose will is free could have been otherwise; he could have done otherwise than to constitute his will as he did. It is a vexed question just how 'he could have done otherwise' is to be understood in contexts such as this one. But although this question is important to the theory of freedom, it has no bearing on the theory of moral responsibility. For the assumption that a person is morally responsible for what he has done does not entail that the person was in a position to have whatever will he wanted.

This assumption *does* entail that the person did what he did freely, or that he did it of his own free will. It is a mistake, however, to believe that someone acts freely only when he is free to do whatever he wants or that he acts of his own free will only if his will is free. Suppose that a person has done what he wanted to do, that he did it because he wanted to do it, and that the will by which he was moved when he did it was his will because it was the will he wanted. Then he did it freely and of his own free will. Even supposing that he could have done otherwise, he would not have done otherwise; and even supposing that he could have had a different will, he would not have wanted his will to differ from what it was. Moreover, since the will that moved him when he acted was his will because he wanted it to be, he cannot claim that his will was forced upon him or that he was a passive bystander to its constitution. Under these conditions, it is quite irrelevant to the evaluation of his moral responsibility to inquire whether the alternatives that he opted against were actually available to him.[9]

In illustration, consider a third kind of addict. Suppose that his addiction has the same physiological basis and the same irresistible thrust as the addictions of the unwilling and wanton addicts, but that he is altogether delighted with his condition. He is a willing addict, who would not have things any other way. If the grip of his addiction should somehow weaken, he would do whatever he could to reinstate it; if his desire for the drug should begin to fade, he would take steps to renew its intensity.

The willing addict's will is not free, for his desire to take the drug will be effective regardless of whether or not he wants this desire to constitute his will. But when he takes the drug, he takes it freely and of his own free will. I am inclined to understand his situation as involving the overdetermination of his first-order desire to take the drug. This desire is his effective desire because he is physiologically addicted. But it is his effective desire also because he wants it to be. His will is outside his control, but, by his second-order desire that his desire for the drug should be effective, he has made this will his own. Given than it is therefore not only because of his addiction that his desire for the drug is effective, he may be morally responsible for taking the drug.

My conception of the freedom of the will appears to be neutral with regard to the problem of determinism. It seems conceivable that it should be causally determined that a person is free to want what he wants to want. If this is conceivable, then it might be causally determined that a person enjoys a free will. There is no more than an innocuous appearance of paradox in the proposition that it is determined, ineluctably and by forces beyond their control, that certain people have free wills and that others do not. There is no incoherence in the proposition that some agency other than a person's own is responsible (even *morally* responsible) for the fact that he enjoys or fails to enjoy freedom of the will. It is possible that a person should be morally responsible for what he does of his own free will and that some other person should also be morally responsible for his having done it.[10]

On the other hand, it seems conceivable that it should come about by chance that a person is free to have the will he wants. If this is conceivable, then it might be a matter of chance that certain people enjoy freedom of the will and that certain others do not. Perhaps it is also conceivable, as a number of philosophers believe, for states of affairs to come about in a way other than by chance or as the outcome of a sequence of natural causes. If it is indeed conceivable for the relevant states of affairs to come about in some third way, then it is also possible that a person should in that third way come to enjoy the freedom of the will.

NOTES

[1] P. F Strawson, *Individuals* (London: Methuen, 1959), 101–2. Ayer's usage of 'person' is similar: 'it is characteristic of persons in this sense that besides having various physical properties . . . they are also credited with various forms of consciousness' (A. J. Ayer, *The Concept of a Person* (New York: St. Martin's, 1963), 82). What concerns Strawson and Ayer is the problem

of understanding the relation between mind and body, rather than the quite different problem of understanding what it is to be a creature that not only has a mind and a body but is also a person.

[2] For the sake of simplicity, I shall deal only with what someone wants or desires, neglecting related phenomena such as choices and decisions. I propose to use the verbs 'to want' and 'to desire' interchangeably, although they are by no means perfect synonyms. My motive in forsaking the established nuances of these words arises from the fact that the verb 'to want', which suits my purposes better so far as its meaning is concerned, does not lend itself so readily to the formation of nouns as does the verb 'to desire'. It is perhaps acceptable, albeit graceless, to speak in the plural of someone's 'wants'. But to speak in the singular of someone's 'want' would be an abomination.

[3] What I say in this paragraph applies not only to cases in which 'to X' refers to a possible action or inaction. It also applies to cases in which 'to X' refers to a first-order desire and in which the statement that 'A wants to X' is therefore a shortened version of a statement—'A wants to want X'—that identifies a desire of the second order.

[4] It is not so clear that the entailment relation described here holds in certain kinds of cases, which I think my fairly be regarded as non-standard, where the essential difference between the standard and the non-standard cases lies in the kind of description by which the first-order desire in question is identified. Thus, suppose that A admires B so fulsomely that, even though he does not know what B wants to do, he wants to be effectively moved by whatever desire effectively moves B, without knowing what B's will is, in other words, A wants his own will to be the same. It certainly does not follow that A already has, among his desires, a desire like the one that constitutes B's will. I shall not pursue here the questions of whether there are genuine counter-examples to the claim made in the text or of how, if there are, that claim should be altered.

[5] Creatures with second-order desires but no second-order volitions differ significantly from brute animals, and, for some purposes, it would be desirable to regard them as persons. My usage, which withholds the designation 'person' from them, is thus somewhat arbitrary. I adopt it largely because it facilitates the formulation of some of the points I wish to make. Hereafter, whenever I consider statements of the form 'A wants to want to X' I shall have in mind statements identifying second-order volitions and not statements identifying second-order desires that are not second-order volitions.

[6] In speaking of the evaluation of his own desires and motives as being characteristic of a person, I do not mean to suggest that a person's second-order volitions

necessarily manifest a *moral* stance on his part toward his first-order desires. It may not be from the point of view of morality that the person evaluates his first-order desires. Moreover, a person may be capricious and irresponsible in forming his second-order volitions and give no serious consideration to what is at stake. Second-order volitions express evaluations only in the sense that they are preferences. There is no essential restrictions on the kind of basis, if any, upon which they are formed.

[7]'Freedom and Action', in *Freedom and Determinism*, ed. Keith Lehrer, (New York: Random House, 1966), 11–44.

[8]I am not suggesting that the alleged difference between these two states of affairs is unverifiable. On the contrary, physiologists might well be able to show that Chisholm's conditions for a free action are not satisfied, by establishing that there is no relevant brain event for which a sufficient physical cause cannot be found.

[9]For another discussion of the considerations that cast doubt on the principle that a person is morally responsible for what he has done only if he could have done otherwise, see my 'Alternate Possibilities and Moral Responsibility'. *Journal of Philosophy*, 1969, 829–39.

[10]There is a difference between being *fully* responsible and being *solely* responsible. Suppose that the willing addict had been made an addict by the deliberate and calculated work of another. Then it may be that both the addict and this other person are fully responsible for the addict's taking the drug, while neither of them is solely responsible for it. That there is a distinction between full moral responsibility and sole moral responsibility is apparent in the following example. A certain light can be turned on or off by flicking either of two switches, and each of these switches is simultaneously flicked to the 'on' position by a different person, neither of whom is aware of the other. Neither person is solely responsible for the light's going on, nor do they share the responsibility in the sense that each is partially responsible; rather, each of them is fully responsible.

Recommended Readings on Persons, Minds, and Free Will

A. **Persons and Minds**

Anderson, A. R., ed. *Minds and Machines.* Englewood Cliffs, N.J.: Prentice-Hall, 1964.

Armstrong, D. M. *A Materialist Theory of the Mind.* London: Routledge and Kegan Paul, 1968.

Block, Ned, ed. *Readings in the Philosophy of Psychology,* 2 vols. Cambridge, Mass.: Harvard University Press, 1980.

Borst, C. V., ed. *The Mind/Brain Identity Theory.* New York: St. Martin's Press, 1970.

Broad, C. D. *The Mind and Its Place in Nature.* London: Routledge and Kegan Paul, 1925.

Campbell, Keith. *Body and Mind.* Garden City, N.Y.: Doubleday, 1970.

Changeux, J.-P. *Neuronal Man: The Biology of Mind.* New York: Oxford University Press, 1985.

Chappell, V. C., ed. *The Philosophy of Mind.* Englewood Cliffs, N.J.: Prentice-Hall, 1962.

Churchland, Paul. *Matter and Consciousness,* 2d ed. Cambridge, Mass.: The MIT Press, 1987.

Cornman, James. *Materialism and Sensations.* New Haven: Yale University Press, 1971.

Dennett, D. C. *Brainstorms: Philosophical Essays on Mind and Psychology.* Cambridge, Mass.: The MIT Press, 1978.

Ducasse, C. J. *Nature, Mind, and Death*. LaSalle, Ill.: Open Court, 1951.

Fodor, Jerry. *Representations*. Cambridge, Mass.: The MIT Press, 1981.

Glover, Jonathan, ed. *The Philosophy of Mind*. New York: Oxford University Press, 1976.

Gunderson, Keith. *Mentality and Machines*. Garden City, N.Y.: Doubleday, 1971.

Haugeland, John, ed. *Mind Design*. Cambridge, Mass.: The MIT Press, 1982.

Hofstadter, D. R., and D. C. Dennett, eds. *The Mind's I*. New York: Basic Books, 1981.

Hook, Sidney, ed. *Dimensions of Mind*. New York: Macmillan, 1960.

LeDoux, Joseph, and William Hirst, eds. *Mind and Brain*. Cambridge: Cambridge University Press, 1986.

Lycan, William. *Consciousness*. Cambridge, Mass.: The MIT Press, 1987.

Miller, Jonathan. *States of Mind*. New York: Pantheon, 1983.

Popper, Karl, and John Eccles. *The Self and Its Brain*. New York: Springer Verlag, 1977.

Putnam, Hilary. *Representation and Reality*. Cambridge, Mass.: The MIT Press, 1988.

Russell, Bertrand. *The Analysis of Mind*. London: Allen and Unwin, 1921.

Ryle, Gilbert. *The Concept of Mind*. London: Hutchinson, 1949.

Searle, John. *Minds, Brains, and Science*. Cambridge, Mass.: Harvard University Press, 1984.

Strawson, P. F. *Individuals*. London: Methuen, 1959.

Wooldridge, D. E. *Mechanical Man: The Physical Basis of Intelligent Life*. New York: McGraw-Hill, 1968.

B. *Persons and Free Will*

Ayers, M. R. *The Refutation of Determinism*. London: Methuen, 1968.

Berofsky, Bernard. *Determinism*. Princeton: Princeton University Press, 1972.

Berofsky, Bernard, ed. *Free Will and Determinism*. New York: Harper and Row, 1966.

Dworkin, Gerald, ed. *Determinism, Free Will, and Moral Responsibility*. Englewood Cliffs, N.J.: Prentice-Hall, 1970.

Hampshire, Stuart. *Freedom of the Individual*. New York: Harper and Row, 1965.

Honderich, Ted, ed. *Essays on Freedom of Action*. London: Routledge and Kegan Paul, 1973.

Kenny, Anthony. *Freewill and Responsibility*. London: Routledge and Kegan Paul, 1978.

Lehrer, Keith, ed. *Freedom and Determinism*. New York: Random House, 1966.

Melden, A. I. *Free Action*. London: Routledge and Kegan Paul, 1961.

Morgenbesser, Sidney, and James Walsh, eds. *Free Will*. Englewood Cliffs, N.J.: Prentice-Hall, 1962.

Pears, David, ed. *Freedom and the Will*. London: Macmillan, 1963.

Strawson, Galen. *Freedom and Belief*. Oxford, Oxford University Press, 1987.

Thorp, John. *Free Will*. London: Routledge and Kegan Paul, 1980.

Van Inwagen, Peter. *An Essay on Free Will*. Oxford: Oxford University Press, 1983.

Watson, Gary, ed. *Free Will*. Oxford: Oxford University Press, 1982.

IV

Universals, Essences, and Natural Kinds

This section consists of two subsections: *Universals and Abstract Entities* and *Essences and Natural Kinds*. The essays in the first subsection focus on a question that has vexed philosophers since Plato's time: are there universals? Philosophers in the tradition of Plato have regarded *universals* as existing entities that are essentially different from individual objects. The essential difference, on the Platonist view, consists in the fact that universals can be exemplified, or instantiated, by *more than one* individual object. For instance, two or more barns can exemplify the property of "redness." And two or more women can exemplify the relation of "being a sister of someone." Platonism about universals is often called *realism* about universals, since it affirms that universals exist independently of human conceivers. In contrast, *nominalism* states that there are only individuals, and *conceptualism* states that universals exist only as constructs of a human conceiver. The traditional problem of universals is basically the problem of answering whether, and if so how, universals exist. The essays in the first subsection represent opposing views on the status of universals.

In "The World of Universals," Bertrand Russell defends Platonism about universals. Russell claims that "we can prove that there must be *relations*, i.e., the sort of universals generally represented by verbs and prepositions." In asking whether something is white, we naturally choose a particular patch of white, and say that something is white if it has the right sort of *resemblance* to our chosen particular. Russell claims that the resemblance required here must

307

be a universal. For "since there are many white things, the resemblance must hold between many pairs of particular white things; and this is the characteristic of a universal." Russell denies that universals exist in the same way that thoughts and physical objects exist. His view is that universals do not exist in time. Russell calls the timeless existence of universals *subsistence* in order to draw a contrast with temporal existence.

In "On What There Is," W. V. Quine begins by explaining how we can meaningfully use names, such as 'Pegasus', without supposing that the apparently named entities actually exist. Here Quine relies on Bertrand Russell's famous theory of descriptions, according to which we can understand names as complex descriptions. One of Quine's lessons is that we should not confuse meaning with naming.

Turning to the problem of universals, Quine draws the related lesson that our meaningful use of predicates such as 'red' or 'is red' need not be regarded as naming a single universal entity: redness. And regarding meaningfulness itself, Quine denies that it commits us to universals called "meanings."

Quine also explains the basis for an *ontology* (a theory of what there is). He claims that our acceptance of an ontology should be similar to our acceptance of a scientific theory: "we adopt, at least insofar as we are reasonable, the simplest conceptual scheme into which the disordered fragments of raw experience can be fitted and arranged." Quine provides a simple standard by which we can decide what the ontological commitments of a theory are: "to be is to be the value of a bound variable." The basic idea here is that a theory makes an ontological commitment *only* by its implying that *there is something* (of a certain sort).

In "A World of Individuals," Nelson Goodman defends a version of *nominalism* according to which there are no classes (or sets). Goodman objects to Platonism on the ground that it generates classes of atoms, classes of classes of atoms, classes of classes of classes of atoms, and so on ad infinitum. On Goodman's nominalism, "no two distinct things have the same atoms; only from different atoms can different things be generated." Goodman devotes much of his essay to answering likely objections to such nominalism.

In "Empiricism, Semantics, and Ontology," Rudolf Carnap explains why our apparent talk of abstract entities does not commit us to Platonism about universals. Carnap calls our system of ways of speaking our *linguistic framework.* Relative to our linguistic framework, Carnap distinguishes two kinds of questions of existence: *internal* and *external* questions.

Internal questions are questions of the existence of certain entities *within our linguistic framework. External questions* are questions of the existence of entities that *transcend our linguistic framework*. The concept of reality involved in internal questions is empirical and non-metaphysical, whereas the concept of reality in external questions is non-empirical and metaphysical.

To accept the world of things from an internal standpoint "means nothing more than to accept a certain form of language, in other words, to accept rules for forming statements and for testing, accepting, or rejecting them." In contrast, Carnap takes a statement of the external reality of a system of entities to be "a pseudo-statement without cognitive content." On Carnap's view, the problem of abstract entities becomes the problem of whether we should accept certain abstract linguistic forms in our overall theory of science. In general, Carnap apparently holds that external questions, in contrast with internal questions, are merely linguistic issues that we typically use pragmatic criteria of some sort (i.e., criteria of usefulness) to assess.

In "Universals and Family Resemblances," Renford Bambrough argues that Ludwig Wittgenstein (1889–1951) solved the problem of universals. Wittgenstein noted that we tend to look for something in common to all the entities that we subsume under a general term. He explained: "We are inclined to think that there must be something in common to all games, say, and that this common property is the justification for applying the term 'game' to the various games; whereas games form a *family* the members of which have family likenesses." Some family members have similar hair; others have similar facial structure; and still others walk the same. But there need not be anything common to all the members, other than their being members of the same family.

This approach to family resemblances underlies Wittgenstein's solution to the problem of universals. Bambrough argues that our use of general terms is meaningful in virtue of the family resemblance relations between the items signified by those terms. He argues also that Wittgenstein's theory of family resemblances provides a superior alternative to both traditional realism and traditional nominalism.

The second subsection of Part IV consists of three essays on *essences* and *natural kinds*. The metaphysical problem of essences is basically the question of whether, and if so, in what way, an object has a special set of features that makes it what it *really* is, and that survives certain changes that the object undergoes. For instance, do you remain who you really are after you get a haircut? And does a tree remain what it really is after a single leaf falls? Typically, essentialists about persons and trees answer yes, on the ground that the relevant *essential* features remain intact.

The philosophical problem of natural kinds is basically the question of whether, and if so, in virtue of what, objects other than artifacts divide up into *kinds* of things. Apparently objects can be similar in some ways and dissimilar in others. Is the similarity of certain objects a mind- and language-independent feature of those objects, and does it provide for those objects' being of one kind? A theory of natural kinds must answer such difficult questions.

In "Essence and Accident," Irving Copi presents an account of essential and accidental (nonessential) features that derives mainly from Aristotle. Following Aristotle, Copi distinguishes between *substantial* and *nonsubstantial* change. An object does not survive a substantial change, but does survive a nonsubstantial change. This distinction between substantial and nonsubstantial change parallels the Aristotelian distinction between *essential* and *accidental* features.

On an Aristotelian view, a feature is essential to an object if and only if its loss would entail the destruction of the object. If a feature is not essential, it is accidental. Copi compares Aristotle's theory of essences to John Locke's corresponding theory, in order to answer whether essences are relative to human language and interests. On Copi's view, real essences can be investigated independently of any linguistic classifying, and science seeks to discover real essences. In fact, Copi claims that both essences and accidents are knowable by science. (For a sharply contrasting view, see the essay by Putnam in Part I above.)

In "Natural Kinds," W. V. Quine opposes both (a) the attempt to define the notion of similarity of things by the notion of a kind, and (b) the attempt to define the notion of a kind by the notion of similarity of things. Quine argues that the notion of similarity or kind changes as science develops, and that the notion of similarity or kind disappears in a mature science. On Quine's view, "the brute irrationality of our sense of similarity, its irrelevance to anything in logic and mathematics, offers little reason to expect that this sense is somehow in tune with the world—a world which, unlike language, we never made." Quine emphasizes that we often revise our notions of similarity or natural kind in light of new scientific theory. But he denies that such notions play any essential role in advanced science.

In "Meaning and Reference," Hilary Putnam presents a view of meaning that has definite implications for natural-kind terms. On Putnam's view, natural-kind "words like 'water' have an unnoticed indexical component: water is stuff that bears a certain similarity relation to the water *around here*." Putnam denies that the extension (or, the set of referents) of natural-kind terms is determined just by concepts that a person associates with those terms. He argues that the meaning of such terms is determined indexically (by our causal relations to certain paradigm-cases with which we are presented, such as the actual water on this planet) and socially (due to the relevant knowledge possessed by the relevant experts, such as the chemist's knowledge of what constitutes water on this planet). If Putnam is right, the semantics of natural-kind terms is more complex than most philosophers have assumed.

Universals and Abstract Entities

The World of Universals*

Bertrand Russell

. . . such entities as relations appear to have a being which is in some way different from that of physical objects, and also different from that of minds and from that of sense-data. In the present chapter we have to consider what is the nature of this kind of being, and also what objects there are that have this kind of being. We will begin with the latter question.

The problem with which we are now concerned is a very old one, since it was brought into philosophy by Plato. Plato's 'theory of ideas' is an attempt to solve this very problem, and in my opinion it is one of the most successful attempts hitherto made. The theory to be advocated in what follows is largely Plato's, with merely such modifications as time has shown to be necessary.

The way the problem arose for Plato was more or less as follows. Let us consider, say, such a notion as *justice*. If we ask ourselves what justice is, it is natural to proceed by considering this, that, and the other just act, with a view to discovering what they have in common. They must all, in some sense,

partake of a common nature, which will be found in whatever is just and in nothing else. This common nature, in virtue of which they are all just, will be justice itself, the pure essence the admixture of which with facts of ordinary life produces the multiplicity of just acts. Similarly with any other word which may be applicable to common facts, such as 'whiteness' for example. The word will be applicable to a number of particular things because they all participate in a common nature or essence. This pure essence is what Plato calls an 'idea' or 'form.' (It must not be supposed that 'ideas', in his sense, exist in minds, though they may be apprehended by minds.) The 'idea' *justice* is not identical with anything that is just: it is something other than particular things, which particular things partake of. Not being particular, it cannot itself exist in the world of sense. Moreover it is not fleeting or changeable like the things of sense: it is eternally itself, immutable and indestructible.

Thus Plato is led to supra-sensible world, more real than the common world of sense, the unchangeable world of ideas, which alone gives to the world of sense whatever pale reflection of reality may belong to it. The truly real world, for Plato, is the world of

*Reprinted by permission, from Russell, *The Problems of Philosophy*, pp. 91–100. Oxford: Oxford University Press, 1912.

313

ideas; for whatever we may attempt to say about things in the world of sense, we can only succeed in saying that they participate in such and such ideas, which, therefore, constitute all their character. Hence it is easy to pass on into a mysticism. We may hope, in a mystic illumination, to *see* the ideas as we see objects of sense; and we may imagine that the ideas exist in heaven. These mystical developments are very natural, but the basis of the theory is in logic, and it is as based in logic that we have to consider it.

The word 'idea' has acquired, in the course of time, many associations which are quite misleading when applied to Plato's 'ideas'. We shall therefore use the word 'universal' instead of the word 'idea', to describe what Plato meant. The essence of the sort of entity that Plato meant is that it is opposed to the particular things that are given in sensation. We speak of whatever is given in sensation, or is of the same nature as things given in sensation, as a *particular*; by opposition to this, a *universal* will be anything which may be shared by many particulars, and has those characteristics which, as we saw, distinguish justice and whiteness from just acts and white things.

When we examine common words, we find that, broadly speaking, proper names stand for particulars, while other substantives, adjectives, prepositions, and verbs stand for universals. Pronouns stand for particulars, but are ambiguous; it is only by the context or the circumstances that we know what particulars they stand for. The word 'now' stands for a particular, namely the present moment; but like pronouns, it stands for an ambiguous particular, because the present is always changing.

It will be seen that no sentence can be made up without at least one word which denotes a universal. The nearest approach would be some such statement as 'I like this'. But even here the word 'like' denotes a universal, for I may like other things, and other people may like things. Thus all truths involve universals, and all knowledge of truths involves acquaintance with universals.

Seeing that nearly all the words to be found in the dictionary stand for universals, it is strange that hardly anybody except students of philosophy ever realizes that there are such entities as universals. We do not naturally dwell upon those words in a sentence which do not stand for particulars; and if we are forced to dwell upon a word which stands for a universal, we naturally think of it as standing for some one of the particulars that come under the universal. When, for example, we hear the sentence, 'Charles I's head was cut off', we may naturally enough think of Charles I, of Charles I's head, and of the operation of cutting off *his* head, which are all particulars; but we do not naturally dwell upon what is meant by the word 'head' or the word 'cut', which is a universal. We feel such words to be incomplete and insubstantial; they seem to demand a context before anything can be done with them. Hence we succeed in avoiding all notice of universals as such, until the study of philosophy forces them upon our attention.

Even among philosophers, we may say, broadly, that only those universals which are named by adjectives or substantives have been much or often recognized, while those named by verbs and prepositions have been usually overlooked. This omission has had a very great effect upon philosophy; it is hardly too much to say that most metaphysics, since Spinoza, has been largely determined by it. The way this has occurred is, in outline, as follows: Speaking generally, adjectives and common nouns express qualities or properties of single things, whereas prepositions and verbs tend to express relations between two or more things. Thus the neglect of prepositions and verbs led to the belief that every proposition can be regarded as attributing a property to a single thing, rather than as expressing a relation between two or more things. Hence it was supposed that, ultimately, there can be no such entities as relations between things. Hence either there can be only one thing in the universe, or, if there are many things, they cannot possibly interact in any way, since any interaction would be a relation, and relations are impossible.

The first of these views, advocated by Spinoza and held in our own day by Bradley and many other philosophers, is called *monism*; the second, advocated by Leibniz but not very common nowadays, is called *monadism*, because each of the isolated things is called a *monad*. Both these opposing philosophies, interesting as they are, result, in my opinion, from an undue attention to one sort of universals, namely the sort represented by adjectives and substantives rather than by verbs and prepositions.

As a matter of fact, if any one were anxious to deny altogether that there are such things as universals, we would find that we cannot strictly prove that there are such entities as *qualities*, i.e. the universals represented by adjectives and substantives, whereas we can prove that there must be *relations*, i.e. the sort of universals generally represented by verbs and prepositions. Let us take in illustration the universal *whiteness*. If we believe that there is such a universal, we shall say that things are white because they have the quality of whiteness. This view, however, was strenuously denied by Berkeley and Hume, who have been followed in this by later empiricists. The form which their denial took was to deny that there are such things as "abstract ideas". When we want to think of whiteness, they said, we form an image of some particular white thing, and reason concerning this particular, taking care not to deduce anything concerning it which we cannot see to be equally true of any other white thing. As an account of our actual mental processes, this is no doubt largely true. In geometry, for example, when we wish to prove something about all triangles, we draw a particular triangle and reason about it, taking care not to use any characteristic which it does not share with other triangles. The beginner, in order to avoid error, often finds it useful to draw several triangles, as unlike each other as possible, in order to make sure that his reasoning is equally applicable to all of them. But a difficulty emerges as soon as we ask ourselves how we know that a thing is white or a triangle. If we wish to avoid the universals

whiteness and *triangularity*, we shall choose some particular patch of white or some particular triangle, and say that anything is white or a triangle if it has the right sort of resemblance to our chosen particular. But then the resemblance required will have to be a universal. Since there are many white things, the resemblance must hold between many pairs of particular white things; and this is the characteristic of a universal. It will be useless to say that there is a different resemblance for each pair, for then we shall have to say that these resemblances resemble each other, and thus at last we shall be forced to admit resemblance as a universal. The relation of resemblance, therefore, must be a true universal. And having been forced to admit this universal, we find that it is no longer worth while to invent difficult and unplausible theories to avoid the admission of such universals as whiteness and triangularity.

Berkeley and Hume failed to perceive this refutation of their rejection of 'abstract ideas', because, like their adversaries, they only thought of *qualities*, and altogether ignored *relations* as universals. We have therefore here another respect in which the rationalists appear to have been in the right as against the empiricists, although, owing to the neglect or denial of relations, the deductions made by rationalists were, if anything, more apt to be mistaken than those made by empiricists.

Having now seen that there must be such entities as universals, the next point to be proved is that their being is not merely mental. By this is meant that whatever being belongs to them is independent of their being thought of or in any way apprehended by minds.

Consider such a proposition as 'Edinburgh is north of London'. Here we have a relation between two places, and it seems plain that the relation subsists independently of our knowledge of it. When we come to know that Edinburgh is north of London, we come to know something which has to do only with Edinburgh and London: we do not cause the truth of the proposition by coming to know it, on the contrary we merely apprehend a fact which was there before we knew it. The part of the earth's surface where Edinburgh stands would be north of the part where London stands, even if there were no human being to know about north and south, and even if there were no minds at all in the universe. This is, of course, denied by many philosophers, either for Berkeley's reasons or for Kant's. But we have already considered these reasons, and decided that they are inadequate. We may therefore now assume it to be true that nothing mental is presupposed in the fact that Edinburgh is north of London. But this fact involves the relation 'north of', which is a universal; and it would be impossible for the whole fact to involve nothing mental if the relation 'north of', which is a constituent part of the fact, did involve anything mental. Hence we must admit that the relation, like the terms it relates, is not dependent upon thought, but belongs to the independent world which thought apprehends but does not create.

This conclusion, however, is met by the difficulty that the relation 'north of' does not seem to *exist* in the same sense in which Edinburgh and London exist. If we ask 'Where and when does this relation exist?' the answer must be 'Nowhere and nowhen'. There is no place or time where we can find the relation 'north of'. It does not exist in Edinburgh any more than in London, for it relates the two and is neutral as between them. Nor can we say that it exists at any particular time. Now everything that can be apprehended by the senses or by introspection exists at some particular time. Hence the relation 'north of' is radically different from such things. It is neither in space nor in time, neither material nor mental; yet it is something.

It is largely the very peculiar kind of being that belongs to universals which has led many people to suppose that they are really mental. We can think *of* a universal, and our thinking then exists in a perfectly ordinary sense, like any other mental act. Suppose, for example, that we are thinking of whiteness. Then *in one sense* it may be said that whiteness is 'in our mind'. In the strict sense, it is not whiteness that is in our mind, but the act of thinking of whiteness. The connected ambiguity in the word 'idea', which we noted at the same time, also causes confusion here. In one sense of this word, namely the sense in which it denotes the *object* of an act of thought, whiteness is an 'idea'. Hence, if the ambiguity is not guarded against, we may come to think that whiteness is an 'idea' in the other sense, i.e. an act of thought; and thus we come to think that whiteness is mental. But in so thinking, we rob it of its essential quality of universality. One man's act of thought is necessarily a different thing from another man's; or man's act of thought at one time is necessarily a different thing from the same man's act of thought at another time. Hence, if whiteness were the thought as opposed to its object, no two different men could think of it, and no one man could think of it twice. That which many different thoughts of whiteness have in common is their *object,* and this object is different from all of them. Thus universals are not thoughts, though when known they are the objects of thoughts.

We shall find it convenient only to speak of things *existing* when they are in time, that is to say, when we can point to some time *at* which they exist (not excluding the possibility of their existing at all times). Thus thoughts and feelings, minds and physical objects *exist.* But universals do not exist in this sense; we shall say that they *subsist* or *have being,* where 'being' is opposed to 'existence' as being timeless. The world of universals, therefore, may also be described as the world of being. The world of being is unchangeable, rigid, exact, delightful to the mathematician, the logician, the builder of metaphysical systems, and all who love perfection more than life. The world of existence is fleeting, vague, without sharp boundaries, without any clear plan or arrangement, but it contains all thoughts and feelings, all the data of sense, and all physical objects, everything that can do either good or harm, everything that makes any difference to the value of life and the world. According to our temperaments, we shall

Universals and Abstract Entities

prefer the contemplation of the one or of the other. The one we do not prefer will probably seem to us a pale shadow of the one we prefer, and hardly worthy to be regarded as in any sense real. But the truth is that both have the same claim on our impartial attention, both are real, and both are important to the metaphysician.

On What There Is*

W. V. Quine

A curious thing about the ontological problem is its simplicity. It can be put in three Anglo-Saxon monosyllables: 'What is there?' It can be answered, moreover, in a word—'Everything'—and everyone will accept this answer as true. However, this is merely to say that there is what there is. There remains room for disagreement over cases; and so the issue has stayed alive down the centuries.

Suppose now that two philosophers, McX and I, differ over ontology. Suppose McX maintains there is something which I maintain there is not. McX can, quite consistently with his own point of view, describe our difference of opinion by saying that I refuse to recognize certain entities. I should protest, of course, that he is wrong in his formulation of our disagreement, for I maintain that there are no entities, of the kind which he alleges, for me to recognize; but my finding him wrong in his formulation of our disagreement is unimportant, for I am committed to considering him wrong in his ontology anyway.

When *I* try to formulate our difference of opinion, on the other hand, I seem to be in a predicament. I cannot admit that there are some things which McX countenances and I do not, for in admitting that there are such things I should be contradicting my own rejection of them.

It would appear, if this reasoning were sound, that in any ontological dispute the proponent of the negative side suffers the disadvantage of not being able to admit that his opponent disagrees with him.

This is the old Platonic riddle of nonbeing. Nonbeing must in some sense be, otherwise what is it that there is not? This tangled doctrine might be nicknamed *Plato's beard;* historically it has proved tough, frequently dulling the edge of Occam's razor.

It is some such line of thought that leads philosophers like McX to impute being where they might otherwise be quite content to recognize that there is nothing. Thus, take Pegasus. If Pegasus *were* not, McX argues, we should not be talking about anything when we use the word; therefore it would be nonsense to say even that Pegasus is not. Thinking to show thus that the denial of Pegasus cannot be coherently maintained, he concludes that Pegasus is.

McX cannot, indeed, quite persuade him-

*Originally published in *The Review of Metaphysics,* Volume 2, number 1 (September 1948), 21–28. Reprinted with permission of the editor.

self that any region of space-time, near or remote, contains a flying horse of flesh and blood. Pressed for further details on Pegasus, then, he says that Pegasus is an idea in men's minds. Here, however, a confusion begins to be apparent. We may for the sake of argument concede that there is an entity, and even a unique entity (though this is rather implausible), which is the mental Pegasus-idea; but this mental entity is not what people are talking about when they deny Pegasus.

McX never confuses the Parthenon with the Parthenon-idea. The Parthenon is physical; the Parthenon-idea is mental (according anyway to McX's version of ideas, and I have no better to offer). The Parthenon is visible, the Parthenon-idea is invisible. We cannot easily imagine two things more unlike, and less liable to confusion, than the Parthenon and the Parthenon-idea. But when we shift from the Parthenon to Pegasus, the confusion sets in—for no other reason than that McX would sooner be deceived by the crudest and most flagrant counterfeit than grant the nonbeing of Pegasus.

The notion that Pegasus must be, because it would otherwise be nonsense to say even that Pegasus is not, has been seen to lead McX into an elementary confusion. Subtler minds, taking the same precept as their starting point, come out with theories of Pegasus which are less patently misguided than McX's, and correspondingly more difficult to eradicate. One of these subtler minds is named, let us say, Wyman. Pegasus, Wyman maintains, has his being as an unactualized possible. When we say of Pegasus that there is no such thing, we are saying, more precisely, that Pegasus does not have the special attribute of actuality. Saying that Pegasus is not actual is on a par, logically, with saying that the Parthenon is not red; in either case we are saying something about an entity whose being is unquestioned.

Wyman, by the way, is one of those philosophers who have united in ruining the good old word 'exist'. Despite his espousal of unactualized possibles, he limits the word 'existence' to actuality—thus preserving an illusion of ontological agreement between himself and us who repudiate the rest of his bloated universe. We have all been prone to say, in our common-sense usage of 'exist', that Pegasus does not exist, meaning simply that there is no such entity at all. If Pegasus existed he would indeed be in space and time, but only because the word 'Pegasus' has spatio-temporal connotations, and not because 'exists' has spatio-temporal connotations. If spatio-temporal reference is lacking when we affirm the existence of the cube root of 27, this is simply because a cube root is not a spatio-temporal kind of thing, and not because we are being ambiguous in our use of 'exist'.[1] However, Wyman, in an ill-conceived effort to appear agreeable, genially grants us the nonexistence of Pegasus and then, contrary to what *we* meant by nonexistence of Pegasus, insists that Pegasus *is*. Existence is one thing, he says, and subsistence is another. The only way I know of coping with this obfuscation of issues is to *give* Wyman the word 'exist'. I'll try not to use it again; I still have 'is'. So much for lexicography; let's get back to Wyman's ontology.

Wyman's overpopulated universe is in many ways unlovely. It offends the aesthetic sense of us who have a taste for desert landscapes, but this is not the worst of it. Wyman's slum of possibles is a breeding ground for disorderly elements. Take, for instance, the possible fat man in that doorway; and, again, the possible bald man in that doorway. Are they the same possible man, or two possible men? How do we decide? How many possible men are there in that doorway? Are there more possible thin ones than fat ones? How many of them are alike? Or would their being alike make them one? Are no *two* possible things alike? Is this the same as saying that it is impossible for two things to be alike? Or, finally, is the concept of identity simply inapplicable to unactualized possibles? But what sense can be found in talking of entities which cannot meaningfully be said to be identical with themselves and distinct from one another? These elements are well-nigh incorrigible. By a Fregean therapy of individual concepts, some effort might be made at rehabilitation; but I feel we'd do better simply to clear Wyman's slum and be done with it.

Possibility, along with the other modalities of necessity and impossibility and contingency, raises problems upon which I do not mean to imply that we should turn our backs. But we can at least limit modalities to whole statements. We may impose the adverb 'possibly' upon a statement as a whole, and we may well worry about the semantical analysis of such usage; but little real advance in such analysis is to be hoped for in expanding our universe to include so-called *possible entities*. I suspect that the main motive for this expansion is simply the old notion that Pegasus, for example, must be because otherwise it would be nonsense to say even that he is not.

Still, all the rank luxuriance of Wyman's universe of possibles would seem to come to naught when we make a slight change in the example and speak not of Pegasus but of the round square cupola on Berkeley College. If, unless Pegasus were, it would be nonsense to say that he is not, then by the same token, unless the round square cupola on Berkeley College were, it would be nonsense to say that it is not. But, unlike Pegasus, the round square cupola on Berkeley College cannot be admitted even as an unactualized *possible*. Can we drive Wyman now to admitting also a realm of unactualizable impossibles? If so, a good many embarrassing questions could be asked about them. We might hope even to trap Wyman in contradictions, by getting him to admit that certain of these entities are at once round and square. But the wily Wyman chooses the other horn of the dilemma and concedes that it is nonsense to say that the round square cupola on Berkeley College is not. He says that the phrase 'round square cupola' is meaningless.

Wyman was not the first to embrace this alternative. The doctrine of the meaninglessness of contradictions runs away back. The tradition survives, moreover, in writers who seem to share none of Wyman's motivations. Still, I wonder whether the first temptation to such a doctrine may not have been substantially the motivation which we have observed in Wyman. Certainly the doctrine has no intrinsic appeal; and it has led its devotees to such quixotic extremes as that of challenging the method of proof by *reductio ad absurdum*—a challenge in which I sense a *reductio ad absurdum* of the doctrine itself.

Moreover, the doctrine of meaninglessness of contradictions has the severe methodological drawback that it makes it impossible, in principle, ever to devise an effective test of what is meaningful and what is not. It would be forever impossible for us to devise systematic ways of deciding whether a string of signs made sense—even to us individually, let alone other people—or not. For it follows from a discovery in mathematical logic, due to Church, that there can be no generally applicable test of contradictoriness.

I have spoken disparagingly of Plato's beard, and hinted that it is tangled. I have dwelt at length on the inconveniences of putting up with it. It is time to think about taking steps.

Russell, in his theory of so-called singular descriptions, showed clearly how we might meaningfully use seeming names without supposing that there be the entities allegedly named. The names to which Russell's theory directly applies are complex descriptive names such as 'the author of *Waverley*,' 'the present King of France', 'the round square cupola on Berkeley College'. Russell analyzes such phrases systematically as fragments of the whole sentences in which they occur. The sentence 'The author of *Waverley* was a poet', for example, is explained as a whole as meaning 'Someone (better: something) wrote *Waverley* and was a poet, and nothing else wrote *Waverley*'. (The point of this added clause is to affirm the uniqueness which is implicit in the word 'the', in '*the* author of *Waverley*'.) The sentence 'The round square cupola on Berkeley College is pink' is explained as 'Something is round and square and is a cupola on Berkeley College and is pink, and nothing else is round and square and a cupola on Berkeley College'.

The virtue of this analysis is that the seeming name, a descriptive phrase, is paraphrased *in context* as a so-called incomplete symbol. No unified expression is offered as an analysis of the descriptive phrase, but the statement as a whole which was the context of that phrase still gets its full quota of meaning—whether true or false.

The unanalyzed statement 'The author of *Waverley* was a poet' contains a part, 'the author of *Waverley*', which is wrongly supposed by McX and Wyman to demand objective reference in order to be meaningful at all. But in Russell's translation, 'Something wrote *Waverley* and was a poet and nothing else wrote *Waverley*', the burden of objective reference which had been put upon the descriptive phrase is now taken over by words of the kind that logicians call bound variables, variables of quantification, namely, words like 'something', 'nothing', 'everything'. These words, far from purporting to be names specifically of the author of *Waverley*, do not purport to be names at all; they refer to entities generally, with a kind of studied ambiguity peculiar to themselves. These quantificational words or bound variables are, of course a basic part of language, and their meaningfulness, at least in context, is not to be challenged. But their meaningfulness in no way presupposes there being either the author of *Waverley* or the round square cupola on Berkeley College or any other specifically preassigned objects.

Where descriptions are concerned, there is no longer any difficulty in affirming or denying being. 'There *is* the author of *Waverley*' is explained by Russell as meaning 'Someone (or, more strictly, something) wrote *Waverley* and nothing else wrote *Waverley*'. 'The author of *Waverley* is not' is explained, correspondingly, as the alternation 'Either each thing failed to write *Waverley* or two or more things wrote *Waverley*'. This alternation is false, but meaningful; and it contains no expression purporting to name the author of *Waverley*. The statement 'The round square cupola on Berkeley College is not' is analyzed in similar fashion. So the old notion that statements of nonbeing defeat themselves goes by the board. When a statement of being or nonbeing is analyzed by Russell's theory of descriptions, it ceases to contain any expression which even purports to name the alleged entity whose being is in question, so that the meaningfulness of the statement no longer can be thought to presuppose that there be such an entity.

Now what of 'Pegasus'? This being a word rather than a descriptive phrase, Russell's argument does not immediately apply to it. However, it can easily be made to apply. We have only to rephrase 'Pegasus' as a description, in any way that seems adequately to single out our idea; say, 'the winged horse that was captured by Bellerophon'. Substituting such a phrase for 'Pegasus', we can then proceed to analyze the statement 'Pegasus is', or 'Pegasus is not', precisely on the analogy of Russell's analysis of 'The author of *Waverley* is' and 'The author of *Waverley* is not'.

In order thus to subsume a one-word name or alleged name such as 'Pegasus' under Russell's theory of description, we must, of course, be able first to translate the word into a description. But this is no real restriction. If the notion of Pegasus had been so obscure or so basic a one that no pat translation into a descriptive phrase had offered itself along familiar lines, we could still have availed ourselves of the following artificial and trivial-seeming device: we could have appealed to the *ex hypothesi* unanalyzable, irreducible attribute of *being Pegasus*, adopting, for its expression, the verb 'is-Pegasus', or 'pegasizes'. The noun 'Pegasus' itself could then be treated as derivative, and identified after all with a description: 'the thing that is-Pegasus', 'the thing that pegasizes'.

If the importing of such a predicate as 'pegasizes' seems to commit us to recognizing that there is a corresponding attribute, pegasizing, in Plato's heaven or in the minds of men, well and good. Neither we nor Wyman nor McX have been contending, thus far, about the being or nonbeing of universals, but rather about that of Pegasus. If in terms of pegasizing we can interpret the noun 'Pegasus' as a description subject to Russell's theory of descriptions, then we have disposed of the old notion that Pegasus cannot be said not to be without presupposing that in some sense Pegasus is.

Our argument is now quite general. McX and Wyman suppose that we could not meaningfully affirm a statement of the form 'So-and-so is not', with a simple or descriptive singular noun in place of 'so-and-so', unless so-and-so is. This supposition is now seen to be quite generally groundless, since the singular noun in question can always be expanded into a singular description, trivially or otherwise, and then analyzed out *à la* Russell.

We commit ourselves to an ontology containing numbers when we say there are prime numbers larger than a million; we commit ourselves to an ontology containing centaurs when we say there are centaurs; and we commit ourselves to an ontology containing Pegasus when we say Pegasus is. But we do not commit ourselves to an ontology containing Pegasus or the author of *Waverley* or the round square cupola on Berkeley College when we say that Pegasus or the author of *Waverley* or the cupola in question is *not*. We need no longer labor under the delusion that the meaningfulness of a statement containing a singular term presupposes an entity named by the term. A singular term need not name to be significant.

An inkling of this might have dawned on Wyman and McX even without benefit of Russell if they had only noticed—as so few of us do—that there is a gulf between *meaning* and *naming* even in the case of a singular term which is genuinely a name of an object. The following example from Frege will serve. The phrase 'Evening Star' names a certain large physical object of spherical form, which is hurtling through space some scores of millions of miles from here. The phrase 'Morning Star' names the same thing, as was probably first established by some observant Babylonian. But the two phrases cannot be regarded as having the same meaning; otherwise that Babylonian could have dispensed with his observations and contented himself with reflecting on the meanings of his words. The meanings, then, being different from one another, must be other than the named object, which is one and the same in both cases.

Confusion of meaning with naming not only made McX think he could not meaningfully repudiate Pegasus; a continuing confusion of meaning with naming no doubt helped engender his absurd notion that Pegasus is an idea, a mental entity. The structure of his confusion is as follows. He confused the alleged *named object* Pegasus with the *meaning* of the word 'Pegasus', therefore concluding that Pegasus must be in order that the word have meaning. But what sorts of things are meanings? This is a moot point; however, one might quite plausibly explain meanings as ideas in the mind, supposing we can make clear sense in turn of the idea of ideas in the mind. Therefore Pegasus, initially confused with a meaning, ends up as an idea in the mind. It is the more remarkable that Wyman, subject to the same initial motivation as McX, should have avoided this particular blunder and wound up with unactualized possibles instead.

Now let us turn to the ontological problem of universals: the question whether there are such entities as attributes, relations, classes, numbers, functions. McX, characteristically enough, thinks there are. Speaking of attributes, he says: "There are red houses, red roses, red sunsets; this much is prephilosophical common sense in which we must all agree. These houses, roses, and sunsets, then, have something in common; and this which they have in common is all I mean by the attribute of redness." For McX, thus, there being attributes is even more obvious and trivial than the obvious and trivial fact of there being red houses, roses, and sunsets. This, I think, is characteristic of metaphysics, or at least of that part of metaphysics called ontology: one who regards a statement on this subject as true at all must regard it as trivially true. One's ontology is basic to the conceptual scheme by which he interprets all experiences, even the most commonplace ones. Judged within some particular conceptual scheme—and how else is judgment possible?—an ontological statement goes without saying, standing in need of no separate justification at all. Ontological statements follow immediately from all matter of casual statements of commonplace fact, just as—from the point of view, anyway, of McX's conceptual scheme—'There is an attribute' follows from 'There are red houses, red roses, red sunsets'.

Judged in another conceptual scheme, an ontological statement which is axiomatic to McX's mind way, with equal immediacy and triviality, be adjudged false. One may admit that there are red houses, roses, and sunsets, but deny, except as a popular and misleading manner of speaking, that they have anything in common. The words 'houses', 'roses', and 'sunsets' are true of sundry individual entities which are houses and roses and sunsets, and the word 'red' or 'red object' is true of each of sundry individual entities which are red houses, red roses, red sunsets; but there is not, in additon, any entity whatever, individual or otherwise, which is named by the word 'redness', nor, for that matter, by the word 'household', 'rosehood', 'sunsethood'. That the houses and roses and sunsets are all of them red may be taken as ultimate and irreducible, and it may be held that McX is no better off, in point of real explanatory power, for all the occult entities which he posits under such names as 'redness'.

One means by which McX might naturally have tried to impose his ontology of universals on us was already removed before we turned to the problem of universals. McX cannot argue that predicates such as 'red' or 'is-red', which we all concur in using, must be regarded as names each of a single universal entity in order that they be meaningful at all. For we have seen that being a name of something is a much more special feature than being meaningful. He cannot even charge us—at least not by *that* argument—with having posited an attribute of pegasizing by our adoption of the predicate 'pegasizes'.

However, McX hits upon a different strategem. "Let us grant," he says, "this distinction between meaning and naming of which you make so much. Let us even grant that 'is red', 'pegasizes', etc., are not names

of attributes. Still, you admit they have meanings. But these *meanings*, whether they are *named* or not, are still universals, and I venture to say that some of them might even be the very things that I call attributes, or something to much the same purpose in the end."

For McX, this is an unusually penetrating speech; and the only way I know to counter it is by refusing to admit meanings. However, I feel no reluctance toward refusing to admit meanings, for I do not thereby deny that words and statements are meaningful. McX and I may agree to the letter in our classification of linguistic forms into the meaningful and the meaningless, even though McX construes meaningfulness as the *having* (in some sense of 'having') of some abstract entity which he calls a meaning, whereas I do not. I remain free to maintain that the fact that a given linguistic utterance is meaningful (or *significant*, as I prefer to say so as not to invite hypostasis of meanings as entities) is an ultimate and irreducible matter of fact; or, I may undertake to analyze it in terms directly of what people do in the presence of the linguistic utterance in question and other utterances similar to it.

The useful ways in which people ordinarily talk or seem to talk about meanings boil down to two: the *having* of meanings, which is significance, and *sameness* of meaning, or synonymy. What is called *giving* the meaning of an utterance is simply the uttering of a synonym, couched, ordinarily, in clearer language than the original. If we are allergic to meanings as such, we can speak directly of utterances as significant or insignificant, and as synonymous or heteronymous one with another. The problem of explaining these adjectives 'significant' and 'synonymous' with some degree of clarity and rigor—preferably, as I see it, in terms of behavior—is as difficult as it is important. But the explanatory value of special and irreducible intermediary entities called meanings is surely illusory.

Up to now I have argued that we can use singular terms significantly in sentences without presupposing that there are the entities which those terms purport to name. I have argued further that we can use general terms, for example, predicates, without conceding them to be names of abstract entities. I have argued further that we can view utterances as significant, and as synonymous or heteronymous with one another, without countenancing a realm of entities called meanings. At this point McX begins to wonder whether there is any limit at all to our ontological immunity. Does *nothing* we may say commit us to the assumption of universals or other entities which we may find unwelcome?

I have already suggested a negative answer to this question, in speaking of bound variables, or variables of quantification, in connection with Russell's theory of descriptions. We can very easily involve ourselves in ontological commitments by saying, for example, that *there is something* (bound variable) which red houses and sunsets have in common; or that *there is something* which is a prime number larger than a million. But this is, essentially, the *only* way we can involve ourselves in ontological commitments: by our use of bound variables. The use of alleged names is no criterion, for we can repudiate their namehood at the drop of a hat unless the assumption of a corresponding entity can be spotted in the things we affirm in terms of bound variables. Names are, in fact, altogether immaterial to the ontological issue, for I have shown, in connection with 'Pegasus' and 'pegasize', that names can be converted to descriptions, and Russell has shown that descriptions can be eliminated. Whatever we say with the help of names can be said in a language which shuns names altogether. To be assumed as an entity is, purely and simply, to be reckoned as the value of a variable. In terms of the categories of traditional grammar, this amounts roughly to saying that to be is to be in the range of reference of a pronoun. Pronouns are the basic media of reference; nouns might better have been named propronouns. The variables of quantification, 'something', 'nothing', 'everything', range over our whole ontology, whatever it may be; and we are convicted of a particular onto-

logical presupposition if, and only if, the alleged presuppositum has to be reckoned among the entities over which our variables range in order to render one of our affirmations true.

We may say, for example, that some dogs are white and not thereby commit ourselves to recognizing either doghood or whiteness as entities. 'Some dogs are white' says that some things that are dogs are white; and, in order that this statement be true, the things over which the bound variable 'something' ranges must include some white dogs, but need not include doghood or whiteness. On the other hand, when we say that some zoölogical species are cross-fertile we are committing ourselves to recognizing as entities the several species themselves, abstract though they are. We remain so committed at least until we devise some way of so paraphrasing the statement as to show that the seeming reference to species on the part of our bound variable was an avoidable manner of speaking.

Classical mathematics, as the example of primes larger than a million clearly illustrates, is up to its neck in commitments to an ontology of abstract entities. Thus it is that the great mediaeval controversy over universals has flared up anew in the modern philosophy of mathematics. The issue is clearer now than of old, because we now have a more explicit standard whereby to decide what ontology a given theory or form of discourse is committed to: a theory is committed to those and only those entities to which the bound variables of the theory must be capable of referring in order that the affirmations made in the theory be true.

Because this standard of ontological presupposition did not emerge clearly in the philosophical tradition, the modern philosophical mathematicians have not on the whole recognized that they were debating the same old problem of universals in a newly clarified form. But the fundamental cleavages among modern points of view on foundations of mathematics do come down pretty explicitly to disagreements as to the range of entities to which the bound variables should be permitted to refer.

The three main mediaeval points of view regarding universals are designated by historians as *realism*, *conceptualism*, and *nominalism*. Essentially these same three doctrines reappear in twentieth-century surveys of the philosophy of mathematics under the new names *logicism*, *intuitionism*, and *formalism*.

Realism, as the word is used in connection with the mediaeval controversy over universals, is the Platonic doctrine that universals or abstract entities have being independently of the mind; the mind may discover them but cannot create them. *Logicism*, represented by Frege, Russell, Whitehead, Church, and Carnap, condones the use of bound variables to refer to abstract entities known and unknown, specifiable and unspecifiable, indiscriminately.

Conceptualism holds that there are universals but they are mind-made. *Intuitionism*, espoused in modern times in one form or another by Poincaré, Brouwer, Weyl, and others, countenances the use of bound variables to refer to abstract entities only when those entities are capable of being cooked up individually from ingredients specified in advance. As Fraenkel has put it, logicism holds that classes are discovered while intuitionism holds that they are invented—a fair statement indeed of the old opposition between realism and conceptualism. This opposition is no mere quibble; it makes an essential difference in the amount of classical mathematics to which one is willing to subscribe. Logicists, or realists, are able on their assumptions to get Cantor's ascending orders of infinity; intuitionists are compelled to stop with the lowest order of infinity, and, as an indirect consequence, to abandon even some of the classical laws of real numbers. The modern controversy between logicism and intuitionism arose, in fact, from disagreements over infinity.

Formalism, associated with the name of Hilbert, echoes intuitionism in deploring the logicist's unbridled recourse to universals. But formalism also finds intuitionism unsatisfactory. This could happen for either of two opposite reasons. The formalist might, like the logicist, object to the crippling of classical mathematics; or he might, like the *nominalists* of old, object to admitting abstract entities at all, even in the restrained sense of mind-made entities. The upshot is the same: the formalist keeps classical mathematics as a play of insignificant notations. This play of notations can still be of utility—whatever utility it has already shown itself to have as a crutch for physicists and technologists. But utility need not imply significance, in any literal linguistic sense. Nor need the marked success of mathematicians in spinning out theorems, and in finding objective bases for agreement with one another's results, imply significance. For an adequate basis for agreement among mathematicians can be found simply in the rules which govern the manipulation of the notations—these syntactical rules being, unlike the notations themselves, quite significant and intelligible.

I have argued that the sort of ontology we adopt can be consequential—notably in connection with mathematics, although this is only an example. Now how are we to adjudicate among rival ontologies? Certainly the answer is not provided by the semantical formula "To be is to be the value of a variable"; this formula serves rather, conversely, in testing the conformity of a given remark or doctrine to a prior ontological standard. We look to bound variables in connection with ontology not in order to know what there is, but in order to know what a given remark or doctrine, ours or someone else's, *says* there is; and this much is quite properly a problem involving language. But what there is is another question.

In debating over what there is, there are still reasons for operating on a semantical plane. One reason is to escape from the predicament noted at the beginning of this essay: the predicament of my not being able to admit that there are things which McX countenances and I do not. So long as I adhere to my ontology, as opposed to McX's, I cannot allow my bound variables to refer to entities which belong to McX's ontology and not to mine. I can, however, consistently describe our disagreement by characterizing the statements which McX affirms. Provided merely that my ontology countenances linguistic forms, or at least concrete inscriptions and utterances, I can talk about McX's sentences.

Another reason for withdrawing to a semantical plane is to find common ground on which to argue. Disagreement in ontology involves basic disagreement in conceptual schemes; yet McX and I, despite these basic disagreements, find that our conceptual schemes converge sufficiently in their intermediate and upper ramifications to enable us to communicate successfully on such topics as politics, weather, and, in particular, language. In so far as our basic controversy over ontology can be translated upward into a semantical controversy about words and what to do with them, the collapse of the controversy into question-begging may be delayed.

It is no wonder, then, that ontological controversy should tend into controversy over language. But we must not jump to the conclusion that what there is depends on words. Translatability of a question into semantical terms is no indication that the question is linguistic. To see Naples is to bear a name which, when prefixed to the words 'sees Naples', yields a true sentence; still there is nothing linguistic about seeing Naples.

Our acceptance of an ontology is, I think, similar in principle to our acceptance of a scientific theory, say a system of physics: we adopt, at least insofar as we are reasonable, the simplest conceptual scheme into which the disordered fragments of raw experience can be fitted and arranged. Our ontology is determined once we have fixed upon the over-all conceptual scheme which is to accommodate science in the broadest sense; and the considerations which determine a reasonable construction of any part of that conceptual scheme, for example, the biological or the physical part, are not different in kind from the considerations which determine a reasonable construction of the whole. To whatever extent the adoption of any system of scientific theory may be said to be a matter of language, the same—but no more—may be said of the adoption of an ontology.

But simplicity, as a guiding principle in constructing conceptual schemes, is not a clear and unambiguous idea; and it is quite capable of presenting a double or multiple standard. Imagine, for example, that we have devised the most economical set of concepts adequate to the play-by-play reporting of immediate experience. The entities under this scheme—the values of bound variables—are, let us suppose, individual subjective events of sensation or reflection. We should still find, no doubt, that a physicalistic conceptual scheme, purporting to talk about external objects, offers great advantages in simplifying our over-all reports. By bringing together scattered sense events and treating them as perceptions of one object, we reduce the complexity of our stream of experience to a manageable conceptual simplicity. The rule of simplicity is indeed our guiding maxim in assigning sense data to objects: we associate an earlier and a later round sensum with the same so-called penny, or with two different so-called pennies, in obedience to the demands of maximum simplicity in our total world-picture.

Here we have two competing conceptual schemes, a phenomenalistic one and a physicalistic one. Which should prevail? Each has its advantages; each has its special simplicity in its own way. Each, I suggest, deserves to be developed. Each may be said, indeed, to be the more fundamental, though in different senses: the one is epistemologically, the other physically, fundamental.

The physical conceptual scheme simplifies our account of experience because of the way myriad scattered sense events come to be associated with single so-called objects; still there is no likelihood that each sentence about physical objects can actually be translated, however deviously and complexly, into the phenomenalistic language. Physical objects are postulated entities which round out and simplify our account of the flux of experience, just as the introduction of irrational numbers simplifies laws of arithmetic. From the point of view of the conceptual scheme of the elementary arithmetic of rational numbers alone, the broader arithmetic of rational and irrational numbers would have the status of a convenient myth, simpler than the literal truth (namely, the arithmetic of rationals) and yet containing that literal truth as a scattered part. Similarly, from a phenomenalistic point of view, the conceptual scheme of physical objects is a convenient myth, simpler than the literal truth and yet containing that literal truth as a scattered part.

Now what of classes or attributes of physical objects, in turn? A platonistic ontology of this sort is, from the point of view of a strictly physicalistic conceptual scheme, as much a myth as that physicalistic conceptual scheme itself is for phenomenalism. This higher myth is a good and useful one, in turn, in so far as it simplifies our account of physics. Since mathematics is an integral part of this higher myth, the utility of this myth for physical science is evident enough. In speaking of it nevertheless as a myth, I echo that philosophy of mathematics to which I alluded earlier under the name of formalism. But an attitude of formalism may with equal justice be adopted toward the physical conceptual scheme, in turn, by the pure aesthete or phenomenalist.

The analogy between the myth of mathematics and the myth of physics is, in some additional and perhaps fortuitous ways, strikingly close. Consider, for example, the crisis which was precipitated in the foundations of mathematics, at the turn of the century, by the discovery of Russell's paradox and other antinomies of set theory. These contradictions had to be obviated by unintuitive, *ad hoc* devices; our mathematical myth-making became deliberate and evident to all. But what of physics? An antinomy arose between the undular and the corpuscular accounts of light; and if this was not as out-and-out a contradiction as Russell's paradox, I suspect that the reason is that physics is not as out-and-out as mathematics. Again, the second great modern crisis in the foundations of mathematics—precipitated in 1931 by Gödel's proof that there are bound to be undecidable statements in arithmetic—has its companion piece in physics in Heisenberg's indeterminacy principle.

In earlier pages I undertook to show that some common arguments in favor of certain ontologies are fallacious. Further, I advanced an explicit standard whereby to decide what the ontological commitments of a theory are. But the question what ontology actually to adopt still stands open, and the obvious counsel is tolerance and an experimental spirit. Let us by all means see how much of the physicalistic conceptual scheme can be reduced to a phenomenalistic one; still, physics also naturally demands pursuing, irreducible *in toto* though it be. Let us see how, or to what degree, natural science may be rendered independent of platonistic mathematics; but let us also pursue mathematics and delve into its platonistic foundations.

From among the various conceptual schemes best suited to these various pursuits, one—the phenomenalistic—claims epistemological priority. Viewed from within the phenomenalistic conceptual scheme, the ontologies of physical objects and mathematical objects are myths. The quality of myth, however, is relative; relative, in this case, to the epistemological point of view. This point of view is one among various, corresponding to one among our various interests and purposes.

NOTES

[1]The impulse to distinguish terminologically between existence as applied to objects actualized somewhere in space-time and existence (or subsistence or being) as applied to other entities arises in part, perhaps, from an idea that the observation of nature is relevant only to questions of existence of the first kind. But this idea is readily refuted by counterinstances such as 'the ratio of the number of centaurs to the number of unicorns'. If there were such a ratio, it would be an abstract entity, viz. a number. Yet it is only by studying nature that we conclude that the number of centaurs and the number of unicorns are both 0 and hence that there is no such ratio.

A World of Individuals*

Nelson Goodman

1. INDIVIDUALS AND CLASSES

For me, as a nominalist, the world is a world of individuals. But this simple statement, I have learned from bitter experience, can be misunderstood in numberless ways. Some misunderstandings have arisen from inadequacies in my own explanations. Other misunderstandings have arisen from inadequate attention to those explanations. Conflicting arguments in bewildering variety have been brought forward to show that nominalism is bad. This paper is one more attempt to make clear what I mean by nominalism and why I think nominalism is good.

A certain amount of trouble can be blamed on emotions attaching to the word "individual". One writer[1] calls it an 'honorific' word; and I am often criticized for applying the term "individual" to something or other that is unworthy of it. Use of a different word, even a coined one, might have been advisable in order to forestall such complaints.

*Copyright ©1956 by University of Notre Dame Press. Reprinted by permission, from *The Problem of Universals*, pp. 13–31. Notre Dame: University of Notre Dame Press, 1956.

Nevertheless, I am prepared to defend the choice of the term "individual" as entirely in accord with a common practice of adapting ordinary language to technical purposes. In some cases, what I take as an individual may indeed lack many characteristics usually associated with the term "individual", and may not count as an individual according to common usage. But the situation with respect to the term "class" is exactly parallel. According to the layman's prelogical usage, children in a schoolroom make up a class, and so do people at a given social level, but Plato and this sheet of paper and the Taj Mahal do not. The term "set" in ordinary usage is perhaps even more restricted than the term "class". Yet by the logician's usage any things whatever make up a class or set. The contention that a genuine whole or individual cannot consist of widely scattered and very unlike parts misses the point as completely as would the contention that a genuine class cannot consist of widely scattered and very unlike members. In the case of "individual" as in the case of "class", a technical usage is explicated with the help of a calculus, and the divergence from ordinary usage is expressly noted. A class for

Boole need not have social cohesion; and an individual for me need not have personal integration.

Confusion of another kind has resulted from the incautious opening sentence of my joint article[2] with Quine. Although the statement "We do not believe in abstract entities" was intended more as a headline than as final doctrine, and although some reservations concerning it were almost immediately indicated[3], it has been fair game for critics ever since. Neither of us would write that sentence today, but neither of us would so change it as to affect anything beyond the first paragraph of the article in question. Quine has recently written that he would "now prefer to treat that sentence as a hypothetical statement of conditions for the construction in hand."[4] My own change would not be from the categorical to the hypothetical, but from the vaguely general to the more specific. I do not look upon abstractness as either a necessary or a sufficient test of incomprehensibility; and indeed the line between what is ordinarily called "abstract" what is ordinarily called "concrete" seems to me vague and capricious. Nominalism for me consists specifically in the refusal to recognize classes.

What has not always been noticed is that essentially this revision is made in my book,[5] published four years later than the joint article. A key principle in this later formulation is that the nominalist rejects classes as incomprehensible, but may take anything whatever as an individual. Some misguided criticism would have been obviated had enough attention been paid to this statement; but I suspect that some of my critics feel they do me a kindness by not taking it seriously. Further explanation may help.

Nominalism as I conceive it (and I am not here speaking for Quine) does not involve excluding abstract entities, spirits, intimations of immortality, or anything of the sort; but requires only that whatever is admitted as an entity at all be construed as an individual. A given philosopher, nominalist or not, may impose very stringent requirements upon what he will admit as an entity; but these requirements, however sound they may be and however intimately associated with traditional nominalism, are quite independent of nominalism in my sense. The nominalism I have described demands only that all entities admitted, no matter what they are, be treated as individuals. Just what this means, I shall explain in the following sections; but for the moment we may suppose that to treat entities as individuals for a system is to take them as values of the variables of lowest type in the system.

Incidentally, several of my critics have confused themselves by lumping together, without due attention to context, passages from different parts of my book. In Chapter VI, I discuss the choice of elements for a certain constructional system; but this does not turn upon the propriety of construing certain entities as individuals. Whatever we are willing to recognize as an entity at all may be construed as an individual. But in building a system, we must consider carefully what entities we are willing to recognize at all—or better, what terms we are willing to interpret as denoting and what terms we want to interpret syncategorematically. Important as the question is, nominalism does not decide it. I have never suggested that nominalism is enough to make a system acceptable. I have suggested only that platonism is enough to make it unacceptable. But more of this later.

Now, however, is nominalism consequential at all? If the nominalist is free to construe anything he pleases as an individual, can't he even construe a class as an individual?

Whatever can be construed as a class can indeed be construed as an individual, and yet a class cannot be construed as an individual. If this seems paradoxical, it can perhaps be clarified by means of an analogy. Suppose that in a certain game a player is to begin by dealing each card from his hand onto the table at either his left or his right; he may put any card on either side and may move a card from side to side if he likes. Then while it is quite true that he is free to put any card on either side, he can never get a left-hand card on the right-hand side; for a card is a left-hand card or a right-hand card according as it lies on his left or his right. Similarly, a table is an individual, or the class of its legs and top, or the class of its molecule-classes of atoms, according to the way it is construed in a system. And whether the Great Dipper is an individual or a class of stars depends upon the system we are using. We can construe anything as an individual (and aside from nominalistic scruples we can construe anything as a class); but we can no more construe a class as an individual than we can get a left-hand card on the right-hand side.

2. THE PRINCIPLE OF NOMINALISM

In brief, while the nominalist may construe anything as an individual, he refuses to construe anything as a class. But just what is the principle of this refusal? In my book I said that, roughly speaking, the nominalist sticks at a distinction of entities without a distinction of content; and some of my critics have overlooked the more explicit formulation that soon followed. The nominalist denies that two different entities can be made up of the same entities. Let us suppose, for example, that a nominalist and a platonist start with the same minimal, atomic elements[6] for their systems; merely for comparative purposes take the number of these atoms as 5. The nominalist admits also all wholes or individual sums comprised of these, and so has a universe of 2^5-1, or 31, entities. He cannot concoct any more; for whatever individuals among the 31 are added together, the result is another individual among those 31. Our platonist, we may suppose, admits no sums of atoms but admits all classes of them. This, not counting the null and unit classes, gives him also 31 entities. But he further admits all classes of classes of atoms; and by this single step he welcomes into his universe 2^{31}-1, or over two billion, additional entities. And he has no thought of stopping there. He also admits all classes of classes of classes of atoms, and so on *ad infinitum*, climbing up through an explosively expanding universe towards a prodigiously teeming Platonic Heaven. He gets all these extra entities out of his original five by a magical process that enables him to make two or more distinct entities from exactly the same entities. And it is just here that the nominalist draws the line.

In the nominalist's world, if we start from any two distinct entities and break each of them down as far as we like (by taking parts, parts of parts, and so on), we always arrive at some entity that is contained in one but not the other of our two original entities. In the platonist's world, on the contrary, there are at least two different entities that we can so break down (by taking members, members of members, and so on) as to arrive at exactly the same entities. For instance, suppose K has two members: the class of a and b, and the class of c and d; and suppose L has two members: the class of a and c, and the class of b and d. Then although K and L are different classes, they alike break down into a, b, c, and d. Again K breaks down into the same entities as does the class having K and L as its members. These are clear cases of what the nominalist objects to as a distinction of entities without distinction of content.

This discloses the relationship between nominalism and extensionalism, which spring from a common aversion to the unwanted multiplication of entities. Extensionalism precludes the composition of more than one entity out of exactly the same entities by membership; nominalism goes further, precluding the composition of more than one entity out of the same entities by any chains of membership. For the extensionalist, two entities are identical if they break down into the same members; for the nominalist, two entities are identical if they break down in any way into the same entities. The extensionalist's restriction upon the generation of entities is a special case of the nominalist's more thoroughgoing restriction.

Nominalism describes the world as composed of individuals. To explain nominalism we need to explain not what individuals are but rather what constitutes describing the world as composed of them. So to describe the world is to describe it as made up of entities no two of which break down into exactly the same entities. What this means I have just explained, but a somewhat more technical formulation may be helpful.

Suppose we have two constructional systems, having one or more (but not necessarily the same or even the same number of) atoms. Entities other than atoms are generated in system *I* as classes, and in system *II* as sum-individuals. Let us now obliterate all purely notational differences between the two systems. We may suppose from the start that each system uses but one style of variable.[7] Then let us remove all remaining telltale signs from system I other than "ε" by expansion in terms of "ε", and similarly let us remove all peculiar signs of system II other than "≪" by expansion in terms of "≪". Finally, let us put "*R*" in for every occurrence of "ε", "ε/ε", "ε/ε/ε", etc. in system I, and for every occurrence of "≪" in system II. No purely notational distinction between the two systems remains; and "*R*" in each is irreflexive, asymmetric, and transitive. Will anything now reveal which system is which?

For each system, *x* is an atom if and only if nothing stands in the relation *R* to x[8]; and *x* is an atom of *y* (symbol: "*Axy*") if and only if *x* is an atom and is identical with or bears the relation *R* to *y*. Now in a nominalistic but not in a platonistic system, entities are the same if their atoms are the same. Thus the disguised systems will be distinguishable from each other by the fact that the nominalistic system satisfies, while the platonistic system violates, the principle:

$$(x) \, (Axy \equiv Axz) \supset y = z.^{9}$$

Obviously the disguised I will violate this principle if the system acknowledges more than $2^{n}-1$ entities, where *n* is the number of its atoms; or again, if I acknowledges any unit-classes, since the unit-class and its member will have the same atoms. But even if I is a platonistic system so restricted as to be distinguished on neither of these two scores, it will still be detectable in its disguised version through violation of the stated principle. And if I admits no two such classes, then indeed it is not platonistic at all, regardless of its notation.

This, I think, disposes of the charge that the distinction between nominalism and platonism is a mere matter of notation,[10]

and also clarifies the nominalist's dictum: "No distinction of entities without distinction of content." For a nominalistic system, no two distinct things have the same atoms; only from different atoms can different things be generated; all non-identities between things are reducible to non-identities between their atoms.

The further question must be raised whether the distinction between nominalism and platonism can be made *purely* formal? In the case we just considered, the problem was how to determine whether a given system is nominalistic or platonistic when we know that a given one of its relations is either ε* or ≪. Suppose now that we are confronted with a system without knowing anything about the interpretation of its predicates; or better, suppose we are given only the arrow-diagrams of the relations of the system. Can we determine whether the system is nominalistic or platonistic? The answer is *no*. We need to know either which elements are atoms of the system or—what amounts to the same thing—which relation is the 'generating' relation[11] of the system. Take, for example, the following diagram for a system with a single relation:

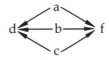

If we know that *a*, *b*, and *c* are the atoms of the system, or that the relation mapped is a generating one, then we know that the system is platonistic—since the distinct elements *d* and *f* then have exactly the same atoms. On the other hand, if we know that *a*, *b*, *c*, *d*, and *f* are all atoms of the system, then we know that the system is nominalistic. But if we do not know what the atoms are or whether the relation is a generating relation, we cannot tell whether the system is platonistic or nominalistic. Notice, though, that without such knowledge, *neither* can we tell whether a system is *extensional* or not. The system diagrammed is extensional if the relation is that of child to parent but surely not extensional if the relation is that of member to class.[12] Lest anyone gleefully welcome the apparent opportunity to dismiss both "nominalistic" and "extensional" as not purely formal characterizations of systems, I hasten to point out that no characterization of systems is purely formal in the sense implied. For if we are given just an arrow-diagram, without any interpretative information whatever, then we do not even know that the arrows represent relationships or that the letters represent elements. We can tell nothing at all about the system in question or even that there *is* a system in question; the diagram might be a hex sign or a complex character serving as the proper name of a single element. A classification of symbolic systems becomes significant only when at least some restrictions are imposed upon the interpretation of the symbols. The criterion for nominalism is formal to the same rather high degree as the usual criterion for extensionality.

What I have tried to do so far is to explain my version of nominalism. In outline, I have said that the nominalist insists on the world being described as composed of individuals, that to describe the world as composed of individuals is to describe it as made up of entities no two of which have the same content, and that this in turn is to describe it by means of a system for which no two distinct entities have exactly the same atoms.

Now, by way of justifying and defending the nominalism thus explained, I want to consider a number of objections to it.

3. ANSWERS TO OBJECTIONS

(i) Objection: The nominalism described is not really nominalism in the traditional sense.

Answer: Doubtless a good many different theses are equally legitimate descendants of earlier nominalism. I claim no more than the principle I have set forth is one reasonable formulation of the traditional injunction against undue multiplication of entities. And I willingly submit this claim to Father Bochenski for adjudication. If he

rules against me, he deprives me of nothing but a label that incites opposition.

(ii) Objection The principle of nominalism set forth is false as a statement, and groundless as a stipulation; for we know from everyday experience that different things often *are* made out of the same material, or the same particles, at different times.

Answer: The catch here is the phrase "at different times". Of course, different figures are often made out of the same lump of clay at different times; and of course, the same atoms often combine into different articles at different times. Likewise, different rooms are, so to speak, often made out of the same building at different places; and the same roads sometimes make up different crossings at different places. Admittedly, it is (spatially) different parts of the building or of the roads that are comprised in the two different rooms or the two different crossings; but so likewise, it is (temporally) different parts of the clay or the atoms that are comprised in the different figures or the different articles. We are at liberty to disregard the temporal or any other dimension we please; but if we were to rule out the spatial divisibility of buildings, or of roads, then we would not very consistently speak of the building, or a road, at different places. Similarly, if we rule out temporal divisibility, then we cannot very consistently speak of the clay, or of the atoms, *at different times*. The common experience of (different temporal parts of) the same clay making up different figures no more discredits the principle of nominalism than does the common experience of (different spatial parts of) the same building make up different rooms.

A variation on this objection points to ordered pairs like *Washington, Lincoln* and *Lincoln, Washington* as clearly illustrating the composition of different entities out of the same individuals.[13] To be pertinent, of course, this objection must not rest on any appeal to the logician's usual manner of defining these ordered pairs as distinct classes of classes; for the legitimacy of such multiple generation of classes out of the same

Universals and Abstract Entities

individuals is just what is in question. Rather the argument must be that, regardless of how ordered pairs are defined in any formal system, we have here an everyday instance of distinct things being composed of the same things. But surely this claim is not true. Normally we no more conclude that we describe different composite entities when we name two people in different order than we conclude that a house from top to bottom and the house from bottom to top are different entities, or that the capital of Massachusetts and the largest city in New England are different things. We do not take the varied histories of the Battle of Bull Run as recounting different occurrences. In daily life a multiplicity of descriptions is no evidence for a corresponding multiplicity of things described.

Thus I find in common experience nothing discordant with the principle of nominalism.

(iii) Objection: Observance of the stated principle of nominalism is no sufficient guarantee of soundness or sense in a philosophical system; for trash of almost any kind can still be brought in on the ground floor as admitted atoms of the system.

Answer: Granted. Nominalism no more guarantees philosophical soundness than the refusal to eat poison guarantees physical well-being. Many additional rules must be observed if we are to achieve either philosophical or mental health. Indeed, in some cases a moderately platonistic system with a wholesome atomic ontology may be a lesser evil than a nominalistic system that takes monstrous vacuities as its atoms—just as a very tiny dose of poison may be less harmful than a bullet in the head.

Nominalism is a necessary rather than a sufficient condition for an acceptable philosophic system. To build well we must also exercise the most scrupulous care in choosing our raw materials. A given philosopher's choice of atoms may very likely be guided by attitudes or principles that are associated with nominalism by temperament or tradition; but such associated principles are independent of nominalism as I have defined it. Nominalism does not protect us from starting with ridiculous atoms. It does protect us from manufacturing gimcracks out of sound atoms by the popular devices of platonism. Nominalism, in other words, is a restrictive rule of processing that won't select our raw materials or help us make good things out of bad materials but will help keep us from making bad things out of good materials.

(iv) Objection: To keep the rule of nominalism by generating wholes, rather than classes, of individuals costs as much as it pays; for it often means forcing the imagination to accept as individuals some scattered or heterogeneous conglomerations that are never in practice recognized as single units and are surely incomprehensible if classes are.[14]

Answer: This is perhaps the most chronic complaint against nominalism: that a progressively and in the end hopelessly strained analogy is involved in extending the application of such terms as "part", "whole", and "individual" beyond the realm of well-demarcated spatio-temporally continuous lumps. Yet as I have suggested earlier, I think this objection can be flatly and finally answered. The terminology of a system is irrelevant to the classification of the system as nominalistic or platonistic by the criterion I have explained. So long as a system admits no two distinct entities having exactly the same atoms, it is nominalistic no matter whether its generating relation is called "ε^*" or "$\ll$" or just "R", and no matter whether the values of its variables are called "classes" or "individuals" or just "entities". The words and symbols used in a system do not make it platonistic; it becomes platonistic only when it admits different entities having just the same atoms.

Thus a nominalistic system cannot put any burden on the imagination that a platonistic system does not. For the nominalist's apparatus is simply part of the platonist's apparatus. A nominalistic system can be mapped into a platonistic one. A nominalistic system is a platonistic system curtained in a specific way.

Whatever new charges may be brought against nominalism, this best-loved of all objections now deserves to be laid to rest.

(v) Objection: Nominalism is trivial for a finitist and pointless for a non-finitist, since any system with a finite ontolgy can easily be made nominalistic while a system with an infinite ontology is repugnant to any nominalist.

Answer: Take the last point first. The nominalist is unlikely to be a non-finitist only in much the way a bricklayer is unlikely to be a ballet dancer. The two things are at most incongruous, not incompatible. Obviously, by the stated criterion for nominalism, some systems with infinite ontologies are nominalistic, and some systems with finite ontologies are platonistic.

But now, Hao Wang argues,[15] any finitistic platonistic system can be easily nominalized. He does not suppose that this can be done by any immediately obvious method, but refers to an ingenious device invented by Quine.[16] Now for the moment let us suppose that this device is entirely successful. Does this mean that the nominalistic program is thereby rendered pointless and trivial? On the contrary it means that an important part of the nominalistic program has been accomplished. The nominalist, after all, is looking for a nominalistic translation of everything that seems to him worth saving. The more he succeeds in finding ways of supplanting platonistic constructions by nominalistic ones, the fewer will be the cases where platonistic apparatus need be eschewed; for we can use without qualms whatever we know how to eliminate. When Wang in effect says: "So you see these occurrences of platonism are harmless after all," he completely discounts the fact that only the nominalist's efforts removed the sting. One might as well say that the program for eradicating smallpox in the United States is trivial because there

is no smallpox around. In one sense, of course, any completed program is trivial—in just the sense that the goal of any program is to trivialize itself.

Unfortunately, however, the nominalistic program has not been so fully accomplished for all finite systems. Quine, after presenting his device, explicitly points out its fatal defects. The device can never be used in a system with an ontology embracing the entire universe; for more inscriptions will be needed to write out even a single universally quantified statement than there are things in the universe. Quine offers his device as an interesting but unsuccessful attempt, and drops it forthwith.

Thus Wang is wrong about the facts concerning Quine's device; and even if the facts were as Wang supposes, they would not support the conclusion he tries to draw.

(vi) Objection: Nominalism is impossible.

Answer: This neatly complements the charge of triviality just discussed. Call a program impossible until it is completed, and call it trivial afterwards, and you have a well-rounded defense against it. In the formal sciences we have proofs that certain problems cannot be solved—for example, the trisection of angles with straight-edge and compass alone. But nothing even resembling proof is available for the impossibility of nominalism. And parts of the program that were once confidently cited as impossible have recently been accomplished; in particular the nominalistic and even finitistic treatment of most of classical mathematics, including general definitions for "proof" and "theorem."[17]

Even if full realization of the nominalistic program ultimately does turn out to be impossible, the efforts expended on it may not be unfruitful. The impossibility of trisecting the angle with straight-edge and compass hardly detracts from the value of Euclidean geometry, or leads us to conclude that Euclid was too frugal in his choice of tools.

In the end, the nominalist may not be quite able to live within his means, but he is going to keep on trying as long as he can. Before he resorts to larceny he wants to make very sure that, and how much, he needs to steal.

(vii) Objection: Nominalism would hamper the development of mathematics and the other sciences by depriving them of methods they have used and are using to achieve some of their most important results.[18]

Answer: Not at all. The nominalist does not presume to restrict the scientist. The scientist may use platonistic class constructions, complex numbers, divination by inspection of entrails, or any claptrappery that he thinks may help him get the results he wants. But what he produces then becomes raw material for the philosopher, whose task is to make sense of all this: to clarify, simplify, explain, interpret in understandable terms. The practical scientist does the business but the philosopher keeps the books. Nominalism is a restraint that a philosopher imposes upon himself, just because he feels he cannot otherwise make real sense of what is put before him. He must digest what is fed him before he can assimilate it; but he does not expect it all to be pre-digested.

All the same, the advantages to the scientist of abundant and intricate apparatus are easily overestimated. Paucity of means often conduces to clarity and progress in science as well as in philosophy. Some scientists indeed—for example, certain workers in structural linguistics[19]—have even imposed the full restriction of nominalism upon themselves in order to avoid confusion and self-deception. The policy of 'no holds barred' may be exhilarating, but it can sometimes result in a terrible tangle.

(viii) Objection: Nominalism is bigoted. In adopting or rejecting systematic apparatus or a system-form, we ought to be governed not by a supposed insight into its intrinsic merits and defects but solely by the results we are enabled to achieve. Language and system-forms are instruments, and instruments are to be judged by how well they work. The philosopher must not handicap himself by prejudiced or dogmatic repudiations of anything that will serve his purpose.

Answer: This point is strongly urged by Carnap[20] and seems also to have been responsible for Quine's somewhat tentative defection from nominalism. But surely the nominalist does not want to exclude anything that will serve the purpose of philosophy. His critics seem to conceive of that purpose as consisting of correct prediction and the control of nature. These are certainly among the major concerns of daily life, technology, and science; but they do not constitute the primary goal of philosophy—nor, I think, of science in its more philosophical aspects. Obviously a system that predicted future events correctly but reported past events erroneously would be quickly dropped by any theoretical scientist or philosopher in his right mind. But even a true and detailed account of facts past, present, and future will leave the philosopher's work undone. As I suggested a moment ago, his task is to interrelate, systematize, interpret, explain. He is driven not by practical needs but by an impractical desire to understand. He, too, will judge a system by how well it works; but a system works for him only to the extent that it clarifies. The nominalist shuns platonistic devices precisely because he feels that their use would defeat rather than serve the purpose of philosophy. A clear story cannot be told in unintelligible language.

The nominalist cannot demonstrate the need for the restrictions he imposes upon himself. He adopts the principle of nominalism in much the same spirit that he and others adopt the principle of extensionality or that logical philosophers in general adopt the law of contradiction. None of these is amenable to proof; all are stipulated as prerequisites of soundness in a philosophic system. They are usually adopted because a philosopher's conscience gives him no choice in the matter. This does not mean that he need deny that he might some time change his mind. If the neopragmatist pushes me hard enough, I will even concede that I might some day give up the law of contradiction in the interest of getting better results—although if I should give up the law I am puzzled about what the difference would then be between getting results and not getting results. But I make this concession only if the pragmatist concedes in return that we might some day even give up his Law of Getting Results. Or does he want to exempt this as constituting the essence of the human mind?

Carnap protests eloquently against what he considers narrowmindedness in philosophy, concluding with the exhortation: "*Let us be cautious in making assertions and critical in examining them but tolerant in permitting linguistic forms*"; and Quine agrees that "the obvious counsel is tolerance and an experimental spirit."[21] Reluctant as I am to cast a shadow on all this sweetness and light, there are limits to my tolerance of tolerance. I admire the statesman tolerant of divergent political opinions, and the person tolerant of racial and educational differences; but I do not admire the accountant who is tolerant about his addition, the logician who is tolerant about his proofs, or the musician who is tolerant about his tone. In every activity, satisfactory performance requires meticulous care in some matters; and in philosophy, one of these matters is the choice of systematic apparatus or 'linguistic form'. Thus in place of Carnap's exhortation, I propose another: "*Let us, as philosophers, be utterly fastidious in choosing linguistic forms.*"

What choices fastidiousness will dictate varies with the individual philosopher. But if that were good reason for indifference, then variations in taste and belief would be good reason for indifference about quality in art and about truth in science.

4. AU REVOIR

I have explained my version of nominalism, and dealt with objections to the effect that it is not nominalism at all, that it is false or groundless, that it is too weak, that it is too strong, that it is trivial, that it is impossible, that it cripples the sciences, and that it is bigoted. Yet I by no means suppose that I have answered all the criticisms that will be or even all that have been made. Nominalism generates few entities but it arouses endless objections. The nominalist is looked upon as an intellectual vandal; and all the good neighbors rush to protect the family heirlooms against him. But the nominalist can go about his business undismayed; for his position is virtually unassailable. Every device he uses, every step he takes, is acceptable to his opponents; he makes no move that is not entirely legitimate by platonistic standards. When the nominalist and the platonist say *au revoir*, only the nominalist can be counted on to comply with the familiar parting admonition they may exchange: "Don't do anything I wouldn't do."

NOTES

[1]Victor Lowe on p. 125 of "Professor Goodman's Concept of an Individual" in the *Philosophical Review*, vol. 62 (1953), pp. 117–126.

[2]"Steps Towards a Constructive Nominalism", *Journal of Symbolic Logic*, vol. 12 (1947), pp. 105–122.

[3]See the third paragraph and the second footnote of the joint article.

[4]*From a Logical Point of View*, Harvard University Press, 1953, pp. 173–4.

[5]*The Structure of Appearance*, Harvard University Press, 1951, see especially p. 35. Incidentally (as explained in the book and later in the present article) since any nominalistic system is readily translated into a platonistic one, acceptance of most of the book by no means depends upon an acceptance of nominalism. This has been explicitly acknowledged by most of my critics.

[6]An atomic element—or atom—of a system is simply an element of the system but contains no lesser elements for the system. Depending on the system, an electron or a molecule or a planet might be taken as an atom.

[7]The aim is to take systems as nearly alike as possible, in order to isolate the critical difference.

[8]Any null class of system *I* will thus appear simply as one of the atoms of the disguised version of *I*, and thus leave no revealing trace.

[9]Both systems will satisfy the converse principle; under nominalism and platonism alike, if *x* and *y* are identical they have the same atoms.

[10] E.g. by Wang on p. 416 of "What is an Individual?" in the *Philosophical Review*, vol. 62 (1953), pp. 413–420.

[11] Given the atoms of the system, a *generating* relation is one such that if and only if x is a non-atomic element of the system will there be some element y that stands in that relation to x. *The generating relation G of a system is the relation that obtains between two elements x and y of the system if and only if x and y are connected by a chain in which each linked pair belongs to a generative relation of the system.*

[12] The system diagrammed, in fact, is extensional only if it is nominalistic, although obviously this is not true of all systems. Every system, of course, is nominalistic only if it is extensional.

[13] *Cf.* p. 110 of C.G. Hempel's article "Reflections on Nelson Goodman's *The Structure of Appearance*", in the *Philosophical Review*, vol. 62 (1953), pp. 108–116.

[14] This objection is urged, for example, by Lowe in the article cited in footnote 1 above; and is also put forth by Quine on p. 559 of his review of *The Structure of Appearance*, in the *Journal of Philosophy*, vol. 48 (1951), pp. 556–563.

[15] See the article cited in footnote 10 above.

[16] In Quine's article "On Universals" in the *Journal of Symbolic Logic*, vol. 12 (1947) pp. 74–84.

[17] In the joint article "Steps Towards a Constructive Nominalism", cited in footnote 2 above.

[18] E.g. see p. 40 of Carnap's "Empiricism, Semantics and Ontology" in the *Revue Internationale de Philosophie*, vol. 4 (1950) pp. 20–40. (Reprinted in *Semantics and the Philosophy of Language*, ed. Linsky, University of Illinois Press 1952, pp. 208–228 and in this volume).

[19] In particular, Zellig Harris and Noam Chomsky. See, for instance, the latter's "Systems of Syntactic Analysis" in the *Journal of Symbolic Logic*, vol. 18 (1953), pp. 242–256.

[20] In the article cited in footnote 18 above.

[21] *From a Logical Point of View* (see footnote 4 above), p. 19.

Empiricism, Semantics, and Ontology*

Rudolf Carnap

1. THE PROBLEM OF ABSTRACT ENTITIES

Empiricists are in general rather suspicious with respect to any kind of abstract entities like properties, classes, relations, numbers, propositions, etc. They usually feel much more in sympathy with nominalists than with realists (in the medieval sense). As far as possible they try to avoid any reference to abstract entities and to restrict themselves to what is sometimes called a nominalistic language, i.e., one not containing such references. However, within certain scientific contexts it seems hardly possible to avoid them. In the case of mathematics, some empiricists try to find a way out by treating the whole of mathematics as a mere calculus, a formal system for which no interpretation is given or can be given. Accordingly, the mathematician is said to speak not about numbers, functions, and infinite classes, but merely about meaningless symbols and formulas manipulated according to given formal rules. In

physics it is more difficult to shun the suspected entities, because the language of physics serves for the communication of reports and predictions and hence cannot be taken as a mere calculus. A physicist who is suspicious of abstract entities may perhaps try to declare a certain part of the language of physics as uninterpreted and uninterpretable, that part which refers to real numbers as space-time coordinates or as values of physical magnitudes, to functions, limits, etc. More probably he will just speak about all these things like anybody else but with an uneasy conscience, like a man who in his everyday life does with qualms many things which are not in accord with the high moral principles he professes on Sundays. Recently the problem of abstract entities has arisen again in connection with semantics, the theory of meaning and truth. Some semanticists say that certain expressions designate certain entities, and among these designated entities they include not only concrete material things but also abstract entities, e.g., properties as designated by predicates and propositions as designated by sentences.[1] Others object strongly to this procedure as violating the basic principles of empiricism and leading back to a metaphysical ontology of the Platonic kind.

It is the purpose of this article to clarify this controversial issue. The nature and implications of the acceptance of a language referring to abstract entities will first be discussed in general; it will be shown that using such a language does not imply embracing a Platonic ontology but is perfectly compatible with empiricism and strictly scientific thinking. Then the special question of the role of abstract entities in semantics will be discussed. It is hoped that the clarification of the issue will be useful to those who would like to accept abstract entities in their work in mathematics, physics, semantics, or any other field; it may help them to overcome nominalistic scruples.

2. LINGUISTIC FRAMEWORKS

Are there properties, classes, numbers, propositions? In order to understand more clearly the nature of these and related problems, it is above all necessary to recognize a fundamental distinction between two kinds of questions concerning the existence or reality of entities. If someone wishes to speak in his language about a new kind of entities, he has to introduce a system of new ways of speaking, subject to new rules; we shall call this procedure the construction of a linguistic *framework* for the new entities in question. And now we must distinguish two kinds of questions of existence: first, questions of the existence of certain entities of the new kind *within the framework*; we call them *internal questions*; and second, questions concerning the existence or reality *of the system of entities as a whole*, called *external questions*. Internal questions and possible answers to them are formulated with the help of the new forms of expressions. The answers may be found either by purely logical methods or by empirical methods, depending upon whether the framework is a logical or a factual one. An external question is of a problematic character which is in need of closer examination.

The world of things. Let us consider as an example the simplest kind of entities dealt with in the everyday language: the spatio-temporally ordered system of observable things and events. Once we have accepted the thing language with its framework for things, we can raise and answer internal questions, e.g., "Is there a white piece of paper on my desk?", "Did King Arthur actually live?", "Are unicorns and centaurs real or merely imaginary?", and the like. These questions are to be answered by empirical investigations. Results of observations are evaluated according to certain rules as confirming or disconfirming evidence for possible answers. (This evaluation is usually carried out, of course, as a matter of habit rather than a deliberate, rational procedure. But it is possible, in a rational reconstruction, to lay down explicit rules for the evaluation. This is one of the main tasks of a pure, as distinguished from a psychological, epistemology.) The concept of reality occurring in these internal questions is an empirical, scientific, non-metaphysical concept. To recognize something as a real thing or event means to succeed in incorporating it into the system of things at a particular space-time position so that it fits together with the other things recognized as real, according to the rules of the framework.

From these questions we must distinguish the external question of the reality of the thing world itself. In contrast to the former questions, this question is raised neither by the man in the street nor by scientists, but only by philosophers. Realists give an affirmative answer, subjective idealists a negative one, and the controversy goes on for centuries without ever being solved. And it cannot be solved because it is framed in a wrong way. To be real in the scientific sense means to be an element of the system; hence this concept cannot be meaningfully applied to the system itself. Those who raise the question of the reality of the thing world itself have perhaps in mind not a theoretical question as their formulation seems to suggest, but rather a practical question, a matter of a practical decision concerning the structure of our language. We have to make the choice whether or not to accept and use the forms of expression in the framework in question.

In the case of this particular example, there is usually no deliberate choice because we all have accepted the thing language early in our lives as a matter of course. Nevertheless, we may regard it as a matter of decision in this sense: we are free to choose to continue using the thing language or not; in the latter case we could restrict ourselves to a language of sense-data and other "phenomenal" entities, or construct an alternative to the customary thing language with another structure, or, finally, we could refrain from speaking. If someone decides to accept the thing language, there is no objection against saying that he has accepted the world of things. But this must not be interpreted as if it meant his acceptance of a *belief* in the reality of the thing world; there is no such belief or assertion or assumption, because it is not a theoretical question. To accept the thing world means nothing more than to accept a certain form of language, in other words, to accept rules for forming statements and for testing, accepting, or rejecting them. The acceptance of the thing language leads, on the basis of observations made, also to the acceptance, belief, and assertion of certain statements. But the thesis of the reality of the thing world cannot be among these statements, because it cannot be formulated in the thing language or, it seems, in any other theoretical language.

The decision of accepting the thing language, although itself not of a cognitive nature, will nevertheless usually be influenced by theoretical knowledge, just like any other deliberate decision concerning the acceptance of linguistic or other rules. The purposes for which the language is intended to be used, for instance, the purpose of communicating factual knowledge, will determine which factors are relevant for the decision. The efficiency, fruitfulness, and simplicity of the use of the thing language may be among the decisive factors. And the questions concerning these qualities are indeed of a theoretical nature. But these questions cannot be identified with the question of realism. They

are not yes-no questions but questions of degree. The thing language in the customary form works indeed with a high degree of efficiency for most purposes of everyday life. This is a matter of fact, based upon the content of our experiences. However, it would be wrong to describe this situation by saying: "The fact of the efficiency of the thing language is confirming evidence for the reality of the thing world"; we should rather say instead: "This fact makes it advisable to accept the thing language".

The system of numbers. As an example of a system which is of a logical rather than a factual nature let us take the system of natural numbers. The framework for this system is constructed by introducing into the language new expressions with suitable rules: (1) numerals like "five" and sentence forms like "there are five books on the table"; (2) the general term "number" for the new entities, and sentence forms like "five is a number"; (3) expressions for properties of numbers (e.g., "odd", "prime"), relations (e.g., "greater than"), and functions (e.g., "plus"), and sentence forms like "two plus three is five"; (4) numerical variables ("m", "n", etc.) and quantifiers for universal sentences ("for every n, . . .") and existential sentences ("there is an n such that . . .") with the customary deductive rules.

Here again there are internal questions, e.g., "Is there a prime number greater than a hundred?" Here, however, the answers are found, not by empirical investigation based on observations, but by logical analysis based on the rules for the new expressions. Therefore the answers are here analytic, i.e., logically true.

What is now the nature of the philosophical question concerning the existence or reality of numbers? To begin with, there is the internal question which, together with the affirmative answer, can be formulated in the new terms, say, by "There are numbers" or, more explicitly, "There is an n such that n is a number". This statement follows from the analytic statement "five is a number" and is therefore itself analytic. Moreover, it is rather trivial (in contradistinction to a statement like "There is a prime number greater than a million", which is likewise analytic but far from trivial), because it does not say more than that the new system is not empty; but this is immediately seen from the rule which states that words like "five" are substitutable for the new variables. Therefore nobody who meant the question "Are there numbers?" in the internal sense would either assert or even seriously consider a negative answer. This makes it plausible to assume that those philosophers who treat the question of the existence of numbers as a serious philosophical problem and offer lengthy arguments on either side, do not have in mind the internal question. And, indeed, if we were to ask them: "Do you mean the question as to whether the framework of numbers, *if* we were to accept it, would be found to be empty or not?", they would probably reply: "Not at all, we mean a question *prior* to the acceptance of the new framework". They might try to explain what they mean by saying that it is a question of the ontological status of numbers; the question whether or not numbers have a certain metaphysical characteristic called reality (but a kind of ideal reality, different from the material reality of the thing world) or subsistence or status of "independent entities". Unfortunately, these philosophers have so far not given a formulation of their question in terms of the common scientific language. Therefore our judgment must be that they have not succeeded in giving to the external question and to the possible answers any cognitive content. Unless and until they supply a clear cognitive interpretation, we are justified in our suspicion that their question is a pseudo-question, that is, one disguised in the form of a theoretical question while in fact it is non-theoretical; in the present case it is the practical problem whether or not to incorporate into the language the new linguistic forms which constitute the framework of numbers.

The system of propositions. New variables, "*p*", "*q*", etc., are introduced with a rule to the effect that any (declarative) sentence may be substituted for a variable of this kind; this includes, in addition to the sentences of the original thing language, also all general sentences with variables of any kind which may have been introduced into the language. Further, the general term "proposition" is introduced. "*p* is a proposition" may be defined by "*p* or not *p*" (or by any other sentence form yielding only analytic sentences). Therefore, every sentence of the form ". . . is a proposition" (where any sentence may stand in the place of the dots) is analytic. This holds, for example, for the sentence:

(a) "Chicago is large is a proposition."

(We disregard here the fact that the rules of English grammar require not a sentence but a that-clause as the subject of another sentence; accordingly, instead of (*a*) we should have to say "That Chicago is large is a proposition".) Predicates may be admitted whose argument expressions are sentences; these predicates may be either extensional (e.g., the customary truth-functional connectives) or not (e.g., modal predicates like "possible", "necessary", etc.) With the help of the new variables, general sentences may be formed, e.g.,

(b) "For every *p*, either *p* or not-*p*".
(c) "There is a *p* such that *p* is not necessary and not-*p* is not necessary".
(d) "There is a *p* such that *p* is a proposition".

(*c*) and (*d*) are internal assertions of existence. The statement "There are propositions" may be meant in the sense of (*d*); in this case it is analytic (since it follows from (*a*)) and even trivial. If, however, the statement is meant in an external sense, then it is non-cognitive.

It is important to notice that the system of rules for the linguistic expressions of the propositional framework (of which only a few rules have here been briefly indicated) is sufficient for the introduction of the framework. Any further explanations as to the nature of the propositions (i.e., the elements of the system indicated, the values of the variables "*p*", "*q*", etc.) are theoretically unnecessary because, if correct, they follow from the rules. For example, are propositions mental events (as in Russell's theory)? A look at the rules shows us that they are not, because otherwise existential statements would be of the form: "If the mental state of the person in question fulfils such and such conditions, then there is a *p* such that . . .". The fact that no references to mental conditions occur in existential statements (like (*c*), (*d*), etc.) shows that propositions are not mental entities. Further, a statement of the existence of linguistic entities (e.g., expressions, classes of expressions, etc.) must contain a reference to a language. The fact that no such reference occurs in the existential statements here, shows that propositions are not linguistic entities. The fact that in these statements no reference to a subject (an observer or knower) occurs (nothing like: "There is a *p* which is necessary for Mr. *X*"), shows that the propositions (and their properties, like necessity, etc.) are not subjective. Although characterizations of these or similar kinds are, strictly speaking, unnecessary, they may nevertheless be practically useful. If they are given, they should be understood, not as ingredient parts of the system, but merely as marginal notes with the purpose of supplying to the reader helpful hints or convenient pictorial associations which may make his learning of the use of the expressions easier than the bare system of the rules would do. Such a characterization is analogous to an extrasystematic explanation which a physicist sometimes gives to the beginner. He might, for example, tell him to imagine the atoms of a gas as small balls rushing around with great speed, or the electromagnetic field and its oscillations as quasi-elastic tensions and vibrations in an ether. In fact, however, all that can accurately be said about atoms or the field is implicitly contained in the physical laws of the theories in question.[2]

The system of thing properties. The thing language contains words like "red", "hard", "stone", "house", etc., which are used for describing what things are like. Now we may introduce new variables, say "*f*", "*g*", etc., for which those words are substitutable and furthermore the general term "property". New rules are laid down which admit sentences like "Red is a property", "Red is a color", "These two pieces of paper have at least one color in common" (i.e., "There is an *f* such that *f* is a color, and . . ."). The last sentence is an internal assertion. It is of an empirical, factual nature. However, the external statement, the philosophical statement of the reality of properties—a special case of the thesis of the reality of universals—is devoid of cognitive content.

The systems of integers and rational numbers. Into a language containing the framework of natural numbers we may introduce first the (positive and negative) integers as relations among natural numbers and then the rational numbers as relations among integers. This involves introducing new types of variables, expressions substitutable for them, and the general terms "integer" and "rational number".

The system of real numbers. On the basis of the rational numbers, the real numbers may be introduced as classes of a special kind (segments) of rational numbers (according to the method developed by Dedekind and Frege). Here again a new type of variables is introduced, expressions substitutable for them (e.g., "$\sqrt{2}$"), and the general term "real number".

The spatio-temporal coordinate system for physics. The new entities are the space-time points. Each is an ordered quadruple of four real numbers, called its coordinates, consisting of three spatial and one temporal coordinates. The physical state of spatio-temporal point or region is described either with the help of qualitative predicates (e.g., "hot") or by ascribing numbers as values of a physical magnitude (e.g., mass, temperature, and the like). The step from the system of things (which does not contain space-time points but only extended objects with spatial and temporal relations between them) to the physical coordinate system is again a matter of decision. Our choice of certain features, although itself not theoretical, is suggested by theoretical knowledge, either logical or factual. For example, the choice of real numbers rather than rational numbers or integers as coordinates is not much influenced by the facts of experience but mainly due to considerations of mathematical simplicity. The restriction to rational coordinates would not be in conflict with any experimental knowledge we have, because the result of any measurement is a rational number. However, it would prevent the use of ordinary geometry (which says, e.g., that the diagonal of a square with the side 1 has the irrational value $\sqrt{2}$) and thus lead to great complications. On the other hand, the decision to use three rather than two or four spatial coordinates is strongly suggested, but still not forced upon us, by the result of common observations. If certain events allegedly observed in spiritualistic séances, e.g., a ball moving out of a sealed box, were confirmed beyond any reasonable doubt, it might seem advisable to use four spatial coordinates. Internal questions are here, in general, empirical questions to be answered by empirical investigations. On the other hand, the external questions of the reality of physical space and physical time are pseudo-questions. A question like "Are there (really) space-time points?" is ambiguous. It may be meant as an internal question; then the affirmative answer is, of course, analytic and trivial. Or it may be meant in the external sense: "Shall we introduce such and such forms into our language?"; in this case it is not a theoretical but a practical question, a matter of decision rather than assertion, and hence the proposed formulation would be misleading. Or finally, it may be meant in the following sense: "Are our experiences such that the use of the linguistic forms in question will be expedient and fruitful?" This is a theoretical question of a factual, empirical nature. But it concerns a matter of degree;

therefore a formulation in the form "real or not?" would be inadequate.

3. WHAT DOES ACCEPTANCE OF A KIND OF ENTITIES MEAN?

Let us now summarize the essential characteristics of situations involving the introduction of a new kind of entities, characteristics which are common to the various examples outlined above.

The acceptance of a new kind of entities is represented in the language by the introduction of a framework of new forms of expressions to be used according to a new set of rules. There may be new names for particular entities of the kind in question; but some such names may already occur in the language before the introduction of the new framework. (Thus, for example, the thing language contains certainly words of the type of "blue" and "house" before the framework of properties is introduced; and it may contain words like "ten" in sentences of the form "I have ten fingers" before the framework of numbers is introduced.) The latter fact shows that the occurrence of constants of the type in question—regarded as names of entities of the new kind after the new framework is introduced—is not a sure sign of the acceptance of the new kind of entities. Therefore the introduction of such constants is not to be regarded as an essential step in the introduction of the framework. The two essential steps are rather the following. First, the introduction of a general term, a predicate of higher level, for the new kind of entities, permitting us to say of any particular entity that it belongs to this kind (e.g., "Red is a *property*", "Five is a *number*"). Second, the introduction of variables of the new type. The new entities are values of these variables; the constants (and the closed compound expressions, if any) are substitutable for the variables.[3] With the help of the variables, general sentences concerning the new entities can be formulated.

After the new forms are introduced into the language, it is possible to formulate with their help internal questions and possible answers to them. A question of this kind may be either empirical or logical; accordingly a true answer is either factually true or analytic.

From the internal questions we must clearly distinguish external questions, i.e., philosophical questions concerning the existence or reality of the total system of the new entities. Many philosophers regard a question of this kind as an ontological question which must be raised and answered *before* the introduction of the new language forms. The latter introduction, they believe, is legitimate only if it can be justified by an ontological insight supplying an affirmative answer to the question of reality. In contrast to this view, we take the position that the introduction of the new ways of speaking does not need any theoretical justification because it does not imply any assertion of reality. We may still speak (and have done so) of "the acceptance of the new entities" since this form of speech is customary; but one must keep in mind that this phrase does not mean for us anything more than acceptance of the new framework, i.e., of the new linguistic forms. Above all, it must not be interpreted as referring to an assumption, belief, or assertion of "the reality of the entities". There is no such assertion. An alleged statement of the reality of the system of entities is a pseudo-statement without cognitive content. To be sure, we have to face at this point an important question; but it is a practical, not a theoretical question; it is the question of whether or not to accept the new linguistic forms. The acceptance cannot be judged as being either true or false because it is not an assertion. It can only be judged as being more or less expedient, fruitful, conducive to the aim for which the language is intended. Judgments of this kind supply the motivation for the decision of accepting or rejecting the kind of entities.[4]

Thus it is clear that the acceptance of a linguistic framework must not be regarded as implying a metaphysical doctrine concerning the reality of the entities in question. It seems to me due to a neglect of this important distinction that some contempo-

rary nominalists label the admission of variables of abstract types as "Platonism".[5] This is, to say the least, an extremely misleading terminology. It leads to the absurd consequence, that the position of everybody who accepts the language of physics with its real number variables (as a language of communication, not merely as a calculus) would be called Platonistic, even if he is a strict empiricist who rejects Platonic metaphysics.

A brief historical remark may here be inserted. The non-cognitive character of the questions which we have called here external questions was recognized and emphasized already by the Vienna Circle under the leadership of Moritz Schlick, the group from which the movement of logical empiricism originated. Influenced by ideas of Ludwig Wittgenstein, the Circle rejected both the thesis of the reality of the external world and the thesis of its irreality as pseudo-statements;[6] the same was the case for both the thesis of the reality of univerals (abstract entities, in our present terminology) and the nominalistic thesis that they are not real and that their alleged names are not names of anything but merely *flatus vocis*. (It is obvious that the apparent negation of a pseudo-statement must also be a pseudo-statement.) It is therefore not correct to classify the members of the Vienna Circle as nominalists, as is sometimes done. However, if we look at the basic anti-metaphysical and pro-scientific attitude of most nominalists (and the same holds for many materialists and realists in the modern sense), disregarding their occasional pseudo-theoretical formulations, then it is, of course, true to say that the Vienna Circle was much closer to those philosophers than to their opponents.

4. ABSTRACT ENTITIES IN SEMANTICS

The problem of the legitimacy and the status of abstract entities has recently again led to controversial discussions in connection with semantics. In a semantical meaning analysis certain expressions in a language are often said to designate (or name or denote or signify or refer to) certain extra-linguistic entities.[7] As long as physical things or events (e.g., Chicago or Caesar's death) are taken as designata (entities designated), no serious doubts arise. But strong objections have been raised, especially by some empiricists, against abstract entities as designata, e.g., against semantic statements of the following kind:

1. "The word 'red' designates a property of things";
2. "The word 'color' designates a property of properties of things";
3. "The word 'five' designates a number";
4. "The word 'odd' designates a property of numbers";
5. "The sentence 'Chicago is large' designates a proposition".

Those who criticize these statements do not, of course, reject the use of the expressions in question, like "red" or "five"; nor would they deny that these expressions are meaningful. But to be meaningful, they would say, is not the same as having a meaning in the sense of an entity designated. They reject the belief, which they regard as implicitly presupposed by those semantic statements, that to each expression of the types in question (adjectives like "red", numbers like "five", etc.) there is a particular real entity to which the expression stands in the relation of designation. This belief is rejected as incompatible with the basic principles of empiricism or of scientific thinking. Derogatory labels like "Platonic realism", "hypostatization", or " 'Fido'-Fido principle" are attached to it. The latter is the name given by Gilbert Ryle to the criticized belief, which, in his view, arises by a naïve inference of analogy: just as there is an entity well known to me, viz. my dog Fido, which is designated by the name "Fido", thus there must be for every meaningful expression a particular entity to which it stands in the relation of designation or naming, i.e., the relation exemplified by "Fido"-Fido. The belief criticized is thus a case of hypostatization, i.e., of treating as names expressions which are not

names. While "Fido" is a name, expressions like "red", "five", etc., are said not to be names, not to designate anything.

Our previous discussion concerning the acceptance of frameworks enables us now to clarify the situation with respect to abstract entities as designata. Let us take as an example the statement:

(a) " 'Five' designates a number".

The formulation of this statement presupposes that our language L contains the forms of expressions which we have called the framework of numbers, in particular, numerical variables and the general term "number". If L contains these forms, the following is an analytic statement in L:

(b) "Five is a number".

Further, to make the statement (a) possible, L must contain an expression like "designates" or "is a name of" for the semantic relation of designation. If suitable rules for this term are laid down, the following is likewise analytic:

(c) " 'Five' designates five".

(Generally speaking, any expression of the form " '. . .' designates . . ." is an analytic statement provided the term ". . ." is a constant in an accepted framework. If the latter condition is not fulfilled, the expression is not a statement.) Since (a) follows from (c) and (b), (a) is likewise analytic.

Thus it is clear that *if* someone accepts the framework of numbers, then he must acknowledge (c) and (b) and hence (a) as true statements. Generally speaking, if someone accepts a framework for a certain kind of entities, then he is bound to admit the entities as possible designata. Thus the question of the admissibility of entities of a certain type or of abstract entities in general as designata is reduced to the question of the acceptability of the linguistic framework for those entities. Both the nominalistic critics, who refuse the status of designators or names to expressions like "red", "five", etc., because they deny the existence of abstract entities, and the skeptics, who express doubts concerning the existence and demand evidence for it, treat the question of existence as a theoretical question. They do, of course, not mean the internal question;

the affirmative answer to *this* question is analytic and trivial and too obvious for doubt or denial, as we have seen. Their doubts refer rather to the system of entities itself; hence they mean the external question. They believe that only after making sure that there really is a system of entities of the kind in question are we justified in accepting the framework by incorporating the linguistic forms into our language. However, we have seen that the external question is not a theoretical question but rather the practical question whether or not to accept those linguistic forms. This acceptance is not in need of a theoretical justification (except with respect to expediency and fruitfulness), because it does not imply a belief or assertion. Ryle says that the "Fido"-Fido principle is "a grotesque theory". Grotesque or not, Ryle is wrong in calling it a theory. It is rather the practical decision to accept certain frameworks. Maybe Ryle is historically right with respect to those whom he mentions as previous representatives of the principle, viz. John Stuart Mill, Frege, and Russell. If these philosophers regarded the acceptance of a system of entities as a theory, an assertion, they were victims of the same old, metaphysical confusion. But it is certainly wrong to regard *my* semantic method as involving a belief in the reality of abstract entities, since I reject a thesis of this kind as a metaphysical pseudo-statement.

The critics of the use of abstract entities in semantics overlook the fundamental difference between the acceptance of a system of entities and an internal assertion, e.g., an assertion that there are elephants or electrons or prime numbers greater than a million. Whoever makes an internal assertion is certainly obliged to justify it by providing evidence, empirical evidence in the case of electrons, logical proof in the case of the prime numbers. The demand for a theoretical justification, correct in the case of internal assertions, is sometimes wrongly applied to the acceptance of a system of entities. Thus, for example, Ernest Nagel asks for "evidence relevant for affirming with warrant that there are such entities as infinitesimals or propositions". He characterizes the evidence required in these cases—in distinction to the

empirical evidence in the case of electrons—as "in the broad sense logical and dialectical". Beyond this no hint is given as to what might be regarded as relevant evidence. Some nominalists regard the acceptance of abstract entities as a kind of superstition or myth, populating the world with fictitious or at least dubious entities, analogous to the belief in centaurs or demons. This shows again the confusion mentioned, because a superstition or myth is a false (or dubious) internal statement.

Let us take as example the natural numbers as cardinal numbers, i.e., in contexts like "Here are three books". The linguistic forms of the framework of numbers, including variables and the general term "number", are generally used in our common language of communication; and it is easy to formulate explicit rules for their use. Thus the logical characteristics of this framework are sufficiently clear (while many internal questions, i.e., arithmetical questions, are, of course, still open). In spite of this, the controversy concerning the external question of the ontological reality of the system of numbers continues. Suppose that one philosopher says: "I believe that there are numbers as real entities. This gives me the right to use the linguistic forms of the numerical framework and to make semantical statements about numbers as designata of numerals". His nominalistic opponent replies: "You are wrong; there are no numbers. The numerals may still be used as meaningful expressions. But they are not names, there are no entities designated by them. Therefore the word "number" and numerical variables must not be used (unless a way were found to introduce them as merely abbreviating devices, a way of translating them into the nominalistic thing language)." I cannot think of any possible evidence that would be regarded as relevant by both philosophers, and therefore, if actually found, would decide the controversy or at least make one of the opposite theses more probable than the other. (To construe the numbers as classes or properties of the second level, according to the Frege-Russell method, does, of course, not solve the controversy, because the first philosopher would affirm and the second deny the existence of the system of classes or properties of the second level.) Therefore I feel compelled to regard the external question as a pseudo-question, until both parties to the controversy offer a common interpretation of the question as a cognitive question; this would involve an indication of possible evidence regarded as relevant by both sides.

There is a particular kind of misinterpretation of the acceptance of abstract entities in various fields of science and in semantics, that needs to be cleared up. Certain early British empiricists (e.g., Berkeley and Hume) denied the existence of abstract entities on the ground that immediate experience presents us only with particulars, not with universals, e.g., with this red patch, but not with Redness or Color-in-General; with this scalene triangle, but not with Scalene Triangularity or Triangularity-in-General. Only entities belonging to a type of which examples were to be found within immediate experience could be accepted as ultimate constituents of reality. Thus, according to this way of thinking, the existence of abstract entities could be asserted only if one could show either that some abstract entities fall within the given, or that abstract entities can be defined in terms of the types of entity which are given. Since these empiricists found no abstract entities within the realm of sense-data, they either denied their existence, or else made a futile attempt to define universals in terms of particulars. Some contemporary philosophers, especially English philosophers following Bertrand Russell, think in basically similar terms. They emphasize a distinction between the data (that which is immediately given in consciousness, e.g., sense-data, immediately past experiences, etc.) and the constructs based on the data. Existence or reality is ascribed only to the data; the constructs are not real entities; the corresponding linguistic expressions are merely ways of speech not actually designating anything (reminiscent of the nominalists' *flatus vocis*). We shall not criticize here this general conception. (As far as it is a principle of accepting certain entities and not accepting others, leaving aside any ontological, phenomenalistic and nominalistic

pseudo-statements, there cannot be any theoretical objection to it.) But if this conception leads to the view that other philosophers or scientists who accept abstract entities thereby assert or imply their occurrence as immediate data, then such a view must be rejected as a misinterpretation. References to space-time points, the electromagnetic field, or electrons in physics, to real or complex numbers and their functions in mathematics, to the excitatory potential or unconscious complexes in psychology, to an inflationary trend in economics, and the like, do not imply the assertion that entities of these kinds occur as immediate data. And the same holds for references to abstract entities as designata in semantics. Some of the criticisms by English philosophers against such references give the impression that, probably due to the misinterpretation just indicated, they accuse the semanticist not so much of bad metaphysics (as some nominalists would do) but of bad psychology. The fact that they regard a semantical method involving abstract entities not merely as doubtful and perhaps wrong, but as manifestly absurd, preposterous and grotesque, and that they show a deep horror and indignation against this method, is perhaps to be explained by a misinterpretation of the kind described. In fact, of course, the semanticist does not in the least assert or imply that the abstract entities to which he refers can be experienced as immediately given either by sensation or by a kind of rational intuition. An assertion of this kind would indeed be very dubious psychology. The psychological question as to which kinds of entities do and which do not occur as immediate data is entirely irrelevant for semantics, just as it is for physics, mathematics, economics, etc., with respect to the examples mentioned above.[8]

5. CONCLUSION

For those who want to develop or use semantical methods, the decisive question is not the alleged ontological question of the existence of abstract entities but rather the question whether the use of abstract linguistic forms or, in technical terms, the use of variables beyond those for things (or phenomenal data), is expedient and fruitful for the purposes for which semantic analyses are made, viz. the analysis, interpretation, clarification, or construction of languages of communication, especially languages of science. This question is here neither decided nor even discussed. It is not a question simply of yes or no, but a matter of degree. Among those philosophers who have carried out semantical analyses and thought about suitable tools for this work, beginning with Plato and Aristotle and, in a more technical way on the basis of modern logic, with C. S. Peirce and Frege, a great majority accepted abstract entities. This does, of course, not prove the case. After all, semantics in the technical sense is still in the initial phases of its development, and we must be prepared for possible fundamental changes in methods. Let us therefore admit that the nominalistic critics may possibly be right. But if so, they will have to offer better arguments than they have so far. Appeal to ontological insight will not carry much weight. The critics will have to show that it is possible to construct a semantical method which avoids all references to abstract entities and achieves by simpler means essentially the same results as the other methods.

The acceptance or rejection of abstract linguistic forms, just as the acceptance or rejection of any other linguistic forms in any branch of science, will finally be decided by their efficiency as instruments, the ratio of the results achieved to the amount and complexity of the efforts required. To decree dogmatic prohibitions of certain linguistic forms instead of testing them by their success or failure in practical use, is worse than futile; it is positively harmful because it may obstruct scientific progress. The history of science shows examples of such prohibitions based on prejudices deriving from religious, mythological, metaphysical, or other irrational sources, which slowed up the developments for shorter or longer periods of time. Let us learn from the lessons of history. Let us grant to those who work in any special field of investigation the freedom to use any form of expression which seems useful to them; the work in the field will sooner or later lead to the elimination of those forms which have no useful function. *Let us be cautious in making assertions and critical in examining them, but tolerant in permitting linguistic forms.*

NOTES

[1] The terms "sentence" and "statement" are here used synonymously for declarative (indicative, propositional) sentences.

[2] In my book *Meaning and Necessity* (Chicago, 1947) I have developed a semantical method which takes propositions as entities designated by sentences (more specifically, as intensions of sentences). In order to facilitate the understanding of the systematic development, I added some informal, extra-systematic explanations concerning the nature of propositions. I said that the term "proposition" "is used neither for a linguistic expression nor for a subjective, mental occurrence, but rather for something objective that may or may not be exemplified in nature. . . . We apply the term 'proposition' to any entities of a certain logical type, namely, those that may be expressed by (declarative) sentences in a language" (p. 27). After some more detailed discussions concerning the relation between propositions and facts, and the nature of false propositions, I added: "It has been the purpose of the preceding remarks to facilitate the understanding of our conception of propositions. If, however, a reader should find these explanations more puzzling than clarifying, or even unacceptable, he may disregard them" (p. 31) (that is, disregard these extra-systematic explanations, not the whole theory of the propositions as intensions of sentences, as one reviewer understood). In spite of this warning, it seems that some of those readers who were puzzled by the explanations, did not disregard them but thought that by raising objections against them they could refute the theory. This is analogous to the procedure of some laymen who by (correctly) criticizing the ether picture or other visualizations of physical theories, thought they had refuted those theories. Perhaps the discussions in the present paper will help in clarifying the role of the system of linguistic rules for the introduction of a framework for entities on the one hand, and that of extra-systematic explanations concerning the nature of the entities on the other.

[3] W. V. Quine was the first to recognize the importance of the introduction of variables as indicating the

acceptance of entities. "The ontology to which one's use of language commits him comprises simply the objects that he treats as falling . . . within the range of values of his variables."

[4] For a closely related point of view on these questions see the detailed dicussions in Herbert Feigl, "Existential Hypotheses", *Philosophy of Science*, 17 (1950), 35–62.

[5] Paul Bernays, "Sur le platonisme dans les mathématiques" (*L'Enseignement math.*, 34 (1935), 52–69).

[6] See Carnap, *Scheinprobleme in der Philosophie; das Fremdpsychische und der Realismusstreit*, Berlin, 1928. Moritz Schlick, *Positivismus und Realismus*, reprinted in *Gesammelte Aufsätze*, Wien, 1938.

[7] See *Meaning and Necessity* (Chicago, 1947). The distinction I have drawn in the latter book between the method of the name-relation and the method of intension and extension is not essential for our present discussion. The term "designation" is used in the present article in a neutral way; it may be understood as referring to the name-relation or to the intension-relation or to the extension-relation or to any similar relations used in other semantical methods.

[8] Wilfrid Sellars ("Acquaintance and Description Again", in *Journal of Philosophy*, 46 (1949), 496–504; see pp. 502 f.) analyzes clearly the roots of the mistake "of taking the designation relation of semantic theory to be a reconstruction of *being present to an experience*".

Universals and Family Resemblances*

Renford Bambrough

I believe that Wittgenstein solved what is known as "the problem of universals", and I would say of his solution, as Hume said of Berkeley's treatment of the same topic, that it is "one of the greatest and most valuable discoveries that has been made of late years in the republic of letters."

I do not expect these claims to be accepted by many philsophers.

Since I claim that Wittgenstein solved the problem I naturally do not claim to be making an original contribution to the study of it. Since I recognise that few philosophers will accept my claim that Wittgenstein solved it, I naturally regard it as worth while to continue to discuss the problem. My purpose is to try to make clear what Wittgenstein's solution is and to try to make clear that it is a solution.

Philosophers ought to be wary of claiming that philosophical problems have been finally solved. Aristotle and Descartes and Spinoza and Berkeley and Hume and the author of the *Tractatus Logico-Philosophicus* lie at the bottom of the sea not far from this rock, with the skeletons of many lesser men to keep them company. But nobody suggests that their journeys were vain, or that nothing can be saved from the wrecks.

In seeking for Wittgenstein's solution we must look mainly to his remarks about "family resemblances" and to his use of the example of games. In the *Blue Book* he speaks of "our craving for generality" and tries to trace this craving to its sources:

> This craving for generality is the resultant of a number of tendencies connected with particular philosophical confusions. There is—
>
> (*a*) The tendency to look for something in common to all the entities which we commonly subsume under a general term.—We are inclined to think that there must be something in common to all games, say, and that this common property is the justification for applying the general term "game" to the various games; whereas games form a *family* the members of which have family likenesses. Some of them have the same nose, others the same eyebrows and others again the same way of walking; and these likenesses overlap. The idea of a general concept being a common prop-

*Copyright © The Aristotelian Society 1960. Reprinted by permission of the Editor, from *Proceedings of the Aristotelian Society* 60 (1960–61), 207–22.

erty of its particular instances connects up with other primitive, too simple, ideas of the structure of language. It is comparable to the idea that *properties* are *ingredients* of the things which have the properties; *e.g.*, that beauty is an ingredient of all beautiful things as alcohol is of beer and wine, and that we therefore could have pure beauty, unadulterated by anything that is beautiful.

(*b*) There is a tendency rooted in our usual forms of expression, to think that the man who has learnt to understand a general term, say, the term "leaf", has thereby come to possess a kind of general picture of a leaf, as opposed to pictures of particular leaves. He was shown different leaves when he learnt the meaning of the word "leaf"; and showing him the particular leaves was only a means to the end of producing "in him" an idea which we imagine to be some kind of general image. We say that he sees what is in common to all these leaves; and this is true if we mean that he can on being asked tell us certain features or properties which they have in common. But we are inclined to think that the general idea of a leaf is something like a visual image, but one which only contains what is common to all leaves. (Galtonian composite photograph.) This again is connected with the idea that the meaning of a word is an image, or a thing correlated to the word. (This roughly means, we are looking at words as though they all were proper names, and we then confuse the bearer of a name with the meaning of the name.) (Pp. 17–18).

In the *Philosophical Investigations* Wittgenstein again speaks of family resemblances, and gives a more elaborate account of the similarities and differences between various games:

66. Consider for example the proceedings that we call "games". I mean board-games, card-games, ball-games, Olympic games, and so on. What is common to them all?—Don't say: "there *must* be something common, or they would not be called 'games'—but *look and see* whether there is anything common to all. — For if you look at them you will not see something that is common to *all*, but similarities, relationships, and a whole series of them at that. To repeat: don't think, but look!—Look for example at board-games, with their multifarious relationships. Now pass to card-games; here you find many correspondences with the first group, but many common features drop out, and others appear. When we pass next to ball-games, much that is common is retained, but much is lost.—Are they all "amusing"? Compare chess with noughts and crosses. Or is there always winning and losing, or competition between players? Think of patience. In ball-games there is winning and losing; but when a child throws his ball at the wall and catches it again, this feature has disappeared. Look at the parts played by skill and luck; and at the difference between skill in chess and skill in tennis. Think now of games like ring-a-ring-a-roses; here is the element of amusement, but how many other characteristic features have disappeared! And we can go through the many, many other groups of games in the same way; can see how similarities crop up and disappear.

And the result of this examination is: we see a complicated network of similarities overlapping and criss-crossing: sometimes overall similarities, sometimes similarities of detail.

67. I can think of no better expression to characterise these similarities than "family resemblances"; for the various resemblances between the members of a family: build, features, colour of eyes, gait, temperament, etc. etc. overlap and criss-cross in the same way.—And I shall say: "games" form a family.

Wittgenstein expounds his analogy informally, and with great economy. Its power can be displayed in an equally simple but more formal way by considering a situation that is familiar to botanical taxonomists.[1] We may classify a set of objects by reference to the presence or absence of features *ABCDE*. It may well happen that five objects *edcba* are such that each of them has four of these properties and lacks the fifth, and that the missing feature is different in each of the five cases. A simple diagram will illustrate this situation:

e	*d*	*c*	*b*	*a*
ABCD	*ABCE*	*ABDE*	*ACDE*	*BCDE*

Here we can already see how natural and how proper it might be to apply the same word to a number of objects between which there is no common feature. And if we confine our attention to any arbitrarily selected four of these objects, say *edca*, then although they all *happen* to have *B* in common, it is clear that it is not in virtue of the presence of *B* that they are all rightly called by the same name. Even if the actual instances were indefinitely numerous, and they all happened to have one or more of the features in common, it would not be in virtue of the presence of the common feature or features that they would all be rightly called by the same name, since the name also applies to *possible* instances that lack the feature or features.

The richness of the possibilities of the family resemblances model becomes more striking still if we set it out more fully and formally in terms of a particular family than Wittgenstein himself ever did. Let us suppose that "the Churchill face" is strikingly and obviously present in each of ten members of the Churchill family, and that when a family group photograph is set before us it is unmistakable that these ten people all belong to the same family. It may be that there are ten features in terms of which we can describe "the family face" (high forehead, bushy eyebrows, blue eyes, Roman nose, high cheekbones, cleft chin, dark hair, dimpled cheeks, pointed ears and ruddy complexion). It is obvious that the unmistakable presence of the family face in every single one of the ten members of the family is compatible with the absence from each of the ten members of the family of

one of the ten constituent features of the family face. It is also obvious that it does not matter if it happens that the feature which is absent from the face of each individual member of the family is present in every one of the others. The members of the family will then have no *feature* in common, and yet they will all unmistakably have *the Churchill face* in common.

This example is very artificial, and it may seem at first sight that its artificiality plays into my hands. But on the contrary, the more natural the example is made the more it suits my purpose. If we remember that a family face does not divide neatly into ten separate features, we widen rather than reduce the scope for large numbers of instances of the family face to lack a single common feature. And if we remember that what goes for faces goes for features too; that all cleft chins have nothing in common except that they are cleft chins, that the possible gradations from Roman nose to snub nose or from high to low cheekbones are continuous and infinite, we see that there could in principle be an infinite number of unmistakable Churchill faces which had no feature in common. In fact it now becomes clear that there is a good sense in which *no two* members of the Churchill family need have *any* feature in common in order for *all* the members of the Churchill family to have the Churchill face.

The passages that I have quoted contain the essence of Wittgenstein's solution of the problem of universals, but they are far from exhausting his account of the topic. Not only are there other places where he speaks of games and of family resemblances: what is more important is that most of his philosophical remarks in *The Blue and Brown Books* and in the *Philosophical Investigations* are concerned with such questions as "What is the meaning of a word?" "What is language?" "What is thinking?" "What is understanding?" And these questions are various forms of the question to which theories of universals, including Wittgenstein's theory of universals, are meant to be answers. There is a clear parallel between what Wittgenstein says about games and what he says about reading, expecting, languages, numbers, propositions; in all these cases we have the idea that there is a common element or ingredient, and Wittgenstein shows us that there is no such ingredient or element. The instances that fall under each of these concepts *form a family*.

It is already clear that the point Wittgenstein made with the example of games has a much wider range of application than that example itself. But exactly how wide is its application meant to be? Wittgenstein's own method of exposition makes it difficult to answer the question. In his striving to find a cure for "our craving for generality," in his polemic against "the contemptuous attitude towards the particular case," he was understandably wary of expressing his own conclusions in general terms. Readers and expositors of Wittgenstein are consequently impelled to make use of glosses and paraphrases and interpretations if they wish to relate his work to philosophical writings and doctrines that are expressed in another idiom; that is to say, to most other philosophical writings and doctrines.

I believe that this is why Wittgenstein's solution of the problem of universals has not been widely understood, and why, in consequence, it has not been widely seen to be a solution.[2] In avoiding the generalities that are characteristic of most philosophical discussion he also avoided reference to the standard "problems of philosophy" and to the "philosophical theories" which have repeatedly been offered as answers to them. He talks about games and families and colours, about reading, expecting and understanding, but not about "the problem of universals." He practised an activity which is "one of the heirs of the subject which used to be called 'philosophy' ", but he did not relate the results of his activity to the results of the enquiries to which it was an heir. He did not, for example, plot the relation between his remarks on games and family resemblances and the doctrines of those philosophers who had been called Nominalists and Realists.

When I claim that Wittgenstein solved the problem of universals I am claiming that his remarks can be paraphrased into a doctrine which can be set out in general terms and can be related to the traditional theories, and which can then be shown to deserve to supersede the traditional theories. My purpose in this paper is to expound such a doctrine and to defend it.

But first I must return to my question about the range of application of the point that is made by the example of games, since it is at this crucial first stage that most readers of Wittgenstein go wrong. When we read what he says about games and family resemblances, we are naturally inclined to ask ourselves, "With what kinds of concepts is Wittgenstein *contrasting* the concepts of game, language, proposition, understanding?" I shall consider three possible answers to this question.

The first answer is suggested by Professor Ayer's remarks about games and family resemblances on pp. 10–12 of *The Problem of Knowledge*. Ayer contrasts the word "game" with the word "red", on the ground that the former does not, while the latter does, mark "a simple and straightforward resemblance" between the things to which the word is applied. He claims that, "The point which Wittgenstein's argument brings out is that the resemblance between the things to which the same word applies may be of different degrees. It is looser and less straightforward in some cases than in others." Now this contrast between simple and complicated concepts is important, and the games example is a convenient means of drawing attention to it, but I am sure that this is not the point that Wittgenstein was making with his example. In the *Brown Book* (p. 131) he asks, "Could you tell me what is in common between a light red and a dark red?" and in the *Philosophical Investigations* (Section 73) he asks, "Which shade is the 'sample in my mind' of the colour green—the sample of what is common to all shades of green?" Wittgenstein could as easily have used the example of red things as the example of games to illustrate "the tendency to look for something in common to all the entities which we commonly subsume under a general term." Just as cricket and chess and patience and ring-a-ring-a-roses have nothing in common *except that they are games,* so poppies and blood and pillar-boxes and hunting-coats have nothing in common *except that they are red.*

A second possible answer is implied by a sentence in Mr. P. F. Strawson's *Individuals:* "It is often admitted, in the analytical treatment of some fairly specific concept, that the wish to understand is less likely to be served by the search for a single strict statement of the necessary and sufficient conditions of its application than by seeing its applications—in Wittgenstein's simile—as forming a family, the members of which may, perhaps, be grouped around a central paradigm case and linked with the latter by various direct or indirect links of logical connexion and analogy." (p. 11). The contrast is not now between simple and complex concepts, but between two kinds of complex concepts: those which are definable by the statement of necessary and sufficient conditions and those which are not. But once again the contrast, although it is important, and is one which the family resemblances simile and the example of games are well able to draw, is not the point that Wittgenstein is concerned with. In the sense in which, according to Wittgenstein, games have nothing in common except that they are games, and red things have nothing in common except that they are red, *brothers have nothing in common except that they are brothers.* It is true that brothers have in common that they are male siblings, but their having in common that they are male siblings in their having in common that they are *brothers,* and not their having in common something in addition to their being brothers. Even a concept which can be explained in terms of necessary and sufficient conditions cannot be *ultimately* explained in such terms. To satisfy the craving for an ultimate explanation of "brother" in such terms it would be necessary to define "male" and "sibling", and the words in which "male" and "sibling" were defined, and so on *ad infinitum* and *ad impossibile.*

What then *is* the contrast that Wittgenstein meant to draw? I suggest that he did not mean to draw a *contrast* at all. Professor Wisdom has remarked that the peculiar difficulty of giving a philosophical account of universals lies in this: that philosophers are usually engaged in implicitly or explicitly comparing and contrasting one type of proposition with another type of proposition (propositions about minds with propositions about bodies, propositions of logic with propositions about matters of fact, propositions about the present and the past with propositions about the future, etc.) whereas propositions involving universals cannot be compared or contrasted with propositions that do not involve universals, since *all* propositions involve universals.[3] If we look at Wittgenstein's doctrine in the light of this remark we can understand it aright and can also see why it has been misunderstood in just those ways that I have mentioned. It is because of the very power of the ways of thought against which Wittgenstein was protesting that philosophers are led to offer accounts of his doctrine which restrict the range of its application. They recognise the importance of Wittgenstein's demonstration that *at least some* general terms can justifiably be applied to their instances although those instances have nothing in common. But they are so deeply attached to the idea that there must be something in common to the instances that fall under a general term that they treat Wittgenstein's examples as special cases, as rogues and vagabonds in the realm of concepts, to be contrasted with the general run of law-abiding concepts which *do* mark the presence of common elements in their instances.

Here we come across an ambiguity which is another obstacle to our getting a clear view of the problem of universals and of Wittgenstein's solution of it. Ayer remarks, in the passage to which I have already referred, that, "It is correct, though not at all enlightening, to say that what games have in common is their being games." It is certainly correct, but I strongly deny that it is unenlightening. It is of course trivially and platitudinously true, but trivialities and platitudes deserve emphatic affirmation when, as often in philosophy, they are explicitly or implicitly denied, or forgotten, or overlooked. Now the platitude that all games have in common that they *are* games is denied by the nominalist, who says that all games have nothing in common except that they are *called* games. And it is not only the nominalist, but also his opponent, who misunderstands the central importance of the platitude that all games have in common that they are games. When he is provoked by the nominalist's claim that all games have nothing in common except that they are called games, and rightly wishes to insist that games have something more in common than simply that they are called games, he feels that he must look for something that games have in common apart from *being* games. This feeling is entirely misplaced. The very terms of the nominalist's challenge require only that the realist should point out something that games have in common apart from *being called* games, and this onus is fully discharged by saying that they *are* games.

Although the feeling is misplaced, it is a very natural feeling, as we can see by considering the kinds of case in which we most typically and ordinarily ask what is in common to a set of objects. If I ask you what these three books have in common, or what those four chairs have in common, you will look to see if the books are all on the same subject or by the same author or published by the same firm; to see if the chairs are all Chippendale or all three-legged or all marked "Not to be removed from this room." It will never occur to you to say that the books have in common that they are books or the chairs that they are chairs. And if you find after close inspection that the chairs or the books do not have in common any of the features I have mentioned, and if you cannot see any other specific feature that they have in common, you will say that as far as you can see they have nothing in common. You will perhaps add that you suppose from the form of my question that I must know of something that they have in common. I may then tell you that all the books once belonged to John Locke or that all the chairs came from Ten Rillington Place. But it would be a poor

sort of joke for me to say that the chairs were all chairs or that the books were all books.

If I ask you what *all* chairs have in common, or what *all* books have in common, you may again try to find a feature like those you would look for in the case of *these three* books or *those four* chairs; and you may again think that it is a poor sort of joke for me to say that what all books have in common is that they are books and that what all chairs have in common is that they are chairs. And yet this time it is not a joke but an important philosophical truth.

Because the normal case where we ask "What have all *these* chairs, books or games in common?" is one in which we are not concerned with their all being chairs, books or games, we are liable to overlook the extreme peculiarity of the *philosophical* question that is asked with the words "What do *all* chairs, *all* books, *all* games have in common?" For of course games *do* have something in common. They *must* have something in common, and yet when we look for what they have in common we cannot find it. When we try to say what they have in common we always fail. And this is not because what we are looking for lies deeply hidden, but because it is too obvious to be seen; not because what we are trying to say is too subtle and complicated to be said, but because it is too easy and too simple to be worth saying: and so we say something more dramatic, but something false, instead. The simple truth is that what games have in common is that they are games. The nominalist is obscurely aware of this, and by rejecting the realist's talk of transcendent, immanent or subsistent forms or universals he shows his awareness. But by his own insistence that games have nothing in common except that they are called games he shows the obscurity of his awareness. The realist too is obscurely aware of it. By his talk of transcendent, immanent or subsistent forms or universals he shows the obscurity of his awareness. But by his hostility to the nominalist's insistence that games have nothing in common except that they are called games he shows his awareness.

Universals and Family Resemblances

All this can be more fully explained by the application of what I will call "Ramsey's Maxim." F. P. Ramsey, after mapping the course of an inconclusive dispute between Russell and W. E. Johnson, writes as follows:

Evidently, however, none of these arguments are really decisive, and the position is extremely unsatisfactory to any one with real curiosity about such a fundamental question. In such cases it is a heuristic maxim that the truth lies not in one of the two disputed views but in some third possibility which has not yet been thought of, which we can only discover by rejecting something assumed as obvious by both the disputants. (*The Foundations of Mathematics*, pp. 115–16.)

It is assumed as obvious by both the nominalist and the realist that there can be no objective justification for the application of a general term to its instances unless its instances have something in common over and above their having in common that they *are* its instances. The nominalist rightly holds that there is no such additional common element, and he therefore wrongly concludes that there is no objective justification for the application of any general term. The realist rightly holds that there is an objective justification for the application of general terms, and he therefore wrongly concludes that there *must* be some additional common element.

Wittgenstein denied the assumption that is common to nominalism and realism, and that is why I say that he solved the problem of universals. For if we deny the mistaken premiss that is common to the realist's argument and the nominalist's argument then we can deny the realist's mistaken conclusion and deny the nominalist's mistaken conclusion; and that is another way of saying that we can affirm the true premiss of the nominalist's argument and can also affirm the true premiss of the realist's argument.

The nominalist says that games have nothing in common except that they are called games.

The realist says that games must have something in common, and he means by this that they must have something in common other than that they are games.

Wittgenstein says that games have nothing in common except that they are games.

Wittgenstein thus denies at one and the same time the nominalist's claim that games have nothing in common except that they are called games and the realist's claim that games have something in common other than that they are games. He asserts at one and the same time the realist's claim that there is an objective justification for the application of the word "game" to games and the nominalist's claim that there is no element that is common to all games. And he is able to do all this because he denies the joint claim of the nominalist and the realist that there cannot be an objective justification for the application of the word "game" to games unless there is an element that is common to all games (*universalia in rebus*) or a common relation that all games bear to something that is not a game (*universalia ante res*).

Wittgenstein is easily confused with the nominalist because he denies what the realist asserts: that games have something in common other than that they are games.

When we see that Wittgenstein is not a nominalist we may easily confuse him with the realist because he denies what the nominalist asserts: that games have nothing in common except that they are called games.

But we can now see that Wittgenstein is neither a realist nor a nominalist: he asserts the simple truth that they both deny and he also asserts the two simple truths of which each of them asserts one and denies the other.

I will now try to put some flesh on to these bare bones.

The value and the limitations of the nominalist's claim that things which are called by the same name have nothing in common except that they are called by the same name can be seen if we look at a case where a set of objects literally and undeniably have nothing in common except that they are called by the same name. If I choose to give the name "alpha" to each of a number of miscellaneous objects (the star Sirius, my fountain-pen, the Parthenon, the colour red, the number five, and the letter Z) then I may well succeed in choosing the objects so *arbitrarily* that I shall succeed in preventing them from having any feature in common, other than that I call them by the name "alpha." But this imaginary case, to which the nominalist likens the use of all general words, has only to be described to be sharply contrasted with the typical case in which I apply a general word, say "chair", to a number of the instances to which it applies. In the first place, the *arbitrariness* of my selection of alphas is not paralleled in the case in which I apply the word "chair" successively to the chair in which I am now sitting, the Speaker's Chair in the House of Commons, the chair used at Bisley for carrying the winner of the Queen's Prize, and one of the deck chairs on the beach at Brighton. In giving a list of chairs I cannot just mention anything that happens to come into my head, while this is exactly what I do in giving my list of alphas. The second point is that the class of alphas is a *closed* class. Once I have given my list I have referred to every single alpha in the universe, actual and possible. Although I *might* have included or excluded any actual or possible object whatsoever when I was drawing up my list, once I have in fact made my arbitrary choice, no further application can be given to the word "alpha" according to the use that I have prescribed. For if I later add an object that I excluded from my list, or remove an object that I included in it, then I am making a different use of the word "alpha." With the word "chair" the position is quite different. There are an infinite number of actual and possible chairs. I cannot aspire to complete the enumeration of all chairs, as I can arbitrarily and at any point complete the enumeration of all alphas, and the word "chair," unlike the word "alpha", can be applied to an infinite number of instances without suffering any change of use.

These two points lead to a third and decisive point. I cannot teach the use of the word "alpha" except by specifically attaching it to each of the objects in my arbitrarily chosen list. No observer can conclude any-thing from watching me attach the label to this, that, or the other object, or to any number of objects however large, about the nature of the object or objects, if any, to which I shall later attach it. The use of the word "alpha" cannot be learned or taught as the use of a general word can be learned or taught. In teaching the use of a general word we may and must refer to characteristics of the objects to which it applies, and of the objects to which it does not apply, and indicate which of these characteristics count for the application on the word and which count against it. A pupil does not have to consult us on every separate occasion on which he encounters a new object, and if he did consult us every time we should have to say that he was not *learning* the use of the word. The reference that we make to a finite number of objects to which the word applies, and to a finite number of objects to which the word does not apply, is capable of equipping the pupil with a capacity for correctly applying or withholding the word to or from an infinite number of objects to which we have made no reference.

All this remains true in the case where it is not I alone, but a large number of people, or all of us, who use the world "alpha" in the way that I suggest. Even if everybody always called a particular set of objects by the same name, that would be insufficient to ensure that the name was a general name, and the claim of the name to be a general name would be defeated by just that necessity for reference to the arbitrary choices of the users of the name that the nominalist mistakenly claims to find in the case of a genuinely general name. For the nominalist is right in thinking that if we always had to make such a reference then there would be no general names as they are understood by the realist.

The nominalist is also right in the stress that he puts on the role of human interests and human purposes in determining our choice of principles of classification. How this insistence on the role of human purposes may be reconciled with the realist's proper insistence on the objectivity of the similarities and dissimilarities on which any genuine classification is based can be seen by considering an imaginary tribe of South Sea Islanders.

Let us suppose that trees are of great importance in the life and work of the South Sea Islanders, and that they have a rich and highly developed language in which they speak of the trees with which their island is thickly clad. But they do not have names for the species and genera of trees as they are recognised by our botanists. As we walk round the island with some of its inhabitants we can easily pick out orange-trees, date-palms and cedars. Our hosts are puzzled that we should call by the same name trees which appear to them to have nothing in common. They in turn surprise us by giving the same name to each of the trees in what is from our point of view a very mixed plantation. They point out to us what they called a mixed plantation, and we see that it is in our terms a clump of trees of the same species. Each party comes to recognise that its own classifications are as puzzling to the other as the other's are puzzling to itself.

This looks like the sort of situation that gives aid and comfort to the nominalist in his battle against the realist. But if we look at it more closely we see that it cannot help him. We know already that our own classification is based on similarities and differences between the trees, similarities and differences which we can point out to the islanders in an attempt to teach them our language. Of course we may fail, but if we do it will not be because we *must* fail.

Now *either* (*a*) The islanders have means of teaching us their classifications, by pointing out similarities and differences which we had not noticed, or in which we had not been interested, in which case *both* classifications are genuine, and no rivalry between them, of a kind that can help the nominalist, could ever arise;

or (*b*) Their classification is arbitrary in the sense in which my use of the word "alpha" was arbitrary, in which case it is not a genuine classification.

It may be that the islanders classify trees as "boat-building trees," "house-building trees," etc., and that they are more concerned with the height, thickness and maturity of the trees than they are with the distinctions of species that interest us.

In a particular case of *prima facie* conflict of classifications, we may not in fact be able to discover whether what appears to be a rival classification really *is* a classification. But we can be sure that *if* it is a classification *then* it is backed by objective similarities and differences, and that if it is *not* backed by objective similarities and differences then it is merely an arbitrary system of names. In no case will it appear that we must choose between rival systems of genuine classification of a set of objects in such a sense that one of them is to be recognised as *the* classification for all purposes.

There is no limit to the number of possible classifications of objects (The nominalist is right about this.)[4]

There is no classification of any set of objects which is not objectively based on genuine similarities and differences. (The realist is right about this.)

The nominalist is so impressed by the infinite diversity of possible classifications that he is blinded to their objectivity.

The realist is so impressed by the objectivity of all genuine classifications that he underestimates their diversity.

Of course we may if we like say that there is one complete system of classification which marks all the similarities and all the differences. (This is the realist's summing up of what we can learn by giving critical attention to the realist and nominalist in turn.)

Or we may say that there are only similarities and differences, from which we may choose according to our purposes and interests. (This is the nominalist's summing up.)

In talking of genuine or objective similarities and differences we must not forget that we are concerned with similarities and differences between *possible* cases as well as between actual cases, and indeed that we are concerned with the actual cases only because they are themselves a selection of the possible cases.

Because the nominalist and the realist are both right and both wrong, each is driven into the other's arms when he tries to be both consistent and faithful to our language, knowledge and experience. The nominalist talks of resemblances until he is pressed into a corner where he must acknowledge that resemblance is unintelligible except as resemblance *in a respect*, and to specify the respect in which objects resemble one another is to indicate a *quality* or *property*. The realist talks of properties and qualities until, when properties and qualities have been explained in terms of other properties and other qualities, he can at last do nothing but point to the *resemblances* between the objects that are said to be characterised by such and such a property or quality.

The question "Are resemblances ultimate or are properties ultimate?" is a perverse question if it is meant as one to which there must be a simple, *single* answer. They are both ultimate, or neither is ultimate. The craving for a single answer is the logically unsatisfiable craving for something that will be the ultimate terminus of explanation and will yet itself be explained.

NOTES

[1] I have profited from several discussions with Dr. S. M. Walters on taxonomy and the problems of universals. On the more general topics treated in this paper I have had several helpful discussions with Mr. R. A. Becher. Miss G. E. M. Anscombe kindly lent me the proofs of her essay on Aristotle, which is in *Three Philosophers* by Miss Anscombe and Mr. P. T. Geach.

[2] Of recent writings on this topic I believe that only Professor Wisdom's *Metaphysics and Verification* (reprinted in *Philosophy and Psycho-analysis*) and Mr. D. F. Pears' *Universals* (reprinted in Flew, *Logic and Language*, Second Series) show a complete understanding of the nature and importance of Wittgenstein's contribution.

[3] Professor Wisdom has pointed out to me that further discussion would be necessary to show that claims of the form "This is Jack" are not exceptions to this rule.

[4] Here one may think of Wittgenstein's remark that "Every application of every word is arbitrary," which emphasises that we can always find *some* distinction between any pair of objects, however closely similar they may be. What might be called the principle of the diversity of discernibles guarantees that we can never be *forced* to apply the same word to two different things.

Essences and Natural Kinds

Essence and Accident*

Irving M. Copi

The notions of essence and accident play important and unobjectionable roles in pre-analytic or pre-philosophical thought and discourse. These roles are familiar, and need no elaboration here. Philosophers cannot ignore them, but must either explain them or (somehow) explain them away. My interest is in explaining them.

If they are taken seriously, the notions of essence and accident seem to me the most appropriately discussed within the framework of a metaphysic of substance, which I shall accordingly assume. The account of essence and accident that I wish to set forth and argue for derives very largely from Aristotle, although it is not strictly Aristotelian. Where it differs from Aristotle's account it does so in order to accommodate some of the insights formulated by Locke in his discussion of "real" and "nominal" essences. My discussion is to be located, then, against the background of a substance metaphysic and a realist epistemology. The theory of essence and accident to be proposed seems to me not only to fit the demands of the gen-

*Copyright © 1954 by *The Journal of Philosophy.* Reprinted by permission, from *The Journal of Philosophy* 51 (November 1954), 706–19.

eral philosophical position mentioned, but also to be consistent with the apparent requirements of contemporary scientific development. I wish to begin my discussion with some historical remarks.

The earliest Western philosophers were much concerned with change and permanence, taking positions so sharply opposed that the issue appeared to be more paradox than problem. If an object which changes really changes, then it cannot literally be one and the same object which undergoes the change. But if the changing thing retains its identity, then it cannot really have changed. Small wonder that early cosmologists divided into warring factions, each embracing a separate horn of their common dilemma, the one denying permanence of any sort, the other denying the very possibility of change.

Aristotle discussed this problem in several of his treatises, bringing to bear on it not only his superb dialectical skill but an admirable, common-sense, dogged insistence that some things do maintain their identity while undergoing change. To explain the observed facts he was led to distinguish different kinds of change. A man does retain his identity though his complexion may change from ruddy to pale, or though he may move from one place to another. He is the same man though he become corpulent in middle life or his sinews shrink with age. In these types of change, called *alteration, locomotion, growth,* and *diminution,* the changing thing remains substantially or essentially what it was before changing.

Another type of change, however, was admitted to be more thoroughgoing. To take, for example, an artificial substance, we can say that if a wooden table is not just painted or moved, but destroyed by fire, we have neither alteration, locomotion, growth, nor diminution alone, but *substantial* change. The characteristic mark of substantial change is that the object undergoing the change does not survive that change or persist through it, but is destroyed in the process. The ashes (and gas and radiant energy) that appear in place of the burned table are not an altered, moved, or large or smaller table, but no table at all. In substantial change its essential property of being a table disappears.

It seems clear that distinguishing these different kinds of change involves distinguishing different kinds of attributes. The basic dichotomy between substantial change and other kinds of change is parallel to that between essential attributes or *essences*, and other kinds of attributes, which may be lumped together as accidental attributes or *accidents*. (Here we diverge rather sharply from at least one moment of Aristotle's own terminology, in ignoring the intermediate category of "property" or "proprium.")

Of the various bases that have been proposed for distinguishing between essence and accident, two stand out as most reasonable. The first has already been implied. If we can distinguish the different kinds of change, then we can say that a given attribute is essential to an object if its loss would result in the destruction of that object, whereas an attribute is a mere accident if the object would remain identifiably and substantially the same without it. This basis for distinguishing between essence and accident, although helpful heuristically, is not adequate philosophically, for it seems to me that the distinctions among these kinds of change presuppose those among the different kinds of attributes.

The other, more satisfactory basis for distinguishing essence from accident is an epistemological or methodological one. Knowledge of the essence of a thing is said to be more important than knowledge of its other attributes. In the *Metaphysica* Aristotle wrote: " . . . we know each thing most fully, when we know what it is, e.g. what man is or what fire is, rather than when we know its quality, its quantity, or its place. . . ."[1] It is the essence that is intended here, for a subsequent passage explains that: ". . . the essence is precisely what something *is*. . . ."[2] It is perhaps an understatement to say that Aristotle held knowledge of essence to be "more important" than knowledge of accidents, for he later says explicitly that: ". . . to *know* each thing . . . is just to know its essence. . . ."[3] And if we confine our attention to scientific knowledge, Aristotle repeatedly assures us that there is no knowledge of accidents at all,[4] but only of essences.[5]

Aristotle was led to draw an ontological conclusion from the foregoing epistemological doctrine. If some attributes of objects are epistemologically significant and others are not, the implication is that the former constitute the real natures of those objects, whereas the latter can be relegated to some less ultimate category. I must confess that I am in sympathy with the realist position which underlies and justifies such an inference, but to expound it in detail would take us too far afield.

As a biologist Aristotle was led to classify things into genera and species, holding that things belong to the same species if and only if they share a common essence. In remarking this fact we need not commit ourselves to any position with respect to the systematic or genetic priority of either logic or biology in Aristotle's thought. He apparently believed these species to be fixed and limited, and tended to ignore whatever could not be conveniently classified within them, holding, for example, that "the production of a mule by a horse" was "contrary to nature,"[6] a curious phrase. Some modern writers have tended to regard this shortcom-

Essences and Natural Kinds

ing as fatal to the Aristotelian system. Thus Susan Stebbing wrote: "Modern theories of organic evolution have combined with modern theories of mathematics to destroy the basis of the Aristotelian conception of essence. . . ."[7] It seems to me, however, that the fixity of species is a casual rather than an integral part of the Aristotelian system, which in its broad outlines as a metaphysical framework can be retained and rendered adequate to the most contemporary of scientific developments. A not dissimilar objection was made by Dewey, who wrote that: "In Aristotelian cosmology, ontology and logic . . . all quantitative determinations were relegated to the state of *accidents,* so that apprehension of them had no scientific standing. . . . Observe by contrast the place occupied by measuring in modern knowledge. Is it then credible that the logic of Greek knowledge has relevance to the logic of modern knowledge?"[8] But the Aristotelian notion of essence *can* admit of quantitative determination, as is suggested by Aristotle himself in admitting ratio as essence.[9] Hence I do not think that this criticism of Dewey's can be regarded as any more decisive than that of Miss Stebbing.

Having set forth in outline an Aristotelian philosophy of essence and accident, I propose next to examine what I consider to be the most serious objection that has been raised against it. According to this criticism, the distinction between essence and accident is not an objective or intrinsic one between genuinely different types of attributes. Attributes are really all of the same basic kind, it is said, and the alleged distinction between essence and accident is simply a projection of differences in human interests or a reflection of peculiarities of vocabulary. Let us try to understand this criticism in as sympathetic a fashion as we can.

The distinction between different kinds of change, on this view, is subjective rather than objective. We happen to be interested, usually, in some attributes of a thing more than in others. When the thing changes, we say that it persists through the change provided that it does not lose attributes by whose possession it satisfies our interests.

For example, our interest in tables is for the most part independent of their colors. Hence that interest remains satisfiable by a given table regardless of any alteration it may suffer with respect to color. Paint a brown table green, and it remains substantially or essentially the same; the change was only an accidental one. If our interests were different, the same objective fact would be classified quite differently. Were our interest to lie in *brown* tables exclusively, then the application of green paint would destroy the object of our interest, would change it substantially or essentially from something which satisfied our interest to something which did not. The implication is that attributes are neither essential nor accidental in themselves, but can be so classified only on the basis of our subjective interests in them. Dewey stated this point of view very succinctly, writing: "As far as present logical texts still continue to talk about essences, properties and accidents as something inherently different from one another, they are repeating distinctions that once had an ontological meaning and that no longer have it. Anything is 'essential' which is indispensable in a given inquiry and anything is 'accidental' which is superfluous."[10]

The present criticism lends itself easily to reformulation in more language-oriented terms. That we regard a table as essentially the same despite alteration in color or movement from place to place is a consequence of the peculiar nature and limitations of our vocabulary, which has a single word for tables, regardless of color, but lacks special words for tables of different colors. Suppose that our language contained no word for tables in general, but had instead—say—the word "towble" for brown table and the word "teeble" for green table. Then the application of green paint to a towble would be said to change it essentially, it might be argued, for no towble would remain; in its place would appear a teeble. Or if there were a single word which applied indiscriminately to tables and heaps of ashes, say "tashble," with no special substantive denoting either of them univocally, then perhaps the destruction of a table by fire would not be regarded as an essential change. That which appeared at the end of the process would admittedly be in a different state from what was there at the start, but it would still be identifiably the same tashble. C. I. Lewis regards the difference between essence and accident to be strictly relative to vocabulary, writing: "Traditionally any attribute required for application of a term is said to be of the essence of the thing named. It is, of course, meaningless to speak of the essence of a thing except relative to its being named by a particular term."[11]

I think that for our purpose these two criticisms can be regarded as variants of a single basic one, for the connection between human interests and human vocabulary is a very intimate one. It is an anthropological and linguistic commonplace that the concern of a culture with a given phenomenon is reflected in the vocabulary of that culture, as in the several Eskimo words which denote subtly different kinds of snow. In our own culture new interests lead continually to innovations in vocabulary; and surely it is the decline of interest in certain things that leads to the obsolescence of words used to refer to them.

Both variants of this criticism were formulated long ago by Locke, and developed at considerable length in his *Essay.* Locke paid comparatively little attention to the problem of change, but where he did discuss it his treatment was very similar to Aristotle's. Thus we are assured in the *Essay* that: ". . . an oak growing from a plant to a great tree, and then lopped, is still the same oak; and a colt grown up to a horse, sometimes fat, sometimes lean, is all the while the same horse. . . ."[12] The oak ". . . continues to be the same plant as long as it partakes of the same life . . ."[13] and the identity of animals is explained in similar terms. Personal identity is explained in terms of sameness of consciousness.[14] If we ignore the Cartesian dualism implicit in that last case, and if we are not too critical of the reappearance of the term "same" in the explanation of *sameness,* we can recognize these answers to be the Aristotelian ones, for according to Aristotle the soul is the principle of life,[15] the life of a

plant is the nutritive soul,[16] that of an animal its sensitive soul,[17] and that of man his rational soul,[18] these souls constituting the substantial forms or essences of the respective substances.[19] On the other hand, in his brief discussion of identity as applied to non-living things, Locke construes it very strictly to apply only to things which ". . . vary not at all. . . ."[20] But the following passage has a characteristically Aristotelian flavor: "Thus that which was grass today, is to-morrow the flesh of a sheep; and within a few days after becomes part of man: in all which, and the like changes, it is evident their real essence, i.e. that constitution, whereon the properties of these several things depended, is destroyed, and perishes with them."[21]

Despite this partial similarity of their views, the bases for distinguishing between the essential properties and other properties of a thing are very different for Locke than for Aristotle. For Aristotle, the distinction is twofold: first, the essential properties of an object are those which are retained by it during any change through which the object remains identifiably the same object; and second, the essential properties of an object are most important in our scientific knowledge of it. For Locke, on the other hand, the *real* essence of a thing is a set of properties which *determine* all the other properties of that thing.[22] Since all other properties depend on its real essence, *any* change in an object entails a change in its real essence. Hence for Locke the essential properties of an object are *not* retained by it during any change. This view is very different from Aristotle's, on which the accidents of a thing are not bound to its essence but can change independently of it. The epistemological difference is equally striking. Whereas for Aristotle all scientific knowledge is knowledge of the essence, for Locke there is *no* knowledge of the real essences of things.[23]

Locke was more interested in what he called "nominal essences," which are more nearly analogous to the Aristotelian notion of essence. Our idea of a particular substance, according to Locke, is a complex idea composed of a number of simple ideas

Essences and Natural Kinds

which are noticed to "go constantly together," plus the notion of a substratum "wherein they do subsist."[24] A general or abstract idea of a sort or species of substance is made out of our complex ideas of various particular substances that resemble each other by leaving out "that which is peculiar to each" and retaining "only what is common to all."[25] Such an abstract idea *determines* a sort or species,[26] and is called a "nominal essence,"[27] for "everything contained in that idea is essential to that sort."[28]

The properties contained in the nominal essence of a thing can be distinguished from the other properties of that thing on the same basis as that on which the Aristotelian essence is distinguished from accidents. In the first place, a particular substance of a given species can change with respect to some property whose idea is *not* included in the nominal essence of that species, and will continue to be recognizably the same thing; whereas it must be regarded as a quite different thing if it changes with respect to some property whose idea *is* included in the nominal essence.[29] And in the second place, the nominal essence is more important in knowledge than other properties. To have knowledge of a thing is to know what *sort* of thing it is, and to know the nominal essence is to know the sort. Locke says, moreover, that the leading qualities of a thing, that is, the most observable and hence, for Locke, the most knowable, are ingredients in the nominal essence.[30] Finally, it is argued in the *Essay* that knowledge of nominal essences is required if we are ever to be certain of the truth of any general proposition.[31] Since Locke's nominal essences play so similar a role to that of Aristotle's essences, Locke's arguments intended to prove their subjectivity and relativity to human interests and vocabulary can be interpreted as applying to Aristotle's notion as well as his own.

One fairly minor difference should be noted before going on. Since Locke's nominal essences are abstract *ideas,* they are immediately subjective in a way that Aristotle's essences are not. But that difference is not decisive, for substances may well have objective properties that nominal essences are ideas *of,* or objective *powers* that correspond to them exactly.[32]

Locke urges that essences are subjective in a less trivial sense. Since they are "inventions"[33] or the "workmanship"[34] of the understanding, different persons in fashioning abstract ideas which they signify by the same term can and do incorporate different simple ideas into them. Acts of choice or selection are involved here, and people do make different choices, as proved by the disputes that so frequently arise over whether particular bodies are of certain species or not.[35]

That essences are relative to vocabulary is argued by Locke in terms of an example: "A silent and a striking watch are but one species to those who have but one name for them: but he that has the name watch for one, and clock for the other, and distinct complex ideas, to which those names belong, to him they are different species."[36]

That the ". . . boundaries of species are as men, and not as nature, makes them . . . ,"[37] proved by the verbal disputes already referred to, is explained by the fact that since we have ". . . need of general names for present use . . . "[38] we ". . . stay not for a perfect discovery of all those qualities which would best show us their most material differences and agreements; but we ourselves divide them, by certain obvious appearances, into species. . . ."[39] Nominal essences are made for *use,* and different intended uses or interests will determine different essences. Even the *noticing* of similarities between distinct particulars is relative to our interest in them, so our selection of simple ideas for inclusion in a nominal essence is relative to such interests. These determining interests are not scientific, for as Locke observed, ". . . languages, in all countries, have been established long before sciences."[40] The situation is rather that the terms of ordinary discourse ". . . have for the most part, in all languages, received their birth and signification from ignorant and illiterate people. . . ."[41] And for the purposes or interests of those practical people, the properties selected by them as essential to the objects they deal with are adequate enough. For "Vulgar notions suit vulgar discourses; and both, though confused enough, yet serve pretty well the market and the wake."[42]

Now do these arguments succeed in establishing that the distinction between essence and accident is subjective rather than objective, that is, relative to human interests and vocabulary?

I think that the objections are not utterly destructive of the Aristotelian doctrine, although they do call attention to needed modifications of it. Locke's case, it seems to me, depends upon his distinction between real and nominal essences, and his belief that real essences are unknowable. But his doctrine that real essences cannot be known flows from two peculiarities of his philosophy, which I see no reason to accept. One of the bases for his belief that real essences are unknowable is his view that the only objects of our knowledge are the ideas that we have in our minds.[43] Locke's other basis for his belief that real essences are unknowable is his doctrine that experiment and observation yield only ". . . judgment and opinion, not knowledge. . . ."[44] Here the term "knowledge" is reserved for what is *certain*.

I would reject these two doctrines on the following grounds. The first of them, that knowledge is only of ideas, is the germ of scepticism. Locke's premises lead necessarily to Hume's conclusions, and the partial scepticism we find explicitly set forth in Locke is but a fragment of the complete scepticism that Hume later showed to be implicitly contained there. It seems to me that if a philosophy denies the very possibility of scientific knowledge, then so much the worse for that philosophy. As for reserving the term "knowledge" for what is certain, that usage has but little to commend it. It seems more reasonable to accept the results of experiment and obsevation, although probable rather than demonstrative, as knowledge nonetheless.

It must be admitted that the doctrine of the unknowability of real essences was not an unreasonable conclusion to draw from the relatively undeveloped state of science in Locke's day. For chemistry, at least, if we can believe what is said of it in the *Essay*, was in a very bad way in the seventeenth century. Locke tells us of the "sad experience" of chemists ". . . when they, sometimes in vain, seek for the same qualities in one parcel of sulphur, antimony or vitriol, which they have found in others. For though they are bodies of the same species, having the same nominal essence, under the same name; yet do they often, upon severe ways of examination, betray qualities so different one from another, as to frustrate the expectations of very wary chemists."[45]

Contemporary science, however, presents a quite different picture. Locke characterized the (allegedly unknowable) real essences of things as the ". . . constitution of their insensible parts; from which flow those sensible qualities, which serve us to distinguish them one from another. . . ."[46] Now modern atomic theory is directly concerned with the insensible parts of things. Through the use of his Periodic Table, interpreted as dealing with atomic number and valency, ". . . Mendeléev was enabled to predict the existence *and properties* . . ." of half a dozen elements whose existence had not been previously known or even suspected.[47] And other scientists have subsequently been able to make similar predictions. Modern science seeks to know the *real* essences of things, and its increasing successes seem to be bringing it progressively nearer to that goal.

It must be granted that Locke's distinction between real and nominal essence is a helpful one, even though it is not absolute. The construction of nominal essences is usually relative to practical interests, and the ordinary notion of the essence of a thing is relative to the words used in referring to it. I think that Locke (and Dewey and Lewis) are correct in that contention. Surely different interests lead different people to classify or sort things in different ways, and thus to adopt different nominal essences, the more permanently useful of which receive separate names in ordinary language. Thus it is that: "Merchants and lovers, cooks and taylors, have words wherewithal to dispatch their ordinary affairs. . . ."[48]

The distinction, however, is not absolute.

Not every interest is narrowly practical. The interest of the scientist is in knowledge and understanding. The scientist desires to know how things behave, and to account for their behavior by means of explanatory hypotheses or theories which permit him to predict what will occur under specified conditions. He is interested in discovering general laws to which objects conform, and the causal relations which obtain among them. The scientist's sorting or classifying of objects is relative to this interest, which is not well served by classifying things on the basis of properties which are either most obvious or most immediately practical. It is better served by classifying things in terms of properties which are relevant to the framing of a maximum number of causal laws and the formulation of explanatory theories. Thus a foodstuff and a mineral source of aluminum, common salt and cryolite, are both classified by the chemist as sodium compounds, because in the context of modern chemical theory it is this common characteristic which is most significant for predicting and understanding the behavior of these substances. In the sphere of scientific inquiry, the distinction between real and nominal essence tends to disappear. The scientist's classification of things is intended to be in terms of their *real* essences. And here, too, the process is reflected in vocabulary, not necessarily or even usually in that of the man in the street, but rather in the technical jargon of the specialist.

The essences which science seeks to discover, then, are real essences rather than nominal ones. Since the arguments for subjectivity or relativity to interest or vocabulary were concerned with nominal rather than real essences, they simply do not apply to real essences as either Locke or Aristotle conceived them.

In one passage of his *Essay*, though, Locke does make the further claim that even a real essence relates to a sort and supposes a species.[49] But on Locke's own account of real essence, the real essence of a particular must be that set of its properties on which all of its other properties depend. And that can be investigated independently of any

sorting or classifying we may do—although once its real essence is discovered, that will determine how we should classify it scientifically if the occasion for doing so arises.

At this point let me indicate the direction in which I think the Aristotelian doctrine of essence and accident might well be modified. Aristotle definitely held that there could be no scientific knowledge of accidents,[50] but contemporary science would admit no such limitation. It seems to me that both Locke's and Aristotle's views about unknowability should be rejected. Contrary to Locke, I should hold that real essences are in principle knowable, and contrary to Aristotle, I should hold that non-essential or accidental properties can also be objects of scientific knowledge.

It seems to me also that neither Locke nor Aristotle gives a satisfactory account of the relationship between essence and accident. For Locke, all (other) properties of a thing depend on its "real constitution" or real essence[51]; but it is not clear whether the dependence is supposed to be causal or logico-deductive. The former is obviously the more acceptable doctrine. Aristotle, on the other hand, held that some properties of a thing, namely, its accidents, do not in any way depend upon its essence. I think that Locke's view, understood as asserting a causal dependence of accident on essence, is the more plausible one, and that the Aristotelian doctrine ought to be so modified as to accord with that of Locke in this respect.

Now if both essences and accidents are scientifically knowable, on what basis are they to be distinguished from each other? I suggest that the epistemological or methodological distinction is still valid. For example, common salt has many properties, some more obvious than others, and some more important than others relative to different practical interests. The scientist singles out its being a compound of equal parts of sodium and chlorine as its essential nature. In doing so he surely does not mean to imply that its chemical constitution is more easily observed than its other properties, or more important to either cook, tailor, merchant, or lover. He classifies it as sodium chloride because, within the context of his theory, that property is fundamental. From its chemical formula more of its properties can be inferred than could be from any other. Since the connection is causal rather than logical, the inference from essence to accident must make use of causal law premises or modes of inference as well as strictly logical ones. Hence to derive conclusions about *all* accidental properties of a substance, we should need to know both its real essence and all relevant causal laws. That is an ideal toward which science strives, rather than its present achievement, of course. To the extent to which one small group of properties of a substance can serve as a basis from which its other properties can be causally derived, to that extent we can be justified in identifying that group of properties as its real essence. This view, it should be noted, is in agreement with Aristotle's doctrine that the definition of a thing should state its essence,[52] and that definition is a scientific process.[53]

There is a certain relativity implied in this account, although it is quite different from those previously discussed. Our *notion* of what constitutes the real essence of a thing is relative to the science of our day. Centuries hence, wiser men will have radically different and more adequate theories, and their notions will be closer approximations than ours to the real essences of things. But it will still be the real essences of things that are destined to be known by Peirce's ultimate community of knowers.

There is one other and more radical sense of accident that I would agree to be relative. Each separate science is concerned with only some of the properties or aspects of things which it studies. Those left out will be accidental relative to the special science which ignores them. They will not be derivable from what that science considers to be the real essences of those things, although a different special science might be much concerned with them, and even include them in *its* notion of the thing's real essence. But as (and if) the sciences become more unified, no properties of a thing will be wholly accidental in this sense, and all will be causally derivable from the real essence.

In closing, I should like to refer once again to the topic of change. If all of a thing's properties depend on its real essence, then it would seem to follow that every change is an essential one. In my opinion, that unwelcome conclusion can be evaded in two ways. In the first place, with respect to common-sense, practical usage, our ordinary sortings will continue to be based on nominal rather than real essences, so that changes can continue to be classified as accidental or essential in the traditional way. And in the second place, with respect to scientific usage, we can say the following. The real essence of a thing will consist very largely of powers or, in modern terms, dispositional properties. An essential change in a thing will involve the replacement of some of its dispositions or powers by other dispositions or powers. But a change which is non-essential or accidental would involve no such replacement; it would rather consist in differently actualized manifestations of the same dispositional property or power. Unfortunately, lack of space prevents an adequate development of this suggestion.

NOTES

[1] 1028a37–1028b2. Quotations are from the Oxford translation.

[2] 1030a1.

[3] 1031b20.

[4] 1026b4; 1027a20, 28; 1064b30; 1065a4. Cf. also *Posterior Analytics* 75a18–22.

[5] 75a28–30.

[6] 1033b33. But cf. 770b9–13.

[7] *A Modern Introduction to Logic* (London: Methuen, 1961), p. 433.

[8] *Logic: The Theory of Inquiry* (New York: Holt, 1938), pp. 89–90.

[9] 993a17–20.

[10] *Logic*, p. 138.

[11] *An Analysis of Knowledge and Valuation* (La Salle, Ill.: Open Court, 1946), p. 41.

[12] Bk. 2, ch. 27, §3.

[13] *Ibid.*

[14] Bk. 2, ch. 27, §8, §9, §10, §16, §17, §23.

[15]*De Anima* 406a6, 415b8.

[16]432a29, 434a22–26; cf. also *De Plantis* 815b28–34.

[17]432a30.

[18]*Politics* 1332b5.

[19]*De Anima* 412a20, 412b13, 415b10.

[20]Bk. 2, ch. 27, §1.

[21]Bk. 3, ch. 4, §19. But cf. Bk. 3, ch. 6, §4, §5.

[22]Bk. 3, ch. 3, §15.

[23]Bk. 3, ch. 3, §15, §17, §18; ch. 6, §3, §6, §9, §12, §18, §49; ch. 9, §12; ch. 10, §18.

[24]Bk. 2, ch. 23, §1.

[25]Bk. 3, ch. 3, §7.

[26]Bk. 3, ch. 3, §12.

[27]Bk. 3, ch. 3, §15.

[28]Bk. 3, ch. 6, §2.

[29]Bk. 2, ch. 27, §28.

[30]Bk. 3, ch. 11, §20.

[31]Bk. 4, ch. 6, §4.

[32]Bk. 2, ch. 23, §7.

[33]Bk. 3, ch. 3, §11.

[34]Bk. 3, ch. 3, §12, §13, §14.

[35]Bk. 3, ch. 3, §14; ch. 6, §26, §27; ch. 9, §16; ch. 10, §22; ch. 11, §6, §7.

[36]Bk. 3, ch. 6, §39.

[37]Bk. 3, ch. 6, §30.

[38]*Ibid.*

[39]*Ibid.*

[40]Bk. 3, ch. 6, §25.

[41]*Ibid.*

[42]Bk. 3, ch. 11, §10.

[43]Bk. 2, ch. 1, §1.

[44]Bk. 4, ch. 12, §10; cf. also Bk. 4, ch. 3, §28.

[45]Bk. 3, ch. 6, §8.

[46]Bk. 3, ch. 3, §17.

[47]J. D. Main Smith, in the *Encyclopaedia Britannica* (14th ed.; 1947), Vol. 17, p. 520 (my italics).

[48]Bk. 3, ch. 11, §10.

[49]Bk. 3, ch. 6, §6.

[50]1064b30–1065a25.

[51]Bk. 3, ch. 3, §18.

[52]91a1, 101b21, 38.

[53]1039b32.

Natural Kinds*

W. V. Quine

What tends to confirm an induction? This question has been aggravated on the one hand by Hempel's puzzle of the non-black non-ravens,[1] and exacerbated on the other by Goodman's puzzle of the grue emeralds.[2] I shall begin my remarks by relating the one puzzle to the other, and the other to an innate flair that we have for natural kinds. Then I shall devote the rest of the paper to reflections on the nature of this notion of natural kinds and its relation to science.

Hempel's puzzle is that just as each black raven tends to confirm the law that all ravens are black, so each green leaf, being a non-black non-raven, should tend to confirm the law that all non-black things are non-ravens, that is, again, that all ravens are black. What is paradoxical is that a green leaf should count toward the law that all ravens are black.

Goodman propounds his puzzle by requiring us to imagine that emeralds, having been identified by some criterion other than color, are now being examined one after an-

other and all up to now are found to be green. Then he proposes to call anything *grue* that is examined today or earlier and found to be green or is not examined before tomorrow and is blue. Should we expect the first one examined tomorrow to be green, because all examined up to now were green? But all examined up to now were also grue; so why not expect the first one tomorrow to be grue, and therefore blue?

The predicate "green," Goodman says,[3] is *projectible;* "grue" is not. He says this by way of putting a name to the problem. His step toward solution is his doctrine of what he calls entrenchment,[4] which I shall touch on later. Meanwhile the terminological point is simply that projectible predicates are predicates ζ and η whose shared instances all do count, for whatever reason, toward confirmation of 'All ζ are η'.

Now I propose assimilating Hempel's puzzle to Goodman's by inferring from Hempel's that the complement of a projectible predicate need not be projectible. "Raven" and "black" are projectible; a black raven does count toward "All ravens are black." Hence a black raven counts also, indirectly, toward "No non-black things are non-ravens," since this says the same thing.

But a green leaf does not count toward "All non-black things are non-ravens," nor, therefore, toward "All ravens are black"; "non-black" and "non-raven" are not projectible. "Green" and "leaf" are projectible, and the green leaf counts toward "All leaves are green" and "All green things are leaves"; but only a black raven can confirm "All ravens are black," the complements not being projectible.

If we see the matter in this way, we must guard against saying that a statement 'All ζ are η' is lawlike only if ζ and η are projectible. "All non-black things are non-ravens" is a law despite its non-projectible terms, since it is equivalent to "All ravens are black." Any statement is lawlike that is logically *equivalent* to 'All ζ and η ' for some projectible ζ and η.[5]

Having concluded that the complement of a projectible predicate need not be projectible, we may ask further whether there is *any* projectible predicate whose complement is projectible. I can conceive that there is not, when complements are taken strictly. We must not be misled by limited or relative complementation; "male human" and "non-male human" are indeed both projectible.

To get back now to the emeralds, why do we expect the next one to be green rather than grue? The intuitive answer lies in similarity, however subjective. Two green emeralds are more similar than two grue ones would be if only one of the grue ones were green. Green things, or at least green emeralds, are a kind.[6] A projectible predicate is one that is true of all and only the things of a kind. What makes Goodman's example a puzzle, however, is the dubious scientific standing of a general notion of similarity, or of kind.

The dubiousness of this notion is itself a remarkable fact. For surely there is nothing more basic to thought and language than our sense of similarity; our sorting of things into kinds. The usual general term, whether a common noun or a verb or an adjective, owes its generality to some resemblance among the things referred to. Indeed, learning to use a word depends on a double resemblance: first, a resemblance between the

present circumstances and past circumstances in which the word was used, and second, a phonetic resemblance between the present utterance of the word and past utterances of it. And every reasonable expectation depends on resemblance of circumstances, together with our tendency to expect similar causes to have similar effects.

The notion of a kind and the notion of similarity or resemblance seem to be variants or adaptations of a single notion. Similarity is immediately definable in terms of kind; for, things are similar when they are two of a kind. The very words for "kind" and "similar" tend to run in etymologically cognate pairs. Cognate with "kind" we have "akin" and "kindred." Cognate with "like" we have "ilk." Cognate with "similar" and "same" and "resemble" there are "*sammeln*" and "assemble," suggesting a gathering into kinds.

We cannot easily imagine a more familiar or fundamental notion than this, or a notion more ubiquitous in its applications. On this score it is like the notions of logic: like identity, negation, alternation, and the rest. And yet, strangely, there is something logically repugnant about it. For we are baffled when we try to relate the general notion of similarity significantly to logical terms. One's first hasty suggestion might be to say that things are similar when they have all or most or many properties in common. Or, trying to be less vague, one might try defining comparative similarity—"*a* is more similar to *b* than to *c*"—as meaning that *a* shares more properties with *b* than with *c*. But any such course only reduces our problem to the unpromising task of settling what to count as a property.

The nature of the problem of what to count as a property can be seen by turning for a moment to set theory. Things are viewed as going together into sets in any and every combination, describable and indescribable. Any two things are joint members of any number of sets. Certainly then we cannot define "*a* is more similar to *b* than to *c*" to mean that *a* and *b* belong jointly to more sets than *a* and *c* do. If properties are to support this line of definition where sets do not, it must be because properties do not, like sets, take things in every random combination. It must be that properties are shared only by things that are significantly similar. But properties in such a sense are no clearer than kinds. To start with such a notion of property, and define similarity on that basis, is no better than accepting similarity as undefined.

The contrast between properties and sets which I suggested just now must not be confused with the more basic and familiar contrast between properties, as intensional, and sets as extensional. Properties are intensional in that they may be counted as distinct properties even though wholly coinciding in respect of the things that have them. There is no call to reckon kinds as intensional. Kinds can be seen as sets, determined by their members. It is just that not all sets are kinds.

If similarity is taken simple-mindedly as a yes-or-no affair, with no degrees, then there is no containing of kinds within broader kinds. For, as remarked, similarity now simply means belonging to some one same kind. If all colored things comprise a kind, then all colored things count as similar, and the set of all red things is too narrow to count as a kind. If on the other hand the set of all red things counts as a kind, then colored things do not all count as similar, and the set of all colored things is too broad to count as a kind. We cannot have it both ways. Kinds can, however, overlap; the red things can comprise one kind, the round another.

When we move up from the simple dyadic relation of similarity to the more serious and useful triadic relation of comparative similarity, a correlative change takes place in the notion of kind. Kinds come to admit now not only of overlapping but also of containment one in another. The set of all red things and the set of all colored things can now both count as kinds; for all colored things can now be counted as resembling one another more than some things do, even though less, on the whole, than red ones do.

At this point, of course, our trivial definition of similarity as sameness of kind breaks down; for almost any two things could count now as common members of some broad kind or other, and anyway we now want to define comparative or triadic similarity. A definition that suggests itself is this: *a* is more similar to *b* than to *c* when *a* and *b* belong jointly to more kinds than *a* and *c* do. But even this works only for finite systems of kinds.

The notion of kind and the notion of similarity seemed to be substantially one notion. We observed further that they resist reduction to less dubious notions, as of logic or set theory. That they at any rate be definable each in terms of the other seems little enough to ask. We just saw a somewhat limping definition of comparative similarity in terms of kinds. What now of the converse project, definition of kind in terms of similarity?

One may be tempted to picture a kind, suitable to a comparative similarity relation, as any set which is "qualitatively spherical" in this sense: it takes in exactly the things that differ less than so-and-so much from some central norm. If without serious loss of accuracy we can assume that there are one or more actual things (*paradigm cases*) that nicely exemplify the desired norm, and one or more actual things (*foils*) that deviate just barely too much to be counted into the desired kind at all, then our definition is easy: *the kind with paradigm a and foil b is the set of all the things to which a is more similar than a is to b.* More generally, then, a set may be said to be a *kind* if and only if there are *a* and *b*, known or unknown, such that the set is the kind with paradigm *a* and foil *b*.

If we consider examples, however, we see that this definition does not give us what we want as kinds. Thus take red. Let us grant that a central shade of red can be picked as norm. The trouble is that the paradigm cases, objects in just that shade of red, can come in all sorts of shapes, weights, sizes, and smells. Mere degree of overall similarity to any one such paradigm case will afford little evidence of degree of redness, since it will depend also on shape, weight, and the rest. If our assumed relation of comparative similarity were just comparative chromatic similarity, then our paradigm-and-foil definition of kind would indeed accommodate redkind. What the definition will not do is distill purely chromatic kinds from mixed similarity.

A different attempt, adapted from Carnap, is this: a set is a kind if all its members are more similar to one another than they all are to any one thing outside the set. In other words, each non-member differs more from some member than that member differs from any member. However, as Goodman showed in a criticism of Carnap,[7] this construction succumbs to what Goodman calls the difficulty of imperfect community. Thus consider the set of all red round things, red wooden things, and round wooden things. Each member of this set resembles each other member somehow: at least in being red, or in being round, or in being wooden, and perhaps in two or all three of these respects or others. Conceivably, moreover, there is no one thing outside the set that resembles every member of the set to even the least of these degrees. The set then meets the proposed definition of kind. Yet surely it is not what anyone means by a kind. It admits yellow croquet balls and red rubber balls while excluding yellow rubber balls.

The relation between similarity and kind, then, is less clear and neat than could be wished. Definition of similarity in terms of kind is halting, and definition of kind in terms of similarity is unknown. Still the two notions are in an important sense correlative. They vary together. If we reassess something a as less similar to b than to c, where it had counted as more similar to b than to c, surely we will correspondingly permute a, b, and c in respect of their assignment to kinds; and conversely.

I have stressed how fundamental the notion of similarity or of kind is to our thinking, and how alien to logic and set theory. I want to go on now to say more about how fundamental these notions are to our thinking, and something also about their nonlogical roots. Afterward I want to bring out how the notion of similarity or of kind changes as science progresses. I shall suggest that it is a mark of maturity of a branch of science that the notion of similarity or kind finally dissolves, so far as it is relevant to that branch of science. That is, it ultimately submits to analysis in the special terms of that branch of science and logic.

For deeper appreciation of how fundamental similarity is, let us observe more closely how it figures in the learning of language. One learns by *ostension* what presentations to call yellow; that is, one learns by hearing the word applied to samples. All he has to go on, of course, is the similarity of further cases to the samples. Similarity being a matter of degree, one has to learn by trial and error how reddish or brownish or greenish a thing can be and still be counted yellow. When he finds he has applied the word too far out, he can use the false cases as samples to the contrary; and then he can proceed to guess whether further cases are yellow or not by considering whether they are more similar to the in-group or the out-group. What one thus uses, even at this primitive state of learning, is a fully functioning sense of similarity, and relative similarity at that: a is more similar to b than to c.

All these delicate comparisons and shrewd inferences about what to call yellow are, in Sherlock Holmes's terminology, elementary. Mostly the process is unconscious. It is the same process by which an animal learns to respond in distinctive ways to his master's commands or other discriminated stimulations.

The primitive sense of similarity that underlies such learning has, we saw, a certain complexity of structure: a is more similar to b than to c. Some people have thought that it has to be much more complex still: that it depends irreducibly on *respects*, thus similarity in color, similarity in shape, and so on. According to this view, our learning of yellow by ostension would have depended on our first having been told or somehow apprised that it was going to be a question of color. Now hints of this kind are a great help, and in our learning we often do depend on them. Still one would like to be able to show that a single general standard of similarity, but of course comparative similarity, is all we need, and that respects can be abstracted afterward. For instance, suppose the child has learned of a yellow ball and block that they count as yellow, and of a red ball and block that they do not, and now he has to decide about a yellow cloth. Presumably he will find the cloth more similar to the yellow ball and to the yellow block then to the red ball or red block; and he will not have needed any prior schooling in colors and respects. Carnap undertook to show long ago how some respects, such as color, could by an ingenious construction be derived from a general similarity notion;[8] however, this development is challenged, again, by Goodman's difficulty of imperfect community.

A standard of similarity is in some sense innate. This point is not against empiricism; it is a commonplace of behavioral psychology. A response to a red circle, if it is rewarded, will be elicited again by a pink ellipse more readily than by a blue triangle; the red circle resembles the pink ellipse more than the blue triangle. Without some such prior spacing of qualities, we could never acquire a habit; all stimuli would be equally alike and equally different. These spacings of qualities, on the part of men and other animals, can be explored and mapped in the laboratory by experiments in conditioning and extinction.[9] Needed as they are for all learning, these distinctive spacings cannot themselves all be learned; some must be innate.

If then I say that there is an innate standard of similarity, I am making a condensed statement that can be interpreted, and truly interpreted, in behavioral terms. Moreover, in this behavioral sense it can be said equally of other animals that they have an innate standard of similarity too. It is part of our animal birthright. And, interestingly enough, it is characteristically animal in its lack of intellectual status. At any rate we noticed earlier how alien the notion is to mathematics and logic.

This innate qualitative spacing of stimulations was seen to have one of its human uses in the ostensive learning of words like "yellow." I should add as a cautionary remark that this is not the only way of learning words, nor the commonest; it is merely

the most rudimentary way. It works when the question of the reference of a word is a simple question of spread; how much of our surroundings counts as yellow, how much counts as water, and so on. Learning a word like "apple" or "square" is more complicated, because here we have to learn also where to say that one apple or square leaves off and another begins. The complication is that apples do not add up to an apple, nor squares, generally, to a square. "Yellow" and "water" are mass terms, concerned only with spread; "apple" and "square" are terms of divided reference, concerned with both spread and individuation. Ostension figures in the learning of terms of this latter kind too, but the process is more complex.[10] And then there are all the other sorts of words, all those abstract and neutral connectives and adverbs and all the recondite terms of scientific theory; and there are also the grammatical constructions themselves to be mastered. The learning of these things is less direct and more complex still. There are deep problems in this domain, but they lie aside from the present topic.

Our way of learning "yellow," then, gives less than a full picture of how we learn language. Yet more emphatically, it gives less than a full picture of the human use of an innate standard of similarity, or innate spacing of qualities. For, as remarked, every reasonable expectation depends on similarity. Again on this score, other animals are like man. Their expectations, if we choose so to conceptualize their avoidance movements and salivation and pressing of levers and the like, are clearly dependent on their appreciation of similarity. Or, to put matters in their methodological order, these avoidance movements and salivation and pressing of levers and the like are typical of what we have to go on in mapping the animals' appreciation of similarity, their spacing of qualities.

Induction itself is essentially only more of the same: animal expectation or habit formation. And the ostensive learning of words is an implicit case of induction. Implicitly the learner of "yellow" is working inductively toward a general law of English verbal behavior, though a law that he will never try to state; he is working up to where he can in general judge when an English speaker would assent to "yellow" and when not.

Not only is ostensive learning a case of induction; it is a curiously comfortable case of induction, a game of chance with loaded dice. At any rate this is so if, as seems plausible, each man's spacing of qualities is enough like his neighbor's. For the learner is generalizing on his yellow samples by similarity considerations, and his neighbors have themselves acquired the use of the word "yellow," in their day, by the same similarity considerations. The learner of "yellow" is thus making his induction in a friendly world. Always, induction expresses our hope that similar causes will have similar effects; but when the induction is the ostensive learning of a word, that pious hope blossoms into a foregone conclusion. The uniformity of people's quality spaces virtually assures that similar presentations will elicit similar verdicts.

It makes one wonder the more about other inductions, where what is sought is a generalization not about our neighbor's verbal behavior but about the harsh impersonal world. It is reasonable that our quality space should match our neighbor's, we being birds of a feather; and so the general trustworthiness of induction in the ostensive learning of words was a put-up job. To trust induction as a way of access to the truths of nature, on the other hand, is to suppose, more nearly, that our quality space matches that of the cosmos. The brute irrationality of our sense of similarity, its irrelevance to anything in logic and mathematics, offers little reason to expect that this sense is somehow in tune with the world—a world which, unlike language, we never made. Why induction should be trusted, apart from special cases such as the ostensive learning of words, is the perennial philosophical problem of induction.

One part of the problem of induction, the part that asks why there should be regularities in nature at all, can, I think, be dismissed. *That* there are or have been regularities, for whatever reason, is an established fact of science; and we cannot ask better

than that. *Why* there have been regularities is an obscure question, for it is hard to see what would count as an answer. What does make clear sense is this other part of the problem of induction: why does our innate subjective spacing of qualities accord so well with the functionally relevant groupings in nature as to make our inductions tend to come out right? Why should our subjective spacing of qualities have a special purchase on nature and a lien on the future?

There is some encouragement in Darwin. If people's innate spacing of qualities is a gene-linked trait, then the spacing that has made for the most successful inductions will have tended to predominate through natural selection.[11] Creatures inveterately wrong in their inductions have a pathetic but praiseworthy tendency to die before reproducing their kind.

At this point let me say that I shall not be impressed by protests that I am using inductive generalizations, Darwin's and others, to justify induction, and thus reasoning in a circle. The reason I shall not be impressed by this is that my position is a naturalistic one; I see philosophy not as an a priori propaedeutic or groundwork for science, but as continuous with science. I see philosophy and science as in the same boat—a boat which, to revert to Neurath's figure as I so often do, we can rebuild only at sea while staying afloat in it. There is no external vantage point, no first philosophy. All scientific findings, all scientific conjectures that are at present plausible, are therefore in my view as welcome for use in philosophy as elsewhere. For me then the problem of induction is a problem about the world: a problem of how we, as we now are (by our present scientific lights), in a world we never made, should stand better than random or coin-tossing chances of coming out right when we predict by inductions which are based on our innate, scientifically unjustified similarity standard. Darwin's natural selection is a plausible partial explanation.

It may, in view of a consideration to which I next turn, be almost explanation enough. This consideration is that induction, after all, has its conspicuous failures.

Thus take color. Nothing in experience, surely, is more vivid and conspicuous than color and its contrasts. And the remarkable fact, which has impressed scientists and philosophers as far back at least as Galileo and Descartes, is that the distinctions that matter for basic physical theory are mostly independent of color contrasts. Color impresses man; raven black impresses Hempel; emerald green impresses Goodman. But color is cosmically secondary. Even slight differences in sensory mechanisms from species to species, Smart remarks,[12] can make overwhelming differences in the grouping of things by color. Color is king in our innate quality space, but undistinguished in cosmic circles. Cosmically, colors would not qualify as kinds.

Color is helpful at the food-gathering level. Here it behaves well under induction, and here, no doubt, has been the survival value of our color-slanted quality space. It is just that contrasts that are crucial for such activities can be insignificant for broader and more theoretical science. If man were to live by basic science alone, natural selection would shift its support to the color-blind mutation.

Living as he does by bread and basic science both, man is torn. Things about his innate similarity sense that are helpful in the one sphere can be a hindrance in the other. Credit is due man's inveterate ingenuity, or human sapience, for having worked around the blinding dazzle of color vision and found the more significant regularities elsewhere. Evidently natural selection has dealt with the conflict by endowing man doubly: with both a color-slanted quality space and the ingenuity to rise above it.

He has risen above it by developing modified systems of kinds, hence modified similarity standards for scientific purposes. By the trial-and-error process of theorizing he has regrouped things into new kinds which prove to lend themselves to many inductions better than the old.

A crude example is the modification of the notion of fish by excluding whales and porpoises. Another taxonomic example is the grouping of kangaroos, opossums, and marsupial mice in a single kind, marsupials, while excluding ordinary mice. By primitive standards the marsupial mouse is more similar to the ordinary mouse than to the kangaroo; by theoretical standards the reverse is true.

A theoretical kind need not be a modification of an intuitive one. It may issue from theory full-blown, without antecedents; for instance the kind which comprises positively charged particles.

We revise our standards of similarity or of natural kinds on the strength, as Goodman remarks,[13] of second-order inductions. New groupings, hypothetically adopted at the suggestion of a growing theory, prove favorable to inductions and so become "entrenched." We newly establish the projectibility of some predicate, to our satisfaction, by successfully trying to project it. In induction nothing succeeds like success.

Between an innate similarity notion or spacing of qualities and a scientifically sophisticated one, there are all gradations. Science, after all, differs from common sense only in degree of methodological sophistication. Our experiences from earliest infancy are bound to have overlaid our innate spacing of qualities by modifying and supplementing our grouping habits little by little, inclining us more and more to an appreciation of theoretical kinds and similarities, long before we reach the point of studying science systematically as such. Moreover, the later phases do not wholly supersede the earlier; we retain different similarity standards, different systems of kinds, for use in different contexts. We all still say that a marsupial mouse is more like an ordinary mouse than a kangaroo, except when we are concerned with genetic matters. Something like our innate quality space continued to function alongside the more sophisticated regroupings that have been found by scientific experience to facilitate induction.

We have seen that a sense of similarity or of kinds is fundamental to learning in the widest sense—to language learning, to induction, to expectation. Toward a further appreciation of how utterly this notion permeates our thought, I want now to point out a number of other very familiar and central notions which seem to depend squarely on this one. They are notions that are definable in terms of similarity, or kinds, and further irreducible.

A notable domain of examples is the domain of dispositions, such as Carnap's example of solubility in water. To say of some individual object that it is soluble in water is not to say merely that it always dissolves when in water, because this would be true by default of any object, however insoluble, if it merely happened to be destined never to get into water. It is to say rather that it *would* dissolve if it were in water; but this account brings small comfort, since the device of a subjunctive conditional involves all the perplexities of disposition terms and more. Thus far I simply repeat Carnap.[14] But now I want to point out what could be done in this connection with the notion of kind. Intuitively, what qualifies a thing as soluble though it never gets into water is that it is of the same kind as the things that actually did or will dissolve; it is similar to them. Strictly we can't simply say "*the* same kind," nor simply "similar," when we have wider and narrower kinds, less and more similarity. Let us then mend our definition by saying that the soluble things are the common members of *all* such kinds. A thing is soluble if *each* kind that is broad enough to embrace all actual victims of solution embraces it too.

Graphically the idea is this: we make a set of all the sometime victims, all the things that actually did or will dissolve in water, and then we add just enough other things to round the set out into a kind. This is the water-soluble kind.

If this definition covers just the desired things, the things that are really soluble in water, it owes its success to a circumstance that could be otherwise. The needed circumstance is that a sufficient variety of things actually get dissolved in water to assure their not all falling under any one kind narrower than the desired water-soluble kind itself. But it is a plausible circumstance, and I am not sure that its accidental character is a drawback. If the trend of events had been

otherwise, perhaps the solubility concept would not have been wanted.

However, if I seem to be defending this definition, I must now hasten to add that of course it has much the same fault as the definition which used the subjunctive conditional. This definition uses the unreduced notion of kind, which is certainly not a notion we want to rest with either; neither theoretical kind nor intuitive kind. My purpose in giving the definition is only to show the link between the problem of dispositions and the problem of kinds.

As between theoretical and intuitive kinds, certainly the theoretical ones are the ones wanted for purposes of defining solubility and other dispositions of scientific concern. Perhaps "amiable" and "reprehensible" are disposition terms whose definitions should draw rather on intuitive kinds.

Another dim notion, which has intimate connections with dispositions and subjunctive conditionals, is the notion of cause; and we shall see that it too turns on the notion of kinds. Hume explained cause as invariable succession, and this makes sense as long as the cause and effect are referred to by general terms. We can say that fire causes heat, and we can mean thereby, as Hume would have it, that each event classifiable under the head of fire is followed by an event classifiable under the head of heat, or heating up. But this account, whatever its virtues for these general causal statements, leaves singular causal statements unexplained.

What does it mean to say that the kicking over of a lamp in Mrs. O'Leary's barn caused the Chicago fire? It cannot mean merely that the event at Mrs. O'Leary's belongs to a set, and the Chicago fire belongs to a set, such that there is invariable succession between the two sets: every member of the one set is followed by a member of the other. This paraphrase is trivially true and too weak. Always, if one event happens to be followed by another, the two belong to *certain* sets between which there is invariable succession. We can rig the sets arbitrarily. Just put any arbitrary events in the first set, including the first of the two events we are interested in; and then in the other set put the second of those two events, together with other events that happen to have occurred just after the other members of the first set.

Because of this way of trivialization, a singular causal statement says no more than that the one event was followed by the other. That is, it says no more if we use the definition just now contemplated; which, therefore, we must not. The trouble with that definition is clear enough: it is the familiar old trouble of the promiscuity of sets. Here, as usual, kinds, being more discriminate, enable us to draw distinctions where sets do not. To say that one event caused another is to say that the two events are of *kinds* between which there is invariable succession. If this correction does not yet take care of Mrs. O'Leary's cow, the fault is only with invariable succession itself, as affording too simple a definition of general causal statements; we need to hedge it around with provisions for partial or contributing causes and a good deal else. That aspect of the causality problem is not my concern. What I wanted to bring out is just the relevance of the notion of kinds, as the needed link between singular and general causal statements.

We have noticed that the notion of kind, or similarity, is crucially relevant to the notion of disposition, to the subjunctive conditional, and to singular causal statements. From a scientific point of view these are a pretty disreputable lot. The notion of kind, or similarity, is equally disreputable. Yet some such notion, some similarity sense, was seen to be crucial to all learning, and central in particular to the processes of inductive generalization and prediction which are the very life of science. It appears that science is rotten to the core.

Yet there may be claimed for this rot a certain undeniable fecundity. Science reveals hidden mysteries, predicts successfully, and works technological wonders. If this is the way of rot, then rot is rather to be prized and praised than patronized.

Rot, actually, is not the best model here. A better model is human progress. A sense of comparative similarity, I remarked earlier, is one of man's animal endowments. Insofar as it fits in with regularities of nature, so as to afford us reasonable success in our primitive inductions and expectations, it is presumably an evolutionary product of natural selection. Secondly, as remarked, one's sense of similarity or one's system of kinds develops and changes and even turns multiple as one matures, making perhaps for increasingly dependable prediction. And at length standards of similarity set in which are geared to theoretical science. This development is a development away from the immediate, subjective, animal sense of similarity to the remoter objectivity of a similarity determined by scientific hypotheses and posits and constructs. Things are similar in the later or theoretical sense to the degree that they are interchangeable parts of the cosmic machine revealed by science.

This progress of similarity standards, in the course of each individual's maturing years, is a sort of recapitulation in the individual of the race's progress from muddy savagery. But the similarity notion even in its theoretical phase is itself a muddy notion still. We have offered no definition of it in satisfactory scientific terms. We of course have a behavioral definition of what counts, for a given individual, as similar to what, or as more similar to what than to what; we have this for similarity old and new, human and animal. But it is no definition of what it means really for a to be more similar to b than to c; really, and quite apart from this or that psychological subject.

Did I already suggest a definition to this purpose, metaphorically, when I said that things are similar to the extent that they are interchangeable parts of the cosmic machine? More literally, could things be said to be similar in proportion to how much of scientific theory would remain true on interchanging those things as objects of reference in the theory? This only hints a direction; consider for instance the dimness of "how much theory." Anyway the direction itself is not a good one; for it would make similarity depend in the wrong way on theory. A man's judgments of similarity do and should depend on his theory, on his beliefs; but similarity itself, what the man's judgments purport to be judgments of, purports to be an objective relation in the world. It belongs in the subject matter not of our theory of theorizing about the world, but of our theory of the world itself. Such would be the acceptable and reputable sort of similarity concept, if it could be defined.

It does get defined in bits: bits suited to special branches of science. In this way, on many limited fronts, man continues his rise from savagery, sloughing off the muddy old notion of kind or similarity piecemeal, a vestige here and a vestige there. Chemistry, the home science of water-solubility itself, is one branch that has reached this stage. Comparative similarity of the sort that matters for chemistry can be stated outright in chemical terms, that is, in terms of chemical composition. Molecules will be said to *match* if they contain atoms of the same elements in the same topological combinations. Then, in principle, we might get at the comparative similarity of objects a and b by considering how many pairs of matching molecules there are, one molecule from a and one from b each time, and how many unmatching pairs. The ratio gives even a theoretical measure of relative similarity, and thus abundantly explains what it is for a to be more similar to b than to c. Or we might prefer to complicate our definition by allowing also for degrees in the matching of molecules; molecules having almost equally many atoms, or having atoms whose atomic numbers or atomic weights are almost equal, could be reckoned as matching better than others. At any rate a lusty chemical similarity concept is assured.

From it, moreover, an equally acceptable concept of kinds is derivable, by the paradigm-and-foil definition noted early in this paper. For it is a question now only of distilling purely chemical kinds from purely chemical similarity; no admixture of other respects of similarity interferes. We thus exonerate water-solubility, which, the last time around, we had reduced no further than to an unexplained notion of kind. Therewith also the associated subjunctive

conditional, "If this were in water it would dissolve," gets its bill of health.

The same scientific advances that have thus provided a solid underpinning for the definition of solubility in terms of kinds, have also, ironically enough, made that line of definition pointless by providing a full understanding of the mechanism of solution. One can redefine water-solubility by simply describing the structural conditions of that mechanism. This embarrassment of riches is, I suspect, a characteristic outcome. That is, once we can legitimize a disposition term by defining the relevant similarity standard, we are apt to know the mechanism of the disposition, and so by-pass the similarity. Not but that the similarity standard is worth clarifying too, for its own sake or for other purposes.

Philosophical or broadly scientific motives can impel us to seek still a basic and absolute concept of similarity, along with such fragmentary similarity concepts as suit special branches of science. This drive for a cosmic similarity concept is perhaps identifiable with the age-old drive to reduce things to their elements. It epitomizes the scientific spirit, though dating back to the pre-Socratics: to Empedocles with his theory of four elements, and above all to Democritus with his atoms. The modern physics of elementary particles, or of hills in space-time, is a more notable effort in this direction.

This idea of rationalizing a single notion of relative similarity, throughout its cosmic sweep, has its metaphysical attractions. But there would remain still the need also to rationalize the similarity notion more locally and superficially, so as to capture only such similarity as is relevant to some special science. Our chemistry example is already a case of this, since it stops short of full analysis into neutrons, electrons, and the other elementary particles.

A more striking example of superficiality, in this good sense, is afforded by taxonomy, say in zoology. Since learning about the evolution of species, we are in a position to define comparative similarity suitably for this science by consideration of family trees. For a theoretical measure of the degree of similarity of two individual animals we can devise some suitable function that depends on proximity and frequency of their common ancestors. Or a more significant concept of degree of similarity might be devised in terms of genes. When kind is construed in terms of any such similarity concept, fishes in the corrected, whale-free sense of the word qualify as a kind while fishes in the more inclusive sense do not.

Different similarity measures, or relative similarity notions, best suit different branches of science; for there are wasteful complications in providing for finer gradations of relative similarity than matter for the phenomena with which the particular science is concerned. Perhaps the branches of science could be revealingly classified by looking to the relative similarity notion that is appropriate to each. Such a plan is reminiscent of Felix Klein's so-called *Erlangerprogramm* in geometry, which involved characterizing the various branches of geometry by what transformations were irrelevant to each. But a branch of science would only qualify for recognition and classification under such a plan when it had matured to the point of clearing up its similarity notion. Such branches of science would qualify further as unified, or integrated into our inclusive systematization of nature, only insofar as their several similarity concepts were *compatible;* capable of meshing, that is, and differing only in the fineness of their discriminations.

Disposition terms and subjunctive conditionals in these areas, where suitable senses of similarity and kind are forthcoming, suddenly turn respectable; respectable and, in principle, superfluous. In other domains they remain disreputable and practically indispensable. They may be seen perhaps as unredeemed notes; the theory that would clear up the unanalyzed underlying similarity notion in such cases is still to come. An example is the disposition called intelligence—the ability, vaguely speaking, to learn quickly and to solve problems. Sometime, whether in terms of proteins or colloids or nerve nets or overt behavior, the relevant branch of science may reach the stage where a similarity notion can be constructed capable of making even the notion of intelligence respectable. And superfluous.

In general we can take it as a very special mark of the maturity of a branch of science that it no longer needs an irreducible notion of similarity and kind. It is that final stage where the animal vestige is wholly absorbed into the theory. In this career of the similarity notion, starting in its innate phase, developing over the years in the light of accumulated experience, passing then from the intuitive phase into theoretical similarity, and finally disappearing altogether, we have a paradigm of the evolution of unreason into science.

NOTES

[1] C. G. Hempel, *Aspects of Scientific Explanation and Other Essays* (New York: Free Press, 1965), p. 15.

[2] Nelson Goodman, *Fact, Fiction, and Forecast* (Cambridge, Mass.: Harvard University Press, 1955, or New York: Bobbs-Merrill, 1965), p. 74. I am indebted to Goodman and to Burton Dreben for helpful criticisms of earlier drafts of the present paper.

[3] Goodman, *Fact,* pp. 82f.

[4] *Ibid.,* pp. 95ff.

[5] I mean this only as a sufficient condition of lawlikeness. See Donald Davidson, "Emeroses by other Names," *Journal of Philosophy,* 63 (1966), 778–780.

[6] This relevance of kind is noted by Goodman, *Fact,* first edition, pp. 119f; second edition, pp. 121f.

[7] Nelson Goodman, *The Structure of Appearance,* 2d ed. (New York: Bobbs-Merrill, 1966), pp. 163f.

[8] Rudolf Carnap, *The Logical Structure of the World* (Berkeley: University of California Press, 1967), pp. 141–147 (German edition, 1928).

[9] See my *Word and Object* (Boston: MIT Press, 1960), pp. 83f, for further discussion and references.

[10] See *Word and Object,* pp. 90–95.

[11] This was noted by S. Watanabe on the second page of his paper "Une explication mathematique du classement d'objets," in *Information and Prediction in Science,* ed. by S. Dockx and P. Bernays (New York: Academic Press, 1965).

[12] J. J. C. Smart, *Philosophy and Scientific Realism* (New York: Humanities, 1963), pp. 68–72.

[13] Goodman, *Fact,* pp. 95ff.

[14] Carnap, "Testability and Meaning," *Philosophy of Science,* 3 (1936), 419–471; 4 (1937), 1–40.

Essences and Natural Kinds

Meaning and Reference*

Hilary Putnam

Unclear as it is, the traditional doctrine that the notion "meaning" possesses the extension/intension ambiguity has certain typical consequences. The doctrine that the meaning of a term is a concept carried the implication that meanings are mental entities. Frege, however, rebelled against this "psychologism." Feeling that meanings are *public* property—that the *same* meaning can be "grasped" by more than one person and by persons at different times—he identified concepts (and hence "intensions" or meanings) with abstract entities rather than mental entities. However, "grasping" these abstract entities was still an individual psychological act. None of these philosophers doubted that understanding a word (knowing its intension) was just a matter of being in a certain psychological state (somewhat in the way in which knowing how to factor numbers in one's head is just a matter of being in a certain very complex psychological state).

Secondly, the timeworn example of the two terms 'creature with a kidney' and 'crea-

ture with a heart' does show that two terms can have the same extension and yet differ in intension. But it was taken to be obvious that the reverse is impossible: two terms cannot differ in extension and have the same intension. Interestingly, no argument for this impossibility was ever offered. Probably it reflects the tradition of the ancient and medieval philosophers, who assumed that the concept corresponding to a term was just a conjunction of predicates, and hence that the concept corresponding to a term must *always* provide a necessary and sufficient condition for falling into the extension of the term. For philosophers like Carnap, who accepted the verifiability theory of meaning, the concept corresponding to a term provided (in the ideal case, where the term had "complete meaning") a *criterion* for belonging to the extension (not just in the sense of "necessary and sufficient condition," but in the strong sense of *way of recognizing* whether a given thing falls into the extension or not). So theory of meaning came to rest on two unchallenged assumptions:

(1) That knowing the meaning of a term is just a matter of being in a certain psychological state (in the sense of

*Copyright © 1973 by *The Journal of Philosophy.* Reprinted by permission, from *The Journal of Philosophy* 70 (November 1973), 699–711.

"psychological state," in which states of memory and belief are "psychological states"; no one thought that knowing the meaning of a word was a continuous state of consciousness, of course).

(2) That the meaning of a term determines its extension (in the sense that sameness of intension entails sameness of extension).

I shall argue that these two assumptions are not jointly satisfied by *any* notion, let alone any notion of meaning. The traditional concept of meaning is a concept which rests on a false theory.

ARE MEANINGS IN THE HEAD?

For the purpose of the following science-fiction examples, we shall suppose that somewhere there is a planet we shall call Twin Earth. Twin Earth is very much like Earth: in fact, people on Twin Earth even speak *English*. In fact, apart from the differences we shall specify in our science-fiction examples, the reader may suppose that Twin Earth is *exactly* like Earth. He may even suppose that he has a *Doppelgänger*—an identical copy—on Twin Earth, if he wishes, although my stories will not depend on this.

Although some of the people on Twin Earth (say, those who call themselves "Americans" and those who call themselves "Canadians" and those who call themselves "Englishmen," etc.) speak English, there are, not surprisingly, a few tiny differences between the dialects of English spoken on Twin Earth and standard English.

One of the peculiarities of Twin Earth is that the liquid called "water" is not H_2O but a different liquid whose chemical formula is very long and complicated. I shall abbreviate this chemical formula simply as XYZ. I shall suppose that XYZ is indistinguishable from water at normal temperatures and pressures. Also, I shall suppppose that the oceans and lakes and seas of Twin Earth contain XYZ and not water, that it rains XYZ on Twin Earth and not water, etc.

If a space ship from Earth ever visits Twin Earth, then the supposition at first will be that 'water' has the same meaning on Earth and on Twin Earth. This supposition will be corrected when it is discovered that "water" on Twin Earth is XYZ, and the Earthian space ship will report somewhat as follows. "On Twin Earth the word 'water' means XYZ."

Symmetrically, if a space ship from Twin Earth ever visits Earth, then the supposition at first will be that the word 'water' has the same meaning on Twin Earth and on Earth. This supposition will be corrected when it is discovered that "water" on Earth is H_2O, and the Twin Earthian space ship will report:

"On Earth the word 'water' means H_2O."

Note that there is no problem about the extension of the term 'water': the word simply has two different meanings (as we say); in the sense in which it is used on Twin Earth, the sense of water$_{TE}$, what *we* call "water" simply isn't water, while in the sense in which it is used on Earth, the sense of water$_E$, what the Twin Earthians call "water" simply isn't water. The extension of 'water' in the sense of water$_E$ is the set of all wholes consisting of H_2O molecules, or something like that; the extension of water in the sense of water$_{TE}$ is the set of all wholes consisting of XYZ molecules, or something like that.

Now let us roll the time back to about 1750. The typical Earthian speaker of English did not know that water consisted of hydrogen and oxygen, and the typical Twin Earthian speaker of English did not know that "water" consisted of XYZ. Let Oscar$_1$ be such a typical Earthian English speaker, and let Oscar$_2$ be his counterpart on Twin Earth. You may suppose that there is no belief that Oscar$_1$ had about water that Oscar$_2$ did not have about "water." If you like, you may even suppose that Oscar$_1$ and Oscar$_2$ were exact duplicates in appearance, feelings, thoughts, interior monologue, etc. Yet the extension of the term 'water' was just as much H_2O on Earth in 1750 as in 1950; and the extension of the term 'water' was just as much XYZ on Twin Earth in 1750 as in 1950. Oscar$_1$ and Oscar$_2$ understood the term 'water' differently in 1750 *although they were in* the same psychological state, and although, given the state of science at the time, it would have taken their scientific communities about fifty years to discover that they understood the term 'water' differently. Thus the extension of the term 'water' (and, in fact, its "meaning" in the intuitive preanalytical usage of that term) is *not* a function of the psychological state of the speaker by itself.[1]

But, it might be objected, why should we accept it that the term 'water' had the same extension in 1750 and in 1950 (on both Earths)? Suppose I point to a glass of water and say "this liquid is called water." My "ostensive definition" of water has the following empirical presupposition: that the body of liquid I am pointing to bears a certain sameness relation (say, *x is the same liquid as y*, or *x is the same$_L$ as y*) to most of the stuff I and other speakers in my linguistic community have on other occasions called "water." If this presupposition is false because, say, I am—unknown to me—pointing to a glass of gin and not a glass of water, then I do not intend my ostensive definition to be accepted. Thus the ostensive definition conveys what might be called a "defeasible" necessary and sufficient condition: the necessary and sufficient condition for being water is bearing the relation *same$_L$* to the stuff in the glass; but this is the necessary and sufficient condition only if the empirical presupposition is satisfied. If it is not satisfied, then one of a series of, so to speak, "fallback" conditions becomes activated.

The key point is that the relation *same$_L$* is a *theoretical* relation: whether something is or is not the same liquid as *this* may take an indeterminate amount of scientific investigation to determine. Thus, the fact that an English speaker in 1750 might have called XYZ "water," whereas he or his successors would not have called XYZ water in 1800 or 1850 does not mean that the "meaning" of 'water' changed for the average speaker in the interval. In 1750 or in 1850 or in 1950 one might have pointed to, say, the liquid in Lake Michigan as an example of "water." What changed was that in 1750 we would

have mistakenly thought that XYZ bore the relation *same$_L$* to the liquid in Lake Michigan, whereas in 1800 or 1850 we would have known that it did not.

Let us now modify our science-fiction story. I shall suppose that molybdenum pots and pans *can't* be distinguished from aluminum pots and pans save by an expert. (This could be true for all I know, and, a fortiori, it could be true for all I know by virtue of "knowing the meaning" of the words *aluminum* and *molybdenum*.) We will now suppose that molybdenum is as common on Twin Earth as aluminum is on Earth, and that aluminum is as rare on Twin Earth as molybdenum is on Earth. In particular, we shall assume that "aluminum" pots and pans are made of molybdenum on Twin Earth. Finally, we shall assume that the words 'aluminum' and 'molybdenum' are *switched* on Twin Earth: 'aluminum' is the name of *molybdenum*, and 'molybdenum' is the name of *aluminum*. If a space ship from Earth visited Twin Earth, the visitors from Earth probably would not suspect that the "aluminum" pots and pans on Twin Earth were not made of aluminum, especially when the Twin Earthians *said* they were. But there is one important difference between the two cases. An Earthian metallurgist could tell very easily that "aluminum" was molybdenum, and a Twin Earthian metallurgist could tell equally easily that aluminum was "molybdenum." (The shudder quotes in the preceding sentence indicated Twin Earthian usages.) Whereas in 1750 no one on either Earth or Twin Earth could have distinguished water from "water," the confusion of aluminum with "aluminum" involves only a part of the linguistic communities involved.

This example makes the same point as the preceding example. If Oscar$_1$ and Oscar$_2$ are standard speakers of Earthian English and Twin Earthian English, respectively, and neither is chemically or metallurgically sophisticated, then there may be no difference at all in their psychological states when they use the word 'aluminum'; nevertheless, we have to say that 'aluminum' has the extension *aluminum* in the idiolect of Oscar$_1$

and the extension *molybdenum* in the idiolect of Oscar₂. (Also we have to say that Oscar₁ and Oscar₂ mean different things by 'aluminum'; that 'aluminum' has a different meaning on Earth than it does on Twin Earth, etc.) Again we see that the psychological state of the speaker does *not* determine the extension (*or* the "meaning," speaking preanalytically) of the word.

Before discussing this example further, let me introduce a *non*-science-fiction example. Suppose you are like me and cannot tell an elm from a beech tree. We still say that the extension of 'elm' in my idiolect is the same as the extension of 'elm' in anyone else's, viz., the set of all elm trees, and that the set of all beech trees is the extension of 'beech' in *both* of our idiolects. Thus 'elm' in my idiolect has a different extension from 'beech' in your idiolect (as it should). Is it really credible that this difference in extension is brought about by some difference in our *concepts?* My *concept* of an elm tree is exactly the same as my concept of a beech tree (I blush to confess). If someone heroically attempts to maintain that the difference between the extension of 'elm' and the extension of 'beech' in *my* idiolect is explained by a difference in my psychological state, then we can always refute him by constructing a "Twin Earth" example—just let the words 'elm' and 'beech' be switched on Twin Earth (the way 'aluminum' and 'molybdenum' were in the previous example). Moreover, suppose I have a *Doppelgänger* on Twin Earth who is molecule for molecule "identical" with me. If you are a dualist, then also suppose my *Doppelgänger* thinks the same verbalized thoughts I do, has the same sense data, the same dispositions, etc. It is absurd to think *his* psychological state is one bit different from mine: yet he "means" *beech* when he says "elm," and *I* "mean" *elm* when I say "elm." Cut the pie any way you like, "meanings" just ain't in the *head!*

A SOCIOLINGUISTIC HYPOTHESIS

The last two examples depend upon a fact about language that seems, surprisingly, never to have been pointed out: that there is *division of linguistic labor.* We could hardly use such words as 'elm' and 'aluminum' if no one possessed a way of recognizing elm trees and aluminum metal; but not everyone to whom the distinction is important has to be able to make the distinction. Let us shift the example; consider *gold.* Gold is important for many reasons: it is a precious metal; it is a monetary metal; it has symbolic value (it is important to most people that the "gold" wedding ring they wear *really* consist of gold and not just *look* gold); etc. Consider our community as a "factory": in this "factory" some people have the "job" of *wearing gold wedding rings;* other people have the "job" of selling gold wedding rings; still other people have the job of *telling whether or not something is really gold.* It is not at all necessary or efficient that everyone who wears a gold ring (or a gold cufflink, etc.), or discusses the "gold standard," etc., engage in buying and selling gold. Nor is it necessary or efficient that everyone who buys and sells gold be able to tell whether or not something is really gold in a society where this form of dishonesty is uncommon (selling fake gold) and in which one can easily consult an expert in case of doubt. And it is *certainly* not necessary or efficient that everyone who has occasion to buy or wear gold be able to tell with any reliability whether or not something is really gold.

The foregoing facts are just examples of mundane division of labor (in a wide sense). But they engender a division of linguistic labor: everyone to whom gold is important for any reason has to *acquire* the word 'gold'; but he does not have to acquire the *method of recognizing* whether something is or is not gold. He can rely on a special subclass of speakers. The features that are generally thought to be present in connection with a general name—necessary and sufficient conditions for membership in the extension, ways of recognizing whether something is in the extension, etc.—are all present in the linguistic community *considered as a collective body;* but that collective body divides the "labor" of knowing and employing these various parts of the "meaning" of 'gold'.

This division of linguistic labor rests upon and presupposes the division of *non*linguistic labor, of course. If only the people who know how to tell whether some metal is really gold or not have any reason to have the word 'gold' in their vocabulary, then the word 'gold' will be as the word 'water' was in 1750 with respect to that subclass of speakers, and the other speakers just won't acquire it at all. And some words do not exhibit any division of linguistic labor: 'chair', for example. But with the increase of division of labor in the society and the rise of science, more and more words begin to exhibit this kind of division of labor. 'Water', for example, did not exhibit it at all before the rise of chemistry. Today it is obviously necessary for every speaker to be able to recognize water (reliably under normal conditions), and probably most adult speakers even know the necessary and sufficient condition "water is H_2O," but only a few adult speakers could distinguish water from liquids that superficially resembled water. In case of doubt, other speakers would rely on the judgment of these "expert" speakers. Thus the way of recognizing possessed by these 'expert' speakers is also, through them, possessed by the collective linguistic body, even though it is not possessed by each individual member of the body, and in this way the most *recherché* fact about water may become part of the *social* meaning of the word although unknown to almost all speakers who acquire the word.

It seems to me that this phenomenon of division of linguistic labor is one that it will be very important for sociolinguistics to investigate. In connection with it, I should like to propose the following hypothesis:

HYPOTHESIS OF THE UNIVERSALITY OF THE DIVISION OF LINGUISTIC LABOR: Every linguistic community exemplifies the sort of division of linguistic labor just described; that is, it possesses at least some terms whose associated "criteria" are known only to a subset of the speakers who acquire the terms, and whose use by the other speakers depends upon a struc-

tured cooperation between them and the speakers in the relevant subsets.

It is easy to see how this phenomenon accounts for some of the examples given above of the failure of the assumptions (1 and 2). When a term is subject to the division of linguistic labor, the "average" speaker who acquires it does not acquire anything that fixes its extension. In particular, his individual psychological state *certainly* does not fix its extension; it is only the sociolinguistic state of the collective linguistic body to which the speaker belongs that fixes the extension.

We may summarize this discussion by pointing out that there are two sorts of tools in the world: there are tools like a hammer or a screwdriver which can be used by one person; and there are tools like a steamship which require the cooperative activity of a number of persons to use. Words have been thought of too much on the model of the first sort of tool.

Indexicality and Rigidity

The first of our science-fiction examples—'water' on Earth and on Twin Earth in 1750—does not involve division of linguistic labor, or at least does not involve it in the same way the examples of 'aluminum' and 'elm' do. There were not (in our story, anyway) any "experts" on water on Earth in 1750, nor any experts on "water" on Twin Earth. The example *does* involve things which are of fundamental importance to the theory of reference and also to the theory of necessary truth, which we shall now discuss.

Let W_1 and W_2 be two possible worlds in which I exist and in which this glass exists and in which I am giving a meaning explanation by pointing to this glass and saying "This is water." Let us suppose that in W_1 the glass is full of H_2O and in W_2 the glass is full of XYZ. We shall also suppose that W_1 is the *actual* world, and that XYZ is the stuff typically called "water" in the world W_2 (so that the relation between English speakers in W_1 and English speakers in W_2 is exactly the same as the relation between English speakers on Earth and English speakers on Twin Earth). Then there are two theories one might have concerning the meaning of 'water':

(1) One might hold that 'water' was *world-relative* but *constant* in meaning (i.e., the word has a constant relative meaning). On this theory, 'water' means the same in W_1 and W_2; it's just that water is H_2O in W_1, and water is XYZ in W_2.

(2) One might hold that water is H_2O in all worlds (the stuff called"water" in W_2 isn't water), but 'water' doesn't have the same meaning in W_1 and W_2.

If what was said before about the Twin Earth case was correct, then (2) is clearly the correct theory. When I say "*this* (liquid) is water," the "this" is, so to speak, a *de re* "this"—i.e., the force of my explanation is that "water" is whatever bears a certain equivalence relation (the relation we called "*same*$_L$" above) to the piece of liquid referred to as "this" *in the actual world*.

We might symbolize the difference between the two theories as a "scope" difference in the following way. On theory (1), the following is true:

1'. (For every world W) (For every x in W) (x is water $\equiv$ x bears *same*$_L$ to the entity referred to as "this" in W)

while on theory (2):

2'. (For every world W) (For every x in W) (x is water $\equiv$ x bears *same*$_L$ to the entity referred to as "this" *in the actual world* W_1)

I call this a "scope" difference because in (1') 'the entity referred to as "this" ' is within the scope of 'For every world W'—as the qualifying phrase 'in W' makes explicit— whereas in (2') 'the entity referred to as "this" ' means "the entity referred to as 'this' *in the actual world*,' and has thus a reference *independent* of the bound variable 'W'.

Kripke calls a designator "rigid" (in a given sentence) if (in that sentence) it refers to the same individual in every possible world in which the designator designates. If

we extend this notion of rigidity to substance names, then we may express Kripke's theory and mine by saying that the term 'water' is *rigid*.

The rigidity of the term 'water' follows from the fact that when I give the "ostensive definition": "*this* (liquid) is water," I intend (2') and not (1').

We may also say, following Kripke, that when I give the ostensive definition "*this* (liquid) is water," the demonstrative 'this' is *rigid*.

What Kripke was the first to observe is that this theory of the meaning (or "use," or whatever) of the word 'water' (and other natural kind terms as well) has startling consequences for the theory of necessary truth.

To explain this, let me introduce the notion of a *cross-world relation*. A two-term relation R will be called *cross-world* when it is understood in such a way that its extension is a set of ordered pairs of individuals *not at all in the same possible world*. For example, it is easy to understand the relation *same height as* as a cross-world relation: just understand it so that, e.g., if x is an individual in a world W_1 who is 5 feet tall (in W_1) and y is an individual in W_2 who is 5 feet tall (in W_2), then the ordered pair x,y belongs to the extension of *same height as*. (Since an individual may have different heights in different possible worlds in which that same individual exists, strictly speaking, it is not the ordered pair x,y that constitutes an element of the extension of *same height as*, but rather the ordered pair x-in-world-W_1, y-in-world-W_2.)

Similarly, we can understand the relation *same*$_L$ (same liquid as) as a cross-world relation by understanding it so that a liquid in world W_1 which has the same important physical properties (in W_1) that a liquid in W_2 possesses (in W_2) bears *same*$_L$ to latter liquid.

Then the theory we have been presenting may be summarized by saying that an entity x, in an arbitrary possible world, is *water* if and only if it bears the relation *same*$_L$ (construed as a cross-world relation) to the stuff *we* call "water" in the actual world.

Suppose, now, that I have not yet discovered what the important physical properties of water are (in the actual world)—i.e., I

    Essences and Natural Kinds

don't yet know that water is H_2O. I may have ways of *recognizing* water that are successful (of course, I may make a small number of mistakes that I won't be able to detect until a later state in our scientific development), but not know the microstructure of water. If I agree that a liquid with the superficial properties of "water" but a different microstructure *isn't really water,* then my ways of recognizing water cannot be regarded as an analytical specification of what *it is to be* water. Rather, the operational definition, like the ostensive one, is simply a way of pointing out a standard—pointing out the stuff *in the actual world* such that, for *x* to be water, in *any* world, is for *x* to bear the relation *same$_L$* to the *normal* members of the class of *local* entities that satisfy the operational definition. "Water" on Twin Earth is not water, even if it satisfies the operational definition, because it doesn't bear *same$_L$* to the *local* stuff that satisfies the operational definition, and local stuff that satisfies the operational definition but has a microstructure different from the rest of the local stuff that satisfies the operational definition isn't water either, because it doesn't bear *same$_L$* to the *normal* examples of the local "water."

Suppose, now, that I discover the microstructure of water—that water is H_2O. At this point I will be able to say that the stuff on Twin Earth that I earlier *mistook* for water isn't really water. In the same way, if you describe, not another planet in the actual universe, but another possible universe in which there is stuff with the chemical formula XYZ which passes the "operational test" for *water,* we shall have to say that that stuff isn't water but merely XYZ. You will not have described a possible world in which "water is XYZ," but merely a possible world in which there are lakes of XYZ, people drink XYZ (and not water), or whatever. In fact, once we have discovered the nature of water, nothing counts as a possible world in which water doesn't have that nature. Once we have discovered that water (in the actual world) is H_2O, *nothing counts as a possible world in which water isn't H_2O.*

On the other hand, we can perfectly well imagine having experiences that would con-

vince us (and that would make it rational to believe that) water *isn't* H_2O. In that sense, it is conceivable that water isn't H_2O. It is conceivable but it isn't possible! Conceivability is no proof of possibility.

Kripke refers to statements that are rationally unrevisable (assuming there are such) as *epistemically necessary.* Statements that are true in all possible worlds he refers to simply as necessary (or sometimes as "metaphysically necessary"). In this terminology, the point just made can be restated as: a statement can be (metaphysically) necessary and epistemically contingent. Human intuition has no privileged access to metaphysical necessity.

In this paper, our interest is in theory of meaning, however, and not in theory of necessary truth. Words like 'now', 'this', 'here' have long been recognized to be *indexical,* or *token-reflexive*—i.e., to have an extension which varies from context to context or token to token. For these words, no one has ever suggested the traditional theory that "intension determines extension." To take our Twin Earth example: if I have a *Doppelgänger* on Twin Earth, then when I think "I have a headache," *he* thinks "I have a headache." But the extension of the particular token of 'I' in his verbalized thought is himself (or his unit class, to be precise), while the extension of the token of 'I' in *my* verbalized thought is *me* (or my unit class, to be precise). So the same word, 'I', has two different extensions in two different idiolects; but it does not follow that the concept I have of myself is in any way different from the concept my *Doppelgänger* has of himself.

Now then, we have maintained that indexicality extends beyond the *obviously* indexical words and morphemes (e.g., the tenses of verbs). Our theory can be summarized as saying that words like 'water' have an unnoticed indexical component: "water" is stuff that bears a certain similarity relation to the water *around here.* Water at another time or in another place or even in another possible world has to bear the relation *same$_L$* to our "water" *in order to be water.* Thus the theory that (1) words have "intensions," which are something like concepts associated with the words by speakers; and (2) intension determines extension—cannot be true of natural kind words like 'water' for the same reason it cannot be true of obviously indexical words like 'I'.

The theory that natural kind words like 'water' are indexical leaves it open, however, whether to say that 'water' in the Twin Earth dialect of English has the same *meaning* as 'water' in the Earth dialect and a different extension—which is what we normally say about 'I' in different idiolects—thereby giving up the doctrine that "meaning (intension) determines extension," or to say, as we have chosen to do, that difference in extension is *ipso facto* a difference in meaning for natural kind words, thereby giving up the doctrine that meanings are concepts, or, indeed, mental entities of *any* kind.[2]

It should be clear, however, that Kripke's doctrine that natural kind words are rigid designators and our doctrine that they are indexical are but two ways of making the same point.

We have now seen that the extension of a term is not fixed by a concept that the individual speaker has in his head, and this is true both because extension is, in general, determined *socially*—there is division of linguistic labor as much as of "real" labor—and

because extension is, in part, determined *indexically*. The extension of our terms depends upon the actual nature of the particular things that serve as paradigms, and this actual nature is not, in general, fully known to the speaker. Traditional semantic theory leaves out two contributions to the determination of reference—the contribution of society and the contribution of the real world; a better semantic theory must encompass both.

NOTES

[1]See fn. 2, and the corresponding text.

[2]Our reasons for rejecting the first option—to say that 'water' has the same meaning on Earth and on Twin Earth, while giving up the doctrine that meaning determines references—are presented in "The Meaning of 'Meaning'." They may be illustrated thus: Suppose 'water' has the same meaning on Earth and on Twin Earth. Now, let the word 'water' become phonemically different on Twin Earth—say, it becomes 'quaxel'. Presumably, this is not a change in meaning per se, on any view. So 'water' and 'quaxel' have the same meaning (although they refer to different liquids). But this is highly counterintuitive. Why not say, then, that 'elm' in my idiolect has the same meaning as 'beech' in your idiolect, although they refer to different trees?

Recommended Readings on Universals, Essences, and Natural Kinds

Aaron, R. I. *The Theory of Universals,* 2d ed. Oxford: Oxford University Press, 1967.

Armstrong, D. M. *Universals and Scientific Realism,* 2 vols. Cambridge: Cambridge University Press, 1978.

Bergmann, Gustav. *Meaning and Existence.* Madison: University of Wisconsin Press, 1960.

———. *Realism: A Critique of Brentano and Meinong.* Madison: University of Wisconsin Press, 1967.

Brody, Baruch. *Identity and Essence.* Princeton: Princeton University Press, 1980.

Butchvarov, Panayot. *Being Qua Being: A Theory of Identity, Existence, and Predication.* Bloomington: Indiana University Press, 1979.

———. *Resemblance and Identity.* Bloomington: Indiana University Press, 1966.

Forbes, Graeme. *The Metaphysics of Modality.* Oxford: Clarendon Press, 1985.

French, P. A., T. E. Uehling, and H. K. Wettstein, eds. *Midwest Studies in Philosophy, Vol. 11: Studies in Essentialism.* Minneapolis: University of Minnesota Press, 1987.

Geach, P. T. *Reference and Generality.* Ithaca: Cornell University Press, 1962.

Goodman, Nelson. *The Structure of Appearance.* Cambridge, Mass.: Harvard University Press, 1951.

Kripke, Saul. *Naming and Necessity.* Cambridge, Mass.: Harvard University Press, 1980.

Loux, Michael. *Substance and Attribute.* Dordrecht: D. Reidel, 1976.

Loux, Michael, ed. *Universals and Particulars,* 2d ed. Notre Dame: University of Notre Dame Press, 1976.

————, ed. *The Possible and the Actual.* Ithaca: Cornell University Press, 1979.

Munitz, Milton, ed. *Identity and Individuation.* New York: New York University Press, 1972.

————. *Logic and Ontology.* New York: New York University Press, 1973.

Plantinga, Alvin. *The Nature of Necessity.* Oxford: Clarendon Press, 1974.

Price, H. H. *Thinking and Experience.* London: Hutchinson, 1953.

Putnam, Hilary. *Philosophy of Logic.* New York: Harper and Row, 1971.

Quinton, Anthony. *The Nature of Things.* London: Routledge and Kegan Paul, 1973.

Rescher, Nicholas. *A Theory of Possibility.* Pittsburgh: University of Pittsburgh Press, 1975.

Schwartz, S. P., ed. *Naming, Necessity, and Natural Kinds.* Ithaca: Cornell University Press, 1977.

Wiggins, David. *Identity and Spatio-Temporal Continuity.* Oxford: Basil Blackwell, 1967.

Wolterstorff, Nicholas. *On Universals.* Chicago: University of Chicago Press, 1973.

V

Reality and God

This section consists of four items on the question whether God exists. Traditionally, this has been one of the central questions of metaphysics, and it has been one of the most controversial. *Theism* states that God does exist; *atheism* states that God does not exist; and *agnosticism* recommends that we suspend judgment on the matter, on the ground that we lack sufficient evidence to affirm that God exists *and* to affirm that God does not exist. If one is an agnostic, one is not an atheist; and if one is an atheist, one is not an agnostic. Orthodox Judaism and Christianity endorse a version of theism that identifies God with a creator who is *omnipotent* (all powerful), *omniscient* (all knowing) and *omnibenevolent* (all loving). But these are not the only versions of theism. One longstanding problem in the philosophy of religion is the question of how we should understand the concept of God. The essays in this section take contrasting stands on not only this issue, but also the issue whether God exists.

In "A Defense of Atheism," Ernest Nagel begins with the orthodox Judeo-Christian notion of God, and argues that the traditional arguments for theism fail. Nagel criticizes the traditional cosmological argument, the traditional ontological argument, and the traditional arguments from design. Regarding the arguments from design, Nagel claims that the facts supposedly explained by theism are better explained by Darwinian biology. In addition, Nagel criticizes traditional theism on the ground that we cannot reconcile the alleged omnipotence and omnibenevolence of God with the sort of evil we find in the world.

Nagel identifies three main theses of philosophical atheism. First, there are no disembodied spirits, and incorporeal entities could not exercise causal powers anyway. Second, "controlled sensory observation is the court of final appeal in issues concerning matters of fact." And third, the "final standard" for evaluating a moral ideal is "the satisfaction of the complex needs of the human creature."

In "The Existence of God—A Debate," Bertrand Russell endorses agnosticism (which should not be confused with atheism), and F. C. Copleston endorses traditional theism. Copleston supports his theism with an argument from contingency and an argument from moral and religious experience. The argument from contingency assumes that the world consists of contingent beings that cannot account for their own existence, and concludes that there must be a noncontingent being (viz. God) who accounts for the fact that contingent things exist. Russell questions the intelligibility of the notion of a noncontingent (or necessary) being, and denies that the world as a whole needs an explanation. Copleston's argument from moral experience claims that only the existence of God will make sense of human moral and religious experience. In opposition, Russell argues that we do not need theism to explain moral and religious experience.

In "Theology and Falsification," Anthony Flew, R. M. Hare, and Basil Mitchell take contrasting positions on the supportability, or confirmability, of the claim that God exists. Flew holds that the claim that God exists is meaningless since it cannot be confirmed or disconfirmed. Hare replies that theistic belief is indeed unconfirmable, but proposes that unconfirmable assumptions (what Hare calls *bliks*) are common and are not meaningless. Mitchell contends that there can be, and actually is, evidence that counts somewhat against theistic belief, but he claims that for a true believer in God such evidence cannot count decisively against the claim that God exists.

In "The Presence of God and the Justification of Religious Belief," Gary Gutting defends a version of theism on the basis of religious experience. Gutting begins with an account of the role of experience in supporting claims about the world. One key assumption of his account is that "an 'of-X' experience is veridical only if, supposing it to be veridical, we should expect, in suitable circumstances, the occurrence of certain further experiences." Assuming the veridicality of an experience of a very good and very powerful being, we would expect that those who have had such an experience once would be likely to do so again, and would find themselves aided in their efforts to live morally better lives. Gutting uses this sort of consideration to argue that religious experiences of God's presence do establish the existence of God.

But Gutting distinguishes two aspects of religious belief: (a) the core of belief, which involves not a substantive account of the details of God's nature, but only "the reality of a superhuman power and love in our lives," and (b) the outer belt, which involves the distinctive theological commitments of various specific religions. Gutting claims that we can justify "decisive assent" *only* to the core of religious belief, and not to the outer belt.

Theism, Atheism, and Agnosticism

A Defense of Atheism*

Ernest Nagel

1

I must begin by stating what sense I am attaching to the word "atheism," and how I am construing the theme of this paper. I shall understand by "atheism" a critique and a denial of the major claims of all varieties of theism. And by theism I shall mean the view which holds, as one writer has expressed it, "that the heavens and the earth and all that they contain owe their existence and continuance in existence to the wisdom and will of a supreme, self-consistent, omnipotent, omniscient, righteous, and benevolent being, who is distinct from, and independent of, what he has created." Several things immediately follow from these definitions.

In the first place, atheism is not necessarily an irreligious concept, for theism is just one among many views concerning the nature and origin of the world. The denial of theism is logically compatible with a religious outlook upon life, and is in fact char-

acteristic of some of the great historical religions. For as readers of this volume will know, early Buddhism is a religion which does not subscribe to any doctrine about a god; and there are pantheistic religions and philosophies which, because they deny that God is a being separate from and independent of the world, are not theistic in the sense of the word explained above.

The second point to note is that atheism is not to be identified with sheer unbelief, or with disbelief in some particular creed of a religious group. Thus, a child who has received no religious instruction and has never heard about God, is not an atheist—for he is not denying any theistic claims. Similarly in the case of an adult who, if he has withdrawn from the faith of his fathers without reflection or because of frank indifference to any theological issue, is also not an atheist—for such an adult is not challenging theism and is not professing any views on the subject. Moreover, though the term "atheist" has been used historically as an abusive label for those who do not happen to subscribe to some regnant orthodoxy (for example, the ancient Romans called the early Christians atheists, because the latter

*From Nagel, "Philosophical Concepts of Atheism," in J. E. Fairchild, ed., *Basic Beliefs* (Sheridan House, Inc. 1959), pp. 167–186. Reprinted by permission.

denied the Roman divinities), or for those who engage in conduct regarded as immoral, it is not in this sense that I am discussing atheism.

One final word of preliminary explanation. I propose to examine some *philosophic* concepts of atheism, and I am not interested in the slightest in the many considerations atheists have advanced against the evidences for some particular religious and theological doctrine—for example, against the truth of the Christian story. What I mean by "philosophical" in the present context is that the views I shall consider are directed against any form of theism, and have their origin and basis in a logical analysis of the theistic position, and in a comprehensive account of the world believed to be wholly intelligible without the adoption of a theistic hypothesis.

Theism as I conceive it is a theological proposition, not a statement of a position that belongs primarily to religion. On my view, religion as a historical and social phenomenon is primarily an institutionalized *cultus* or practice, which possesses identifiable social functions and which expresses certain attitudes men take toward their world. Although it is doubtful whether men ever engage in religious practices or assume religious attitudes without some more or less explicit interpretation of their ritual or some rationale for their attitude, it is still the case that it is possible to distinguish religion as a social and personal phenomenon from the theological doctrines which may be developed as justifications for religious practices. Indeed, in some of the great religions of the world the profession of a creed plays a relatively minor role. In short, religion is a form of social communion, a participation in certain kinds of ritual (whether it be a dance, worship, prayer, or the like), and a form of experience (sometimes, though not invariably, directed to a personal confrontation with divine and holy things). Theology is an articulated and, at its best, a rational attempt at understanding these feelings and practices, in the light of their relation to other parts of human experience, and in terms of some hypothesis concerning the nature of things entire.

2

As I see it, atheistic philosophies fall into two major groups: 1) those which hold that the theistic doctrine is meaningful, but reject it either on the ground that, (a) the positive evidence for it is insufficient, or (b) the negative evidence is quite overwhelming; and 2) those who hold that the theistic thesis is not even meaningful, and reject it (a) as just nonsense or (b) as literally meaningless but interpreting it as a symbolic rendering of human ideals, thus reading the theistic thesis in a sense that most believers in theism would disavow. Critiques of theism falling into the second main group are usually based on some form of what is known as "the verifiability theory of meaning," and cannot be evaluated without first examining that theory. The limited space at my disposal makes such an examination impossible, so that the brief comment I will allow myself to make on these criticisms must be stated dogmatically. The versions of the verifiability theory commonly used to show that theism has no cognitive meaning also exclude most scientific theories (e.g., theories about the atomic constitution of matter) as meaningless, and are unacceptable for at least this reason. More generally, I do not find the claim credible that all theistic statements are meaningless nonsense, and I believe that on the contrary theism can be construed as a doctrine which is either true or false and which must therefore be assessed in the light of the arguments advanced for it. In any case, however, most of the traditional atheistic critiques of theism belong to the first rather than the second group of analyses mentioned above.

But before turning to the philosophical examination of the major classical arguments for theism, it is well to note that such philosophical critiques do not quite convey the passion with which atheists have often carried on their analyses of theistic views. For historically, atheism has been, and indeed continues to be, a form of social and political protest, directed as much against institutionalized religion as against theistic doctrine. Atheism has been, in effect, a moral revulsion against the undoubted abuses of the secular power exercised by religious leaders and religious institutions.

Religious authorities have opposed the correction of glaring injustices, and encouraged politically and socially reactionary policies. Religious institutions have been havens of obscurantist thought and centers for the dissemination of intolerance. Religious creeds have been used to set limits to free inquiry, to perpetuate inhumane treatment of the ill and the underprivileged, and to support moral doctrines insensitive to human suffering.

These indictments may not tell the whole story about the historical significance of religion; but they are at least an important part of the story. The refutation of theism has thus seemed to many as an indispensable step not only towards liberating men's minds from superstition, but also towards achieving a more equitable reordering of society. And no account of even the more philosophical aspects of atheistic thought is adequate, which does not give proper recognition to the powerful social motives that actuate many atheistic arguments.

But however this may be, I want now to discuss three classical arguments for the existence of God, arguments which have constituted at least a partial basis for theistic commitments. As long as theism is defended simply as a dogma, asserted as a matter of direct revelation or as the deliverance of authority, belief in the dogma is impregnable to rational argument. In fact, however, reasons are frequently advanced in support of the theistic creed, and these reasons have been the subject of acute philosophical critiques.

One of the oldest intellectual defenses of theism is the cosmological argument, also known as the argument from a first cause. Briefly put, the argument runs as follows. Every event must have a cause. Hence an event A must have as cause some event B, which in turn must have a cause C, and so on. But if there is no end to this backward progression of causes, the progression will be infinite; and in the opinion of those who use this argument, an infinite series of actual events is unintelligible and absurd. Hence there must be a first cause, and this first cause is God, the initiator of all change in the universe.

The argument is an ancient one, and is especially effective when stated within the framework of assumptions of Aristotelian physics; and it has impressed many generations of exceptionally keen minds. The argument is nonetheless a weak reed on which to rest the theistic thesis. Let us waive any question concerning the validity of the principle that every event has a cause, for though the question is important its discussion would lead us far afield. However, if the principle is assumed, it is surely incongruous to postulate a first cause as a way of escaping from the coils of an infinite series. For if everything must have a cause, why does not God require one for His own existence? The standard answer is that He does not need any, because He is self-caused. But if God can be self-caused, why cannot the world itself be self-caused? Why do we require a God transcending the world to bring the world into existence and to initiate changes in it? On the other hand, the supposed inconceivability and absurdity of an infinite series of regressive causes will be admitted by no one who has competent familiarity with the modern mathematical analysis of infinity. The cosmological argument does not stand up under scrutiny.

The second "proof" of God's existence is usually called the ontological argument. It too has a long history going back to early Christian days, though it acquired great prominence only in medieval times. The argument can be stated in several ways, one of which is the following. Since God is conceived to be omnipotent, he is a perfect being. A perfect being is defined as one whose essence or nature lacks no attributes (or properties) whatsoever, one whose nature is complete in every respect. But it is evident that we have an idea of a perfect being, for we have just defined the idea; and since this is so, the argument continues, God who is the perfect being must exist. Why must he? Because his existence follows from his defined nature. For if God lacked the attribute of existence, he would be lacking at least one attribute, and would therefore not be perfect. To sum up, since we have an idea of God as a perfect being, God must exist.

There are several ways of approaching this argument, but I shall consider only one. The argument was exploded by the 18th century philosopher Immanuel Kant. The substance of Kant's criticism is that it is just a confusion to say that existence is an attribute, and that though the *word* "existence" may occur as the grammatical predicate in a sentence no attribute is being predicated of a thing when we say that the thing exists or has existence. Thus, to use Kant's example, when we think of $100 we are thinking of the nature of this sum of money; but the nature of $100 remains the same whether we have $100 in our pockets or not. Accordingly, we are confounding grammar with logic if we suppose that some characteristic is being attributed to the nature of $100 when we say that a hundred dollar bill exists in someone's pocket.

To make the point clearer, consider another example. When we say that a lion has a tawny color, we are predicating a certain attribute of the animal, and similarly when we say that the lion is fierce or is hungry. But when we say the lion exists, all that we are saying is that something is (or has the nature of) a lion; we are not specifying an attribute which belongs to the nature of anything that is a lion. In short, the word "existence" does not signify any attribute, and in consequence no attribute that belongs to the nature of anything. Accordingly, it does not follow from the assumption that we have an idea of a perfect being that such a being exists. For the idea of a perfect being does not involve the attribute of existence as a constituent of that idea, since there is no such attribute. The ontological argument thus has a serious leak, and it can hold no water.

3

The two arguments discussed thus far are purely dialectical, and attempt to establish God's existence without any appeal to empirical data. The next argument, called the argument from design, is different in char-

acter, for it is based on what purports to be empirical evidence. I wish to examine two forms of this argument.

One variant of it calls attention to the remarkable way in which different things and processes in the world are integrated with each other, and concludes that this mutual "fitness" of things can be explained only by the assumption of a divine architect who planned the world and everything in it. For example, living organisms can maintain themselves in a variety of environments, and do so in virtue of their delicate mechanisms which adapt the organisms to all sorts of environmental changes. There is thus an intricate pattern of means and ends throughout the animate world. But the existence of this pattern is unintelligible, so the argument runs, except on the hypothesis that the pattern has been deliberately instituted by a Supreme Designer. If we find a watch in some deserted spot, we do not think it came into existence by chance, and we do not hesitate to conclude that an intelligent creature designed and made it. But the world and all its contents exhibit mechanisms and mutual adjustments that are far more complicated and subtle than are those of a watch. Must we not therefore conclude that these things too have a Creator?

The conclusion of this argument is based on an inference from analogy: the watch and the world are alike in possessing a congruence of parts and an adjustment of means to ends; the watch has a watchmaker; hence the world has a world maker. But is the analogy a good one? Let us once more waive some important issues, in particular the issue whether the universe is the unified system such as the watch admittedly is. And let us concentrate on the question what is the ground for our assurance that watches do not come into existence except through the operations of intelligent manufacturers. The answer is plain. We have never run across a watch which has not been deliberately made by someone. But the situation is nothing like this in the case of the innumerable animate and inanimate systems with which we are familiar. Even in the case of living organisms, though they are generated by their parent organisms, the parents do not "make" their progeny in the same sense in which watchmakers make watches. And once this point is clear, the inference from the existence of living organisms to the existence of a supreme designer no longer appears credible.

Moreover, the argument loses all its force if the facts which the hypothesis of a divine designer is supposed to explain can be understood on the basis of a better supported assumption. And indeed, such an alternative explanation is one of the achievements of Darwinian biology. For Darwin showed that one can account for the variety of biological species, as well as for their adaptations to their environments, without invoking a divine creator and acts of special creation. The Darwinian theory explains the diversity of biological species in terms of chance variations in the structure of organisms, and of a mechanism of selection which retains those variant forms that possess some advantages for survival. The evidence for these assumptions is considerable; and developments subsequent to Darwin have only strengthened the case for a thoroughly naturalistic explanation of the facts of biological adaptation. In any event, this version of the argument from design has nothing to recommend it.

A second form of this argument has been recently revived in the speculations of some modern physicists. No one who is familiar with the facts, can fail to be impressed by the success with which the use of mathematical methods has enabled us to obtain intellectual mastery of many parts of nature. But some thinkers have therefore concluded that since the book of nature is ostensibly written in mathematical language, nature must be the creation of a divine mathematician. However, the argument is most dubious. For it rests, among other things, on the assumption that mathematical tools can be successfully used only if the events of nature exhibit some *special* kind of order, and on the further assumption that if the structure of things were different from what they are mathematical language would be inadequate for describing such structure. But it can be shown that no matter what the world

were like—even if it impressed us as being utterly chaotic—it would still possess some order, and would in principle be amenable to a mathematical description. In point of fact, it makes no sense to say that there is absolutely *no* pattern in any conceivable subject matter. To be sure, there are differences in complexities of structure, and if the patterns of events were sufficiently complex we might not be able to unravel them. But however that may be, the success of mathematical physics in giving us some understanding of the world around us does not yield the conclusion that only a mathematician could have devised the patterns of order we have discovered in nature.

4

The inconclusiveness of the three classical arguments for the existence of God was already made evident by Kant, in a manner substantially not different from the above discussion. There are, however, other types of arguments for theism that have been influential in the history of thought, two of which I wish to consider, even if only briefly.

Indeed, though Kant destroyed the classical intellectual foundations for theism, he himself invented a fresh argument for it. Kant's attempted proof is not intended to be a purely theoretical demonstration, and is based on the supposed facts of our moral nature. It has exerted an enormous influence on subsequent theological speculation. In barest outline, the argument is as follows. According to Kant, we are subject not only to physical laws like the rest of nature, but also to moral ones. These moral laws are categorical imperatives, which we must heed not because of their utilitarian consequences, but simply because as autonomous moral agents it is our duty to accept them as binding. However, Kant was keenly aware that though virtue may be its reward, the virtuous man (that is, the man who acts out of a sense of duty and in conformity with the moral law) does not always receive his just deserts in this world; nor did he shut his eyes to the fact that evil men frequently enjoy the best things this world has to offer. In short, virtue does not always reap happiness. Nevertheless, the highest human good is the realization of happiness commensurate with one's virtue; and Kant believed that it is a practical postulate of the moral life to promote this good. But what can guarantee that the highest good is realizable? Such a guarantee can be found only in God, who must therefore exist if the highest good is not to be a fatuous ideal. The existence of an omnipotent, omniscient, and omnibenevolent God is thus postulated as a necessary condition for the possibility of a moral life.

Despite the prestige this argument has acquired, it is difficult to grant it any force. It is easy enough to postulate God's existence. But as Bertrand Russell observed in another connection, postulation has all the advantages of theft over honest toil. No postulation carries with it any assurance that what is postulated is actually the case. And though we may postulate God's existence as a means to guaranteeing the possibility of realizing happiness together with virtue, the postulation establishes neither the actual realizability of this ideal nor the fact of his existence. Moreover, the argument is not made more cogent when we recognize that it is based squarely on the highly dubious conception that considerations of utility and human happiness must not enter into the determination of what is morally obligatory. Having built his moral theory on a radical separation of means from ends, Kant was driven to the desperate postulation of God's existence in order to relate them again. The argument is thus at best a *tour de force*, contrived to remedy a fatal flaw in Kant's initial moral assumptions. It carries no conviction to anyone who does not commit Kant's initial blunder.

One further type of argument, pervasive in much Protestant theological literature, deserves brief mention. Arguments of this type take their point of departure from the psychology of religious and mystical experience. Those who have undergone such experiences, often report that during the experience they feel themselves to be in the presence of the divine and holy, that they lose their sense of self-identity and become merged with some fundamental reality, or that they enjoy a feeling of total dependence upon some ultimate power. The overwhelming sense of transcending one's finitude which characterizes such vivid periods of life, and of coalescing with some ultimate source of all existence, is then taken to be compelling evidence for the existence of a supreme being. In a variant form of this argument, other theologians have identified God as the object which satisfies the commonly experienced need for integrating one's scattered and conflicting impulses into a coherent unity, or as the subject which is of ultimate concern to us. In short, a proof of God's existence is found in the occurrence of certain distinctive experiences.

It would be flying in the face of well-attested facts were one to deny that such experiences frequently occur. But do these facts constitute evidence for the conclusion based on them? Does the fact, for example, that an individual experiences a profound sense of direct contact with an alleged transcendent ground of all reality, constitute competent evidence for the claim that there is such a ground and that it is the immediate cause of the experience? If well-established canons for evaluating evidence are accepted, the answer is surely negative. No one will dispute that many men do have vivid experiences in which such things as ghosts or pink elephants appear before them; but only the hopelessly credulous will without further ado count such experiences as establishing the existence of ghosts and pink elephants. To establish the existence of such things, evidence is required that is obtained under controlled conditions and that can be confirmed by independent inquirers. Again, though a man's report that he is suffering pain may be taken at face value, one cannot take at face value the claim, were he to make it, that it is the food he ate which is the cause (or a contributory cause) of his felt pain—not even if the man were to report a vivid feeling of abdominal disturbance. And similarly, an overwhelming feeling of being in the presence of the Divine is evidence enough for admitting the genuineness of such feeling; it is no evidence for the claim that a supreme being with a substantial existence independent of the experience is the cause of the experience.

5

Thus far the discussion has been concerned with noting inadequacies in various arguments widely used to support theism. However, much atheistic criticism is also directed toward exposing incoherencies in the very thesis of theism. I want therefore to consider this aspect of the atheistic critique, though I will restrict myself to the central difficulty in the theistic position which arises from the simultaneous attribution of omnipotence, omniscience, and omnibenevolence to the Deity. The difficulty is that of reconciling these attributes with the occurrence of evil in the world. Accordingly, the question to which I now turn is whether, despite the existence of evil, it is possible to construct a theodicy which will justify the ways of an infinitely powerful and just God to man.

Two main types of solutions have been proposed for this problem. One way that is frequently used is to maintain that what is commonly called evil is only an illusion, or at worst only the "privation" or absence of good. Accordingly, evil is not "really real," it is only the "negative" side of God's beneficence, it is only the product of our limited intelligence which fails to plumb the true character of God's creative bounty. A sufficient comment on this proposed solution is that facts are not altered or abolished by rebaptizing them. Evil may indeed be only an appearance and not genuine. But this does not eliminate from the realm of appearance the tragedies, the sufferings, and the iniquities which men so frequently endure. And it raises once more, though on another level, the problem of reconciling the fact that there is evil in the realm of appearance with God's alleged omnibenevolence. In any event, it is small comfort to anyone suffering a cruel

misfortune for which he is in no way responsible, to be told that what he is undergoing is only the absence of good. It is a gratuitous insult to mankind, a symptom of insensitivity and indifference to human suffering, to be assured that all the miseries and agonies men experience are only illusory.

Another gambit often played in attempting to justify the ways of God to man is to argue that the things called evil are evil only because they are viewed in isolation; they are not evil when viewed in proper perspective and in relation to the rest of creation. Thus, if one attends to but a single instrument in an orchestra, the sounds issuing from it may indeed be harsh and discordant. But if one is placed at a proper distance from the whole orchestra, the sounds of that single instrument will mingle with the sounds issuing from the other players to produce a marvellous bit of symphonic music. Analogously, experiences we call painful undoubtedly occur and are real enough. But the pain is judged to be an evil only because it is experienced in a limited perspective—the pain is there for the sake of a more inclusive good, whose reality eludes us because our intelligences are too weak to apprehend things in their entirety.

It is an appropriate retort to this argument that of course we judge things to be evil in a human perspective, but that since we are not God this is the only proper perspective in which to judge them. It may indeed be the case that what is evil for us is not evil for some other part of creation. However, we are not this other part of creation, and it is irrelevant to argue that were we something other than what we are, our evaluations of what is good and bad would be different. Moreover, the worthlessness of the argument becomes even more evident if we remind ourselves that it is unsupported speculation to suppose that whatever is evil in a finite perspective is good from the purported perspective of the totality of things. For the argument can be turned around: what we judge to be a good is a good only because it is viewed in isolation; when it is viewed in proper perspective, and in relation to the entire scheme of things, it is an evil. This is in fact a standard form of the argument for a universal pessimism. Is it any worse than the similar argument for a universal optimism? The very raising of this question is a *reductio ad absurdum* of the proposed solution to the ancient problem of evil.

I do not believe it is possible to reconcile the alleged omnipotence and omnibenevolence of God with the unvarnished facts of human existence. In point of fact, many theologians have concurred in this conclusion; for in order to escape from the difficulty which the traditional attributes of God present, they have assumed that God is not all powerful, and that there are limits as to what He can do in his efforts to establish a righteous order in the universe. But whether such a modified theology is better off, is doubtful; and in any event, the question still remains whether the facts of human life support the claim that an omnibenevolent Deity, though limited in power, is revealed in the ordering of human history. It is pertinent to note in this connection that though there have been many historians who have made the effort, no historian has yet succeeded in showing to the satisfaction of his professional colleagues that the hypothesis of a Divine Providence is capable of explaining anything which cannot be explained just as well without this hypothesis.

6

This last remark naturally leads to the question whether, apart from their polemics against theism, philosophical atheists have not shared a common set of positive views, a common set of philosophical convictions which set them off from other groups of thinkers. In one very clear sense of this query the answer is indubitably negative. For there never has been what one might call a "school of atheism," in the way in which there has been a Platonic school or even a Kantian school. In point of fact, atheistic critics of theism can be found among many of the conventional groupings of philosophical thinkers—even, I venture to add, among professional theologians in recent years who in effect preach atheism in the guise of language taken bodily from the Christian tradition.

Nevertheless, despite the variety of philosophic positions to which at one time or another in the history of thought atheists have subscribed, it seems to me that atheism is not simply a negative standpoint. At any rate, there is a certain quality of intellectual temper that has characterized, and continues to characterize, many philosophical atheists. (I am excluding from consideration the so-called "village atheist," whose primary concern is to twit and ridicule those who accept some form of theism, or for that matter those who have any religious convictions.) Moreover, their rejection of theism is based not only on the inadequacies they have found in the arguments for theism, but often also on the positive ground that atheism is a corollary to a better supported general outlook upon the nature of things. I want therefore to conclude this discussion with a brief enumeration of some points of positive doctrine to which by and large philosophical atheists seem to me to subscribe. These points fall into three major groups.

In the first place, philosophical atheists reject the assumption that there are disembodied spirits, or that incorporeal entities of any sort can exercise a causal agency. On the contrary, atheists are generally agreed that if we wish to achieve any understanding of what takes place in the universe, we must look to the operations of organized bodies. Accordingly, the various processes taking place in nature, whether animate or inanimate, are to be explained in terms of the properties and structures of identifiable and spatiotemporally located objects. Moreover, the present variety of systems and activities found in the universe is to be accounted for on the basis of the transformations things undergo when they enter into different relations with one another—transformations which often result in the emergence of novel kinds of objects. On the other hand, though things are in flux and undergo alteration, there is no all-encompassing unitary pattern

Theism, Atheism, and Agnosticism

of change. Nature is ineradicably plural, both in respect to the individuals occurring in it as well as in respect to the processes in which things become involved. Accordingly, the human scene and the human perspective are not illusory; and man and his works are no less and no more "real" than are other parts or phases of the cosmos. At the risk of using a possibly misleading characterization, all of this can be summarized by saying that an atheistic view of things is a form of materialism.

In the second place, atheists generally manifest a marked empirical temper, and often take as their ideal the intellectual methods employed in the contemporaneous empirical sciences. Philosophical atheists differ considerably on important points of detail in their account of how responsible claims to knowledge are to be established. But there is substantial agreement among them that controlled sensory observation is the court of final appeal in issues concerning matters of fact. It is indeed this commitment to the use of an empirical method which is the final basis of the atheistic critique of theism. For at bottom this critique seeks to show that we can understand whatever a theistic assumption is alleged to explain, through the use of the proved methods of the positive sciences and without the introduction of empirically unsupported *ad hoc* hypotheses about a Deity. It is pertinent in this connection to recall a familiar legend about the French mathematical physicist Laplace. According to the story, Laplace made a personal presentation of a copy of his now famous book on celestial mechanics to Napoleon. Napoleon glanced through the volume, and finding no reference to the Deity asked Laplace whether God's existence played any role in the analysis. "Sire, I have no need for that hypothesis," Laplace is reported to have replied. The dismissal of sterile hypotheses characterizes not only the work of Laplace; it is the uniform rule in scientific inquiry. The sterility of the theistic assumption is one of the main burdens of the literature of atheism both ancient and modern.

And finally, atheistic thinkers have generally accepted a utilitarian basis for judging moral issues, and they have exhibited a libertarian attitude toward human needs and impulses. The conceptions of the human good they have advocated are conceptions which are commensurate with the actual capacities of mortal men, so that it is the satisfaction of the complex needs of the human creature which is the final standard for evaluating the validity of a moral ideal or moral prescription.

In consequence, the emphasis of atheistic moral reflection has been this-worldly rather than other-worldly, individualistic rather than authoritarian. The stress upon a good life that must be consummated in this world, has made atheists vigorous opponents of moral codes which seek to repress human impulses in the name of some unrealizable other-worldly ideal. The individualism that is so pronounced a strain in many philosophical atheists has made them tolerant of human limitations and sensitive to the plurality of legitimate moral goals. On the other hand, this individualism has certainly not prevented many of them from recognizing the crucial role which institutional arrangements can play in achieving desirable patterns of human living. In consequence, atheists have made important contributions to the development of a climate of opinion favorable to pursuing the values of a liberal civilization and they have played effective roles in attempts to rectify social injustices.

Atheists cannot build their moral outlook on foundations upon which so many men conduct their lives. In particular, atheism cannot offer the incentives to conduct and the consolations for misfortune which theistic religions supply to their adherents. It can offer no hope of personal immortality, no threats of Divine chastisement, no promise of eventual recompense for injustices suffered, no blueprints to sure salvation. For on its view of the place of man in nature, human excellence and human dignity must be achieved within a finite life-span, or not at all, so that the rewards of moral endeavor must come from the quality of civilized living, and not from some source of disbursement that dwells outside of time. Accordingly, atheistic moral reflection at its best does not culminate in a quiescent ideal of human perfection, but is a vigorous call to intelligent activity—activity for the sake of realizing human potentialities and for eliminating whatever stands in the way of such realization. Nevertheless, though slavish resignation to remediable ills is not characteristic of atheistic thought, responsible atheists have never pretended that human effort can invariably achieve the heart's every legitimate desire. A tragic view of life is thus an uneliminable ingredient in atheistic thought. This ingredient does not invite or generally produce lugubrious lamentation. But it does touch the atheist's view of man and his place in nature with an emotion that makes the philosophical atheist a kindred spirit to those who, within the frameworks of various religious traditions, have developed a serenely resigned attitude toward the inevitable tragedies of the human estate.

The Existence of God—A Debate*

Bertrand Russell and F. C. Copleston

Copleston: As we are going to discuss the existence of God, it might perhaps be as well to come to some provisional agreement as to what we understand by the term "God." I presume that we mean a supreme personal being—distinct from the world and creator of the world. Would you agree—provisionally at least—to accept this statement as the meaning of the term "God"?

Russell: Yes, I accept this definition.

Copleston: Well, my position is the affirmative position that such a being actually exists, and that His existence can be proved philosophically. Perhaps you would tell me if your position is that of agnosticism or of atheism. I mean, would you say that the non-existence of God can be proved?

Russell: No, I should not say that: my position is agnostic.

Copleston: Would you agree with me that the problem of God is a problem of great importance? For example, would you agree that if God does not exist, human beings and human history can have no other purpose than the purpose they choose to give themselves, which—in practice—is

likely to mean the purpose which those impose who have the power to impose it?

Russell: Roughly speaking, yes, though I should have to place some limitation on your last clause.

Copleston: Would you agree that if there is no God—no absolute Being—there can be no absolute values? I mean, would you agree that if there is no absolute good that the relativity of values results?

Russell: No, I think these questions are logically distinct. Take, for instance, G. E. Moore's *Principia Ethica*, where he maintains that there is a distinction of good and evil, that both of these are definite concepts. But he does not bring in the idea of God to support that contention.

Copleston: Well, suppose we leave the question of good till later, till we come to the moral argument, and I give first a metaphysical argument. I'd like to put the main weight on the metaphysical argument based on Leibniz's argument from "Contingency" and then later we might discuss the moral argument. Suppose I give a brief statement on the metaphysical argument and that then we go on to discuss it?

Russell: That seems to me to be a very good plan.

THE ARGUMENT FROM CONTINGENCY

COPLESTON: Well, for clarity's sake, I'll divide the argument into distinct stages. First of all, I should say, we know that there are at least some beings in the world which do not contain in themselves the reason for their existence. For example, I depend on my parents, and now on the air, and on food, and so on. Now, secondly, the world is simply the real or imagined totality or aggregate of individual objects, none of which contain in themselves alone the reason for their existence. There isn't any world distinct from the objects which form it, any more than the human race is something apart from the members. Therefore, I should say, since objects or events exist, and since no object of experience contains within itself the reason of its existence, this reason, the totality of objects, must have a reason external to itself. That reason must be an existent being. Well, this being is either itself the reason for its own existence, or it is not. If it is, well and good. If it is not, then we must proceed farther. But if we proceed to infinity in that sense, then there's no explanation of existence at all. So, I should say, in order to explain existence, we must come to a being which contains within itself the reason for its own existence, that is to say, which cannot not exist.

RUSSELL: This raises a great many points and it is not altogether easy to know where to begin, but I think that, perhaps, in answering your argument, the best point at which to begin is the question of necessary being. The word "necessary," I should maintain, can only be applied significantly to propositions. And, in fact, only to such as are analytic—that is to say—such as it is self-contradictory to deny. I could only admit a necessary being if there were a being whose existence it is self-contradictory to deny. I should like to know whether you would accept Leibniz's division of propositions into truths of reason and truths of fact. The former—the truths of reason—being necessary.

COPLESTON: Well, I certainly should not subscribe to what seems to be Leibniz's idea of truths of reason and truths of fact, since it would appear that, for him, there are in the long run only analytic propositions. It would seem that for Leibniz truths of fact are ultimately reducible to truths of reason. That is to say, to analytic propositions, at least for an omniscient mind. Well, I couldn't agree with that. For one thing, it would fail to meet the requirements of the experience of freedom. I don't want to uphold the whole philosophy of Leibniz. I have made use of his argument from contingent to necessary being, basing the argument on the principle of sufficient reason, simply because it seems to me a brief and clear formulation of what is, in my opinion, the fundamental metaphysical argument for God's existence.

RUSSELL: But, to my mind, "a necessary proposition" has got to be analytic. I don't see what else it can mean. And analytic propositions are always complex and logically somewhat late. "Irrational animals are animals" is an analytic proposition; but a proposition such as "This is an animal" can never be analytic. In fact, all the propositions that can be analytic are somewhat late in the build-up of propositions.

COPLESTON: Take the proposition "If there is a contingent being then there is a necessary being." I consider that that proposition hypothetically expressed is a necessary proposition. If you are going to call every necessary proposition an analytic proposition, then—in order to avoid a dispute in terminology—I would agree to call it analytic, though I don't consider it a tautological proposition. But the proposition is a necessary proposition only on the supposition that there is a contingent being. That there is a contingent being actually existing has to be discovered by experience, and the proposition that there is a contingent being is certainly not an analytic proposition, though once you know, I should maintain, that there is a contingent being, it follows of necessity that there is a necessary being.

RUSSELL: The difficulty of this argument is that I don't admit the idea of a necessary being and I don't admit that there is any particular meaning in calling other beings "contingent." These phrases don't for me have a significance except within a logic that I reject.

COPLESTON: Do you mean that you reject these terms because they won't fit in with what is called "modern logic"?

RUSSELL: Well, I can't find anything that they could mean. The word "necessary," it seems to me, is a useless word, except as applied to analytic propositions, not to things.

COPLESTON: In the first place, what do you mean by "modern logic"? As far as I know, there are somewhat differing systems. In the second place, not all modern logicians surely would admit the meaninglessness of metaphysics. We both know, at any rate, one very eminent modern thinker whose knowledge of modern logic was profound, but who certainly did not think that metaphysics are meaningless or, in particular, that the problem of God is meaningless. Again, even if all modern logicians held that metaphysical terms are meaningless, it would not follow that they were right. The proposition that metaphysical terms are meaningless seems to me to be a proposition based on an assumed philosophy. The dogmatic position behind it seems to be this: What will not go into my machine is nonexistent, or it is meaningless; it is the expression of emotion. I am simply trying to point out that anybody who says that a particular system of modern logic is the sole criterion of meaning is saying something that is over-dogmatic; he is dogmatically insisting that a part of philosophy is the whole of philosophy. After all, a "contingent" being is a being which has not in itself the complete reason for its existence, that's what I mean by a contingent being. You know, as well as I do, that the existence of neither of us can be explained without reference to something or somebody outside us, our parents, for example. A "necessary" being, on the other hand, means a being that must and cannot not exist. You may say that there is no such being, but you will find it hard to convince me that you do not understand the terms I am using. If you do not understand them, then how can you be entitled to say that

such a being does not exist, if that is what you do say?

RUSSELL: Well, there are points here that I don't propose to go into at length. I don't maintain the meaninglessness of metaphysics in general at all. I maintain the meaninglessness of certain particular terms—not on any general ground, but simply because I've not been able to see an interpretation of those particular terms. It's not a general dogma—it's a particular thing. But those points I will leave out for the moment. And I will say that what you have been saying brings us back, it seems to me, to the ontological argument that there is a being whose essence involves existence, so that his existence is analytic. That seems to me to be impossible, and it raises, of course, the question what one means by existence, and as to this, I think a subject named can never be significantly said to exist but only a subject described. And that existence, in fact, quite definitely is not a predicate.

COPLESTON: Well, you say, I believe, that it is bad grammar, or rather bad syntax to say for example "T. S. Eliot exists"; one ought to say, for example, "He, the author of *Murder in the Cathedral*, exists." Are you going to say that the proposition, "The cause of the world exists," is without meaning? You may say that the world has no cause; but I fail to see how you can say that the proposition that "the cause of the world exists" is meaningless. Put it in the form of a question: "Has the world a cause?" or "Does a cause of the world exist?" Most people surely would understand the question, even if they don't agree about the answer.

RUSSELL: Well, certainly the question "Does the cause of the world exist?" is a question that has meaning. But if you say "Yes, God is the cause of the world" you're using God as a proper name; then "God exists" will not be a statement that has meaning; that is the position that I'm maintaining. Because, therefore, it will follow that it cannot be an analytic proposition ever to say that this or that exists. For example, suppose you take as your subject "the existent round-square," it would look like an analytic proposition that "the existent round-square exists," but it doesn't exist.

COPLESTON: No, it doesn't, then surely you can't say it doesn't exist unless you have a conception of what existence is. As to the phrase "existent round-square," I should say that it has no meaning at all.

RUSSELL: I quite agree. Then I should say the same thing in another context in reference to a "necessary being."

COPLESTON: Well, we seem to have arrived at an impasse. To say that a necessary being is a being that must exist and cannot not exist has for me a definite meaning. For you it has no meaning.

RUSSELL: Well, we can press the point a little, I think. A being that must exist and cannot not exist, would surely, according to you, be a being whose essence involves existence.

COPLESTON: Yes, a being the essence of which is to exist. But I should not be willing to argue the existence of God simply from the idea of His essence because I don't think we have any clear intuition of God's essence as yet. I think we have to argue from the world of experience to God.

RUSSELL: Yes, I quite see the distinction. But, at the same time, for a being with sufficient knowledge it would be true to say "Here is this being whose essence involves existence!"

COPLESTON: Yes, certainly if anybody saw God, he would see that God must exist.

RUSSELL: So that I mean there is a being whose essence involves existence although we don't know that essence. We only know there is such a being.

COPLESTON: Yes, I should add we don't know the essence *a priori*. It is only *a posteriori* through our experience of the world that we come to a knowledge of the existence of that being. And then one argues, the essence and existence must be identical. Because if God's essence and God's existence was not identical, then some sufficient reason for this existence would have to be found beyond God.

RUSSELL: So it all turns on this question of sufficient reason, and I must say you haven't defined "sufficient reason" in a way that I can understand—what do you mean by sufficient reason? You don't mean cause?

COPLESTON: Not necessarily. Cause is a kind of sufficient reason. Only contingent being can have a cause. God is His own sufficient reason; and He is not cause of Himself. By sufficient reason in the full sense I mean an explanation adequate for the existence of some particular being.

RUSSELL But when is an explanation adequate? Suppose I am about to make a flame with a match. You may say that the adequate explanation of that is that I rub it on the box.

COPLESTON: Well, for practical purposes—but theoretically, that is only a partial explanation. An adequate explanation must ultimately be a total explanation, to which nothing further can be added.

RUSSELL: Then I can only say that you're looking for something which can't be got, and which one ought not to expect to get.

COPLESTON: To say that one has not found it is one thing; to say that one should not look for it seems to me rather dogmatic.

RUSSELL: Well, I don't know. I mean, the explanation of one thing is another thing which makes the other thing dependent on yet another, and you have to grasp this sorry scheme of things entire to do what you want, and that we can't do.

COPLESTON: But are you going to say that we can't, or we shouldn't even raise the question of the existence of the whole of this sorry scheme of things—of the whole universe?

RUSSELL: Yes. I don't think there's any meaning in it at all. I think the word "universe" is a handy word in some connections, but I don't think it stands for anything that has a meaning.

COPLESTON: If the word is meaningless, it can't be so very handy. In any case, I don't say that the universe is something different from the objects which compose it (I indicated that in my brief summary of the proof), what I'm doing is to look for the reason, in this case the cause of the objects—the real or imagined totality of which constitute what we call the universe. You say, I think that the universe—or my existence if

Theism, Atheism, and Agnosticism

you prefer, or any other existence—is unintelligible?

RUSSELL: First may I take up the point that if a word is meaningless it can't be handy. That sounds well but isn't in fact correct. Take, say, such a word as "the" or "than." You can't point to any object that those words mean, but they are very useful words; I should say the same of "universe." But leaving that point, you ask whether I consider that the universe is unintelligible. I shouldn't say unintelligible—I think it is without explanation. Intelligible, to my mind, is a different thing. Intelligible has to do with the thing itself intrinsically and not with its relations.

COPLESTON: Well, my point is that what we call the world is intrinsically unintelligible, apart from the existence of God. You see, I don't believe that the infinity of the series of events—I mean a horizontal series, so to speak—if such an infinity could be proved, would be in the slightest degree relevant to the situation. If you add up chocolates you get chocolates after all and not a sheep. If you add up chocolates to infinity, you presumably get an infinite number of chocolates. So if you add up contingent beings to infinity, you still get contingent beings, not a necessary being. An infinite series of contingent beings will be, to my way of thinking, as unable to cause itself as one contingent being. However, you say, I think, that it is illegitimate to raise the question of what will explain the existence of any particular object?

RUSSELL: It's quite all right if you mean by explaining it, simply finding a cause for it.

COPLESTON: Well, why stop at one particular object? Why shouldn't one raise the question of the cause of the existence of all particular objects?

RUSSELL: Because I see no reason to think there is any. The whole concept of cause is one we derive from our observation of particular things; I see no reason whatsoever to suppose that the total has any cause whatsoever.

COPLESTON: Well, to say that there isn't any cause is not the same thing as saying that we shouldn't look for a cause. The statement that there isn't any cause should come, if it comes at all, at the end of the inquiry, not the beginning. In any case, if the total has no cause, then to my way of thinking it must be its own cause, which seems to me impossible. Moreover, the statement that the world is simply there if in answer to a question, presupposes that the question has meaning.

RUSSELL: No, it doesn't need to be its own cause, what I'm saying is that the concept of cause is not applicable to the total.

COPLESTON: Then you would agree with Sartre that the universe is what he calls "gratuitous"?

RUSSELL: Well, the word "gratuitous" suggests that it might be something else; I should say that the universe is just there, and that's all.

COPLESTON: Well, I can't see how you can rule out the legitimacy of asking the question how the total, or anything at all comes to be there. Why something rather than nothing, that is the question? The fact that we gain our knowledge of causality empirically, from particular causes, does not rule out the possibility of asking what the cause of the series is. If the word "cause" were meaningless or if it could be shown that Kant's view of the matter were correct, the question would be illegitimate I agree; but you don't seem to hold that the word "cause" is meaningless, and I do not suppose you are a Kantian.

RUSSELL: I can illustrate what seems to me your fallacy. Every man who exists has a mother, and it seems to me your argument is that therefore the human race must have a mother, but obviously the human race hasn't a mother—that's a different logical sphere.

COPLESTON: Well, I can't really see any parity. If I were saying "every object has a phenomenal cause, therefore, the whole series has a phenomenal cause," there would be a parity; but I'm not saying that; I'm saying, every object has a phenomenal cause if you insist on the infinity of the series—but the series of phenomenal causes is an insufficient explanation of the series. Therefore, the series has not a phenomenal cause but a transcendent cause.

RUSSELL: That's always assuming that not only every particular thing in the world, but the world as a whole must have a cause. For that assumption I see no ground whatever. If you'll give me a ground I'll listen to it.

COPLESTON: Well, the series of events is either caused or it's not caused. If it is caused, there must obviously be a cause outside the series. If it's not caused then it's sufficient to itself, and if it's sufficient to itself it is what I call necessary. But it can't be necessary since each member is contingent, and we've agreed that the total has no reality apart from its members, therefore, it can't be necessary. Therefore, it can't be (caused)—uncaused— therefore it must have a cause. And I should like to observe in passing that the statement "the world is simply there and is inexplicable" can't be got out of logical analysis.

RUSSELL: I don't want to seem arrogant, but it does seem to me that I can conceive things that you say the human mind can't conceive. As for things not having a cause, the physicists assure us that individual quantum transitions in atoms have no cause.

COPLESTON: Well, I wonder now whether that isn't simply a temporary inference.

RUSSELL: It may be, but it does show that physicists' minds can conceive it.

COPLESTON: Yes, I agree, some scientists—physicists—are willing to allow for indetermination within a restricted field. But very many scientists are not so willing. I think that Professor Dingle, of London University, maintains that the Heisenberg uncertainty principle tells us something about the success (or the lack of it) of the present atomic theory in correlating observations, but not about nature in itself, and many physicists would accept this view. In any case, I don't see how physicists can fail to accept the theory in practice, even if they don't do so in theory. I cannot see how science could be conducted on any other assumption than that of order and intelligibility in nature. The physicist presupposes, at least tacitly, that there is some sense in investigating nature and looking for the causes of events, just as the detective presupposes

that there is some sense in looking for the cause of a murder. The metaphysician assumes that there is sense in looking for the reason or cause of phenomena, and, not being a Kantian, I consider that the metaphysician is as justified in his assumption as the physicist. When Sartre, for example, says that the world is gratuitous, I think that he has not sufficiently considered what is implied by "gratuitous."

RUSSELL: I think—there seems to me a certain unwarrantable extension here; a physicist looks for causes; that does not necessarily imply that there are causes everywhere. A man may look for gold without assuming that there is gold everywhere; if he finds gold, well and good, if he doesn't he's had bad luck. The same is true when the physicists look for causes. As for Sartre, I don't profess to know what he means, and I shouldn't like to be thought to interpret him, but for my part, I do think the notion of the world having an explanation is a mistake. I don't see why one should expect it to have, and I think what you say about what the scientist assumes is an over-statement.

COPLESTON: Well, it seems to me that the scientist does make some such assumption. When he experiments to find out some particular truth, behind that experiment lies the assumption that the universe is not simply discontinuous. There is the possibility of finding out a truth by experiment. The experiment may be a bad one, it may lead to no result, or not to the result that he wants, but that at any rate there is the possibility, through experiment, of finding out the truth that he assumes. And that seems to me to assume an ordered and intelligible universe.

RUSSELL: I think you're generalizing more than is necessary. Undoubtedly the scientist assumes that this sort of thing is likely to be found and will often be found. He does not assume that it will be found, and that's a very important matter in modern physics.

COPLESTON: Well, I think he does assume or is bound to assume it tacitly in practice. It may be that, to quote Professor Haldane, "when I light the gas under the kettle, some of the water molecules will fly off as vapor, and there is no way of finding out which will do so," but it doesn't follow necessarily that the idea of chance must be introduced except in relation to our knowledge.

RUSSELL: No it doesn't—at least if I may believe what he says. He's finding out quite a lot of things—the scientist is finding out quite a lot of things that are happening in the world, which are, at first, beginnings of causal chains—first causes which haven't in themselves got causes. He does not assume that everything has a cause.

COPLESTON: Surely that's a first cause within a certain selected field. It's a relatively first cause.

RUSSELL: I don't think he'd say so. If there's a world in which most events, but not all, have causes, he will then be able to depict the probabilities and uncertainties by assuming that this particular event you're interested in probably has a cause. And since in any case you won't get more than probability that's good enough.

COPLESTON: It may be that the scientist doesn't hope to obtain more than probability, but in raising the question he assumes that the question of explanation has a meaning. But your general point then, Lord Russell, is that it's illegitimate even to ask the question of the cause of the world?

RUSSELL: Yes, that's my position.

COPLESTON: If it's a question that for you has no meaning, it's of course very difficult to discuss it, isn't it?

RUSSELL: Yes, it is very difficult. What do you say—shall we pass on to some other issue?

RELIGIOUS EXPERIENCE

COPLESTON: Let's. Well, perhaps I might say a word about religious experience, and then we can go on to moral experience. I don't regard religious experience as a strict proof of the existence of God, so the character of the discussion changes somewhat, but I think it's true to say that the best explanation of it is the existence of God. By religious experience I don't mean simply feeling good. I mean a loving, but unclear, awareness of some object which irresistibly

seems to the experiencer as something transcending the self, something transcending all the normal objects of experience, something which cannot be pictured or conceptualized, but of the reality of which doubt is impossible—at least during the experience. I should claim that cannot be explained adequately and without residue, simply subjectively. The actual basic experience at any rate is most easily explained on the hypothesis that there is actually some objective cause of that experience.

RUSSELL: I should reply to that line of argument that the whole argument from our own mental states to something outside us, is a very tricky affair. Even where we all admit its validity, we only feel justified in doing so, I think, because of the consensus of mankind. If there's a crowd in a room and there's a clock in a room, they can all see the clock. The fact that they can all see it tends to make them think that it's not an hallucination: whereas these religious experiences do tend to be very private.

COPLESTON: Yes, they do. I'm speaking strictly of mystical experience proper, and I certainly don't include, by the way, what are called visions. I mean simply the experience, and I quite admit it's indefinable, of the transcendent object or of what seems to be a transcendent object. I remember Julian Huxley in some lecture saying that religious experience, or mystical experience, is as much a real experience as falling in love or appreciating poetry and art. Well, I believe that when we appreciate poetry and art we appreciate definite poems or a definite work of art. If we fall in love, well, we fall in love with somebody and not with nobody.

RUSSELL: May I interrupt for a moment here. That is by no means always the case. Japanese novelists never consider that they have achieved a success unless large numbers of real people commit suicide for love of the imaginary heroine.

COPLESTON: Well, I must take your word for these goings on in Japan. I haven't committed suicide, I'm glad to say, but I have been strongly influenced in the taking of two important steps in my life by two biographies. However, I must say I see little resemblance between the real influence of those books on me and the mystic experience proper, so far, that is, as an outsider can obtain an idea of that experience.

RUSSELL: Well, I mean we wouldn't regard God as being on the same level as the characters in a work of fiction. You'll admit there's a distinction here?

COPLESTON: I certainly should. But what I'd say is that the best explanation seems to be the not purely subjectivist explanation. Of course, a subjectivist explanation is possible in the case of certain people in whom there is little relation between the experience and life, in the case of deluded people and hallucinated people, and so on. But when you get what one might call the pure type, say St. Francis of Assisi, when you get an experience that results in an overflow of dynamic and creative love, the best explanation of that it seems to me is the actual existence of an objective cause of the experience.

RUSSELL: Well, I'm not contending in a dogmatic way that there is not a God. What I'm contending is that we don't know that there is. I can only take what is recorded as I should take other records and I do find that a very great many things are reported, and I am sure you would not accept things about demons and devils and what not—and they're reported in exactly the same tone of voice and with exactly the same conviction. And the mystic, if his vision is veridical, may be said to know that there are devils. But I don't know that there are.

COPLESTON: But surely in the case of the devils there have been people speaking mainly of visions, appearances, angels or demons and so on. I should rule out the visual appearances, because I think they can be explained apart from the existence of the object which is supposed to be seen.

RUSSELL: But don't you think there are abundant recorded cases of people who believe that they've heard Satan speaking to them in their hearts, in just the same way as the mystics assert God—and I'm not talking now of an external vision, I'm talking of a purely mental experience. That seems to be an experience of the same sort as mystics' experience of God, and I don't see that from what mystics tell us you can get any argu-

ment for God which is not equally an argument for Satan.

COPLESTON: I quite agree, of course, that people have imagined or thought they have heard or seen Satan. And I have no wish in passing to deny the existence of Satan. But I do not think that people have claimed to have experienced Satan in the precise way in which mystics claim to have experienced God. Take the case of a non-Christian, Plotinus. He admits the experience is something inexpressible, the object is an object of love, and therefore, not an object that causes horror and disgust. And the effect of that experience is, I should say, borne out, or I mean the validity of the experience is borne out in the records of the life of Plotinus. At any rate it is more reasonable to suppose that he had that experience if we're willing to accept Porphyry's account of Plotinus's general kindness and benevolence.

RUSSELL: The fact that a belief has a good moral effect upon a man is no evidence whatsoever in favor of its truth.

COPLESTON: No, but if it could actually be proved that the belief was actually responsible for a good effect on a man's life, I should consider it a presumption in favor of some truth, at any rate of the positive part of the belief if not of its entire validity. But in any case I am using the character of the life as evidence in favor of the mystic's veracity and sanity rather than as a proof of the truth of his beliefs.

RUSSELL: But even that I don't think is any evidence. I've had experiences myself that have altered my character profoundly. And I thought at the time at any rate that it was altered for the good. Those experiences were important, but they did not involve the existence of something outside me, and I don't think that if I'd thought they did, the fact that they had a wholesome effect would have been any evidence that I was right.

COPLESTON: No, but I think that the good effect would attest your veracity in describing your experience. Please remember that I'm not saying that a mystic's mediation or interpretation of his experience should be immune from discussion or criticism.

RUSSELL: Obviously the character of a

412   *Theism, Atheism, and Agnosticism*

young man may be—and often is—immensely affected for good by reading about some great man in history, and it may happen that the great man is a myth and doesn't exist, but the boy is just as much affected for good as if he did. There have been such people. Plutarch's *Lives* take Lycurgus as an example, who certainly did not exist, but you might be very much influenced by reading Lycurgus under the impression that he had previously existed. You would then be influenced by an object that you'd loved, but it wouldn't be an existing object.

COPLESTON: I agree with you on that, of course, that a man may be influenced by a character in fiction. Without going into the question of what it is precisely that influences him (I should say a real value) I think that the situation of that man and of the mystic are different. After all the man who is influenced by Lycurgus hasn't got the irresistible impression that he's experienced in some way the ultimate reality.

RUSSELL: I don't think you've quite got my point about these historical characters—these unhistorical characters in history. I'm not assuming what you call an effect on the reason. I'm assuming that the young man reading about this person and believing him to be real loves him—which is quite easy to happen, and yet he's loving a phantom.

COPLESTON: In one sense he's loving a phantom, that's perfectly true, in the sense, I mean, that he's loving X or Y who doesn't exist. But at the same time, it is not, I think, the phantom as such that the young man loves; he perceives a real value, an idea which he recognizes as objectively valid, and that's what excites his love.

RUSSELL: Well, in the same sense we had before about the characters in fiction.

COPLESTON: Yes, in one sense the man's loving a phantom—perfectly true. But in another sense he's loving what he perceives to be a value.

THE MORAL ARGUMENT

RUSSELL: But aren't you now saying in effect, I mean by God whatever is good or the sum total of what is good—the system of what is good, and, therefore, when a young man loves anything that is good he is loving God. Is that what you're saying, because if so, it wants a bit of arguing.

COPLESTON: I don't say, of course, that God is the sum total or system of what is good in the pantheistic sense; I'm not a pantheist, but I do think that all goodness reflects God in some way and proceeds from Him, so that in a sense the man who loves what is truly good, loves God even if he doesn't advert to God. But still I agree that the validity of such an interpretation of a man's conduct depends on the recognition of God's existence, obviously.

RUSSELL: Yes, but that's a point to be proved.

COPLESTON: Quite so, but I regard the metaphysical argument as probative, but there we differ.

RUSSELL: You see, I feel that some things are good and that other things are bad. I love the things that are good, that I think are good, and I hate the things that I think are bad. I don't say that these things are good because they participate in the Divine goodness.

COPLESTON: Yes, but what's your justification for distinguishing between good and bad or how do you view the distinction between them?

RUSSELL: I don't have any justification any more than I have when I distinguish between blue and yellow. What is my justification for distinguishing between blue and yellow? I can see they are different.

COPLESTON: Well, that is an excellent justification, I agree. You distinguish blue and yellow by seeing them, so you distinguish good and bad by what faculty?

RUSSELL: By my feelings.

COPLESTON: By your feelings. Well, that's what I was asking. You think that good and evil have reference simply to feeling?

RUSSELL: Well, why does one type of object look yellow and another look blue? I can more or less give an answer to that thanks to the physicists, and as to why I think one sort of thing good and another evil, probably there is an answer of the same sort, but it hasn't been gone into in the same way and I couldn't give it you.

COPLESTON: Well, let's take the behavior of the Commandant of Belsen. That appears to you as undesirable and evil and to me too. To Adolf Hitler we suppose it appeared as something good and desirable. I suppose you'd have to admit that for Hitler it was good and for you it is evil.

RUSSELL: No, I shouldn't quite go so far as that. I mean, I think people can make mistakes in that as they can in other things. If you have jaundice you see things yellow that are not yellow. You're making a mistake.

COPLESTON: Yes, one can make mistakes, but can you make a mistake if it's simply a question of reference to a feeling or emotion? Surely Hitler would be the only possible judge of what appealed to his emotions.

RUSSELL: It would be quite right to say that it appealed to his emotions, but you can say various things about that; among others, that if that sort of thing makes that sort of appeal to Hitler's emotions, then Hitler makes quite a different appeal to my emotions.

COPLESTON: Granted. But there's no objective criterion outside feeling then for condemning the conduct of the Commandant of Belsen, in your view?

RUSSELL: No more than there is for the color-blind person who's in exactly the same state. Why do we intellectually condemn the color-blind man? Isn't it because he's in the minority?

COPLESTON: I would say because he is lacking in a thing which normally belongs to human nature.

RUSSELL: Yes, but if he were in the majority, we shouldn't say that.

COPLESTON: Then you'd say that there's no criterion outside feeling that will enable one to distinguish between the behavior of the Commandant of Belsen and the behavior, say, of Sir Stafford Cripps or the Archbishop of Canterbury.

RUSSELL: The feeling is a little too simplified. You've got to take account of the effects of actions and your feelings towards those effects. You see, you can have an argument about it if you say that certain sorts of occurrences are the sort you like and certain others the sort you don't like. Then you have to take account of the effects of actions. You can very well say that the effects of the actions of the Commmandant of Belsen were painful and unpleasant.

COPLESTON: They certainly were, I agree, very painful and unpleasant to all the people in the camp.

RUSSELL: Yes, but not only to the people in the camp, but to outsiders contemplating them also.

COPLESTON: Yes, quite true in imagination. But that's my point. I don't approve of them, and I know you don't approve of them, but I don't see what ground you have for not approving of them, because after all, to the Commandant of Belsen himself, they're pleasant, those actions.

RUSSELL: Yes, but you see I don't need any more ground in that case than I do in the case of color perception. There are some people who think everything is yellow, there are people suffering from jaundice, and I don't agree with these people. I can't prove that the things are not yellow, there isn't any proof, but most people agree with me that they're not yellow, and most people agree with me that the Commandant of Belsen was making mistakes.

COPLESTON: Well, do you accept any moral obligation?

RUSSELL: Well, I should have to answer at considerable length to answer that. Practically speaking—yes. Theoretically speaking I should have to define moral obligation rather carefully.

COPLESTON: Well, do you think that the word "ought" simply has an emotional connotation?

RUSSELL: No, I don't think that, because you see, as I was saying a moment ago, one has to take account of the effects, and I think right conduct is that which would probably produce the greatest possible balance in intrinsic value of all the acts possible in the circumstances, and you've got to take account of the probable effects of your action in considering what is right.

COPLESTON: Well, I brought in moral obligation because I think that one can approach the question of God's existence in that way. The vast majority of the human race will make, and always have made, some distinction between right and wrong. The vast majority I think has some consciousness of an obligation in the moral sphere. It's my opinion that the perception of values and the consciousness of moral law and obligation are best explained through the hypothesis of a transcendent ground of value and of an author of the moral law. I do mean by "author of the moral law" an arbitrary author of the moral law. I think, in fact, that those modern atheists who have argued in the converse way "there is no God; therefore, there are no absolute values and no absolute law," are quite logical.

RUSSELL: I don't like the word "absolute." I don't think there is anything absolute whatever. The moral law, for example, is always changing. At one period in the development of the human race, almost everybody thought cannibalism was a duty.

COPLESTON: Well, I don't see that differences in particular moral judgments are any conclusive argument against the universality of the moral law. Let's assume for the moment that there are absolute moral values, even on that hypothesis it's only to be expected that different individuals and different groups should enjoy varying degrees of insight into those values.

RUSSELL: I'm inclined to think that "ought," the feeling that one has about "ought," is an echo of what has been told one by one's parents or one's nurses.

COPLESTON: Well, I wonder if you can explain away the idea of the "ought" merely in terms of nurses and parents. I really don't see how it can be conveyed to anybody in other terms than itself. It seems to me that if there is a moral order bearing upon the human conscience, that that moral order is unintelligible apart from the existence of God.

RUSSELL: Then you have to say one or other of two things. Either God only speaks to a very small percentage of mankind—which happens to include yourself—or He deliberately says things that are not true in talking to the consciences of savages.

COPLESTON: Well, you see, I'm not suggesting that God actually dictates moral precepts to the conscience. The human being's idea of the content of the moral law depends certainly to a large extent on education and environment, and a man has to use his reason in assessing the validity of the actual moral ideas of his social group. But the possibility of criticizing the accepted moral code presupposes that there is an objective standard, that there is an ideal moral order, which imposes itself (I mean the obligatory character of which can be recognized). I think that the recognition of this ideal moral order is part of the recognition of contingency. It implies the existence of a real foundation of God.

RUSSELL: But the law-giver has always been, it seems to me, one's parents or someone like. There are plenty of terrestrial law-givers to account for it, and that would explain why people's consciences are so amazingly different in different times and places.

COPLESTON: It helps to explain differences in the perception of particular moral values, which otherwise are inexplicable. It will help to explain changes in the matter of the moral law in the content of the precepts as accepted by this or that nation, or this or that individual. But the form of it, what Kant calls the categorical imperative, the "ought," I really don't see how that can possibly be conveyed to anybody by nurse or parent because there aren't any possible terms, so far as I can see, with which it can be explained. It can't be defined in other terms than itself, because once you've defined it in other terms than itself you've explained it away. It's no longer a moral "ought." It's something else.

RUSSELL: Well, I think the sense of "ought" is the effect of somebody's imagined disapproval, it may be God's imagined disapproval, but it's somebody's imagined disapproval. And I think that is what is meant by "ought."

COPLESTON: It seems to me to be external customs and taboos and things of that sort which can most easily be explained simply through environment and education, but all that seems to me to belong to what I call the matter of the law, the content. The idea of the "ought" as such can never be conveyed to a man by the tribal chief or by anybody else, because there are no other terms in which it could be conveyed. It seems to me entirely—— [Russell breaks in].

RUSSELL: But I don't see any reason to say that—I mean we all know about conditioned reflexes. We know that an animal, if punished habitually for a certain sort of act, after a time will refrain. I don't think the animal refrains from arguing within himself, "Master will be angry if I do this." He has a feeling that that's not the thing to do. That's what we can do with ourselves and nothing more.

COPLESTON: I see no reason to suppose that an animal has a consciousness of moral obligation; and we certainly don't regard an animal as morally responsible for his acts of disobedience. But a man has a consciousness of obligation and of moral values. I see no reason to suppose that one could condition all men as one can "condition" an animal, and I don't suppose you'd really want to do so even if one could. If "behaviorism" were true, there would be no objective moral distinction between the emperor Nero and St. Francis of Assisi. I can't help feeling, Lord Russell, you know, that you regard the conduct of the Commandant at Belsen as morally reprehensible, and that you yourself would never under any circumstances act in that way, even if you thought, or had reason to think, that possibly the balance of the happiness of the human race might be increased through some people being treated in that abominable manner.

RUSSELL: No. I wouldn't imitate the conduct of a mad dog. The fact that I wouldn't do it doesn't really bear on this question we're discussing.

COPLESTON: No, but if you were making a utilitarian explanation of right and wrong in terms of consequences, it might be held, and I suppose some of the Nazis of the better type would have held that although it's lamentable to have to act in this way, yet the balance in the long run leads to greater happiness. I don't think you'd say that, would you? I think you'd say that that sort of ac-

tion is wrong—and in itself, quite apart from whether the general balance of happiness is increased or not. Then, if you're prepared to say that, then I think you must have some criterion of right and wrong, that is outside the criterion of feeling, at any rate. To me, that admission would ultimately result in the admission of an ultimate ground of value in God.

RUSSELL: I think we are perhaps getting into confusion. It is not direct feeling about the act by which I should judge, but rather a feeling as to the effects. And I can't admit any circumstances in which certain kinds of behavior, such as you have been discussing, would do good. I can't imagine circumstances in which they would have a beneficial effect. I think the persons who think they do are deceiving themselves. But if there were circumstances in which they would have a beneficial effect, then I might be obliged, however reluctantly, to say—"Well, I don't like these things, but I will acquiesce in them," just as I acquiesce in the Criminal Law, although I profoundly dislike punishment.

COPLESTON: Well, perhaps it's time I summed up my position. I've argued two things. First, that the existence of God can be philosophically proved by a metaphysical argument; secondly, that it is only the existence of God that will make sense of man's moral experience and of religious experience. Personally, I think that your way of accounting for man's moral judgments leads inevitably to a contradiction between what your theory demands and your own spontaneous judgments. Moreover, your theory explains moral obligation away, and explaining away is not explanation. As regards the metaphysical argument, we are apparently in agreement that what we call the world consists simply of contingent beings. That is, of beings no one of which can account for its own existence. You say that the series of events needs no explanation: I say that if there were no necessary being, no being which must exist and cannot not exist, nothing would exist. The infinity of the series of contingent beings, even if proved, would be irrelevant. Something does exist; therefore, there must be something which accounts for this fact, a being which is outside the series of contingent beings. If you admitted this, we could then have discussed whether that being is personal, good, and so on. On the actual point discussed, whether there is or is not a necessary being, I find myself, I think, in agreement with the great majority of classical philosophers.

You maintain, I think, that existing beings are simply there, and that I have no justification for raising the question of the explanation of their existence. But I would like to point out that this position cannot be substantiated by logical analysis; it expresses a philosophy which itself stands in need of proof. I think we have reached an impasse because our ideas of philosophy are radically different; it seems to me that what I call a part of philosophy, that you call the whole, insofar at least as philosophy is rational. It seems to me, if you will pardon my saying so, that besides your own logical system—which you call "modern" in opposition to antiquated logic (a tendentious adjective)—you maintain a philosophy which cannot be substantiated by logical analysis. After all, the problem of God's existence is an existential problem whereas logical analysis does not deal directly with problems of existence. So it seems to me, to declare that the terms involved in one set of problems are meaningless because they are not required in dealing with another set of problems, is to settle from the beginning the nature and extent of philosophy, and that is itself a philosophical act which stands in need of justification.

RUSSELL: Well, I should like to say just a few words by way of summary on my side. First, as to the metaphysical argument: I don't admit the connotations of such a term as "contingent" or the possibility of explanation in Father Copleston's sense. I think the word "contingent" inevitably suggests the possibility of something that wouldn't have this what you might call accidental character of just being there, and I don't thing this is true except in the purely causal sense. You can sometimes give a causal explanation of one thing as being the effect of something else, but that is merely referring one thing to another thing and there's no—to my mind—explanation in Father Copleston's sense of anything at all, nor is there any meaning in calling things "contingent" because there isn't anything else they could be. That's what I should say about that, but I should like to say a few words about Father Copleston's accusation that I regard logic as all philosophy—that is by no means the case. I don't by any means regard logic as all philosophy. I think logic is an essential part of philosophy and logic has to be used in philosophy, and in that I think he and I are at one. When the logic that he uses was new—namely, in the time of Aristotle, there had to be a great deal of fuss made about it; Aristotle made a lot of fuss about that logic. Nowadays it's become old and respectable, and you don't have to make so much fuss about it. The logic that I believe in is comparatively new, and therefore I have to imitate Aristotle in making a fuss about it; but it's not that I think it's all philosophy by any means—I don't think so. I think it's an important part of philosophy, and when I say that, I don't find a meaning for this or that word, that is a position of detail based upon what I've found out about that particular word, from thinking about it. It's not a general position that all words that are used in metaphysics are nonsense, or anything like that which I don't really hold.

As regards the moral argument, I do find that when one studies anthropology or history, there are people who think it their duty to perform acts which I think abominable, and I certainly can't, therefore, attribute Divine origin to the matter of moral obligation, which Father Copleston doesn't ask me to; but I think even the form of moral obligation, when it takes the form of enjoining you to eat your father or what not, doesn't seem to me to be such a very beautiful and noble thing; and, therefore, I cannot attribute a Divine origin to this sense of moral obligation, which I think is quite easily accounted for in quite other ways.

The Existence of God—A Debate   **417**

Theology and Falsification*

Anthony Flew, R. M. Hare, and Basil Mitchell

ANTHONY FLEW

Let us begin with a parable. It is a parable developed from a tale told by John Wisdom in his haunting and revelatory article 'Gods'. Once upon a time two explorers came upon a clearing in the jungle. In the clearing were growing many flowers and many weeds. One explorer says, 'Some gardener must tend this plot'. The other disagrees, 'There is no gardener'. So they pitch their tents and set a watch. No gardener is ever seen. 'But perhaps he is an invisible gardener'. So they set up a barbed-wire fence. They electrify it. They patrol with bloodhounds. (For they remember how H. G. Wells's *The Invisible Man* could be both smelt and touched though he could not be seen.) But no shrieks ever suggest that some intruder has received a shock. No movements of the wire ever betray an invisible climber. The bloodhounds never give cry. Yet still the Believer is not convinced. 'But

*Reprinted with permission of Macmillan Publishing Company, from *New Essays in Philosophical Theology*, eds. A. Flew & A. MacIntyre. Copyright © 1955 by Anthony Flew and Alasdair MacIntyre, renewed 1963.

there is a gardener, invisible, intangible, insensible to electric shocks, a gardener who has no scent and makes no sound, a gardener who comes secretly to look after the garden which he loves'. At last the Sceptic despairs, 'But what remains of your original assertion? Just how does what you call an invisible, intangible, eternally elusive gardener differ from an imaginary gardener or even from no gardener at all?'

In this parable we can see how what starts as an assertion, that something exists or that there is some analogy between certain complexes of phenomena, may be reduced step by step to an altogether different status, to an expression perhaps of a 'picture preference'. The Sceptic says there is no gardener. The Believer says there is a gardener (but invisible, etc.). One man talks about sexual behaviour. Another man prefers to talk of Aphrodite (but knows that there is not really a superhuman person additional to, and somehow responsible for, all sexual phenomena). The process of qualification may be checked at any point before the original assertion is completely withdrawn and something of that first assertion will remain (Tautology). Mr. Wells's invisible man could not, admittedly, be seen, but in all other respects he was a man like the rest of us. But though the process of qualification may be, and of course usually is, checked in time, it is not always judiciously so halted. Someone may dissipate his assertion completely without noticing that he has done so. A fine brash hypothesis may thus be killed by inches, the death by a thousand qualifications.

And in this, it seems to me, lies the peculiar danger, the endemic evil, of theological utterance. Take such utterances as 'God has a plan', 'God created the world', 'God loves us as a father loves his children'. They look at first sight very much like assertions, vast cosmological assertions. Of course, this is no sure sign that they either are, or are intended to be, assertions. But let us confine ourselves to the cases where those who utter such sentences intend them to express assertions. (Merely remarking parenthetically that those who intend or interpret such utterances as crypto-commands, expressions of wishes, disguised ejaculations, concealed ethics, or as anything else but assertions, are unlikely to succeed in making them either properly orthodox or practically effective.)

Now to assert that such and such is the case is necessarily equivalent to denying that such and such is not the case. Suppose then that we are in doubt as to what someone who gives vent to an utterance is asserting, or suppose that, more radically, we are sceptical as to whether he is really asserting anything at all, one way of trying to understand (or perhaps it will be to expose) his utterance is to attempt to find what he would regard as counting against, or as being incompatible with, its truth. For if the utterance is indeed an assertion, it will necessarily be equivalent to a denial of the negation of that assertion. And anything which would count against the assertion, or which would induce the speaker to withdraw it and to admit that it had been mistaken, must be part of (or the whole of) the meaning of the negation of that assertion. And to know the meaning of the negation of an assertion, is as near as makes no matter, to know the meaning of that assertion. And if there is nothing which a putative assertion denies then there is nothing which it asserts either: and so it is not really an assertion. When the Sceptic in the parable asked the Believer, 'Just how does what you call an invisible, intangible, eternally elusive gardener differ from an imaginary gardener or even from no gardener at all?' he was suggesting that the Believer's earlier statement had been so eroded by qualification that it was no longer an assertion at all.

Now it often seems to people who are not religious as if there was no conceivable event or series of events the occurrence of which would be admitted by sophisticated religious people to be a sufficient reason for conceding 'There wasn't a God after all' or 'God does not really love us then'. Someone tells us that God loves us as a father loves his children. We are reassured. But then we see a child dying of inoperable cancer of the throat. His earthly father is driven frantic in his efforts to help, but his Heavenly Father reveals no obvious sign of concern. Some qualification is made—God's love is 'not a merely human love' or it is 'an inscrutable love', perhaps—and we realize that such sufferings are quite compatible with the truth of the assertion that 'God loves us as a father (but, of course, . . .)'. We are reassured again. But then perhaps we ask: what is this assurance of God's (appropriately qualified) love worth, what is this apparent guarantee really a guarantee against? Just what would have to happen not merely (morally and wrongly) to tempt but also (logically and rightly) to entitle us to say 'God does not love us' or even 'God does not exist'? I therefore put to the succeeding symposiasts the simple central questions, 'What would have to occur or to have occurred to constitute for you a disproof of the love of, or of the existence of, God?'

R. M. HARE

I wish to make it clear that I shall not try to defend Christianity in particular, but religion in general—not because I do not believe in Christianity, but because you cannot understand what Christianity is, until you have understood what religion is.

I must begin by confessing that, on the ground marked out by Flew, he seems to me to be completely victorious. I therefore shift my ground by relating another parable. A certain lunatic is convinced that all dons want to murder him. His friends introduce him to all the mildest and most respectable dons that they can find, and after each of them has retired, they say, 'You see, he doesn't really want to murder you; he spoke to you in a most cordial manner; surely you are convinced now?' But the lunatic replies, 'Yes, but that was only his diabolical cunning; he's really plotting against me the whole time, like the rest of them; I know it I tell you'. However many kindly dons are produced, the reaction is still the same.

Now we say that such a person is deluded. But what is he deluded about? About the truth or falsity of an assertion? Let us apply Flew's test to him. There is no behaviour of dons that can be enacted which he will accept as counting against his theory; and therefore his theory, on this test, asserts nothing. But it does not follow that there is no difference between what he thinks about dons and what most of us think about them—otherwise we should not call him a lunatic and ourselves sane, and dons would have no reason to feel uneasy about his presence in Oxford.

Let us call that in which we differ from this lunatic, our respective *bliks*. He has an insane *blik* about dons; we have a sane one. It is important to realize that we have a sane one, not no *blik* at all; for there must be two sides to any argument—if he has a wrong *blik*, then those who are right about dons must have a right one. Flew has shown that a *blik* does not consist in an assertion or system of them; but nevertheless it is very important to have the right *blik*.

Let us try to imagine what it would be like to have different *bliks* about other things than dons. When I am driving my car, it sometimes occurs to me to wonder whether my movements of the steering-wheel will always continue to be followed by corre-

sponding alterations in the direction of the car. I have never had a steering failure, though I have had skids, which must be similar. Moreover, I know enough about how the steering of my car is made, to know the sort of thing that would have to go wrong for the steering to fail—steel joints would have to part, or steel rods break, or something—but how do I know that this won't happen? The truth is, I don't know; I just have a *blik* about steel and its properties, so that normally I trust the steering of my car; but I find it not at all difficult to imagine what it would be like to lose this *blik* and acquire the opposite one. People would say I was silly about steel; but there would be no mistaking the reality of the difference between our respective *bliks*—for example, I should never go in a motor-car. Yet I should hesitate to say that the difference between us was the difference between contradictory assertions. No amount of safe arrivals or bench-tests will remove my *blik* and restore the normal one; for my *blik* is compatible with any finite number of such tests.

It was Hume who taught us that our whole commerce with the world depends upon our *blik* about the world; and that differences between *bliks* about the world cannot be settled by observation of what happens in the world. That was why, having performed the interesting experiment of doubting the ordinary man's *blik* about the world, and showing that no proof could be given to make us adopt one *blik* rather than another, he turned to backgammon to take his mind off the problem. It seems, indeed, to be impossible even to formulate as an assertion the normal *blik* about the world which makes me put my confidence in the future reliability of steel joints, in the continued ability of the road to support my car, and not gape beneath it revealing nothing below; in the general non-homicidal tendencies of dons; in my own continued well-being (in some sense of that word that I may not now fully understand) if I continue to do what is right according to my lights; in the general likelihood of people like Hitler coming to a bad end. But perhaps a formulation less inadequate than

Theism, Atheism, and Agnosticism

most is to be found in the Psalms: 'The earth is weak and all the inhabiters thereof: I bear up the pillars of it'.

The mistake of the position which Flew selects for attack is to regard this kind of talk as some sort of *explanation*, as scientists are accustomed to use the word. As such, it would obviously be ludicrous. We no longer believe in God as an Atlas—*nous n'avons pas besoin de cette hypothèse.** But it is nevertheless true to say that, as Hume saw, without a *blik* there can be no explanation; for it is by our *bliks* that we decide what is and what is not an explanation. Suppose we believed that everything that happened, happened by pure chance. This would not of course be an assertion; for it is compatible with anything happening or not happening, and so, incidentally, is its contradictory. But if we had this belief, we should not be able to explain or predict or plan anything. Thus, although we should not be *asserting* anything different from those of a more normal belief, there would be a great difference between us; and this is the sort of difference that there is between those who really believe in God and those who really disbelieve in him.

The word 'really' is important, and may excite suspicion. I put it in, because when people have had a good Christian upbringing, as have most of those who now profess not to believe in any sort of religion, it is very hard to discover what they really believe. The reason why they find it so easy to think that they are not religious, is that they have never got into the frame of mind of one who suffers from the doubts to which religion is the answer. Not for them the terrors of the primitive jungle. Having abandoned some of the more picturesque fringes of religion, they think that they have abandoned the whole thing—whereas in fact they still have got, and could not live without, a religion of a comfortably substantial, albeit highly sophisticated, kind, which differs from that of many 'religious people' in little more than this, that 'religious people' like to sing Psalms about theirs—a very natural and

*We have no need of this hypothesis.

proper thing to do. But nevertheless there may be a big difference lying behind—the difference between two people who, though side by side, are walking in different directions. I do not know in what direction Flew is walking; perhaps he does not know either. But we have had some examples recently of various ways in which one can walk away from Christianity, and there are any number of possibilities. After all, man has not changed biologically since primitive times; it is his religion that has changed, and it can easily change again. And if you do not think that such changes make a difference, get acquainted with some Sikhs and some Mussulmans of the same Punjabi stock; you will find them quite different sorts of people.

There is an important difference between Flew's parable and my own which we have not yet noticed. The explorers do not *mind* about their garden; they discuss it with interest, but not with concern. But my lunatic, poor fellow, minds about dons; and I mind about the steering of my car; it often has people in it that I care for. It is because I mind very much about what goes on in the garden in which I find myself, that I am unable to share the explorers' detachment.

BASIL MITCHELL

Flew's article is searching and perceptive, but there is, I think, something odd about his conduct of the theologian's case. The theologian surely would not deny that the fact of pain counts against the assertion that God loves men. This very incompatibility generates the most intractable of theological problems—the problem of evil. So the theologian *does* recognize the fact of pain as counting against Christian doctrine. But it is true that he will not allow it—or anything—to count decisively against it; for he is committed by his faith to trust in God. His attitude is not that of the detached observer, but of the believer.

Perhaps this can be brought out by yet another parable. In time of war in an occupied country, a member of the resistance meets one night a stranger who deeply impresses him. They spend that night together in conversation. The Stranger tells the partisan that he himself is on the side of the resistance—indeed that he is in command of it, and urges the partisan to have faith in him no matter what happens. The partisan is utterly convinced at that meeting of the Stranger's sincerity and constancy and undertakes to trust him.

They never meet in conditions of intimacy again. But sometimes the Stranger is seen helping members of the resistance, and the partisan is grateful and says to his friends, 'He is on our side'.

Sometimes he is seen in the uniform of the police handing over patriots to the occupying power. On these occasions his friends murmur against him: but the partisan still says, 'He is on our side'. He still believes that, in spite of appearances, the Stranger did not deceive him. Sometimes he asks the Stranger for help and receives it. He is then thankful. Sometimes he asks and does not receive it. Then he says, 'The Stranger knows best'. Sometimes his friends, in exasperation, say, 'Well, what *would* he have to do for you to admit that you were wrong and that he is not on our side?' But the partisan refuses to answer. He will not consent to put the Stranger to the test. And sometimes his friends complain, 'Well, what *would* he have to do for you to admit that you were wrong and that he is not on our side?' But the partisan refuses to answer. He will not consent to put the Stranger to the test. And sometimes his friends complain, 'Well, if *that's* what you mean by his being on our side, the sooner he goes over to the other side the better'.

The partisan of the parable does not allow anything to count decisively against the proposition 'The Stranger is on our side'. This is because he has committed himself to trust the Stranger. But he of course recognizes that the Stranger's ambiguous behaviour *does* count against what he believes about him. It is precisely this situation which constitutes the trial of his faith.

When the partisan asks for help and doesn't get it, what can he do? He can (a) conclude that the stranger is not on our side or; (b) maintain that he is on our side, but that he has reasons for withholding help.

The first he will refuse to do. How long can he uphold the second position without its becoming just silly?

I don't think one can say in advance. It will depend on the nature of the impression created by the Stranger in the first place. It will depend, too, on the manner in which he takes the Stranger's behaviour. If he blandly dismisses it as of no consequence, as having no bearing upon his belief, it will be assumed that he is thoughtless or insane. And it quite obviously won't do for him to say easily, 'Oh, when used of the Stranger the phrase "is on our side" *means* ambiguous behaviour of this sort'. In that case he would be like the religious man who says blandly of a terrible disaster 'It is God's will'. No, he will only be regarded as sane and reasonable in his belief, if he experiences in himself the full force of the conflict.

It is here that my parable differs from Hare's. The partisan admits that many things may and do count against his belief: whereas Hare's lunatic who has a *blik* about dons doesn't admit that anything counts against his *blik*. Nothing *can* count against *bliks*. Also the partisan has a reason for having in the first instance committed himself, viz. the character of the Stranger; whereas the lunatic has no reason for his *blik* about dons—because, of course, you can't have reasons for *bliks*.

This means that I agree with Flew that theological utterances must be assertions. The partisan is making an assertion when he says, 'The Stranger is on our side'.

Do I want to say that the partisan's belief about the Stranger is, in any sense, an explanation? I think I do. It explains and makes sense of the Stranger's behaviour: it helps to explain also the resistance movement in the context of which he appears. In each case it differs from the interpretation which the others put upon the same facts.

'God loves men' resembles 'the Stranger is on our side' (and many other significant statements, e.g. historical ones) in not being conclusively falsifiable. They can both be treated in at least three different ways:

(1) As provisional hypotheses to be discarded if experience tells against them; (2) As significant articles of faith; (3) As vacuous formulae (expressing, perhaps, a desire for reassurance) to which experience makes no difference and which make no difference to life.

The Christian, once he has committed himself, is precluded by his faith from taking up the first attitude: 'Thou shalt not tempt the Lord thy God'. He is in constant danger, as Flew has observed, of slipping into the third. But he need not; and, if he does, it is a failure in faith as well as in logic.

ANTHONY FLEW

It has been a good discussion: and I am glad to have helped to provoke it. But now it must come to an end: and the Editors of *University* have asked me to make some concluding remarks. Since it is impossible to deal with all the issues raised or to comment separately upon each contribution, I will concentrate on Mitchell and Hare, as representative of two very different kinds of response to the challenge made in 'Theology and Falsification'.

The challenge, it will be remembered, ran like this. Some theological utterances seem to, and are intended to, provide explanations or express assertions. Now an assertion, to be an assertion at all, must claim that things stand thus and thus; *and not otherwise.* Similarly an explanation, to be an explanation at all, must explain why this particular thing occurs; *and not something else.* Those last clauses are crucial. And yet sophisticated religious people—or so it seemed to me—are apt to overlook this, and tend to refuse to allow, not merely that anything actually does occur, but that anything conceivably could occur, which would count against their theological assertions and explanations. But in so far as they do this their supposed explanations are actually bogus, and their seeming assertions are really vacuous.

Mitchell's response to this challenge is admirably direct, straightforward, and understanding. He agrees 'that theological utterances must be assertions'. He agrees that if they are to be assertions, there must be something that would count against their truth. He agrees, too, that believers are in constant danger of transforming their would-be assertions into 'vacuous formulae'. But he takes me to task for an oddity in my 'conduct of the theologian's case. The theologian surely would not deny that the fact of pain counts against the assertion that God loves men. This very incompatibility generates the most intractable of theological problems, the problem of evil'. I think he is right. I should have made a distinction between two very different ways of dealing with what looks like evidence against the love of God: the way I stressed was the expedient of qualifying the original assertion; the way the theologian usually takes, at first, is to admit that it looks bad but to insist that there is—there must be—some explanation which will show that, in spite of appearances, there really is a God who loves us. His difficulty, it seems to me, is that he has given God attributes which rule out all possible saving explanations. In Mitchell's parable of the Stranger it is easy for the believer to find plausible excuses for ambiguous behaviour: for the Stranger is a man. But suppose the Stranger is God. We cannot say that he would like to help but cannot: God is omnipotent. We cannot say that he would help if he only knew: God is omniscient. We cannot say that he is not responsible for the wickedness of others: God creates those others. Indeed an omnipotent, omniscient God must be an accessory before (and during) the fact to every human misdeed; as well as being responsible for every non-moral defect in the universe. So, though I entirely concede that Mitchell was absolutely right to insist against me that the theologian's first move is to look for an *explanation*, I still think that in the end, if relentlessly pursued, he will have to resort to the avoiding action of *qualification.* And there lies the danger of that death by a thousand qualifications, which would, I agree, constitute 'a failure in faith as well as in logic'.

Hare's approach is fresh and bold. He confesses that 'on the ground marked out by Flew, he seems to me to be completely victorious.' He therefore introduces the concept of *blik*. But while I think that there is room for some such concept in philosophy, and that philosophers should be grateful to Hare for his invention, I nevertheless want to insist that any attempt to analyse Christian religious utterances as expressions or affirmations of a *blik* rather than as (at least would-be) assertions about the cosmos is fundamentally misguided. *First*, because thus interpreted they would be entirely unorthodox. If Hare's religion really is a *blik*, involving no cosmological assertions about the nature and activities of a supposed personal creator, then surely he is not a Christian at all. *Second*, because thus interpreted, they could scarcely do the job they do. If they were not even intended as assertions then many religious activities would become fraudulent, or merely silly. If 'You ought *because* it is God's will' asserts no more than 'You ought', then the person who prefers the former phraseology is not really giving a reason, but a fraudulent substitute for one, a dialectical dud cheque. If 'My soul must be immortal *because* God loves his children, etc.' asserts no more than 'My soul must be immortal', then the man who reassures himself with theological arguments for immortality is being as silly as the man who tries to clear his overdraft by writing his bank a cheque on the same account. (Of course neither of these utterances would be distinctively Christian: but this discussion never pretended to be so confined.) Religious utterances may indeed express false or even bogus assertions: but I simply do not believe that they are not both intended and interpreted to be or at any rate to presuppose assertions, at least in the context of religious practice; whatever shifts may be demanded, in another context, by the exigencies of theological apologetic.

One final suggestion. The philosophers of religion might well draw upon George Orwell's last appalling nightmare *1984* for the concept of *doublethink*. 'Doublethink means the power of holding two contradictory beliefs simultaneously, and accepting both of them. The party intellectual knows that he is playing tricks with reality, but by the exercise of *doublethink* he also satisfied himself that reality is not violated' (*1984*, p. 220). Perhaps religious intellectuals too are sometimes driven to doublethink in order to retain their faith in a loving God in face of the reality of a heartless and indifferent world. But of this more another time, perhaps.

Theism, Atheism, and Agnosticism

The Presence of God and the Justification of Religious Belief*

Gary Gutting

1. EXPERIENCES OF GOD

At least since William James' classic work, it has been a commonplace that there are many varieties of religious experience. Oddly, however, philosophical analysts of religious experiences have often ignored this diversity and treated exceptional instances—mystical experiences and physical visions—as typical or even exhaustive of the type. By contrast, I propose to center my discussion on a particular type of religious experience that, though paid little explicit attention by philosophers, is one of the most common and most important in the lives of believers. This is the sort of experience that psychologists of religion call "direct awareness of the presence of God." James gives the following general characterization of such experiences:[1]

*Copyright © 1982 by the University of Notre Dame Press. Reprinted by permission, from Gutting, *Religious Belief and Religious Skepticism*, pp. 141–76. Notre Dame: University of Notre Dame Press, 1982.

We may lay it down as certain that in the distinctively religious sphere of experience, many persons (how many we cannot tell) possess the objects of their belief, not in the form of mere conceptions which their intellect accepts as true, but rather in the form of quasi-sensible realities directly apprehended [*The Varieties of Religious Experience*, p. 65].

James cites a number of instances of this sort of experience:

There was not a mere consciousness of something there, but fused in the central happiness of it, a startling awareness of some ineffable good. Not vague either, not like the emotional effect of some poem, or scene, or blossom, or music, but the sure knowledge of the close presence of a sort of mighty person, and after it went, the memory persisted as the one perception of reality. Everything else might be a dream, but not that [p. 63].

I remember the night, and almost the very spot on the hilltop, where my soul opened out, as it were, into the Infinite, and there was a rushing together of the two worlds, the inner and the outer. . . . I stood alone with Him who had made me, and all the beauty of the world, and love, and sorrow, and even temptation. I did not seek Him, but felt the perfect unison of my spirit with His. . . . The darkness held a presence that was all the more felt because it was not seen. I could not any more have doubted that *He* was there than that I was. I felt myself to be, if possible, the less real of the two [p. 67].

Of the following statement, James says, "Probably thousands of unpretending Christians would write an almost identical account":

God is more real to me than any thought or thing or person. I feel his presence positively, and the more as I live in closer harmony with his laws as written in my body and mind. I feel him in the sunshine or rain. . . . I talk to him as to a companion in prayer and praise, and our communion is delightful. He answers me again and again, often in words so clearly spoken that it seems my outer ear must have carried the tone, but generally in strong mental impressions [p. 70].

Finally, a few brief statements taken, James says, at random:

God surrounds me like the physical atmosphere. He is closer to me than my own breath. In him literally I live and move and have my being.

There are times when I seem to stand in his very presence, to talk with him. Answers to prayers have come, sometimes direct and overwhelming in their revelation of his presence and powers. . . .

I have the sense of a presence, strong, and at the same time soothing, which hovers over me. Sometimes it seems to enwrap me with sustaining arms [p. 71].

More systematic studies reveal the same phenomenon. A recent example is a survey of a random sample of a hundred British university students, two-thirds of whom said they have had religious experiences of some sort, with about one-fourth describing their experiences as "awareness of the presence of God."[2] The following are some representative comments by students reporting such experiences:

It was just about dark and I was looking out of the library window. . . . I was aware of everything going on around me, and I felt that everybody had rejected me—and I felt very alone. But at the same time I was aware of something that was giving me strength and keeping me going . . . protecting me ["Religious Experience Amongst a Group of Post-Graduate Students," p. 168].

It's something that is there all the time. One's awareness of it is limited by one's willingness to submit to it [p. 168].

When I pray . . . I am not praying in a vacuum; there is a response and I feel that at the time of praying, otherwise I think I'd eventually give it up [p. 170].

At university I began to feel the 'gay' life had nothing to offer, life seemed meaningless and all came to a climax about a month before 1st year exams. I was feeling pretty anxious. One night in my room, as I was going to bed, things were at a bursting point. I said, 'I give you my life, whoever you are.' I definitely felt somebody was there and something had been done. I felt relief but not much else, emotionally. It was like a re-direction and this was a gradual thing [pp. 172–73].

There is every reason to believe that at least a very large number of such reports are candid, that the experiences reported did in fact take place. The crucial question is whether any of the experiences are veridical, whether there is reason to think that there really is a powerful and benevolent nonhuman being experienced by people reporting religious experiences. But before discussing this issue, we need to become as clear as possible about the nature of the experiences in question. This is especially important because, as noted above, many philosophical critics of religious experience have simply ignored the existence of the sorts of experiences I have cited. Alasdair MacIntyre, for example, begins his discussion of religious experience by reducing all such experiences ("visions" in his terminology) to two classes:

> . . . first, those visions which can properly be called such, that is, those where something is *seen;* and second, those where the experience is of a feeling-state or of a mental image, which are only called visions by an honorific extension of the term.[3]

He then goes on to argue that religious experiences of the second type could never provide evidence for religious claims because "an experience of a distinctively 'mental' kind, a feeling-state or an image cannot of itself yield us any information about anything other than experience" ("Visions," p. 256). With regard to visions properly speaking, MacIntyre argues that they of course cannot be themselves literally of God, since he cannot be seen, and that we are never warranted in inferring from an X that we see to a Y that we do not see unless we have on other occasions experienced a correlation between X and Y. Whatever we may think of MacIntyre's arguments here (and the second seems particularly weak), it is clear that they do not apply to religious experiences of the sort we are concerned with, since these are neither reports of mere feeling-states or mental images nor claims to have literally seen saints, angels, or the like. Rather, they are experiences that are both *perceptual* (i.e., purporting to be of something other than the experiencer) and *nonsensory* (not of some object of the special senses). As such, they fall into neither of MacIntrye's two classes and so escape the objections he raises.

Similarly, Wallace Matson[4] raises difficulties first for the veridicality of experiences of "voices and visions" and second for

"mystical" experiences (i.e., extraordinary encounters that cannot be intelligibly described to those who have not had them). We have already noted that the experiences with which we are concerned are not of "visions or voices." But neither are they the mystic's ineffable raptures. Although they sometimes have aspects their subjects feel cannot be fully described, they can all be adequately if not completely expressed by saying that they are of a very powerful and very good nonhuman person who is concerned about us. Accordingly, Matson's objections to the veridicality of mystical experiences—which all derive from their apparently peculiar ineffability—are irrelevant to the experiences we are concerned with. These, to summarize, are not given as mere feelings or images, nor are they literal physical visions or ineffable mystical insights. Rather, they are perceptual but nonsensory experiences, purporting to be of a good and powerful being concerned with us.

But are these experiences actually of such a being? A first crucial point is that no experience that purports to be of an external object, taken simply by itself, makes it reasonable to believe that there is such an object. There are no "phenomenological" features of an experience that will mark it off as of something real. (This is the valid core of Descartes' dream argument: there may be no intrinsic differences between a veridical and a nonveridical perceptual experience.) Given an experience that purports to be of X, we need to know more before we are entitled to believe that X exists. A useful way of putting this point is as follows: given an experience with X as its *intentional object*, we may still ask if it is reasonable to believe that X exists (that X is a real object). However, for this language not to be misleading, we need to note that saying "E has X as its intentional object" does not mean that X exists in some special nonreal way; rather it means that E has the internal character of being an "of-X" experience; i.e., it is the sort of experience that, if veridical, is of a really existing X.

Given that a religious experience does not wear its veridicality on its sleeve, the central question is how we can move from the experience to its veridicality. Among critics of religious experience, the most common view is that the mere subjective occurrence of an of-God experience is in itself no evidence for God's existence; the fact that the experience has occurred must be supplemented by further premises to form an argument (deductive or inductive) that entails "God exists." Thus, Anthony Flew after noting that "the mere fact of the occurrence of subjective religious experience does not by itself warrant the conclusion that there are any objective religious truths," goes on to say:

> . . . those who propose to rest a lot of weight upon the evidence of religious experience [should] take it as their first and inescapable task to answer the basic question: How and when would we be justified in making inferences from the facts of the occurrence of religious experience, considered as a purely psychological phenomenon, to conclusions about the supposed objective religious truths. . . . [5]

Here Flew misrepresents the epistemic connection between an "of-X" experience and the claim that X exists. This can be most readily seen from the following parody of his statement about religious experience and religious belief:

> . . . those who propose to rest a lot of weight upon the evidence of experiences of material objects should take it as their first and inescapable task to answer the basic question: How and when would we be justified in making inferences from the facts of the occurrence of experiences of material objects, considered as a purely psychological phenomenon, to conclusions about the supposed objective truths about material objects. . . .

We have been no more successful at inferring truths about material objects from the subjective occurrence of sense experiences than we have been at inferring truths about God from the subjective occurrence of religious experiences. But no doubts should arise about our belief that sense experiences yield knowledge of material objects, because such experiences do not support these knowledge claims by providing a premise for some master argument against skepticism regarding the senses. Similarly, the failure of religious experiences to ground such an argument does not count against their veridicality. Flew has based his objection on a faulty analysis of the way experiences support objective truth claims.

How, then, do of-X experiences support the claim that X exists? Richard Swinburne[6] has recently suggested that such an experience provides *prima facie* evidence for the claim, evidence that will be decisive if there is not some overriding reason in our background knowledge for questioning the experience's veridicality. He formulates this suggestion in a "Principle of Credulity": "I suggest that it is a principle of rationality that (in the absence of special considerations) if it seems (epistemically) to a subject that X is present, then probably X is present; what one seems to perceive is probably so" (*The Existence of God*, p. 245). The "special considerations" that can impugn the veridicality of an of-X experience are of four sorts. There can be considerations that show: (1) "that the apparent perception was made under conditions or by a subject found in the past to be unreliable" (p. 260); (2) "that the perceptual claim was to have perceived an object of a certain kind in circumstances where similar perceptual claims have proved false" (p. 261); (3) "that on background evidence it is probable that X was not present" (p. 261); (4) "that whether or not X was there, X was probably not a cause of the experience of its seeming to me that X was there" (pp. 263–64). Swinburne argues that none of these conditions are conditions under which we have religious experiences (or receive reports of such experiences); so he concludes that the Principle of Credulity warrants the conclusion that God exists.

Swinburne is right in thinking that to understand properly the epistemic relation between of-X experiences and claims that X exists we need to recognize that the experience is *prima facie* evidence for the claim. But I think he misconstrues the sense in which the experience is *prima facie* evidence. He takes "*prima facie*" to mean that the evidence of the experience is by itself decisive unless there is some overriding consideration in our background knowledge. But this claim is too strong.

Suppose, for example, I walk into my study one afternoon and seem to see, clearly and distinctly, my recently deceased aunt sitting in my chair. We may assume that the conditions of this experience (my mental state, the lighting of the room, etc.) are not ones that we have reason to think produce unreliable perceptions. Thus, the first of Swinburne's defeating conditions does not hold. Nor, given normal circumstances, does the second condition hold. Most likely, I have no knowledge at all of circumstances in which experiences of the dead by apparently normal persons have turned out to be nonveridical. (We may even assume that I have never heard of anyone I regard as at all reliable reporting such an experience.) Further, knowing nothing at all about the habits or powers of the dead, I have no reason to think that my aunt could not now be in my study or, if present, could not be seen by me. So Swinburne's third and fourth conditions do not hold for this case. But, although none of the four defeating conditions Swinburne recognizes apply, it is obvious that I am not entitled, without further information, to believe that I have in fact seen my aunt. To be entitled to the belief I would need much more evidence—for example, numerous repetitions of the experience, other people having the same or similar experiences, a long visit in which the appearance behaved in ways characteristic of my aunt, information from the appearance that only my aunt had access to, etc. The mere experience described above provides some slight support for the claim that my aunt is in my room, but, even in the absence of defeating conditions, not nearly enough to warrant believing it.

As this example suggests, an of-X experience in general provides *prima facie* evidence of X's existence only in the sense of supplying some (but not sufficient) support for the claim that X exists. For belief in the claim to be warranted, the solitary of-X experience requires supplementation by additional corroborating experiences. It, along with the additional corroboration, provides an adequate cumulative case for the claim. In cases of kinds of objects of which we have frequently had veridical experiences, we can of course rightly believe that they exist, without further corroboration beyond our seeming to see them. But this is because we have good inductive reason to expect that the further corroborations will be forthcoming. With relatively unfamiliar objects—from elves to deceased aunts to divine beings—this sort of inductive reason is not available; and warranted assent must await further corroboration.[7]

Thus, neither Flew's suggestion that an of-X experience by itself has no evidential force, nor Swinburne's that it has sufficient force in the absence of defeating conditions, is adequate. Rather, we should think of an individual of-God experience as providing significant but not sufficient evidence for God's existence, needing to be included in a cumulative body of diverse evidence that can warrant the claim that God exists.

C. B. Martin endorses the sort of view of experiential evidence I am suggesting.[8] He does not require a one-dimensional inference from a subjective experience to its veridicality, but he does insist on the relevance of further "checking procedures" if a subjective experience is claimed to yield an objective truth. For the case of ordinary sense perception (e.g., of a sheet of blue paper), we can, he says, make two sorts of claims. The first is just that the experience as a subjective episode is occurring: "There seems to be a sheet of blue paper." Here the experience is "self-authenticating"; that is, the mere fact of its occurrence is sufficient to establish the truth of the claim based on it. The second sort of claim is that the experience correctly represents an objective state of affairs: "There is a sheet of blue paper." Here, Martin notes, more than just the occurrence of the experience is relevant to the truth of the claim:

The presence of a piece of blue paper is not to be read off from my experience of a piece of blue paper. Other things are relevant: What would a photograph reveal? Can I touch it? What do others see? It is only when I admit the relevance of such checking procedures that I can lay claim to apprehending the paper, and, indeed, the admission of the relevance of such procedures is what gives meaning to the assertion that I am apprehending the paper. [p. 77].

Presumably, Martin does not mean that, when I have the experience of seeing a piece of paper, I am never entitled to believe that there actually is a piece of paper unless I have in fact carried out further checking procedures. As we have seen, the inductive background of ordinary experience usually obviates the need for such checking. But to claim that the paper is objectively present is to admit the relevance in principle of such checking procedures in the following sense: if such checking procedures should happen not to support the claim, then it becomes questionable; and, if for some reason, the claim is questioned, the procedure can and should be invoked to support it.

It seems to me that Martin, unlike Flew and Swinburne, is employing an essentially correct account of the role of experience in the establishment of objective-truth claims. The main elements of this account are: (1) an "of-X" experience is veridical only if, supposing it to be veridical, we should expect, in suitable circumstances, the occurrence of certain further experiences; (2) if these further experiences do not occur (given the suitable circumstances), we have no basis for accepting the experience as veridical; (3) if, in the relevant circumstances, the experiences occur, we do have a basis for accepting the experience as veridical; (4) if there is some reason for questioning the veridicality of the experience, then appeal to further expected experiences is needed before accepting the experience as veridical.

Since religious beliefs in general and the veridicality of religious experiences in particular are not rationally unquestionable, re-

ligious experiences need further corroboration. So here we must, contrary to Swinburne, insist on the need to support the veridicality claim by further checking procedures. Such checking procedures are not further premises in a one-dimensional proof of God's existence; rather, they contribute to a many-dimensional, cumulative experiential case for his reality.

Given this, Martin goes on to claim that in the case of religious experiences of God no further checking procedures are available: "There are no tests agreed upon to establish genuine experience of God and distinguish it decisively from the ungenuine" ("A Religious Way of Knowing," p. 79). Because this is so, he concludes, religious experiences cannot be rightly taken as establishing the objective reality of God; they show nothing besides the existence of certain human psychological states.

What is puzzling here is Martin's assumption that the need for further checking immediately excludes accepting the veridicality of religious experiences. For surely, at least for the class of experiences we are discussing, there are further experiences that would be expected, given their veridicality. Given the veridicality of the typical experience of a very good and very powerful being concerned about us, we would, for example, expect that: (1) those who have had such experiences once would be likely to have them again; (2) other individuals will be found to have had similar experiences; (3) those having such experiences will find themselves aided in their endeavors to lead morally better lives. All these expectations follow from the nature of the experienced being and its concern for us. If the being has soothed, inspired, or warned me once, it is reasonable to expect that it will do so again in appropriate circumstances. If it is concerned enough to contact *me*, it is reasonable to think that it will contact others in similar situations. Most important, if it is indeed an extraordinarily good, wise, and powerful being, there is reason to think that intimate contact with it will be of great help in our efforts to lead good lives (just as such contact with a human being of exemplary character and wisdom would be likely to have such a result).[9] Further, for some religious experiences, all these expectations are fulfilled to a very high degree. (1) Many people have numerous "of-God" experiences and some even find themselves having a continual sense of the divine presence. (2) "Of-God" experiences are reported from almost every human culture, and the institutional traditions (e.g., churches) they sustain have been among the most enduring in human history. (3) In very many cases, those having "of-God" experiences undergo major moral transformations and find a purpose and strength of will they previously lacked.

It seems, then, that we can argue that religious experiences of God's presence do establish his existence. The experiences themselves give *prima facie* warrant to the claim that he exists, and the fulfillment of the expectations induced by the assumption that the experiences are veridical provides the further support needed for ultimate warrant. This form of an argument from religious experience could be impressively developed by employing detailed illustrations from the literature of religious experience. But here I want to proceed in a different direction, to examine the underpinnings of the argument by developing and discussing the major philosophical challenges to it.

2. REDESCRIBING THE EXPERIENCES

The most fundamental way of attacking the above appeal to direct perceptions of God is to question its assumption that the experiences referred to are in fact perceptual; i.e., that, as they occur, the experiences purport to be of an external divine object. There is no doubt that many say this is the nature of their experience and, similarly, no doubt that they have had something very impressive happen to them. But they could, after all, be misdescribing the subjective content of their own experience. And there might seem to be a very good reason for concluding that they are; namely, that there

could, in principle, be no experiences of the sort they claim to have had. There are two ways of developing such an objection: (1) by trying to show that no experience could have the sort of object these experiences are said to have; (2) by trying to show that the alleged experiences of God are so different from our paradigmatic experiences of persons (namely, experiences of other humans) that they cannot be properly described as encounters with a person.

(1) There are some descriptions of God under which it might seem very odd to say that we had directly experienced him. How, for example, could we claim to have experienced him as the creator of the universe or as omniscient, omnipotent, and all-good? Surely, it might be thought, such attributes would have to be inferred from or read into an experience, not directly given in it. How, for example, could an experience of the creator of the entire universe differ from one of the creator of everything except one planet? Or an experience of an all-loving being from an experience of a being who loved everything except Gallo Hearty Burgundy? Of course, the experiences we are concerned with are not typically claimed to be of God as creator, omnipotent, etc.; but they are claimed to be of someone encountered as far more powerful and good than any human being. How could even such lesser properties be given in an immediate experience? They might be inferrable from the nature of a person's interventions in the world, but not just from an awareness of a person's presence.

The assumption of the objections raised in the above paragraph is that some properties can be directly experienced by us whereas others cannot. This may well be true; but, if so, how do we know it? How, for example, do we know that we can ascertain the eye-color but not the total cash worth of a person by direct experience? One relevant consideration is whether experiencers can be reasonably thought to be in causal contact with states of affairs expressing the information they are said to know by direct experience. Thus, we might reject the claim that someone knows my total cash worth just by looking at me, on the grounds that the information is not available in my physical features or behavior. In the case of God, however, there is every reason to think that he can causally interact with anyone at any time. But given the causal accessibility of an object, surely the only way of knowing whether or not it can be experienced is to see if people actually do experience it. This, for example, is how most of us know that football referees' whistles, but not dog whistles, can be heard by human ears. There are no intrinsic characteristics of certain properties by which we can judge *a priori* that they can or cannot be directly perceived. Consequently, the assumption that divine qualities—even in the strong form of omnipotence, and the like—cannot be directly experienced could be justified only by showing that they are not experienced. Since this last claim is just what is at stake in discussions of religious experience, it is apparent that the present objection must beg the question.

(2) The second line of criticism has been interestingly developed by Ronald Hepburn.[10] He begins with the idea, put forward especially by Martin Buber and theologians influenced by him, that an encounter with God would have to be essentially different from our ordinary encounters with material things and even with human persons because all these encounters are with *objects* (*Its*), the presence of which can be checked for by the effects of their behavior in the world. For, according to this view:

> God . . . never becomes an *It*, an object: he is eternally a *Thou* only. There is no detecting *his* presence by bumps on the stair or even a whispered word or a glimpse of a face. We cannot, with *him*, point or glance in this or that direction and say, 'There, he is coming now.' We have only that felt sense of personal meeting, a sense of addressing and being addressed. He leaves no marks of his presence such that we might say—'This proves he is with us' [*Christianity and Paradox*, p. 25].

The obvious question is, If an "encounter" with God is so different from our experience of objects, why even call it an experience of something? Because, it is said, we find in some of our experiences of human persons significant, though imperfect, analogies to an encounter with God. Specifically, it is possible to move from our ordinary, mundane encounters with other people, in which we regard them as little more than things equivalent to their behavioral effects in the world, to intimate experiences in which behavioral cues are of minimal significance and our apprehension of the other person becomes close to a direct *acquaintance* unmediated by knowledge of behavioral effects. Thus, we find in human relations degrees of "purity" of personal encounters, corresponding to a decreasing dependence of the encounters on behavioral cues. From this, we can make sense of a totally pure "I-Thou" encounter with God.

Hepburn's objection to this view is that in fact it cannot make good on the claim that there are *any* encounters that even approach the ideal of a pure, unmediated awareness of personal presence. He considers several cases of human encounters, ranging from someone's studying my bodily movements in order to mimic them, to an intimate conversation, punctuated by long but pregnant pauses, with a close friend. Reflecting on these cases, he notes that in even the most intimate encounter it is entirely possible for me to be mistaken in my "sense" of the other's presence (e.g., I may still "sense" John's presence in the dark room where we have been speaking, even though he has slipped out during one of the pregnant pauses). Given this, Hepburn comments:

> The fact that we can make occasional mistakes about encounters with human beings . . . would not necessarily make nonsense of the scale of 'purity'. What *does* upset it is . . . the continuing importance of 'knowledge about' or 'knowledge that' in even the most intimate relationships. My ease of mind during John's silence is inductively justified by my memory of the countless times he has ended such a

Theism, Atheism, and Agnosticism

silence with words that showed he had been meditating on something I said to him. . . . The longer one has known somebody, the more experience one has gathered of him, the longer the gaps that one can allow between checking in various ways upon his reaction to what is being said and done. In *this* sense one is not so dependent on information *about* him. . . . But, again, this is so only because we assume consistency in our friend's personality. Whereas, the actual forms that his consistent behavior takes we have had to learn by watching, asking, and listening [pp. 35–36].

Hepburn's conclusion, accordingly, is that we have no ordinary analogues to the alleged "purely personal" encounter with God and so are not at all entitled to speak of these encounters as perceptual experiences.

However, even if Hepburn's assessment of "I-Thou" encounters with God is correct, his conclusion does not seem to apply to the sort of religious experience that concerns us. For the cases we have cited do not describe experiences of a person with no mediation via experiences of the person's activities. Rather, God is encountered as responding to the experiencer, aiding and comforting him, expressing his love. So these experiences meet Hepburn's condition that a perceptual experience of a person must involve an awareness of the person via "behavioral cues." Of course, the behavioral cues in this case are not sensorily perceived bodily states or activities. But to assume that the cues must be of this sort just begs the question by ruling out *a priori* the possibility of encountering nonembodied persons.

Further, Hepburn's argument does not even seem telling against a purported experience of a person unmediated by behavioral cues. For it is obvious that not everything we perceive is perceived mediately. In the case of our perception of human beings, for example, the behavior through which we perceive them is itself, in some cases, perceived directly, not by perceiving some further cue of the behavior. (Thus, I perceive Edward by hearing his words, but I do not

hear his words by means of any further perception.) But, as we argued above, given the "causal availability" of a person, there is no *a priori* way of determining whether he can or cannot be directly perceived. Even if we know from experience that human persons cannot be directly perceived, it does not follow that the same is true of nonhuman persons. As noted above, the only way of finding out is to see what people have in fact perceived.

I suspect that Hepburn's real difficulty is not with the idea of directly perceiving a person, but with the claim that such a perception is self-authenticating and so cannot be checked by further experiences. Certainly, he sees the theologians he is criticizing as thinking that direct personal encounters with God are self-authenticating. Thus, in summarizing the view of H. H. Farmer, he says: "Encounter with God . . . is self-authenticating, 'known only through direct perception not describable in other terms' " (p. 40). But though this may be the view of Hepburn's opponents, there is no need to tie direct perception to self-authentification. After all, I may directly perceive that you have long blonde hair, and still revise my judgment when I see you removing a wig. Similarly, I might have a direct experience of God's presence and later rightly reject its veridicality on the grounds that it was drug-induced or had a negative moral effect on my life. It is true that in cases of direct perception *one* source of further checking is not available: we cannot ask if an error was made regarding the behavioral cues. But there can still be other sorts of checks, such as compatibility with subsequent experiences.

I conclude, then, that attempts to redescribe presence-of-God experiences as nonperceptual are not successful.

3. EXPLAINING THE EXPERIENCES AWAY

When we are presented with the claim that a given religious experience is truly a revelation of the divine, we are often inclined to point out that the occurrence of the experience can be as well or better explained without the assumption that it was in fact produced by an encounter with God. Thus, we make reference to Freudian projections and wish fulfillments, group-induced expectations, schizophrenic personalities, and even the biochemistry of puberty to account for various religious experiences. Do such explanations truly impugn the veridicality of the experiences they try to account for? An adequate answer requires some reflection on the logic of explanation.

A first crucial point is that no explanation is acceptable unless there is reason to think that the explanandum it yields is true. There are no acceptable explanations of why there are only seven planets. Here there are two importantly different cases. In the first, the above condition is readily satisfied because we have good independent grounds for thinking that the premises of the explanation (the explanans) are true and so can conclude by a sound argument from them to the truth of the explanandum. In the second case, we do not have adequate independent support for the explanans, but rather hope that its successful explanation of the explanandum will help provide such support. In this case, we are justified in regarding the explanation as adequate only if we have good independent reason to think that the explanandum is true.

Let us now apply these comments to attempts to explain away the veridicality of an experience. To claim that an explanation of an experience shows that it is not veridical is to propose an explanans that yields an explanandum asserting the nonveridicality of the experience. The assertion will be justified only if there is reason to think the explanation is adequate, and this will be so only if there is reason to think the explanandum is true. In the first of the cases distinguished in the preceding paragraph, we can rightly regard the explanans itself as establishing the truth of the explanandum, and so the claim that the explanation has shown the nonveridicality of the experience is warranted. Thus, if we know on independent grounds that Jean-Paul has been taking mescaline and that taking mescaline usually causes him to have hallucinations of menacing crustaceans, then we have an explanation of his experience of menacing crustaceans that shows it to be nonveridical. But in the second case this conclusion may not be drawn. If we have no independent support for the claims of the explanans about Jean-Paul's drug use and its probable effects, then, in order to accept the explanation as adequate, we need to have independent support for the claim that Jean-Paul's experiences are nonveridical. In this case, then, the proposed explanation cannot be used to show that the experience it explains is nonveridical.

Our conclusion then must be that we can "explain away" a religious experience only by means of an explanans whose truth we can establish independently of its purported explanatory power. With this in mind, let us examine some standard attempts to explain away religious experiences.

It will be useful to distinguish two sorts of such attempts. The first are based on peculiarities of the individuals who have religious experiences; for example, it may be pointed out that a particular religious mystic shows signs of a psychosis that is typically associated with religious hallucinations. The second are based on traits common to everyone (or at least everyone belonging to some very broad class); thus, a Freudian might note that we all have unconscious desires to believe in the divine reality allegedly revealed in religious experiences.

The first sort of attempt to explain away religious experiences faces the initial difficulty of severe limitation in scope of application. Even if the "of-God" experiences of some people can be discounted because of their psychological abnormalities, the large number of apparently normal people reporting such experiences makes it extremely unlikely that such an approach could explain away all or even most of these experiences. The approach would be successful only if we had independent reason for thinking that the experiences were nonveridical and could then use this fact to support the hypothesis that there are hidden abnormalities in those who have them. But then, of course, the psychological explanation would presuppose

Theism, Atheism, and Agnosticism

rather than establish the nonveridicality of the experiences it explained.

Furthermore, it is not even clear that the independent establishment of an individual's psychological or physiological abnormalities would ordinarily impugn the veridicality of his religious experiences. The presence of psychotic traits or a history of use of hallucinatory drugs will often impugn the reliability of an individual's sense experiences, because we know that such conditions cause sensory distortions. But it is not so obvious that factors suggesting the unreliability of a person's sense experiences suggest a similar unreliability of his nonsensory experiences. *A priori*, there is just as much reason to think that the abnormalities that inhibit perceptions of material objects might enhance perception of nonmaterial objects.[11] Of course, we might discover correlations between certain psychological traits and the nonveridicality of the religious experiences of those who have them. But this would require some means, other than the appeal to psychological explanations, of determining the nonveridicality of religious experiences; and there is little likelihood that everyone reporting religious experiences would have the traits in question. So there is little reason to think that this first approach to explaining away religious experiences will be successful.

What about explanations of religious experiences on the basis of traits common to all human beings? Freud, for example, claims that "religious ideas . . . are fulfillments of the oldest, strongest and most urgent wishes of mankind." For example:

> . . . the benevolent rule of a divine Providence allays our fear of the dangers of life; the establishment of a moral world-order ensures the fulfillment of the demands of justice . . .; and the prolongation of earthly existence in a future life provides the local and temporal framework in which these wish-fulfillments shall take place.[12]

Given that we so deeply desire the truth of religious claims, it is not surprising that many people have experiences that seem to support their truth. For, as common sense suggests and depth psychology shows, there are mechanisms whereby the mind is capable, in certain circumstances, of seeing or othewise experiencing what it wants to. Hence, from a Freudian perspective, there is a relatively straightforward explanation of religious experiences. Moreover, the premises of this explanation (that we desire religious claims to be true, that the mind can produce experiences fulfilling its wishes) have strong support apart from their role in explaining religious experiences. So shouldn't we conclude that this sort of account does undermine the veridicality of religious experiences?

No. The difficulty is this: even if we do have independent knowledge of the existence and the nature of the mechanisms of wish fulfillment, the Freudian explanation of any specific religious experience requires not only that these mechanisms exist as *capacities* but that they be actually operative in the occurrences of the experiences being explained. But there is no way of seeing the actual operation of wish-fulfillment mechanisms; we can only postulate them as the best explanation of the occurrence of delusory experiences. Hence, to be entitled to assert the actual operation of wish-fulfillment mechanisms, we must first have good reason to think that the experiences they explain are nonveridical. So the Freudian attempt to explain away religious experience is inevitably question-begging.

The same sort of difficulty faces Marxist explanations, based, for example, on the ideas that religious beliefs support the power of the ruling class and that there are socioeconomic forces capable of causing individuals to have experiences supporting these beliefs. We would need to know that these forces were in fact operative in a given case and to know this independent of information about the nonveridicality of the experiences. Similar strictures apply to any other attempts at general explanations (via social, economic, psychological or other causes) of religious experiences and beliefs. It is not sufficient to show just that such causes *could* produce the experiences and beliefs. It must also be shown that they are in fact operative in given cases; and it is very hard to see how this can be done without assuming ahead of time that the experiences and beliefs are nonveridical.

It is sometimes suggested—by both Freudians and Marxists—that *all* experiences are psychologically or economically determined. If we knew this to be so, then we would be justified in appealing to economic or psychological causes to explain religious experiences. It is hard to see what evidence could be put forward for these claims of universal determinism. But, given any such claim, we must surely allow that experiences can be veridical (and known to be so) in spite of their being determined, or else fall into an extreme skepticism. But then the mere fact that a religious experience is psychologically or economically determined does not undermine its veridicality.

A final difficulty facing Freudian and Marxist critiques of religious experience—and critiques based on any other general views of human reality and its place in the world—is that their own basic beliefs and the "evidence" they are said to be based on seem at least as susceptible to being explained away as are religious beliefs and experiences. There are after all Freudian explanations of Marxism and the Marxist explanations of Freudianism. (Not to mention the possibility of religious explanations of both.) The attempt to discredit general worldviews by proposing explanations themselves based on rival worldviews is a two-edged sword that can easily be turned against those who wield it.

So far we have been considering the possibility of showing religious experiences to be nonveridical by appealing to specific scientific (or purportedly scientific) theories that explain them. However, there is another way in which scientific explanation might seem to call religious experiences into question. Science, it might be argued, is ultimately our only source of reliable information about what there is. We begin, admittedly, with a commonsense view of the furniture of the universe, derived from

our ordinary sense experience—the view Sellars calls "the manifest image." But this view is subject to correction and even ultimate replacement by the view of things—"the scientific image"—that results from the careful scrutiny of our world by the methods of postulational empirical science. To cite some standard examples, we have learned, contrary to manifest appearances, that color is not an intrinsic quality of external material objects, and that such objects are not homogeneous units but multitudinous aggregates of elementary particles. Of course science is far from having achieved a complete account of what there is; nonetheless, there is no basis for accepting the existence of entities and processes that show no sign of having a place in the ultimate scientific scheme of things. Nor is it just that immaterial agents such as God seem to have no place in this scheme. It also seems that the scientific study of the human mind and brain suggests no extrasensory faculties by which we might perceive such agents. From this point of view, the objection to religious experiences is not that they can be explained away by science but that there are no prospects for a positive scientific account of their veridicality. Since the view that these experiences are veridical finds no place in our scientific account of world, it is reasonable to abandon it and to suppose that religious experiences are in fact the delusive products of one or another of the mechanisms capable of producing them.

Many religious believers will be inclined to simply dismiss this line of argument because of its apparently gratuitous assumption that science alone is capable of giving a complete account of what there is. In my opinion, such a dismissal ignores the very powerful case that can be made for a strong form of scientific realism.[13] In any case, it will not impress the nonbeliever who is committed to the primacy of science or even the believer who hesitates to make factual claims that go beyond or conflict with established scientific results. However, I do not think that the defense of religious experiences needs to reject the claims of scientific realism. We can both agree that "science is the measure of what there is" *and* claim that we have true encounters with God.

The reconciliation of scientific realism and religious experience depends, however, on a proper understanding of the import of realism. Realism is indeed a vain pretension if it claims that all truths are scientific truths and that nonscientific categories such as 'person', 'meaning', and 'good' must be either translated into scientific terms or else rejected as having no applications. Rather, such categories—and the truths expressed in their terms—must be regarded as valid and irreducible to science. Scientific realism is just the assertion that their validity does not derive from their reference to some special realm of entities that supplements those discovered by scientific inquiry.

This version of scientific realism has been brilliantly developed and defended by Wilfrid Sellars. He has, in particular, argued that an acceptance of realism does not require rejecting the framework of persons. Thus, at the end of his essay "Philosophy and the Scientific Image of Man,"[14] Sellars says:

> To say that a certain person desired to do A, thought it his duty to do B but was forced to do C, is not to *describe* him as one might describe a scientific specimen. One does indeed describe him, but one does something more. And it is this something more which is the irreducible core of the framework of persons [p. 39; Sellars's emphasis].

He goes on to suggest that this irreducible "something more" is the recognition of the person as belonging to a community with us: "Thus, to recognize a featherless biped or dolphin or Martian as a person is to think of oneself and it as belonging to a community" (ibid.). Sellars further argues that a community is defined by the most general *intentions* that are shared by its members. As a result, recognizing someone "as a person requires that one think thoughts of the form, 'We (one) shall do . . . actions of kind A in circumstances of kind C.' " Further, he emphasizes, "To think thoughts of this kind is not to *classify* or *explain*, but to rehearse an intention." Accordingly, he concludes:

> . . . the conceptual framework of persons is not something that needs to be *reconciled with* the scientific image, but rather something to be *joined* to it. Thus, to complete the scientific image we need to enrich it *not* with more ways of saying what is the case, but with the language of community and individual intentions [p. 40; Sellars's emphasis].

Supposing that this approach to the framework of persons can be adequately developed (and Sellars has carried it a long way in various directions), we can accept a Sellarsian version of scientific realism and still maintain that there are irreducible truths about persons and their interrelations.

Sellars, of course, is concerned only with the framework of human persons. Does his account also allow for the recognition of a divine person? One apparent obstacle to such a recognition is this: Although the category of 'human person' is irreducible to scientific categories, the existence of truths about specific human persons depends on the existence of certain scientifically describable physical systems; namely, the scientific counterparts of what in the manifest image we call the person's body. Without such a system as the person's physical locus, talk of a person will lack the minimal ontological foothold it needs to be appropriate. Now it would seem that God is regarded as precisely a person who has no body and hence no physical locus, and so could not be countenanced by even Sellars's nonreductive scientific realism. However, it seems to me that orthodox religious thought allows and even suggests (by its claim that God is present everywhere in the world) the identification of the physical world as a whole as God's physical locus in the sense required by the Sellarsian account of persons. This is not pantheism: there is no suggestion that God is identical with his physical locus. Nor is there any need to accept a divine hylomorphism by thinking of God as having the world as his body in the sense that human beings have bodies. For though, like our bodies for us, the world is the vehicle whereby God communicates to human beings, there is no need to think that God's nature depends on the world the way that human nature depends on human bodies. Talk of the divine person could express truths that would hold regardless of the state of the physical world.

Another apparent difficulty: it might seem that, on the Sellarsian view, there could be truths about God only to the extent that we choose to recognize him as a person, by deciding to think of him and ourselves as members of a common community. But it is just as possible that the community in which God has his reality as a person exists most fundamentally in virtue of *his* intentions toward us, not vice versa (just as infants are included in the human community in virtue of the intentions of adults).

A final objection: Won't the Sellarsian view at least entail that God cannot exist if the universe does not, and so be inconsistent with God's autonomy and role as creator of all that is? For even Sellars's realism cannot admit the existence of a person with no physical locus, since this would mean that there was a reality in no way accessible to scientific discovery. Here I think a certain retreat from the strict realist ontological view might be necessary, but it is not a retreat that rejects the central insights that motivate realism. Realism, as I am considering it, is essentially a claim about the methods of inquiry whereby we can arrive at a true account of reality. It holds that scientific methods of inquiry are the only ones that we can rely on to produce a complete and accurate account of what there is. If, however, as religious experiences suggest, the world is the physical locus of a divine person with whom we have direct perceptual contact, there arises the possibility of obtaining information about what there is from this person. Such information could not contradict what we do or could know by pursuit of scientific inquiry. But it could supplement what is so known; for example, by telling us that the divine person exists in essential in-dependence of the physical universe. Our coming to know this would refute a realist claim that we can have no knowledge of what there is apart from science. But since the knowledge would have been given to us by authoritative revelation and not obtained by any human methods of inquiry, it would be consistent with the essential realist view that there are no methods except those of science whereby we can, *on our own authority,* rightly assert anything about what there is.

4. RELIGIOUS EXPERIENCES AND RELIGION

So far the objections we have considered have derived from epistemological considerations quite separate from, if not opposed to, the content of religious beliefs. In this section we turn to objections derived from religion itself. I will first examine the suggestion that the true God's transcendence and utter uniqueness make it impossible for him to be the object of a human experience (at least of the relatively straightforward perceptual experiences with which we are concerned).

More precisely, the difficulty can be formulated in this way: any object given in our experience must be properly characterizable in terms of our concepts. (On a Kantian view, the experience is possible only if the object is given under our concepts; on an empiricist view, we could abstract the concepts from the object as experienced.) But it is an essential feature of God that none of our concepts are properly applicable to him.[15] For, if they were, he would be just another thing in our world, even if a preeminent one, and not the creator of this world. So, if a being is given as an object of our experience, one thing we can surely conclude is that it is not the God who created us and whom we worship. We may, on this view, allow for special "mystical experiences" that are not encounters with an external object but rapturous unions with God that, as the mystics insist, cannot be described in human language and concepts. But these are very different from the percep-

Theism, Atheism, and Agnosticism

tions of God that are our focus here. Indeed, to the extent that mystical experiences are accepted as true manifestations of God, they show that our more mundane perceptions of a powerful and good person are not.

There are at least three important lines of response to this difficulty. First, it should be noted that the objection does not in fact question the veridicality of experiences of a good and powerful person concerned about us. At best, it shows that there is another religiously relevant being, not encountered in these experiences. If it is true that this unexperienceable being is the primary focus of religious belief, then our "of-God" experiences do not ground the central claim of religion. Nonetheless, the existence of the sort of being revealed in these experiences must be of very great importance for us. Second, even religious views that most emphasize the utter transcendence of God (e.g., some versions of Christianity and Hinduism) allow for the role of mediators (angels, lesser gods) between God and man. So even if our experiences are not strictly of God, they may still be important factors in our relation to him. Finally, there is the possibility—at the heart of Christianity in the doctrine of incarnation—that even a transcendent God might reveal himself to us by taking on a human form. Christians who hold that a man living among us was the transcendent God can hardly reject the possibility that this God could reveal himself to us in nonsensory experiences. This possibility is further supported by the fact that, even if none of our concepts are properly applicable to God, there must be some that are more adequate than others to his reality. Thus, it is surely less of a mistake to say that God is good and powerful than to say that he is neurotic and deciduous. But if this is so, there would seem to be room for an experience—although imperfect—of God in terms of the concepts most appropriate to him.

Another objection drawn from religion is based on the alleged wide diversity in the content of experiences of God and the apparent dependence of this content on the religious traditions of the experiencers. This di-versity is undeniable if we take account of the entire range of religious experiences; but it is by far most prominent in the extreme cases of literal visions and the "private revelations" of the most advanced mystics. The Virgin Mary does not appear to Hindus; Moslems do not have mystical encounters with the Trinity. But at best this sort of diversity shows that religious experience does not establish the superiority of one religious tradition over others. The fact remains that in all traditions there are countless experiences of a superhuman loving power concerned about us; and even the otherwise divergent physical and mystical visions share this essential core of content.

There are, it is true, two crucial questions on which there are differences between and even within traditions: Is the divine reality truly other than that of the experiencer? And is the divine reality personal or impersonal? However, the difference between those who answer these questions affirmatively and those who answer them negatively is not so great as it might seem. Even those who emphasize the unity of God and self admit that God is other than the ordinary mundane self of our everyday life. So in spite of their insistence that there is an ultimate unity, they agree that the divine is other than the "finite" or "illusory" self that is transcended in rapturous union with the divine. Given this, they could surely also admit the possibility of an essentially veridical, although incomplete, encounter of the finite self with God. Similarly, those who encounter God as "impersonal" do not claim that he is more like a rock than a human being, but that even the category of 'person' is not adequate to his reality. Even so, there is no reason that an encounter with God as a person could not be partially revelatory of the divine nature or perhaps an experience of a mediator between us and God. So, despite the manifest diversity of religious experiences, there remains a content common to them all; and, apart from very uncommon instances of highly specific revelations via visions or mystical insights, it is possible to accept consistently the essential features of almost all religious experiences.

5. RELIGIOUS EXPERIENCES AND THE JUSTIFICATION OF RELIGIOUS BELIEF

People candidly report that they have directly experienced the presence of a good and powerful nonhuman being concerned about us. The experiences are not isolated events in their lives but are followed by other and more intimate encounters with this being, sometimes even to the point of an abiding sense of its presence. These encounters are a source of moral strength and comfort, even more than we would expect from prolonged and intimate contact with the most admirable human. Further, similar experiences with similar effects are reported by great numbers of people from diverse times and places. There is no reason to think that these experiences do not have the perceptual character attributed to them, and there are no explanations of them (as a whole) as delusory that are not question-begging. Further, there are few if any other religious experiences that contradict their central content. Surely, we then have very good reason to believe that at least some of these experiences are veridical and hence that there is a good and powerful being, concerned about us, who has revealed himself to human beings. So much, I think, is established by our discussion so far.

To what extent does this conclusion justify religious belief? If we have in mind the beliefs of the great majority of religious people, the answer is: very little. Typically, religious belief includes substantive accounts of the nature of God (e.g., that he is omnipotent, omniscient, all-good, the creator of all things, triune, etc.), of his relations to man (e.g., that he became man to save us, that this salvation is carried out by sacramental acts within specific religious communities), of the moral ideals (self-sacrifice, love for all men) that should animate our lives, and of an afterlife dependent on the moral quality of our lives here on earth. Hardly anything of any such accounts is justified by knowing that there is a powerful and good being concerned about us. We can sum up the situation by saying that "of-God" experiences

provide us much more with *access to* than with *accounts of* God. Of course, this access necessarily involves some minimal description of what is encountered, but this description falls far short of what is asserted by any major religion and of what is held by almost all believers.

However, these experiences still have very great significance. First and most importantly, they establish the crucial claim that religion as a pervasive phenomenon of human life is based on a genuine contact with a reality beyond ourselves. As C. D. Broad said after a characteristically judicious assessment of the veridicality of religious experiences:

> The claim of any particular religion or sect to have complete or final truth on these subjects seems to me to be too ridiculous to be worth a moment's consideration. But the opposite extreme of holding that the whole religious experience of mankind is a gigantic system of pure delusion seems to me to be almost (though not quite) as farfetched.[16]

Further, the fact that the religious beliefs of mankind derive to at least some extent from an access to the divine warrants our taking seriously the major beliefs of the great world religions. These beliefs have been formed (in part at least) by the sustained and intimate contact of generations of people with a superhuman power; and so, even if they are not to be believed without question, they ought to be carefully and respectfully scrutinized as potential sources of truth. Finally, given the fact that the great world religions seem to be the main loci and sustainers of our access to God, there is good reason for anyone interested in attaining such access or in more deeply understanding what it reveals to take part in the life of some established religious community. (And to these considerations many can add the happiness and moral inspiration they find in the fellowship of a particular religious tradition.)

So it seems that accepting the veridicality of religious experiences can provide good reasons for associating ourselves with the great religious traditions of mankind. There is no *a priori* reason why this association must be with one particular tradition or even a specific church. But for many people there will be specific psychological and social factors that make their participation in just one tradition or church most valuable. Moreover, the richness and diversity of the religious life of any one major tradition suggests that most of us will lose little by so restricting our primary commitment. On the contrary, a refusal to participate fully in some specific "form of religious life" may lead to an abstract and superficial religiosity that will fall far short of profiting from what the religious experiences of humankind have to offer. So, for many people at least, there is good reason for a commitment to a particular religious community.

But there is a serious question about the nature of this commitment. If my participation in the life of a religious community is not to be hypocritical, I surely must share the *beliefs* on which this life is based. But, since hardly any of these beliefs are justified by the appeal to religious experience (or, it would seem, by any other standard apologetic arguments), how can I in all honesty accept them?

One possible approach here is an appeal to a version of the pragmatic defense of religious belief. I know that great personal benefits are available to me if I participate fully in the life of a specific religious community, and that this full participation requires sharing the beliefs of this community. So, for the sake of the benefits, I am entitled to hold certain beliefs even though I have no reasons supporting their truth. This will be a sound argument, supposing that the benefits of believing can in fact be shown to take precedence over the epistemic value (or even obligation) of guiding belief by evidence. But even if sound, such a pragmatic argument represents an unfortunate need to subordinate our search for *knowledge* (i.e., belief justified by reasons relevant to the truth of what is believed) to other values. And there is the very real possibility (supported by Nietzsche's critique of religious

belief) that the soundness of the pragmatic argument derives from the weakness of those for whom it applies. For isn't the argument based on the idea that our happiness requires the crutch of beliefs not known to be true, and wouldn't stronger psyches be able to thrive merely on what they can show to be true?

This challenge can be met by the Millian argument that the interests of truth itself are best served by debates between those who are genuinely committed to opposing views. Our best chance of eventually reaching the truth about questions to which different religions give different answers is to see to it that there are continuing discussions of these questions, and that at least some of those taking part in the discussions defend with all their resources beliefs they themselves hold. In this way, the pragmatic justification for a commitment to a specific set of religious beliefs can be shown to be entirely in accord with our epistemic obligation to further the search for truth based on evidence.

However, this defense of a specific set of religious beliefs has the same limitations as a defense of beliefs by appeal to methodological conservatism: it warrants only interim, not decisive, assent to the beliefs in question. That is, they are rightly assented to, but only with the understanding that there is epistemic need for continuing discussion of their truth status. As I argued earlier, a merely interim assent is not sufficient for the sort of commitment that seems to be involved in religious belief. However, the decisive assent needed for such a commitment is appropriate to the belief, warranted by religious experience, in the existence of a divine being as the object of that experience. Accordingly, it seems to me that we must make an important distinction between two aspects of religious belief. First, there is what we might call a "core" of belief to which decisive assent is given. Such assent should not be given to any substantive account of the details of God's nature and his relations with us (such as those offered by the creeds and theologies of religions), but only to the reality of a superhuman power and love in our lives, as this has been revealed by religious experiences of the presence of God. Second, there is an "outer belt" of belief (similar to what James calls "overbelief") to which only interim assent is appropriate.[17] Here are included almost all the content of the creeds and theologies that express the distinctive commitments of specific religions.

This distinction of a core and an outer belt of belief makes good sense of the idea, often put forward by believers, that their faith is not so much a matter of believing that certain propositions are true as it is of believing in a person. Of course, belief in a person does require belief that the person exists and has a basic set of identifying properties. But the core of religious faith has only a very minimal propositional content, and consists primarily of living with an awareness of and an openness to the power and goodness of a divinity that remains essentially mysterious to us. The greatest cognitive failure of religions throughout history has been their confusion, due to a fundamental self-misunderstanding, of the core and the outer belt of their commitment. This confusion leads to demands for decisive assent to claims that at best deserve interim assent. These demands are rightly rejected as intellectually irresponsible, with the result that religion is regarded as a thoroughly unreasonable commitment. The separation of a core of belief from the outer belt of overbelief provides the basis for a rehabilitation of the cognitive claims of religion.

We should not, however, fall into the opposite error of thinking that what I have called the outer belt is an unimportant part of religious belief. As we have already noted, such beliefs do originate from sustained and intimate contacts with God, and so at least point in the direction of important truths. We have also seen that a commitment to them is an integral part of full participation in the life of religious communities. Moreover, the outer belt is relevant to the justification of the core of religious belief. The reason is that the appeal to religious experiences of the divine will be (rightly) rejected out of hand if there are no coherent and intelligible ways of including a divine reality in our best available accounts of man and his world. If, for example, the only way we had today of thinking of the divine were in terms of a literal understanding of the ancient Greek or Norse myths, then we would have every reason to reject the veridicality of religious experiences on the grounds that there is independent reason to think that their purported objects do not exist. Consequently, the viability of the core of religious belief requires that the idea of a divine reality be formulated in ways that show it to be a significant possibility in terms of our best available general accounts of reality. Such formulations maintain religious belief as a "live option" in the general cultural context in which the believer lives. They do not themselves justify the core of belief, but they make essential intellectual room for beliefs based on religious experience. The detailed doctrinal formulations (inevitably carried out in terms of available secular intellectual resources) that I have called the "outer belt" of religious belief perform just this function. They make the idea of a divine presence in the world the central assertion of a comprehensive and detailed account of man and his world. This account goes far beyond what is justified by our experiences of the divine; but, properly developed, it should present an intellectually respectable worldview when judged in the context of our best secular accounts. In this way the outer belt plays an essential role in the justification of religious belief.

NOTES

[1] W. James, *The Varieties of Religious Experience* (New York: Mentor Books, 1958; originally published 1902). Page references are given in the text.

[2] D. Hay, "Religious Experience Amongst a Group of Post-Graduate Students—A Qualitative Study," *Journal for the Scientific Study of Religion* 18 (1979) pp. 164–82.

[3] "Visions," in A. Flew and A. MacIntyre, eds., *New Essays in Philosophical Theology* (London: Macmillan, 1955), pp. 254–55.

[4] W. Matson, *The Existence of God* (Ithaca, N.Y.: Cornell University Press, 1965).

[5] A. Flew, *God and Philosophy* (New York: Harcourt, Brace & World, 1966), p. 129.

[6] R. Swinburne, *The Existence of God* (New York: Oxford University Press, 1979). References will be given in the text.

[7] I am saying in effect that there is inductive basis for applying the Principle of Credulity to ordinary experiences but not to religious ones. Swinburne considers this suggestion but rejects it on the following grounds:

> . . . an induction from past experiences to future experiences is only reliable if we correctly recall our past experiences. And what grounds do we have for supposing that we do? Clearly not inductive grounds—an inductive justification of the reliability of memory claims would obviously be circular. Here clearly we must rely on the principle that things are the way they seem as a basic principle not further justifiable. . . . And if it is justifiable to use [this principle] when other justifications fail in memory cases, what good argument can be given against using it in other kinds of cases when other justifications fail? (*The Existence of God*, p. 256).

But in fact it is not clear that memory claims admit of no justification apart from an appeal to the Principle of Credulity. A memory claim might, for example, be supported by its coherence with an immense body of other memory claims and present experiences; or it might be properly regarded as basic. Neither of these moves is appropriate to support the veridicality of religious experiences.

[8] C. B. Martin, "A Religious Way of Knowing," in A. Flew and A. MacIntyre, eds., *New Essays in Philosophical Theology* (London: Macmillan, 1955). Page references will be given in the text.

[9] All the expectations mentioned presuppose that the being encountered in religious experience would act in ways that we would (or should) in similar circumstances. Therefore, there can be no support from the fulfillment of these expectations for the omniscience of the being encountered (because we would not expect an omniscient being to act as we would, with our very limited knowledge). If, however, the experience has been of the being as omniscient and other aspects of the experience are corroborated, then some support is provided for the claim that the being is omniscient, because there is support for the overall reliability of the experience. Further, an experience of a being as omniscient would be corroborated by subsequent experiences of its great knowledge (e.g., by its predicting unexpected events or revealing profound truths about human nature that we were unlikely to have discovered ourselves). Similarly, experiences of a being as omnipotent and all-good can be corroborated by subsequent experiences of its power and benevolence. It seems, however, that most presence-of-God experiences present him simply as very wise, powerful, and good, and do not support strict doctrines of omniscience, omnipotence, and omnibenevolence. If so, these doctrines belong to what I will call the "outer belt" of belief, not to its "core."

[10] R. Hepburn, *Christianity and Paradox* (London: C. A. Watts & Co., 1958). Page references will be given in the text.

[11] C. D. Broad makes this point in *Religion, Philosophy and Psychical Research* (London: Routledge & Kegan Paul, 1953), p. 198.

[12] Sigmund Freud, *The Future of an Illusion* (Garden City, N.Y.: Doubleday, 1964), pp. 47–48.

[13] For a defense of scientific realism, see my paper "Scientific Realism," in J. C. Pitt, ed., *The Philosophy of Wilfrid Sellars: Queries and Extensions* (Dordrecht: Reidel, 1978).

[14] Wilfrid Sellars, *Science, Perception, and Reality* (New York: Humanities Press, 1963). Page references will be given in the text.

[15] The literal claim that none of our concepts apply to God is absurd. Someone defending the view discussed in the text would have to formulate it on the basis of the thesis that anything we experience must properly (e.g., literally) fall under our concepts. When this modification is made, the thesis is at least not obviously true.

[16] Broad, op. cit., pp. 200–201.

[17] The terms "core" and "outer belt" are adapted from Lakatos's philosophy of science, which distinguishes the "hard core" and "protective belt" of scientific research programs ("The Methodology of Scientific Research Programmes," in I. Lakatos and A. Musgrave, eds., *Criticism and the Growth of Knowledge* [New York: Cambridge University Press, 1970]). The meaning I have given the terms is similar to, but by no means essentially the same as, that given them by Lakatos.

Recommended Readings on the Existence of God

Audi, Robert, and William Wainwright, eds. *Rationality, Religious Belief, and Moral Commitment.* Ithaca: Cornell University Press, 1986.

Brody, Baruch, ed. *Readings in the Philosophy of Religion.* Englewood Cliffs, N.J.: Prentice-Hall, 1974.

Burrill, D. R., ed. *The Cosmological Arguments.* Garden City, N.Y.: Doubleday, 1967.

Cahn, Steven, and David Shatz, eds. *Contemporary Philosophy of Religion.* Oxford: Oxford University Press, 1982.

Delaney, C. F., ed. *Rationality and Religious Belief.* Notre Dame: University of Notre Dame Press, 1979.

Hick, John, ed. *The Existence of God.* New York: Macmillan, 1964.

Hick, John, and A. C. McGill, eds. *The Many-Faced Argument.* New York: Macmillan, 1967.

Kenny, Anthony. *The God of the Philosophers.* Oxford: Oxford University Press, 1979.

Mackie, J. L. *The Miracle of Theism.* Oxford: Clarendon Press, 1982.

Matson, W. I. *The Existence of God.* Ithaca: Cornell University Press, 1965.

Mavrodes, George. *Belief in God.* New York: Random House, 1970.

Mitchell, Basil, ed. *The Philosophy of Religion.* Oxford: Oxford University Press, 1971.

Morris, Thomas, ed. *The Concept of God.* Oxford: Oxford University Press, 1987.

Plantinga, Alvin. *God, Freedom, and Evil.* New York: Harper and Row, 1974.

———. *God and Other Minds.* Ithaca: Cornell University Press, 1967.

———, ed. *The Ontological Argument.* Garden City, N.Y.: Doubleday, 1965.

Plantinga, Alvin, and Nicholas Wolterstorff, eds. *Faith and Rationality.* Notre Dame: University of Notre Dame Press, 1983.

Rowe, William. *Philosophy of Religion.* Belmont, Cal.: Wadsworth, 1978.

Swinburne, Richard. *The Coherence of Theism.* Oxford: Oxford University Press, 1977.

———. *The Existence of God.* Oxford: Oxford University Press, 1979.

The Origins of the Essays

This book reprints the following essays by permission of the relevant copyright holders.

1. "Yes, Virginia, There is a Real World," by William P. Alston. From *Proceedings and Addresses of the American Philosophical Association* 52, #6 (1979), 779–808.

2. "Why There Isn't a Ready-Made World," by Hilary Putnam. From Putnam, *Realism and Reason* (*Philosophical Papers, vol. 3*), pp. 205–28. Cambridge: Cambridge University Press, 1983.

3. "Realism vs. Anti-Realism," by Nicholas Wolterstorff. From *Realism* (*Proceedings and Addresses of the American Catholic Philosophical Association, vol. 59*), ed. D. O. Dahlstrom, pp. 182–205. Washington, D.C.: The American Catholic Philosophical Association, 1984.

4. "The Scope and Language of Science," by W. V. Quine. From Quine, *The Ways of Paradox*, 2d ed., pp. 228–45. Cambridge, Mass.: Harvard University Press, 1976.

5. "Arguments Concerning Scientific Realism," by Bas van Fraassen. From van Fraassen, *The Scientific Image*, pp. 6–25, 32–40. Oxford: Oxford University Press, 1980.

6. "Scientific Realism versus Constructive Empiricism: A Dialogue," by Gary Gutting. From *The Monist* 65 (1983), 336–49.

7. "Space, Time, and Space-Time," by W. H. Newton-Smith. From *The Nature of Time*, eds. Raymond Flood and Michael Lockwood, pp. 22–35. Oxford: Basil Blackwell, 1986.

8. "Three Steps Toward Absolutism," by J. L. Mackie. From *Space, Time, and Causality*, ed. Richard Swinburne, pp. 3–22. Dordrecht: D. Reidel, 1983.

9. "The Meaning of Time," by Adolf Grünbaum. From *Basic Issues in the Philosophy of Time*, eds. Eugene Freeman and Wilfrid Sellars, pp. 195–228. La Salle, Ill: Open Court, 1971.

10. "Causality: Critique of Hume's Analysis," by C. J. Ducasse. From Ducasse, *Nature, Mind, and Death*, pp. 91–100. La Salle, Ill.: Open Court, 1951.

11. "Causation and Recipes," by Douglas Gasking. From *Mind* 64 (1955), 479–87.

12. "Causation," by Richard Taylor. From *The Monist* 47 (1963), 287–313.

13. "The Traditional Problem of Body and Mind," by C. D. Broad. From Broad, *The Mind and Its Place in Nature*, pp. 95–121. London: Routledge and Kegan Paul, 1925.

14. "Materialism," by J. J. C. Smart. From *The Journal of Philosophy* 60 (1963), 651–62.

15. "A Nonreductive Identity Thesis about Mind and Body," by James Cornman. From *Reason and Responsibility*, 5th ed., ed. Joel Feinberg, pp. 285–96. Belmont, Cal.: Wadsworth, 1981.

16. "Mind-Body Identity, Privacy, and Categories," by Richard Rorty. From *The Review of Metaphysics* 19 (1965), 24–54.

17. "The Mind-Body Problem," by Jerry Fodor. From *Scientific American* 244 (January 1981), 114–23.

18. "Free Will and Psychoanalysis," by John Hospers. From *Readings in Ethical Theory*, eds. Wilfrid Sellars and John Hospers, pp. 560–75. New York: Appleton-Century-Crofts, 1952.

19. "Freedom and Determinism," by Richard Taylor. From Taylor, *Metaphysics*, 2d ed., pp. 39–57. Englewood Cliffs: Prentice-Hall, 1974.

20. "Acting Freely," by Gerald Dworkin. From *Nous* 4 (1970), 367–83.

21. "Freedom of the Will and the Concept of a Person," by Harry Frankfurt. From *The Journal of Philosophy* 68 (1971), 5–20.

22. "The World of Universals," by Bertrand Russell. From Russell, *The Problems of Philosophy*, pp. 91–100. Oxford: Oxford University Press, 1912.

23. "On What There Is," by W. V. Quine. From *The Review of Metaphysics* 2 (1948), 21–28.

24. "A World of Individuals," by Nelson Goodman. From *The Problem of Universals*, pp. 13–31. Notre Dame: University of Notre Dame Press, 1956.

25. "Empiricism, Semantics and Ontology," by Rudolf Carnap. From *Revue Internationale de Philosophie* 4 (1950), 20–40.

26. "Universals and Family Resemblances," by Renford Bambrough. From *Proceedings of the Aristotelian Society* 60 (1960–61), 207–22.

27. "Essence and Accident," by Irving M. Copi. From *The Journal of Philosophy* 51 (1954), 706–19.

28. "Natural Kinds," by W. V. Quine. From *Essays in Honor of Carl G. Hempel*, ed. Nicholas Rescher, pp. 5–23. Dordrecht: D. Reidel, 1970.

29. "Meaning and Reference," by Hilary Putnam. From *The Journal of Philosophy* 70 (1973), 699–711.

30. "A Defense of Atheism," by Ernest Nagel. From "Philosophical Concepts of Atheism," in *Basic Beliefs*, ed. J. E. Fairchild. New York: Sheridan House, 1959.

31. "The Existence of God—A Debate," by Bertrand Russell and F. C. Copleston. From *Humanitas* (1948).

32. "Theology and Falsification," by Anthony Flew, R. M. Hare, and Basil Mitchell. From *New Essays in Philosophical Theology*, eds. A. Flew and A. MacIntyre, pp. 96–108. New York: Macmillan, 1955.

33. "The Presence of God and the Justification of Religious Belief," by Gary Gutting. From Gutting, *Religious Belief and Religious Skepticism*, pp. 141–76. Notre Dame: University of Notre Dame Press, 1982.

Index

A

Absolute future/past, 139
Absolute rotation, 127
Absolutism, 110, 122–34
  absolute acceleration, 125–28
  absolute duration, 128–30
  absolute motion and rest, 130–34
  general arguments, 122–25
  varieties of, 123
Abstract entities, 71
  problem of, 338–39
  in semantics, 344–47
Abstract linguistic forms, acceptance/rejection of, 348
Acceleration, absolute, 125–28
Accidents, and essences, 361–69
Acting freely, 282–92
  See also Free will
Addicts, as wanton creatures, 297–98
The Affluent Society (Galbraith), 206
Agency, theory of, 184, 279–81
Agnosticism, 391
Alston, W. 3, 18–33
Analysis of causality, 157
  failure of, 157–58
Andronicus of Rhodes, 1
Anisotropy of time, distinction between temporal becoming and, 136–40
Anscombe, 286
Anti anti-realist argument, 27–28
Anti-realism:
  creative anti-realism, 55
  existential anti-realism, 55

in Middle Ages, 55
radical creative anti-realism, 55
versus realism, 50–64, 81
See also Realism
Anti-realists, 18–33
  attack on correspondence theory of truth, 52–53
  definition of truth by, 25
  thesis concerning world-constitution, 56
"An A Priori Argument for Realism" (McGinn), 20
A priori knowledge, 9
  as metaphysical knowledge, 2
Aristotle, 3, 9, 282, 289, 310, 348, 350, 362–63
  Metaphysics, 1, 362
  Physics, 1
  view of metaphysics, 1–2
Assertibility conditions, 42
Assertoric utterances, 60
Atheism:
  association with sheer unbelief, 395–96
  basis for judging moral issues, 403
  basis of rejection of theism, 402
  categories of, 396–97
  defense of, 395–404
  philosophical concepts of, 396
Attribute-specificity, in relation to events at other times, 149
Autarchic fiction, 260
Ayer, A. J., 4, 5, 263, 353

B

"Bad Newton," 116–117
Baier, K., 231, 233–35

449

Bambrough, R., 309
Barrow, I., 113–14
Bayesians, 87
Becoming:
  and conflict between determinism and
    indeterminism, 146–51
  denial of, 144
  mind-dependence of, 140–46
  critique of objections to, 143–46
  tensed variety of, 139
Becominglessness, of physical events, 144
Bergman, H., 148
Bergon, H., 147
Berkeley, G., 3, 45, 250, 315, 350
Between Science and Philosophy (Smart), 87–88, 94
Blanshard, B., 20
Block universe theory, 144
The Blue and Brown Books (Wittgenstein), 352
Blue Book (Wittgenstein), 350–51
Body/mind, traditional problem of, 187–99
Boltzmann, L., 77
Bondi, H., 147, 148–49
Boyd, R., 78, 93
Bradley, F. H., 10, 20, 25, 27
Broad, C. D., 181–82, 187–99, 208, 210–11
Broad construal of metaphysics, 3–8
  objections to justifiability of, 4–8
Brouwer, L. E. J., 235
The Brown Book (Wittgenstein), 353
Buber, M., 432
Burnyeat, M., 45
Butler, S., 264

C

Cambridge theory, 116
Cantor, G., 325
Capek, M., 144, 149, 150
Carnap, R., 4, 5, 82, 308, 325, 335, 336, 373, 377, 381
Cartwright, R., 57
Cassirer, E., 50–51, 54
Causal necessity, versus logical necessity, 272–73
"Causal powers", 40
Causal relations, 38, 251
  among psychological states, 251
Causation, 38–41, 155–78
  causes as necessary and sufficient conditions, 171–74
  compared to reference, 45
  contemporaneous causes and effects, 176–78
  event-event causation, 243
  Hume's analysis, 156–60
  laws, 170–71
  mental causation, 208–11
  metaphysics of, 169
  moral causation, 288–89

necessity, 168–69
  versus invariable sequence, 169–70
  "non-humean" causation, 40–41
  power, 168
  and recipes, 161–66
  time and efficacy, 174–76
  See also Mental causation
Central-state identity theory, *See* Mind-body identity
  theory
Ceteris paribus qualifications, of putative laws, 89
Characterization of "now," 141–42
Chisholm, R., 300–301
Christianity and Paradox (Hepburn), 432
Chroust, A. H., 10
Church, A., 325
Clarke, S., 109, 114
Classes, individuals and, 328–30
Clock paradox, 129–30
Closed sentences, scientific language, 72–73
Coherent ontology, 42, 47
Commonsense physical world language-game, 30
Compatibilism, 184
Compound sentences, 71
Conceiver-relative, 5
Conceptualism, 307, 325
Conceptualized conscious experienes, 110
Conservation of Energy principle, 191–93
Constructive empiricism, 15, 80–82
Contemporaneous causes and effects, 176–78
Copernican revolution, 51
Copernicus, 88
Copi, I. M., 310, 361–69
Copleston, F. C., 392, 405–17
Cornman, J., 182, 208–21
Correspondence theory of truth, 13, 19–20, 34
Counterfactuals, "similarity metric" and, 41–42
Creative anti-realism, 55
Cross-world relation, 386

D

Darwin, C., 375, 399
Daveney, T. V., 283
Death, neutral identity theory and, 220–21
De facto event-properties, of future events, 150
Diliberation, 270–72
Demand for explanation, 99
  limits of, 87–89
Demons:
  analogy between sensations and, 224–26
  as hallucinations, 235–36
Denial of essences, as denial of intrinsic structure, 35
Denial of interaction, 196–98
Denial of physical becoming, 144
Denial of theism, 395

Gasking, D., 111, 161–66
General Theory of Relativity, 120–21, 131
Glymour, C., 94
God, *See* Existence of God
Gödel, K., 48
Goodman, N., 40, 41, 47, 54, 308, 328–49, 370–71, 376
"Good Newton," 116–17
Grammatical fictions, 204
Grünbaum, A., 110, 135–54
Gutting, G., 15–16, 96–105, 392, 425–43

H

Hallucinations, 225, 229–30
  devils as, 235–36
Hancock, R., 10
Hard determinism, 184
Hare, R. M., 392, 419–21
Harman, G., 85
Hegel, G. W. F., 25, 51
Hegel (Taylor), 51
Heisenberg uncertainty principle, 410
Hempel, C. G., 370
Hepburn, R., 432–33
Here-NOW event, 139
Hertz, H., 77
Higher-level epistemic judgments, realism and, 26
Hilbert, D., 325
"History of Metaphysics" (Hancock), 10n
Hobbes, T., 139–40, 213
Holding a theory, definition of, 96–97
Hospers, J., 184, 254–66
Hume, D., 110–11, 127, 156, 169, 190, 250, 315, 350, 366, 377
  analysis of causality, 157
    failure of, 157–58
  on ascertainment of causation by single experiment, 158–59
  "rules by which to judge of causes and effects", 159–60
  skepticism, 156–57
Huxley, T., 211, 411
Hypostatization, 345

I

Ideal tests, notion of, 58
Ideas:
  misleading associations, 314
  theory of, 313–17
Illicit spatialization of time, 137–38
Inanimate objects, extending responsibility to, 263
Indeterminacy of translation, 21
Indeterminism, 184

simple indeterminisim, 276–79
  as theory, 277–79
Indeterministic quantum world:
  lack of attribute-specificity, 149
  physical events of, 150
Indeterministic universe, distinctive feature of, 147
Indicator words, 70–71
Individuals, 328–49
  and classes, 328–30
  principle of nominalism, 330–32
Individuals (Strawson), 354
Induction, 374–75
Inductively justified generalizations, 99
Inference, 85–87
  and observation, 83
  rule of inference to best explanation, 85–87
  and unobservable entities, 85
Inscrutability of reference, 21
Instrumentalism, 80
Instrumentalist views, 87
Interaction, 187
  argument against, 189
  arguments in favor of, 198–99
  denial of, 196–98
  dualistic interactionism, 181, 182, 208
  problem of, 187
  telegram argument, 198–99
  See also Two-sided interaction
Internal questions, 308, 339
Intrinsic attribute-specificity, of future events, 149
Intuition:
  fixed intuitive certainties, realism and, 22
  underlying functionalsim, 245
Intuitionism, 325

J

James, W., 20, 25, 143, 198, 250, 425–26
Johnson, W. E., 356

K

Kant, I., 2, 3, 36–37, 45, 47, 54, 55, 62, 250, 288, 398, 399
  metaphysics of experience, 3
  view of metaphysics, 2
Kinds, *See* Natural kinds
Klein, F., 380
Knowledge institution, 40
Kripke, S., 42–44, 48, 60, 386

L

Language, reality independent of, 69–70
Language-game approach, 23–25, 30
Law of Getting Results, 336

Neutral identity theory (*cont.*)
  extrasensory perception and minds distinct from bodies, 219–20
  implausibility of only brains with psychological properites, 218–19
  implication of something meaningless, 216–18
Newton, I., 47–48, 113, 115, 116, 125, 147
Newton-Smith, W. H., 109, 113–21
Nominal essences, 365
Nominalism, 55, 307, 308, 325
  answers to objections, 332–36
  bigotry of, 335–36
  development of mathematics and, 335
  finitistic platonistic systems, 334
  refusal to recognize classes, 329
"Non-humean" causation, 40–41
Nonreductive identity thesis, 208–21
"Nothing but", 213–14
Noumena, coherent theory of, 47
Noumenal world, 40
"Now-contents" of awareness, 139

O

Objects, essences and, 42–44
Observable:
  definition of, 84
  distinction between unobservable and, 103–5
Observation, and inference, 83
Observation language, explanatory failure of, 98
Observation terms, eliminability of, 226–31
Occurrence-status, of future events, 149
"Of-God" experiences, 431, 434
Omnipotence, fiction of, 260–61
Omnipotence-complex, 260
"One-sided action of body on mind" theory, 211
Ontological presupposition, 324
Ontological relativism, 21
"The Ontological Status of Theoretical Entities" (Maxwell), 82, 94
Ontology, 308, 318, 326, 338–49
  possible worlds ontology, 43
Open sentences, scientific language, 72
Operationalist principle, 125
Oppenheim, F., 282–83, 290
"The Origin of Metaphysics" (Chroust), 10
Ostensive learning, 374–75
Overridable justifiability, verifiability and, 6

P

Panpsychism, 218
Particulars:
  proper names as, 314
  universals and, 314
Passage of time, 135

Peirce, C. S., 20, 25, 26, 78, 348
Perceptual realism, 20
Phenomenological fallacy, of materialism, 201
Phillips, D. Z., 23
Philosophical account, of how things are, 7–8
Philosophical Investigations (Wittgenstein), 203–4, 351, 352
Philosophy of Logic (Putnam), 90–91, 95n
Philosophy and the Mirror of Nature (Rorty), 22
"Philosophy and the Scientific Image of Man" (Sellars), 437–38
Physicalization of states of mind, 74–75
Physical ontology, 74
Place, U. T., 201
Plamenatz, J. P., 283
Plantinga, A., 55, 57
Plato, 307, 313–14, 348
"Platonic" realism, 20
Platonic realism, 345
Plato's beard doctrine, 318
Poincare, H., 325
Positivism, 80
Power, causation and, 268
Presence of God:
  direct awareness of, 425
  and justification of religious belief, 425–43
  See also Existence of God
Present, transiency of, 135
The "Present" in Physics (Dobbs), 143
Principia (Newton), 117
Principle of Credulity, 428–29
Principle of sufficient reason, 124
Private subject-matter, definition of, 235
The Problem of Knowledge (Ayer), 353
Prolegomena to Any Future Metaphysics (Kant), 2
Psychological states, causal relation among, 251
Ptolemy, 88
Putnam, H., 13–14, 19, 34–49, 50–52, 56, 59, 78, 87, 90–91, 93, 95, 310, 381–88

Q

Qualitative psychological content, 183
Qualities, as universals, 315
Quantum theory, and theory of the big bang, 8
Quine, W. V., 14–15, 30, 45, 66–76, 308, 310, 318–27, 329, 334, 335, 336, 370–80
  ontological relativism, 21, 30
Quotation, non-extensionality of, 73–74

R

Radical behaviorism, 241–42
Radical creative anti-realism, 55
Ramsey, F. P., 356
Ramsey's Maxim, 356

System of numbers, 340–41
System of propositions, 341–42
System of real numbers, 342
Systems of integers and rational numbers, 342
System of thing properties, 342

T

Tarskian paradigm, 32n
Taylor, C., 51
Taylor, R., 111, 167–78, 184, 267–81
Telegram argument, in favor of interaction, 198–99
Temporal becoming, distinction between anisotropy of
　time and, 136–40
Terminating judgments, 29
Theism, 391, 396
　atheism as basis of rejection of, 402
　denial of, 395
　as theological proposition, 396
Theological realism, 97
Theology, and falsification, 418–24
Theoretical relation, 383
Theories, indispensability of, 101
Theory of agency, 184, 279–81
Theory and Evidence (Glymour), 94
Theory of ideas, 313
Theory/observation dichotomy, 82–85
Time:
　illicit spatialization of, 137–38
　meaning of, 135–54
Time and efficacy, causation and, 174–76
Time-like separation of events, 144
Time simpliciter, 134
Token physicalism, 244
Topic-neutral experiences, 182
Topic-neutral language, 183, 223
Transcendental Deduction (Kant), 37
Transcendental realism, 35
Translation form, mind-body identity theory, 223
Treatise (Hume), 156–57
Truth:
　anti-realists' theory of, 56
　defined by anti-realists, 25
　realistic conception of, 18
Truth-conditions, 52–53, 57, 60
Truth and Other Enigmas (Dummett), 95
Turing machines, 183, 247–48
Two-sided interaction, 181, 208–11
　philosophical arguments against, 188–91
　scientific arguments against, 191–95
　　argument from energy, 191–94
　　argument from structure of nervous system, 194–95
Type physicalism, 244

U

Ultimate Argument, 92–93
Universality of the division of linguistic labor, 385
Universals:
　abstract entities and, 312–59
　and family resemblances, 350–59
　particulars, 314
　qualities as, 315
　words as, 314
Unobservable entities, and inference, 85
Utterances:
　assetoric utterances, 60
　correctness of, 60

V

Vague predicates, 83
Vaihinger, H., 90–91
van Fraassen, B., 15, 77–95
The Varieties of Religious Experience (James), 425
Verbal Behavior (Skinner), 31
Verificationism, 23–25, 91–92, 132
　theory of meaning, 124
Verification principle, 4
Vienna Circle, 344
Visions, 427–28

W

Wang, H., 334
Wanton creatures, 185
　distinction between a person and, 297
　essential characteristic of, 296
　second-order volitions and, 296–97
　wanton addicts, 297–98
Watson, J. B., 241
Ways of Worldmaking (Goodman), 54
Weinberg, S., 36
Wells, H. G., 418
Weyl, H., 144, 325
"What Is Mathematical Truth" (Dummett), 92
Whitehead, A., 235
Whitrow, G. J., 144–45, 147, 150–51
Will, F., 40
Winch, P., 23
Wittgenstein, L., 23, 37, 61, 203–5, 309, 344, 350–59ff
Wittgenstein on Rules and Private Languages (Kripke), 60
Wolterstorff, N., 14, 50–64
Words, as universals, 314
World-constitution thesis, 53, 56, 61